OXFORD JUNIOR ENCYCLOPAEDIA

VOLUME I
MANKIND

OXFORD JUNIOR ENCYCLOPAEDIA

GENERAL EDITORS
LAURA E. SALT & GEOFFREY M. BOUMPHREY
ILLUSTRATIONS EDITOR: HELEN MARY PETTER

VOLUME I
MANKIND

OXFORD UNIVERSITY PRESS

Oxford University Press, Ely House, London W.1

GLASGOW NEW YORK TORONTO MELBOURNE WELLINGTON
CAPE TOWN IBADAN NAIROBI DAR ES SALAAM LUSAKA ADDIS ABABA
DELHI BOMBAY CALCUTTA MADRAS KARACHI LAHORE DACCA
KUALA LUMPUR SINGAPORE HONG KONG TOKYO

FIRST PUBLISHED 1948
REPRINTED WITH CORRECTIONS 1949, 1952, 1955, 1960
REVISED AND RESET 1974

PHOTOSET BY OLIVER BURRIDGE FILMSETTING LTD, CRAWLEY
AND PRINTED IN GREAT BRITAIN
AT THE UNIVERSITY PRESS, OXFORD
BY VIVIAN RIDLER
PRINTER TO THE UNIVERSITY

PREFACE

IN authorizing the preparation of this work the Delegates of the Oxford University Press had foremost in mind the need to provide a basic book of reference for school libraries. In form it was to be a genuine encyclopaedia, in treatment and vocabulary suitable for the young reader. To many children (and indeed to many adults) reading is not a natural activity: they do not turn to books for their own sake. But they can be trained to go to books for information which they want for some particular purpose—and thus, very often, to form a habit which will be of lifelong value. Their capacity to read continuously for any length of time being limited, they can absorb knowledge better if they get it in small quantities: therefore they will often read reference books when they may reject the reading of more extended matter. Again, it is probably true to say of such readers that their approach is from the particular to the general, and from the application to the principle, rather than the reverse, that their main interest is in the modern world around them, and that since they are not very good at conceiving things outside their own experience, their capacity for grasping abstract ideas is limited. On the other hand, once their interest is aroused, they will often pursue a subject to remarkable lengths, so long as its development is logical and the treatment avoids dullness.

But such generalizations can easily be overdone: many children using the books will not be of this type. Moreover, it was evident from the first that a project involving so great an amount of work, however exactly it might meet its principal mark, would be fully justified only if it could be of service to a far wider circle of readers. Even for the age-group first in mind, anything like 'writing down to children' must plainly be taboo—but clear exposition and simple language are no bad qualities in writing for any audience. Here, then, it seemed was the opportunity to provide a work of reference suitable for many readers to whom the large, standard encyclopaedias are too heavy and technical, and the popular alternatives for the most part neither sufficiently complete nor authoritative. The fact that the plan allowed for an exceptionally large proportion of illustrations to text (between one-quarter and one-third of the total space) is an advantage to any reader, since pictures may, in many instances, save whole paragraphs of involved explanation. With these secondary aims well in mind, then, the General Editors have ventured to hope that the encyclopaedia may find usefulness not only among certain younger children, but also among older students in clubs, libraries, and Young People's Colleges, and even to no small extent among their parents and other adults who may wish for a simple approach to some unfamiliar or forgotten subject.

SCOPE AND EMPHASIS. Within certain limits the OXFORD JUNIOR ENCY-CLOPAEDIA purports to be reasonably comprehensive, though (in common with all general encyclopaedias) not exhaustive. Chief among these limits is that matter already easily available in school text-books is included only so far as its presence is necessary for the proper understanding of the subject under discussion. Thus, although an immense field of history is surveyed, it will be found mainly under headings dealing with its effects, or in the biographies of those who lived to make it. Purely technical or scientific subjects, also, are omitted except when they have some general interest. In natural history and kindred studies the immense variety of forms necessarily led at times either to their treatment by groups or to their omission on purely arbitrary decisions as to which species would, in all probability, never be looked for, or because there was nothing particularly interesting to say of them. In point of general balance the stress is laid rather on the modern world, though due space is given to the factors which have shaped it, no less than to those which are changing it.

ARRANGEMENT. The Encyclopaedia is planned to consist of twelve volumes and an index. Each of the twelve main volumes is arranged alphabetically, and each deals with a particular range of related subjects (see PLAN OF VOLUMES, p. xii). Within its terms of reference, then, each volume is self-contained, and, owing to the great number of single-line cross-references, can well be used alone. The Index covers all entries in the Encyclopaedia. This arrangement, which has the incidental advantage of making the Encyclopaedia easier to revise, arose mainly from one consideration. If articles were to be kept really short—and, in fact, few approach and very few exceed 2,000 words—many subjects could be dealt with comprehensively only be referring the reader to other relevant articles—itself a desirable thing to do. It was clearly preferable for these to be under his hand, rather than be dispersed through any of the twelve volumes at the caprice of the alphabet. This the present arrangement achieves to a great extent. If it has led to a small amount of overlapping, that again is not without its advantages.

Cross-references, then, play an indispensable part in the make-up of the encyclopaedia. They are of two kinds: references in the text to further articles amplifying the particular point under review, and references at the end of an article to others taking the whole subject farther. Therefore, a reader looking up any wide subject, such as MYTHOLOGY, and following up its cross-references either in the text or at the end of the article, can discover under what main headwords the subject is treated. These, again, will refer him to any subsidiary articles, as also, in many cases, to those of a complementary nature. Thus he may be guided either from the general to the particular or vice versa. It is believed that the titles of the twelve volumes (see p. xii), in conjunction with their sub-titles, will usually lead the reader straight to the volume containing the information he wants. In selecting headwords, the rules generally followed have been to prefer the familiar, or even the colloquial, reserving the technical alternative for a single-line entry, and to group narrow subjects under a headword of wider scope. Thus, for HOMO SAPIENS, *see* FOSSIL MAN; for METAPHYSICS, *see* PHILOSOPHY; for MANCHUS, *see* CHINESE PEOPLES; and for YOGA, *see* HINDUISM, section I.

L. E. S., G. M. B.

Oxford

LIST OF CONTRIBUTORS

ADVISORY EDITOR

PROF. DARYLL FORDE. Ph.D., Professor of Anthropology, London University

PRINCIPAL CONTRIBUTORS

Prehistory

JACQUETTA HAWKES

PROF. STUART PIGGOTT, Abercromby Professor of Prehistoric Archaeology, Edinburgh University

A. G. SHERRATT, Ashmolean Museum, Oxford

Early Civilizations

PROF. S. H. HOOKE, B.D., F.S.A.

H. J. BRAUNHOLTZ, Keeper of the Dept. of Ethnography, British Museum

JACQUETTA HAWKES

ANNE LONSDALE, Lecturer in Chinese, St. Anne's College, Oxford

Religion

PROF. E. O. JAMES, D.Litt., Ph.D., Hon.D.D., F.S.A., Professor of Philosophy of Religion, London University

REV. A. C. BOUQUET, D.D., Hon. C.F., Lecturer in History and Comparative Study of Religion, Cambridge University

REV. JOHN FOSTER, D.D., Professor of Ecclesiastical History, Glasgow University

Mythology and Primitive Beliefs

LORD RAGLAN

Folklore

EDWARD A. ARMSTRONG

Races and Peoples

A. HINGSTON QUIGGIN (general)

E. W. ARDENER, M.A., Fellow of St. John's College, Oxford (Africa)

DR. G. M. FRITERS, L. et D. ès Sc.P., Geneva (Central Asia)

F. J. RICHARDS (India)

MALCOLM D. DEAS, M.A., Fellow of St. Antony's College, Oxford (South America)

OTHER CONTRIBUTORS

J. BAINES, Griffith Institute, Oxford

BEATRICE BLACKWOOD, B.Sc., M.A., F.S.A., Lecturer in Ethnology in the University of Oxford

C. H. C. BLOUNT, M.A., Senior History Master, King Edward's School, Birmingham

G. H. S. BUSHNELL, Ph.D., F.B.A.

REV. G. W. BUTTERWORTH, Litt.D., Bodington Memorial Fellow of Leeds University

MALCOLM CALDWELL

J. K. CAMPBELL, D.Phil., Fellow of St. Antony's College, Oxford

MEYRICK H. CARRÉ, Lecturer, University of Bristol

WENDY CULL

H. A. DAVIES, Headmaster of Quaker's Yard Grammar School

PHYLLIS DEANE, M.A., Newnham College, Cambridge

ADRIAN DIGBY, Dept. of Ethnography, British Museum

C. C. EDWARDS

R. D. FINLAYSON

P. M. FITZGERALD

GRATTAN FREYER, Ph.D.

JOHN B. GILLINGHAM, B.Phil., L.S.E.

RICHARD GOMBRICH, D.Phil., Fellow of Wolfson College, Oxford

G. M. HENRY

EDWARD HODGKIN

MARY HOLDSWORTH, M.A., Principal St. Mary's College, Durham University

CHRISTINA HOLE

J. HUSSEY, B.Litt., Ph.D., London

J. H. HUTTON, C.I.E., D.Sc.

International Society For Educational Information, Tokyo, Inc.

R. K. JAIN, Ph.D., Lecturer in Indian Sociology, Oxford

E. J. E. JEFFES

PRESIDENT CLIFTON G. M. KERR, British Mission, Church of Jesus Christ Latter Day Saints

ADAM J. KUYPER

HON. M. LAMBERT

PROF. W. G. LAMBERT, Dept. of Ancient History, University of Birmingham

H. T. LAMBRICK, C.I.E., M.A., Fellow of Oriel College, Oxford

G. L. LEWIS, M.A., D.Phil., Senior Lecturer in Turkish in the University of Oxford

SIR HARRY LUKE, K.C.M.G., D.Litt.

AUDREY M. MALAN

REV. T. W. MANSON, D.D., F.B.A.

ELIZABETH MONROE, C.M.G.

T. W. MOODY, Fellow of Trinity College, and Professor of Modern History, University of Dublin

URGUNGE ONON, Leeds University

R. V. PENNINGTON

D. PETRIE

JEAN PETRIE

HELEN MARY PETTER

O. POSTGATE

P. POSTGATE

C. H. ROBERTS, C.B.E., F.B.A., Fellow of St. John's College, Oxford

RICHARD ROBINSON, B.Litt., M.A., Fellow and Lecturer in Philosophy, Oriel College, Oxford

W. ROBSON

CECIL ROTH

JOHN RUDDLE

PROF. P. E. RUSSELL, M.A., King Alfonso XIII Professor of Spanish Studies in the University of Oxford

FRANK SAVERY, C.B.E., H.M. Consul General, Warsaw, 1919–39

A. N. SHERWIN-WHITE, M.A., F.B.A., Fellow and Lecturer in Ancient History, St. John's College, Oxford

ANDRÉ SINGER

R. B. SMITH, Ph.D., S.O.A.S., London

T. E. SMITH, Inst. of Commonwealth Studies

D. SPARROW

O. H. K. SPATE, Ph.D., formerly Lecturer in Geography, Rangoon University

IAN STEPHENS, C.I.E., M.A.

ANNE SUTHERLAND, Dept. of Anthropology, University of Durham

D. WALKER

R. A. F. WALLIS

MARY WARNOCK, Talbot Research Fellow, Lady Margaret Hall, Oxford

MARTIN WIGHT

G. D. N. WORSWICK, M.A., Director, National Institute of Economic and Social Research

ACKNOWLEDGEMENTS

THE EDITORS wish to thank all those who have helped in any way in compiling this volume. They are particularly indebted to the following for lending photographs: the Director of the British Museum and the Keeper of the Department of Ethnography, British Museum; the Director of the National Gallery; the Librarian of the Haddon Library, University Museum of Archaeology and Ethnology, Cambridge; the Curator of the Pitt Rivers Museum, Oxford; the Visitors of the Ashmolean Museum, Oxford; and the Librarian of the Bodleian Library, Oxford.

The Editors are indebted also to the Keeper of Antiquities, Ashmolean Museum, Oxford, for help in revising the articles on ancient civilizations of the Near East; to Ravi Dayal, O.U.P., Delhi, and I. M. Owen, O.U.P., Toronto, for their help in the revision of articles on the Commonwealth nations; and to the many Embassies and High Commissions who supplied information and help in the revision of articles on both foreign and Commonwealth countries.

COLOUR PLATES

PLAN OF VOLUMES

HOW TO USE THIS BOOK

THIS VOLUME is one of twelve, each on a separate group of subjects, the whole set forming what is called an encyclopaedia, or work from which you can find out almost anything you want to know. (The word comes originally from the Greek *enkuklios*, circular or complete, and *paideia*, education.) Each of the twelve volumes is arranged alphabetically within itself, as twelve dictionaries would be.

The difference between a dictionary and an encyclopaedia is that, while the first gives you no more than the meanings and derivations of words, the second tells you a very great deal more about their subjects. For instance, from a dictionary you could learn that a BUSHMAN is a native of South Africa, and little more; but an encyclopaedia will tell you what Bushmen are like, how they eat grubs and insects, and can find water in deserts where white men would die of thirst—and many other things about them. Then a dictionary contains nearly every word in the language; but an encyclopaedia deals only with words and subjects about which there is something interesting to be said, beyond their bare meanings. So you should not expect to find every word in an encyclopaedia—every subject is there, but not every word.

There are two ways in which you can find a subject in the OXFORD JUNIOR ENCYCLOPAEDIA. The first way is to make use of the Index. The second way is to study the Plan of Volumes on the opposite page, and then to decide in which volume the subject comes.

Very often you will be able to tell from the title alone which volume contains the information you need; but if not, the list of sub-headings on the plan opposite will help to direct you. For example, if you want to find out about an animal or plant, you would look it up in Volume II, Natural History; but if you want to know to what uses man has put that animal or plant in something like stock breeding or agriculture, or by what means he has destroyed it as a pest, you would find it in Volume VI. If your subject were something in nature that does not have life—such as the sun, or a particular country or river, or a kind of stone—you would find it in Volume III, with tides, earthquakes, the weather, and many other things. Matters connected with communication of any kind—of people, or goods, or even of ideas—are in Volume IV. So you would look there for languages, and printing, and broadcasting, as well as for ships, and trains, and roads. But if it is the engineering side of any of these things that interests you, Volume VIII,

Engineering, is the place to try. Business and trade are in Volume VII; and how we are governed and protected by the State, the law, and the armed forces is in Volume X. All kinds of sport and games, as well as hobbies, pets, and entertainments, are in Volume IX; and Volume XI deals with almost everything connected with our homes, from the building and furnishing of the house to the clothes and health of those who live in it. The titles of Volumes V and XII, Great Lives and The Arts, explain themselves; and a rather fuller account of the volume you are reading now is given on page xv. If you cannot find your subject readily by this means, then you must make use of the Index. An article on page xv of the Index Volume will tell you how to do this.

To find your subject in Volume I, think of its ordinary name, and then look it up just as though you were using a dictionary—the As on the first page and the Zs on the last. If you cannot find it, try a more general word. For instance, if you want to know what are the duties of an Anglican bishop and cannot find an article with that title, try the more general title CLERGY. If you cannot think of a more general word, you should at once use the Index.

As you read any article, you will probably come across the titles of other articles in some way connected with what you are reading. You will know that they are titles of other articles because they will be printed in capital letters. Either they will be followed by (q.v.) in brackets (this is short for the Latin *quod vide*, and means 'which see'), or else they themselves will be in brackets, with the word *see* in front of them. You can look up these other articles at once if you want to know more about the particular point dealt with, or you can save them up until you have finished the article you are reading. At the end of any article you may find the words 'See also', followed by one or more titles in small capital letters. If you look these titles up, they will tell you still more about the subject that interests you. These last 'cross-references' are very useful if you want to look up a particularly wide subject (such as EVOLUTION or FOLKLORE), because they show you at once the titles of all the main articles dealing with it. You can then decide for yourself which to read.

WHAT YOU WILL FIND IN THIS VOLUME

THIS VOLUME IS ABOUT MAN, THE WAY HE HAS LIVED AT DIFFERENT TIMES AND IN DIFFERENT PLACES, AND THE THINGS HE HAS BELIEVED

PREHISTORIC MAN AND ANCIENT CIVILIZATIONS. You can read how man developed by EVOLUTION through many stages until FOSSIL MAN appeared (for his earliest remains are so old that the bones have become fossilized). You can read what ARCHAEOLOGY has discovered about how men lived before history was written, and how the great civilizations rose, flourished, and disappeared.

RACES AND PEOPLES. Man has spread all over the world, sometimes moving in large MIGRATIONS, settling in the places where conditions suited his way of life. You can read about the different races, such as the NEGROES in Africa, the AMERICAN INDIANS in America, or the various kinds of PACIFIC ISLANDERS. You can follow the history of our own civilization from the DARK AGES, through the RENAISSANCE, up to the present day. There is a separate article on the history and customs of each nation, and of many of the primitive peoples of the world.

RELIGION AND PHILOSOPHY. The beliefs of man are as varied as the types of people. You can read how ideas about GOD have developed and have become embodied in the great religions of the world. The growth of CHRISTIANITY is described, and there are articles on the various branches of the CHRISTIAN CHURCH. Other articles show how the peoples of the ancient civilizations expressed their ideas on RELIGION through RITUAL, and how MYTHOLOGY grew up from the ritual.

FOLKLORE. The beliefs in MAGIC formed part of primitive belief from earliest times, and can still be seen in the customs of people all over the world. Articles on such things as GIANTS, FAIRIES, SPELLS AND CHARMS, and on BIRTH, DEATH, and MARRIAGE CEREMONIES tell how these beliefs and customs came into being in the dim past and still remain alive, although their original meanings may have been lost.

The words in small capitals are the headings of some of the general articles.

ALTERNATIVE NAMES AND SPELLINGS

NAMES of places and foreign words which have come into general use are often spelt in various ways. Sometimes a people or a country or a town has two quite different names. The list below gives some of the forms which are used in this volume with their alternatives in brackets.

Bagdad (Baghdad)
Bedouin (Beduin, Badawin)
Celt (Kelt)
Constantinople (Istanbul)
Druze (Druse, Druge)
Ecuador (Equador)
Eskimo (Esquimau), Eskimos (Esquimaux)
Ethiopia (Abyssinia)
Fellaheen (Fellahin)
Freya (Frigg)
Genghis Khan (Chinggis Khan)
Gypsies (Gipsies)
Iraqi (Iraki)
Khalifa (Caliph)
Knossos (Cnossus, Gnossus)
Koran (Qur'an)

Manchuria (Manchukuo)
Mogul (Moghul, Mughal)
Muhammadan (Mohammedan, Musselman)
Muslim (Moslem)
Odin (Woden)
Peking (Peiping)
Persia (Iran)
Pygmy (Pigmy)
Rumania (Romania, Roumania)
Shiva (Siva)
Sinhalese (Cingalese)
Taboo (Tabu)
Thailand (Siam)
Tsar (Czar, Tzar)
Tyr (Tiu)
Yugoslavia (Jugoslavia)

A

ACHAEANS, *see* GREEK CIVILIZATION, Section 2 a.

AEGEAN CIVILIZATION, *see* MINOAN CIVILIZATION; MYCENEAN CIVILIZATION.

AFGHANS. The people of Afghanistan are made up of various ethnic groups, including Afghans, Turks, Persians, and Mongols; but one factor unifies fundamentally their outlook and different ways of life—they are all proud Muslims (*see* ISLAM).

The Afghans have been famed as warriors since the first we know of them in A.D. 982; and the British have experienced their valour and cunning during three Afghan Wars and in frequent raids across the Indian North-West Frontier. These lithe men with flowing robes, white turbans, nail-studded shoes with turned-up toes, rifles, and cartridge belts, are mainly farmers and herders belonging to various tribes.

The east and south-east mountains of Afghanistan, which are nomad strongholds, are arid and infertile, and the inhabitants have been forced to wander far and wide, with their black tents transported on camels, to find grazing for the great herds of fat-tailed sheep which are their principal wealth. It is seldom now that they raid the Khyber Pass—where their deadly hidden rifle fire used to be the terror of merchant caravans and of travellers making their way from India to Kabul, the Afghan capital; but passage through the Pass is still forbidden after sunset. Reservations for winter grazing have now been allotted to them in the plains of West Pakistan, so that they no longer have to take it by force.

The most proud and independent of the Afghan tribes is, perhaps, the Ghilzai, whose centre is Ghazni, where the embroidered sheepskin coats and waistcoats (*pustins*) are made.

Tall, slender, bearded, and fair-skinned, with aquiline features and piercing eyes, they look like Old Testament warriors and prophets.

The Turks of Afghanistan live to the north of the Hindu Kush range, on the plains divided from the steppes of Russian Turkestan by the Amu Darya (Oxus) river. Besides the Durranis of Herat, they include the Uzbeks, who came over from Uzbekistan in Soviet Russia and settled in north Afghanistan. They live mainly by breeding horses, camels, and sheep, though latterly they have taken to cultivating cotton and rice. Unlike the Afghans, they have ruddy skins, blue eyes, fair or red hair and beards, and wear gay cretonne quilted coats.

Different from the roving peoples are the village-dwelling Persians, or Tadjiks. Probably they lived in all the fertile regions in their village communities before the Afghans surged westwards from the mountains. The Tadjiks are still the merchants and artisans in the towns, and have remained as tenants of land which the Afghans took from them (*see* SOVIET CENTRAL ASIAN PEOPLES, Section 4).

The Hazaras, a Mongol people, probably came into Afghanistan in the 13th century with the armies of Genghis Khan and settled in the mountains south of the Hindu Kush. They are industrious farmers, and used to make excellent soldiers in the pioneer regiments of the Indian Army. They belong to a different sect of Islam from the Afghans, who despise and oppress them.

In some wild, almost inaccessible valleys of the Hindu Kush live the Sia-Push (black-clad) and Safed-Push (white-clad) peoples of Nuristan. Divided into tribes, shut away in remote valleys, and isolated by high mountain ranges, they play little part in Afghan affairs.

Some thirty languages are spoken in Afghanistan today. Dari (Persian) and Pushtu are the main languages, though Uzbeks speak Turkish,

GHILZAI TRIBESMEN

Camera Press

and the Nuristanis speak four different Indo-Iranian languages. Pushtu is the official language of the country (*see* PERSIAN LANGUAGES, Vol. IV).

The history of Afghanistan has been shaped largely by the fact that it lay on the overland route into India, used by a sequence of invaders through the ages. The first of importance was the Persian king, CYRUS, who conquered most of what is now Afghanistan in 600 B.C. The next conquerors were the Greeks under ALEXANDER THE GREAT in 328 B.C. The Greeks continued in Afghanistan for nearly 300 years, and Greek coins and Buddhist sculptures strongly marked by Greek influence have been discovered there. BUDDHISM (q.v.) came into east Afghanistan from India in the 3rd century B.C. The next important invader was GENGHIS KHAN, the ruthless Mongol conqueror, who, in A.D. 1220, massacred whole populations and laid waste areas, many of which have remained deserts ever since. After this came the Turk, TAMBURLAINE (qq.v. Vol. V), who invaded Afghanistan on his way to India in A.D. 1398. By 1747 the Turkish Durrani tribe had become the most powerful in the country, and one of its members, Ahmed Khan, was elected the first king of an independent and more or less united Kingdom of Afghanistan.

The First and Second Afghan Wars with Great Britain in 1839 and 1878 were really caused by Britain's fear of a Russian invasion of India through Afghanistan. The first war ended in a disastrous withdrawal of British troops from the country. As a result of the second war the British claimed control of Afghan foreign policy and established a powerful amir, Abdur Rahman, on the throne. Abdur Rahman gained control of the entire country and brought tribal warfare to an end. His son ended slavery and founded a college run on European lines. The Third Afghan War broke out in 1919 when the Amir demanded complete freedom from Britain. The Afghans were quickly defeated, but were granted their freedom.

The next amir, Amanulla, determined to modernize Afghanistan, and tried to introduce universal education, European clothing, and the unveiling of women. The conservative and fanatically Muslim tribesmen were outraged, and, led by the *mullahs* (priests), drove Amanulla from the country. Fortunately there arose a great leader, Mohammed Nadir, who in the four years before he was assassinated put Afghanistan on a firm foundation. He set up a constitutional government with an elected parliament. His son, Zahir Shah, who succeeded him was overthrown by a coup in 1973. To weld together the European-educated Afghans and the conservative tribesmen into something more like a modern nation remains a problem.

See also Vol. III: AFGHANISTAN.
See also INDEX, p. 133.

Camera Press

UZBEK WOMEN WEAVING CARPETS IN KABUL

PEOPLES OF AFRICA

AFRICANS. Africa south of the Sahara is occupied mainly by black peoples. There is, however, as much variation in physique and culture as among the inhabitants of other continents. The 'Negroid' physical type is popularly seen as the characteristic one. Considerable regional differences exist; many names for these ('Bantu', 'Hamitic') really refer to language rather than 'race'. Two exceptions are the PYGMIES and the BUSHMEN (qq.v.) who were once widely distributed through the continent. Bushmen and HOTTENTOTS (q.v.) speak Khoi-San languages, in which the famous 'click' sounds occur.

The most ancient black African cultures probably lay among the WEST AFRICANS (q.v.). In Nigeria the Nok culture began several hundred years B.C. It was succeeded by the rich Ife and Benin cultures whose artistic traditions survived to the present day. Traces of even earlier cultures have been found in the Sahara. The many languages spoken in West Africa are distantly related to the 'ancestor' of the present Bantu languages (*see* AFRICAN LANGUAGES, Vol. IV).

The speakers of Bantu languages are not a 'race'. They are found as far north as Cameroon, Zaïre, Uganda and Kenya, as well as among the SOUTHERN AFRICANS (q.v.). On the East African coast the Swahili Bantu speakers established an Islamic civilization. Their language was written in Arabic characters. In Rhodesia the great stone-works at Zimbambwe were built a thousand years ago.

Most Africans were agricultural iron-users before the colonial period. Cattle-herding was also characteristic of the West African savannah (e.g. Fulani) and of many Eastern and Southern African peoples. Social systems were highly adaptable. Elaborate kingdoms were found in all parts of the continent (*see* ASHANTI, ZULU). Some, like Benin (Nigeria) or Buganda (Uganda) could be autocratic. Everywhere the extended family and other kinsfolk formed the basis for co-operation.

There was great variety in African religions. Some had many gods, as in Greece. Reverence for the ancestors (*see* ANCESTOR WORSHIP), and especially for royal ancestors was common. Witchcraft beliefs were less destructive than in Europe, and MAGIC (q.v.) and medicine were closely linked. African beliefs were not simple, and a very complicated view of the world was found among the Dogon of West Africa. The influence of ISLAM has been felt for up to 1,000 years in the Savannah areas and among many EAST AFRICANS (qq.v.). Christianity has spread widely elsewhere, mainly in the last century, although ETHIOPIANS (q.v.) have been Christians since the 4th century A.D.

The present-day independent African nations are very rarely of one 'tribe'. Like Belgium, Switzerland, or the United Kingdom, they combine several languages and cultures. The boundaries of the former colonies of European countries have not been changed much since independence. This is partly because each colony had its own administrative and economic structure. The old colonial languages are frequently used by educated people for government and administration.

Nowadays an important difference between the African states lies in whether they are French-speaking (Francophone) or English-speaking (Anglophone). The French-speaking countries especially stress cultural links with France. The English-speaking countries are somewhat richer and more populous on average. Although they are mostly linked with Britain in the Commonwealth, they often act independently of each other.

Outside these two main groups lie: Ethiopia (because of its ancient independence); Somalia and Sudan (because of their connections with the Arab world); Liberia (because of its original independence as a settlement of Black Americans); Rhodesia and the Republic of South Africa (under white rule); Lesotho, Botswana and Swaziland (in economic dependence on South Africa); the formerly Spanish Equatorial Guinea; and the Portuguese colonies of Angola, P. Guinea, and Mozambique. Zaïre (Congo) and the Malagasy Republic (Madagascar) look towards the Francophone group.

See also Vol. III: AFRICA.

AFRIKANERS, *see* SOUTH AFRICANS.

AGNOSTIC, 'a man who does not know'. This word was coined in 1869 by HUXLEY (q.v. Vol. V) at a time when Darwin's theory of evolution was causing many thoughtful men to question accepted beliefs about God. An agnostic says 'he does not know' whether God exists or not. He cannot prove the existence of God by the use of his reason; nor can he apprehend God by the use of his five senses. These are the implements by which a scientist tries to discover the nature of everything else in the Universe, but since these long-trusted tools fail to reveal to the agnostic either the nature or the existence of God, he finds himself in a state of 'honest doubt' about God's presence in our world. If one asserts that God exists, one is a theist; if one denies that God exists, one is an atheist; if one suspends judgement on this matter, one is an agnostic.

See also RATIONALISM; GOD; EVOLUTION OF MAN.

AINUS, *see* JAPANESE.

ALBANIANS. The little country of Albania, one of the Balkan countries on the Adriatic, north of Greece, has a population of about two millions. The Albanians vary a good deal in appearance,

Royal Geographical Society

NORTH ALBANIAN CHIEFTAINS

some being dark, some fair. But most of them have strong regular features, long oval faces, long necks, and broad shoulders. They walk with an upright carriage and a proud air and, as a nation, they are extremely tough, brave, and fiercely patriotic.

The Albanians are mainly an agricultural people who, partly because of the mountains and inaccessible nature of their country, still retain customs and a way of life discarded by their neighbours.

In remoter mountain villages they remain loyal to their tribal traditions in which correct behaviour may often appear fanatical and violent by western standards. An attitude of neutrality is hardly known among them. The members of each tribal group believe that they are descended in the male line from an original common ancestor. So strong is the sense of tribal solidarity and feeling of personal dignity that a personal insult—even quite a small one—can only be wiped out by bloodshed, and all members of the tribe are responsible for exacting vengeance. Indeed, to avoid an accidental blow, it was the custom, until recently, for men to walk a rifle's length apart and women a distaff's length apart. Tribal customs were ruled by the law of Lek, and

enforced by tribal elders. This was an unwritten law attributed to Lek Dukagjin who lived about 1387.

Every district has its characteristic native costume for men and women. A mountaineer wears white trousers braided with black and a gaily coloured sash which he uses as a pocket. His jacket of rich-coloured velvet, often embroidered with gold, is only used on rare occasions. He wears sandals, and on his head a white cap with often a scarf wrapped round it. Over all he wears for protection a rough shaggy mantle and hood made of goat-hair cloth or coarse wool. He makes a spectacular figure on his fine horse, for most Albanians are good horsemen.

The Albanians speak an Indo-European language which may be a descendant of ancient Illyrian. It has two principal dialects, Gheg in the north and Tosk in the south. Gheg communities are more distinctively tribal in their organization and live in rugged and often remote mountain country. Those who speak the Tosk dialect live mainly in the farming villages of the more fertile areas in the south of Albania and in the past had more frequent contacts with the worlds outside and a less flexible social code. The majority of Albanians (approximately 70%) are Muslims (*see* ISLAM). But there are also important Christian minorities of Roman Catholics (10%) in the north and Eastern Orthodox believers (20%) in the south.

The Albanians resisted the attacks of the Ottoman Turkish Empire with great success under their famous leader, George Castriot (Scanderbeg); but after his death, towards the end of the 15th century, they came under Turkish domination, which lasted, at least nominally, until the establishment of an independent kingdom in 1912. But in fact they have had much independence since the time of Ali Pasha (1714–1822), an enterprising and ruthless Albanian leader who loosened the Turkish hold.

On Good Friday, 1939, Albania was occupied by the Italians under Mussolini, and remained under Italian rule until October 1944 when, after their resistance forces had liberated three-quarters of the national territory, a provisional government dominated by communists was established. Later, in January 1946, it proclaimed Albania a People's Republic.

Since 1944 the communists have struggled to transform their traditional society into a modern communist state. Many of the results have been entirely beneficial. Illiteracy has fallen from 80% before 1939 to about 10% in 1970. The majority of villages now have electricity and radios. The general standard of living is higher. But the price of change has also been high. By 1960, 86·3% of the cultivated land had been forced into collective farms. Women were recruited into the new factories, built with Soviet Russian assistance. Such innovations were intensely unpopular in a traditional society where family control over property and women was a basic principle. To force through its social reconstruction the régime has had to act extremely repressively.

In the years after Stalin's death (1953) Soviet Russia gradually adopted a more liberal policy at home, and abroad improved her relations with Albania's neighbour Yugoslavia, and later even with Greece. None of these changes was welcomed by Albania's leader, Enver Hoxha, and in 1960 Albania moved into a permanent alignment with China in the growing opposition between that country and Soviet Russia.

See also Vol. III: ALBANIA; INDEX, p. 133.

ALLAH, *see* ISLAM; GOD, Section b.

AMAZONS. A legendary nation of women-warriors who are supposed to have lived in ancient times somewhere near the Black Sea. Their name means 'without breast'; for the legend tells that they removed their right breasts

British Museum
AMAZON WARRIORS
Painting from a Greek Vase *c.* 500 B.C.

in order that they might shoot better with bow and arrows. They came to the help of the TROJANS (q.v.) in their struggle against Greece. It was said also that at one time they attacked Greece, but were repelled by the King Theseus who captured their queen, Hippolyta. One of the ten labours of Heracles was to secure the girdle of this Queen Hippolyta of the Amazons. Most of the accounts of the Amazons come in the works of the Greek historian HERODOTUS (q.v. Vol. V).

AMERICAN INDIANS. When Columbus, sailing in search of India in 1492, discovered new islands and a new mainland, he thought he had reached India; so he called the inhabitants 'Indians'. American Indians are related to the Mongoloid peoples of China and Siberia, for man did not evolve in the Americas (*see* EVOLUTION OF MAN) but entered these continents in the distant past from Asia. They came across the land bridge which then existed at the Bering Straits, perhaps pursuing migrating herds of game. It is probable that the migrations began in the second half of the last Ice Age, some 25,000 years ago, and continued at widely separated intervals. There were probably other later migrations by sea—perhaps from Japan about 3000 B.C. and from Africa about 500 B.C. The American Indians show considerable diversity of racial types, possibly because of the need to adapt to the many differences of climate occurring between northern Greenland and Tierra del Fuego at the extreme south.

The earliest inhabitants were nomadic hunters of big game on the Great Plains of the western United States and the grasslands of South America. By the end of the last Ice Age about 10,000 years ago the mammoth, the ground sloth, and many other big game animals were extinct and their hunters were forced to turn to fishing, gathering shellfish, seeds and nuts, and hunting smaller game and birds. By 5000 B.C. this was the way of life in many American Indian settlements along the coasts and river banks of North and South America. Plant collecting led to farming, of two types: Tropical Forest root-crop agriculture in South America (yams, manioc, etc.); and the Desert Pattern of corn, beans, and squash agriculture in Mexico. The spread of the latter pattern into the Central Andes, upper Central America, and throughout Mexico had a profound effect. Populations became big enough and rich enough to support priests, artists and architects, and finally, the elaborate civil service and military specialists necessary for empires. It was in these areas of high civilization and dense population that the largest numbers of American Indians survived the contact with European diseases and European exploitation, and it is in these regions today that Indians make up the greatest part of the populations. In the temperate zones of North America and southern South America the sparser Indian populations were swamped by the influx of Europeans.

See also Vol. IV: AMERICAN INDIAN LANGUAGES.

AMERICAN INDIANS, CENTRAL AND SOUTH. 1. When the Spaniards first came to South America they found peoples there at very different stages of cultural development, ranging from simple hunting bands, such as the Ona, to complex empires such as that of the Inca. The preceding article, AMERICAN INDIANS, suggests reasons for this unequal development. The articles AZTEC CIVILIZATION, INCA CIVILIZATION, and PERU, CIVILIZATION OF, describe the highly-developed cultures existing in Central and South America before the European contact. There are articles in this volume on the peoples of the South and Central American states. This article is concerned with the peoples who lived there before the Europeans arrived, by hunting, by gathering, or by primitive agricultural methods.

2. HUNTERS. A hunting way of life was common throughout the grasslands of the pampas and Patagonia, where the ostrich-like rhea was hunted with the bola, a weapon consisting of a ball or balls attached to a strong cord which entangled the victim at which it was thrown. The

Dr. A. J. Butt Colson

TROPICAL FOREST, SOUTH AMERICAN INDIANS, GUYANA

The woman is weaving a sling of locally grown cotton, which she will wear for carrying a baby in

brave Araucanians were one of these peoples, now absorbed into the Chilean nation. Another important hunting group survived until recent times, the Ona of northern Tierra del Fuego, who hunted the llama-like guanaco. By and large, the hunting people lived in groups of a few families related through the father, roaming within their own hunting territory, and killing any trespassers. Guanaco skin served both as clothing and as material for a primitive dwelling. Men were dominant in these groups, holding women in subjugation.

3. SHELLFISH GATHERERS. Only a few such groups of coastal peoples still survived by the time of European contact, notably in southern Tierra del Fuego and the nearby coast of Chile. Their food consisted of shellfish, sea birds, and sea mammals. They lived in small groups, staying in one place as long as the mussel beds held out, then travelling on by canoe. The men were the hunters, while the women dived for shellfish in the freezing cold water. In spite of the cold, they had devised little clothing or shelter.

4. PLANT GATHERERS. In the Gran Chaco, now within northern Argentina, western Paraguay, and eastern Bolivia, a large population lived partly by hunting, partly by collecting the nutritious wild vegetable foods of the savannah lands. The introduction of animals from Europe, especially the horse, affected their simple lives profoundly. Some tribes became proficient cavalrymen and enslaved their neighbours. The wars between these equestrian Indians and the Spanish were long-lasting and bloody.

5. PRIMITIVE FARMERS. In the highlands of eastern Brazil people cultivated sweet potatoes and yams in narrow strips along the streams, and also hunted and collected wild foods in the adjoining grasslands. They lived in villages of about 400 people, in houses laid out in a wheel-like pattern. Their social and work life was highly communal; for instance, each day began with group singing.

6. TROPICAL FOREST PEOPLES. Many peoples cultivated root vegetables in jungle areas of lowland South America. Those who lived near

FAMILY NEAR LAKE TITICACA, WITH BALSAM BOATS

Camera Press

streams were also fishermen and they usually lived in villages of one or two thousand people. Those who were far from streams lived in smaller groups and hunted. Many tropical forest groups were warriors. Some used blowpipes with poisonous darts. Some of the Tupi-speaking peoples of the Brazilian coast and Central Amazon would make war for the sole purpose of capturing prisoners whom they brought back to the village to provide a cannibal feast. Far up the Amazon, in the interior of Ecuador, the head-hunting Jivaro used to shrink the heads of enemies killed in battle and keep them as trophies.

The more advanced tropical forest groups lived in thatched frame houses. They invented hammocks, woven from the bark of the hamaca tree. These, slung between the house poles, served as beds. They wore little clothing but much jewellery and had elaborate head-dresses of feathers. They practised 'slash and burn' agriculture, very suitable to tropical soils of low fertility; they cleared a patch of jungle, dried and burned the slash, grew crops there for two or three years till the soil was exhausted, and then cleared another bit of jungle. The tropical forest peoples for the most part have been either exterminated or assimilated by their neighbours —for example, the Tupi-Guarani form the Indian element in Paraguay; but a few in remote areas of the Amazon Basin still live in their traditional way.

In the Greater Antilles the most advanced cultures, based on the cultivation of a root-crop called manioc, were those of the Arawaks and Caribs in the Caribbean area; Arawak peoples of Hispaniola and Cuba had developed relatively large kingdoms. These peoples were almost exterminated by the European conquerors and the diseases they brought with them (*see* WEST INDIANS).

7. SEED-CROP FARMERS. Indians whose farming was based on the crops corn, bean, and squash, and who spoke a Nahua language, developed the AZTEC CIVILIZATION: the Mayan-speaking people developed the MAYA CIVILIZATION in the tropical forests and mountains of Guatemala, Honduras, and the south of Mexico, and Quechua-speaking Indians produced the INCA CIVILIZATION (qq.v.) which extended through much of Peru, Bolivia, northern Chile, northwest Argentina, and most of Ecuador. Many other seed-crop peoples were scattered through lower Central America and the northern

Andes of Columbia and Ecuador, living in small kingdoms under monarchs they worshipped as gods. The Chibchas of the Northern Andes are among the best known of them. These peoples produced beautiful ceramics and remarkable gold work.

See also Vol. III: SOUTH AMERICA; CENTRAL AMERICA.

AMERICAN INDIANS, NORTH. There were in 1970 over three-quarters of a million AMERICAN INDIANS (q.v.) in the United States, and about a quarter of a million in Canada. About a quarter of a million lived in three U.S. states—Oklahoma, Arizona, and New Mexico, the others being distributed throughout the U.S. More than half live in tribal units, usually in Indian reservations, but many others live the life of modern citizens. It is usual to group the North American Indians at the time of European contact according to the five main regions and occupations which greatly influenced their cultures.

1. CARIBOU INDIANS. Caribou (Indian for reindeer) roamed in herds from one feeding-ground

Smithsonian Institute

MAH-TO-TOH-PA, THE FOUR BEARS, SECOND CHIEF OF THE MANDAN INDIAN TRIBE OF THE MISSOURI RIVER

Painting by George Catlin, about 1830

to the next in the forests and on the plains extending to the Arctic coasts of North America; they were hunted by the Eskimos in the summer and by the Indians farther south in the winter. Before the days of guns, the Indians caught them in traps or pitfalls, they drove them over soft snow and pursued them on snow-shoes, or they drove them into the water and speared them from their spruce-bark canoes. For a big drive they set up rows of stakes and drove them into ambushes. They stored the dried flesh in pits or caches; no hunter would ever rifle the cache of another. Much of the flesh was pounded into pemmican and packed in fat, in which condition it would keep for months.

These Indians made their shirts, leggings or trousers, and moccasins of skins. Women wore much the same clothes as the men, only of softer materials—often doeskin—and their clothes were more richly decorated with shells, dyed porcupine quills, or feathers. Wealthy men wore robes of beaver, wolf, bear, or coyote fur.

Like the ESKIMOS (q.v.) to the north and the Plains Indians to the south, the Caribou Indians grew no grain or vegetables, though the women collected roots and berries, mashed them, and used them for food and flavouring. They had no pottery in earlier days, so they used to make square cooking-pots of birch bark or round ones of finely plaited basketry lined with pitch. As these would burn if they were placed on the fire, they dropped heated stones into the pot full of water, and so brought it to the boil, and in this way they could stew meat and berries.

During the winter many Indians lived in solid wooden houses, sometimes partly underground for warmth; and in some parts they built a large 'ceremonial lodge', about 15 metres long, for feasts, dances, and great occasions. In many parts there were no permanent settlements, and the Indians, when they were hunting, lived in their bark wigwams which were easily moved.

Each hunting group managed its own affairs, recognizing as its leader or chief the most skilful or wealthy hunter of the group. Girls often were betrothed very young, and the parents arranged the marriages. In some parts a boy proposed to a girl by asking, 'Will you pack my beaver snares for me?' If she accepted, he handed over his beaver snares, she set up the tent, and they were recognized as man and wife. If she refused, it was in the conventional phrase, 'No, there are plenty of women, ask another.'

2. NORTHERN FISHERMEN. The Indians of the north-west coast depended mainly on fish, and especially on SALMON (q.v. Vol. II). Each of the large rivers has a heavy annual run of salmon. To capture them one tribe, the Yurok, built a huge weir to block the width of the Klamath river. In other areas they speared and harpooned the fish singly, and dried and smoked the flesh, sometimes making it into a paste which they stored in finely-plaited baskets. The Indians built large plank houses of redwood or cedar from the great forests, splitting the planks by means of whalebone or elk antler wedges. The villages generally consisted of thirty or more houses set in a line facing the sea along a sheltered part of the coast. The houses used to be large, solid, and rectangular, about 15 metres long. In each house several related families lived together. In front they set up 'totem poles', carved with the crests of animals linked in mythical tales with the particular clan and family (see TOTEMISM).

Close-fitting clothing was not needed in this mild coastal region—men often went barefoot, wearing nothing but a loincloth. Cloaks were made of skins, fibre matting, and beautiful blankets woven of wool and hair. Women had long garments of dressed skins, often decorated with beads and shells. A man's social importance depended largely on his wealth, and, in a high-class marriage, the bridegroom had to pay a large bride-price to his bride's parents. In the north, chiefs vied with each other in 'potlatch'—competitive gift-giving for the sake of prestige.

3. EASTERN WOODSMEN. East of the Mississippi, the white man's influence was early felt, disrupting the patterns of Indian life, which are therefore not so clearly known. In the north-east the Indians lived by hunting; in the east they both farmed and hunted and along the rivers they practised intensive farming.

The hunting way of life is best exemplified by the Algonquins of eastern Canada, who hunted moose, beaver, and bear. They lived in villages in conical tents covered in skin or bark, and wore fitted skin jackets and trousers, and snowshoes. One remarkable achievement of theirs was a very manoeuvrable frame canoe, covered in birch-bark.

Among the peoples of mixed agricultural, hunting, and gathering economy, the five tribes of the war alliance known as the League of the Iroquois are the most famous—the Mohawk, Oneida, Onondaga, Cayuga, and Seneca. The

Smithsonian Institute

PLAINS INDIANS: MANDAN VILLAGE ON THE MISSOURI
The Mandan were more settled than other Plains Indians and lived in stockaded villages

League could defeat surrounding tribes. They brought war captives back to their villages, for ceremonial death after torture (often by the women). They were valuable allies to the British during the American Revolution. The Iroquois lived in the fertile parklands which stretch from Lake Huron eastwards to Lake Champlain, where they built small palisaded villages, round which they grew large fields of Indian corn (maize). Their dwellings were 'longhouses'—pole structures with peaked or curved roofs, covered with elm-bark, each housing several families. The women were responsible for the cultivation of crops, which included beans and squash as well as corn; and government was a sort of constitutional matriarchy in which the sachems (village captains) were chosen by the senior women. Many Iroquois now specialize in steel work on city skyscrapers.

The people who practised intensive farming also produced excellent works of art and a highly organized society, as the ruins of a great city, Cahokia, across the Mississippi from modern St. Louis, bear witness. Their towns had a large central plaza flanked by pyramids of earth crowned by temples and palaces. The Natchez people of the Mississippi Valley were ruled by a sacred monarch called the Great Sun, and had a complete and rigid structure of ranks, determined on a hereditary basis.

4. PLAINS INDIANS. Tribes whose names are famous in history—Blackfoot, Crow, Dakota, Assiniboin, Arapaho, and Cheyenne—hunted the bison, called 'buffalo', on the treeless prairies of North America, between the Mississippi and the Rocky Mountains. They had lived by growing corn, beans, squash, and occasional hunting until the Spaniards introduced the horse into the continent. Then they stalked the bison and surrounded them on horseback, shooting them with bows and arrows, or trapping them. Most groups of Plains Indians became nomadic bison-hunters. Moreover, forest tribes who were hunters such as the Cree, moved out of the Canadian woodlands into the Plains, as well as seed-gathering groups from the Great Basin, such as the Comanche. From this mixture of tribes the Plains way of life emerged. Everything had to be portable, so they used skin containers instead of pottery, and conical skin-covered tepees, easily dismantled as the Indians moved from place to place, served as houses. They used the tepee poles as the shafts of the travois, a wheel-less carrying device, dragged by a horse, on which all the family possessions were loaded. They made their tepees, and also bags and outer garments, from bison skins, carefully cured, scraped, and softened. They used deerskins for most other clothing—often decorated with heavy fringes and embroidered at first with porcupine quill, and later with beadwork. They ate bison meat and used the hair of the bison for stuffing, its paunch as a water-bucket, its sinews for string, its horns for spoons, and its bones for tools.

The most serious crime was to hunt a solitary bison which might cause the herd to move off and to be lost to the whole tribe. The offender had his horses confiscated and his tepee and weapons smashed. If he resisted, he was killed. Horses were the major form of wealth, so the Indian started systematically raiding the horses of enemy tribes. This form of raiding warfare, generally with the capture of horses as its object, increased greatly and developed a definite technique. The weapons they used were circular

THUNDER BIRD

B. Blackwood

The totem of a dead man, placed above his grave. It is made of wood, carved, and painted in bright colours. Kwakiutl Tribe, Vancouver Islands, B.C.

shields of hide, bows and arrows, and heavy wooden lances. There were few pitched battles and not as a rule great loss of life; but there was great rivalry to perform the boldest deeds of daring: a man's reputation and status in his tribe depended much on this, and there grew up elaborate conventions about what could be counted a brave deed. These deeds were recorded in picture-writing on the tepees or on the hero's bison robes, and when he took part in social or ritual ceremonies he started by recounting his deeds.

The object of religion was for a man to get in touch with a powerful supernatural being who would henceforth be his guardian. To achieve this he would fast, and perhaps torture himself, as in the Sun Dance where a man, to increase his spiritual strength, hooked skewers through his back and shoulders, suspended himself on the Sun Dance Lodge, and then worked free by forcing the skewers to tear his muscles.

With the advent of the white man, the introduction of guns, and the coming of the railway, the bison had little chance of survival. The U.S. army subjugated the Plains Indians after bitter warfare, but today their descendants are relatively numerous, nearly 100,000.

5. PUEBLO INDIANS. The Spanish word *pueblo* (town) indicates that these Indians of the Mexico area, unlike most North American Indians, lived in large settlements. Their multi-storied houses, built of stone or sun-dried bricks, often on cliffs, presented high blank walls to the outside, and were entered by means of a ladder from the flat roof. They faced inwards on plazas where larger ceremonial buildings stood. There are some surviving examples, one of which, Oraibi in Arizona, has been occupied continuously since the 13th century; but most Pueblo towns are now built with individual unit houses.

Their economy was and still is based on the growing of corn, beans, and squash. Long before the arrival of the Spanish, cotton was grown and woven, always by the men of the tribe. The women made, and the Hopi people still make, attractive pottery, and harden it in open fires. They collect the fine clay, prepare it by sifting, kneading, and moistening, and roll it out into sausage-like strips which are built spirally from the base. Then they add a coating of thin clay, black, red, yellow, or white, and burnish the surface before the pot is fired. In some villages pots are painted with yellows and blacks in

B. *Blackwood*

ACOMA PUEBLO, NEW MEXICO
The round structures in the foreground are bread-ovens

striking designs, representing mountains, thunder, clouds or rain, and animals. This pottery is made without a potter's wheel, with no more complex tools than the women's fingers, bits of a broken pot for a scraper, a water-worn pebble for a polisher, and a frayed stalk for a paint-brush. The women also make baskets of dyed strips of leaves and stems decorated with the same type of design. (*See* Colour Plate opp. p. 32.)

For the Hopi tribes the spirit world is peopled with many diverse, grotesque forms, known as 'katchinas'; villagers disguise themselves as katchinas and visit children to frighten them into good behaviour. When young men are initiated into full clan membership, they learn who the katchinas really are.

In this dry area the priests, since they are believed to be the rain-makers, are of great importance. Each clan in a *pueblo* has its *kiva* or ceremonial chamber, often partly underground. Here throughout the year they hold elaborate ceremonies with masked dances, the purpose of which is to obtain a good rainfall, good crops, and general good fortune for the village.

Pueblo Indians have been less affected by their contact with white men than any other North American group. The social and religious life of the surviving villages still functions in the traditional way.

AMERICAN NEGROES. In 1970 there were nearly 23 million Negroes in the United States of America—over 11% of the total U.S. population. About two-fifths of them still live in the southern states, compared with about two-thirds in 1950 and 90% in 1910. They now average nearly 20% of all residents of the Southern States, but 30% in South Carolina and 36% in Mississippi. During the two world wars the demand for Negro labour in the northern factories caused great migrations from the country districts of the South; the numbers of the northern Negroes are still increasing, mainly because of migrations from the South but also because of a high birth-rate. In the big cities the increase is most striking; between 1950 and 1970 the percentage of Negro residents rose thus: New York, 9·5% to 21·2%; Chicago, 13·6% to 32·7%; Detroit, 16·2% to 43·7%; Philadelphia, 18·2% to 33·6%; Washington, 35% to 71%. In New York most of the 1,666,600 Negroes live in Harlem.

Nearly all Negroes now living in the States were born there, and all are of African descent (*see* NEGRO AFRICANS). In 1619 a Dutch sea-captain brought a ship-load of Negroes from western Africa to the recently founded colony of Virginia. The planters bought them as 'servants', and later started the slave system which

Camera Press

A CLASS OF SIX-YEAR-OLDS IN AMERICA
State schools offer education to all children

was destined to have a fateful influence on American history. The trade remained small at first, but between 1680 and 1786 two million slaves were brought to America and the West Indies. In 1808 their importation into the United States was prohibited; but they continued to be imported illegally despite the increasingly severe measures brought against the smugglers. The Northern States sought to abolish slavery throughout the Union, but the Southern States, being dependent upon slave labour to cultivate their vast cotton and tobacco plantations, declared their right to keep slaves and to break away from the Union. This was the issue upon which the AMERICAN CIVIL WAR (q.v. Vol. X) was fought; and it was only with the defeat of the Southern States that slavery was completely abolished in 1865.

After freedom, the Southern Negroes had to compete for jobs with a large, poor white group who became bitterly anti-Negro. After the Reconstruction Period, during which the federal government had tried to protect the rights of the newly emancipated Negroes, the Southern whites passed local state laws known as the 'Black Codes', which provided unequal treatment for Negroes. They could neither rent nor own land; they could not move about freely; they were virtually excluded from voting; they were forced to travel in separate railway carriages and could not attend certain schools and universities. SECRET SOCIETIES (q.v. Vol. X), notably the Ku Klux Klan, arose to threaten and even lynch individuals who did not submit.

The position of the Negroes since then has gradually improved, particularly since the end of the Second World War. The United States Supreme Court has banned the segregation of Negroes and whites on buses. In 1955 it banned similar segregation in state schools, and directed the University of Alabama to admit two Negro students, thus setting a precedent for similar admissions. A notable Negro leader in the struggle for integration, Martin Luther King, was assassinated in 1968.

The development of education is a powerful influence towards the sweeping away of remaining inequalities. The 19th-century Negro leader, BOOKER WASHINGTON (q.v. Vol. V), urged his people to seek redress through education. In 1865 nearly 95% of the Negro population was illiterate; in 1969 illiteracy was 3·6%, compared with 0·9% among white Americans. Negroes are still improving their position not only in education but on many social and political fronts, for example, in obtaining equal voting rights. The Negro vote has become very important in the cities, and Negroes now hold office on all levels of city, state, and national government as attorneys, judges, and administrators.

Negroes, while retaining their own culture as in the rhythm of the blues, in NEGRO SPIRITUALS (q.v. Vol. XII), and in folklore, have also contributed much to the general culture as writers, scientists, artists, and musicians. They have also distinguished themselves greatly as singers and athletes. A Negro, Ralph Bunche, was awarded the Nobel Peace Prize in 1950, and became Under-Secretary of the United Nations in 1954.

AMERICANS (U.S.A.). There were over 206·5 million people living in the United States of America (1971), of whom over a quarter live in the large cities, another quarter in rural areas and one half in towns of less than 100,000 inhabitants. There are some 792,000 North AMERICAN INDIANS (q.v.) most of whom live on 200 'reservations'.

A SMALL TOWN IN NEW ENGLAND

U.S.I.S.

Then there are nearly 23 million AMERICAN NEGROES (q.v.), two-fifths of whom live in the Southern States, where they still lack some of the privileges and rights of the white population. The rest of the people of the States are of very mixed origin—British, French, German, Scandinavian, Russian, Finnish, people from the Balkans, Italians, Dutchmen, Greeks, Poles, Jews, even Chinese and Japanese. Evidence of this mixture of nationalities appears in American surnames and names of towns, and in the physical appearance of some places such as German towns in Texas, Italian communities in California, and the Chinese quarters in San Francisco. But all these different peoples eventually become Americans, learn to speak English, and in the course of two, or at most three, generations completely lose contact with their countries of origin. During the two world wars of the present century, Ameri-

cans whose ancestors came from enemy countries were quite as loyal as those of British or French descent. The Commander-in-Chief of the united allied armies in the Second World War, General Eisenhower, was himself of German descent.

The British were not the first Europeans to land in America: they were preceded by CHRISTOPHER COLUMBUS (q.v. Vol. V), an Italian, sailing under the flag of Spain, and by JOHN CABOT (q.v. Vol. V), another Italian who sailed from Bristol in 1497. It is probable also that the Vikings reached America about A.D. 1000. The first settlers were, however, British—people like SIR WALTER RALEIGH (q.v. Vol. V), John Smith, who, following Raleigh, successfully colonized Virginia, the oldest state of the Union, and the Pilgrim Fathers, religious refugees who landed on the bleak New England coast in 1620. Some of the early colonists were Dutchmen who settled in the states now known as New York, New Jersey, and Delaware—states which became English colonies in consequence of a war between England and Holland.

The early settlers were almost all people in search of freedom or opportunity. There were adventurers like the original colonists of Virginia; there were people driven by religious persecution to seek lands where they could worship as they pleased, such as the Puritans of New England, the QUAKERS (q.v.) of Pennsylvania, and the Roman Catholics of Maryland and the Carolinas. Many others crossed the ocean in the hope of a freer and happier life than Europe had offered them, as, for example, those who followed General Oglethorpe to Georgia, intending to make it a refuge for debtors and other poor people for whom there was no hope in England.

In 1775 there were thirteen colonies on the eastern seaboard of America, all owing nominal allegiance to the British Crown, very loosely bound together, often at variance, and differing widely in many ways from one another. The southern colonies had large rice, cotton, and tobacco estates worked by Negro slaves imported from Africa, while the people of the North were mainly engaged in farming and shipbuilding. The AMERICAN WAR OF INDEPENDENCE (q.v. Vol. X) with Great Britain, from 1775 to 1783, not only gained the colonists their independence, but also taught them the urgent necessity of union, without which their new-won freedom would not have lasted long. Those Americans, such as BENJAMIN FRANKLIN, the scientist, and ALEXANDER HAMILTON and James Madison who helped to frame the constitution of the United States, have as strong a claim to the grateful regard of their countrymen as GEORGE WASHINGTON, the great leader who became the first President, and THOMAS JEFFERSON who drew up the Declaration of Independence in 1776 (qq.v. Vol. V).

There are fifty states in the American Union, Alaska and Hawaii having been admitted in 1958 and 1959 respectively. The government is a Federal Government, in which the powers of the central government and those of the separate states are clearly defined. Each state has a parliament of its own which makes laws relating to local matters and raises taxes for the state's special needs. The people of each state also elect representatives to a national parliament called Congress, which sits in Washington, D.C. This Parliament makes laws binding on the whole nation, raises taxes for national purposes, and decides matters of the greatest importance, such as the declaration of war. It has two houses, the Senate and the House of Representatives; two Senators are elected to represent each state; a total of 435 Representatives are elected, the numbers being apportioned on the basis of the population of each state. The head of the government is the President, who is elected for a period of four years (see AMERICAN CONSTITUTION, Vol. X). FRANKLIN ROOSEVELT (q.v. Vol. V) was elected four times, but in 1951 an amendment to the Constitution was ratified whereby no President may be elected more than twice. Roosevelt, in fact, was the only President re-elected so often; only ten others have been elected to a second term. Some of the great presidents, such as GEORGE WASHINGTON, ABRAHAM LINCOLN (qq.v. Vol. V), and the two Roosevelts, have done much to shape the course of American history.

There has been only one serious threat to the Union—the AMERICAN CIVIL WAR (q.v. Vol. X) of 1861 to 1865 between the Northern and Southern States. The triumph of the North made certain the continuance of the United States and the end of Negro slavery. Even while the war was being fought and afterwards, hardy pioneers were extending the boundaries of the country westward until the Pacific Coast had been reached. The sense of equality which came from common struggles against wild and ruthless Nature had a very great effect upon the development of American character. From these experiences the Americans learnt respect for manual skill, forthrightness of manner, open handed hospitality, and a progressive habit of mind, all of which remain typically American characteristics.

The American is a great believer in education. Almost all children between the ages of 7 and 15 attend one of the many kinds of elementary or primary schools. Most are enrolled in the state or public schools, but others go to private schools, the best of which are state inspected. State schools are co-educational and divided into twelve grades, each grade corresponding to a year in a child's life. The last four years are spent in a high school where students may prepare for more advanced study in a university or learn a trade. At the completion of twelve years' study, the student is presented with a graduation diploma at a somewhat elaborate ceremony

U.S.I.S.

NEW YORK CITY

The World Trade Centre, composed of twin towers, is the world's tallest building (411 metres)

known as 'Commencement'. Then, if he chooses and if his work is of a sufficiently high quality, he may enter a university. Some American universities are state and some privately controlled. Certain ones, such as Harvard, Yale, Princeton, and Columbia, although young compared with the ancient universities of Europe, are recognized all over the world for their fine scholarship. Students may also attend a two-year 'junior' college, where academic studies are combined with preparation for a specific career. There are also schools which train people to be barbers, airline hostesses, salesmen, radio mechanics, and the like. As a rule AMERICAN EDUCATION (q.v. Vol. X) emphasizes the practical rather more than does British education.

It is natural that in the greatest industrial country in the world there should be many great inventors and scientists. Thomas EDISON (q.v. Vol. V), who came from Ohio, invented the phonograph and, jointly with Eastman, another American, was the inventor of motion pictures and many useful electrical devices. American scientists, in collaboration with British and Canadian, were the first to discover a means of using atomic energy, a discovery likely to affect civilization as profoundly as the invention of the steam-engine. Americans played a big part in the conquest of the air: two of them, Wilbur and Orville Wright, were the first to fly in a free heavier-than-air machine. Americans competed with the Russians in SPACE EXPLORATION (q.v. Vol. IV), launching their first satellite in 1958, and by 1969 achieving the dramatic feat of landing the first ever men on the moon.

In art, literature, and music Americans have the vitality and enthusiasm of a young nation, and their spoken language reflects the same vigour. The works of American authors such as EMERSON, Poe, WHITMAN, Mark TWAIN, Melville, Hemingway, and Faulkner (qq.v. Vol. V) are widely read by English-speaking peoples. American symphony orchestras, theatres, operahouses, museums, and libraries receive enthusiastic popular support. America early took the lead in the development of the cinema, and many of the world's most famous films were made at Hollywood in California. The Americans are also pre-eminent in outdoor activities; they excel in many forms of sport, particularly baseball, American football, athletics, lawn tennis, and boxing.

The Americans are a people who are mentally very much alive. They have always stood for the great principles of liberty and democracy, although there are among them great variations of wealth. An occasional clash between labour and management testifies to the once bitter conflict between them. The almost proverbial spirit of free enterprise stimulates initiative and imagination, although it may lead Americans to put too high a value on financial and material success. In his political relations the American sometimes shows intolerance, but in religion there is the widest toleration: everyone has a right to worship as he pleases. There are more than 250 religious sects in the country; although Protestants predominate, Catholics and Jews are increasing in numbers. There are some sects of purely American origin, such as the CHRISTIAN SCIENTIST CHURCH and the MORMON religion of Utah (qq.v.). Diversity of religion is greater in the United States than in any other country in the world except India.

See also Vol. III: UNITED STATES OF AMERICA.
See also Vol. IV: AMERICAN LANGUAGE.
See also Vol. XII: AMERICAN ART, AMERICAN LITERATURE.
See also INDEX, p. 158.

ANCESTOR WORSHIP is a very ancient widespread religious practice, perhaps the most ancient of all. It is of many different types, ranging from simple reverence for one's family ancestors to the more elaborate worship of ancestral heroes, chieftains, and kings. Ancient as it is, ancestor worship is still practised today, in New Guinea for instance. Perhaps the reason for the importance of this form of worship in early religions is that, in a world where men felt insecure against forces which they could not control or understand, it was natural to pay respect to the powers of such outstanding human beings as kings and chieftains—especially as the life-force in these persons was believed to continue, and become increasingly mysterious and perhaps more powerful, after death and detachment from the body. Ancestors also stand for life as a thing which goes on from age to age; and it may well be that early man, like many people today, felt this, believing it possible to ensure life and well-being by paying respect to and relying on those who had gone before. Worshippers of ancestors certainly feel in awe of them and wish to keep them friendly. One other thing is certain: they have no doubt that these ancestors survive. They take this for granted and their ceremonies of ancestor worship are as natural to them as conversation with their own next-door neighbours.

Here is a short account of a ceremony such as used to be held among the Min Chia, of Yunnan in western China. Every family had a domestic altar, usually placed in the principal room. On it stood three ancestral tablets, representing the heads of the family for the last three generations, and these were flanked by vases of flowers with an incense-burner in front. Sometimes there was also the image of a Buddhist saint. On the wall behind the altar were pasted red paper strips bearing the Chinese characters for Heaven and Earth. Before the morning and evening meals one of the male members of the household, usually the son of the house, would come to the altar, strike a gong, light a stick of incense in the burner before the tablets, and bow. He then fetched the bowls containing the morning meal, placed them on the altar, again struck the gong, and waited with downcast eyes for about a minute. Then he bowed again, took

ANCESTRAL FIGURE FROM NEW GUINEA
Painted wood about 4·2 metres high

FIGURE USED FOR ANCESTOR WORSHIP IN WEST AFRICA
Wood, overlaid with bronze and copper, about 60 cm high

the bowls away, and the food was eaten. This simple rite was intended to link the life of the ancestors with the daily life of their descendants, and to ensure their well-being. But sometimes more elaborate ceremonies took place. During the first fortnight in August the departed spirits were supposed to come back to the old home for a short stay. The night before they were due to depart again an altar was set up in the courtyard of the house, covered with red cloth, and spread with a number of dishes and six cups of rice wine. In the centre of the altar stood an incense-burner, flanked by two candles, and in front was a wood fire in a brazier. The head of the family read from a pile of cards the names of all the family ancestors, and then handed the cards one by one to one of the children, who burnt them in the brazier. When all the names had been read, the head of the family rose and bowed three times to the altar, and then all the family, even to the youngest child, passed in front of the altar and bowed three times with the head to the ground. The wine was then poured out on the ground and on the fire, and some pinches of the food were scattered on the ground and burned in the brazier. Finally, the family went out to the street gate and let off crackers as a farewell to the departing spirits. Everybody was extremely reverent and solemn.

In certain parts of New Guinea the tribal 'clubhouse' of the men contains curious wooden shield-like objects, each of which symbolizes an ancestor and is the object of certain ceremonies. Among the Nagas, hill-tribes of Assam, large upright stones fulfil the same end. Indeed, if a Naga were to see an English churchyard or cemetery, he would probably think that our tombstones were meant for this purpose. Here is an example of a custom which has lasted in two widely separated parts of the world.

ANCIENT CIVILIZATIONS. In recent centuries Europeans have been exploring unknown countries and meeting with peoples who were still entirely uncivilized, peoples living on wild animals and plants and with only the simplest possessions. Five thousand years ago the inhabitants of Britain were no more advanced than this, and there seems no reason why Britain should not have remained as backward as Central Africa had not invaders and explorers brought with them civilized ideas which had first grown up in the lands now known as Egypt and Mesopotamia.

It was in the great river valleys of the Nile and the Tigris and Euphrates, valleys which careful farming and irrigation could make very fertile, that the earliest-known civilizations of the world were made. It was in these valleys that men came to live together in ordered societies where all had their specialized duties, as farmer, builder, metal-worker, merchant, priest, scribe, and so forth, forming a community which could be prosperous and secure under accepted laws. This, roughly, is what is meant by civilization, although we also expect a civilized community to develop its arts, to produce poets and musicians, painters, sculptors, and fine craftsmen. Civilization of this sort would not have been possible had not men already taken that earlier great step forward, the development of farming.

Farming, which also began in the Middle East, although not in the river valleys, enabled individuals to produce more food than their own families could eat. The extra food could be used to feed specialist workers, craftsmen, and others whose products were wanted by the community.

This specialization of duties within the community is an essential part of civilization. As such specialists find it more convenient to live close together for many reasons, civilized societies commonly develop towns and cities. In fact, many of the cities which grew up in Mesopotamia some time before 3000 B.C. stood on the sites of older villages, the homes of simple farming communities.

One of the oldest known farming communities grew up by a natural spring in the valley of the river Jordan. By about 9,000 years ago these people were already living in close-packed houses defended by stone walls and towers. This ancient township has been discovered by archaeologists beneath the ruined city of Jericho which was captured by Joshua and the Israelites nearly 6,000 years after its foundation.

The Anatolian peninsula (modern Turkey) was another region where farming began very early and people were able to live together in large, settled communities. At Catal Huyuk, for instance, there was a town of neat mud-brick houses covering 12 hectares flourishing by 6000 B.C. It had shrines with sacred images and walls painted with ritual scenes of men and animals.

It is interesting to follow the growth of civilization in a single place. Erech, (or Uruk) on the lower Euphrates, is a good example. If a visitor had gone there in the middle of the 4th millennium B.C. he would have found a village street lined with the small houses of peasant farmers and simple craftsmen and perhaps a modest place of worship. Returning some six centuries later he could wander through the streets of a city with a population of tens of thousands and splendid temples towering against the sky. It would be ruled over by a king as steward of the gods and by his court officials. More significant still, priestly scribes were developing the art of writing so that they could keep account of the great wealth of the temples.

Erech shows how civilization grew in one of its earliest centres, the rich land of the SUMERIANS (q.v.). By 3000 B.C. town life of a kind was developing also in Egypt, although there by the Nile society remained more rural (*see* EGYPTIAN CIVILIZATION). In another 500 years or so true city life had spread to a third great river valley, that of the Indus in Pakistan and India (*see* INDIAN CIVILIZATIONS). There the streets were laid out on a grid plan as in modern American cities.

Civilization is like a spreading fire: from these most ancient centres it was to extend further and further afield. Partly it was carried by merchants who might establish trading posts that grew into towns, much as the British established Hong Kong and Singapore. Sometimes when farming was spread by people seeking fresh land, urban life might develop locally. It was by these means, and also by direct military conquest, that civilization radiated from Mesopotamia, Egypt, and India. One of the most natural lines for it to follow from the delta lands of Sumer was north-westward up the Tigris and Euphrates valleys. Thus we find Semites founding Assur, which long after was to be the capital city of the ASSYRIANS (q.v.), in the plateau country of the northern Tigris basin.

By 2400 B.C. Semitic peoples who were settled in Akkad, the country immediately north of the Delta, under their great leader Sargon conquered the Sumerians. Six hundred years later another great Semitic ruler, Hammurabi, who had his capital in the hitherto modest city of Babylon, welded together Assyria, Akkad, and Sumer into one—the BABYLONIAN empire (q.v.), whose capital city became the richest and perhaps the most beautiful in western Asia. But before very long Assyria broke away and again became an independent state—and from that time onward for many centuries there was rivalry and frequent warfare between Assyria and Babylonia. The Assyrians sacked Babylon at the beginning of the 7th century B.C. A little later they conquered Egypt. Fortune turned rapidly against them, however, and by the end of the same century Assyrian power had been ended by the combined armies of the Babylonians and Medes. It was after this success that the Medes and PERSIANS (q.v.) began their conquests, until in the 5th century B.C. the Persian Empire included all the ancient centres of civilization from western India to Egypt. It was the Greeks who prevented the Persians from pushing even farther west, into Europe.

To return to earlier times, another region where civilization was destined quite soon to be established was that lying between the two ancient centres of Egypt and Mesopotamia, the lands forming a relatively fertile strip along the eastern margin of the Mediterranean, where in time the Amorites and CANAANITES, the PHOENICIANS and HEBREWS (qq.v.) were to have their own important history. This region, through which traffic between Egypt and Mesopotamia passed, was bound always to be a warring ground between these two great countries, sometimes one and sometimes the other gaining control. The Egyptians had early trading-posts on the coast, a famous one being at Byblos in Lebanon which handled, among other goods, the famous cedar wood of the Lebanon. The Phoenicians themselves became among the greatest trading and seafaring peoples of ancient times. Their adventurous traders pushed as far westward as the Atlantic; they established colonies, including the famous Carthage, and they perfected the ALPHABET (q.v. Vol. IV) that was to be adapted by the Greeks and so become the parent of our own. To the north were a mixed indigenous and Indo-European people, the HITTITES (q.v.), whose territory extended into the high plateau lands of Asia Minor. At the times of their greatest strength the Hittites pushed southwards, dominated the Canaanites and other peoples of Syria and Palestine, and were involved in conflict with Egypt.

So in the 2nd millennium B.C. there were civilized peoples living all around the eastern end of the Mediterranean, from Egypt to Asia Minor, all more or less in touch and affecting one another both by warfare and trade. But already, long before this, a first foothold of civilization had been established in Europe. Farming communities had been established in the island and some of the neighbouring shores of the Aegean for thousands of years and were improving their craftsmanship, housing and trade. Then about 3000 B.C., probably helped on by contacts with the eastern Mediterranean and Egypt, Crete moved ahead of the rest of the Aegean. Ruling families began to live in fine palaces with an elegant court where the fine arts flowered. This MINOAN CIVILIZATION (q.v.) of Crete was in many ways a very brilliant one, as is well shown by the famous palace of Knossos. The island became the centre of a seafaring civilization which naturally soon spread to the islands and shores of the Aegean. It was carried to the mainland of Greece, where the later civilization is known as MYCENAEAN (q.v.) after the great city of Mycenae, ruled by the earliest known Greek-speaking people, the Achaeans of Homer's poems. It seems that in about 1900 B.C. northern invaders may have begun to enter Greece and the Aegean—uncivilized peoples coming from the heart of the European continent and probably

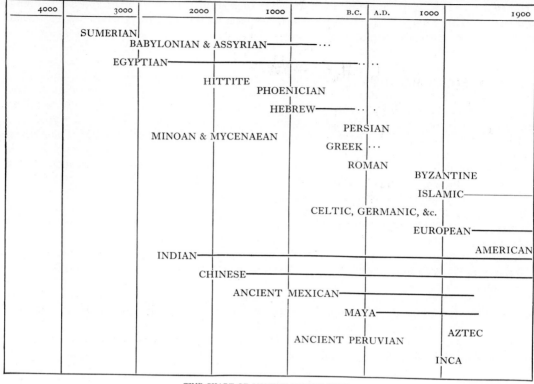

4000	3000	2000	1000	B.C.	A.D.	1000	1900

SUMERIAN
BABYLONIAN & ASSYRIAN———— ...
EGYPTIAN——————————— .. ..
HITTITE
PHOENICIAN
HEBREW—————— .. .
PERSIAN
MINOAN & MYCENAEAN
GREEK |...
ROMAN
BYZANTINE
ISLAMIC————
CELTIC, GERMANIC, &c.
EUROPEAN———
AMERICAN
INDIAN—————————————
CHINESE——————————
ANCIENT MEXICAN————
MAYA———
AZTEC
ANCIENT PERUVIAN
INCA

TIME CHART OF ANCIENT CIVILIZATIONS

This chart shows only approximately when the chief civilizations of the world flourished, for it is often impossible to date the beginning and end of a civilization accurately

speaking an Indo-European language from which the Greek tongue grew. It was from a mixture of northern invaders and aboriginal inhabitants that the classical GREEK CIVILIZATION (q.v.) was to develop a thousand years later.

During the 4th millennium B.C. the basic ideas on which all civilizations rest were beginning to spread towards western and northern Europe. These ideas were, of course, those concerned with farming, knowledge of which was gradually carried along the shores of the Mediterranean and Atlantic and along the Danube valley until at last it reached Britain and Scandinavia.

But although agriculture was now practised all over Europe, and bronze-working and other technical skills were developed, it still took an immensely long time for any of the more advanced elements of the Eastern civilizations to follow. Indeed, it was left to the Greeks and Romans to introduce civilized life to western Europe. Greek traders, establishing colonial cities along the Mediterranean, greatly influenced all the countries with which they made contact. The Etruscans, who were establishing their own unusual civilization in northern Italy, owed much to them, and the Etruscans in turn played an important part in the foundation of the ROMAN state (q.v.) in the 6th and 5th centuries B.C. Greek ideas, too, spreading both from their own trading cities and by way of Italy, helped to develop the still barbarous but in many ways splendid life of the CELTS (q.v.). Civilization had come slowly to the West; yet it was from the West, not from the East, that fresh waves of explorers, traders, and colonists were to set out to carry it to America, to Africa, and to the Pacific. In this way, during recent centuries, ideas and ways of life which originated by the Tigris, Euphrates, and Nile have been spread throughout the entire planet.

When the Spaniards invaded South and Central America in the 16th century they discovered that there already existed well-advanced civilizations which had been developing independently of the civilizations of the Old World.

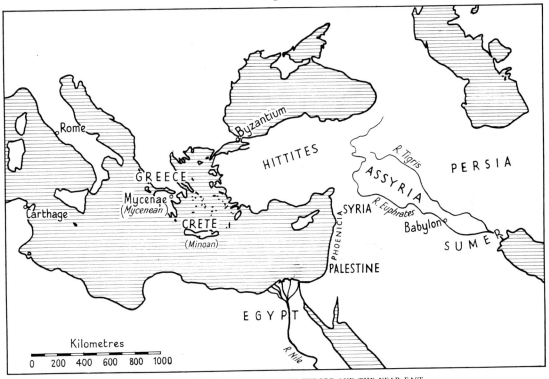

MAP OF THE ANCIENT CIVILIZATIONS OF EUROPE AND THE NEAR EAST

This map shows the approximate positions of the centres of the chief civilizations, regardless of the periods at which they flourished

The culture of ANCIENT MEXICO (q.v.), though probably not as old as that of Mesopotamia or Egypt, is now thought to date back to many centuries before Christ. That in ANCIENT PERU (q.v.) also goes back to about 1000 B.C. These were followed up by the great civilizations of the MAYA, the AZTECS, and the INCAS (qq.v.). It is interesting to note that, advanced as these people were in many directions—for instance, in social organization, in mathematical calculations, and in many forms of art—they were, even by the 15th century A.D., without some inventions known in the East for thousands of years. Thus the wheel was not known anywhere in America until the Europeans came; and the Incas had no form of writing.

In the Far East, in China, another independent civilization grew up in another river valley, the Yellow River or Hwang-ho in north China. CHINESE CIVILIZATION (q.v.) is not so old as that of Mesopotamia or Egypt; but it is the oldest civilization still continuing today, and it has lasted, with only temporary breaks, for some 4000 years or more.

See also ARCHAEOLOGY.

ANDAMAN ISLANDERS. The earliest account we have of the Negritoes of the Andaman Islands in the Bay of Bengal comes from some Arab travellers about A.D. 870. They reported that the islanders were black, with woolly hair and most terrifying expressions, that they were quite naked, had feet almost a span long, and that they ate human flesh quite raw. Marco Polo some 400 years later gave an equally bad report, describing them as 'most brutish and savage' with heads, eyes, and teeth resembling dogs. 'Their dispositions are cruel and every person not of their own nation that they can lay hands on they kill and eat.' It is no wonder that the islands were feared and avoided.

Their evil reputation is, however, quite undeserved. They are a pygmy people, the men usually not much over 1·5 metres. Their hair is black and frizzy and seldom more than 5 to 8 cm long, and their skin is very black, like a well-polished black-leather shoe. They have slender bodies and small hands and feet. They are not naturally quarrelsome, and their anger soon cools. Husbands and wives show much devotion to each other and to their children, who are

British Museum

NATIVE OF THE ANDAMAN ISLANDS USING AN ADZE

generally given whatever they want, however unsuitable.

They live in small bands, spend much of their time in games and sports, and they have a passion for dancing. Dances are held on all ceremonial occasions, such as the beginning of a new season, a marriage, or the end of mourning, as well as at any time of general rejoicing. They dance and sing for hours by moonlight or by the blaze of the camp fires to the accompaniment of beating on a curved piece of wood.

Food is their chief interest in life, and as they have no cultivated crops they depend on hunting, fishing, and collecting forest produce. They collect shellfish round the coast, they spear turtles and shoot fish with bows and arrows, and they hunt game, especially pigs, in the forest. The men make excellent canoes from hollowed-out tree trunks, some of them up to 9 metres long.

In their hot moist climate, where the thermometer seldom drops below 27°C, there is no need for clothes, but the Andamanese wear such a wealth of circlets, garters, bracelets, waistbands, necklaces and strings of shells and bones that they cannot be called naked. On special occasions they are almost covered with strips of palm-leaves, and they also paint their bodies with elaborate patterns on ceremonial occasions.

Until the coming of Europeans there was no knowledge of iron in the islands, and shell was used instead. The axe or adze had a shell blade, spears and arrows had shell tips, and knives were of sharpened bamboo. The Andamanese had great difficulty in making fire; so they had to keep their fires always burning and, when travelling, they carried a smouldering torch from one camp to another.

Their huts are quickly made from poles and thatched with palm-leaves. They are usually open at the sides, but can keep out the heaviest rains. Several of these huts in a circle round a central dancing-ground form the village. But there is no permanent settlement, as the whole community moves from camping-ground to camping-ground according to the season and the food supplies.

The Andamanese have no chiefs, but as with most hunting groups, whoever has most experience acts as leader. Beyond this all are free and equal, the only restraint being public opinion. They worship the spirits, some good and some bad, of the sun, moon, winds, rocks, and creatures of the forest who, as they believe, were once men and women (*see* ANIMISM). There are no priests, but some men know more about the spirits than ordinary folk, and these are respected and feared, being credited with ability to foretell the future, to cure illnesses, and to control the weather.

See also PYGMIES.
See also Vol. III: ANDAMAN ISLANDS.

ANGEL. This word is used in the Bible for a divine messenger sent by God to minister to human beings on earth. Though the Jews believed that Jehovah was the One True God, they recognized angels as messengers sent by Him to guide and comfort His chosen people. He alone was to be worshipped as the Lord of the Land, jealously demanding the sole allegiance of His people. But so high and exalted was He that the Hebrews came to regard Him much as they would have regarded a powerful eastern monarch surrounded by vassal princes whom He had conquered. It is thus possible that the idea of angels originally represented in the Hebrew mind the conquest of the old gods and spirits of heathen Palestine by the One True God. Jehovah in this way gathered round Him an increasingly large

THE SEVEN ANGELS OF THE APOCALYPSE
Illumination from a 13th-century Apocalypse

'court' composed of the 'cherubim', represented with outspread wings, the 'seraphim' or flying serpents with flaming wings, and the archangels, such as Gabriel, Michael, Raphael, Phanuel, and Uriel, who, as His princes, continually await God's commands. Thus, 'all the host of heaven stood by Him on His right hand and on His left'.

There were also angels who presided over the workings of nature, such as the motions of the stars, the rain, and the hail. Others looked after the different nations, while every human being had his own particular guardian or helper, just as in Persia each individual was assigned a 'double', or *fravashi*, at birth. There were, again, angels who recorded the deeds of men, keeping an account of everything said and done by each individual. Finally, there was the angel of death who sooner or later was destined to visit everybody, good and bad alike, and announce that their last hour had come.

In the New Testament we find much the same beliefs. It was the archangel Gabriel, the 'mighty man of God', who is said to have been sent to Zacharias, the father of John the Baptist, and to Mary the mother of Jesus, to explain to them how God was going to visit and redeem the world. When the long-expected Messiah was born at Bethlehem, the glad tidings were proclaimed to the shepherds by a 'heavenly host'. At the end of the period of temptation in the desert, and after the great struggle in the garden of Gethsemane, an angel ministered to Jesus, and both His resurrection and ascension were declared by angelic messengers. Apart from these special occasions, every child is said to have a guardian helper watching over him, as has every member of the Church. The apostles we are told, were delivered from prison by an angel, and by the same heavenly messengers Philip was shown where to go and St. Paul

National Gallery

THE ARCHANGEL RAPHAEL LEADING TOBIAS ON HIS JOURNEY
Italian Painting, 15th century, School of Verrocchio

times offered to angels, they were never worshipped as gods. This was strictly forbidden, lest they should be confused with the pagan gods they had replaced.

There has been a good deal of discussion about the nature, shape, and characteristics of angels. Some have claimed that they were invisible spirits without any bodily form; others, that they have a thin rather ghost-like or fiery appearance. But all are agreed that they are created beings like man, and since some of them are said to have fallen away from God before the world was made, it has been generally supposed that they are capable of sinning and therefore must have free will. Their life and work consist wholly and solely in serving God in their several ways, but, as John of Damascus very wisely declared in summing up his description of an angel, 'the form and character of its substance God alone knows who created it'. It is perhaps a pity that later writers and thinkers were not content to leave it at that, since there is no way of finding out exactly what an angel is like. But in the Middle Ages much time was spent on speculations which really did not throw any light on the problem. After the Reformation in northern Europe, angels were just taken for granted; but except in the Roman Catholic Church no prayers were made to them or asked from them; so that they have tended to fall into the background, having lost their original purpose as divine messengers. Nevertheless, the fall of Lucifer and the other angels who rebelled against God gave John Milton a dramatic theme for the greatest of English epic poems, PARADISE LOST (q.v. Vol. XII).

Besides Jews and Christians, the third community who recognize the existence of angels are the Muslims (*see* ISLAM). When the prophet Muhammad in the 7th century A.D. began his movement in Arabia, the Arabs were acquainted with a great company of inferior spirits. These he took over and, borrowing a good many of his ideas from Jewish and Christian sources, he made the good spirits the servants of God (Allah), as angels, and the bad spirits the servants of Satan, as demons. Both, he taught, were formed from one single substance and were given the power of reason, life, and speech. The angels neither eat nor drink and are without sex, their function being to act as the bodyguard of God, and obey His commands fully. Most of their time is spent in repeating the sacred name

what to do when he was shipwrecked. Therefore, like the Jews, the Christians thought that they were guided and helped by the ministry of angels and that angels would carry their prayers to God, just as at the last they would bear their souls to Paradise and separate the wheat from the tares (i.e. the righteous from the wicked) when they reaped the harvest of the world on the Day of Judgement.

As the Church spread from Palestine into eastern Europe the angels took the place of the old pagan gods and spirits. Villages, towns, and countries, as well as individuals, were assigned guardians to protect them from the powers of evil. So numerous, in fact, became the heavenly host that it was divided into ranks and offices on much the same plan as were the officials of the Roman Empire. Dionysius the Areopagite arranged them in three hierarchies containing three choirs each: Seraphim, Cherubim, and Thrones; Dominions, Virtues, and Powers; Principalities, Archangels, and Angels. Of these only the last two choirs had an immediate mission to men. Although prayers were some-

'Allah'; but whatever they do is done to His glory. Chief among them are the four throne-bearers, the first of whom prays for all true believers, the second for tame animals, the third for birds, and the fourth for wild beasts. Then come the cherubim who day and night do nothing but repeat the words 'glory to Allah' and live in a particular part of the sky.

Of the four Archangels—Michael, Gabriel, Azra'il, and Israf'il—Michael carried the revelation recorded in the Koran to Muhammad, and has since been responsible for providing food for the body and knowledge for the mind, while his assistants watch over the world for good, and control the forces of nature. His form, however, is so wonderful that it is known only to Allah. Azra'il is the angel of death. So terrible is his appearance that, when the rest of the company first saw him, they fainted and did not recover consciousness for a thousand years. It is he who carries away the souls of men and delivers them either to the 'angels of compassion', or to the 'angels of punishment', according to whether the dying person is a believer or an unbeliever. Israf'il, on the other hand, puts the souls into the body at birth, and he will blow the trumpet at the Last Day and at the general resurrection. At the gate of Paradise an angel called Ridwan is stationed and another terrible being, known as Malik, guards hell.

Every Muslim is protected from evil spirits (jinn) by four angels, two guarding him by day and another two by night. These, it is thought, change places at sunrise and sunset, and keep a record of his doings. The Jinn were created 2,000 years before Adam, but sinned against God and were degraded from their high estate. The greatest among them was Iblis (*see* SATAN), who was formed of smokeless fire, and has control over the rest of the fallen angels. But although angels play such a prominent part in Muhammadan belief, they are generally thought to be inferior to human believers as they do not share in the delights of Paradise.

See also HEAVEN.

ANGLICAN CHURCH, *see* CHURCH OF ENGLAND.

ANGLO-CATHOLICS, *see* CHURCH OF ENGLAND.

ANGLO-SAXONS, *see* BRITISH PEOPLES.

ANIMISM. This word was originally used to describe the belief that the development of all living things arises from more than merely material causes—that there is, in fact, such a thing as soul or spirit (Latin: *anima*). To this extent, then, all Christians or people of any religion may be called animists; so, too, may anyone who believes in ghosts. But the word has more recently been used in a special sense to describe a primitive form of religion which peoples the world with countless spirits—varying, of course, in size and importance. All sorts of visible objects, and not merely human beings and animals, are thought of as alive: not only is there a great spirit in the sun and in the moon, but there is a smaller one in the tree at your door, and another in the stream. Not everything is, in practice, believed to be animated by a spirit: many things, such as a bit of flint, a club or spear, are not treated as containing individual spirits in ordinary circumstances. But on occasions when such objects are used in actions beyond man's ordinary power—when, for instance, the spear strikes powerfully from a long distance—then the object is thought of as being animated by a spirit.

One form of animism, known as fetishism or *juju*, is strongly developed in West Africa. In South Nigeria, for example, there are believed to be *jujus* in tools and weapons, in lakes, rivers, and springs, in the farmland, house, and hearth, and also in specially made objects (fetishes or *jujus*). Such objects—the smallpox *juju*, for example—are worshipped because spirits also called *jujus* are supposed to inhabit them. The *juju* is believed to cause the good or ill fortune connected with the object; and special ceremonies must be used to appeal to its goodwill.

The Greeks believed in little spirits that swarmed like midges or bacteria; and the Japanese have any number of them—indeed, a famous convert to Christianity, Uchimura, exclaimed: 'One God, not ten million, that *is* joyful news'. India knows them by the score as *devatas* or godlings, and a large part of the Hinduism of the village populations has been described as 'spirit scaring and spirit squaring'.

It has been argued that there is another primitive religion older than animism. This has therefore been called pre-animism or animatism. It has also been called dynamism, because it is a belief in a vague force, rather like electricity, which inhabits all sorts of things, and makes

British Museum

A WEST AFRICAN FETISH

A nail is stuck into the figure to mark each time a petition is
made to the spirit that inhabits it

them behave as they do. This force is reverenced wherever it occurs. It is certainly the case that in many different parts of the world such a force is believed in, though it is called by a number of different names, *mana* in Polynesia, *orenda* or *wakonda* among some American Indians, in West Africa *orisha*, in Madagascar *andriamanitra*, and perhaps, in Latin, *numen*. But we have no direct evidence as to whether man in the earliest stage of his religious beliefs did in fact develop what we call an 'abstract' idea or use a 'general' term

such as a *force*, or *power*, or *principle*. Early man probably thought rather as a child thinks: a child starts with a single 'concrete' thing, like 'my daddy', 'my doll', 'my shoes', and does not as easily grasp the meaning of such words as 'parenthood', or 'mechanism', or 'footgear'. So it may well be that in the beginning man thought of the power or *mana* in his own particular spear-thrower, or in the bull he owned, or in the volcano just above his village, and only came very much later to think of *power-in-general*. The real question is, did he think of the *mana* or power in his spear-thrower as a living person, or simply as a power? If the former, then he was an animist. If the latter, then he was a dynamist.

APOCRYPHA, *see* BIBLE; SACRED BOOKS, Section 6.

ARABS. The term 'Arab' is applied firstly to the inhabitants of the Arabian Peninsula, and secondly to people, wherever they live, who speak Arabic and claim descent from the Arab conquerors of North Africa, Syria, and Mesopotamia.

The Arabs are often spoken of as members of the Semitic race; but they are, even those in Arabia, of mixed origin, and it is better to use the term 'Semitic' only for the group of languages to which Arabic belongs (*see* SEMITIC LANGUAGES, Vol. IV). This group includes Hebrew, Syriac, and Aramaic, the last being the language of Babylonia which was adopted by the Jews in place of Hebrew during the captivity. It is probable that before the time of Muhammad the Arabic language was confined to central and southern Arabia; but as a result of the Muslim conquests in the 7th century A.D. it became the language of Syria (including Palestine), Mesopotamia (now called Iraq), Egypt, and the North African coast as far as Morocco. It spread later to parts of the northern Sudan.

The great majority of the people of these countries are Muslim (*see* ISLAM); but in Egypt there are many Christian Arabs known as COPTS (q.v.), and in the Lebanon there is a large body of Maronites who acknowledge the authority of the Pope, though their clergy are married. There used to be large and flourishing Jewish communities in most Arab countries, but since the establishment of ISRAEL (q.v.) most of them have preferred to go there, so today there are only a few thousands left. There are also many sects which, though Muslim in name, are outside orthodox Islam. The best known of these are the Druzes who live in the Lebanon and in part of Syria (*see* SYRIANS).

The great Arab conquests of the 7th century began with the rise of the faith of Islam under the leadership of MUHAMMAD (q.v. Vol. V). At this time there was no power anywhere strong enough to withstand the amazing outburst of vitality and energy among the Arab people. The Khalifas (or Caliphs) who followed Muhammad were capable military leaders and rulers, and according to the standards of the day were tolerant as conquerors. The Arabs, in spite of continual fighting, increased enormously in numbers, taking the women of those they had killed, and the children of these captives were reckoned as pure-bred Arabs. They were in this way able to keep in the field large armies. In the west they pushed on to the Straits of Gibraltar and in A.D. 709 crossed into Spain (*see* MOORS). In the east they gradually overran Persia, much of central Asia, and western India.

As well as military conquests the Arabs also carried with them to the lands they overran their religious faith and their culture. At a time when art and learning were at a low ebb in Europe, the Arabs were directing their great vigour and zeal to science, literature, and art, as well as fighting. They absorbed the culture of Greece and Persia and made it their own, and, when Christian Europe was hardly emerging from the gloom and barbarism of the Dark Ages, the Arab cities of Bagdad (in Iraq), Cairo (in Egypt), and Cordova (in Spain) were centres of a brilliant civilization.

During the 7th and 8th centuries, after periods of civil war, the centre of Arab power was moved first to Damascus and then to Bagdad (of *Arabian Nights* fame). In course of time Persian and Turkish officials began to replace Arabs; and as the Turks became more and more powerful, the Khalifas declined into being little more than their tools, until in 1258, when Mongol hordes from central Asia invaded Persia and sacked Bagdad, the last of them was murdered. From then until 1918, after the First World War, the eastern Arab countries were either in fact or in name part of the Turkish Empire, although Egypt enjoyed a considerable degree of freedom after Mohammed Ali founded the reigning dynasty in 1805.

When the Turkish empire collapsed in 1918 a

J. Allan Cash

WORKING AMONG DATE-PALMS IN SAUDI ARABIA

number of new Arab countries were set up, some of them (Iraq and Palestine) under the protection (or 'mandate') of Britain, and others (Syria and Lebanon) under the mandate of France. The Second World War brought all Arab countries complete independence. Nationalist feelings everywhere grew stronger, particularly because of what Arabs felt was the unjust creation of a Jewish state (Israel) in what they regarded as Arab land. A League of Arab states was founded in 1945, and often since then Arab governments have tried to unite with each other to make themselves stronger. But so far all these efforts have come to nothing.

The modern Arabs are divided into three main classes—the townsmen, the peasants, and the BEDOUIN (q.v.). We hear much more of the Bedouin than is warranted by either their numbers or importance. They never intermarry with either the townsmen or the peasants. The townsmen are much the same from Tangier to Basra. They are traders and craftsmen, clerks and government officials. As a rule they can read and write, and they wear European clothes. If they can afford it they will often try to send their sons—and even their daughters—to Europe or America to complete their education. It is

MARKET DAY AT TOZEUR, TUNISIA

Tunisian Embassy

very rare for a townsman to have more than one wife. In an Arab town all the makers and sellers of a particular class of goods live in the same street or quarter, as they used to do in London in the Middle Ages.

The towns on the Arabian peninsula are much less europeanized, except for the ones closely connected with the oil industry, such as Kuwait, Bahrain, and Dhahran. From the point of view of Muslim Arabs everywhere the most important towns are the Holy Cities of Mecca (where the Prophet Muhammad was born) and Medina (where he died). Every year thousands of people from all over the Muslim world go on pilgrimage to these cities, which no non-Muslims are ever allowed inside.

The great majority of the Arabs, however, are peasants (*fellaheen*). They are often confused with the Bedouin, whom they resemble in many ways. They dress very much like Bedouin, and their women are unveiled. Mostly illiterate, they are organized in tribes and observe tribal law in matters connected with blood feuds. But between the peasants and the Bedouin there is a great gulf fixed, each usually regarding the other with hatred and contempt. The peasants live in

villages. Their sheikhs are landowners, often employing many ploughmen; but the majority of the peasants are smallholders, who scratch a bare living by toiling from dawn to dusk on their holdings, often with primitive implements. In Egypt many crops, particularly cotton and sugar-cane, are grown by means of irrigation; but over most of the Arab world the crops depend on the rain. The chief crops grown are wheat and barley; but in many parts there are also olives and vines.

The peasants own many camels which they use entirely for transport, never riding them. (*See* Colour Plate opp. p. 256.) They usually buy these from the Bedouin. The sheikhs ride thoroughbred mares, of which they are very proud. The peasants ride donkeys. All ploughing is done with oxen, as it was in England up to about 200 years ago, and the ploughs do not turn the soil over, but merely push through it to break it up. The corn is brought into the villages on camels and piled on the threshing-floors. It is then, in many parts, threshed by means of sledges. These, which are studded with spikes, are drawn by donkeys and driven round and round the threshing-floors by small boys. The corn is then separated from the chaff by winnowing. The peasants also own some cattle and sheep, which, apart from the plough-oxen, are usually put in charge of herdsmen belonging to the smaller and poorer Bedouin tribes.

Unlike the townsmen, the richer peasants often marry up to four wives. These are fully employed in attending to the wants of their large households and the guests whom they often entertain. All rich Arabs keep open house and, though often extremely astute in money matters, like to have a reputation for hospitality.

See also EGYPTIANS; IRAQIS; MOORS; SYRIANS.
See also Vol. III: ARABIA; EGYPT; IRAQ; SYRIA.
See also Vol. IV: ARABIC LANGUAGE.
See also Vol. XII: ARABIC LITERATURE; ISLAMIC ART.

ARCHAEOLOGY. Archaeology is the study of the past. An archaeologist looks for and studies all kinds of traces left by ancient peoples—anything from a whole city to a single sherd of pottery. When an historian investigates the past, he studies mostly written documents; these are his primary sources. An archaeologist is interested in material things, and from studying them and asking himself questions about them he builds up a picture of the life of the people who made and used them. The prehistoric period in any area is the period of human settlement before the first written records, and most archaeologists are interested in the remote past. But, since written records do not tell us everything we would like to know about the life of literate peoples, there is also plenty of scope for the archaeologist within the historic period. His findings make what is recorded in words more real and vivid to us, and contemporary documents, when they exist, help him to interpret his findings. It is rare for him to be responsible for discovering written sources, though this can happen. For example, archaeologists have found the Linear B tablets in Crete, quantities of Roman and Greek inscriptions, and CUNEIFORM WRITING (q.v. Vol. IV), in the Near East.

The problems of studying any particular period of the past are very specialized; there are many different branches of archaeology, such as Prehistoric, Classical, or Medieval. The main periods of the past are subdivided, and archaeologists specialize by period (for example,

Lockley's Archaeological Society photo, John Dettmar

WELWYN, HERTFORDSHIRE: ARCHAEOLOGISTS EXCAVATING THE ROMAN BATH HOUSE
This site was discovered when the motorway was being made. It is now preserved in a steel vault underneath the motorway embankment

Palaeolithic (Old Stone Age) archaeology within the Prehistoric period), and often by area (New World Archaeology, Near Eastern Archaeology and so forth). Other archaeological specializations develop from the pursuit of a particular kind of evidence demanding particular skills: thus, Marine Archaeology involves the scientific exploration and recovery mainly of ancient shipwrecks and their contents but sometimes also of ancient sites inundated by rising sea-levels. Underwater explorers, notably Jacques-Ives Cousteau, have devised new helpful techniques (see BATHYSCAPHE, Vol. IV). Several shipwrecks of prehistoric age are now known, a famous example being the find at Cape Gelidonya in Turkey of a sunk Bronze Age merchant ship with intact cargo. Industrial archaeology is concerned with recording, while they still survive, buildings, machines and communications of the Early Industrial period—in Britain, notably those of the INDUSTRIAL REVOLUTION (q.v. Vol. VII).

Archaeologists' methods of study are also very varied. Excavation to recover new evidence is only one approach, though a very important one. It is an extremely careful and scientific process. A site may contain several settlements of different ages, each built upon and disturbing the ruins of its predecessor, and each producing a different set of artefacts—tools, weapons, ornaments, jewellery, pottery and utensils, coins, furnishings of all kinds—not to mention building debris, burials, food refuse, scattered or in rubbish pits, and natural soil accumulation. Amongst all this the archaeologist may find objects imported from elsewhere. If similar objects have been dated at known sites in other areas or other countries, this may help him to date the new finds, or the new layer he is working on. So he must recover all objects with great care, and record their true position in the sequence of deposits at the site. He has to understand how the series of strata or layers was formed, and discover whether it has remained undisturbed. In any simple, undisturbed stratified sequence, the oldest layers must always be at the bottom and the youngest at the top. But the sequence is rarely so simple, since disturbances may be profound; for example one of the 'tells' (settlement mounds) of the Near East, such as Jericho, may show many phases of destruction and rebuilding, with intervening periods of desertion. In a long sequence, the earliest levels may be several tens of metres below the modern surface.

The amount of information the archaeologist can achieve depends on the conditions of survival at the site he is excavating. At prehistoric sites, sometimes only the very durable materials like stone or pottery may survive. Perfectly dry sites and waterlogged sites are best for preserving soft materials such as skin, textiles, leather, wood or plant remains. The rich finds from TUTANKHAMEN's TOMB (q.v. Vol. XII) offer an example of fine preservation in dry conditions, while waterlogging is well illustrated by the survival of objects at several Neolithic LAKE DWELLINGS sites (q.v.) in Switzerland. In Siberia, complete mammoths (skin, hair, soft parts of the body, bone, and ivory)—were preserved from Late Pleistocene times in deep-frozen ground.

Not all archaeologists excavate: others specialize in the study, identification, comparison and interpretation of archaeological finds, especially different kinds of artefacts, notably pottery, and implements of stone or of different metals. Such study may involve taking many precise measurements, analyzing raw materials, studying traces of wear under a microscope, or programming a computer to carry out mathematical or statistical comparisons of sets of objects. This is often essential to the building up of a proper sequence of stages in the history of occupation of an area.

It is not only the artefacts and structures which are important for an understanding of man's past, but also all changes in the natural background—climate, landforms, resources of animal and plant food, availability of raw material, and so forth. The evidence is there, alongside the cultural material, and interpreting it is called Environmental Archaeology.

In this study specialists from many fields have essential contributions to make: palaeontologists or zoologists help interpret animal bones, botanists study plant remains and pollen grains, geologists or soil-scientists throw light on the natural processes of deposition, alteration and erosion which have been at work while the strata were forming. The identification of contemporary pollen grains preserved in archaeological deposits is one of the most striking ways of reconstructing a former environment, but many other kinds of evidence are needed.

Indeed, the archaeologist can now call on scientific aids at most stages of his work. To help him discover sites, he may use aerial photography or various prospecting methods (like magnetometer or resistivity surveying) to help him locate

A HOPI INDIAN BASKET-MAKER, ARIZONA

buried features. Where ditches have been dug and later filled, or where buried masonry lies below the surface, the crops are tall and rich or poor and stunted respectively, because of the varying depths of soil. From the air, these effects show up by shadow or colour variation.

A major problem has always been the dating of sites and finds. Stratification helps an archaeologist to establish relative dating (that is, to say whether certain settlements or artefact types are older or younger than others), but it does not directly help him to estimate ages in years. Radiocarbon dating is a highly important chronometric method, with a range of at least 40,000 years. This method depends on the fact that all living organic matter contains carbon, of which a fixed proportion is Carbon-14, a RADIO-ACTIVE ISOTOPE (q.v. Vol. VIII). This unstable isotope decays at a known and constant rate, from the death of the organism, since the intake of fresh carbon then ceases. When the archaeologist uncovers some suitable 'dead' organic material such as wood, charcoal, bone or shell, it may be possible under laboratory conditions to 'count' the surviving amount of Carbon-14 in a sample of it and thus establish, with a margin of error, the length of time since the organism died. This usually offers a reasonably good date (in the sense of an estimate of age) for the archaeological layer from which the sample came, provided it was in its correct layer there (another reason for minute care in excavation). Some tens of thousands of radiocarbon dates exist, from all over the world, extending in some areas well back into the Palaeolithic period. Dates have even been obtained for some of the later industries of Neanderthal Man.

Other dating methods depend on radioactive decay of isotopes of other elements, notably of uranium and potassium. The Potassium-Argon method has helped to date some of the earliest human industries of all, including the Old Stone Age finds from East Rudolf in North Kenya which are around $2\frac{1}{2}$ million years old. This method usually applies to rocks or deposits of volcanic origin. Fission-track dating, depending on the decay of a uranium isotope, can be used for both short-range and long-range dating of artificial or natural (volcanic) glass. Thermoluminescence dating is a relatively new method, applicable to pottery and fired clay, derived from their containing various radioactive impurities which start to break down from the time

British Museum

SILVER BOWL FOUND IN THE SAXON BURIAL SHIP AT SUTTON HOO, SUFFOLK

A Saxon chieftain was buried in this ship with weapons, jewellery, and precious vessels. This bowl is Byzantine workmanship

that the pottery is fired at a certain critical temperature.

Archaeology, as a careful study rather than a romantic interest, is not much more than a hundred years old. The major methodological advances began in the second half of the nineteenth century, and the subject has developed at an increasing pace ever since. Dramatic steps forward have been taken since the Second World War; now, if the archaeologist is not himself a scientist, he is at least accustomed to digest and coordinate the contributions of scientist colleagues. The purpose of his work remains the same—to unravel the long and complicated story of man's past in all lands.

ARGENTINES. The Argentine Republic is the largest and richest of the Spanish American republics, and it rivals Brazil for the leadership of South America. It is the most European in character of all the South American states except Uruguay. Its population is almost entirely of European origin.

The great estuary of the Rio de la Plata was discovered by the Spaniards in 1515. In 1536 they built there the city of Buenos Aires, or 'the Port of St. Mary of the Good Airs', which became the capital of the region. But for two hundred years this whole vast expanse of Spanish South America was ruled from Peru, and it was only in the 18th century that the King of Spain appointed a separate viceroy for the Rio de la Plata. In those days Argentina was the least accessible of the Spanish colonies because the main Spanish line of communication ran across the Atlantic to the isthmus of Panama and from there down to the Pacific coast to Peru, instead of round the bulge of Brazil into the South Atlantic. For this reason the Spanish–American War of Independence began later in Argentina than in the more northern countries.

The Wars of Independence (1807-26) were really an offshoot of the Napoleonic Wars in Europe. When Napoleon conquered Spain in 1808 the Spanish colonies had the chance to gain their freedom and independence, like the United States in North America thirty years before. The Argentine Declaration of Independence was in 1816. The leader in Buenos Aires was SAN MARTÍN (q.v. Vol. V), an officer in the Spanish army and a fine soldier. He became the Liberator of the southern half of the continent, as BOLÍVAR (q.v. Vol. V) was the liberator of the northern, and freed all Spanish America up to Peru from Spanish rule. But the Argentines also have a debt of gratitude to the great English minister, Canning, who recognized the independence of the young Spanish-American republics and protected them from being reconquered by Spain. There is a statue of Canning in Buenos Aires in recognition of this.

It was some time after the winning of its independence that the Argentine Republic found peace and stability. For ten years there were disorder and civil war followed by twenty years of dictatorship under Rosas, who destroyed all opposition and united the country by tyranny and force. But in 1853 the Argentines adopted a constitution very similar to that of the United States, and the peaceful development of the Republic began.

The growth and prosperity of Argentina has always depended on the large treeless plains called pampas; but four things were needed to make the pampas fully productive: railways, immigrants, barbed wire, and refrigeration. Railways solved the problem of communications. The pampas are a paradise for railway-makers —the lines can be built there for hundreds of miles with scarcely a curve or a gradient—and a thick railway network grew up, converging on Buenos Aires. Immigrants solved the problem of Argentina's very small population. In the past hundred years great numbers of settlers have flocked from Europe to Argentina as to North America. The most numerous have been Italians, Spaniards, and Poles, but there have been many others—so that Argentina has become a 'melting-pot of nations' no less than the United States. Wire-fencing solved the problem of dividing up the great expanse of the pampas, where there are no natural boundaries, into separate farms and ranches. And the invention of the refrigerator allowed frozen meat to be exported all over the world.

Originally it was sheep-farming that was the chief source of Argentine wealth. This was followed by cattle-raising and beef-production; frozen meat was first exported in 1877. About the beginning of the 20th century, however, wheat became more important than meat. Of recent years Argentina has done much to develop her industries, but she still remains essentially an agricultural country for the purposes of export.

The typical Argentino of the pampas used to be the gaucho or cowboy, a wild figure carrying a lasso and a *boleadoras*, an Indian weapon of leather and stones with which he caught horses and other animals by entangling their legs. Argentine music has been much influenced by gaucho folk-songs, haunting and melancholy, expressing the solitude of the wide open spaces; and the gaucho has also played a romantic part in Argentine literature. Perhaps the greatest of Argentine poems is *Martin Fierro*, by José Hernandez, which has a gaucho for its hero, and describes the feelings of the gauchos as their traditional pastoral way of life disappears before the advance of immigration and industrialism. For, like the American cowboy, the gaucho has almost died out. The herding of cattle today is more likely to be done in a motor-car than on horseback.

Ever since the days of Canning, Argentina has had close relations with Britain. (Indeed, the distance by sea from Buenos Aires to Liverpool is very little farther than that from Buenos Aires to New York.) The British, by the loan of their money and their industrial and engineering skill, played a greater part than any other country in the development of Argentina. Most of the railways were British-built, and British-owned, though they have now been bought up by the Argentine Government. And Britain has

Mansell

GAUCHOS ROUNDING UP HORSES
The horses are caught with lassoes and then tied to a post

been the greatest customer for Argentine exports of wheat, beef, and mutton.

During Perón's dictatorship (1946–55) the Argentines became increasingly nationalist and resented foreign influence in their country. Since his fall, the Army's insistence on keeping him out of politics has created grave political difficulties.

BUENOS AIRES, the capital, where more than a quarter of the population now lives, is the largest city of South America (q.v. Vol. III). With its luxurious shops and brilliant sporting events it rivals the cities of Europe or of the United States, and it possesses two of the world's great newspapers, *La Prensa* and *La Nación*. The language of Argentina is Spanish, but it has developed differently from the Spanish spoken in Spain, just as American has developed differently from English. And though the Argentines are Spanish

in their origin and culture, they have long been a distinct nation. They resemble in many ways a blend between Spaniards and Italians, who have been the most numerous settlers; and Buenos Aires has been described as one of the world's greatest Italian cities. The Argentino has the pride and fiery passion of the Spaniard, combined with the Italian's charm and his theatrical and changeful temperament.

See also Vol. III: ARGENTINA; Vol. IV: SPANISH AND PORTUGUESE LANGUAGES. See also INDEX, p. 133.

ARMENIANS. The ancient country of Armenia lay south of the Caucasus Mountains between the Black Sea and the Caspian Sea. The original Armenians probably migrated there somewhere about 1200 B.C. The Armenians call themselves Hai and claim descent from Haik, great-grandson of Japheth, son of Noah. They were conquered

John Massey Stewart

ARMENIANS IN EREVAN, U.S.S.R.

They are admiring old Armenian manuscripts

successively by the Assyrians, Medes, Persians, and Romans. They became Christians in the early 4th century, and for a time the Armenian Church was the centre of Asiatic Christianity. After a period of independence and prosperity, they fell under the Greeks, then the Turks, and then the Mongols. For a long time Turkey and Persia fought for control, and by the 16th century the Ottoman Turks held all of the country. In the 18th century Russia became a contender, and in the early 19th century took part of Armenia north of Mount Ararat.

The Armenians suffered continuous persecution and massacres, especially in Turkish Armenia. These reached a fearful climax in 1915 when Russia and Turkey were enemies in the First World War, and many Armenians were pro-Russian. Turkey deported one-third of the Armenians; another third escaped, many to Russia; and the remaining third were massacred or died of starvation. Those living in Russia's Armenian territory suffered further losses in the 1917 Revolution. In 1922 a Soviet Republic was formed embracing Armenia, Georgia, and Azerbaijan, but in 1936 it was dissolved, and one part of it became the present Armenian Socialist Republic. There are over 3 million Armenians in the U.S.S.R., mostly in Armenia. Those engaged in agriculture live in collectives. Armenia was traditionally famous for its wine, and for the carpets and lace woven by the women.

Nearly another million Armenians are scattered throughout the world. The largest group, 200,000, live in the United States; about 100,000 in France; 60,000 in Turkey; and others in the Middle East, South America, India, and the Far East. Typically, they are tall, handsome people with black hair and brownish skin, broad skulls and high foreheads. They have often been compared with the JEWS (q.v.) because both peoples have suffered centuries of persecution, and both have shown special talents in finance and trade. See also Vol. III: ARMENIA.

ARTHURIAN LEGEND. This takes three forms. In the first Arthur is a fabled leader of the Britons against the Saxons; in the second he is a purely mythical character; in the third he is a hero of romance. The origin of all three was probably a Celtic war-god.

The first known mention of Arthur occurs in the *History of the Britons,* by Nennius, who probably lived about A.D. 800, and describes Arthur as having lived about 300 years earlier. Nennius calls Arthur the 'war-leader of the kings of Britain', and credits him with twelve glorious victories over the Saxons, in which 'no one overthrew them but he alone'. In one battle he killed 960 men with his own hand. This has obviously no historical value.

Apart from the Welsh Annals, which merely copy and exaggerate Nennius, the only other 'history' which mentions Arthur is Geoffrey of Monmouth's *History of the Kings of Britain,* written in 1136. He represents Arthur as a hero-king of Britain who not only defeats the Scots, Picts, and Saxons, but also conquers a great part of Europe.

Arthur as a purely mythical character is to be found in a number of Welsh poems and legends of uncertain date. From these it would seem that he was still regarded by laymen as a god, but by the priests as a demon. The former tell of his fights with magic weapons against giants and monsters, but never against the Saxons. The latter tell of his encounter with saints, in which he always gets the worst of it.

Bib. Nat. Paris

KING ARTHUR AND THE KNIGHTS OF THE ROUND TABLE
Illumination from a late 15th-century French MS

In 1155 the Anglo-Norman poet Wace of Jersey retold Geoffrey of Monmouth's story in French verse, adding some details—for instance, the 'Round Table' makes its first appearance in his work. The English writer Layamon in his *Brut*, a verse chronicle of 'the noble deeds of England', based his version of Arthur on Wace's.

It is as a hero of romance that Arthur is now best known. He owes his position as a hero of romance to Chrétien of Troyes, a French court poet who lived at the end of the 12th century (*see* ROMANCE LITERATURE, Vol. XII). At this time the ideas of CHIVALRY (q.v. Vol. X) and courtly love were developing in western Europe. Chrétien found an inspiring subject in the realm of Arthur and the exploits of his knights. He collected material from Celtic legend, from earlier romances, and from his own readings of the Roman poets, and he combined it all into fresh romances so skilfully, and so much in accord with the sentiments of the time, that he not only gave the highest satisfaction to the court ladies, but also set for all time a fashion for chivalrous romance. His King Arthur is a combination of the figures of Celtic myth with Charlemagne and various Greek heroes, particularly Agamemnon. Many of Chrétien's heroes bear Celtic names, and some of the incidents are from Celtic sources. But probably more are drawn from the classics: many stories told about Lancelot remind us of Achilles, and many about

Guinevere remind us of Helen of Troy. But the French romance poets did not only chronicle events, they brought out the significance of these events, and interpreted the motives and the conflicts of the characters. There are many French versions of the stories of Lancelot, Merlin, the death of Arthur, and the Quest of the Holy Grail. This last story is also called *Perceval* and was the subject of the opera *Parzival* by the 19th-century German composer, Richard WAGNER (q.v. Vol. V). In general, the French poets as well as the 13th-century French writer of the Arthurian Prose Cycle known as *Lancelot* were concerned more with Lancelot than Arthur.

The great English version of Sir Thomas Malory first appeared in 1485, printed by William CAXTON (q.v. Vol. V). We now know that Caxton abridged and edited it heavily. In 1934 a Malory manuscript was discovered in Winchester College, and was first published in 1965, nearly 500 years after it was written; so we can now read the text that Malory wrote. Malory's work comprises: The Tale of King Arthur; The Tale of the Noble King Arthur and Emperor Lucius; The Noble Tale of Sir Launcelot; The Tale of Sir Gareth; The Book of Sir Tristram; The Grail; The Book of Sir Launcelot and Queen Guinevere; and the Morte Arthur (Death of Arthur). The Morte Arthur reads like a novel. Launcelot is caught between his devoted, self-denying love for Guinevere, Arthur's Queen, and the code of chivalry which enjoins him to loyalty to his fellow knights. To protect her he kills Gawain's brothers, and thus incurs Gawain's enmity.

Many later poets have taken the Arthurian Legend as the basis of their own creations, the best known of these being Tennyson's *Idylls of the King*.

See also Vol. XII · ARTHURIAN LITERATURE.

ARYAN (Sanskrit *arya* = noble). This is the name of a very large group of languages, more usually known as the Indo-European languages. The original speakers probably came from the Russian Steppe country. Their descendants occupied north Iran and Turkestan, and about 1500 B.C. some settled in north India, where they spread their language (*see* INDIAN CIVILIZATIONS). Some time before the Iron Age the Aryan people seem to have spread over Europe, probably introducing the horse and the bronze sword. No trace of them remains except in the languages. In spite of this the Nazis claimed Aryan origin for the German race, in order to assert the idea of its supremacy.

See also Vol. IV: INDO-EUROPEAN LANGUAGES.

ASCETICISM.

ASCETICISM. This word has an interesting origin. It comes from a Greek verb, *askein*, which means 'to do athletic exercises' or 'to train the body'. The noun for this is *askēsis* or discipline. In I Corinthians ix. 24-27 St. Paul describes this sort of process as being closely akin to what a Christian has to do in order to bring his bodily passions and appetites under control. So asceticism connotes a process through which the body is brought under control, is conditioned to moderation, and is subordinated to the life of the spirit.

Asceticism, in some form or another, is a prominent feature of all higher religions, including BUDDHISM, CHRISTIANITY, HINDUISM, JUDAISM, and ISLAM (qq.v.). All schools of asceticism, however varied, are based upon two fundamental doctrines that they hold in common. The first of these is the belief in the dualism of the physical and the spiritual, or of body and soul. The second is the conviction that the body is essentially inferior to the soul and stands somehow as a hindrance or a threat to man's proper spiritual development. Ascetics have differed widely in their interpretation of these doctrines. Some have held that the body is altogether sinful and corrupt, and that man can attain goodness only by the strictest repression of his bodily appetites. Others have held, more moderately, that the body is essentially good, and needs only to be made into a healthy and faithful vessel for the soul. But all ascetic doctrines have taught the necessity for the control of the flesh in the interest of the spirit.

The purpose of such a discipline is to develop virtue on the one hand, and on the other to lessen temptation, to avoid evil, to moderate passion, and to eliminate such disorders as those Christianity lists as 'the seven deadly sins': pride, covetousness, lust, envy, gluttony, anger, sloth. This denial and mortification of the body, through such practices as abstinence, continence, and withdrawal from the world, may be treated as an end in itself. If it is, it tends to be carried to extremes. Jesus, Buddha, Muhammad, and most other great religious leaders condemned extreme practices because such practices show a contempt for the totality of God's creation and often lead to self-righteousness.

In the first three centuries Christian asceticism was expressed mainly in the preparation of Christians for martyrdom and in the ideal of virginity. Withdrawal from the world was also practised. From about A.D. 320 onwards we find a great increase in the number of people of both sexes who left the towns and cities and went to live in out-of-the-way spots, such as the Nubian desert in Egypt. Some of these were solitary hermits; others lived in groups—it is from the latter that the institutions which we call 'monasteries' developed. The first two great organizers of Egyptian groups of ascetics were called Pachomius and Anthony: in their societies each individual lived a solitary life although he was the member of a group. Later, however, other communities came into existence which were more like colleges or schools, and which had a fair degree of social intercourse. These were mainly due to the pioneer work of ST. BENEDICT (q.v. Vol. V) in Italy at Monte Cassino. At the other extreme were the complete hermits who gave up all contact with other human beings and often went in for the greatest extremes of harsh discipline and self-torture, most commonly the beating of the body which they regarded as a mystical sharing in the scourging of Christ.

Asceticism is still widely practised in the Christian church: many sects observe days of fasting; monks and nuns live celibate lives; and

Pitt-Rivers Museum
AN INDIAN ASCETIC WEARING AN IRON COLLAR

some sects, especially those who lay great stress on the sinful and corrupt nature of man, believe that salvation can be won only by avoiding the ordinary pleasures of life, and practising a strict self-discipline.

It is the doctrine of asceticism that man is really a pilgrim of eternity, that his highest element is his soul, and that his true purpose in this life is spiritual discipline and cultivation, in order to prepare and fit himself for the better life to come. All of the positive practices of asceticism are aimed at this end. These practices include prayer, meditation, devotion, and the dedication of one's life to the service of God. Systematic techniques involving varying degrees of asceticism for achieving spiritual development were devised by the yogi in India, and are practised by many Hindus, Buddhists, and Jains not only in India but also in Sri Lanka, Japan, Korea, and South-east Asia. These techniques differ in the various Yoga schools. A well-known system is the 'royal Yoga' of eight stages: the practice of continence; fulfilling charitable obligations; correct sitting posture for meditation; breath control, withdrawal of the mind from the exterior world; intuitive knowledge of the deity, or other object of meditation; retaining this object of meditation exclusively; and merging of the mind with the object of meditation. The achievement of this final state brings release from the cycle of births and deaths (*see* HINDUISM).

See also FRIAR; MONK.

ASHANTI (AFRICANS). The Ashanti are one of the Negro peoples of Ghana, a Commonwealth State of West Africa. They are fairly typical of the larger and more progressive communities of West Africa. The Ashanti belong to a group of peoples called the Akan who all have similar customs and languages. They may have migrated to their present area from the North, but there is little evidence about their history before about the 17th century.

The Ashantis were, in the 18th and 19th centuries, a great warrior people under a paramount chief, the Asantehene. The symbol of his authority is the Golden Stool, a wooden stool covered with gold, which is considered to contain the soul of the Ashanti nation and thus represents its unity. Under the Asantehene are chiefs of the different states which originally came together to form the Ashanti confederacy. The chief of each state is always elected from the 'royal family' of

R. S. Rattray coll., Pitt-Rivers Museum

ASHANTI GOLD-WEIGHT

The Ashanti made elaborate little sculptures to use in place of weights on scales for weighing gold-dust. This one depicts two old impoverished friends, Amoaku and Adu, meeting after many years of separation

the state and his authority is represented by his 'stool'. This marks not only political but religious authority; thus all chiefs are both political leaders and religious heads of their communities and the guardians of custom. All chiefs act on the advice of councils; that of the Asantehene includes the Queen Mother and the chiefs of the confederate states. In recent years the Government of Ghana has been transferring many of the political functions of the chiefs and councils to itself and to local government bodies, which have been set up on the model of those of Britain. The state councils have been left mainly with ceremonial and judicial tasks, hearing and judging cases involving native law and custom. Respect for the Asantehene and the other chiefs remains strong, so that the transition from the traditional to the new form of government has not always been easy.

In social and economic customs the Ashanti have proved a progressive people, many taking advantages of opportunities offered by European civilization. Kumasi, the capital of Ashanti, is a large town, with electric light, wide streets, and a modern water-supply. Most of the population, however, live in villages. Corrugated iron roofs have nearly everywhere replaced the traditional ones made of palm-thatch, whilst many people

West African Review

STOOLS CARVED AND PLATED WITH METAL, CARRIED IN A
PROCESSION AT KUMASI, GHANA

build their house walls of cement and not of mud and sticks. A typical village consists of two to three hundred compounds—the rooms of the houses being built round central courtyards. The family group living in a compound is much larger than an English family and may include cousins, uncles, and aunts, though each woman has a room and a kitchen for herself and her small children.

The Ashanti people are nearly all farmers; besides growing food crops for themselves, they grow cocoa for sale to the agents of European firms. Much of the world's cocoa comes from Ghana. The cultivated fields are often scattered round the village for five or six kilometres, but they are not easy to see, for there are no hedges or fences, and the thick undergrowth, or 'bush', often surrounds them on all sides. The fields of members of one household may be scattered about in different parts of the land round the village. The farmers often employ labourers, who come in to live and work on the farms from the poorer Northern Territories and from the neighbouring French colonies. Between the coco-trees the men grow coco-yams, maize, and ground-nuts; their wives also grow food-stuffs, including pepper, okra, and plantains.

The chief food is *fufu*—a mixture of yam and plantain, pounded together in a mortar and dipped in a palm-oil stew. Sometimes the Ashanti catch fish in the river or eat dried fish sent up from the coast. No cattle can live in their country because of the tsetse-fly, but they keep sheep, goats, and fowls. Increasingly nowadays they buy tinned food, corned beef, milk, and sardines with the money they earn from their cocoa.

The clothing of the Ashanti people consists of a long, gaily-coloured cloth, which the men wear slung over the shoulder. If they wish to pay a mark of respect to a superior, they lower the cloth from the shoulder as an Englishman would touch his cap. The women wear a loose blouse with a cloth wrapped round the waist like a skirt. Small girls wear their cloth wrapped tightly round under the armpits, leaving their shoulders bare, and boys cross the two ends of the cloth round their neck and tie it at the back.

Children are named after the day of the week on which they are born—just as Man Friday was named after the day of the week on which Robinson Crusoe found him—and descent is traced chiefly through the mother's family. An Ashanti mother generally carries her small child on her back whenever she goes to the farm or to the market.

Nearly every village has its own small school. Usually there are more boys and girls wanting to go to school than the buildings can hold, and the schoolchildren and their teachers often build new classrooms themselves. The best pupils can go on to the secondary schools in the large towns, and finally to one of the country's three universities.

The Ashanti people have many forms of amusement. Nearly every village now has a football ground; the boys play with bare feet, but they are able to kick the ball very hard. The elder men like to play draughts and *warri*, a game played with beans or beads on a wooden board. On special occasions a big dance is held in which all the villagers can join. But the Ashanti do not dance together in couples like the Europeans: men and women dance in separate groups, each having their own dances. The Ashanti have, in common with the other Akan peoples, a great collection of folk tales about animals, of whom the most famous is Ananse, the spider.

There are many skilled craftsmen among the Ashantis. The goldsmiths have long worked the gold that comes from mines in Ashanti—these gave Ghana its former name of the Gold Coast.

Besides the goldsmiths, there are blacksmiths, silversmiths, and wood-carvers. Especially beautiful work is found in the ornamented stools of the chiefs. Nowadays many carpenters are making furniture in European style. Weaving is still practised today, and many beautiful designs are woven. Pottery-making is in the hands of the women; and though they do not use the potter's wheel they are skilful in shaping round pots entirely by hand.

See also Vol. III: GHANA.
See also Vol. IV: AFRICAN LANGUAGES.

ASSYRIAN CIVILIZATION. It is not easy to make a sharp distinction between the Assyrian and BABYLONIAN (q.v.) civilizations of Mesopotamia. The peoples of both countries belonged to the western Semites, and both borrowed the main elements of their civilization from the SUMERIANS (q.v.), who had settled long before them in the Tigris–Euphrates valley, in what is now Iraq. The history of the two peoples is very closely connected, and their language, laws, religion, and social organization have strong resemblances. Nevertheless, there is a difference between them which is due partly to the different contacts they had with outside peoples, partly to the different geographical and climatic conditions of the two countries, and partly to the different elements of which the populations of the two countries were composed.

Assyria sprang, like Rome, from very small beginnings. At the outset of its history the land of Assyria was less than 160 km from north to south, and about 60 km at its greatest breadth from east to west. It consisted of a narrow strip of fertile soil on each side of the river Tigris, stretching north to the foot-hills. Archaeologists think that the first permanent villages were established by the late seventh millenium B.C.: the fall of Nineveh and the final collapse of the Assyrian Empire took place in 612 B.C.

In the early period of their history the dwellers of Assyria seem to have been completely dominated by the Sumerians, from whom they received their cuneiform, or wedge-shaped writing, their religion, and much else of their material culture. But Sumerian rule in Assyria came to an end about 2370 B.C., and for 250 years Assyria was under the power of a line of Akkadian kings founded by the great warrior, Sargon.

Recorded Assyrian history begins with a

British Museum
ASHUR-NAZIR-PAL II
King of Assyria, 885–860 B.C.

governor appointed to rule at Assur, the main city of the region, by a ruler of the 3rd Dynasty of Ur, about 2000 B.C. In the following century or so many inscribed clay tablets reveal the great activity of Assyrian merchant traders in eastern Turkey, but tell virtually nothing of the country's history. Then, at the end of the 19th century B.C., a man of foreign origin seized power in Assur and ruled with great effect as Samsi-Adad I (c. 1813–1781 B.C.). A man of conspicuous energy and initiative he created a unified state with authority over much of northern Mesopotamia, largely inhabited by nomadic and semi-nomadic tribes with quite different traditions of government. When he died this empire collapsed.

While the kings of Assyria were thus laying the foundations of her greatness, the hitherto unknown city of Babylon, under a new line of kings, had risen to the first place among the city-states of Mesopotamia. It is probable that for a period Assyria was under the domination of Babylon; but about 1600 B.C. this first Babylonian Empire came to an end, and Assyria was able to establish her independence. During the

THE CAPTURE OF A CITY BY TIGLATH PILESER III

Families are evacuated in bullock carts, their flocks are driven away by the captors, and scribes make up the accounts of the spoil. Relief from the Palace of Tiglath Pileser III (745–727 B.C.)

following centuries, with various changes of fortune, Assyria built herself up as a military power, holding control of the trade-routes to the south and west and of the principal source of iron in Asia Minor. By 911 B.C. and the accession of King Adad-nirari II, she had become a compact, well-armed, well-organized military state. Until the fall of Nineveh, the chief city in Assyria, in 612 B.C., she pursued her course of expansion and conquest, gaining the undisputed mastery of Elam, Mesopotamia, Syria, Palestine, the Arabian marches, and finally of Egypt.

This period of Assyrian history falls into two parts. The first begins with the successes of King Ashur-nazir-pal II, whose long reign (883–859 B.C.) was spent in unceasing warfare. Assyrian warlike exploits were for the first time vividly set forth on the magnificent bas-relief carvings of the reign of Ashur-nazir-pal, and in consequence this king is credited with the introduction of 'frightfulness' into ancient warfare. But there can be little doubt that the barbarous practices represented on his bas-reliefs and described on his monuments were characteristic of all warfare in those times. Egyptian monuments show similar cruelties and mutilations as practised by the Egyptians in war. Shalmaneser III continued the warlike policy of his father, but directed his attacks specially against the Syrian states. Ahab, King of Israel, is mentioned in Shalmaneser's account of the important battle of Qarqar (853 B.C.), where the advance of the Assyrians clearly received a setback. At the close

of his reign in 824 B.C. the fortunes of Assyria were temporarily beginning to decline.

The second and final period of Assyrian ascendancy began with the reign of King Tiglath Pileser III (744–727 B.C.). A series of brilliant conquerors and rulers followed him: Sargon, Sennacherib, Esarhaddon, and Ashur-bani-pal, of whose reigns and achievements we have full historical records, and who raised Assyria to the highest summit of her glory. In 671 B.C. the Assyrian army conquered Egypt; but the conquest brought them no good, and the strain which it threw upon the resources of the state was one of the causes which brought about the sudden and dramatic collapse of the great empire. In 612 a combined army of Babylonians and Medes attacked the great city of Nineveh, and burnt it to the ground.

The civilization of Assyria depended mainly on foreign trade and on military conquest resulting in the control of the great trade-routes and access to the Mediterranean. The three main classes of Sumerian society—the rulers, priests, freemen (merchants, farmers, and craftsmen), and slaves—are found both in Assyria and in Babylonia; but in some ways Assyrian law and customs appear to have developed along independent lines. Assyrian law made special provisions for the dependents of common soldiers in case of death or imprisonment in foreign countries—an important law in a country where military service played so great a part. There was a tendency to make the king supreme in matters of law, and for the administration to become national instead of local. These special characteristics all helped to build Assyria into a compact centralized military state governed by the king and a body of officials responsible only to him.

In the matter of architecture, stone, which was very hard to obtain in Babylonia, was abundant in Assyria, and, in consequence, Assyrian buildings were often built or faced with stone. Also, because the climate was much colder, Assyrian houses were built on a different plan from the Babylonian—they had their main entrance at the end of the side-wall instead of in the middle. The Assyrians developed a style of sculpture, the vigour and naturalness of which is excelled only in Crete. Their hunting scenes show a knowledge of anatomy and a power of depicting swift movement which not even the Greeks surpassed. The Assyrians produced no literature of their own. Their myths and sagas were borrowed from Babylonia (*see* BABYLONIAN MYTHS); but their later kings were very active in collecting all the literary material available in Mesopotamia—indeed, our knowledge of Mesopotamian civilization is largely due to the vast collection of tablets which King Ashur-bani-pal brought from every corner of his empire to his great library at Nineveh. But the principal achievement of Assyrian civilization, as of Roman, lay in administration and organization.

Sennacherib's great aqueduct, the oldest known in the world, which brought water to the city of Nineveh from the mountains 48 km away, is an example of their efficiency. Our idea of the Assyrians has been unduly influenced by the descriptions given in the Old Testament by the prophets. To the Hebrews the Assyrians were the incarnation of mere brute force, just as the Romans seemed to the Jews of a later time; but other evidence goes to show that, while they were ruthlessly efficient as a military power, they organized the trade and commerce of their empire with equal efficiency; they developed artistic skill of a very high order, and collected and arranged the literary material of their time in a way which could only have been done by a highly civilized people.

See also ANCIENT CIVILIZATIONS; SUMERIANS; BABYLONIANS.

See also Vol. XII: ASSYRIAN ART.

ASTROLOGY is the mock science which claims to be able to trace a connexion between human affairs and the movements of the stars and planets. It must not be confused with ASTRONOMY (q.v. Vol. III), a science becoming more exact every year, which deals only with the nature and movements of the heavenly bodies. To compare the merits of the two, we need only observe that astronomers are accustomed to predict such events as eclipses centuries ahead with great precision, whereas no modern astrologer

British Museum

A LION HUNT
Relief from the Palace of Ashur-bani-pal (668–626 B.C.)

foretold so world-shaking an event as the outbreak of the Second World War even a few weeks in advance. Nevertheless, just as modern chemistry is founded on the painstaking researches of the early alchemists, striving to turn base metals to gold, so modern astronomy owes an immense amount to the observations of astrologers. The movements they noted in the heavens were often stated with astonishing accuracy; it was in their attempts to relate these to human destinies that they failed.

With the background of knowledge and the increasing belief in reason which we possess today, it seems absurd to educated people that the position of the stars at the moment of a man's birth should have any influence on his physique, character, or life, or that the destinies even of great nations should be traceable in the heavens. And yet it is easy to see how the superstition arose. The influence of the sun on living things was obvious; that of the moon on the tides at least must soon have been noticed—why should the influence of the heavens end there? Above all, there was man's great and abiding desire to explain things. He did not like feeling that he was at the mercy of events, that catastrophes such as plagues, famines, wars, and even the death of the individual should come upon him without apparent reason. If he could explain them, it was at least something: if he could foretell them, it would be an immense gain. And so people have always been willing to believe many forms of fortune-telling (*see* DIVINATION). The accidental coincidence of one eclipse with some great event in human affairs would convince him—since he was only too eager to be convinced.

The belief in astrology was widespread among early peoples centuries, if not thousands of years, before Christ. It flourished among the Chinese (whose astrologers were expected to foretell solar eclipses well in advance, so that suitable measures could be taken to prevent 'the dragon swallowing the sun' entirely), among the Babylonians, the Egyptians, the Etruscans, the Greeks, the Hindus, and the Arabs (as the *Arabian Nights* shows well). It is still very prevalent in the East. The early Christian fathers differed among themselves as to its truth—though its influence is clearly seen in the charming Bible story of the wise men of the East who were guided by a star which 'moved before them' and led them to the manger at Bethlehem. In western Europe it was

at its height in the 14th and 15th centuries, though it flourished until well into the 17th century. Among educated people its death-knell was sounded by the astronomical theories of NEWTON (q.v. Vol. V); and yet, in Britain and America today, hundreds of thousands of people read the astrological predictions in certain of the Sunday newspapers each week, with at least a certain measure of belief, and the sales of almanacs containing prophecies based on astrology still reach a very high figure every year.

It was chiefly the BABYLONIANS (q.v.) who worked out the 'principles' of astrology, although they believed the planets to be actual gods, rather than the mere 'influences' to which they later declined. The basis of the whole system was the subdivision of the celestial sphere (or whole expanse of sky enveloping the earth) into twelve Houses of Heaven, named after the twelve signs of the zodiac. These houses may be thought of as the outer skin of a peeled orange, each 'quarter' or 'pig' of the fruit being a house. According to the system most commonly practised, the top and bottom of the orange lay above the North and below the South poles respectively. To an observer on the Earth here—like a pip at the centre of the orange, six houses would always be visible, the remaining six being below the horizon. Each of the different houses touched upon a special subject covering: (1) life, (2) riches, (3) brethren, (4) parents, (5) children, (6) health, (7) marriage, (8) death, (9) religion, (10) dignities, (11) friends, (12) enemies. Their power varied according to their position at the particular moment of interest, being strongest when they were 'in the ascendant' or just about to rise over the horizon on the astrologer's right as he faced south. Each planet, too, had certain properties, and each the particular house of which it was 'lord'. When it was actually in its own house, its power for good or ill was greatly magnified. On this fantastic framework a vast fabric of superstition was gradually erected until almost everything on earth and every aspect of life was linked in some way with the stars. Animals, metals, colours, stones, drugs, and many other things each had its planet. The zodiac itself was held to parallel the parts of the human body, the first sign Aries, the Ram, being the head, and the Fishes, or 'Pisces', the last, being the feet, while of the remaining signs each claimed its own part of the anatomy.

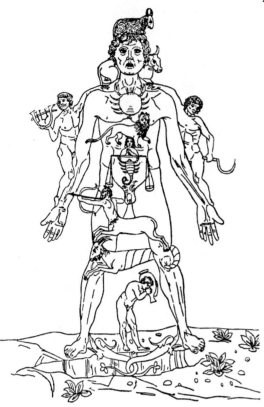

THE ZODIAC MAN

Italian engraving, 1495. The figure shows the parts of the body under the domination of the signs of the Zodiac. Early medicine was greatly influenced by astrology, and doctors would only attempt to cure their patients if the stars were propitious

To cast a horoscope, the astrologer would find out the exact hour and date of his client's birth and then calculate from his tables the position of the heavenly bodies at that time. The particular house in the ascendant would be ascertained and note taken as to whether its influence was strengthened or weakened by the position of its lord. But this was no more than the beginning. Immensely complicated calculations could be made on the relative positions of the houses and planets, those of the sun and moon being by no means omitted. Influences could be estimated to wax or wane in power according to whether planets were in 'conjunction' or 'opposition', or forming the corners of various geometrical figures. The same process was followed in deciding whether a day would be auspicious or inauspicious for joining battle, for starting on a journey, or for beginning any other important enterprise. The opportunities for error in so

intricate a series of calculations were great, and were not lessened by the wide variations between the systems used. But beyond all this lies the fact that modern science has been quite unable to find any basis in reason for the principles of astrology. Certain astrologers, notably Nostrodamus (1503–66), appear to have made occasional prophecies of almost miraculous accuracy; but against these must be set the many millions of predictions which have proved false. No one, perhaps, did more to kill the superstition than Swift in his feud with Partridge the almanac-maker; but it is astonishing how the superstition lingers on. We may look forward to a day when increasing confidence in the power of reason to mould the future will leave of astrology only those words which we use so frequently, forgetful of their origin—such as 'disastrous', 'ill-starred', 'influence', and 'ascendancy'—and the many picturesque allusions to the subject in literature.

ATHEISM, *see* RATIONALISM.

ATHENIANS, *see* GREEK CIVILIZATION.

AUGURY, *see* DIVINATION.

AUSTRALIAN ABORIGINES. When the first settlers arrived in Australia in 1788, there were approximately 300,000 Aboriginal people there. It was a sparse population, divided into about 500 tribal associations, with as many separate languages and 600 dialects.

In the ensuing years vast numbers of the Aboriginal population were wiped out by diseases introduced by the Europeans, by planned massacre, and, above all, by the effects of apathy in the face of overwhelming problems created by the white invasion of Aboriginal territory. Land was life to the Aborigine; each tribe had clearly defined territory, which was both his source of food and his spiritual home. With European occupation of tribal grounds, the dispossessed Aborigines had to retreat inland, creating problems of territorial rights. The Aborigines were a nomadic people. As water and food were distributed unevenly and seasonally, the hunter had to move within his tribal boundaries following the food supply.

Although there was considerable difference in physique, with tall, dark people to the north, and shorter, fairer people in the central desert,

OLD MEN OF A CENTRAL AUSTRALIAN TRIBE SING SACRED SONGS BEFORE A CORROBOREE

the customs and culture were similar over most of the continent. There was little martial organization and great wars were unknown, although there were occasional tribal skirmishes. All tribes hunted by similar methods, loved music, song, and dancing, had similar ideas of property and government, and had religious and social structures with much in common.

The men hunted kangaroos, lizards, birds, snakes, and emus with spear, boomerang, and woomera. They fished with spear and net, and had axes of hard stone, chipped stone knives set in handles of gum, and wooden clubs and shields. The woman's chief tool was the digging stick, used mainly for finding roots for food; she also collected seeds, edible grubs, insects, and frogs; coastal tribes would also eat shellfish.

Aborigines had many ingenious ways of getting water, and could journey over dry tracts where a European would die of thirst. They drained moisture from the roots of eucalyptus trees, sucked water from the wet sand, collected it from underground tubers, and even on occasion from the bodies of frogs which, after drinking, buried themselves to withstand drought.

For household equipment they would have a few wooden or bark trays, some baskets, stone knives for cutting up food, and grinding-stones to pulverize roots and seeds. They made fire by rubbing two pieces of wood together, and cooked in hot ashes. They built no houses, but made huts that were little more than a row of branches set up to keep off the wind, covered with sheets of bark or skins for extra protection. They often sheltered in caves.

They wore few clothes, and personal decoration was limited to cuts in the skin and designs in paint and grease over the face and body. Some tribes added tufts of down on special occasions; the men might wear nose-pins of bone, necklaces of shells or teeth, and ornamented headbands.

In contrast to the simplicity of daily life, social rules were extremely complicated. The relationships between and within tribal groups controlled marriage and inheritance. There were elaborate ceremonies connected with the totems of the different groups (*see* TOTEMISM), the purpose of which was to maintain and increase the food supply, and to keep the various tribal divisions in close and friendly contact. The older men

Australian Information Bureau

YOUNG ABORIGINES LEARNING TREE-PLANTING

generally had great control over the younger men and women. The medicine man was believed to be able to cause or cure disease by magical powers. The INITIATION CEREMONIES (q.v.) were used to impress on the younger people, by myth and drama, the importance of respecting the traditional rules of society.

They usually included circumcision of the boys, knocking out of two of their lower teeth, and decoration with cuts in the skin, rubbed with ashes so that the patterns would stand out. Among some tribes there were ceremonies for girls before they were married.

Children were well-treated and never punished, but in spite of this they had a hard time. Food was often scarce, so a sick child might be abandoned when the tribe moved camp. Boys and girls began to help the women and to hunt for food at an early age. The girls were often betrothed at birth, and married at thirteen or fourteen. A man could acquire as many wives as he wished, providing they were of the right class of relationship.

It was impossible for hunting and pastoral ways of life to exist side by side. By the 1880s a great many tribes had been obliterated. The aborigines were dispersed and dispossessed, and the squatters (the men taking up land for cattle and sheep grazing) took advantage of them. They rapidly became excellent stockmen, their wives worked around the homestead, and were paid 'in kind' with basic foodstuffs, cast-off clothes, blankets, and tobacco. Others went to live on church mission stations.

Loss of tribal lands and the break in tribal structure drew the Aborigines to the European settlements, where they were treated with indifference, or with paternalist charity. The powerless native of Australia rapidly lost self-respect and dignity.

Neglect, ill-health, and exploitation decimated the population: an Aborigine killed one or two cattle for food, a party of white horsemen might seek revenge by wholesale slaughter. The relationship between white and black deteriorated, and there were attacks on both sides. By the 1930s public feeling was aroused by these atrocities, and a policy of protection was formed.

Mission and government reserves were set up and still exist; on some the Aborigines can live an almost traditional life, but others provide no more than subsistence-level charity.

It was not until the 1960s that all Aboriginal adults received the vote, and that discriminatory laws were abolished. The Aborigines are now increasing in number, and by the end of the century they should once again number approximately 300,000.

Many Aborigines today live in slum conditions in the cities, often unemployed and living on government pensions. There is, however, a growing awareness of their problem. It is realized that to offer them equality of rights and opportunity will not be effective without some moulding of national educational and economic policies to suit Aboriginal needs. The aim now is for development rather than protection.

See also AUSTRALIANS; RACES AND PEOPLES.

AUSTRALIANS. The majority of the thirteen million people living in Australia are of British or European origin, most of them Australian born. The British, however, were not the first to migrate to the southern continent. The earliest inhabitants, it is thought, were the AUSTRALIAN ABORIGINES (q.v.), whose ancestors travelled probably from South-East Asia some 30,000 years ago.

It is strange that neither the Asiatic navigators nor the Polynesians appear to have touched Australian shores. From old maps it does seem likely that the Portuguese had seen a great deal of the west Australian coast more than 400 years ago. The Dutch had reached the country in 1606, and by 1644 they had roughly charted much of the northern, western, and southern coasts of what they called New Holland. The first British visitors were shipwrecked on the coast in 1622. In 1688 and again in 1699 WILLIAM DAMPIER (q.v. Vol. V) landed, and formed an unfavourable view of the land and its inhabitants.

JAMES COOK (q.v. Vol. V) visited Botany Bay in 1770 and undertook the first major exploration with his charting of the eastern coastline. Joseph Banks came with Cook and made the first great collection of Australian plants. It was Banks who suggested the use of Botany Bay as a prison colony (see TRANSPORTATION, Vol. X). In 1788 the First Fleet, under Captain Arthur Phillip, carrying 726 convicts and their guards, arrived at Sydney Cove on 26th January, subsequently celebrated as Foundation Day.

At first the new colony lived on the ragged edge of hunger and hardship. Expansion inland was slow. Rich pasture lands round Parramatta and Windsor were developed, but it was twenty-years before any explorers found their way over the precipitous Blue Mountains which rise eighty kilometres inland from Sydney. Most of the early coastal settlers were whalers and sealers. Until 1833 whale oil and whale-bone made up more than half of Sydney's exports; but whaling grounds were rapidly exhausted, and the industry lost importance.

John MacArthur began rearing merino sheep in 1805, and during his lifetime he proved that Australia could grow the fine wool that Britain needed. Tasmanian sheepmen crossed the Bass Strait and began to develop the pastures of Victoria. Pioneers with carts loaded with supplies drove sheep and cattle overland into South Australia and Queensland to make new settlements, and bullock-teams, usually of eight, ploughed the land and hauled timber out of the forests. As the sheep industry flourished, the invaluable oxen drew wool-wagons to the ports, distances of up to 800 km, from where the wool was carried to London by fast sailing CLIPPER SHIPS (q.v. Vol. IV). The first fleet of convicts had taken 8 months to reach Australia; the clipper cut down the time of the passage until the *Thermopylae* ran from London to Melbourne in 61 days 17 hours. Now, flying time between east coast Australia and London has been reduced to less than 24 hours.

By 1850, Australia's European population had reached 405,000, mainly sheep-farmers. Most of the labour was convict. Between 1788 and 1867, 160,000 convicts were sent to Australia often convicted of quite trivial crimes. They became shepherds, shearers, and bullock-drivers; they farmed, built houses, churches, and government buildings; they made roads and bridges, and even taught children and acted as police. Most of the bushrangers, the outlaws of Australia's history, were runaway convicts.

Signs of gold were first found in 1823. Other finds followed, but discoveries were not publicized for fear of public commotion, convict escapes, and general disruption to farming, trading, and industry. Then in 1851, Edward Hargreaves, returning from the Californian goldfields, found traces of gold over a wide area in New South Wales. The goldrush developed at

Camera Press

MOLONG, A SHIPPING AND RAIL CENTRE IN AUSTRALIAN 'BACK COUNTRY'
The goods train is loaded with wheat

enormous speed; would-be miners poured in from the British Isles, Europe, America, China, and other countries. The goldfields of Victoria and New South Wales, Bendigo, Ballarat, Sofala, and Ophir were famed around the world. The 1850s were Australia's golden age. Melbourne particularly went ahead with a great building boom, erecting vast public edifices in the then popular neo-Gothic style. By 1860 the European population had increased to 1,145,000.

In 1853 the first railway was opened, and in 1854 sea voyages under steam began. The eastern states suffered in the world-wide economic depression of the 1890s, but in western Australia gold was found in enormous quantities, and the boom that followed lasted almost until the First World War. Australian mineral resources brought international speculation again in the 1960s, when vast deposits of iron, nickel, and other valuable ores were found in western Australia, Queensland, and the Northern Territory.

Until 1901 the country consisted of six separate colonies. There was very little united planning; for instance, the railways in the different colonies had different gauges, varying from 5 ft. 3 in. to 3 ft. 6 in., a blunder that is still costing millions of dollars to put right. However, in 1900 arrangements were finalized for the six states to form a federal union with one Commonwealth Government. This Government took over Papua in 1906 and the mandated territory of New Guinea after the First World War. In 1930 it annexed 5,890,000 square km of Antarctica, where Australia now has a common frontier, some 2,000 km long, with the Norwegian antarctic territories. No one lives in Antarctica, but the seas just to the north of it are the world's chief whaling grounds. Other Australian territories include Norfolk, Cocos, and Christmas Islands.

Australia exports large quantities of wool, meat, butter and other dairy products, wheat, fruit, and other foodstuffs, but most Australians do not live and work in the country. The use of modern machinery has reduced the rural labour force, so that approximately 75% of the population is concentrated in the major cities and provincial urban areas. As industry increases, more and more people move to the cities, and it has become important to decentralize—that is, to encourage more people to live in smaller towns away from the great urban areas, thereby spreading the population over the entire country. Although much of the arid country in central and western Australia is almost uninhabited, the development of mineral resources is taking people inland. Since the 1960s, mining towns have been constructed, complete in themselves, with houses, shops, schools, churches, and entertainment facilities.

The population of Australia has become more cosmopolitan since the Second World War, and 'New Australians' have brought great cultural diversity and colour to the community. There has been an influx of European migrants, particularly from Britain and the Mediterranean countries, Italy, Greece, and Yugoslavia. Many come from Germany, Holland, Malta, and Poland, and in lesser numbers, from other European countries, the Middle East, and the United States. The largest immigrant group continues to come from Britain. Australia has had a policy of selective immigration, known until recently as the 'White Australia' policy. This limited, almost to the point of total exclusion, settlement by persons of non-European origin, but today there is a move towards a less exclusive policy.

Australia, like New Zealand and Canada, is an independent nation within the Commonwealth. She played an important part in the two World Wars, especially in the Second, where the entry of Japan brought the fighting into the Pacific area. In recent years, however, the traditional links with Britain have become more tenuous, and with Britain's entry into the European Economic Community, trading ties between the two countries will be considerably lessened. In 1971 Japan provided the largest market for Australian exports, followed by the United States and Britain. China is now the largest purchaser of Australian wheat.

The increasing ease of international travel and communication has made Australians more aware both of other countries and of their own national identity. Australia is no longer merely the world's greatest sheep farm or cattle station. It has made valuable contributions to world science, particularly in medicine, radio-astronomy, and aviation, and has produced many singers, actors, and sportsmen of international repute. Outstanding painters, such as Sidney Nolan, and novelists, notably Patrick White, have interpreted to the world the life and strange landscapes of their country. The most significant architectural achievement of this century is the Sydney Opera House.

Most people live near the coast. Popular sports are swimming and surfing, tennis, cricket, golf, and four different kinds of football. The standard of living is high: most people own their own house, one in three their own car. There are excellent health services, with the Royal Flying Doctor Service providing medical care for thousands of people in isolated parts of the country; and educational provisions at all levels are of a high standard.

Australia today is a prosperous, growing, and independent nation. The Eastern countries are of great importance to her from the trading and economic point of view; the United States is the most important ally in matters of defence; and Britain's influence as founder of the nation remains. The established legal and constitutional systems, both part of the British heritage, and the traditional link with the Crown, ensure that Australia's social structure remains essentially British in character. But with her isolated geographical position, proximity to Asia, and various other alliances, it is difficult to forecast Australia's future role in international affairs.

See also TASMANIANS.
See also Vol. III: AUSTRALIA.
See also INDEX, p. 133.

AUSTRIANS. Austria, a landlocked country of Central Europe, is mainly a land of picturesque mountains and narrow river valleys. It was inhabited in ancient times by the Illyrians, conquered by the Celts in about 400 B.C., and flourished under the Roman Empire for nearly four centuries from the 1st century B.C. Then it was overrun in turn by Germanic tribes, Huns, and Avars, till at the close of the 8th century it became part of the HOLY ROMAN EMPIRE (q.v.). Later invading Magyars from Hungary were defeated in 955, and for two centuries Austria enjoyed peaceful development under the Babenberg family.

J. Allan Cash

BAND WEARING TRADITIONAL TYROLESE COSTUME

theatre, and they have a long tradition of excellence in decor and production. The opening of the rebuilt Vienna State Opera House in 1955 was a gala occasion.

Austrians are traditionally tolerant of other peoples; indeed, they are probably unique amongst Central Europeans in not having very strong nationalist feeling. This perhaps explains why many Austrians during the 1930s advocated a union with Germany as the best way out of their economic distress. Hitler's occupation, however, by arousing violent anti-German feeling, made Austrians much more conscious of their separate nationality.

In 1972 there are more than seven million Austrians, nine-tenths of whom are Roman Catholics, and nearly a quarter of whom live in VIENNA (q.v. Vol. III), a most beautiful capital city, long noted for the vigour of its intellectual and artistic life. There used to be a considerable Jewish community in Austria, especially in Vienna; but with the coming of Hitler many Jews fled to Western Europe and the United States. Many others perished in Nazi concentration camps.

Over one-third of the land is forested, and barely a half can be used for food production. About 20% of the population are engaged in agriculture; they are mainly cattle and dairy farmers in the mountainous regions, but in the flatter lands of the east they also grow root and cereal crops. Each province has its own traditional costumes and local customs. Vineyards thrive in various regions, and sampling the new wine is a special Austrian entertainment (*Heurigen*). The friendliness and gaiety of the ordinary people make them excellent hosts in a country to some extent dependent upon a summer and winter-sports tourist trade.

There are also many industrial workers living in towns such as Graz, Linz, and Leoben, occupied in heavy industries and other manufactures, and organized in the Austrian trade unions movement. The basic industries of the Republic have been nationalized since 1946.

See also Vol. III: AUSTRIA.
See also INDEX, p. 134.

The Hapsburgs ruled Austria from 1276 to 1918. By conquest, marriage, and clever diplomacy the Hapsburgs acquired a mighty empire, which in 1555 included a very large part of Europe (*see* INDEX, p. 54). Before its fall in 1918, it included present Czechoslovakia, Hungary, and parts of Yugoslavia, Rumania, Italy, and Poland, as well as Austria proper. With the Revolution of 1918 came the fall of the Hapsburg dynasty, and Austria, as the result of defeat and the Treaty of St. Germain, lost all the non-Germanic provinces of her empire.

Present-day Austrians are racially very mixed and, like the English, are rather proud of it. They speak German with a soft inflexion. They are easy-going, good-humoured people, and very gifted artistically, particularly in music. MOZART, SCHUBERT, STRAUSS (qq.v. Vol. V), and Schönberg, to name only a few, were all Austrians. Their national temperament reveals itself in their most successful style of architecture, the Baroque, which is full of gaiety and exuberance (*see* BAROQUE ARCHITECTURE, Vol. XII); and a similar love of ornament is found in their Biedermeyer style of furniture, and in the beautiful wrought-iron work to be seen, for example, at Innsbruck. The Viennese are very fond of the

AVEBURY is one of the most impressive and interesting prehistoric monuments in all Europe. It stands on the north Wiltshire Downs a few kilometres west of Marlborough, and is a sacred enclosure which may be likened to

AVEBURY FROM THE AIR

Ashmolean Museum

The village has grown up along the road which cuts through the prehistoric site. The circular bank can be clearly seen, and within it some of the standing stones

STONEHENGE (q.v.) and to many other circles built in Britain during the Bronze Age. In the past this great monument has been damaged by builders who wished to split up its stones, and by farmers who found that they got in the way of the plough; but excavation, helped by old records, has rediscovered the original plan. It has even been possible to set up again many stones which had been buried and forgotten.

Avebury, in the final form in which its makers left it, was a very complicated affair indeed and so large that a great part of the present-day village is enclosed within it. First there is an encircling bank no less than 390 metres across and with a ditch on the inner side. Inside this again, standing along the lip of the ditch, is a ring of enormous stones, once about a hundred in number. This large stone circle encloses a pair of smaller ones, standing side by side, and each originally made up of twenty-five to thirty stones. At their centres there were, originally, other large upright stones. This sacred area of the stone circles could be approached by four entrances through the bank and ditch; and from the southern one an imposing 'avenue', a double line of standing stones, led away for over a mile to Overton Hill where there was

another much smaller stone circle. The Overton circle had quite disappeared, but it has been found by excavation and marked out with concrete blocks; many stones of the avenue, on the other hand, are preserved and make a fine sight flanking the roadside towards the great enclosure itself. There may have been another avenue leading from the west entrance; but there is no trace of it today, and only excavation can show if it ever existed. Excavation has shown the way in which the stones were originally set up. A small hole was dug to receive the base of the stone, which was then slid into it with the help of a sloping ramp. The stone had then to be levered and heaved upright, and to prevent it from tipping right over while this was being done a line of stakes was driven in along the farther side of the hole.

Avebury is one of the largest of a class of monuments called *Henges* which seem to be important tribal gathering-places built at the end of the Neolithic period about 2000 B.C. when copper was first beginning to be used in Britain. Their builders belonged to the *Beaker culture*, named after their characteristic decorated pottery.

Very many of the Avebury stones are immensely heavy, and the outer bank must have stood 16 metres above the bottom of its ditch—a height as great as a five- or six-storey building. The making of such a place, all carried out with the simplest stone and bone tools, must have taken a very great deal of labour. It suggests that it must have served quite a large number of people living over a wide area, and we can imagine how, on days when special religious ceremonies were being held, tribesmen came to Avebury from all parts of the downs.

See also PREHISTORIC MAN.

AZTEC CIVILIZATION. When the Spaniards, under the leadership of CORTÉS (q.v. Vol. V) conquered Mexico at the beginning of the 16th century, they found established there the remarkable civilization of the Aztecs, which was at the height of its political and cultural development. A small band of Europeans was able to conquer them partly by first subduing and then allying themselves with some of their hereditary enemies, and partly by reason of the advantages they derived from horses and fire-arms. In addition, the morale of their ruler, Moctezuma (or Montezuma) II, was shattered by the belief that Cortés was the god Quetzalcoatl returning in fulfilment of an ancient prophecy to claim his own. Contemporary accounts give us a very vivid picture of the life and achievements of the Aztecs, who, like the INCAS of Peru (q.v.), are thus far better known to us than their predecessors.

The Aztecs were the latest of a series of civilizations in Mexico (*see* MEXICAN ANCIENT CIVILIZATIONS). They were a band of wandering hunters, who arrived in the Valley of Mexico from the north-west in the wake of others to find all the best lands occupied. Here they lived precariously, first as vassals of established states or as mercenaries, until they settled on some inhospitable islands in the swamps surrounding the lake on whose dried-up bed Mexico City now stands, in a year Two Reed, corresponding to 1325 or 1344. Here they founded their capital, Tenochtitlán, and when their ruler, Itzcoatl, acceded in 1427, they had become a powerful and aggressive state. They were an extremely warlike people, and first in alliance with other small states and finally as the dominant partner, they gradually extended their power over much of Mexico and far beyond it into Central America.

As the nation became more powerful, the

British Museum

STONE MASK OF XIPE, GOD OF SOWING AND PLANTING

Victims were sacrificed to him by flaying and he is usually clad in a human skin

warriors and the nobility increased their importance at the expense of the peasants and took more and more control of society. Itzcoatl had a very powerful chief minister, Tlacaelel, who caused the old records to be burnt because they made too much of the Aztec's barbarian origin, and rewrote Aztec history. Succeeding rulers assumed more and more the character of divine kings, as the deference with which Moctezuma II was treated at the time of the Conquest showed. In the meantime, the population increased, and local sources of food were insufficient to feed them, hence more and more conquests were undertaken to obtain tribute.

British Museum

PAINTED POTTERY VASE FROM CHOLULA

It is decorated in red on orange and cream. Height 11·5 cm

THE FIRE GOD XIUHTECUTLI
Stone figure 1·2 metres high

the sacred ball game, and a rack for the skulls of sacrificial victims. The principal shrine was a pair of temples dedicated to Huitzilopochtli, god of war and the sun, and Tlaloc, the rain god, standing side by side on the largest pyramid. There was a temple to the feathered serpent god, Quetzalcoatl, who was also the wind god, and this was circular so as not to impede the course of the wind. The temples were periodically enlarged, generally at the end of every 52 years, the older pyramid being covered with a fresh casing of stone and provided with new stairways and temples. The last time the main temple was enlarged, in 1487, it is believed that 20,000 victims were sacrificed.

Like other Mexican peoples the Aztecs had a complicated calendar. There were 18 months of 20 days, with a 5-day unlucky period at the end. At the same time ran a series of 260-day cycles composed of thirteen numbers and 20 named days (*see* illus., p. 55). When the 365-day cycle and the 260-day cycle are combined, each day is designated by two names and two numbers, a combination which recurs every 52 years. When such a cycle ended, special precautions had to be taken lest the world should come to an end. Every month there were festivals in honour of particular gods, usually involving extremely brutal human sacrifice. The victim had to mount the temple stairway, was seized at the top and stretched over a convex stone by four priests, his chest was cut open with a flint knife by another, and his heart torn out. The most efficacious victims were brave warriors taken in battle, and special wars (Wars of Flowers) were arranged to obtain them, but children and slaves were also sacrificed. Human blood and particularly human hearts were needed to nourish the gods, a belief which goes back to Toltec times, but it got more and more exaggerated under the Aztecs. Victims offered to the god Xipe, a god of fertility, were flayed after sacrifice and the skin was worn by a priest, symbolizing the covering of young vegetation on the earth in spring. Other victims were bound to a scaffold and shot with arrows so that the blood would fertilize the earth.

The Aztecs, like other Mexican peoples, used an elaborate kind of picture writing in colours. Some of their books, or codices, have been preserved, but some of the best belonged to the Mixtecs of Oaxaca, including Codex Nuttall which is in the British Museum. They were made of long strips of bark paper or deer skin, sized

Underneath the foundations of the modern city of Mexico lie the ruined remains of Tenochtitlán. The old town, dominated by its temples and white buildings, must have been a splendid sight. It was crossed by many canals, along which boats came with merchandise. Three stone causeways, with defensive bridges at intervals, ran across the lake to the shores. The sacred enclosure, which occupied the site of the present Cathedral and central square, contained many temples standing on lofty pyramids, a court for

THE GREAT CALENDAR STONE

It represents the disk of the sun. In the centre is the face of the sun-god, surrounded by the names of the 4 previous suns in square panels. In the next band are the 20-day signs of the Aztec calendar. The outermost circle is formed by 2 serpents, each with a human head in its jaws Diameter 3·65 metres

with lime and concertina-folded. The Aztecs, like the MAYA (q.v.), counted by twenties; dots stood for units and other symbols were used for 20, 400, and 8,000. Names of places were indicated by picture symbols. For instance, the town Caltepec would be shown by drawing a house symbol (*calli*) on a mountain symbol (*tepetl*). Some of the books were written soon after the Spanish conquest, and the meaning of the pictures and symbols is explained by Spanish translations written alongside. Some books were sacred almanacs and were used for divining

lucky and unlucky days; others were chronicles telling of early wanderings and conquests, and others genealogies. Others illustrated more personal matters, such as the diet and education of children, who were carefully and severely brought up. Tribute rolls form an important section.

Nearly all the young men, except those destined for the priesthood, were trained as soldiers, and for this purpose they were grouped into different wards, each under its own military chief. Warfare was their greatest glory—warriors killed in battle were believed to go to heaven.

They fought with bows, lances, and clubs or swords, edged with sharp flakes of obsidian, a kind of volcanic glass. They carried skin-covered wicker-work shields and wore wooden helmets with feather plumes.

They carried on trade mainly by barter, though as a substitute for money they used cacao beans and quills containing gold dust which had a fixed standard of value. They cultivated maize and many crops long known to the Mexicans. They made chocolate from cacao beans and a fermented drink from the juice of the Mexican aloe, called *pulque*, which is still popular. They were fond of flowers, which were grown in the water-gardens of Xochimilco (as they are today), and used them at ceremonies or served them up at banquets to provide sweet scents between the courses of food. They caught fish in the lakes. There was no other form óf transport except boats, as the wheel was unknown in America until the arrival of the Europeans, nor were there any draught animals. Dogs and turkeys were bred for food. We owe our turkeys to the American Indians, as well as tomatoes and chocolate.

Aztec art includes some excellent work, although some of the best was made by Mixtec workmen, and either traded or sent as tribute to Tenochtitlán. This includes the mosaics of turquoise, pyrite, and shell, encrusting wooded masks, a human skull, and the wooden handle of a stone sacrificial knife, all now in the British Museum. The knife-handle represents an eagle knight, a member of one of the orders—eagles and jaguars—who formed the élite of the Aztec army. The Aztecs sculptured the hardest stones, both in low relief and in the round, using stone tools and abrasives, and produced some very powerful massive statues of gods, besides an abundance of smaller objects. One of the most famous relief carvings is the calendar stone, which in its present damaged state is 3·6 metres in diameter and weighs 20 tonnes. The potter's wheel was not known in ancient America, but the Aztecs made large quantities of attractive hand-modelled pottery, delicately painted in black or grey on an orange or red ground. The brilliant polychrome pottery, often found in

British Museum

MASK OF TURQUOISE AND SHELL MOSAIC ON WOODEN BASE
It probably represents Tonatiuh, the sun-god

Aztec sites, came as tribute from Cholula in the Mixtec country (*see* illus., p. 53). Archaeologists have also found admirably carved log drums, used at sacrifices, and at least one upright war drum, with eagles and other carvings of a quality recalling European heraldry of the best period. Again, the best examples can be ascribed to the Mixtecs. The Aztecs were skilled weavers of cotton textiles and used feathers with great effect for head-dresses and for designs on shields.

The Maya of Central America and the Aztec of Mexico have sometimes been compared to the Greeks and the Romans in the development of their civilizations. The comparison cannot be pressed too far; but it is true that the early Maya, like the Athenians of Greece, had a special genius for art and mathematical science, while the Aztecs more nearly resembled the Romans in their military skill and capacity for political organization.

See also Vol. III: MEXICO.

B

BABYLONIAN CIVILIZATION. In the early period of its history Babylon, whose name Babili means 'Gate of God', was an unimportant city situated on the left bank of the Euphrates, just below the point where the rivers Tigris and Euphrates are only about 56 km distant from each other, 80 km south of Baghdad. Babylon owed her greatness to the fact that she lay at the meeting-point of two important trading routes, the one connecting her with northern Syria, the Mediterranean, and Egypt, and the other leading northward to Asia Minor and the Black Sea. She also controlled a third route leading into Persia.

Babylon first became leader of the city-states of Mesopotamia in 1894 B.C., when the kings of what is called the First Amorite Dynasty rose to power. This period lasted until the fall of the Amorite Dynasty about 1600 B.C. The most famous king of this dynasty was the great Hammurabi, who is best known for his collection of the ancient laws and customs of the country, now called the Hammurabi Code. The Code was engraved on a pillar of black basalt rock, at the head of which was carved a picture of Hammurabi receiving the laws from the hand of the Sun-god, Shamash. A copy of this pillar is in the British Museum.

The second stage of Babylonian history lasts from 1600 B.C. up to the fall of Nineveh in 612 B.C. During this period Babylon was conquered by a barbaric highland people called Kassites and then fell under the power of ASSYRIA (q.v.). When the Assyrians were conquered by the Medes and Chaldeans and their capital Nineveh was captured, Babylon rose again under Nebuchadnezzar II to an even greater height of power and splendour than she had yet enjoyed—a period known as the Neo-Babylonian Empire. It did not, however, last long: in 539 B.C. the Persian King, CYRUS the Great (q.v. Vol. V), entered Babylon in triumph, and the power of Babylon came to a shameful end.

But through all the changes of fortune which Babylon experienced, she remained the chief centre of civilization in Mesopotamia, much as the imperial city of Rome remained the centre of European civilization even after the Roman Empire had lost its power. The civilization of Babylon, like that of her great rival and conqueror, Assyria, rested upon the foundation of the ancient SUMERIAN CIVILIZATION (q.v.) which they followed. The three classes into which Babylonian society was divided were taken over from the Sumerian pattern of social life. They consisted of the *amelu*—the King and the nobles, together with the warrior class and state officials;

Giraudon

PILLAR INSCRIBED WITH THE LAWS OF HAMMURABI

the *mushkenu*—people who might be called the 'commoners', that is, merchants, craftsmen, farmers, fishermen, and so forth; and lastly, the *wardu*—the slaves, the foundation upon which the whole social structure rested, as it did in Greek and Roman society. There was an old Babylonian proverb which ran: 'The man is the shadow of the god; the slave is the shadow of the man; but the king is the equal of the god.' The King occupied a very special place as the representative of the god, and in the early period of kingship the King was generally made into a god, either after death, or in some cases during his lifetime. The ritual for making King Lipitish-tar into a god has been preserved. As the representative of the god, the King was regarded as the owner of the land, or as the god's tenant-in-chief. All holders of land paid rent to the temple in the form of cattle, grain, fish, wine, and other products of the land. The earliest written records found in the excavation of the temple of Ishtar at Erech consist of the temple accounts, which give details of dues paid in kind to the priests for the goddess. The King also played a very important part in the central event of the Babylonian religious year, the great New Year Festival in the spring. This lasted for eleven days and was a most elaborate and splendid ceremony. Each day had its special prayers and RITUALS (q.v.). Some of the rituals were carried out in secret by the priests; but most of them were performed in the great court of the temple of the god Marduk, in the presence of the whole population of Babylon. The central acts of the Festival were a dramatic representation of the death and resurrection of the god; a sacred combat in which the god vanquished a figure representing the primeval chaos-dragon, Tiamat; a triumphal procession through the city along the Sacred Way; and, as the climax of the ceremonies, a sacred marriage, in which the god, represented by the King, was married to the goddess, represented by a royal princess or a priestess. In all these proceedings the King played a central part, representing the god in his various acts. This festival continued to be celebrated as late as the 2nd century B.C., long after Babylon had ceased to have any political importance. Even when Babylon had come under Assyrian rule the Assyrian kings did not consider themselves properly enthroned until they had performed the ceremony of 'taking the hand of god' at the New Year Festival in Babylon.

DEMON OF DISEASE   *British Museum*

Babylonian terra cotta amulet, *c.* 9th century B.C.

The gods of the Babylonian religion had been taken over from the Sumerians, and many of their names were kept. The high god was Anu, the sky-god, corresponding to the Greek Zeus; next to him came Enlil, originally a wind-god, but later regarded as the earth-god; he was gradually replaced by the chief god of Babylon, Marduk; the third of the three principal gods was Ea, the god of the watery deep and the inventor of magic. Although there was an ancient mother-goddess, worshipped under various names, the goddess most widely worshipped in Mesopotamia was Ishtar, who had temples in most of the great cities of Assyria and Babylonia. In addition to these great gods, every city had its own special god. All these gods had wives and large families, and many lesser gods as servants and messengers. So the Babylonian pantheon, or assembly of gods, was a vast affair, running into thousands. Moreover, besides the gods great and small, there were hosts of evil spirits, many of them with special names, such as Lamashtu, a female demon who was particularly dangerous to pregnant women. Several classes of priests had as their main business the task of performing the spells and incantations intended to protect people from the attacks of these hostile demons. Babylonian tablets give us pictures of these horrible creatures, half-beast, half-human; and many of the magical spells and rituals used against

to collect and arrange for his great library in Nineveh tablets from every part of his empire relating to all kinds of subjects, especially religious. Hence we now can read not only the diplomatic correspondence of the Assyrian kings, but also thousands of business documents, magical tablets, liturgies, omen-tablets, the great myths of Babylon, chronicles, and so forth. History, however, in the modern sense is hardly represented in what has come down to us of Babylonian literature.

See also ANCIENT CIVILIZATIONS; SUMERIANS; ASSYRIAN CIVILIZATION.

See also Vol. XII: BABYLONIAN ART.

BABYLONIAN MYTHS. About 2000 B.C. the southern part of Mesopotamia, which had been the home of Sumerian civilization, was taken over by the Babylonians. These people adopted much from the SUMERIANS (q.v.), and myths were no exception. These were stories about the gods, the origin of the universe, of battles with monsters, and such like (*see* MYTHOLOGY). Often the Babylonians took over such stories from the Sumerians and rewrote them in other words, but some of their myths are more original. They are written on clay tablets, and these have been found in the ruins of both Babylonian and Assyrian cities, since the Assyrians mostly used Babylonian myths. Normally these stories were recited to audiences, since few people could read or write. Some examples of Babylonian myths will illustrate the kind of story and its meaning.

The *Descent of Ishtar* is about Ishtar, goddess of love. For reasons not given she decided to go down to the underworld, where her sister, Ereshkigal, ruled over the dead. This was a dangerous undertaking, since anyone who went down was not allowed to come up again. Ishtar boldly approached the gate and told the doorman that he must open to her, otherwise she would break down the door and let the dead escape. The doorman asked her to wait until he had announced her arrival to Ereshkigal, who was much alarmed to receive this news. However, she instructed the doorman to let Ishtar in, but on the usual conditions. This meant that she was let through the seven gates which led down to the underworld, but at each one a piece of her clothing was taken away, so that she finally arrived in front of her sister naked. At once she was handed over to Namtar, the demon of diseases, and was soon dead. Her absence above ground was noticed by her messenger who, on the advice of the god Ea, sent down to the underworld a specially-created being to rescue her. This creature entertained Ereshkigal by some kind of performance, which pleased her so much

A GOD WITH FORKED LIGHTNING PURSUING A MONSTER

A relief from the palace of King Ashur-nazir-pal II of Assyria, who is shown standing on the left

that she promised whatever the creature might ask. To her dismay the creature asked for Ishtar. So the body was revived, and Ishtar was allowed to return to the upper world through the seven gates, receiving back her clothing at each gate.

Ishtar's descent in the myth into the underworld symbolizes the coming on of autumn and winter, and her return to the upper world symbolizes spring and summer, when plants grow and animals have their young. She is identified with the power behind this growth and multiplying.

A different kind of myth is called *Atra-hasis* after the hero of the flood. It begins at the time when only gods lived on earth, and they had to work for their daily bread. They disliked this so much that after some years they went on strike and surrounded the house of Enlil, the chief god on earth. He called a conference of Anu, the god of heaven, and Ea, the god of the waters which were thought to exist beneath the earth. The gods who had stopped work were asked to explain their conduct, and when they described how much they disliked the hard labour, a plan was eventually worked out whereby Ea and the Mother Goddess were asked to create beings to do all the hard work of the universe. Ea proposed the details: one god, probably the ringleader of the strikers, was to be killed, and from his flesh and blood, mixed with clay, man was to be formed.

By various stages and processes fourteen human figures were made from the mixture, and these emerged as the first seven human pairs. They multiplied, dug irrigation canals, and generally worked as expected. However, one unplanned result was that, as their numbers increased, they made so much noise that Enlil could not sleep. Accordingly he sent plague to reduce their numbers, and this began to take effect. At this time Atra-hasis seems to have been king of the humans. His personal god was Ea, who, having created the human race, was not happy to see it die out through plague. So he advised Atra-hasis how humans might placate the god of plague, Namtar, and so save themselves. Atra-hasis followed Ea's advice, and once more the human race and their noise multiplied. Enlil, again unable to sleep, decided to reduce numbers by causing a drought. But again Ea advised Atra-hasis how the storm god, Adad, could be placated, and Atra-hasis persuaded Adad furtively to send mist and dew so that the crops should grow without Enlil's noticing anything.

By now Enlil suspected that a god was frustrating his plans; so he called a conference. He persuaded all the gods to agree to send a great flood that would wipe out the human race once and for all, and he bound them by oath to carry out his plan. Ea, however, though unable, because of his oath, to prevent the flood, warned his servant Atra-hasis to build a boat. Atra-hasis did this, and just before the rains began he, his family, and birds and animals went aboard. When the flood subsided, and the boat was seen, Enlil became very angry. However, the destruction brought about by the flood had caused such panic among the gods that Enlil was persuaded to allow the human race to continue, though he insisted that Ea and the Mother Goddess must control them better.

Two different things are done in this story. The first part of the myth explains how conditions in the world came about. In ancient Mesopotamia people built temples and offered regular meals, like their own, before the statues of the gods. Thus the myth is trying to explain how man was first created in order to serve the gods. Then a flood was a natural theme to take in a country where floods were common, and where occasionally very severe floods caused much damage. So the story of the great flood reflects, no doubt, an actual historical flood. The story of Noah and the ark in Genesis is certainly connected with the Babylonian myth.

The *Epic of Creation* is a later myth of the origin of the universe. It begins at a time before even the gods existed. The universe consisted of only two kinds of water: Apsû, the male, who was thought of as the water under the earth; and Tiamat, the female, whose name means 'Sea'. These two mixed their waters together and thereby started a process of creation. The result was generations of gods, but also of disharmony, for the younger gods disturbed the older ones by their noise and games. The older generation prepared to wipe out the younger; but Ea stepped in and killed Apsû so putting an end to these plans. Tiamat, now urged to take action, created a host of monsters to fight for her under her new spouse, Qingu. The younger gods, having tried in vain to confront Tiamat and her army, tried to think what to do next. Then Ea suggested that his son Marduk might take up the

A SUMERIAN MYTH

British Museum

The sun-god rises from the underworld between the mountains of the East, assisted by the water-god and Ea and his two-faced vizier, Usmu, and awaited by Ishtar, the morning and evening star. Seal of Adda the scribe, 2300–2150 B.C.

challenge. Marduk agreed so long as, if he defeated Tiamat, he might become chief of the gods. The younger gods accepted the conditions, and Marduk set out, suitably armed. At first glance, the opposing host of monsters terrified Marduk, but he recovered his nerve and went on to win.

After his victory he split Tiamat's body into two parts, making the upper part the sky, and the lower part the earth. He then organized all the parts of the universe to his liking. The gods gave him presents to celebrate his victory. Marduk suggested building Babylon as the central point in the universe, where all the gods would assemble for meetings. The gods agreed, but it was hinted that some way might be found of provisioning the temples without involving the gods in any toil. Marduk, therefore, with the advice and help of Ea, made man from the blood of Qingu, Tiamat's spouse; and the other gods in gratitude built Marduk's temple in Babylon, presented it to him at a banquet, and at the same time gave him a series of fifty different names.

Several things are being done in this myth. As in the myths already recounted, the origins of things are being explained: in this case, the origins of the various parts of the universe, the gods, the human race, and Babylon. Also this myth explains how Marduk, the god of Babylon, who had been quite insignificant, became chief of the gods; Babylon too had been a very un-

important place until the great king Hammurabi made it the capital of his empire. When this happened, Marduk entered the ranks of the 'great gods'. His change in status was simply a reflection of the changed position of the city of Babylon. He became more and more important until, about 1100 B.C., he was generally acknowledged as the most important god of all. In fact, the *Epic of Creation* is mainly concerned with explaining and justifying the position of Marduk, a junior god, as the head of the pantheon, that is, of all the gods.

There are many other myths, and none of these strange stories are the product of wild imagination. They are serious attempts of an intelligent people who had no scientific knowledge to explain the universe and its workings and powers.

See also BABYLONIAN CIVILIZATION; MYTHOLOGY.
See also Vol. XII: BABYLONIAN ART.

BAPTISM, *see* SACRAMENTS.

BAPTIST. A Baptist is a Protestant Christian of a tradition whose adherents do not baptize infants, but only those who are old enough to make a personal profession of faith in Jesus Christ. This they call 'Believers' Baptism'. The person to be baptized goes right into the water, instead of being sprinkled, as in most churches. Baptists claim that in practising baptism by immersion they follow the example of Jesus Christ whom St. John the Baptist baptized in the River Jordan.

The Baptist Church is evangelical, that is, it sets greater store by the Bible than by ceremonies. The sermon is the most important part of the service. Baptists have traditionally been defenders of freedom of conscience and religious liberty.

The first Baptist congregation in London was formed in 1611, under the guidance of John Smyth and Thomas Helwys, who were perhaps influenced by the principles of the Anabaptists, an extreme sect formed in Zurich at the time of the Reformation. John BUNYAN (q.v. Vol. V), the author of *Pilgrim's Progress*, was an outstanding English 17th-century Baptist preacher, who advocated open membership and co-operation and fellowship with fellow Christians. The Baptist movement has been divided at times between those churches open to all comers and the Strict Baptist Churches who limited their congregations to baptized believers. In organization the Baptists resemble the CONGREGATIONAL-ISTS (q.v.).

Baptists from England, Wales, and Germany in the 17th century established congregations in the American colonies. One English Baptist, Roger Williams (1603-83), founded the first settlement in Rhode Island in 1636 and framed a notably liberal constitution; but in 1639 he severed his church connexions. He remained a Christian believer, as well as an apostle of religious toleration, and liberal democracy.

The Baptist Missionary Society, formed in 1792 in England at the call of William Carey (1761-1834), inspired missionary zeal in Protestant churches generally and led to a great expansion of the Baptist community, particularly in America. Among the famous Baptist missionaries were Carey himself who served in India, George Grenfell (1849-1906) in the Congo, and Timothy Richard (1845-1919) in China.

Today there are over 31,000,000 members in at least 130 countries; the great majority, more than 27,000,000, are in the United States.

See also CHRISTIAN CHURCH.

BARROWS AND CAIRNS. Scattered across the landscape in many parts of Europe are the remains of mounds or piles of stones marking ancient burial-places. Most of these belong to the farming groups of prehistoric times, from the New Stone Age onwards (starting in Britain

around 2500 B.C.). A few are of Roman date, while some were built by the pagan Saxons. Those built of earth are called barrows, while heaps of stone are called cairns.

Of the prehistoric ones, the earliest types (3500 B.C.-2500 B.C.) are long barrows which cover collective burials and possibly belonged to one family or lineage. Some of these had stone-built chambers which could be periodically re-opened for new burials. The method of using large stones in building these chambers is called the megalithic construction technique (*see* MEGA-LITHS), and this naturally occurs only where there was building stone in massive slabs. In other areas, a simple mound with a wooden chamber (or without a chamber at all) was used, as on the English chalklands; though where stone was abundant the whole mound might consist of stones cleared from the fields. Some of the bodies buried in these tombs had been 'exposed'— that is, left for the flesh to rot from the bones before burial.

Quite different are the smaller mounds covering individual burials called round barrows. These circular mounds are surrounded by one or more shallow ditches. They often occur in whole cemeteries as groups or lines of mounds, usually on the crests of hills. Such barrows became very common at the end of the New Stone Age when copper was first beginning to be worked in Britain, around 2000 B.C. Small copper knives found in these barrows are among the earliest finds of metal in Britain. These belong to the Beaker period, called after the drinking-cups which often accompany the skeletons. The skeletons are often found crouched on their side, and it has been suggested that this is because the bodies were carried in a cloth bundle.

A little later than this, when true bronze (copper mixed with tin) was being used, we find especially rich burials with gold ornaments and fine regalia. These are some of the first evidence for chiefs or kings.

Because these tombs were covered with mounds, they are easier to find than remains of the houses and villages in which their makers actually lived. For many periods in prehistory, therefore, archaeologists depend on excavating burial mounds to see what kinds of weapons and ornaments were made at the time. However, this can sometimes give a wrong impression because only special objects might be put in graves.

Ashmolean Museum

NEW STONE AGE LONG BARROW AND BRONZE AGE ROUND BARROWS AT WINTERBOURNE STOKE, WILTS.

In Britain many barrows have been destroyed by ploughing, though even then they may show up as greener rings in growing corn, where the ditch allows roots to penetrate deeply into the soil. Most of the barrows which do survive are on the chalk downlands or in heathlands such as the New Forest, which have not been ploughed for thousands of years. They are marked on Ordnance Survey maps by the Latin word *tumulus*.

BASQUES. The Basques are a people who live on either side of the Pyrenees, some in Navarre and the Basque Provinces of Northern Spain, some in three departments of Southern France. Their origin is unknown, but they are probably the oldest western race living in Europe today. In the early Middle Ages they were notorious as a wild people who robbed pilgrims journeying to the shrines in Spain. Their subsequent history is one of gradual subjection to their most powerful neighbours, such as the Kings of Castile. Basques are now either Spanish or French citizens.

Their racial distinctiveness, however, is still preserved in their language, which in 1957 was spoken by about half a million people, and in their native game, PELOTA (q.v. Vol. IX). The Basque language is not related to any other language: it is a very difficult one to learn for its nouns have more than fifteen cases: its verbal system is even more complicated. Very little literature has been written in it. There are seven chief dialects in Basque.

BASUTOS, *see* SOUTHERN AFRICANS.

BAVARIANS, *see* GERMANS.

BEDOUIN. The word is the French spelling of Arabic Badāwīn, 'nomads'. The Bedouin inhabit a large area of the Middle East, including SAUDI ARABIA, JORDAN, IRAQ, SYRIA, EGYPT (qq.v. Vol. III), Yemen, United Arab Emirates, Qatar, Oman and Kuwait (*see* ARABIA, Vol. III). They formed an important part of the army that swept out of Arabia in the 7th century, bearing the new religion of ISLAM (q.v.). Their descendants brought Islam to North Africa. The Bedouin are Muslims, they speak Arabic, and belong to the Caucasian stock. Their exact numbers are difficult to discover. For Saudi Arabia it is estimated that two-thirds of the population are nomads.

The Bedouin are herdsmen and move with their one-humped camels or dromedaries, sheep, and goats on a seasonal round within demarcated tribal territories. Their movements are determined by the availability of water and pasture. They live in tents woven from goats' hair; each tent contains separate quarters for men, women, and children. Their material culture—tents, clothing, leather goods, domestic equipment—is simple and designed for mobility. Their animals supply them with milk, cheese, and meat as well as wool, hair, and leather from which they make their domestic articles. They use camels for transportation, and the number owned determines a family's wealth and status. These one-humped camels do not exist in the wild state, and their origin is unknown.

The Bedouin reckon descent through the father's line; they move in bands of kinsmen who regard themselves as members of larger tribal groupings formed on the basis of descent. Family ties are close, and marriage between cousins is usual, particularly with the father's brother's daughter. Kinsmen help one another and pay fines if a relative commits a crime or inflicts an injury, the payment usually being made in animals. Inter-tribal conflicts arise because of violation of pasture rights. Each tribal section owes allegiance to the *shaikhs* of successively larger sections of the tribe, but governs itself through a council of family heads or elders. A *shaikh*, who is elected by the heads of the leading families, rules in consultation with the elders and in allegiance to the government of the country. An important *shaikh* usually has a large herd of livestock and camels, a large tent, and several wives.

Western influences are slowly affecting the Bedouin way of life. Today some of them have settled jobs in oil fields and in industry, and some have risen to high offices in the various Arab countries. But the Bedouin in general have resisted the attempts that have been made in some countries to settle them as farmers, and prefer to remain herdsmen and tent-dwellers.

See also SAHARA, PEOPLES OF.

See also Vol. IV: ARABIC LANGUAGE.

A GROUP OF BEDOUIN

Haddon Library, Cambridge

When they travel from one grazing ground to another, the Bedouin carry all their belongings on the backs of their camels

BELGIANS. In Roman times Belgium was that part of Gaul known as Gallia Belgica and was inhabited mainly by Celtic tribes. However, by the 5th century, when the FRANKS (q.v.) became rulers, immigrations from the north had changed its populations largely to Germanic. Both the Celtic and Germanic elements are to be found in Belgium: the Walloons, a people of Celtic origin, live in the south-east of the country and speak Walloon, a dialect of the ancient French; while in the north are the Flemish, a Germanic people speaking their own Flemish language. Both French and Flemish are the official and business languages of Belgium (*see* FRENCH AND GERMAN LANGUAGES, Vol. IV). Most of the people belong to the Roman Catholic Church.

After several centuries of rule by the Franks the country split into independent duchies, counties, and free cities. In Flanders especially, free merchant cities developed, and played an important part in medieval life. There was a flourishing trade between the Flemish cloth merchants and England in the Middle Ages. Bruges was the chief wool market of northern Europe. Bruges, Ghent, and Ypres were famed for their prosperity and civic pride, and the wealth of the merchants is reflected in the magnificent 15th century buildings and in the brilliant painting of the time. By a series of conquests and alliances the Netherlands or Low Countries, as Belgium and Holland (*see* DUTCH) were then called, became part of the Empire of Maximilian of Austria in 1477. Later they became part of the Spanish Empire; but in 1598 Belgium became for a short time an independent kingdom. Between 1621, when it fell again under Spanish rule, and 1815, when it became one state with Holland, Belgium was governed by a succession of countries. In 1831 it separated from Holland, and set up an independent kingdom.

Today Belgium is the most densely populated country in Europe; it has great manufacturing industries and is very intensely cultivated: about one third of the population live by agriculture and horticulture. Brussels has become the seat of NATO and of the European Economic Community, better known as the Common Market. Since the importance of coal has declined, Belgium has developed a vast petrochemical industry, especially around the port of Antwerp, ideally situated as an outlet to the sea. Other important modern industries are: steel, non-ferrous metals, mechanical engineering, textiles,

Belgian Embassy

BRUGES: GOTHIC ROOM, TOWN HALL

Session of the international College of Europe

and glass. With Holland and Luxemburg, Belgium has created the Benelux Economic Union, the fourth largest export group in the world.

See also Vol. III: BELGIUM; BRUSSELS.
See also Vol. XII: FLEMISH ART.
See also INDEX, p. 134.

BENEDICTINE, *see* MONK.

BENGALIS. The Bengalis inhabit the new state of Bangladesh and the adjacent Indian state of West Bengal; their mother-tongue, Bengali, is one of the richest languages in Asia. In 1971 it was estimated that the populations of Bangladesh and West Bengal were about 75 millions and 45 millions respectively, that of Bangladesh being largely Muslim and that of West Bengal largely Hindu. However, both areas contain sizable minority religious groups. From 1947 until its emergence as an independent state in 1971, the Bangladesh region formed East Pakistan; but its people have comparatively little in common with those of Pakistan (*see* PAKISTANIS). They are mostly of indigenous origin, Muslims descended from Bengali Hindus who embraced ISLAM (q.v.) during the centuries when India was under Muslim rule. The capital of Bangladesh is Dacca, a historic city and older than Calcutta, in West Bengal.

Both Bangladesh and West Bengal are heavily and densely populated areas, with an average population of over 510 people per square kilometre. About 10% of the inhabitants of Bangladesh live in cities; the majority in rural areas live not so much in villages but rather in closely-linked, small farms scattered over the countryside. These farms often contain two or three matting huts with high-pitched gabled roofs; and because of the prevalence of streams and lakes created by inundation, each homestead is built on a raised island, surrounded by a patch of vegetables, tobacco plants, and mango trees—the garden of the Bengali peasant. The fertile plains of West Bengal are slightly drier, its hills considerably richer in minerals, and over 25% of the population of this Indian state is urban, concentrated mainly in and around Calcutta and the coalfields of the Damodar river valley.

The Bengalis are an intellectual, subtle, and artistic people. Their greatest writer in modern times, Rabindranath TAGORE (q.v. Vol. V), was awarded the Nobel Prize in 1913, the first Asian to gain such a distinction. However, as with other peoples in the region, the common man is mainly engaged in traditional occupations: agriculture (mostly rice cultivation), fishing, and boat traffic on the waterways of the Ganges-Brahmaputra. The jute and textile industries of Bangladesh and West Bengal also provide employment. Moreover West Bengal is one of the major industrial centres of India and the factories particularly around Calcutta produce a wide range of goods.

See also INDEX, p. 134.

BERBERS, *see* MOORS; SAHARA, PEOPLES OF.

BIBLE. 1. One of the materials on which men wrote in the ancient world was made from a kind of reed called Papyrus or Byblus (*see* WRITING, HISTORY OF, Vol. IV). From the first name comes our word 'paper', from the second 'Bible', meaning 'books'. When Greek Christians spoke of *Tà Βιβλία* (*ta Biblia*), 'The Books', they meant the sacred books of their religion. It is well to remember that the Greek word was plural. The Bible is not a book, but two collections of books. One collection is the Old Testament, the sacred books of JUDAISM (q.v.). The other is the New Testament.

2. THE OLD TESTAMENT. Its language is

BANGLADESH: JUTE CUTTING

Camera Press

British Museum

TWO PAGES FROM THE CODEX SINAITICUS (LUKE xix. 13–xx. 34)

An early MS. of the Bible written in Greek probably in the first half of the 4th century. It was found in a convent on Mount Sinai in the 19th century and given to the Tsar of Russia. It is now in the British Museum

Hebrew. It consists of thirty-nine books which the Jews divided into three groups:

The Law—Genesis to Deuteronomy, also called Pentateuch, or five books.

The Prophets—Joshua to 2 Kings, and Isaiah to Malachi (omitting Daniel and Lamentations).

The Writings—the rest of the books, including Daniel and Lamentations.

It may help more to make our own division, according to what the books are about.

History—God and His People. This is set out, not just as a record of events, but as the mighty acts of God, who is preparing a People for Himself, whose work is still going on, to lead to even greater things in the future.

It is God who makes all things in the beginning (Genesis). It is against Him that men do evil. From among all mankind He chooses the family of Abraham. When this family, now grown to a tribe, is in slavery in Egypt, God raises up Moses as leader and makes a Way Out (Exodus). Thus they come to Palestine, under Moses' successor (Joshua). They believe that God gave them the Law, to shape the life of their tribe (Leviticus, Numbers, Deuteronomy).

Under various tribal leaders (Judges) they try to get a firmer footing in their new country. The greatest of these leaders (Samuel) answers their demand for a King. The greatest King is David. Others succeed to the throne (Kings). About 933 B.C. the kingdom divides into Israel, the Northern part, and Judah, the Southern. Israel falls before the Assyrians in 722 B.C. and Judah before the Babylonians in 586 B.C. Parts of this same story are told from a different point of view in Chronicles.

Some of the Hebrews deported to Babylon return late in the 6th century B.C. and more the following century (Ezra and Nehemiah).

Prophecy—God's Will for His People. Many people think of prophesying as *fore*telling what is going to happen. More often it is *forth*-telling, proclaiming what God wants men to do now. The PROPHET (q.v.) is someone who feels that he has a message from God for the times. The earliest Hebrew prophets to leave their message in writing in our Old Testament belong to the 8th century B.C. The 8th-century prophets, Amos, Hosea, Isaiah, and Micah, speak of the social wrongs of their time, as well as the false idolatry. God is righteous, and His People should show they are His by their conduct. Judgement is about to come for all their evil. The Assyrians will invade Palestine. But this sinful and suffering nation is still God's people.

About 586 B.C. Jeremiah in Jerusalem sees still more certain doom coming from Babylon. He is equally sure of the future, that the nation, after a period of misfortune, will make a fresh start.

In Ezekiel's time the doom has come; he is one of the exiles, looking to the reformed and holy nation of the future. The author of Isaiah, Chapters xl–lv, belongs to this time, with his message of comfort and hope. Here is the mysterious figure of the Suffering Servant. It seems likely that the prophet meant God's people who had to suffer because the world was so full of sin. Jesus used these chapters to explain why He must suffer and die.

Haggai and Zechariah, about 520 B.C., stimulate and strengthen both the returning exiles from Babylon and the remnant who had been left in Palestine under enemy occupation in their task of rebuilding God's Temple. Malachi and Obadiah belong to the middle of the next century.

Poetry—the Songbook of the People. The book of Psalms is by far the most important part. It is a collection of hymns. Lamentations is five bitter laments connected with the Fall of Jerusalem, 586 B.C. The Song of Songs is a cluster of marriage lyrics.

Other Literature—Problems of the People. Job is poetic drama about the problem of innocent suffering. Jonah is a parable showing that God's people ought to preach to heathen nations. Ruth also shows God's care for the foreigner. Proverbs is a collection of wise sayings about conduct. Ecclesiastes is the musings of a man who is tempted to doubt if life is worth living.

Daniel belongs to a late type of Jewish writing which seems as though the writer is telling of strange things seen in a dream. The purpose is to show that God's will does in the end triumph over the evils of the world.

The first Christians continued to read in their services and in their homes these Old Testament Scriptures of the Jews, but they saw new meanings in many of these books. The People whom God had been preparing for Himself, they saw fulfilled in the Christian Church, and boldly claimed themselves to be the True Israel. God's will for His people they found to point to Jesus and His followers—for many prophets had spoken of the Chosen People as having a duty as well as a privilege, the duty of enlightening other nations. Some prophets had spoken in times of suffering of a deliverance, some of a Deliverer whom God would send—the Messiah (Anointed One) in Hebrew, the Christ in Greek. They saw all these prophecies fulfilled in Jesus, and the mysterious words about the Suffering Servant fulfilled in His sufferings, death, and resurrection. The poetry of the Old Testament, especially the Psalms, became the Christians' first hymnbook. The Christians' own literature, the New Testament, is only to be understood against the background of the Old.

3. NEW TESTAMENT. These additional twenty-seven books, most of them letters, were written over the greater part of a hundred years and were not at first thought of as forming a new holy book. The writers use the colloquial Greek of their day. They all have one great subject, Jesus Christ. The first part of the New Testament, the four Gospels, sets out His birth, life, teaching, death, and resurrection. But this is, in the words of St. Luke, only 'what Jesus *began* to do'. The rest of the books go on to show how, although now unseen, He is still with His People, and still enables men to live triumphantly.

The earliest of the writings are the two letters of the Thessalonians—though some think that the letter to the Galatians may have been even earlier. Paul, the missionary, wrote about A.D. 53, because the young Church had misunderstood some points of Christian teaching, especially about the coming again of the Lord Jesus. During the next few years St. Paul wrote to Christians in Corinth, Galatia (part of Asia Minor), and Rome. The letters to Corinth and Galatia were written because false teachers were leading his converts astray; that to Rome is the most weighty of all the epistles—perhaps the most important letter ever written. It was to the Church already founded in the capital of the Western World—and it set out the central doctrines of the Christian faith concerning Salvation. A few years later St. Paul wrote the letters to the Colossians, Ephesians, Philippians, and Philemon, in Asia Minor. He wrote from prison in Rome, and he wrote of the universal Church, through which Christ acts, and through which He will triumph. He called the Church Christ's Body.

Both Peter and Paul had nearly reached the end of their lives when the first Gospel appeared. It was written about A.D. 63 by Mark, who had often been interpreter for Peter, who could speak no Greek, and remembered his word-pictures of Jesus. At this time there was also a written collection of 'sayings of Jesus', such as the first Christians had been in the habit of learning by heart and reciting. A little later two people independently decided to combine this early collection and Mark's book into a fuller Gospel. Matthew's Gospel comes from one who was a Jew, and who emphasized that Jesus fulfils all the Old Testament promises; Luke is the only New Testament writer who was a Gentile. He wrote of Jesus as the Saviour of the world.

At the end of the 1st century St. John's Gospel was written by an old man of great spiritual wisdom. His life of Jesus is different from the others, and has been compared to a great artist's painting, which is different from the best of photographs. Finally, apart from ten books of shorter letters, we can mention three other books. The Epistle to the Hebrews represents among the letters what Matthew's Gospel does among the Gospels—Jesus as the crown of Jewish religion. The Acts of the Apostles is a second volume by St. Luke, telling the history of the early Church, from its small beginnings in Jerusalem until St. Paul's arrival at the world's capital, Rome. The Book of Revelation is in the New Testament what the book of Daniel is in the Old. In the language of strange visions it pictures the final triumph of Christ and His followers, and the glories of the Church Triumphant in Heaven.

See also CHRISTIANITY; JESUS OF NAZARETH; SACRED BOOKS; PROPHECY. See also INDEX, pp. 103–112.

See also Vol. XII: TRANSLATIONS, Section 2.

BIRTH CEREMONIES. The principal observances and ceremonies which take place when a child is born may be divided into two groups: (1) those which have as their object driving off evil spirits, frustrating witchcraft, and bringing blessing and good fortune, and (2) those which are concerned with the reception of the child as a new member of the community.

THE WARDING-OFF OF EVIL. The birth of a child is an occasion when primitive people feel anxiety and awe, as well as joy. Afraid that a kind of magical unluckiness may spread from those connected with the mysterious event, they take precautions to prevent this. Before having their babies, women are often considered to be in a state of TABOO (q.v.), and amongst primitive people are isolated in special huts. This sometimes applies to husbands as well as wives. Thus, during the last month before a birth

Pitt-Rivers Museum

SOUTHERN SUDAN: THE CEREMONY OF ADMISSION INTO THE COMMUNITY

A fire is lighted at the threshold, and the newborn child is handed out over it

amongst the Dyaks of Borneo, neither the man nor his wife may approach a fire or eat fruit or bore holes or dive into water, as any of these acts would, it is believed, injure the child. One of the strangest customs connected with these ideas is called the 'couvade' and is found in places as far apart as South America, China, and the Pacific islands. When the baby is born the father takes to his bed, sometimes dressed as a woman, as if he, and not his wife, had borne the baby—and he may stay there for days or even weeks. There are indications that the 'couvade' used to be observed even in England and Ireland. The custom is partly due to ideas of sympathetic MAGIC (q.v.). Thus, a Winnebago Indian or an Australian native keeps on the move at the time of childbirth in order, as he believes, to help the child to be born. At times of anxiety civilized people often say 'How helpless I feel!' Primitive people work off this feeling of helplessness by doing something similar to what they want to happen, and so feel they are helping it to happen. In ancient Greece the father used to run round the hearth after a child was born; in Estonia he ran round the church while the baby was being baptized. Active efforts are commonly made to keep evil spirits away and to banish witchcraft both before and after a child is born. In parts of the Philippine Islands the husband stands on top of the house brandishing a sword. It is a common practice for amulets or charms to be fastened to the new-born babe to protect it from the powers of evil.

The attacks of evil spirits are believed to be most dangerous and persistent in the interval between birth and the ceremony by which the child is received into membership of the community. The naming ceremony is often associated with the admission ceremony, as in Christian baptism and Jewish circumcision. In the British Isles it used to be thought that there was special danger that the fairies would steal an unbaptized infant, and therefore a piece of iron or some salt was placed at the foot of the bed or a lighted candle was carried around it. In Germany a knife was stuck into the door or a horseshoe placed in the cradle; the Jews rubbed a new-born baby with salt (Ezekiel xvi. 4); a Muslim baby is carried about accompanied by girls bearing lighted candles, and salt is sprinkled on the floor to protect the child from the evil eye (*see* MAGIC). When a Hindu child is born an iron article is placed in the room, and a fire is kept burning in a corner for four or five days. It can be seen from these instances that the power of fire, iron, and salt to drive off evil was very widely believed in, as was the value of particular life-giving or luck-bringing charms. Such beliefs spread from one people to another in ancient times.

In England an egg was sometimes given to an unchristened child, and in China red and white hard-boiled eggs are placed in the baby's bath. Eggs, as our own Easter eggs, are connected with the idea of rebirth. The appearance of a chicken out of what looks like a stone symbolizes life coming out of a dead thing. In ancient times gold was thought of as a life-giving charm, and it is recorded that the Jews in Bulgaria and Rumania put a gold coin in the child's cap. In ancient India a baby was held over some object of gold. It is still a common practice in Yorkshire for a baby to be given a coin. Sometimes a child is held up to the moon, a widespread custom which probably goes back to very ancient times, for moon worship was a very early form of religion. Probably the idea was that, as the moon grows, so should the baby grow.

THE ADMISSION INTO THE COMMUNITY. By far the most important ceremony in connexion with a birth, around which other rites tend to gather, is the giving of the name. Primitive folk believe that a person's name is a part of that person—perhaps the most important part (*see* SPELLS AND CHARMS). The Eskimos, for example, say that a man is made up of body, soul, and name—the name being the part which survives death. So a child without a ceremonially-given name is not a complete personality. There is a widespread belief that if a child is not soon given a name it will pine away. It was also supposed to be unwise to tell a baby's name before it was christened, as the fairies or evil spirits might steal it.

A common idea is that a baby is an ancestor reborn, so the parents have to find out its name rather than choose it. One of the ways adopted for doing this is to hold up the baby while it is crying, and repeat to it a list of names: the name being pronounced at the moment it stops crying is its true name. Ideas sometimes are rather confused. In a South African tribe, although people may regard a baby as an incarnation of its grandfather and give it his name, they will still go on worshipping the spirit of the grandfather (*see* ANCESTOR WORSHIP). There is often a fixed date after birth for the name-giving ceremony. The ancient Greeks held it on the tenth day. In south Germany there was a belief that a soul flies around between rebirths as a butterfly; in Nidderdale, in Yorkshire, it is said that babies which die unchristened become those strange nocturnal birds called nightjars. Another idea was that they joined the fairies. In China, to make sure that the baby will not be spirited away, an open lock is moved over its body and closed when it reaches the ground, so anchoring the child to this world. A new-born baby is often presented before the gods, and communion established between it and the ancestors.

One of the most widespread practices is some form of baptism. As well as in Christian lands, such rites are found in Central America, Papua, Tibet, and many other parts of the world. Water, especially running water, since it is life-giving and also purifying, is considered specially suitable for birth ceremonies.

There is sometimes a ceremony of readmission of the mother into the tribe after her time of seclusion. A Hopi Indian mother cannot go out until five days have elapsed after the birth. On the twentieth day the child is presented to the sun, and the mother becomes again a full member of the community. In England the custom is often observed that a mother does not go out until she has been 'churched'. A birth is, of course, the occasion for such expressions of joy and goodwill as feasting and the giving of presents.

See also FOLKLORE.

BLACK FELLOWS, *see* AUSTRALIAN ABORIGINES.

BOERS, *see* SOUTH AFRICANS.

BOHEMIANS, *see* CZECHOSLOVAKS.

BOLIVIANS. Though Bolivia is four times the size of the British Isles, its population of five million is less than a tenth of the population of Britain. Three-quarters of the people live on the highland plateau to the east of the Andes Mountains, and most of the rest of Bolivia, particularly the low, hot forest lands to the north, is very thinly peopled. In spite of some immigration, including about 3,000 Germans, the country is under-populated. If Bolivia is to take its place among the South American Republics it needs more people, for much of the wealth of the country has not yet been exploited, and the eastern valleys in particular are very fertile and rich.

The Indian population of Bolivia is descended from the great pre-Spanish Indian civilizations (*see* INCA). They now form the majority of the people. Although their standard of living is still low, their lot has been somewhat improved by the reforms of President Victor Paz Estenssoro that followed the Revolution of 1952, when peasants seized the land. Conditions in the mines are, however, still very bad, and mining is an important industry, tin being the principal export of the country.

Like most of South America, Bolivia became part of the Spanish Empire in the 16th century. For a time the silver-mining city of Potosi was the richest city in the world. In the early 19th century came the great wars of liberation under the leadership of the Venezuelan soldier-statesman, BOLIVAR (q.v. Vol. V); and in 1825 the state, called Bolivia in honour of Bolivar, was separated from Peru and established as an independent republic. In a war with Chile (1879–83) she lost her stretch of Pacific coastline and became a completely land-locked country. In 1932, in an attempt to force an outlet to the Atlantic south-east, she engaged in a disastrous war of much blood and horror with Paraguay. But she gained no outlet to the sea.

Bolivia's social and political difficulties are the result of her geographical isolation and consequent economic stagnation.

See also Vol. III : BOLIVIA.
See also INDEX, p. 135.

Camera Press

WOMEN QUEUE OUTSIDE A STATE-OWNED SHOP

BRAHMINS, *see* CASTE.

BRAZILIANS. Although the South American state of Brazil has an area more than thirty-five times the size of Great Britain, its total population is not much more than one and a half times that of Britain—some 93 million. Most of this population lives along the coasts and in the eastern highlands. In the tropical forest regions of the Amazon there are large areas where the population is only one man per 2 or 3 sq. km.

The people of Brazil are very mixed in origin. First there are the aboriginal Indians, many of whom were killed by the early settlers or died under forced labour in the gold-mines. There are still many tribes of Indians in the forests of the interior who have had little or no contact with the white man, and continue their tribal life of hunting and fishing. Many an expedition has come to an untimely end through meeting parties of these Indians with their poisoned arrows, and it is still considered dangerous to travel through some parts of the Amazon headwaters because of these tribal raids. As in other countries bordering on the Amazon basin, the retaliation of the 'civilized' has often been to massacre the Indians (*see* AMERICAN INDIANS, CENTRAL AND SOUTH).

The white population are descendants of the early Portuguese settlers and of the big European immigrants of fortune-seekers, especially during the 19th century. Brazil is the only South American republic where Portuguese, rather than Spanish, is the official language.

The third element in the Brazilian population is the Negro, the descendants of the slaves brought over from West Africa in the 17th century to replace the Indians, first in the sugar plantations and then in the gold- and diamond-mines. There is no segregation in Brazil. Though it is still true that most poor Brazilians are black and that most Black Brazilians are poor, the relations between people of all colours are easy by this world's standards.

A further immigrant element has been the Japanese, who have flourished as farmers around the City of São Paulo, said to be the fastest growing city in the world.

The Portuguese first came to Brazil in 1500. They found there the brazilwood tree, which produced a much-prized red dye called brazil, and from this came the name of the country. The early settlers fought with the Indians and enslaved them ruthlessly, making them work too hard in miserable conditions. The only people to consider the welfare of the Indians were the Jesuit missionaries, who made expeditions into the interior of the country, risking hardship and death to bring a better way of life to the Indian tribes. They fought against the slave-gatherers, and did what they could to protect the Indians against the slave-trade.

In 1807 Napoleon attacked Portugal; and the King of Portugal, with many of the best families of nobles, fled from Europe to Brazil, settling in Rio de Janeiro. They brought with them works of art, books, and customs, which had a considerable effect on the culture of the Brazilians. When Napoleon was defeated, the King returned to Portugal, but his son, Pedro, remained behind. Shortly afterwards Brazil separated from Portugal and Pedro became the first emperor. His son, Pedro II, who reigned from 1831 to 1889, was a progressive, liberal-minded ruler, and built up Brazil on something like democratic lines. By 1888 most of the slave owners had freed their slaves, and in that year slavery was officially abolished. When, in 1889, the country decided on a republic, Pedro abdicated, and the revolution was carried through without a struggle. Much money has since been spent in developing modern ports, railways, airways, industries, and other facilities of a modern state, and in improving sanitation, so doing away with the plagues of yellow fever.

Throughout its history Brazil has been through a series of booms and depressions resulting in sudden changes and the making and losing of great fortunes. These have been caused by the exploitation and collapse of one major product after another. The first settlers put all their efforts into sugar plantations. Then followed the great gold and diamond rush. In 1900 the possibilities of rubber were discovered, and a great rubber boom followed. But rubber seeds had been smuggled out of the country, and new rubber plantations in the East Indies stole the market. In 1754 a Franciscan monk planted some coffee seeds in his monastery; and from this grew the great coffee industry, now the major source of Brazil's exports and the largest supplier to the world. There are other sources of great wealth in Brazil waiting to be exploited: the richness of the Amazon forests, in which almost every known tree flourishes; the great iron-ore deposits, the possibilities of stock-breeding in the

J. Allan Cash

A COFFEE PLANT NURSERY IN BRAZIL

Brazilian highlands—all these offer prospects of a more stable national economy. Since the Second World War Brazil has industrialized at a very rapid rate.

In 1964 the Army put an end to democratic government in Brazil, which had entered a very confused and demagogic phase. Military rule has had some success in running the economy, but a high price has been paid in the loss of personal freedom.

See also Vol. III: BRAZIL; INDEX, p. 135.

BRETONS, a Celtic people of Brittany. *See* CELTIC CIVILIZATIONS; FRENCH.

BRITISH ISRAELITE. In 1649 a certain John Sadler wrote a book called *The Rights of the Kingdom*, in which he suggested that the name of Britain was derived from two Syrian words *berat anak*—the land of tin and lead; and he drew attention to the resemblances between Hebrew and English law and custom—though, in fact, these are due to the influence of the Bible, and not to any racial connexions. Then between 1757 and 1824 a retired naval officer, Richard Brothers, wrote fifteen volumes on the descent of the British from the Hebrews, claiming himself to be descended from King David. He died insane. From 1840 onwards a number of writers, including C. P. Smyth, Astronomer Royal for Scotland, developed the idea that the British are the descendants of the so-called lost ten tribes. An organized movement called the British-Israel World Federation developed.

The most serious objection to the British-Israel theory is the now well-established fact that the ten tribes never were 'lost'. Right to the end of the Bible the Twelve Tribes are spoken of as still existing. The verse in the apocryphal book 2 Esdras xiii. 40, quoted by British Israelites is a mistranslation. Josephus in his History (A.D. 93) knows nothing of these 'lost' tribes.

It is officially denied by the College of Arms that the present British sovereign is descended from David, as the British Israelites declare.

The British Israelites filled whole books with calculations of the proportions of the Great Pyramid of Egypt in inches, upon which are based alleged revelations by God regarding the future history of the world. Their methods are mistaken; the 'inch' of British measurement was not used in the construction of the pyramid.

BRITISH PEOPLES. Five thousand years ago farming tribes who came from Europe were

THE ROYAL COAT OF ARMS

already living in settled communities in the British Isles. Between about 3000 B.C. and the time of Christ further waves of invaders reached Britain from the continent of Europe. Archaeologists can give us only a hazy picture of these remote peoples, but they included a seafaring race from the Western Mediterranean who sailed up the coast of France and settled in western England, Wales, Ireland, and Scotland and left as evidence of their technical skill and religious beliefs the standing stones or *megaliths* so common in western Britain. Later came the Celts, a more advanced people from northern France who, by the time of the Roman conquest (43 A.D.), had reached some degree of political organization and a very high level of artistic achievement in bronze, iron, and pottery.

Properly recorded British history begins with the Romans, who conquered and held for almost 400 years England and Wales, but never subjugated Scotland or Ireland. The Romans built impressive towns and roads and introduced some of the British to civilized Roman habits, such as the daily bath. They gave Britain 400 years of peace, but their presence had remarkably little lasting effect on the people, except that, near the end of the occupation, the Christian religion spread to Britain, where it was warmly received and transmitted even to those Britons not subject to Rome.

After the departure of the Romans and the collapse of the Roman Empire in the West, came new waves of invaders from Europe. These were the Anglo-Saxons, pagan warriors from north-west Germany and Holland, who settled in what is now England. The Celtic peoples were either driven westwards into Wales and Cornwall or enslaved by the newcomers. The Celts in the west retained their Christian religion and, in the 7th century, played an important part in converting the Anglo-Saxons, or 'English' to Christianity.

Anglo-Saxon England was divided into six or seven warring petty kingdoms, such as Northumbria, Mercia, and Wessex. By the 9th century, however, the kings of Wessex, of whom ALFRED THE GREAT (q.v. Vol. V) is the most famous, were becoming recognized as national leaders. But yet another influx of foreigners was beginning, this time from Scandinavia. Viking raiders from Norway looted and pillaged all parts of the British coasts and finally settled, mainly in Scotland and Ireland. England's main worry was the Danes, who managed to conquer much of the east of the country; in the 11th century the whole of England was united under the Danish King Cnut. Although the Danes became local leaders and landowners, they formed only a minority of the population and did not substantially change the language or culture of the people.

The last major foreign incursion into Britain, the Norman Conquest of 1066, was similar to the Danish invasion in that it gave England a new aristocracy, this time from northern France. The Normans brought their own military, political, and legal system, feudalism, and, despite occasional civil wars, they gave England sound, if harsh government. The successors of the Norman kings subjugated Wales and began the conquest of Ireland, but failed in their attempts to overcome the Scots. The union between England and Scotland came about only when the king of Scotland, James VI, succeeded to the English throne in 1603.

England in the Middle Ages was linked closely to France, and most of the wars of the period stemmed from attempts by English kings to extend or defend their possessions there. In the 15th century the English were expelled from France, and the accompanying civil wars in England were ended only the strong, ruthless Tudor monarchs, one of whom, HENRY VIII, began the breach between England and the Roman Catholic Church. Another, QUEEN ELIZABETH I (qq.v. Vol. V), saw the growth of

English sea-power and the defeat, in 1588, of the Spanish Armada.

Modern British political institutions began to develop in Tudor times, although their roots go back further. In the 17th century came several conflicts between the Tudors' successors and Parliament, which at that time represented only the more wealthy people. The issue was decided in favour of Parliament, with the result that Britain has ever since been a constitutional monarchy. In the 19th and 20th centuries pressure from working-class leaders and others caused the right to elect members of the House of Commons to be extended to all men and, later still, women. Britain, therefore, although it still has a Queen who can trace her descent from William the Conqueror and Alfred the Great, can rightly claim to be a democracy.

The several parts of the British Isles were brought together into a single political unit under English domination partly by conquest (in the case of Wales and Ireland), partly by an accident of inheritance (in Scotland's case).

Whereas English, SCOTS, and WELSH lived in harmony, the IRISH (qq.v.) never accepted English rule willingly and, in the late 19th and early 20th centuries, struggled, often violently, for their independence. A compromise of 1922 gave independence to most of Ireland (later to become the Irish Republic) and kept the six counties of Northern Ireland within the United Kingdom. But even this settlement has not pleased everyone: violence erupted again in Northern Ireland in 1969.

Until 1066 the British Isles had lain open to foreign invasion for at least 4,000 years. From then onwards the growing strength of England in particular and lessening pressure from would-be invaders have meant that there have been no large-scale infusions of new blood. English, or British, governments have been able to decide whether to admit strangers or not. Thus Edward III invited Flemish weavers to settle in England and late 17th-century governments welcomed the French HUGUENOTS (q.v.) fleeing from religious persecution. The Flemings

John Hilleson

CEREMONY: A ROYAL WEDDING IN WESTMINSTER

COUNTRYSIDE: A FARM IN ROSEDALE, YORKSHIRE   *J. Allan Cash*

and Huguenots, however, amounted to only a minute fraction of the total population. Nor did the late 19th-century influx of Russian Jews and German businessmen make much impact. In the 20th century some political refugees have sought asylum in Britain (Germans escaping from Hitler's tyranny, Poles unwilling to return to their homeland after 1945, and Hungarian exiles after the revolt of 1956), but the total number of Europeans seeking British nationality has always been small.

Last in the lengthy catalogue of people who have come to the British Isles from abroad are the West Indians, Indians, Pakistanis, and other Commonwealth peoples who were admitted in the 1950s and 1960s, and the Ugandan Asians who sought refuge there in 1972. Although more numerous than most recent groups of immigrants, these 'black Britons' are only a small proportion of the whole population, which remains, in the east and south, predominantly Anglo-Saxon and, in the west and north, a mixture of Celtic, Anglo-Saxon, and Scandinavian.

The language of the British people is an indication of their mixed origin. The pre-Roman Britons spoke a variety of Celtic dialects. The Anglo-Saxon invaders had their own entirely different language, related to the ancestors of modern German and Dutch. The Celtic languages died out in the areas of Anglo-Saxon settlement, but survived in the west: modern WELSH, IRISH, GAELIC (qq.v. Vol IV), Manx, and the now extinct Cornish are thus links with Britain's remote past. Anglo-Saxon, or Early English, was the main root of modern English and remained the principal language of most of England until the Norman Conquest. It produced its own literature, of which the poem *Beowulf* is the finest example. For at least two centuries after the Conquest, two distinct languages appear to have been spoken, the Norman French of the barons and knights and the Early English of the peasants. By the 14th century the two were fusing into the 'Middle English' of Chaucer's *Canterbury Tales*. From this modern English developed, reaching something like its present form at the time of Queen Elizabeth I and Shakespeare. Just as England became politically dominant in the British Isles, so English became the language of most of the British people (*see* ENGLISH LANGUAGE, Vol. IV).

J. Allan Cash

CITY: SHEFFIELD CITY CENTRE AND PARKLAND

Even though virtually everyone in the British Isles speaks English, they do not all speak in the same way; dialect and accent distinguish the various regions. These differences were until recently so marked that people from, for example, Norfolk and Cumberland might not be able to understand each other. Radio, television, and popular education have somewhat lessened the 'dialect barrier', but a traveller still notices a pronounced change in speech as he moves around the country.

Just as successive migrations to Britain account for the composition of the British people, so migration from the British Isles explains the spread of the English language and British institutions and culture to many parts of the world. From the 17th to the 19th centuries large numbers of English, Scots, and Irish emigrated to what were first the British North American colonies and later the United States of America. Migrations of the 19th and 20th centuries have given Australia, New Zealand, and most of Canada their predominantly British character, while other British settlers have made new homes in South Africa, Rhodesia, Kenya, the West Indies, and elsewhere.

There have also been numerous population movements within the British Isles. The Scots, for example, came to Scotland from Ireland at the same time as the Anglo-Saxons were arriving in England, and the present-day Protestant population of Northern Ireland can trace its ancestry back to settlements by English and Scottish families in Ulster in the 16th and 17th centuries. Within the last two centuries London and the industrial towns of northern and central England have attracted large numbers of people from the poorer parts of the British Isles. There are more Scots in London than in Edinburgh and many English families can point to Irish, Welsh, or Scottish forbears.

In the 19th century the British were the richest and strongest nation in the world. They had acquired, by discovery and conquest, an Empire embracing a quarter of the world's population, including India, Canada, Australia, New Zealand, many West Indian islands, and a large part of Africa. That so small an island had become so powerful was due to the enterprise of its merchants and manufacturers. Brave and ruthless seafarers, who in the days of Drake and Hawkins were little more than pirates,

SPORTS: A CRICKET HERO PURSUED BY ADMIRERS

Central Press

had by the 18th century grabbed a large share of the highly profitable trade in slaves and West Indian sugar. The British navy had mastery of the seas, and British gold financed European armies in a series of wars against the French. Then in the late 18th and early 19th centuries a spate of inventions relating to the textile, iron, and coal-mining industries, accompanied by the first successful harnessing of steam power, led to a massive expansion of British industry, the movement of population from countryside to town, and the transformation of the landscape. By about 1850 the INDUSTRIAL REVOLUTION (q.v. Vol. VII) was well advanced and Britain's industrial lead over other nations gave her the right to claim the title 'workshop of the world'.

This economic pre-eminence, on which Britain's wealth and power depended, was not to last, however. Other nations began to catch up. The United States and Germany, both of whom had bigger populations and greater resources, had overtaken Britain by the beginning of the 20th century. Britain's wealth was based on industries such as cotton, coal-mining, and heavy engineering, in which she had given the world a lead, but the new industries of the 20th century, such as the manufacture of motor vehicles and aeroplanes and the electrical and chemical industries, had been pioneered by foreigners. Britain had to face increasingly fierce competition and reconcile herself to a smaller share of world trade. Two world wars consumed a large part of her accumulated wealth and forced her to abandon her role of world power. Her governments, manufacturers, and people have, however, adapted themselves to the challenge of the late 20th century. They have not tried to live on the nation's past glories, but have built up the new industries vital to a modern state in a competitive world.

The overall prosperity of a nation affects, but does not determine, the living standards of the people. A great deal depends on how the wealth is divided. During Britain's 19th-century heyday the mass of the working people enjoyed a standard of living little, if at all, higher than their peasant ancestors, mainly because wages were low and governments did not consider that it was their duty to provide pensions, sickness benefit, or any of the other amenities of the Welfare State. During the present century, on the other hand, when Britain has experienced a comparative decline, the standard of living has improved enormously. This change, which has come about mainly since the Second World War, is due to the success of powerful trade unions in compelling employers to pay higher wages, to a recognition by manufacturers that well-paid workers are good customers, and to government policies to keep down unemployment. The state now also provides a range of social services which guarantee the people free medical treatment and education, give pensions for the aged, and, in a variety of ways, attempt to eliminate poverty and hardship.

The British people are more numerous than ever before. They are also better fed, clothed, housed, and cared for than their forefathers. Whether their standards will continue to rise depends on their own abilities and efforts. They are a proud and defiant nation, as they proved in 1940 when they stood behind Churchill in stubborn resistance to Hitler. They are resourceful and inventive, as their industrial history demonstrates. They have repeatedly extricated themselves from crisis, but they often have to reach the brink of disaster before they realize their predicament.

See also Vol. III: ENGLAND; SCOTLAND; WALES; IRELAND; INDEX, p. 141.
See also Vol. IV: ENGLISH LANGUAGE.
See also Vol. XII: BRITISH ART; ENGLISH LITERATURE.

BRONZE AGE, *see* PREHISTORIC MAN, Section 5.

BUDDHISM ranks with ISLAM and HINDUISM (qq.v.) as one of the most influential non-Christian religions in the world. The name Buddhist comes from a Sanskrit adjective *buddha*, which means the enlightened one—'a person who has woken up to some great truth'. It is the title given to GAUTAMA (q.v. Vol. V), the founder of the Buddhist faith.

Siddhārtha Gautama was born in about 560 B.C. on the borders of what is now the state of Nepal on the northern frontier of India. His people were local princes, and he was of the *Kshatriya* or ruling caste (*see* CASTE). He grew up at a time when the belief in many gods and their worship by sacrifice were beginning to seem inadequate to Indians of deep religious sensibility—just as, at about the same time they were beginning to dissatisfy similar people in Greece, Iran, and China.

Gautama was not the first to experiment with a better way—there had been philosophers in north India for generations, living in the forests and jungles and training disciples. One group of these who had completely broken away from established religion, came to be called JAINS (q.v.), and their teachings probably influenced Gautama. At this time the more profound teachers were convinced that the ordinary religion was futile. There was, they felt, only one Self in the whole universe, and the object of life ought to be to discover one's relation to that Self within one's own little self, and then to go on to improve it. But so far the teachers had only suggested that this should be done by bludgeoning the body into obedience (*see* ASCETICISM) and by tricks of technique (Yoga) and meditation. Gautama did not entirely reject these, but he thought that they were inadequate and that, in particular, self-torture went too far. So he proceeded to plan a new movement which could be shared by everybody —and not simply by the priestly caste—in which the body's basic needs should be satisfied, and moral conduct, especially kindness to others, including animals, should play a leading part. The end aimed at was a completely happy state in which the individual ceased to bother about himself and his future, and aimed only at achieving a condition of perfect selfless tranquillity, referred to as *nirvāna*, namely, 'cessation' of all bad thoughts.

Gautama died at the age of 80, after a ministry of 45 years, during which he founded many groups of disciples to whom he preached regularly. Even during his lifetime it became clear that a real follower of the Buddha had to live very much as monks and nuns do. So the Buddha founded the world's first order of monks and nuns, who were to live by begging food, and it was the duty of a Buddhist layman to help to support them.

At first Buddhism developed within the general Indian religious tradition (*see* HINDUISM); but later on, missionaries carried it outside India, and it extended north, south, and east—till today it is the main religion in Sri Lanka, Burma, Thailand, and Indo-China. Most Japanese call themselves Buddhists, though they have more than one religion at a time and only use Buddhism for certain purposes; and before the Communist government, the same was true of very many Chinese. The communists have also put an end to most of the Buddhism in Tibet and

A COLOSSAL STATUE OF THE BUDDHA NEAR YOKOHAMA, JAPAN

Mongolia. There are hardly any Buddhists in India now, but some in Nepal and Bangladesh.

Buddhism has split into two main parts. The larger one we call Northern Buddhism, but it calls itself Mahāyāna (the Great Way). Some Mahāyāna Buddhists call the smaller southern community Hīnayāna (the Lesser Way); but the latter think themselves more faithful to the original teaching of Gautama. Actually, both are developments, and perhaps neither exactly represents the original message of the Buddha. This was exceedingly practical and kept clear of speculation and theology. What the Buddha certainly taught was that most of life was full of unhappiness and tension; that this was caused by people's thirst for all sorts of unsatisfying things; that to get rid of the unhappiness you must get rid of the thirst; and that to do this the best way was to follow his system of meditation and disciplined conduct. This is summarized as the Four Noble Truths. The Mahāyāna developed a theory that Gautama was one of a series of incarnations of the Supreme Being or Buddha-Spirit. These incarnate individuals, who are rather like the Christian saints, are known as *Bodhisattvas,* and are held to have deliberately stopped short

of attaining final happiness in order to help and teach other human beings. There are a great many of them—and some are certainly not real historical characters, since whenever Mahāyāna Buddhism has been established in a country it has tended to turn the gods of that country into Buddhist saints, so that people can keep on worshipping them. Southern Buddhism does not recognize most of these Bodhisattvas or saints.

Japanese Buddhism has some very distinctive sects; one of them teaches that salvation can be obtained and Paradise (which is called the Pure Land) reached by trusting in the merits and reciting the name of a particular Bodhisattva called Amidha.

For missionary purposes Buddhist teaching has been summarized in the Four Noble Truths, mentioned above, and in the scheme of practice known as the Noble Eightfold Path, comprising 'correct' views, aspiration, speech, behaviour, livelihood, effort, mindfulness, and concentration. But these are rather meaningless, unless you know what Gautama meant by 'correct'. For example, he said that nobody might earn his living by taking life; this should stop a Buddhist from being a soldier or a gamekeeper. Right behaviour means keeping the equivalent of the sixth, seventh, eighth, and ninth commandments in the Bible, as well as being a total abstainer from alcohol. None of the teaching attributed to Gautama was committed to writing till two or three centuries after his death, so that it is difficult to say how much of the Buddhist scriptures—the *Tripitaka* or *Three Baskets of Tradition*—is really his teaching (*see* SACRED BOOKS). The same kind of comment might be made about Christianity, except that the teaching and life of Jesus were recorded in writing about 40 years after he had left this earth.

Here is a description of a Buddhist meeting in Thailand, where Buddhism is very much alive. The *wat* or temple has at one end an altar with statues of the Buddha and saints and with lights and flowers. About one-third of the way to the door is the preacher's throne or pulpit. On the occasion described there were about twenty monks in front of the pulpit and a congregation of about forty-five behind it, all seated on mats. Behind the pulpit was a candle-rack for offerings of candles to the Buddha. While waiting for the service to begin the congregation were chatting,

The goal to be aimed at in all Buddhism is a state of mind called *nirvāna*, which was described by one Buddhist monk as 'bliss unspeakable'. Literally the word means 'blowing out' or 'cessation', i.e. 'the cessation of fanning a fire so as to let it die out'. This fire is the fire of 'greed, hatred, and delusion', which causes one to be reborn eternally unless it is stilled. The main point on which all Buddhists seem to be agreed is that the sense of being an individual is an illusion to be got rid of, chiefly by meditation. Gautama's disciples may have carried this side of his thought farther than he did himself. The main experience sought after is the feeling of 'release' from illusion into the fullness and freedom of understanding the Truth; this is also release from rebirth.

In theory Buddhists stress the virtue of kindness. But some Christians think that Buddhists are often so concerned with the uprooting of all desire that they seem to be rather indifferent to the needs and sufferings of others and therefore uninterested in social service and social co-operation. But perhaps the same might be said of some Christian societies. Buddhism, like other faiths, is still changing and is sensitive to criticism. There are those who say that it has rendered Asia somewhat the same service that Christianity has rendered Europe. Buddhism has been in the past a good deal like those types of Christianity which give up the world as a bad job; but it is not much like those which seek to reform or improve the world.

BULGARIANS. The Bulgars were a conquering nomadic tribe which came into Europe from the lower regions of the river Volga in Russia. By the 8th century they had settled in their present home and mixed with the Slavonic-speaking peoples there, adopting their language but retaining their own traditions. They fell under the domination of the Ottoman Empire (*see* Turks) in 1393 and remained under Turkey until they gained a semi-independence in 1908. There is still a considerable Turkish minority, though the Bulgarians themselves belong to the Orthodox Eastern Church (q.v.). In the First and Second World Wars Bulgaria fought on the side of Germany, but in 1944 the country signed an armistice with the U.S.S.R., and Bulgarian communists gained control of the government.

Bulgaria emerged from five centuries of

J. Allan Cash

PRIEST OF ALL THE MAHĀYĀNA BUDDHISTS, WITH PRAYER WHEEL, AT BOUDHA, NEPAL

chewing betel-nut, drinking tea, and some even smoking. A few were praying. The service began with chanting in unison by the monks for about 10 minutes, followed by a reading of a lesson for about 20 minutes, first in Pāli, the language of their scriptures, then in a Thai translation. When the preacher left the pulpit there was more chanting, and finally everybody bowed low till their heads touched the ground. Then the monks rose and filed out, the congregation drank more tea and, after a little conversation, dispersed, each member putting a coin in the alms box at the door as he went out. The readings are generally from the records of the discourses of the Buddha and are listened to with great reverence and attention. Buddhist prayer is, for the most part, what we should call meditation. There is no asking; but sometimes the meditation, or the saying of a series of texts from the sacred books of Buddhism, is undertaken with the idea that credit is earned this way. Since to the Buddhist the Universe is strictly ruled by cause and effect, credit gained by prayer may be applied to the benefit of the worshipper himself or of anyone he particularly wishes to help.

Royal Geographical Society

BULGARIAN TRADITIONAL PEASANT COSTUME

Since 1944 the Bulgarian constitution and state economy have followed a Soviet pattern. Various five-year plans, partly supported by Soviet Russian capital, have resulted in the creation of new industries which include steel mills, chemical plants, and electricity power stations. Virtually all productive land is held by vast collective farms.

Peasant workers on the collective farms are allowed to keep small private plots for grazing a cow or goat and growing their own vegetables. With these resources and frugal habits the rural population live relatively well despite modest wages. By the end of the 1960s essential goods were available everywhere in a reasonable variety. But in the towns, where between 1946 and 1971 the urban proportion of the population had increased from 25 per cent to 52 per cent of the total, housing was generally inadequate. Higher education, on the other hand, has been greatly expanded, particularly in technology, and is available to all students who reach the required standards.

The transformation of a backward Balkan state into a relatively prosperous modern communist state has been made at the cost of a severe regimentation of almost all aspects of life, including artistic expression. The Bulgarian government in faithfully following every change in Soviet Russian policy has allowed some degree of liberalization since 1956. This has not satisfied many younger Bulgarians who, although they do not oppose the system, nevertheless copy Western styles in pop music and dress and in doing so often outrage the authorities.

See also Vol. III: BULGARIA; INDEX, p. 135.
See also Vol. IV: SLAVONIC LANGUAGES.

Turkish domination as an impoverished and backward state, with few good roads, few large towns, and with almost no development of her natural resources. Eighty-five per cent. of the population were peasant farmers whose land was often so barren that a living could be wrested from it only by constant toil. Though villagers wore their gay national costume, village life was ruled by stern and puritanical elders, who gave or withheld permission for young people to marry. The puritanical tradition was even more striking in city life.

The Bulgarian capacity for hard work and careful living is accompanied by a rather unexpected fanaticism which has shown itself many times in their history. In the 10th century thousands were martyred for their fanatical devotion to Bogomilism, a heretical movement which disputed the moral teaching of the gospels and insisted that all material things were of the Devil. And in more recent history many Bulgarian Communists died for their beliefs before their party came to power in 1944, just as after that date their opponents were persecuted with equal severity.

BURMESE. Two-thirds of Burma's twenty-eight million people are the real Burmese; the rest include mountain tribes above the Irrawaddy valley and Indian and Chinese immigrants. These jungle people for the most part still live primitive lives and have primitive ideas. A few people, such as the Was on the Chinese border, are still head-hunters—not so much because they are ferocious by nature, but because sacrifices are thought necessary to ensure good crops; there are strict rules as to how and whom and when to head-hunt. One often hears of the scores of languages of India and Burma; but it must be remembered that most are spoken by very few people—for instance, the Padaungs,

G. E. Harvey

A SHAN GIRL

whose women wear brass rings on their necks, number only a few thousands.

In the north and west are the Nagas and Kachins. On the open grassy plateau in the east are the more civilized Shans, one of the largest groups: they practise BUDDHISM (q.v.) and are a very likeable people and great gamblers. They are divided into small tribes, some of only a few hundred people occupying tiny patches of land. Farther south, in the wild Salween country, are the hill Karens. Like most of the hill people, they follow ANIMISM (q.v.). The territory of each of these peoples is now a political division of the Union of Burma. Burma proper comprises over half the country. The States, which each has its own State Government are, in order of size: Shan State, Kachin State, Kawthoolei (formerly Karen) State, Hazah States, and the Chin Division.

The ruling classes of the Burmese came from southern China about 1,000 years ago. Their first great king Anawrahta (about A.D. 1066) founded the beautiful city of Pagan, which was sacked by Kublai Khan's Mongols. There followed long wars with the Siamese and other peoples. Sometimes a great leader would unite the country for a while. One of the greatest, Alaungpaya, was a simple village headman (rather like a combination of William Wallace and Robert Bruce) who rallied his people and, when he died in 1760, had built a strong kingdom again. After him there was one really good and wise ruler, Mindon Min; but most of the kings were weak or tyrannical. As a result of three wars with the British (in which there was much injustice on both sides) Burma became a province of India. In 1937 it was separated, and in 1948 become completely independent. The new state tried to achieve parliamentary democracy, but failed. In 1962 General Ne Win overthrew the government and replaced it by a Revolutionary Council, with himself as Chairman. This Council is still the supreme body in Burma.

Most people in Burma are farmers, living in small villages of thatched houses. The house-walls are often woven like patterned basket work in strips of bamboo: bamboo, indeed, is used for all sorts of things from beds to smiths' bellows. The houses are raised off the ground on posts, and the space beneath is used as a shed for bullocks, carts, or even boats, as a work-room where the girls do hand-loom weaving, and not least as a playground for the children. Most houses are half-veranda and, even in the towns, are gay with flowers and creepers. Nearly every village has a white pagoda or Buddhist shrine, while large ones have a monastery or two, generally big wooden buildings with elaborately carved gables and corrugated iron roofs, guarded by gaudily painted statues of beasts like sphinxes sitting up, of elephant-headed geese, and other queer legendary bests. The monks or *pongyis* wear bright orange or yellow robes and in the morning go through the villages in single file collecting gifts of food in beautiful polished black bowls. On the outskirts of the village is usually a big shady banyan tree, with a little wooden shrine, in which there are candles, fruit, and flowers offered to the local *nat* or spirit; and often there are big jars of water and a bamboo shelter for weary travellers.

Burma no longer has a European community. The English used to consider Burma one of the pleasantest countries in the East, perhaps because family life and the position of women were more like those of the English than those of most Eastern peoples—Burmese women ran much of the business of the country. The Burmese are fond of flowers, bright colours, and children, but they are rather hot-tempered. Both men and women wear gaily-coloured skirts or *lungy*, and the women wear white muslin jackets. A Burmese holiday crowd is a mass of vivid, but never clashing, colour. No Burman is happy without a bath in the cool of the evening, and children like to splash about in the river or ride on huge water buffaloes.

Most of the people are engaged in agriculture —especially rice cultivation—fishing, mining, and forestry. Rubies, diamonds, sapphires, teak,

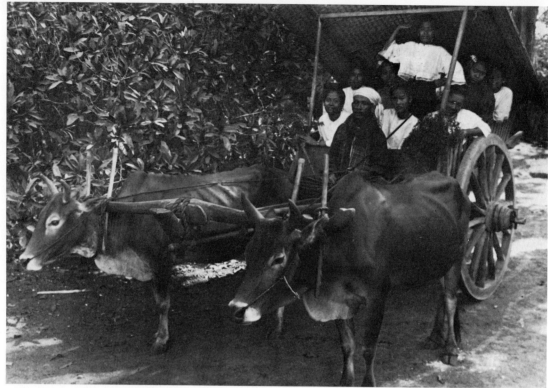

Paul Popper

A TRADITIONAL BULLOCK CART IN SOUTH BURMA

and Chinese birds' nests are among the exotic products. Although the literacy rate is high for Asia, the people have not lost their skill in crafts; Burmese pottery, wood and ivory carving, and silk and cotton weaving are outstanding.

See also Vol. III: Burma; Index, p. 135.
See also Vol. IV: Chinese Languages.

BURYATS, *see* Siberian Peoples, Section 3.

BUSHMEN are a hunting and gathering people who live in south-west Africa, in the Kalahari desert area, and the north-west corner of the Republic of South Africa. They keep no domestic animals and cultivate no crops, but live solely by hunting and food gathering. They look different from the Negro, being small in stature with yellowish-brown skins which wrinkle early. Their hair is extremely tightly curled, their faces flat with broad noses, bulging foreheads, and narrow slanting eyes.

The Bushmen were once found over the whole of south Africa; but they were caught between the southern movement of the Bantu peoples and the northward advance of the European settlers, and were gradually driven back into the barren desert region, so that today they are found in only a very small area.

They live in small unstable bands, varying from 20 to 100 people, which intermarry with one another. Each band is composed of a number of distinct families. Generally the men have only one wife, and the children belong to the father. Each band has its own particular territory where it hunts.

The Bushmen are expert hunters and use bows and poisoned arrows, spears, or traps. When an animal is hit by an arrow they follow it until the poison takes effect; then they cut off the flesh around the wound and eat the rest. The hunters are skilled in stalking and have very keen sight. Sometimes they dress up in animal skins to approach the animal they are stalking; sometimes they imitate the cries of animals to attract their prey closer. Other hunters make traps and set nooses to snare small game. Generally the men hunt alone or with their sons, but sometimes the whole group combines in a hunting drive. Fences are built across a valley, and openings are left in front of which deep pits are dug. The beaters then drive the large animals into the valley so that they fall into the pits beside which are the hunters waiting to kill them. In the wet season the men drive the animals into swampy ground, where they are caught in the mud and can be easily killed. While the men get food by hunting, the women collect roots, berries, and insects for food, using digging-sticks —long sticks pointed at the end. They are especially fond of termites (white ants) and their eggs, called 'Bushman rice'. Vegetable food is scarce in this barren district, and the Bushmen have to make use of anything edible. They hardly make any attempt to store food, but eat plentifully when they are lucky and go hungry when there is no food.

Even in apparently harsh desert conditions, however, they generally manage to live comfortably enough with little labour. Despite the cultural emphasis on hunting, their main source of food is in fact wild nuts, roots, and berries.

When the young people grow up they have to pass through INITIATION CEREMONIES (q.v.). The boys are kept apart for a month and are instructed in tribal knowledge and in hunting. Girls have to remain in their huts and observe certain food taboos (*see* TABOO). The Bushmen have no chiefs, but their older and more experienced men act as leaders in hunting. Medicine men play an important part, for they are supposed to be able to bring rain; they look after the boys' initiation ceremonies and act as doctors for the community.

Haddon Library, Cambridge
A BUSHMAN FAMILY

The people have very little clothing. The men wear a three-cornered piece of skin tied round the waist and drawn between the legs, and a kaross, a patchwork cloak made of skins scraped and stretched till they are soft, which is worn over the shoulder by day and as a blanket by night. The women wear small aprons of skin. They make their implements for hunting from wood and bone, their arrows from reeds, bowstring from the sinews, and bowshafts from the leg bones of animals. Their houses are semicircular in shape and are made of branches stuck in the ground and tied at the top.

During the dry season water is often a more pressing need than food. The Bushman can locate underground water, which he sucks up from a patch of wet sand through a reed. He uses ostrich egg-shells for carrying and storing water.

The Bushmen are very fond of dancing and have dances in which they imitate animals, and for which they decorate themselves elaborately. These dances often involve treatment of illness by specialists who achieve a state of trance. They have musical instruments, such as pipes, drums, and the musical bow—a gourd rind with strings stretched across. Their ancestors may have painted on the walls of caves and rock shelters, but the present-day Bushmen have lost the art. They have an abundance of folk-tales, chiefly animal stories, hunting adventures, and myths of sun, moon, and stars.

Although it was once thought that the Bushmen were dying out, the population managed to achieve an equilibrium in its remaining terri-

Paul Popper
A BUSHMAN MAKING FIRE

He lights dry tinder by twisting in it an arrow from which the steel point has been removed

tories, and their numbers are now on the increase.

See also SOUTHERN AFRICANS.

BYZANTINE EMPIRE.

When the western half of the Roman Empire went to pieces before the barbarian invaders in the 4th and 5th centuries A.D., the eastern half kept up the traditions of Rome, and its citizens liked to call themselves 'Romans'. Its capital was Constantinople, 'the Second Rome', which CONSTANTINE (q.v. Vol. V), the first Christian Roman Emperor, founded in A.D. 330 on a first-class site commanding the crossroads of Europe and Asia where the old Greek city of Byzantium used to be. This eastern half of the Roman Empire, which is called the Eastern Roman or Byzantine Empire, lasted throughout the Middle Ages. It was constantly protecting the rest of the Christian world from various attacks. The Slavs, who crossed the Danube from the north and settled in the Balkans, never succeeded in conquering Constantinople, but finally became Christians and members of the ORTHODOX EASTERN CHURCH (q.v.) and learnt a great deal from Byzantine civilization. There were threats also from wandering Mongolian tribes such as the HUNS (q.v.) and the Bulgars, who were always making raids across the Danube. In the east, first the Persians and then the Arabs tried to eat up the Byzantine provinces and master 'the great city'. By the 8th century the Byzantines had lost Egypt, Syria, North Africa, and a good deal of Italy. But they kept parts of Italy, Sicily, Greece, parts of the Balkans, and, most important of all to them, Asia Minor with its prosperous cities round the coast and its great highlands, which provided the Empire with men and supplies. This smaller empire was in some ways a more workable unit; and from the 9th to the 12th centuries the Byzantine Empire was at its greatest. But during the 11th century a new enemy, the Seljuk Turks, appeared and began to attack the provinces of Asia Minor. The emperors, already hard-pressed elsewhere, asked

Anderson

THE BYZANTINE EMPEROR JUSTINIAN WITH A PRIEST, ADMINISTRATORS, AND SOLDIERS

The magnificence of the brilliantly coloured mosaic and the impressive dignity of the figures express the idea of the Emperor as Christ's representative on earth. Mosaic from S. Vitale, Ravenna, 6th century

western Europe to help drive back the Turks. The answer came in the form of the First Crusade. Vast hordes of pilgrims and soldiers from all parts of the West thronged eastwards; but they were not so much interested in saving Asia Minor for the Byzantine Empire as in reaching Jerusalem or establishing kingdoms for themselves in Syria and Palestine. The Byzantines never regained complete control of Asia Minor, and this was the first great blow to their power. The second was the capture of Constantinople in 1204 by the Fourth Crusade, another expedition from the West that was supposed to be going to protect the Holy Land. The reason for this scandalous attack of Christian on Christian was partly that the Western countries were jealous of the political and commercial power of the Byzantine Empire, and partly a desire to end the split between the Roman Catholic Church and the Orthodox Eastern Church—though this was not a likely way to bring about a union (*see* CRUSADES). From 1204 to 1261 there was a Latin Emperor in Constantinople, and small Latin states were set up in such of the Byzantine provinces as the crusaders could seize—mostly in Greece and the Greek islands. The Byzantine Emperor retreated to Nicaea in Asia Minor. In 1261 he managed to regain Constantinople and some of the lost territory in the Balkans and Greece; but the Byzantines were so weakened by the attacks of Western Christendom as well as by revolts among the Balkan principalities that they were unable to deal with a new danger which threatened them—the rise of the Ottoman Turks. From the end of the 13th century the Turks were establishing themselves in Asia Minor, and by the mid-14th century had got a foothold in Europe. Neither the Byzantines nor the other Christian rulers in the Balkans could drive them back. Constantinople was captured in 1453 and the Eastern Roman Empire fell.

The secret of Byzantine success throughout the thousand years and more of its existence lay in the strength of its imperial tradition and in its underlying belief in the validity of the Christian religion. The Christian Emperor at Constantinople was the mainspring of Byzantine life, and although there were many other factors to be taken into account—the army, the senate, heads of government departments, the people of Constantinople—all real authority, in both administration and foreign policy, lay with the Emperor.

British Museum

ST. JOHN THE EVANGELIST DICTATING TO A SCRIBE

Illumination from an 11th–12th century Byzantine MS. on the Lives of Saints. B.M. Add. MS. 11870

He was regarded as being Christ's regent on earth, and he had a very special place in court ceremonies and church services. He usually worked very closely with the head of the Byzantine Church, the Patriarch of Constantinople. Together with the church councils at which he presided, he was responsible for seeing that right doctrine was taught and good order kept in the Church. This close relation between Church and State, which is so marked a feature of Byzantine life, is best described as one of interdependence.

In educational matters the Byzantine Empire preserved the fine Greek traditions of learning, and so there was no need to rebuild a system of education with the help of the Church, as in the West. The Empire had schools in its provinces and a state-subsidized university founded at Constantinople as early as A.D. 425. At first both the Greek and Latin languages were used, as in the old Roman Empire, but gradually Latin fell out, and Greek became the tongue of the Byzantines. There was a lively interest in learning and education. In better class families girls often got as good an education as their brothers.

It used to be thought that the Byzantine Empire preserved rather than created, but this is not true, for it did both. It preserved, because it admired the works of ancient Greek historians and dramatists, poets and orators, and made copies of their writings; but the Byzantines themselves produced original works of value. For instance, they wrote first-class histories and memoirs, and they also wrote many lives of saints—often vivid, pithy, racy accounts which are almost the equivalent of our novels. They had a strong legal sense: they not only codified earlier Roman law, but from time to time modified codes in use to meet the need of a new generation. But their greatest achievements lay in art and religion, and in both these they were outstandingly original and creative. They were great architects, and built churches, palaces, aqueducts, public buildings, and private houses; and they produced beautiful decoration for everything they made, from the mosaics and paintings in their cathedrals and parish churches to the designs of their dress materials. Their passionate devotion to Christianity is reflected in the achievements of their Church. The Church services, for instance, became gradually enriched during the early Middle Ages, and in the later period there were great developments in the Church music. Many men entered monasteries or lived as hermits, and some of the writings of these 'friends of God' are still widely read today in the Orthodox Church and elsewhere. One can get some idea of what Christian worship meant to the Byzantines by going to present-day services in an Orthodox Eastern Church, which are to be found in most large English cities having a number of Greek residents.

Apart from its major contributions to civilization, the Byzantine Empire must have been interesting to live in. It was a cosmopolitan world full of vitality, a great trading-centre, a half-way house between East and West, where one could visit the City and enjoy a good ballet or a learned argument, or watch the magnificent imperial processions or the races in the Hippodrome. One could go into the countryside and take part in May-day revels or harvest celebrations, and find old customs lingering on in vineyards and fishing-villages. Byzantium, through its allegiance to Christianity, thought a good deal about the next world, but it also knew how to live to the full in this world, and its relish for life was a reminder of its pagan past.

See also CHRISTIAN CHURCH.
See also Vol. XII: BYZANTINE ART.

C

CALVINIST. A Calvinist is a member of the group of Protestant Churches which look back to JOHN CALVIN of Geneva (1509-64) (q.v. Vol. V) as their Reformation leader. These churches are known in the British Isles as 'Presbyterian' and on the mainland of Europe as 'Reformed'. In North America the name of the denomination indicates its British or continental origin.

Calvin was a Frenchman whose book, *Institutes of the Christian Religion* (1536) made people recognize him, at the early age of 26, as the most important scholar of the Reformation. He spent most of his life in Switzerland. The Reformation had already begun there, but only in a negative way. As Calvin rebuilt it, the Church in Geneva became a model for many other reformers. One enthusiast of those times described it as 'the most perfect school of Christ that ever was on the earth since the days of the Apostles'. Six thousand refugees (including Englishmen who fled from Mary's persecution) were to be found there. These spread Calvinism far and wide.

Calvinism, as a system of Christian teaching, has as its basic belief the sovereignty of God. God is King. God's will is the cause, and God's glory the end, of all things. So Calvin taught that God had fixed beforehand who was to be saved and who was to be damned, a doctrine that is called predestination; but few even among Calvinists hold so extreme a view now.

Calvinism had a very wide influence on all branches of Protestantism, including Congregationalists, Baptists, and some of the more Protestant members of the Church of England.

PRESBYTERIANISM. In the British Isles the state church of Scotland takes the lead among Presbyterian Churches. JOHN KNOX (q.v. Vol. V) had been a disciple of Calvin in Geneva. On his return to Scotland in 1559 he became leader of the Scottish Reformation. English Presbyterianism began with the Puritans of the 16th century. The Presbyterian Church in Ireland dates from 1642; and that in Wales springs from a religious revival in the 18th century.

Presbyterians emphasize the authority of the Bible as the Word of God. The sermon takes a prominent part in the Sunday Service. The ministers are well trained in biblical study and are theologically among the best educated of the Protestant clergy. Holy Communion, also, is accompanied by a sermon. It is held infrequently because it is a great occasion, only to be approached after due preparation.

There are no bishops in the Presbyterian Church. The Ministry is of one order only, that of Presbyter. Elders (laymen) representing the congregation share with the minister in the work and government of the church and form the 'session' (Scotland 'kirk session'). Ministers and elders of a wide area meet in Presbytery, and those elected from the whole nation in the annual General Assembly. At the head of the General Assembly is the Moderator, who is appointed for one year only. In 1843 a large section of Scottish Presbyterians claiming spiritual independence abandoned the state connexion. They resigned their livings and organized the Free Church of Scotland. In 1929, however, the divisions were healed, and the reunited Church of Scotland has become a truly national Church, but enjoying so large a measure of spiritual independence that it is not cramped by its State connexion.

Calvinist Churches (Presbyterian and Reformed) are to be found in most countries of Europe, in the Dominions, and the U.S.A., and, through missionary work in the last hundred and fifty years, in many parts of Asia and Africa. Those in Holland and the Protestant cantons of Switzerland enjoy some state support; that in Scotland is the established Church.

See also REFORMATION.

CAMBODIANS. The Khmers, or Cambodians, once ruled a large empire in South East Asia, centred upon the famous temples of Angkor which flourished from the 9th to the 14th centuries. That empire declined, and the Khmers lost territory to neighbouring Thailand (Siam) and Vietnam, leaving the present country with a population of about six million inhabitants. It was conquered by the French in 1862, and recovered its independence only in 1954. Since 1970, its life has been seriously disrupted by civil war and by incursions of both North and South Vietnamese troops.

The Khmers, smaller and darker than the neighbouring Vietnamese, are mostly country-dwellers. The population of Phnom-Penh, the capital, includes some Khmers but also a large number of Chinese and Vietnamese immigrants. Cambodians belong to the Theravada branch of BHUDDHISM (q.v.), and every village has its *wat* or monastery, with yellow-robed monks. The country is dominated by the Mekong river, whose tributary includes the vast lake, Tonlé Sap; the river and lake are important for transport, for irrigating ricefields and for providing fish, which in time of peace are adequate to support the population.

See also Vol. III: CAMBODIA.
See also INDEX, p. 136.

CAMPS, PREHISTORIC, *see* EARTHWORKS AND HILL-FORTS.

CANAANITES. This is a name given in ancient cuneiform and Egyptian documents to the Semitic inhabitants of the coastal cities of Syria and Palestine and some of the towns and villages in the Jordan and other fertile valleys inland. The Canaanites were really exactly the same people as the PHOENICIANS (q.v.), but it was only the Greeks, from about the 8th century B.C., who applied the latter name to them; the Canaanites themselves never used it. The Hebrew writers of the Old Testament often used the expression 'Land of Canaan' in a loose way meaning the whole of Palestine; and 'Canaanites' to denote all its non-Israelite inhabitants.

See also HEBREW CIVILIZATION.

CANADIANS. Though the easternmost parts of the land we now call Canada were claimed for England in 1497 by JOHN CABOT and for France in 1534–5 by JACQUES CARTIER (qq.v. Vol. V), there was no attempt at settlement until the 17th century. In 1604 the Frenchman Champlain started a fur-trading post in Acadia (now Nova Scotia). It failed, and he turned his attention to Canada, a name which then meant simply the land watered by the St. Lawrence River and its tributaries. In 1608 he built the trading post of Québec, from which he made important journeys into the interior, forming alliances with the Algonkian and Huron Indian nations. A devout Roman Catholic, he encouraged Jesuit missionaries to come in, and in the course of their heroic efforts to convert the natives they carried on the work of exploration.

Fur-trading and settlement are hostile to each other, and Champlain's company did not support his efforts to populate the shores of the St. Lawrence. But in 1663 LOUIS XIV (q.v. Vol. V) made New France a royal province. He sent troops in 1665 to end the threat of attacks from the Iroquois, who were Indian allies of the English. Now that the serious work of building the colony could begin, New France soon grew strong and prospered, and the banks of the St. Lawrence became lined with farms. Meanwhile in the forests to the north-west adventurers carried on the work of the fur-trade in the face of a new challenge from England. In 1670 the HUDSON'S BAY COMPANY (q.v. Vol. VII) established posts on the shore of Hudson Bay to draw off the trade of the Indians from far-away Montreal. There followed a long struggle. In 1710 the British seized most of Acadia, renaming it Nova Scotia; but the first real settlement there, Halifax, began only in 1749. In 1759 the victory of WOLFE (q.v. Vol. V) at Québec ended French power in North America. But the valley of the St. Lawrence remained French in language and customs.

When the American colonies rebelled against Britain, three remained loyal; Nova Scotia, Newfoundland (first successfully settled in 1637), and Canada. After the war, some 40,000 Loyalists left the United States to find new homes in Nova Scotia and what is now southern Ontario. So that the French-Canadians could continue to use French laws and customs and the Loyalists to govern themselves in the British manner, Canada was divided into two provinces, Upper and Lower Canada (now Ontario and Québec). In 1867, partly for reasons of security, Nova Scotia, New Brunswick, Québec, and Ontario joined to form one Dominion under the name of Canada. Soon Prince Edward Island and British Columbia also joined; Canada took over from the Hudson's Bay Company the great North-western interior, out of which the provinces of Manitoba, Saskatchewan, and Alberta were later formed; and in 1949 Newfoundland completed the list by entering Canada. Since 1931 Canada has been a completely independent kingdom, whose sovereign is always the same

C.G.T.B.

WHEAT-CUTTING ON THE CANADIAN PRAIRIES

person as the King or Queen of Great Britain (*see* CANADA, GOVERNMENT OF, Vol. X).

Canada, in spite of its vast size, has less than 22 million inhabitants (1972). Nearly half its area consists of the great Canadian Shield, a rocky plain with little soil, which though often beautiful, is inhospitable to settlement. Another large area that is hardly inhabited at all, and part of which is underlain by the Shield, is the barren land of the Arctic. Roughly eighty per cent of the population, in fact, lives within 320 km of the U.S. border: in the Atlantic provinces; in the rich and fertile Lower Lakes and St. Lawrence Lowland where most of the big cities are; on the western prairies, which yield wheat, beef, and oil; and in the mild climate of the British Columbian valleys and coast.

Although Canada has vast stretches of farming and forest land, more than three-quarters of the population live in cities and towns—nearly one-third of them in the four largest cities: MONTREAL (q.v. Vol. III), Toronto, Vancouver, and Winnipeg. Canada has a great wealth of natural resources that derive from the country's immense open spaces—lumber, pulpwood for paper, electric power from rapids and waterfalls, metals from the rocks of the Canadian Shield, wheat and oil from the prairies. These industries do not require many people to do their work; and, like the fur trade in the early days, most of them exist in areas that are sparsely settled. The majority of Canadians are dependent for their livelihood on various manufacturing and service industries, most of which are found in large urban centres.

The origins of the people are still mainly British (over 8 million) and French (nearly 6 million). But there are descendants of most of the nations of Europe, notably Germans, Italians, Ukrainians, and Dutch. There are small numbers of people of Asiatic and African descent, and 244,000 AMERICAN INDIANS and some 17,000 ESKIMOS (qq.v.).

Since 1947 immigration has varied from a low of 64,000 per year in 1947 to a high of 282,000 in 1957. Since 1967 the number of immigrants has been declining. In 1971 it was 122,000, with the majority coming from the U.S.A., the United Kingdom and Ireland, the West Indies, and Portugal. Because there has also been a decline in the birth rate, from a high of 2.5% in the late 1950s to approximately 1.7% in 1972, the rate of Canada's growth in the 1970s has been slowing down.

Among such a mixed population it is natural to find a variety of religions. The largest group (of which the majority is French speaking) is Roman Catholic, followed by the United Church (a union of Presbyterians and Methodists) and the Anglican Church. Besides these there are Presbyterians, Baptists, Greek Catholics and Greek Orthodox, Lutherans, and Jews.

Canadian High Commissioner

SKATING AMONG THE ICE SCULPTURES ON DUFFERIN TERRACE, QUEBEC CITY

Canadians have been slow to develop a marked national character and the things that go with it, such as a distinctive literature and art. Canada is closely linked by friendship, economics, and geography to three older and much more populous countries—Britain, the United States, and France. English-speaking Canadians naturally read American and British books and magazines and see American films and television shows; while French-speaking Canadians are similarly influenced by the literature of France. With so relatively small a population and with two official languages, writers do not easily find a large market for their work in Canada alone. But in spite of this, Canada has had some fine painters, and, especially since the 1960s, there has been some outstanding literary work in both English and French. In science, especially in the work on DIABETES (q.v. Vol. XI) and in the development of nuclear power for peaceful uses, Canada has contributed much. The famous world's fair,

Expo 67, held in Montreal in 1967, the hundredth anniversary of the forming of the confederation, not only displayed Canada's creative energy but stimulated her national pride.

Everyone has heard of the famous Royal Canadian Mounted Police—the Mounties of story and film. Today, in fact, they are 'mounted' on cars, aircraft, and even ships, rather than horses, and they may patrol the lonely lands of the North by dog-sled or on snow shoes (*see* Section 5, POLICEMAN, Vol. X).

Canadian nationalism has complex elements. Owing to differences in language and culture, Québec, where most French-speaking Canadians live, has developed rather differently from the rest of Canada. The parish priests, most of whom wished to preserve the way of life of the old French colony, dominated Québec's politics and education, while the English-speaking minority controlled industry and finance. But in the early 1960s new forces began to assert the need of the French-speaking 'Québécois' to be 'masters in our own house'. This led on the one hand to a separatist movement, demanding that Québec be a nation on its own, and on the other hand to a growing official recognition of Québec's particular needs. The Federal Government implemented many domestic reforms and discussed with all the provinces possible changes in the constitution concerning the federal-provincial relationship. Most Canadians, whether French-speaking or otherwise, now believe that Québec can maintain a dynamic and progressive society within the Confederation.

Meanwhile Canada has become increasingly fearful of American domination, both economically and culturally. After the Second World War, investment flowed freely into Canada from the U.S.A. until, by the end of the 1950s more than half the Canadian manufacturing industry and even a larger percentage of natural resources were owned or controlled by Americans. The government was under pressure to take steps to increase the proportion of Canadian ownership, but had to balance these demands with the need for new capital to stimulate industrial growth. American cultural domination is difficult to check, since it is not easy to prevent the inevitable absorption of cultural influences from so close a neighbour.

In spite of French-Canadian nationalism and fear of American domination, Canada has survived as a federal state for over a hundred years in an era of narrow nationalism. It is now in the process of fashioning a new kind of co-operative federalism to meet the needs of the future.

See also Vol. III: CANADA; INDEX, p. 136.

CANNIBALISM. People eat human flesh either because they are hungry or because by so doing they are fulfilling a religious rite. Individual people and whole societies have been driven to eat human flesh by extreme hunger, caused by shipwreck, siege, or famine. But there have been tribes who ate human flesh not only because they needed the meat to supplement their mainly vegetable diet but also because they enjoyed its taste. In the past, human flesh was part of the diet of the Maoris of New Zealand and other Polynesians, West and Central Africans, and some American Indians, including the Caribs of the West Indies, from a 16th-century Spanish variant of whose name the word cannibal is said to be derived.

In discussing ritual cannibalism we can distin-guish between the eating of friends and relatives who have died, and the eating of slaves or enemies. Some Australian aborigines eat parts of their dead relatives as a sign of affection or of honour. A widespread motive is to obtain the courage, strength, or other virtues of the dead person. A brave enemy was sometimes eaten for the same purpose. More often, however, enemies were eaten as an insult, or out of revenge, or because the spirit was thought thereby to be prevented from returning to plague the killer. The bodies of criminals, murderers, and those accused of being sorcerers or witches were similarly eaten to destroy their harmful powers. Marco Polo found this in Central Asia, and it is reported from parts of Africa and from many islands of the South Seas. Some peoples, for example, the AZTECS of pre-Conquest Mexico (q.v.), regarded human sacrifice as a necessary accompaniment of important religious or social ceremonies, the victims being usually prisoners of war or slaves, parts of whom were sometimes eaten. In Africa and Melanesia ritual canni-balism accompanied ceremonies celebrating the accession or death of a chief, or the completion of some important enterprise, and were a part sometimes of fertility rites. On such occasions the eating of human flesh was probably often confined to certain persons, such as chiefs or priests.

There is some archaeological evidence that cannibalism may have been practised in pre-historic Europe. From the classics we know that it occasionally occurred in its ritual aspect in ancient Greece, and there are indications of its former existence in the myths and legends of many other European and Asian peoples. At the present day it is practised only in a few remote places. Accusations of cannibalism are sometimes brought by one group against another with which it is on bad terms, so that reports of its existence have to be verified before being accepted.

CARIBS, *see* WEST INDIANS; AMERICAN INDIANS, CENTRAL AND SOUTH.

CARTHAGINIANS, *see* PHOENICIANS.

CASTE. Indian society is arranged in a system of closed hereditary groups, which are usually called by the Portuguese word 'castes' (literally, 'lineages') or by the Hindu word *jati* (literally, 'species'). In this system each group or caste

INDIAN SCULPTURE FROM PESHAWAR

The caste mark is in the middle of the forehead

ranks above or below the others. Observers of Indian society find it a very complex system. It shares many features of hierarchial groupings in other parts of the world, but it also possesses certain unique characteristics.

The classical division of Hindu society into four classes is described by the word *varna* (literally, 'colour'). The four classes are Brahman (priest); Kshatriya (warrior); Vaishya (merchant); and Shudra (servant). Most Indian castes can roughly be divided into these four classes, and those not within the *varna* scheme are known as untouchables. The lowest-ranking groups of the Hindus are called outcastes as they are formed from groups of people who for some reason have been excommunicated from their own caste. Even the non-Hindus of India, namely, Muslims, Christians, Sikhs, Jains, and Parsis, are divided into groups resembling castes and assigned a place either within the *varna* scheme or outside it. The Indians find the *varna* scheme convenient to establish the social identities of individuals and groups belonging to widely separated regions of the country.

The caste system is quite rigid in the sense that one is born into a caste and cannot normally change it. All castes of the Brahman *varna* are the highest and those of the Shudra *varna* the lowest, while castes of the two middle classes have intermediate rank and status. With each status go certain typical customs, occupations, and accepted kinds of behaviour. Yet, the traditional divisions do not always fix the occupations of the people. With recent economic and political changes, there is an increasing degree of flexibility. It is common to see a Brahman doctor or an office clerk who is really a member of the goldsmiths' caste.

A persistent feature of the caste system is that the members of a caste arrange marriages within their caste. In actual practice people may not marry outside an even smaller subdivision of the caste, known as the subcaste or *jati*. Though in cosmopolitan cities highly-educated people may ignore the subcaste limits for marriage, it is true to say that the majority of marriages in modern India are still arranged by parents within the caste or the subcaste.

Also, in many villages of India there are councils of elders, known as 'panchayat', working as keepers of law and order within their subcastes. These councils often send representatives to caste associations based in a city or a town. Since discrimination on the basis of caste is illegal under the Indian constitution, matters like marriage outside one's subcaste, or acceptance of food from the hands of a lower caste person, cannot be taken up and judged by the governmental machinery of law and order. Such subjects are tackled by the panchayat at village level and by the caste associations in towns. By and large, caste panchayats and associations have ceased to play an important role outside the restricted sphere of matters pertaining to family disputes, marriage regulations, and the preservation of cultural heritage.

See also HINDUISM.

CATHOLIC CHURCH, *see* CHRISTIAN CHURCH; ROMAN CATHOLIC CHURCH.

CAVE MAN. This expression is a legacy from the old days of archaeology and is now rather meaningless and misleading. When in the last century many spectacular remains of Old Stone Age man were found in caves in France and England, it was assumed that caves were the constant and permanent dwellings of these peoples, and the term 'Cave Man' was invented.

THE EMPEROR CH'EN HOU-CHOU SEEKING INSPIRATION
FOR A POEM

Chinese painting of the Ming Dynasty (1368–1644)

French Tourist Bureau

CAVE PAINTING OF A BULL

Old Stone Age, from Lascaux, Dordogne, France

As we now realize, caves (at least the front parts, where it was reasonably light) were used by ancient man as temporary or semi-permanent shelters at all times (in England, as a matter of fact, there is more archaeological evidence of the use of caves in the Roman period than at any other time!); and the recent discoveries in south Russia and Siberia have brought to light well-built houses half-dug into the ground, obviously the winter dwellings of late Old Stone Age man. Like many modern primitive peoples, Old Stone Age man lived a seasonal life varying according to the time of year. There are drawings on cave walls of summer huts made of light brushwood or skins on a frame; in the winter caves would be used by those groups of people who lived in a region where suitable holes in rocks occur, and who did not dig and build winter houses of the Russian kind. Sometimes burials were made in caves by digging a grave in the accumulated litter of earlier occupants.

Although early man used caves occasionally in the sub-tropical regions where he first evolved, they became of special importance only when men spread to the tundra areas surrounding the ice-sheets in Europe and Asia. This happened during the last glacial phase, beginning some 70,000 years ago, during the Neanderthal stage of human evolution. Areas such as the Dordogne in southern France—a limestone region with many caves—thus give some of the best evidence of the life of Old Stone Age man.

Caves are, of course, a very permanent form of dwelling, remaining intact for thousands of years; and so we have been able to excavate the accumulated rubbish of countless centuries of occupation from their floors, often separated one from another by the stalactite that forms from the water dripping in limestone caverns. Moreover, the walls in caves in south and west France and in Spain were used by late Old Stone Age man as the surface for his drawings, paintings, and engravings of animals and these pictures have remained there since they were first painted many thousands of years ago.

See also PREHISTORIC MAN.

See also Vol. XII: PREHISTORIC ART, Section 4.

CELTIC CIVILIZATION. It is very difficult to define exactly what is meant by Celtic civilization or to limit it either in time or place. For the Celtic peoples, whom we know of in western Europe as the Gauls and Britons, and whose language is still spoken in various forms in Wales, Ireland, and Scotland, grew gradually out of the mixture of prehistoric peoples who had settled in western and central Europe during the New Stone and Bronze Ages (*see* PREHISTORIC MAN). The centres of their later civilization were north-east France, south-west Germany, and Bohemia. It was here that the La Tène culture first developed—the name La Tène is given to the civilization of the Celts during the centuries when they were most powerful and important, roughly from 400 B.C. until the Roman conquest of Britain in the middle of the 1st century after Christ. The whole history of the Celts of this time was shaped by the fact that their homeland lay between the Germans to the north and the various Mediterranean peoples, including the Romans to the south. After 1000 B.C. the Germans were almost continuously trying to push southward from their own homelands in the extreme north of Europe, which meant, of course, that they were pushing against their Celtic neighbours in an attempt to occupy their land.

It was partly this pressure from the Germans that made the Celts in their turn start a series of warlike migrations which carried them over much of Europe and brought them into conflict with the Greeks and Romans. In about 400 B.C. Celtic tribes crossed the Alps into northern Italy, settled there, and made savage raids against the Romans. Meanwhile other groups of Celts had pushed into Spain, westward into Britain, and eastward along the Danube, making settlements as far east as Asia Minor. In the 3rd century they were raiding also in Greece.

British Museum

CELTIC SHIELD

Found in the Thames at Battersea. Bronze decorated with coloured enamel

artists were able to see things that came from Greece and other countries—painted wine cups, for instance, and fine bronze vessels—and to make use of what they saw in the development of their own work. But they did not copy the Greek forms and designs: they changed them into something that was Celtic, something entirely different from any other art in the world before or since. Unlike the Greeks and Romans, the Celts were interested not in representing nature, but in making curious patterns, abstract forms. They used these designs to ornament their most treasured possessions, incising or embossing them, or picking them out in coloured enamels. When, occasionally, they represented living things, a horse, bird, boar, or human face, they did not make them look realistic, but exaggerated certain features until they appeared altogether strange and haunting.

It is interesting to notice what types of object were decorated in this way, for this will suggest which of their possessions the Celts thought to be the most important, and hence what sort of people they were and the kind of life they led. Much of the art is found on personal ornaments —on necklets, armlets, brooches, and many other things in bronze or gold—and it is clear therefore that this was a people who loved to dress up and make a splendid display. But most often the Celtic artists were employed to decorate fighting equipment—helmets and shields, swords, spears, horse-trappings, and battle-chariots. Evidently, then, the Celts were a most warlike people. Having no central government and very little idea of being a nation, their many different tribes were for ever fighting.

The tribes were led by chiefs or kings, and sometimes one of these might succeed in defeating his neighbours and so building up quite a large kingdom. This was done, for example, by the British King Cunobelin (Shakespeare's Cymbeline), who at the beginning of the first century A.D. was ruling over the whole of south-eastern England. But such conquests seldom lasted: other rulers, growing jealous, tried to destroy them.

As well as in their arms and armour, the Celtic love of fighting is shown in their fortifications. The strongholds which they built, most often on hill-tops, are indeed much the most conspicuous of the remains which they have left behind for us to see today. In Britain alone there are hundreds of them. Sometimes the ramparts

Thus at the time of their greatest extent, the Celts held vast territories all the way from Ireland to Galatia (Asia Minor). After 200 B.C., however, their power was gradually destroyed: they were pressed by the Germans in the north, and from the south by the Romans who took one Celtic land after another, adding them to their expanding empire. The last territory to be conquered in this way was Britain—so that Ireland and Scotland were then left as the only countries where Celts could maintain their independence and something of their civilization.

We must now consider this civilization, the La Tène culture, which the migrating Celts took with them wherever they went. During the earlier part of the European Iron Age the Celtic peoples between north-east France and Bohemia began to receive new ideas brought by traders from the Mediterranean. In this way Celtic

Ashmolean Museum

MAIDEN CASTLE, DORSET

One of the largest Celtic fortifications belonging to the early Iron Age. It was built on the site of an earlier New Stone Age fortification, which the Celts enlarged and improved. The castle was also used later by the Romans

were made from piled-up chalk or other softer soils; but in rocky country the walls were usually built with stone blocks. These forts might be put up against a foreign enemy such as the Germans, or against other Celts, either hostile neighbouring tribes or migrating bands. Some of these strongholds became more than mere places of refuge; they were also tribal centres with permanent settlements inside their walls. Indeed by the 1st century B.C. actual towns were beginning to grow up among the Celts, although they never became anything like such an important part of their civilization as they were for Mediterranean peoples like the Greeks and Romans.

The Celts could be good farmers—in Britain, for instance, they grew enough corn to export some to the Continent—but cattle were even more important to them, particularly to migrating tribes, since these must have depended almost entirely on the great herds which they could drive with them as they moved about Europe.

The Celtic priests, or Druids, are famous, yet very few facts are known about them (*see* RELI-GION, PREHISTORIC). They seem to have been a curious mixture, for while they practised philosophy and poetry, they also engaged in savage and cruel rites, including human sacrifice. Such a contrast is, indeed, characteristic of the Celts. Their love of display, their reckless bravery and lack of discipline in war, their uncouth homes where they ate and drank far too much, as well as the brutality of some of their customs, justified the Romans in regarding them as barbarians. Yet we are right to speak of Celtic civilization, for they had a great and distinctive achievement of their own. The great works of fortification, still so impressive after 2,000 years, prove their energy and skill in military architecture; they were sensitive to poetry and other literature; above all they produced brilliantly gifted artists and craftsmen. It was a tradition too, which did not come to an end with prehistoric times, but survived to make the largest contribution to the rich and important IRISH civilization (q.v.) in the early Christian period.

See also ANCIENT CIVILIZATIONS; Vol. IV: CELTIC LANGUAGES; Vol. XII: PREHISTORIC ART.

CENTRAL AFRICA, PEOPLES OF. This region of Central Africa, corresponding roughly to the Congo basin, has about 50 million inhabitants, of whom almost a half live in Zaïre (Congo).

Nearly all these people are of the great Bantu language family, which is believed to originate in this area. They are agricultural, with two common traits: they practise shifting cultivation, and the women do much of the agricultural work. In the forest they grow yams, cassava, groundnuts, beans, and other food crops; maize is important all over the region. In savannah areas, northern Cameroon and Rwanda for example, they rear cattle. Traditionally they live in small villages.

There are scores of Bantu-speaking tribes. In Zaïre the large groups of tribes (see Map, p. 3) include the Kongo; the Luba; the Lunda; the Kuba, famous for their sculptures; and the Mongo. In Angola the main groups are the Ovimbunda and Kimbunda. Ovimbunda is a common language in much of Angola; so is Lingala in the west of Zaïre, and Swahili further east in that country, and Sango in the Central African Republic (*see* AFRICAN LANGUAGES, Vol. IV). Bantu peoples in northern Zambia include notably the Bemba and the Ndembu. Rwanda and Burundi are the homes of the Hutu, a Bantu farming people, and the Tutsi, a smaller group who traditionally ruled them; recent history has been bloodstained, with Hutu uprisings successful in Rwanda and unsuccessful in Burundi.

The PYGMIES (q.v.) are different from other Congo Basin peoples. There are also non-Bantu-speaking peoples in the region, notably the Azande in north-east Zaïre, and the Fulani in north Cameroon.

Traditional religions vary greatly, as do witch-craft and magical customs, everywhere important. God is traditionally called Nzambi by many tribes. Chieftancy varies greatly also, and while some peoples always lived in small units, the Kongo and Lunda had big kingdoms for centuries.

Today millions are Christians, mostly Catholics in Zaïre and the Congo. Protestant Missions have converted many Angolans and Zambians, and independent Protestant churches flourish notably among the Kongo. There are some Muslims, mainly in the north and east.

The Congo Basin peoples were greatly affected by the European and Arab SLAVE TRADES (q.v. Vol. VII), and then by colonization. Many millions have now moved to towns, above all Kinshasa, and to industrial centres, notably the Katanga and Zambian mines. Others have turned to cash crops, particularly oil palms and coffee. Recent troubles have caused migrations within Zaïre and from Angola and Rwanda. Through widespread education, the people have adopted some European ways, and many speak the French language. But African languages and customs remain dominant.

See also Vol. III: AFRICA; ANGOLA; ZAMBIA.

CENTRAL AMERICANS. There are six Central American countries: Guatemala, Salvador, Honduras, Nicaragua, Costa Rica, and Panama. Each of them stretches across Central America from the Caribbean Sea to the Pacific, except Salvador, which is entirely on the Pacific side. These are independent republics. But Central America also includes the British colony of British Honduras, on the Caribbean coast, which is bordered inland by Mexico and Guatemala.

On his first voyage in 1492 Columbus discovered the Caribbean islands of Hispaniola and Cuba (*see* WEST INDIANS). On his fourth voyage ten years later he crossed the Caribbean as well as the Atlantic and discovered the mainland of Central America. Thus Central America became the middle section of the vast Spanish Empire, between 'New Spain' (Mexico) in the north and 'New Granada' (Columbia) in the south. All the Central American states, except Panama, formed the Spanish captaincy-general of Guatemala. The captaincy-general declared its independence of Spain in 1821, along with

CENTRAL AMERICA

Camera Press

GUATEMALA: INDIANS ON THE STEPS OF SANTO TOMAS CHURCH, CHICHICASTENANGO

Mexico; but it was some years before its five provinces became five distinct republics. At first they tried to combine in a Central American Union, and this idea is still not altogether dead; but the communications between them are very bad—it was only Spanish rule that had held them together; and in due course they split apart into separate nations.

The republic of Panama came into existence much later. Originally it was part of the South American republic of Colombia. But in 1903 the United States encouraged Panama to declare its independence, because the Americans wanted to build a canal through the Panama isthmus. The new government of Panama allowed them to do so; and the Canal was opened in 1914. The building of this Canal through the fever-infested tropical jungles and mountains is one of the greatest engineering feats in history. It cut across the narrowest part of the isthmus in the middle of the Panama Republic. The Canal and a strip of land on either side of it are together called the Canal Zone, and belong to the United States (*see* PANAMA CANAL, Vol. IV).

Central America is very thinly populated: all the six republics together have not as many inhabitants as London. They are mainly Indian countries, like Mexico. In Salvador, Honduras, Nicaragua, and Panama, the people are mostly of mixed Indian and European blood, and in Guatemala the majority are pure Indian. Remains of the ancient Indian civilization of the MAYA people (q.v.), much of which has only recently been discovered, are to be found in Central America, especially in Guatemala and Yucatan. For most of their history these countries have been ruled by dictators. Their peoples are poor. The official language is Spanish, but the Indians still speak their own dialects, of which there are an astonishing variety. The dominant religion is Roman Catholic. From all over Central America the Indians go on pilgrimage to the famous image of the Black Christ of Esquipulas, in Guatemala. In the towns there are splendid churches and houses built by the Spaniards during colonial times; but in the country-side, among the neat villages of the Indians, and on the mountain slopes where every scrap of level soil has been tilled for centuries, there has been little change since before the Spaniards came.

One of the Central American countries is a contrast to the rest. This is Costa Rica. Its population is mainly white, with very few

Indians. The land is divided up among many farmers instead of being collected in great estates; and the country is one of the most progressive in Latin America. It has been called 'a small oasis of democracy amidst a desert of Central American dictators'.

See AMERICAN INDIANS, CENTRAL AND SOUTH.
See also Vol. III: CENTRAL AMERICA; PANAMA.
See also INDEX, pp. 138, 142, 143, 151, 152, 154.

CEYLONESE. The inhabitants of Sri Lanka (Ceylon) are called Ceylonese. Sinhalese form about two-thirds of the population, Tamils about a fifth, while the remainder consists of Moormen (descendants of Arab and Tamil parents), Burghers (descendants of Dutch and Ceylonese parents), and a handful of other peoples. The official language is Sinhala, and Tamil is used for some official purposes. English is a major second language. The Sinhalese, an Aryan people from Bengal, colonized Ceylon in the 6th century B.C., driving the aboriginal VEDDAS (q.v.) into the jungle districts. A few centuries later the Sinhalese adopted BUDDHISM (q.v.) as their religion, which it still is. Under their long line of kings, a high civilization developed; and the ruins of great cities, with magnificent palaces, monasteries, and dagabas (bell-shaped brick monuments enclosing sacred relics) remain to this day. They built vast dams in the northern and eastern lowlands to collect rainfall during the short rainy season, and irrigate rice fields during the dry season. These great reservoirs, repaired during the last century, are again in use.

The Sinhalese, weakened by malaria, invasions, and civil wars, neglected their irrigation and allowed the jungle gradually to engulf their ancient cities and fertile land. They moved further south where the rainfall is more regular and abundant, and malaria less rampant. Here the centre of government became Kandy, a town in the hills well protected by mountain ranges, dense jungles, and the river Mahaweli Ganga. The Portuguese, who arrived in 1505, soon obtained control of the maritime provinces where the strong Roman Catholic element and surnames such as 'Fernando' and 'de Silva' still reflect their influence. In 1656 the Portuguese were ousted by the Dutch, seeking commerce, especially in spices. After about 140 they were conquered by the British, who made the island their premier colony, and in 1948 it became a self-governing state within the British Commonwealth of Nations. Under British rule excellent roads were built, about 1700 km of railway connected all important places, and the great planting of tea and rubber took place. The population grew tremendously and education, fostered by Christian missionaries, flourished.

The highland Sinhalese (Kandyans) still cling to some of their ancient laws and feudal traditions. On ceremonial occasions, Kandyan chiefs wear a very distinctive and ornamental dress. The principal occasion is the Perahera, a great annual pageant in Kandy, when a relic, reputed to be a tooth of Gautama Buddha, is carried about the town in grand procession on the back of a gorgeously caparisoned elephant to the accompaniment of tom-toms and fifes, numerous other elephants, male dancers, and torch-bearers. Another annual event, which lasts several months, is a great pilgrimage to the top of Adam's Peak (2241 m), where a small shrine encloses a shallow depression in the rock, reputed to be a footprint of the Buddha.

Apart from the city of COLOMBO (q.v. Vol. III) and a few small towns, the bulk of the Sinhalese live in villages scattered throughout the island. Most of the village houses are wattle-and-daub huts of two or three rooms, thatched with coconut-leaf mats. Each hut stands in its own little garden, embowered in coconut and other palms, and surrounded by jak-fruit trees, banana plants, and a small vegetable garden. A paddy (rice) field in the neighbourhood supplies the staple food. The men wear a skirt-like garment and a simple cotton shirt, the women a length of calico wrapped around and tucked in at the waist, and a cotton bodice. Kandyan women wear a garment like the Indian sari, with an end draped over one shoulder.

The Sinhalese are handsome people with regular features, brown eyes and skin, and black hair. They tend to be proud and independent, hospitable and courteous to strangers, light-hearted and easy-going. But lawyers thrive among them, because they love litigation.

The Tamils in Sri Lanka form two groups. In the northern and eastern maritime districts they are descendants of Tamil invaders from South India. They live by agriculture, cultivating rice, palmyra palms, and coarse tobacco, and by fishing and sea-trading. The other group consists of Tamil labourers imported by European planters in the last century to work the planta-

The Times

THE PERAHERA, AN ANNUAL FESTIVAL IN KANDY

tions. They contributed greatly to Sri Lanka's prosperity. The Tamils are of Dravidian stock, usually darker in colour than the Sinhalese and of somewhat coarser features. They are industrious and enterprising. The majority are Hindus. In dress the men differ little from the Sinhalese, but the women wear the sari and are very fond of jewellery, especially silver ear-rings. Sinhalese and Tamils seldom intermarry, and the Tamils fear that their interests and culture are liable to be crushed by the dominant Sinhalese.

The next most important racial groups are the Moormen who are all Muslims and mainly small traders, and the Burghers who belong to the Dutch Reformed Presbyterian Church and do most of the professional and clerical work.

Owing to the conquest of malaria during and since the 1939–45 war, the death-rate has been so reduced that the population of this beautiful country has risen rapidly. This poses a problem, and Sri Lanka has to import rice and other foodstuffs.

See also Vol. III: CEYLON; INDEX, p. 137.
See also Vol. IV: INDIAN LANGUAGES.

CHALDEANS, *see* SUMERIANS.

CHILEANS. The people of Chile are probably the most progressive of the Latin-American countries. The population is relatively small, about ten millions, almost 90% of whom live in the fertile central valley.

The country was first colonized in the 16th century by Spaniards from Peru. The journey was a severe one, since the invading expedition had to cross the arid northern desert; and the first expedition in 1535 failed. In 1541 Pedro de Valdivia made a successful invasion and founded the city of Santiago. The climatic conditions of extreme heat and cold and the continuous attacks of the many independent tribes of Indians made the lot of the earlier settlers no easy one, and consequently they became virile, hard-working people, always on the alert.

Before the arrival of the Spaniards the interior parts of the country were inhabited by scattered Indian tribes, who lived by hunting and fishing, and who have now almost disappeared. Towards the south, however, in the district now called Araucania, lived more hardy and intelligent Indian tribes who practised agriculture. These tribes had learnt many useful arts and industries, including the working of silver, from the INCAS of Peru (q.v.). They put up a valiant struggle against the Spaniards for some 250 years until, in 1882, a final peace treaty was signed. During this time the Spaniards had learnt to respect the bravery of the Indians: in fact the old Indian leaders, Lautaro and Caupolican, rank among the most famous of Chile's heroes. The Spanish poet, Alonso de Ercilla, wrote a long poem, *La Araucana*, about their exploits. Today all citizens of the Republic, Indian and Spanish, have equal rights.

Chile owed her independence from Spain largely to the efforts of Bernardo O'Higgins, the son of an Irish immigrant and a Spanish lady. The elder O'Higgins had come from Peru and won the respect of whites and Indians alike by his useful public services, mainly in engineering works. His son, Bernardo, put himself at the head of the independence movement in Chile and, with the help of SAN MARTÍN, the liberator of the Argentine (q.v. Vol. V), outmanoeuvred and outfought the Spanish forces. Bernardo was elected first president of the Chile republic.

The modern Chilean has benefited from the fact that the early colonists never depended on slavery. There was little aristocracy and a democratic outlook from the beginning. The colonists and the Indians intermarried a good deal, building up a class of *mestizos* (half Spanish, half Indian). Many immigrants came in, especially during the 19th century, and these included thousands of Germans—practical, hard-working, farming people who own the neat, efficient farms in the south of the country. Most of the agriculture was carried on in enormous estates, called *fundos*, but these have disappeared with the agrarian reforms of Presidents Frei (Christian Democrat) and Allende (Socialist). In the country districts there are

Camera Press
CHILE: POVERTY AND POLITICAL SLOGANS

still to be seen the heavy wagons drawn by teams of oxen, the farmers' high two-wheeled carts, and strings of horses and mules with barrels of local wine slung on either side of the saddle.

Chile became the focus of world attention after the victory of Salvador Allende in 1970, at the head of a coalition of socialists, communists, and radicals. His well-wishers hope that he will succeed in carrying out a socialist revolution, without the oppresssion and disruption that mar some socialist régimes.

See also AMERICAN INDIANS, CENTRAL AND SOUTH.
See also Vol. III: CHILE.
See also INDEX, p. 137.

CHINESE CIVILIZATION: China's is the oldest surviving civilization in the world today. Of course civilizations emerged in Mesopotamia and Egypt far earlier than in China, for the first Chinese period to produce written records is dated as late as 1500 B.C. But Egypt and Babylon fell long since, while Chinese civilization has remained recognizably the same to this day. Moreover, it has had an enormous influence on the whole of South-east Asia. Japan, Korea, Tibet and Vietnam have borrowed widely from China, and both the Chinese and INDIAN CIVILIZATIONS (q.v.) have influenced the life of Burma, Thailand, Malaysia, and Indonesia.

People lived in the area we now know as China

long before 1500 B.C. Very early human remains, nearly half a million years old, have been found near Peking (*see* FOSSIL MAN). This early man, known as Peking Man, was a primitive hunter who knew the use of fire. Agriculture in China began before 3000 B.C., and wheel-turned pottery by 2000 B.C. Different ideas and styles sprang up in various parts of China, identifiable by their different styles of pottery. The art of bronze-casting was discovered before 1500 B.C. and almost simultaneously a way of life arose in the Yellow River valley around the modern towns of Chenghow and Anyang which we can identify as truly Chinese. The remains of these cities show square city-walls with streets inside built on a grid-system and a north-south orientation, just like later Chinese towns. Their inhabitants knew how to make silk, their fine bronze vessels were copied and recopied throughout Chinese history, and, above all, their system of writing is recognizably the same as that still in use today. This early writing was not understood until the beginning of this century, when strange bones, previously thought to be 'dragon bones' and used for medicines, because of the patterns in which they were covered, came to the attention of historians and archaeologists from China and the West. Excavations on the early city-sites yielded yet more inscribed bones, and the task of deciphering them began. This early script is closer to real pictures than the later, more stylized Chinese script (*see* CHINESE LANGUAGES, Vol. IV) but there are enough similarities for it to be deciphered quite easily. One very important thing about this script was that it enabled archaeologists to confirm by their new records the earliest written accounts the Chinese had made of their own past. The inventors of the early script were identified as the people of the Shang dynasty, said by tradition to have ruled from 1766–1122 B.C.

Chinese history is usually divided into periods by the names of these dynasties, or ruling families. There are legends of an even earlier dynasty, the Hsia, but there is only shadowy archaeological evidence that it existed. The Chinese tell stories of a whole series of purely mythical emperors: Shen Nung is said to have invented agriculture; and Huang Ti, the Yellow Emperor, is supposed to have invented many arts including pottery and music. An interesting character in these early legends is Yü the Great, a hero chosen by the Emperor Shun to curb the

terrible floods which had overtaken North China. The Yellow River, which flows through the North China plain, is so heavy with silt that it floods dangerously and often; therefore, the people who lived in the valley had to build dykes. To do this they formed work groups, which were a first step towards organizing themselves into larger social units. The people in North China and to a lesser extent in the Yangtze River valley have always had to co-operate to achieve flood-control and irrigation works, even up to the present day.

The Shang dynasty people, being farmers dependent on the right seasons for planting and harvesting, had developed a very accurate calendar. They kept detailed astronomical records, and some early Chinese records are so good that they help astronomers today to date super-nova explosions and other phenomena which took place over 3,000 years ago. They practised a primitive religion: they used the bones and tortoise-shells on which their writing is preserved for divination by applying a red-hot needle and interpreting the pattern of heat-cracks. The questions and answers then inscribed on the bones were about every sort of problem, for instance, the luckiest days for hunting and war. Divination of various sorts were practised throughout Chinese history: to find lucky days for marriages, perhaps; or, by a process called Feng-shui (Wind-and water), to determine the best site for a new house or a tomb.

The Shang were hunters as well as farmers. At that time the Yellow River valley was thickly forested and elephants, rhinoceroses, and tigers were found there. As the population grew and more farming land was needed, trees were cut down and the forest disappeared, leaving the North China Plain the bare, windswept place it is today, vulnerable to sandstorms which often blow away the topsoil in places. The climate also changed with the disappearance of the forests and became colder and harsher. Meanwhile, the Shang under its priest-emperors in its well-planned cities had come to dominate many smaller tribes in the North China Plain. But in about 1100 B.C. a younger, stronger nation invaded China from the West, and the Shang dynasty fell.

The conquerors set up what is known as the Chou dynasty; under their 700 year rule North China reached the peak of her classical development, and the area covered by Chinese culture extended south of the Yangtze and down the eastern seaboard. The use of iron became widespread both for weapons and for farm implements, causing a rise in production which in turn brought a rise in population. At first the Chou fought from war-chariots as their predecessors had done; but repeated border fighting with the nomad tribes on the north and west, who fought with cavalry, taught the Chinese, too, the use of the stirrup and the art of using the bow and arrows on horseback, as the Parthians had done.

The Chou ruled at first by a fairly strict feudal system—members of the Chou royal house held different cities and their surrounding farmlands in the Yellow River valley in fief for the Chou king in his capital near modern Sian. In 776 B.C. this Chou power was shattered by barbarian invasions from the west. The capital was sacked, and the Chou forced to move east and build a new capital at Loyang. Although the feudal lords remained nominally subordinate to the Chou king, his authority became almost purely religious, and real power lay in the hands of a succession of rulers in the different states which made up the Chou kingdom, Ch'i, Chin, and Ch'u among others. It was in this period that CONFUCIUS (q.v. Vol. V) lived, and many other schools of philosophy flourished in response to the political and social changes that were taking place. Even the nominal religious control of the Chou king had dwindled away by 400 B.C., and the next 150 years were a period of bitter fighting and short-lived alliances.

Then another power from the west, the state of Ch'in, imposed its rule on all China, founding the first Chinese empire in 221 B.C. Ch'in Shih Huang Ti, the first emperor, put through many new measures; for example, he standardized the coinage, the weights and measures, and writing. Without such steps the control of a unified empire would have been impossible. But the infamy of Ch'in Shih Huang Ti's black deeds brought dishonour to his name. Later Chinese historians recorded his cruelty in destroying thousands of peasant-labourers, who were forced to construct roads and palaces for him and above all to build the Great Wall of China (q.v.) as a boundary against the Hsiung Nu, or Huns, always pressing in from Central Asia. In his desire for glory he had all books except technical treatises, and the records of his own feats destroyed and 300 Confucian scholars buried

alive. This Burning of the Books need not have been so serious in its effects, for he kept a copy of every book in the Imperial library. But this in turn was burnt down, and many books were lost for ever in the civil wars that occurred between the fall of his empire and the founding of the Han dynasty, 202 B.C.–A.D. 221.

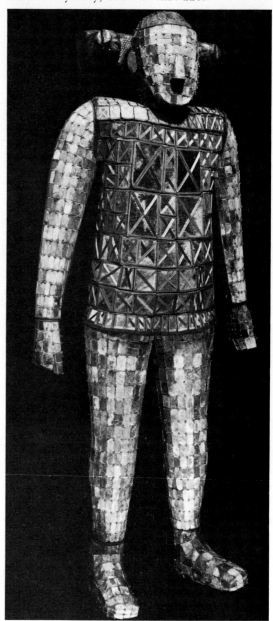

Robert Harding

JADE SUIT FROM QUEEN TOU'S TOMB

Pieces of jade, symbol of eternity, are joined with gold wire. The royal corpse it encased had turned to dust. Han Dynasty

Under the Han the Chinese empire spread south to Canton and west across Central Asia. China at this period was the only country which knew how to produce silk, and silk garments were much prized in the west, particularly at Rome. The Romans bought silk from the land they knew as Serica, although no formal contact was ever made between the two great empires of Rome and China. At home the Chinese created a civil service to which the emperor could delegate his powers instead of the hereditary feudal nobility of the Chou period, and they set up a system of schools and universities to prepare candidates for the examinations by which the civil servants were chosen. Paper was invented and BUDDHISM (q.v.) was introduced into China via Central Asia from India.

The peace and prosperity of the Han gradually crumbled away, with the revenues from taxation at home decreasing and with nomad tribes pressing on the western frontiers. For over 300 years China split into several states, some ruled by 'foreign' races from the North, in a period known as the Six Dynasties. In A.D. 589 the Sui ruling house founded a new dynasty which was to reunite China as the Ch'in had done in 221 B.C. and just as quickly to collapse and be replaced by a powerful and long-lasting dynasty, the T'ang A.D. 618–906. China's frontiers again stretched far out into Central Asia and to the South; literature, especially poetry, music, painting, pottery and sculpture all flourished at the courts of such great patrons of the arts as Hsuan Tsung (A.D. 712–755). The capital city of Ch'ang-an was at that time the largest city in the world, filled with fine buildings, parks and palaces where travellers and traders gathered from all over Asia. Printing was invented, the earliest dated printed book being the *Diamond Sutra* of A.D. 868.

Historians in China and the west often talk of a 'dynastic cycle' in China, a natural rise, decadence and fall within every dynasty; this was certainly true of the T'ang, although the heights of its power were long past when it fell in A.D. 906 from much the same causes (lack of money in the Treasury and external pressure, this time from Korea and Tibet) as brought down the Han. After a period of disunion, known as the Five Dynasties, the Sung dynasty emerged successfully in A.D. 960 and ruled a united China until A.D. 1126. In 1126 the incursions of the Chin Tartars finally proved too

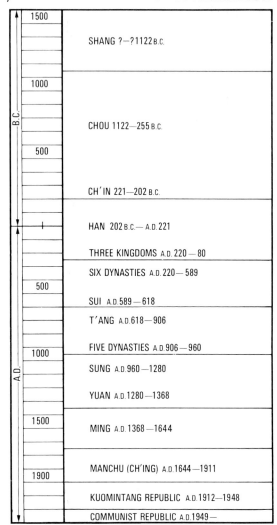

THE CHINESE DYNASTIES

much for the young Sung emperor. The court fled south and the Southern Sung dynasty continued in power with its capital at Hangchow, south of the Yangtze, until A.D. 1279. This whole period was a time for re-examining the purpose and method of imperial government, reorganizing the bureaucracy, its methods of recruitment, and the education of its members. Philosophers, most notably Chu Hsi, turning back to the teachings of Confucius and reinterpreting them after centuries in which Taoism and Buddhism (*see* CHINESE RELIGION) had also come to have profound influences on Chinese thought, produced a new blend of ethics and metaphysics which we call Neo-Confucianism.

This was to remain the orthodox interpretation of the classics and the required body of knowledge for schoolboys and examination-candidates until the introduction of western education in the 19th century.

At this time the use of printing became widespread several centuries before the art reached Gutenberg and Caxton in the West. But the Sung, though an extremely civilized dynasty, was not a very powerful one. In A.D. 1206 GENGHIS KHAN (q.v. Vol. V) led an invasion into Northern China and by 1279 all resistance to the Mongol invaders from the North-west had disappeared. The Sung dynasty fell and China came under the control of a foreign Mongol dynasty known as the Yuan. We know quite well what Yuan China was like because at this time MARCO POLO made his famous journey to China and took service under KUBLAI KHAN (qq.v. Vol. V), the greatest of the Yuan rulers. But the Chinese resented their foreign masters and while some retreated to live as hermits, others organized revolt. In 1368 the Mongols were driven out and a new Chinese dynasty, the Ming, was founded, to survive until it, in turn, was overthrown by another foreign power, the Manchu, in 1644. The Ming was a highly cultured, but politically rather stagnant period for China, for many of the most interesting writers and thinkers of the time preferred not to become involved in political life and several emperors fell under the power of the unscrupulous eunuchs who served them at court. But it was at this time that the Yung Lo emperor rebuilt the walls, palaces and temples of Peking many of which are still standing today, and ordered the compilation of the Great Encyclopaedia, a work of over a million pages.

In 1644 the Manchus, who had been pressing on Northern China for some time under their leader Nurhachi, finally destroyed the Ming power. Under the Manchu dynasty, known as the Ch'ing, China regained her furthest west boundaries in Central Asia, and claimed control over Tibet. Two of the great Ch'ing emperors, K'ang Hsi and Ch'ien Lung, who each reigned for sixty years were among the most powerful and cultivated that China ever had. But by Ch'ien Lung's reign, the causes of Ch'ing decay were already beginning to be clear. Pressure from European merchants, first Portuguese, then Dutch, English and French, to gain better conditions for their trade had been mounting through the late 18th century, culminating in the embassy led by Lord Macartney in 1793 to Ch'ien Lung himself. But China was self-sufficient and imported only luxury goods while the European demand for tea and other fashionable items like porcelain meant that the balance of trade at this time was very much in China's favour. In the 19th century England, in particular, forced on China a trade in the drug opium which altered the balance in England's favour and became a drain on China's silver reserves. China resisted the trade and in 1841 the first Opium War was fought. Intermittent fighting over this and other trade concessions continued until 1860 when England and France marched on Peking, burned the Summer Palace, and made a more lasting peace on their own terms. Hong Kong island had already been ceded to Britain as a trading base and the city of Shanghai grew up near the mouth of the Yangtze as a great international trading port.

Meanwhile internal pressures, especially the Tai-p'ing rebellion (1850–64), were also hastening the decline and fall of the Ch'ing empire. In 1908 the emperor, then a child of five, abdicated some of his powers, and in 1912 a Republic was set up, at first under Yuan Shih-k'ai, who himself had dynastic ambitions, and then after his death in 1916, under SUN YAT-SEN (q.v. Vol. V) a Republican reformer from Southern China. Sun Yat-sen realized that, after centuries of rule by emperors, China was not ready for a full democratic government. He aimed at a one-party government under the 'Kuomintang', or National Party, and based his policies on the 'San Min Chu I', the 'Three Principles of the People'. Nationalism; People's democracy; and the socializing and improving of the People's livelihood. Nearly twenty years of disruption and civil war passed before the new Republic was properly established. Sun Yat-sen had invited the Russian communist party to help with the revolution after it came to power in Russia in 1919, but the Chinese communist party which was formed soon clashed with the Kuomintang. A great deal of fighting followed and when the right-wing Kuomintang party got control under Chiang Kai-shek, the Communists under Mao Tse-tung escaped from the Kuomintang troops which encircled them and after the famous Long March in 1934, from South-east China all the way to Yenan in the north-west, they set up a rival soviet state there.

Just before Japan's attack on China in 1936,

the communist leaders and Chiang Kai-shek made an agreement to form a common front, although Chiang would have preferred to wipe out the communist bases before turning his attention to the foreign enemy. After ten years of bitter fighting, the victory over Japan in 1945 allowed the old differences to flare up again. After civil war between the Communists and the Kuomintang, in which Chiang Kai-shek's forces were beaten and forced to remove to the island of Taiwan, the new People's Republic of China led by Mao Tse-tung was proclaimed on 1st October 1949 in Peking.

In 1955-58 the Communist government reorganized agricultural communities for COL-LECTIVE FARMING (q.v. Vol. VI) first in co-operatives and then in the larger communes, often the size of English counties. With such pooling of resources and manpower, bigger projects of irrigation, land reclamation and public works could be carried out. The Yellow River's flooding was finally tamed by the building of the San Men dam, the Yangtze was bridged at Nanking, and huge areas of loess soil in the Yellow River valley and the north-west were reafforested to anchor the topsoil and maintain fertility. In 1958 the Great Leap Forward, and in 1966 the Cultural Revolution helped to jolt the traditional pattern of working and thinking that had been followed in China for centuries and make her people more readily adaptable to new demands. In 1971 mainland China became a member of the United Nations, unseating Taiwan, which had continued to represent China since 1949.

See also ANCIENT CIVILIZATIONS.
See also Vol. III : CHINA.
See also Vol. IV : CHINESE LANGUAGE.
See also Vol. XII : CHINESE ART ; CHINESE LITERATURE.

CHINESE PEOPLES. In 1972 there were over 700 million people in the People's Republic of China. They form by far the biggest group of human beings in the world in the sense of a people united by ancestry, language, and everyday life. (For comparison, in 1972 India had about 538 millions, Russia 242 millions, and the U.S.A. 203 millions.) The Chinese and their neighbours are of Mongolian type (*see* RACES AND PEOPLES), that is, they have straight, dark hair, yellowish skin, round heads, and dark, often narrow eyes. But within the broad racial type there are vast differences. China is such a huge country and within her borders geo-

graphical and climatic conditions differ so much that there is naturally as much physical difference among the inhabitants as there is in Europe between, for example, Swedes and Italians. The Northern Chinese in general are tall, sturdy, and well-built, with a slower steadier temperament, while the Southern Chinese are often very slight in build, agile, and of a more excitable nature.

The first Chinese were groups of clans living in the Yellow River valley. As they grew and spread southwards through China, many other tribes who differed from them culturally but not racially were absorbed and became 'Chinese' themselves. The Chinese did not differentiate between themselves and 'foreigners' so much on racial grounds, but rather on the basis of language and culture. This made them very tolerant of Arab or Jewish traders in their midst who chose to live in a Chinese manner and hence were often assimilated. But some groups of non-Chinese tribesmen remain unassimilated to this day, particularly in South and West China, still retaining their own languages and customs, while there are Mongol-Turkish tribes in the west and north-west, and a large Muslim population in Sinkiang and Chinese Turkestan. They are now referred to as China's National Minorities, while the Chinese themselves are called Han Chinese, after one of their earliest and greatest dynasties. Our name for them comes from the Ch'in dynasty, the first and one of the most hated of their imperial houses.

By the 19th century China was becoming over-populated and many enterprising Chinese, particularly from the south, moved out into South-east Asia, Singapore, Malaysia, Thailand, Burma, and Borneo and across to the west coast of America. There are now over 20 million 'Overseas Chinese', and many of the old Chinese customs such as New Year celebrations, which are disappearing in mainland China, are still kept up abroad.

China has always been a nation of peasant-farmers. Cut off from the west by great mountain ranges, its most densely populated areas are towards the Pacific coast, in the alluvial valleys of the great rivers and along the coastal plains. In the half-century before the Second World War great cities grew up on the eastern seaboard—Shanghai, Canton, Tientsin, and, along the Yangtze, notably Wuhan.

J. Allan Cash

THE IMPERIAL PALACE, PEKING: THE HALL OF MIDDLE HARMONY

J. Allan Cash

RICE FIELDS NEAR CANTON

During the war with the Japanese, the more backward provinces of the west were much developed and overland communications with the rest of S.E. Asia were improved. Since the founding of the People's Republic in 1949 there has also been considerable industrial development, notably in the new Tatung oilfields of the distant north-west and the iron and steel centre of Anshan in Manchuria. This too has been accompanied by a tremendous growth of communications. Lanchow, which used to be a small, medieval frontier city, is now a great railway centre, with one of its lines linking the Chinese to the Russian Turksib railway. Roads have been built connecting Lhasa, the Tibetan capital, with Chengtu in south-west China and with the Indian frontier. Most of the remote inaccessible parts of China are gradually being linked by new roads and railways, or by air.

Nevertheless, it is still true that more than three-quarters of the immense population find their livelihood in agriculture—some of the most intensive land cultivation in the world. Only north of the Great Wall are the farmers satisfied with one crop per year. Even as far north as Peking they obtain either three crops in two years, or even two crops in one year off the same plot of land, while in south China three crops can be grown annually.

Let us take a village in the great north plain through which the Yellow River runs. The landscape is brown and featureless except when the crops such as millet, kaoliang, wheat, and soya beans are above ground. Vegetables are widely grown but there is little livestock except pigs, hens, and flocks of ducks. Many villages have fishponds in which carp and other fish are raised. There is little to catch the eye except the villages themselves, the larger ones still walled, dyked for protection against floods, with a few clumps of pine trees to mark the site of an old burial mound. The fields are sometimes dotted with these grave-mounds, although the practice has now been abandoned and some have been ploughed under to prevent precious cultivable land from being wasted. For the same reason, unless the village is on one of the new motor highways, many roads are just narrow tracks, wide enough for mules and donkeys, wheelbarrows, and bicycles which are often used to pull small carts.

Naturally peasant-life is somewhat different in central and south China. There millet and wheat give way to rice and tea and there is more farming of silkworms. The mule and the donkey are largely replaced by the bad-tempered water-buffalo in the paddyfields and by porters tramp-in the flagstone hill paths on foot, and lorries winding up hairpin mountain roads in the far south and west. In the deltas of the great rivers, canals (some 40,000 km of them in the Yangtze delta alone) take the place of roads. In these parts also there are thousands of 'boat people' whose only homes are their barges on the water.

Formerly the family strip of land was so small, taxes so heavy, and floods or droughts so widespread that the farmer could scrape only the barest existence from the soil. The communist government improved the lot of the peasants to some extent by abolishing the landlord class and redistributing the land among the poorer farmers. But this measure was inadequate to increase production and put into practice any large-scale programme to improve the land. First a co-operative system was introduced, and finally the People's Communes were organized in 1958 (see COLLECTIVE FARMING, Vol. VI).

The communes, covering areas as large as English counties, can be effectively organized into large work-forces for the busy seasons of sowing, transplanting rice-seedlings, and harvesting, and for construction-works such as terracing hillsides, digging irrigation canals, and building new roads, houses, and hospitals. The work force can also be divided into smaller units of production, working on the land, making and mending farm equipment, and processing the particular crops of the area such as tea and cotton. Machines have now replaced animal and human labour for many tasks. Most communes use electric water-pumps for their irrigation system, and many have tractors and mechanical rice-transplanters to help with their regular work. But heavy machinery, such as the large bulldozers used for road-building, is still scarce and human labour takes its place.

Everyone contributes to the life of the commune and in return everyone is fed and housed, the children are educated at least to the primary level, and there are medical teams to care for the sick. The same sort of organization exists in the towns, where members of a factory are often housed in the same blocks of flats, with their own nurseries and schools and their own sports facilities. Ping-pong and basket-ball are very popular, while groups of people still

J. Allan Cash

MOTHER AND SON IN THEIR HOME IN A CHINESE COMMUNE

In winter a fire is lit under the sleeping bench on which they are sitting

regularly do exercises together, the older ones using the old Taoist shadow-boxing movements. The Chinese used to divide the year into 10-day periods, but early this century they adopted the western calendar, with a week of 7 days and Sunday as a rest-day. In the towns there are theatres, concert-halls, exhibitions, and cinemas, parks and playgrounds for the children, as well as museums and fine old buildings, for the Chinese take a great interest in their past as a valuable lesson for the present. In the countryside travelling teams of actors, singers, or musicians, or travelling film teams put on performances. Many communes have their own broadcasting network in addition to the national ones, and there are television stations in the big cities.

The material standard of life in China is still lower than in the West, but the Chinese hope to avoid developing into the European type of consumer society with all the problems of pollution and unemployment which this brings. Their emphasis on agriculture and on the reusing of waste products and their refusal to undertake large-scale production—for instance of cars, so that China's streets are still half-empty—is all part of this policy.

See also CHINESE CIVILIZATION.
See also Vol. III: CHINA; INDEX, p. 137.
See also Vol. IV: CHINESE AND ALLIED LANGUAGES.

CHINESE RELIGION. The three great religions of China, Confucianism, Taoism, and Buddhism, are also known in China as the Three Philosophies. All of them can be treated as offering explanations of the world, which are open to discussion, or as ethical teachings about how people should behave in daily life, or as religious faiths in which people believe and worship.

Confucianism is probably the most philosophical of the three, for it offers no theories about an afterlife. It was founded on the doctrines of CONFUCIUS (q.v. Vol. V), who lived under the Chou dynasty from 550 to 479 B.C. In his day the old feudal order of society was breaking down, and he was chiefly interested in reminding people of the virtues on which he thought the ideal society of the past had been based. He treated moral questions in terms of particular relationships (the way a father should treat a son, or a husband his wife) rather than as general theories of The Good Life, and his chief moral precept was 'shu', or Reciprocity —do as you would be done by. Confucius never succeeded in his ambition to become a Chief Minister and advise a king on virtuous government, and he had only a handful of disciples. But his teachings were collected by his grandson and other followers and passed down by his greatest disciple Mencius at the beginning of the Han dynasty (202 B.C.–A.D. 220). At this time the Chinese were finding ways of ruling the whole of China as one empire instead of in several small kingdoms, and a system of bureaucracy and of delegating duties was devised. For such a system Confucianism was ideal, with its belief in responsibility and public service, its vision of the state as a family and the Emperor as its father and mother, and its stress on the importance of the virtuous minister. From that time with a few interruptions Confucianism remained the official doctrine of Imperial China. Confucian rites were bound up with the Imperial rituals and with ANCESTOR WORSHIP (q.v.), a most important feature of Chinese religion. Only sons could carry on a family's sacrifices, so families often adopted sons to ensure that the supply would not cease and leave a family of hungry ghosts. Confucius himself was venerated as a great Sage, or Wise Man, and his spirit-tablet was honoured in temples erected to his memory all over China.

Taoism (pronounced Dowism), the second great religion of China, originated like Confucianism in the breakdown of society at the end of the Chou dynasty and the accompanying civil wars. Its founder, Lao Tzu, is a mythical figure said to have taught Confucius himself and to be the author of a book, the *Tao Te Ching*, which cannot really have been compiled before the 3rd century B.C. It is full of oracular advice, for instance on how to survive in troubled times by imitating water which always seeks the lowest place and can yet be very

London Missionary Society

CONFUCIAN TEMPLE AT CHUFOO, SHANTUNG PROVINCE

One of the oldest temples still standing, dating from the Yuan Dynasty (1280–1368)

powerful. The *Chuang Tzu*, the second Taoist classic, is named after Chuang Chou, a 3rd-century philosopher. In it he points out what a difference there is between the simple nature of the real world and the complex and often conflicting qualities (height, depth, colour, taste, and above all, goodness and badness) that Man imposes on it. Underneath all these artificial phenomena is Tao, the Way, which cannot be described in words. Chuang Tzu's attempt to convey his vision of this Tao through stories and allegories makes this one of the greatest prose-works in Chinese literature.

Taoism, as we see it in these books, was a philosophy for men who renounced the active teachings of Confucianism and retired from the world. But there was also a religious side of Taoism close to mysticism. The introduction of Buddhism in the 1st–3rd centuries A.D. led Taoists to copy the services, priests, monasteries, and scriptures (or 'sutras') of the Buddhist church. Taoists had already begun a search for a drug of immortality which would bring them eternal life. Often these drugs were made from dangerous substances like mercury or arsenic, so that far from bestowing eternal life, they

THE TEMPLE OF HEAVEN, PEKING, 15TH–16TH CENTURY

A ceremony was held in this temple every year at which the Emperor offered sacrifices to the Heavenly Spirits

poisoned those who took them. Taoists also tried chemical ways of turning base metals to gold, like the alchemists of Western Europe. Religious Taoism early degenerated into a super- stitious worship full of charms, spells, and rituals, while the ideas of philosophical Taoism became so well-known that most learned men in China would make use of them quite unconsciously.

BUDDHISM (q.v.) was the only foreign religion ever absorbed by the Chinese. This was partly because certain Buddhist beliefs, like the worth- lessness and unreality of fame and power, echoed Taoist teachings, and partly because the Chinese often selected only those ideas they found con- genial. For instance, Buddhists say a man should leave family ties and retire from the world, con- tradicting Confucius' insistence on filial piety. But Buddhists also say that by prayers and good works one can acquire merit for others as well as oneself. So Chinese Buddhists could still be filial sons by following the second teaching rather than

the first. Strict Buddhists say this world is just illu- sion, but they also believe in a series of rebirths as humans or animals, until a state of perfection in Nirvana is reached. From this idea simple people created wonderful tales of this Buddhist Heaven, which were more comforting than the Confucian lack of interest in an afterlife. That is why the Chinese sometimes said that they divided their three religions like this: Confucianism for every- day life; Taoism for weddings, fortune-telling, medicine, or magic; and Buddhism for funerals.

Some Chinese were just Confucians perhaps, or just Buddhists; but most believed in a mixture of all three schools combined with the original popular religion of China. To such people Buddha might be the chief god or he might be the Jade Emperor, the Taoist ruler of Heaven whose powers overlapped with the old sky-god, T'ien, or Heaven. Heaven was important to the Imperial cult as well, for only the Emperor, known as Son of Heaven, could perform the midwinter sacrifice to Heaven and the mid-summer sacrifice to Earth which would keep the seasons turning. New gods were often created from real people; for instance, Kuan Ti, a hero of the civil wars after the Han dynasty (202 B.C.–A.D. 221), became the God of War. Gods were all given ranks in the Jade Emperor's court, like the human civil servants at the Emperor's court, and people also believed in an Underworld where ten Judges presided over several Hells. So many officials were needed in Hell that stories said living men were sometimes taken to serve there. For the Chinese had a strong belief in the presence of gods, spirits, ghosts, and demons all around them in this world and found it natural to think of humans travelling just as easily into the Spirit-world. Every hill or river had its god, while animals and ghosts were believed to take human shape to lure men to their doom. Every household had paper door-gods and spirit-screens to keep these spirits out, and was pro-tected by its own hearth-god who reported annually to the Jade Emperor on the behaviour of his family.

Other foreign religions besides Buddhism were introduced into China, but none had the same success. From T'ang times (A.D. 618–906) in-creasing trade across Central Asia meant that Middle Eastern religions such as Manichaeism, or the Syrian form of Christianity known as Nestorianism, or, finally, ISLAM (q.v.) reached China, but there were comparatively few con-verts. The large Muslim population in China was mostly descended from Arab traders or mercenary soldiers, and the numbers of Nestorian Christians in China up till the 13th century were also settlers rather than converts. China was usually tolerant of other religions as long as they did not harm the state. There were, however, occasional persecutions directed chiefly at the wealth of the Buddhist and Taoist monasteries.

The first Christian missionaries from Western Europe were Franciscan friars who had a short-lived success in Peking in the 13th and 14th centuries. In the 17th century the Jesuits led by Matteo Ricci were the first of many Catholic missions to re-enter China, while the first Pro-testant missionary, Robert Morrison, arrived in 1805. Many sects continued their work, founding schools and hospitals as well as churches, until 1951 when foreign missionaries were asked to leave China. The Communist government did not discourage the Protestant Chinese from wor-ship as much as the Catholics, who had become associated with the Japanese in the Sino-Japanese war (1937–1945) and were more hostile to Com-munism. But religious life of any sort was seen as a distraction from the task of building the New China. At present, Marxist-Leninism and the thought of Chairman Mao provide an adequate this-worldly ethic.

See also CHINESE PEOPLES.

CHRIST, *see* JESUS OF NAZARETH.

CHRISTIAN CHURCH. The word Church (Anglo-Saxon *circe*) comes from the Greek *kuriakon* and originally meant 'The Lord's (house)', i.e. the building where Christians gather for worship. The first church in Jerusalem in the year A.D. 29 was a house—perhaps the same in which the Last Supper was eaten (Acts i. 13). House-churches continued for 200 years and more before special churches were built. The word church came to be used also for the com-munity of people who gathered in the church, or all these local churches together—'the whole estate of Christ's Church'. Sometimes the word is used also for all who have belonged, the dead as well as the living.

The first congregation in Jerusalem numbered only about 120 members, the immediate fol-lowers of JESUS OF NAZARETH (q.v.). The leaders were the Apostles—twelve, as there were twelve tribes of Israel. They believed that Jesus had called them to build His Church—a new Israel in which all God's promises to His chosen people would be fulfilled. To enter this com-munity a man must repent and be spiritually reborn by Baptism (*see* SACRAMENT)— the INITIA-TION CEREMONY (q.v.) of the Christian Church. The members joined with each other in repeat-ing the action of Jesus when 'He took bread and brake it' (Matt. xxvi. 26), the sacrament of thanksgiving or Eucharist (*see* SACRAMENT). And this was the central service of the Church.

The first problem which faced the Church was its attitude to the Jewish law. The first Christians were Jews and were bound by the Law. But was it necessary for non-Jewish Chris-tians also to keep the Jewish Law? ST. PAUL (q.v. Vol. V) declared that the Church must be independent of JUDAISM (q.v.) in order that it might fulfil its destiny as a world-religion. About 100 years later, when many of its members wanted to break all Jewish connexions and even throw

CHURCH OF THE NATIVITY, BETHLEHEM

Built in the 4th century, rebuilt in the 6th, used by many denominations. A Greek Orthodox priest is lighting candles by the grotto (right) where, according to legend, Jesus was born

over the authority of the Old Testament, the opposite danger faced the Church—pagan and magical beliefs began to creep in. The leaders of the Church therefore chose out the most trusted Christian writings and declared these to be 'the faith as we received it from the apostles'. In this way, about A.D. 200 the books which we call the New Testament began to be recognized as the standard writings or 'canon' (*see* BIBLE). The early Church made several short and simple creeds or statements of its belief, which are similar to the later version called the Apostles' Creed, widely used in public worship. By the beginning of the 4th century many false doctrines were springing up. The leaders of the Church gathered in a great council at Nicaea and agreed together upon an official creed, which is known as the Creed of Nicaea. This is practically the same as the creed used in the Service of Holy Communion.

During the first 500 years of its life the Christian Church increased in numbers and spread widely, both to the East and the West, in spite of persecution. By A.D. 300 it had reached Armenia, and there was an Armenian State Church. Soon after A.D. 300 the Church was also strong in parts of Egypt (*see* COPT), and had already spread from Syria into Persia (*see* NESTORIAN). A spirit of local independence later caused Christians in these lands to claim independence of the Church of the Roman Empire, and this resulted in the Coptic, Nestorian, and Jacobite divisions. The Church reached south down the Red Sea to the tip of Arabia and down both shores of the Persian Gulf. Probably by the 3rd century it had reached India. In 313, during the reign of the Roman Emperor CONSTANTINE (q.v. Vol. V), Christians in the Roman Empire were freed from persecution, and Christianity soon became recognized as the official religion. There was a vast increase in Church membership, and many churches were built, including the Church of the Nativity at Bethlehem.

The bishops of the historic cities, Jerusalem, Antioch, Alexandria, Rome, and of the 4th-century Christian capital, Constantinople, were recognized as pre-eminent; they were later called Patriarchs. Of these five, four belonged to the East and only one, the Patriarch of Rome (the Pope), belonged to the West. He, therefore, became particularly important: Rome was the city associated with St. Peter and St. Paul, the centre of Western Christendom and the ancient capital of the Roman Empire. This great worldly power which had come to the Church brought with it the temptation of worldliness and a lowering of standards—a temptation to put temporal power and glory before spiritual glory. But some felt that the Christian life should be one of poverty and hardship (*see* ASCETICISM). As early as the 3rd century in Egypt men had begun to go into the desert as hermits. Later, some hermits joined together in communities and adopted a strict rule of life, and so there grew up the monasteries. The standard rule of life for the MONKS (q.v.) in the West was the Rule of St. Benedict, established in 529.

There followed in Europe a period called the DARK AGES (q.v.), during which hordes of barbarians swept over from the east and north and bit by bit broke down the Western Roman Empire and threw much of Europe back into barbarism. When most things Roman were destroyed, the Church remained. When all other life was becoming local and tribal, the Church stood for a larger unity. Unfortunately the Church herself suffered from the ignorance and superstition of the Dark Ages: nevertheless the Christian religion provided the nucleus around which a new civilization began to develop. And the Church won over the barbarians, not only in lands formerly Roman but farther north as well. In the 7th century there arose in Arabia the religion which was to prove Christianity's chief rival—ISLAM (q.v.), the religion founded by Muhammad. Within a century this new religion, carried by the armies of Muslim Arabs, swept over the lands of Christianity's origin and early advance—Syria, Palestine, Egypt, North Africa, and as far as Spain. During the following two or three centuries progress in art and learning belonged more to the Muslim than the Christian world. Indeed Islam has always remained the greatest rival to Christianity all over the world.

When the Western Roman Empire was crumbling before the attacks of Goths and Huns, the Eastern or BYZANTINE EMPIRE (q.v.), centred at Constantinople, remained intact. The breach between the Church of the West and the Eastern Church became wider, especially because the East would not recognize the supremacy of the Pope over their own Patriarchs. When the Byzantine Empire was faced with attacks from the Turks and appealed to the West for help, the tremendous enthusiasm which brought about the CRUSADES (1096–1291) (q.v.) was stirred, not only by the desire to rescue the Holy Land from the infidel Muslim, but also by a desire to bring the Eastern Church under the authority of Rome.

From the 11th and 12th centuries onwards, as Europe became more settled, a new spirit began to grow within the Church—on the one side encouraging learning, on the other bringing religion more into touch with the needs of the people. The orders of FRIARS (q.v.) were founded —the two great orders being the Franciscans (1209) and the Dominicans (1216). Both these orders provided the Church with zealous evangelists at home and abroad, in Muslim Spain, Africa, and Persia, and before the end of the century even as far as China. Then in the 15th century came the RENAISSANCE (q.v.) in Italy, and in the 16th the REFORMATION (q.v.) in the north. The breakdown of the old feudal system, the growing sense of nationality which was awakening in Europe, and the beginnings of democratic government, all constituted threats to the old autocratic absolute monarchy of the Pope as head of the Church. About 1200 Pope Innocent III declared that the Pope was head of a feudal world and that kings held their kingdoms as fiefs from the Pope. But the modern world would no longer accept this: it looked for a Church, no less than a State, managed on a constitutional basis, where national interests would have a chance to be represented. At the same time the earnest, inquiring spirit of the age led men to question things which they had merely accepted before, and to condemn abuses. These two sides to the Reformation, the political and the religious, got a good deal mixed up, and there were both sides to most of the main movements.

The first break came in the early 15th century with John Huss of Bohemia who, influenced by the teaching of WYCLIFFE (q.v. Vol. V), founded the MORAVIAN CHURCH (q.v.). In 1517 Luther started the break from the Pope in Germany. This produced the LUTHERAN CHURCH (q.v.), to which most people in north Germany, Denmark, Norway, and Sweden belong. In 1536 Calvin started the movement which resulted in the CALVINIST CHURCH (q.v.). This spread from Switzerland over western Germany and the Netherlands, and also to Scotland. The English Reformation left medieval church order less disturbed (except for the dissolution of the monasteries), and most of the old forms of service (see PRAYER BOOK) were kept in the CHURCH OF ENGLAND (q.v.). The English bishops maintain the 'Apostolic Succession', bishops appointing bishops from the earliest times by the laying on of hands. The bishops owe their power and authority to that which Christ himself in the first place gave to his Apostles. The nonepiscopal communions emphasize the handing on of the faith, rather than of the office and authority.

In the 16th to 18th centuries groups of English people, dissatisfied with the reformation of the Anglican Church, broke away and formed separate denominations. The Independents or CONGREGATIONALISTS (q.v.) and the BAPTISTS (q.v.) formed separate Nonconformist churches. Bands of Puritans and QUAKERS (q.v.) sought freedom of worship in America. In the 18th century the METHODIST CHURCH (q.v.) was founded by John and Charles WESLEY (q.v. Vol. V). In North America, which was largely colonized by Protestant countries, many different divisions of Protestant Christianity have sprung up in the last two centuries. The chart below shows how the Church has branched out through the centuries, and how all the branches have come from the same root and are part of the one religion.

The Roman Catholic Church met the Reformation with a Counter-Reformation in which it stiffened its own discipline, removing many abuses, and launched a bitter attack against the Protestants (see INQUISITION). This attack, carried on with violence of feeling, resulted in cruelty and bloodshed on both sides. At the same time, with the Jesuits as pioneers in many lands, missionary work carried Roman Catholic Christianity to the New World (America), to parts of West, South, and East Africa, and to India, Ceylon, Burma, Malaya, the East Indies, Japan and China. Protestant missions came into being in the 19th century, and from 1790 to 1840 most of the great missionary societies were founded. During the last century missionaries followed explorers and traders into all parts of the world, so that the Church became at last 'world wide'.

Christians say in their Creed: 'I believe in the holy, catholick Church.' The Church is not yet altogether one, holy, or catholic (universal). There is, however, more concern about unity today than there has been since the Reformation: the World Council of Churches, to which all the main Churches except the Roman Catholic belong, is a step towards that goal. The Church is more nearly Catholic than ever before. In its human weakness the Church often fails to reach great holiness. It has been accused of opposing new ways of human progress, and of persecuting those who sought after truth. Indeed, like most

and, later, particularly in western Europe. There Christianity radically affected the civilization which was developed.

Christianity is hard to describe because there are so many ideas as to what it is. 'A Christian' may mean a person who has a deep personal religious faith. Or it may mean someone connected with one branch of the CHRISTIAN CHURCH (q.v.). Or it may mean someone brought up to

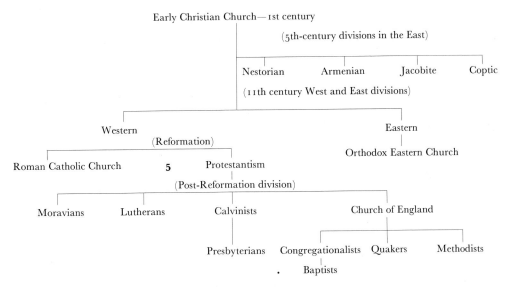

CHART SHOWING HOW THE BRANCHES OF THE CHRISTIAN CHURCH HAVE DEVELOPED

established institutions, the Church has generally been conservative and slow to accept new ideas. But in this conservatism there is a security against the risk of falling victim to false doctrines, though its immediate effect may be unprogressive. And the Church has always accepted ideas which were proved by experience to be true.

See also CHRISTIANITY; CHRISTIAN YEAR.

CHRISTIANITY is the most universal religion. Of the world's population nearly one-third are nominal Christians. While these today are to be found in almost every land under the sun, they are not evenly spread. In Europe, America, and Australasia, two people out of three would call themselves Christians. In Africa it is less than one in ten. Elsewhere the average is little more than one person in a hundred. Yet this religion began not in Europe but in Asia. It just happened that its earliest great triumphs were in the lands around the Mediterranean,

a way of life which was more or less affected by the Christian tradition. Then again in most lands 'Christian' is not a sufficient description; one must say of what kind. And the denominations are bewilderingly many. There are differences of belief, still more differences of organization, and even different standards of 'Christian' conduct. It will be best for us to see what lies behind it all, what it meant to begin with, adding a few remarks as to how it works out in terms of modern life.

'Christians' was not their first name. Followers of this religion used to call each other 'believers', 'disciples', 'saints': believers because they believed certain things about JESUS OF NAZARETH (q.v.), their founder; disciples because they added themselves to the small company which Jesus himself had called together; saints because they began to live a holy life according to the standard Jesus had set up. 'The disciples were called Christians first in Antioch' (Acts xi.

ALLEGORICAL FIGURE OF THE CHURCH

Medieval figure holding the Cross and Chalice, symbols of the Christian faith. Her crown proclaims the triumph of the Church. 13th-century statue on the porch of Strasbourg Cathedral

26), a name given them scornfully by the heathen.

Christianity took over from JUDAISM (q.v.) its scriptures (the Old Testament) and much of its teaching about God: that He is One, Creator of all that is; that His Purposes are to be fulfilled in and through His People, who have come into a special relationship with Him; that He is holy, to be satisfied only by those who do good. The Old Testament was reinterpreted by Christians according to what they had come to believe about Jesus.

The Jews had for hundreds of years believed themselves to be God's chosen people. They were always waiting for the Messiah, the Prophet, Priest and King, who was to bring God's message and deliver them from the hands of their oppressors—for they had been for a long time under the domination of overlords, the Babylonians, the Persians, the Greeks, and finally the Romans. And so the idea had grown up that this Messiah was to be a political leader, a King in the material sense. In A.D. 29 Jesus began his ministry by proclaiming 'The time is fulfilled. The Kingdom of God is at hand.' Later the Apostles assured their hearers that the King had come—even though most of His chosen people had not recognized Him.

The Messiah who came was different from the Messiah whom the Jews had expected. They looked for a prophet. The Apostles declared that Jesus was more than a prophet, hearing and declaring the word of God—that He was the Son of God, or as one Apostle described it, 'The Word became flesh and dwelt among us'. Through Jesus, God was revealed in a human life. This is called the doctrine of the Incarnation (carnis = of the flesh) and is the central teaching of Christianity.

Then Jesus did not save His people in the way the Jews expected. Instead of leading His people in triumph, He was rejected, He suffered, and He died on the cross. The Apostles explained this by reminding the Jews of the prophecies in the Old Testament of the Suffering Servant (Isaiah liii) which the Jews had not thought could refer to the Messiah. The Jews expected a priest. The Apostles declared that Jesus was not only Priest but also Sacrifice, given in atonement for the sins of mankind. In the sacrifice of Jesus is shown the love of God which seeks out and saves sinful man. This is the doctrine of Atonement (at-one-ment) and is the meaning of the simple ceremony of the Last Supper which Jesus told men to repeat in remembrance of His sacrifice and of man's salvation. The Apostles also declared that Jesus had risen from the dead and had returned to be with God, leaving his disciples to bear witness to His resurrection to all the world.

The Jews expected a King. The Apostles declared that there was now a new meaning to the chosen people of God. The Kingdom belonged to all who believed. Entry to the Kingdom was not by being born a Jew but by being reborn by repentance and baptism. Therefore the message the Apostles had for the world was for the Gentile as much as for Jew—everyone had an equal right. It is not surprising that most Jews found this new conception of the Messiah and of their own place in God's Kingdom hard to accept.

Jesus summarized His teaching about life in the new society in various ways: in the two Great Commandments. 'Thou shalt love the Lord thy God with all thy heart, soul, mind, and strength, and thy neighbour as thyself'; in the eight beatitudes (blessings) (Matt. v) which reverse so many worldly values; most strikingly in that command 'Be ye perfect as your Father in Heaven is perfect'. It all sounded an impossible standard. But the Apostles taught that the Christian life was not a matter of striving to keep a new and higher law, but of a new relationship with God and a new power because of that relationship. Jesus promised a sense of power, a spiritual presence to make up for the lack of His bodily presence. The Apostles claimed that this promise was fulfilled in the coming of the Holy Spirit, and that God's Spirit was in His Church.

Christianity, differently expressed in different ages and in different lands, will be found everywhere to have these ideas behind it. Different branches of Christianity may have stressed one or other of these tenets of belief more than the rest, but all Christians believe in one God, Creator and Father; in Jesus Christ as God Incarnate (become man) who sacrificed Himself in atonement for man's sin, rose from the dead and returned to God; and in God's Holy Spirit who gives man a new quality of life. This is expressed in Christianity's classical summary, the Apostles' Creed.

The history of Christianity is a record of splendid achievement mixed with recurring unfaithfulness and failure. Western civilization has been built up in the main on Christian standards and way of life. Even those who belong to no part of the Christian Church are indebted to Christianity for their outlook upon life and for the attitude to moral questions which is revealed in the laws and customs of their country. But although Christianity has influenced Western civilization, a real 'Christian civilization' has never yet been seen. A civilization built up on the two Great Commandments and all that they imply would be something very different from anything humanity has yet achieved.

CHRISTIAN SCIENCE. This entirely modern interpretation of Christianity has nothing to do with any natural science. Taking the Bible as its authority, it claims that Jesus intended his followers to practise the healing of sickness as well as of sin as a part of their Christian faith. Its discoverer and founder was an American, Mary Baker Eddy (1821–1910), whose work *Science and Health with Key to the Scriptures* (1875) is the textbook of this religion.

As a young woman Mary Baker was a member of the Congregational Church and a devoted student of the Bible. She suffered a great deal from illness; and in her search for health, she became aware that the church did not include healing of the sick as part of its ministry.

During the middle years of her life she had a severe fall and was not expected to recover. She relates that three days later, while reading the account of Jesus' healing of the paralyzed man in the book of Matthew, she was instantly healed and walked into the next room, to the astonishment of her friends.

This healing led her to a renewed, intensive study of the Bible to discover what she felt were the spiritual laws underlying Jesus' healing work, which were to be learned through an understanding of God. Such an understanding, she said, would be the Science of Christianity.

Interest in her work and teaching grew, until in 1879 a small group of her students voted to organize a church. In 1892 the church took its present form as The Mother Church, The First Church of Christ, Scientist, in Boston, Massachusetts. By 1970 there were over 3,200 Christian Science branch churches and societies in forty-five countries in the world.

Christian Science teaches that God cannot be any less than totally good, and that consequently

Christian Science Publishing Society

MRS. EDDY

Christian Science is a religion which has no clergy. Church services consist of hymns, prayer, and related readings by two lay Readers from the Bible and from *Science and Health*. The readings for each Sunday—called the Lesson-Sermon—are listed in *The Christian Science Quarterly* so that Christian Scientists may study them during the week preceding the Sunday service. At Wednesday evening meetings, the readings are from the Bible and the Christian Science textbook, selected by individual Readers, and so are different in each church. Also, members of the congregation may give testimonies of healing, guidance, or spiritual regeneration.

Each Christian Science church maintains a Sunday School for pupils up to the age of 20, where the only instructional materials are the Bible and *Science and Health*. They also maintain Christian Science Reading Rooms, open to the public, where Christian Science literature may be studied, borrowed, or purchased.

Aside from the writings of Mrs. Eddy, the chief publications of the Christian Science Church are a monthly, *The Christian Science Journal*, which contains articles, testimonies of healing, and a list of Christian Scientists who are engaged in the public practice of Christian Science healing; a weekly, *The Christian Science Sentinel*; and the international daily newspaper, *The Christian Science Monitor*, which has a world-wide reputation for its high standards of journalism.

He does not create evil of any kind; therefore evil does not have a real or necessary existence. In proportion as this is understood, the evil that seems so real to mortals disappears from experience, according to Christian Science, and this is what is meant by healing—whether it is healing of sin, sickness, grief, poverty, loneliness, troubled human relationship, or any other sort of problem.

Critics of Christian Science are, however, sceptical of the value and consistency of Mrs. Eddy's teaching with regard to the unreality of evil. Her complete rejection of the whole of medical and surgical science as not only worthless but positively harmful seems to many thoughtful people extremely rash and hard to justify. She made up for herself a system of thought which accounted for her experiences, and believed she could find warrant for it in the Bible. She interpreted the woman in Revelation xii, 'arrayed with the sun, with the moon under her feet, and crowned with twelve stars', as being a prophecy of herself, and the 'little book' (Rev. x.2) as her textbook.

CHRISTIAN YEAR. Christianity, like all religions, keeps certain days in the year as holy-days and FESTIVALS (q.v.). Some of these are very old in the history of the Church, others have been added at later times. Some have declined since the Reformation but are still kept by the Church of Rome, and by the Orthodox East.

The Jews, from very early times, kept the seventh day in the week as a sacred day—the Sabbath, the day of rest. The Early Church, however, kept sacred the first day in the week which they called 'The Lord's Day', because it was the day of Christ's Resurrection. It was an early custom to keep a day of fast as preparation before a feast, and the Early Church kept Friday, the day of Christ's Crucifixion, as a partial fast each week.

The Church Year begins, not on 1 January, but on Advent Sunday, four Sundays before Christmas. Advent (coming) is the period in the

Christian Year when the Church prepares for the coming of the Lord at Christmas. Christmas, 25 December, the festival of the Nativity or birth of Christ, was not instituted until the 4th century A.D. In the East 6 January, the Roman winter festival, was the day kept to mark both the birth and baptism of Jesus. The keeping of 25 December as Christ's birthday arose in this way: the Spring Festival held on 25 March, the festival of Creation, when the year springs to life again, had for long been widely kept. The Christians took over the ancient festival and used it for celebrating the feast of the Annunciation, when the Angel announced to Mary that she should conceive God's Son. If Jesus were conceived on 25 March, he would be born nine months later, which is 25 December. 6 January, Epiphany (showing forth) is still kept, but in the West it is thought of as celebrating the visit of the Magi (Wise Men) and the showing forth of Jesus to the Gentiles (non-Jews).

The oldest and greatest festival in the Christian Year is Easter. The word Easter comes from an Old English word *eastre*, the name of a dawn-goddess worshipped in the Spring, but it is now used for the Christian festival of the Resurrection which falls at about the same time, as does also the Jewish Passover. It is kept on the first Sunday after the full moon on or after 21 March. It is the festival of the beginning of new life which is the reason for celebrating it with Easter eggs. Before Easter comes the period of fast called Lent (Old English, Spring), which has varied in length from three to eight weeks but is now fixed in the West at forty days. Lent begins with Ash Wednesday (ashes being a sign of penitence) and ends with Holy Week. Palm Sunday, the Sunday before Easter, is kept in remembrance of Jesus' triumphal entry into Jerusalem. Good Friday in Holy Week, the day of the Crucifixion, is the most important fast in the year, the only day when the Holy Communion is not celebrated.

The Jews held a harvest festival called Pentecost (Greek 'fifty days'), fifty days after Passover. This became from very early times the Christian Whit Sunday (White-Sunday because the newly-baptized wore white robes)—the festival to celebrate the coming of the Holy Ghost as described in Acts ii. Forty days after Easter is the Feast of Christ's Ascension, which has been kept everywhere since the 4th century. Trinity Sunday, one week after Whit Sunday, was not generally

By gracious permission of H.M. the Queen

PAGE FROM A MEDIEVAL CALENDAR

Books of Hours, which contained the forms for the various Church services, usually had a calendar giving all the Feasts and Saints' Days in the Christian Year. This page is for 1–15 July. Every day is a Saint's Day, the most important being written in red. Round the margin are scenes of the occupations of the month, in this case harvesting, and the figures of Amos and St. Philip. Sobieski Book of Hours. French, 15th century

kept till the 14th century, and Corpus Christi (Body of Christ)—the festival in honour of the Holy Eucharist, held on the Thursday after Trinity Sunday—began in the West in 1264. These are the main feast days of the Christian Year.

The days when notable Christians suffered martyrdom were often kept in remembrance of them in early days, and some of these came to be recognized by the Church everywhere. In the 4th century days were allotted to each of the Apostles and other SAINTS (q.v.) so that almost every day in the Calendar commemorates some Christian figure. From about 610, 1 November has been kept as All Saints' Day; and from the year 998 the following day has been kept as a day of prayer for the souls of all the departed, All Souls' Day. Other special days are kept to commemorate important events in the life of Christ, such as the Feast of the Circumcision (1 January), or the Transfiguration (6 August). Some branches of the CHRISTIAN CHURCH (q.v.) pay more attention to these minor feast days, others less; but all branches of the Church celebrate the major festivals such as Easter, Christmas, and Whit Sunday.

CHURCH, CHRISTIAN, *see* CHRISTIAN CHURCH.

CHURCH OF ENGLAND. The earliest mention of CHRISTIANITY (q.v.) in Britain is made by Tertullian about A.D. 200. He wrote about 'places of the Britons, unreached by the Romans, but subject to the law of Christ'. In 314 three bishops, a priest, and a deacon from Britain were present at a Church synod at Arles. In the 5th century the heathen Angles and Saxons invaded Britain and drove the Christian Britons into Wales and Cornwall. England, the land of the Angles, was a heathen country.

In 597 Pope Gregory I sent Saint Augustine and forty monks from Rome to Kent. In 635 a Celtic mission, led by Aidan, came from St. Columba's island of Iona to evangelize Northumbria. Between the two missions the nominal conversion of the whole country was soon secured. Pope Gregory had planned two archbishops under each. In fact it was nine centuries before England was divided into so many dioceses, and the southern see always remained at Canterbury, where Augustine first settled. The Roman missionaries, making the typically Roman contribution of organization, drew English Christianity into touch with the Continent and saved it from insularity. The Celtic missionaries contributed a spirit of independence and missionary zeal, both of which have remained features of the English Church. Even in the first 100 years there arose outstanding native leaders. Caedmon, who was a cowherd at Whitby Abbey, became one of the fathers of English poetry; Cuthbert was the Apostle of the Lowlands; Wilfrid in 664 became first English Bishop of York; BEDE (q.v. Vol. V) was father of English history and a scholar of European reputation; Willibrord went from Ripon as missionary to the Netherlands about 690; Boniface of Crediton joined him in 719 to become Apostle of Germany; Englishmen evangelized Scandinavia in the 11th century.

From the Synod of Whitby 664, which acknowledged the Roman connexion, to the REFORMATION (q.v.) and Henry VIII's break with Rome in 1534, the Church in England was a part of the Church of the West (*see* CHRISTIAN CHURCH). The Supremacy Act of 1534 declared the King to be 'the only supreme head in earth of the Church of England, called *Ecclesia Anglicana*'. This did not mean that the King claimed any spiritual powers, but that the Church came within the sphere of his rule and not under any outside authority such as the Pope in Rome. Under Elizabeth the term 'head' was changed to 'governor'. The Royal Supremacy, i.e. the State connexion, is not unlike the authority exercised by the Board of Governors of a school —oversight as to general well-being, leaving the actual running to those who, by calling and training, are capable of doing it.

In 1536-9 the monasteries were dissolved—the excuse being reform, the real reason greed for

Crown copyright

THE ROYAL COAT OF ARMS

All churches had to display the Royal Arms to show that the Monarch was head of the Church. 17th-century Chancel Screen at Abbeydore, Herefordshire

THE ENTHRONEMENT OF AN ARCHBISHOP OF CANTERBURY

The ceremony at the Chancel Steps, Canterbury Cathedral

their wealth. In 1538 the English Church was told to use the English Bible (*see* TRANSLATIONS, (2) BIBLE, Vol. XII). Under Edward VI in 1549 there was issued the first PRAYER BOOK (q.v.), in English instead of Latin, and with many minor alterations of the medieval services. In 1552 this was revised and made more definitely Protestant, and Forty-Two Articles (later revised to Thirty-Nine), statements as to Protestant belief, were made binding on the clergy. In Elizabeth's reign the third Prayer Book was issued, and permanent independence from Rome was secured.

The English Reformation was different in character from that on the Continent. It was an attempt to purify tradition rather than to change it. There was no break with medieval ways of worship, with the succession of bishops, nor with church order as a whole. The Church of England was designed to include a wide variety, 'low-churchmen' and 'high', and this its twofold nature has enabled it to do. It is at once Protestant in the sense of being truly reformed, and Catholic in the sense of holding an unbroken tradition. But its reforms were not thorough-going enough for many people; and consequently, during the 16th and 17th centuries came the break off of some sections (*see* CONGREGATIONALIST *and* BAPTIST).

In the 18th century a revival of religious zeal, led by JOHN WESLEY (q.v. Vol. V), resulted in the formation of the 'Methodist Societies', at first as a part of the Church of England, later as a separate dominion (*see* METHODIST). This movement influenced one section of the Church of England which became known as Evangelical. The marks of an Evangelical were to treat religion as a deeply personal matter, the experience of conversion opening a religious life which was strict, fervent, full of good works, and directed towards bringing others to the same way. Prominent among the Evangelicals were William WILBERFORCE (q.v. Vol. V), who did so much to abolish the slave trade (1807), Robert Raikes (1735–1811), who was one of the pioneers of popular education about 1780, and Charles

Simeon, a Cambridge vicar, the inspiration behind missionary work which prepared the way for the Church Missionary Society, founded in 1799.

In 1833 began a revival of a different kind, the Oxford Movement. This was a protest against the Church's dependence on the State, and a reassertion that the Church in England was a true part of the Catholic Church—hence came the name Anglo-Catholic. The leaders, nearly all Oxford men, of whom NEWMAN (q.v. Vol. V) is the best known, spread their ideas by writing tracts, so they were sometimes called Tractarians. This movement too brought revived zeal. A few religious communities were begun, doing what the old monastic orders had done up to 1536. Holy Communion was brought into greater prominence and frequency, and worship enriched. Enthusiasm in missionary work also began to revive, expressing itself mainly through the increased work of the Society for the Propagation of the Gospel in Foreign Parts (1701), which (with the S.P.C.K.) is the oldest missionary society.

Until 1784 there was no Anglican bishop overseas. The church in the American colonies was under the care of the Bishop of London. American Independence made this obviously absurd, and Bishop Seabury was consecrated the first bishop for the Protestant Episcopal Church of America. This marked a notable change. The Church of England, at first purely a national Church, was to become, as the result of the worldwide missionary expansion in the following century and a half, not national but universal—as indeed the Church should always be. After the U.S.A. came Nova Scotia, a bishopric in 1787, then Quebec, 1793. In 1814 the first Anglican bishopric in Asia was founded at Calcutta. Now there is even an Anglican Bishop of the Arctic. The Anglican Church literally stretches across the world. Except where the work is in its early stages, or where population is too scattered to make it possible, these extensions of the Anglican Church have developed into separate Provinces, in full communion with Canterbury and York, but administered by their own Church courts and, increasingly, with native bishops and clergy. When nowadays bishops are summoned for consultation at Lambeth once in ten years, the 320 or so bishops include representatives of many colours and races.

See also CLERGY.

CINGALESE, *see* CEYLONESE.

CLERGY. 1. This is the name for those who are separated by ordination for the service (ministry) of the Church, in contrast to the laity, who are the Church's ordinary members. Practically every religion has its PRIESTS (q.v.). This article is concerned only with the clergy of the CHURCH OF ENGLAND (q.v.).

2. ARCHBISHOP. The Church of England is divided into two provinces—Canterbury and York. Canterbury was the first missionary centre in England, and so is always placed first. The Archbishop of Canterbury is (1) Bishop of the diocese of Canterbury (Kent); (2) Archbishop (chief bishop) or Metropolitan of the Southern Province of twenty-nine dioceses, presiding over its Convocation (i.e. 'calling-together' of these twenty-nine bishops and representative clergy); (3) Primate of all England. As Primate it is his duty to crown the Monarch, to advise him or her in Church affairs, to preside over the General Synod (which, in 1970, replaced the Church Assembly as the Parliament of the Church and consists of about 250 clergy and 250 laity from every diocese in England) and over other gatherings which represent the Church of the whole nation. The Archbishop of Canterbury is recognized as head of the Anglican Communion, which includes the Episcopal Church in the U.S.A., the Commonwealth, and many other overseas dioceses; and he presides over the Lambeth Conference of Bishops, which since 1867 has aimed at meeting about every ten years. In this widest of his responsibilities he is what other ancient Churches would call Patriarch.

The Archbishop of York is Bishop of York diocese, Archbishop of the Northern Province of fourteen dioceses, and vice-chairman of the Church Assembly.

3. BISHOP. As Father-in-God of his diocese, he has to secure the right clergy, ordain and institute them, and supervise their work (by visitation at least every three years). He also confirms those who, having been baptized, are ready to become full members of the Church. Bishops were once chosen by the clergy and people of the diocese, and this now happens in overseas dioceses where the Church has no State connexion. In the Middle Ages, when the Bishops became important and powerful, the King generally tried to have a hand in the appointment. Since the Reformation, Bishops in England have been

CLERGY OF THE CHURCH OF ENGLAND

From left to right: Bishop with crozier, in mitre and cope. Bishop in chimere with a white rochet beneath. Priest in surplice and cassock. Priest in chasuble over an alb

appointed by the Crown, which means that the Prime Minister selects a candidate for the King, and the Dean and Chapter confirm the choice. Of the forty-three English bishops twenty-six have seats in the House of Lords. In big dioceses a suffragan or assistant bishop is appointed to help the bishop.

4. DEAN AND CHAPTER. The Dean is responsible for the cathedral, chief church of a diocese, and for its services. In ancient cathedrals he, too, is appointed by the Crown. In newer ones the name of Provost is used, and the appointment is made by the Bishop. The Dean presides over the Cathedral Chapter, a meeting so called because in the Middle Ages they used to read a chapter of the Monastic Rule (*see* MONK). The Chapter consists of Canons (Greek for 'rule', because they used to live together like monks), who are the resident cathedral staff. Sometimes canons are given special responsibility for particular work in the diocese, such as religious education or missionary work. An Honorary Canon is non-resident and has no stipend from the cathedral. A few cathedrals have 'Prebendaries', who, though the word means stipend, are now in fact honorary only.

5. ARCHDEACON. Most dioceses are divided into two or more parts called archdeaconries. As the name implies, the Archdeacon was once a chief deacon, but now he is always in priest's orders. He has always been responsible for the business side of his part of the diocese, but now

he informs, advises, and assists the Bishop in its spiritual care as well.

6. RURAL DEAN. The diocese also has smaller divisions, called rural deaneries, of perhaps as many as forty parishes. The Rural Dean is appointed by the Bishop to keep him informed concerning this group of parishes and to act for him there, for instance, in inducting new vicars.

7. PARISH PRIEST (Parson, Rector, Vicar). In feudal times the lord of the manor would provide a free-holding to support a priest for the people of his domain. The owners of land in the manor paid a tithe (tenth) to support the 'living' (i.e. the income which goes with a church appointment). Patronage is a relic of feudal society. The patron of the living is the person (or in some cases a body such as a monastery) who has the right to choose a priest for appointment by the Bishop. Livings varied and still vary considerably in the income they produce. The priest who has spiritual charge of the parish and the worship of its church is called a Rector (ruler) or Vicar (representative)—a term used if the priest represented, for instance, a monastery to which the living belonged. If the parish is large, the Rector or Vicar has an assistant, called a Curate. In the PRAYER BOOK (q.v.), curate, like the French *curé*, means 'one who has a spiritual charge', i.e. the Rector or Vicar himself. Later it came to mean a substitute, and now it means an assistant.

8. DEACON. Of the three orders of clergy—

bishop, priest, deacon—this is the lowest. The Deacon was an assistant to the priest with especial care for visiting the sick and needy. Now a Deacon is generally on the way to becoming a priest. The Deaconess represents the only ordained ministry of women (except in Hong Kong, where two women have recently been ordained to the priesthood). There were women recognized in the service of the Church in Apostolic times. The Deaconess Order of the Church of England was founded in 1923.

COLOMBIA, PEOPLES OF.

This country in the north of South America is the only country to be named after the discoverer of America, COLUMBUS (q.v. Vol. V), although he himself never reached it. Under Spanish rule Colombia formed part of the viceroyalty of New Granada, together with Venezuela and Ecuador. It was a vitally important part of the Spanish Empire, since it controlled the line of communication between the Atlantic and the Pacific across the isthmus of Panama. At the beginning of the 19th century Colombia, like Venezuela, was liberated from Spanish rule by SIMON BOLIVAR (q.v. Vol. V); and for some years after independence was won, there was a republic of Great Colombia, including Colombia, Venezuela, and Ecuador, which afterwards split up into separate nations. Through most of the 19th century Colombia was in a state of civil war; and at last in 1903 the province of Panama revolted and declared its independence with the help of the United States. Since that time the country has had a period of somewhat more peaceful progress. It has proved itself one of the more truly democratic of the Latin American states, and has not suffered from dictators, though it has suffered much from revivals of the feud between the two old parties, the Liberals and the Conservatives.

The majority of the people are of mixed European and Indian blood, but there are a great many whites of Spanish descent, and smaller numbers of pure Indians and Negroes. The main crop is coffee; next to Brazil, Colombia is the world's largest producer. Mining, forestry, and oil production are important. Life is still very primitive in the more remote places, where such modern luxuries as sanitation and good schools are unknown. Spanish, which is spoken in a very pure form, is the language of the country, but many of the Indians in the jungles

Camera Press

COLOMBIAN PEASANTS ON THEIR WAY TO A LAND REFORM MEETING

still speak only their own native languages. Bogotá, the capital city, was one of the intellectual centres of the Spanish Empire, and is often called the Athens of South America, because of its interest in literature and art, and the scholars, scientists, and poets it has produced. The old town with its fine Spanish buildings and paintings preserves the atmosphere of a city in Spain.

Colombia now has a population of twenty-three million, larger than that of Argentina, and ranking third in Latin America behind Brazil and Mexico.

See also AMERICAN INDIANS, CENTRAL AND SOUTH.
See also Vol. III: COLOMBIA; INDEX, p. 138.

CONFUCIANISM, *see* CHINESE RELIGION.

CONGREGATIONALIST.

A congregationalist is a member of a denomination which is based on the principle that the local, gathered church is the true church and that each local unit should be self-governing under the guidance of the Holy Spirit and so obedient to Christ, the true and only Head of the Church. The worship in such a local church is not governed by a set liturgy. Great emphasis is laid on reading Scripture and on preaching. The Lord's Supper is celebrated normally at least once a month. The members of the local church form the 'congregation', which has always been empowered to call its own minister and to appoint such other officers (e.g. elders and deacons) as it thinks necessary. Although it maintains that each local unit should be self-governing, Congregationalism has from the beginning been well aware of the responsibilities of local congregations to each other.

Congregationalism as a separate movement emerged from the tumult of the English Reformation. In the Elizabethan period the attempt to set up a comprehensive national church had the support of some Puritans; but the more radical Protestants felt that it would be a long and difficult task to persuade the Government to adopt further reforms. They advocated 'Reformation without tarrying for anie'. Many of them were opposed to the idea of a national church in any case. Robert Browne (probably 1550–1633) was one of the earlier leaders; hence the name Brownists. He and his followers were Separatists because they were not content with the parish system; Independents, because of their principle of local government; Nonconformists, because they could not in conscience accept the National Church. Because of these convictions many suffered persecution and exile. Among them were the Pilgrim Fathers, who set sail for America in the Mayflower in 1620.

Congregationalists were deeply involved in the Civil War (*see* CIVIL WAR, ENGLISH Vol. X) and many of them were supporters of Oliver Cromwell, who shared their religious convictions.

When Charles II was restored to the throne in 1660, a further attempt to establish a comprehensive national church was made. In 1662 the Clarendon Code was enforced, which aimed at the abolition of Nonconformity. A number of clergy of Congregational and Presbyterian conviction were dismissed from their livings on August 24th 1662. In 1689, however, the Toleration Act brought an easier period.

In 1795 the London Missionary Society was founded, and this Society, while interdenominational in character, was mainly supported by Congregationalists. Some of its missionaries were famous pioneers; notably Robert Morrison in China (1782–1834), John Williams in the South Seas (1796–1839), and David Livingstone in Africa (1813–73). In the present century the pattern of missionary work has altered a good deal, because the churches founded by the original missionaries have in fact become self-governing, for example the Church of South India. In 1966 the London Missionary Society recast its constitution and became the Congregational Council for World Mission. The newly formed United Reformed Church (see below) is to be one of its constituent members.

Congregationalism has spread through the English-speaking world, but it is scarcely found elsewhere. In Australia, Southern Africa, and the United States of America it has been an influential religious force. Frequently, as in India and Canada, it has been closely associated with moves towards church union. In 1957 the majority of Congregational Churches in the U.S.A. united with the Evangelical and Reformed Church to form the United Church of Christ in U.S.A. In 1891 the International Congregational Church was formed; and in 1970 this body merged with the World Alliance of Reformed Churches (Presbyterian) at a combined assembly in Nairobi. Congregationalists in Great Britain have been closely associated with the Free Church Federal Council, the British Council of Churches, and the World Council of Churches.

The Congregational Union of England and Wales was formed in 1831. It was a voluntary association of local churches; and it was made very clear that it had no legislative authority over its member churches. *A Declaration of Faith, Church Order and Discipline* was published in 1833. Increasingly, however, particularly since 1912, the Union was found to have a useful function in serving the churches; and in 1966 the constitution was changed and the Union became the Congregational *Church in* England and Wales. Interdependence was now wedded to independence.

In 1963 conversations were begun with the Presbyterian Church of England with a view to the union of the two denominations; and in October 1972 there was inaugurated the United Reformed Church, comprising all but two of the Presbyterian congregations and all but about 15 per cent of the Congregational membership. A Congregational Federation, which has been designed largely to revert to the 1831–3 pattern, was also formed in 1972.

See also CHRISTIAN CHURCH; REFORMATION.

COPTIC CHURCH. The word Copt means Egyptian. Its origin from the Greek may be represented in English by shortening 'Egyptian' to 'Gypt' and then softening it to 'Copt'.

The word is used to denote Christians in Egypt. Their tradition is that St. Mark, who wrote the Gospel, was their first missionary. By A.D. 200 Christianity was strong, especially in Alexandria, which became a great centre of (Greek) Christian learning. A century later it had spread to the Egyptian population. The Church became separated from the main body of Christians in the Eastern Roman Empire, about 451, largely because of the spirit of local independence. The Copts suffered much after the Arab invasion (about 640), when ISLAM (q.v.) became the official religion. Soon the majority of the population became Muslims. Today the Church numbers $3\frac{1}{2}$ million members under its Patriarch, the (Coptic) Bishop of Alexandria. Its people speak Arabic, though the liturgy contains some Coptic, i.e. ancient Egyptian. In the 4th century Christianity spread to Ethiopia, entering from the Red Sea coast. There the King was converted, and Christianity remains to this day the official religion. The Ethiopian Church counts itself the daughter of the Coptic. Its liturgy is in the ancient language, Ge'ez, a close relation of Tigre (*see* ETHIOPIANS).

See also CHRISTIAN CHURCH.

CORSICANS, *see* Vol. III: CORSICA.

COSSACKS. These were independent and warlike frontiersmen, consisting at first of fugitives from Russia, Poland, and Lithuania, who settled in the late 15th and 16th centuries, north of the Black Sea, on the banks of the rivers Don and Dnieper. They were magnificent horsemen, as have been most of the peoples living in the steppes of Russia. They lived across the trade-routes from the eastern Mediterranean countries to the Far East, and often attacked and robbed the caravan parties. Later Cossack groups settled along rivers east of the Caspian Sea.

The Cossacks were lovers of freedom, and they organized a remarkably democratic society in times when their neighbours were living under the absolute rule of autocratic princes. Until the 17th century they allowed no class distinctions. All the land belonged to the 'Host' of the community, and was only lent to individual

COSSACKS OF DAGHESTAN

S.C.R.

Cossacks. The community was governed by a popular council called the Circle which had absolute power over the lives and possessions of the population. Its methods were crude, and offenders were punished by being drowned in the river. The leader, the Ataman, was elected by the whole community, and had absolute power only in time of war.

By the 17th century the Cossacks had come under the authority of the Russians or of the Poles. The Russians formed Cossack contingents of light cavalry, which later became a very important part of the Russian Army. They revolted against the Russians in the time of Catherine the Great, but were severely crushed. Fearing Communist interference with their way of life, the Cossacks fought against the Bolsheviks in the Russian Revolution of 1917-20.

The Cossacks, their way of life, their grand horsemanship, and fame as soldiers, have been the subject of much Russian literature. Tolstoy's famous story, *The Cossacks*, gives a vivid description of their way of life in 1852. Pushkin in his story, *The Captain's Daughter*, describes their rebellion against Catherine the Great.

See also RUSSIANS.

CREATION MYTHS, *see* BABYLONIAN MYTHS; HEBREW MYTHS.

CREOLE, descendant of European or Negro settlers in the West Indies (*see* WEST INDIANS).

CRETANS, *see* MINOAN CIVILIZATION.

CROATS, *see* YUGOSLAVS.

CRUSADES. In 1095 Alexius, Emperor of the BYZANTINE EMPIRE (q.v.) appealed to the people of western Europe to help defend his empire against the invasions of the Muslim Turks, and to win back Jerusalem and the Holy Land which had been taken by the Turks in 1076. Jerusalem, indeed, was one of the Holy Places of ISLAM (q.v.). But through the centuries Christians had continued to regard it as the centre of Christendom and a place of PILGRIMAGE (q.v.). Returning pilgrims kept alive the idea that Jerusalem ought to belong to the Christians. Thus many people came to believe that a war to recover Jerusalem would be a Holy War.

The idea that a war could be holy was not new. In the 9th and 10th centuries Europe had been attacked by Vikings, Magyars, and Arabs. Since none of these peoples were Christians, the defence of Europe against them was looked upon as a Holy War. The war against the Arabs in Spain went on through the 11th century. So by 1095 men were thoroughly accustomed to the idea of fighting Muslims in a holy cause.

In response to the Emperor's appeal Pope Urban II called upon both rich and poor to help their Christian brothers in the East. On all sides men flocked to do the Pope's bidding and to 'take the cross'—a piece of cloth cut into the shape of a cross which they wore as a sign that they had taken a vow to go on crusade. The Pope's message was taken up by other preachers—among them, PETER THE HERMIT (q.v. Vol. V). Neither Emperor Alexius nor Pope Urban had foreseen that so many thousands of people, rich and poor, men and women, would volunteer to undertake the long and dangerous journey to the East. But there was something immensely attractive about a journey which was like a Holy War and a pilgrimage combined. People believed that if they went on crusade their sins would be forgiven and they would go to heaven when they died. To the adventurous the Crusades gave a grand opportunity of indulging in the joys and excitement of warfare under cover of a religious duty. Many saw the chance of obtaining riches and land. So from this variety of motives, pious and self-seeking, men sold their possessions to raise enough money to equip themselves and their followers. They then set out for Constantinople.

But the first contingents to go had very few possessions to sell. They were mostly poor peasants roused by the electrifying eloquence of Peter the Hermit. In 1096 several undisciplined hordes left France and Germany to march through Hungary and Bulgaria. On their way they massacred Jews. Only a small fraction of them reached Constantinople, and most of these were wiped out in their first battle with the Turks of Asia Minor.

The second group of armies consisted mainly of knights and soldiers. By different routes they all made their way to Constantinople. There they met Emperor Alexius and then, as one army, they marched towards the Holy Land. There was no commander-in-chief. Instead the leadership was shared among several princes, among them Godfrey of Bouillon and a brilliant general named Bohemund. The crusaders endured great

Philips, Wells, Somerset

A KNIGHT OF THE TIME OF THE CRUSADES

Early 13th-century figure on the West Front of Wells Cathedral

hardships and fought many battles. As in most other wars many cruel and inhuman deeds were done. Eventually, in 1099—3 years after they left home—they captured Jerusalem. Godfrey of Bouillon became the first ruler of the new Christian kingdom of Jerusalem. Other princes seized lands in Syria and Palestine. In this way the crusader states of Antioch, Tripoli and Edessa were established.

The first crusade had been an amazing success, and everybody in Europe was delighted. But the crusaders had been very lucky as well as very brave. The Muslim rulers of Syria and Palestine had been more interested in their own quarrels than in uniting against the newcomers, but once they learned to fight together they easily outnumbered the enemy. The new states were short of fighting men because many crusaders had returned home, as if from a pilgrimage, as soon as they reached Jerusaelem. In 1144 Edessa fell. Clearly, reinforcements were needed and so St. BERNARD (q.v. Vol. V) preached the Second Crusade. This, however, failed to achieve anything worthwhile.

The Muslims now began to preach their own Holy War. This idea helped to unite the Muslim world, and so it was enthusiastically supported by Saladin, the great statesman who rose to be ruler of Egypt and Syria. In 1187 Saladin overran almost the whole of Palestine and captured Jerusalem. Shocked at this news, the Christians of Europe organized the Third Crusade. In King Richard the Lionheart of England the crusaders found an outstanding leader. But although he conquered Cyprus and recovered the coastal plain of Palestine, not even he could recapture Jerusalem. It was while he was on his way home from the crusade that King Richard was captured and imprisoned in a German castle. The legend of how he was discovered by his faithful minstrel, Blondel, is well-known.

The Fourth Crusade was planned by Pope Innocent III. A Venetian fleet was hired to take the crusaders to the Holy Land, but when they gathered at Venice, the crusaders found that they did not have enough money to pay for the fleet. In this embarrassing situation they agreed to do what the Venetians asked—attack the Byzantine Empire. In 1204 they sacked Constantinople. So it was that crusaders learned to make war on fellow-Christians.

In 1212 there occurred the Children's Crusade. The idea arose that only the innocent could free

E. K. Waterhouse

THE CASTLE OF MARQAB, SYRIA
One of the castles built by the Crusaders in the 13th century

the Holy Land. So thousands of children from France and Germany left their homes and marched to the Mediterranean, believing that they would be able to walk across the sea to Jerusalem. They found that they could not, and that they were stranded hundreds of miles from home. Most of them never saw their families again. They died or were sold into slavery. This strange and tragic story is the basis of the legend of the Pied Piper. Further crusades followed, including two led by the saintly French king, Louis IX. But little was achieved, and by 1291 the whole of the Holy Land was back in Muslim hands. Of the Christian conquests only Cyprus remained (until 1571).

There was not much to show for 200 years of crusading. Many lives had been lost. The Christian Byzantine Empire had been torn apart. Relations between Christians and Jews, between Christians and Muslims, and between Christians of the West and of the East were worse than ever before.

See also KNIGHTS, ORDERS OF.

CRYSTAL GAZING, *see* DIVINATION.

CUBA, PEOPLES OF, *see* WEST INDIANS.

CYPRIOTS. The people of the island of Cyprus, at the eastern end of the Mediterranean, can claim the longest continuous political and artistic history of any part of the British Commonwealth. Traces of their civilizations are to be found as early as the 15th century B.C. The Old Testament name Kittium applied both to Cyprus and to the town Kition (Citium), the modern Larnaca, which was a centre of Phoenician civilization as well as the birth-place of the Greek philosopher, Zeno, founder of the Stoic School of philosophy. The island was already prominent artistically in the early Bronze Age and its mythology goes back into some of the earliest beliefs of the human race. People lived here as early as 6000 B.C.

Its position in the centre of eastern Mediterranean civilization caused Cyprus to be the meeting-place and often the battlefield of races, languages, faiths, and civilizations at the very dawn of history. As mythology merged into history, there flourished in Cyprus side by side the cultures, arts, and languages of the three great civilizations of the GREEKS, the PHOENICIANS, and the EGYPTIANS (qq.v.). For centuries the great Temple of Aphrodite in Paphos in the south-west part of the island was the most celebrated shrine of that goddess in the ancient world.

In A.D. 45 St. Paul and St. Barnabas brought Christianity to Cyprus and converted the Roman ruler, Sergius Paulus, so that the island became the first country in the world to be governed by a Christian ruler. When the Roman Empire split, Cyprus belonged to the eastern half, the BYZANTINE EMPIRE (q.v.). For a few years from 1184 the island was independent, and then it was occupied for one year by Richard I of England on his way to take part in the Third Crusade. Then for some 300 years Cyprus was ruled by the kings and queens of the brilliant French dynasty of Lusignan. At this time— perhaps the greatest in the island's history—the port of Famagusta was the busiest in art in the eastern Mediterranean, and vied with Venice in the wealth and luxury of its merchant princes.

In 1489 the Venetian Republic took control of the island in order to fortify it against the advance of the Ottoman Turks (q.v.). In 1571, however, the Turks captured Cyprus and held it till 1878. During the short period of Venetian rule there held office a certain Christoforo Moro, who was the original of Shakespeare's 'Moor of Venice'. The 'Seaport in Cyprus'—the scene of *Othello*—is the Cyprus port of Famagusta.

Hulton Picture Library

A STREET IN NICOSIA, CYPRUS

During the period of Ottoman rule the history of Cyprus was uneventful. In 1878, however, Britain and Turkey agreed that Britain should occupy Cyprus in order that she might assist Turkey in defending herself against Russia. After the First World War, in which Turkey was on the losing side, Cyprus became a British Crown Colony.

In 1955 a Greek Cypriot underground organization (EOKA), led by Colonel Grivas, launched an armed campaign for Enosis (the union of Cyprus with Greece). A state of emergency was declared and lasted until the signature in 1959 of the Zurich and London Agreements. In accordance with these Agreements, the Republic of Cyprus was set up in 1960 and its Constitution guaranteed by Greece, Turkey, and Great Britain. Two small areas of Cyprus remained under British sovereignty for Britain's use as military bases.

The Cypriot people—except for small groups of Maronites in the north-west and Armenians in the capital, Nicosia—fall into two main divisions: four-fifths are Greek-speaking members of the ORTHODOX EASTERN CHURCH (q.v.), while the remaining one-fifth are Turkish-speaking followers of ISLAM (q.v.) who came over with the Turkish conquerors in the 16th century.

The Constitution of the Republic attempted to maintain a balance between the Greek and Turkish communities, but in 1963 the balance broke down and intercommunal fighting broke out. A United Nations peace-keeping force (UNFICYP) was set up in March 1964 and has remained in the island ever since. A second outbreak of serious fighting occurred in 1967, and a Turkish invasion was narrowly averted.

See also Vol. III: CYPRUS.

CZECHOSLOVAKS. The Czechs and the Slovaks are a Slav people belonging to the same language group as the Russians and Poles (*see* SLAVONIC LANGUAGES, Vol. IV). They inhabit a new country, Czechoslovakia, which was formed after the First World War in 1918; but they are a people with a very old and romantic history.

The kingdom of Bohemia, which now forms a part of modern Czechoslovakia, was an important country of the Middle Ages. Prague, the chief city of Bohemia and capital of Czechoslovakia, has the oldest University of central Europe, founded by Charles IV in 1348. One of our own English queens, Anne, wife of

Richard II, came from Bohemia. The country is rich with fairy tales and traditional stories, one of which, the story of good King Wenceslas, is known to everybody. The famous Christian King, who ruled Bohemia in the 10th century and was beloved by his people for his good and just rule, was murdered as he was coming out of church by his pagan brother who was jealous of him. His tomb is still a place of pilgrimage for the Czechoslovak people.

The Czechs and Slovaks first came to Bohemia and the surrounding country in the 6th century, during the course of a general migration of Slav people from the East. About 300 years later, Christianity was brought to them by St. Cyril and other missionaries from Thessalonica. St. Cyril also invented for the Slav people an alphabet which is still called Cyrillic after him, and which was used in Bohemia until they adopted the Latin alphabet. The Cyrillic alphabet is still used in Serbia, Bulgaria, and Russia. In the 15th century the religious teaching of John Wycliffe spread to Bohemia, and was taken up by the great Czech scholar, John Huss. The followers of Huss, called Hussites or MORA-VIANS (q.v.), were bitterly opposed by the Roman Catholics; the people were divided among themselves, and the country was weakened and unable to defend itself against greedy and powerful neighbours. In the 17th century Bohemia was absorbed into the Austrian Empire, under whose rule it remained until after the First World War. The Hussites suffered terrible persecution, and in the 17th century 30,000 of them were driven from their country and wandered homeless across Europe. They lived so much like GYPSIES (q.v.), that they were often confused with them, especially in France, where the gypsies were called Bohemians. In England the word 'Bohemian' came to be used to describe people of an artistic temperament and an unsettled and unconventional way of living.

During the time of their subjection to Austria, the Czechs never lost their sense of nationality or their longing for independence; and their national leaders did all they could to foster unity and patriotism. Political organizations were not allowed, but their rulers could hardly object to societies formed for physical culture. These societies, called Sokols, were a means of banding the young people together and giving them a sense of unity and purpose. The word *Sokol* means falcon, and the members endeavoured to become as swift and strong and fearless as falcons. The Sokols continued to develop after the Czechs gained their independence: great festivals were held at Prague, where as many as 10,000 young men and women would give their gymnastic displays to enormous audiences.

When the First World War broke out in 1914, the Czechs and Slovaks saw their chance. They had the great good fortune to possess a leader of outstanding wisdom and courage in THOMAS MASARYK (q.v. Vol. V). Through a secret society called the Mafia, they gave help to the Allies against the Austrians and Germans, and in return were given their independence at the treaty of Versailles. Under the leadership of the wise Masaryk, a strong democratic republic was built up, and great progress was made towards unity and prosperity.

Unfortunately, a discontented minority of German origin, living in a part of Czechoslovakia, gave the German dictator, Hitler, an excuse for attacking. Masaryk's successor, Dr. Beneš, became head of a government in exile which conducted the war from London until the Germans were defeated and Czechoslovakia was once more free. Early in 1948 a Communist government was formed in Czechoslovakia, and it received the support of 89 per cent of the people in an election at which the alternatives were to vote for the Communist Government candidates or to return a blank vote. In the last competitive elections to take place in Czechoslovakia (in 1946) the Communists had acquired 40 per cent of the votes in the Czech lands of Bohemia and Moravia and 30 per cent support in Slovakia. After 1948 the Czechoslovak political system became closely modelled on that of the Soviet Union and by the 1960s this had led to widespread dissatisfaction and to pressure for reform even from within the ranks of the Communist party. The reform movement reached a climax in 1968 when the head of the Communist Party and Czechoslovak President for the greater part of the post-1948 period, Antonín Novotný, was removed from both these posts and replaced as party head by Alexander Dubček and as President by General Ludvík Svoboda. Changes making for greater democracy within the political system of Czechoslovakia were interrupted by the armed intervention in August, 1968, of the Soviet Union and several of her Warsaw Pact allies. This led to a reversal of the reforms which had been initiated under the leadership of

J. Allan Cash

A FAMOUS CLOCK IN PRAGUE

The Czechs (in particular) and Slovaks are traditionally industrious peoples, and in the period between the world wars they were fast developing the natural riches of their country. Before the Second World War shops in Britain sold many well-designed Czechoslovak goods, notably Bohemian glass and the boots and shoes of the famous Bata brothers. The Bren gun was a Czech invention which probably took its name from that of the town of Brno. The Skoda armament works were among the largest in central Europe. Since 1948 Czechoslovak heavy industry has continued to develop and full employment has been maintained; but her light industry has been less successful, and there have also been occasional shortages of such essential commodities as meat.

Much of the country is mountainous and covered with great forests which are broken by fertile valleys and clearings. In the more remote districts in the south-east, the forests are still the haunts of fierce wild animals. Bears (like the one that killed Antigonus in Shakespeare's *Winter's Tale*) are still a danger to the lonely shepherd, and packs of wolves and wild boars, driven by hunger in the long cold winters, will make ravages on the flocks and even come to the outskirts of the villages. In the plains of Slovakia, bordering the river Danube, huge flocks of geese are to be seen, often in the charge of a boy. Roast goose is the usual dish for any festive occasion. The village people still wear their national costumes with elaborate head-dresses on special occasions.

Dubček (who was replaced as party leader by Gustav Husák in 1969). The only reform to survive (at least in part) the change of leadership and Soviet pressure was the plan to turn Czechoslovakia into a federal state of Czechs and Slovaks. The federation came into formal existence in 1969.

See also Vol. III: CZECHOSLOVAKIA; INDEX, p. 139.

D

DALMATIANS, *see* YUGOSLAVS.

DANES. These are a Scandinavian people, as are their neighbours the SWEDES and NORWEGIANS (qq.v.). The ancestors of all three were the Norsemen or VIKINGS (q.v.). Denmark has existed as a united kingdom since about 985. Though the English king Alfred the Great defeated the Danes on land and sea, England was, for a short period—under the Danish King Canute—part of a kingdom that included Denmark and Norway.

The history of Denmark is closely interlocked with the histories of Sweden and Norway. Sometimes they were friends, sometimes enemies. For a time, in the 14th century, all three were united under a Danish queen, Margaret. Denmark lost its hold over Sweden in 1523 and gave up Norway in 1814. For many years now the three countries have been at peace and closely associated. Denmark's position among nations was much strengthened by the great marriages made by Danish princesses at the end of the 19th century—Princess Alexandra of Denmark became Queen of England and Princess Dagmar (Marie) Empress of Russia, while their brother George was elected King of Greece.

Today Denmark is a democracy with a constitutional monarch. But it was not till 1788 that the Danish peasants were freed from feudalism, and the monarchy was absolutist till 1849. It is the oldest monarchy in Europe, and for 500 years the kings have been named alternately Christian and Frederick. Queen Margrethe II succeeded her father King Frederick IX in 1972. Parliament, consisting of one house called the Folketing, frames the laws, and the Government wields the executive power. The established religion is the Lutheran, introduced in 1536, but there is complete religious toleration.

The state provides free education at all levels.

Since 1814 education has been compulsory between the ages of 7 and 14. There are many secondary schools and specialized colleges, and three universities, Copenhagen, Aarhus, and Odense. A fourth is being built at the ancient royal city of Roskilde where most Danish kings are buried in the cathedral. Adult education has played an important part in Denmark since the founding of the first Folk High School in the world, in 1844. Danes are among the five biggest reading and bookbuying peoples.

The Danes are traditionally a nation of farmers. Most of the farms are smallholdings, but a system of co-operative production and marketing enables the small farmer to get the advantage of large-scale business. Co-operative creameries, meat-packing plants, butter and cheese factories are run by experts for the benefit of producer and consumer. Fishing, too, is an important industry. But farming and fishing now engage only 11·5% of the population, compared with 46% in industry and commerce.

Since the Second World War the Danes have made a new Industrial Revolution, so that the

Royal Danish Embassy

A PEDESTRIAN PRECINCT, HOLSTEBRO, JUTLAND

Royal Danish Embassy

A DANISH FARM

industrial exports are now three times as valuable as the agricultural. They range from machinery, tankers, and electronic equipment to furniture and plastic boats. This fast development has caused a shortage of labour which has been filled by foreign workers, chiefly from Yugoslavia and the Near East. It has also resulted in a rise in the standard of living; one Dane in five has a car, and three out of five own their own house.

Their long tradition of independent nationhood has given the Danes a strong and deep sense of national unity. This showed itself very much during the German occupation in the Second World War, when, though powerless to fight, they put up a most effective passive resistance. They are excellent linguists, German and English being the languages most commonly spoken. They are good mixers. The foreigner quickly feels at home in Denmark, and the Dane as quickly feels at home in other countries. Danish immigrants to the United States and Canada are a valuable part of the population.

See also Vol. III: DENMARK; INDEX, p. 139.
See also Vol. IV: SCANDINAVIAN LANGUAGES.

DARK AGES. The period in European history, from the decline and fall of the great Roman Empire in the 5th and 6th centuries to the beginnings of the medieval revival in the 11th and 12th centuries, is called 'dark', partly because comparatively little is known about it, and partly because it was a time when civilization in Europe was at a low ebb—very dark compared with the brilliant civilizations of GREECE and ROME (qq.v.) which had gone before, and the great period of the RENAISSANCE (q.v.) which was to follow.

During the 4th and 5th centuries invading hordes of HUNS, GOTHS, and VANDALS (qq.v.) swept across Europe, spreading destruction as they went. They established kingdoms in Europe and were constantly at war with each other and with the Roman Empire, whose power they finally broke. During this period the kings were rarely strong enough to enforce law and order, and the local lords, from the great barons down to every petty knight, had their strongholds from which they attacked their neighbours and laid waste their lands.

During the end of the 8th and beginning of the 9th centuries CHARLEMAGNE (q.v. Vol. V) extended the kingdom of the Franks into a great empire, and in A.D. 800 he was crowned Holy Roman Emperor. He conceived of the HOLY ROMAN EMPIRE (q.v.) as a great civilizing influence in Europe; but, unfortunately, when he died there was no great leader to take his place, and Europe fell back again into anarchy.

The CHRISTIAN CHURCH (q.v.) preserved a little of Roman civilization and learning, and the records of churchmen provide us with almost all the knowledge we have of these centuries. The monks wrote chronicles for their monasteries, and some of these have survived. But the Church also was unenlightened in many of its actions, and often its bishops and abbots were wordly men, more concerned with preserving their power in an insecure world than in fostering truth and progress. The influence of Greek civilization, preserved and fostered in the BYZANTINE EMPIRE (q.v.), spread very little into the West during these centuries because of the difficulty of communication, especially after Arab ships got control of the Mediterranean. The civilization of the ARABS (q.v.) was resisted in the West because it was accompanied by the Muslim religion (*see* ISLAM), and Europe had little knowledge of the arts and sciences of the Muslim world except in so far as they spread along North Africa into Spain with the MOORS (q.v.).

DEATH CEREMONIES. Among many primitive peoples, death is believed to be unnatural and to have come into the world because men displeased a supernatural being or disobeyed his command. The Bataks of the Philippine Islands say that their god punished them by sending death because they once deceived him with a shark wrapped up to look like a corpse; and some Australian natives believe that death came when a woman attacked a forbidden tree with a stone axe and disturbed the bat which lived in it. The book of Genesis tells how mankind became subject to death because Adam and Eve ate the fruit of a forbidden tree.

Most people believe in some kind of life after death. This belief was held by Stone Age men (*see* RELIGION, PREHISTORIC), by the peoples of most ancient civilizations, by the greatest Greek philosophers (*see* PLATO; ARISTOTLE; Vol. V), and gives additional meaning and purpose to life for most people today. Ideas differ widely as to what the spirits of the dead are like, but frequently they are thought of as shadowy ghosts. A common idea is that they are born again as other people, animals, or even as stars.

The part of the person which is believed to leave the body at death is imagined in various ways. Some North American Indians think it is a little manikin living in the person's head. There are widespread beliefs that the 'soul' is the breath or the person's shadow and that at death it flies away from the body in the shape of a bird. People open windows after someone has died to let the soul out. The Egyptians combined several of these ideas, believing that a dead man had a spark of intelligence which went back to the gods, a bird-like soul which fluttered round the tomb, a shadow, and a 'double' which rejoined the mummy after 3,000 years when the whole man rose from the dead.

Primitive peoples often take precautions when the corpse is brought out of the house to prevent the spirit's return. All over the world they avoid using the door of the house, hut, or tent. In Holland special 'corpse doors' were even made. Some Siberian tribespeople carry the body out through a corner of the tent; and Pacific Islanders (Melanesians) break down the side of the hut although the door is wide enough. Usually the body is carried out feet foremost, so that the dead man may not see the way, and his ghost be thus prevented from returning; and sometimes the corpse is turned round to confuse the spirit. In parts of Ireland the funeral goes to the cemetery by the longest way; in the Solomon Islands the mourners return by a different route from that by which they went; and in Siberia the order of the returning procession is reversed. To prevent the dead haunting them people bury the body face downwards, stroke the grave with a branch (Melanesia), break the bones (Australia), or tie a clog to it (Ancient India). On one occasion, when a man was murdered in the island of Arran, the police buried his boots below high-water mark to prevent his 'walking'. Sometimes seeds or imitation money are strewn on the road or near the grave, as it is thought that wandering spirits will be delayed counting them. Funerals are sometimes held at night, as it is believed that then the spirits will find it more difficult to capture souls.

It has been very widely believed that the dead have need in the other world of the food, implements, servants, &c., that they have used in this world, and that these things must be provided for them at their burial. As long ago as the Old Stone Age, flint implements and marrow bones were buried with the dead; and still, in many parts of the world, provision is made at the time of the burial or afterwards for the needs of the departed person's spirit. Our knowledge of how the ancient Egyptians lived is largely due to the fact that they placed in the tombs of their kings and other important people for their use after death the things they used in everyday life. The ancient practice in Babylonia, Egypt, and China of sacrificing people to minister to the mighty dead in the Otherworld gave place to the custom of burying models instead. In fact, the idea that models would do instead of real things spread widely. In museums you may see the models of people, ships, and houses found in Egyptian tombs, and still today paper models of people and houses may be carried in Chinese funeral

Griffith Institute
MODEL OF A BOAT FOUND IN THE TOMB OF TUTANKHAMEN

J. Allan Cash

A GRAVE IN THE CONGO
The effigy of the dead man and his possessions

processions and burnt afterwards so that the dead may benefit by them. Amongst Egyptians, Babylonians, Greeks, Celts, Australian natives, and other peoples, there was a belief in Islands of the Dead, and so oars or a miniature boat were buried with the dead to be used on the journey. The Lapps killed a reindeer to help on the journey, which was believed to take as long as three years.

The ritual eating and drinking, which take place after a death, are connected with the custom of providing for the needs of the dead man's soul. During 'wakes', which used to be held in England and are still observed in Ireland and other European countries, the relatives and friends sit up all night by the coffin, eating, drinking, playing games, asking riddles, and telling stories. They are afraid to sleep in the house with a corpse lest they meet its spirit in their dreams and fall ill in consequence: therefore the mourners eat and talk to keep themselves awake, and the dead are often believed also to partake of the meal. In parts of the world as far apart as Ireland and China food is left in the house in case the spirit returns. The Chinese serve regular meals beside the coffin each day until the funeral. On the Festival of the Ancestral Spirits they carry roast pigs to the tombs of their forefathers as a token offering; then they carry them home and feast on them! In north China, on a certain day in autumn, rolls

of paper representing bundles of winter clothing are placed on a bed and the spirit invited to take them. In Babylonia food and drink as well as clothes were left for the use of the dead. Their repose was believed to depend on the sacred breaking of bread by the relatives in a communion SACRIFICE (q.v.) performed monthly. Life-giving charms, such as shells and objects made of gold, were often buried with the dead, and it is probable that the games played and dances performed after a death—often by masked or disguised people—were originally intended to represent gods or spirits and believed to help the dead person in some way.

Amongst many peoples mourners 'rend their garments' or even tear their hair or cut themselves to show their grief, and loud wailing cries are uttered by the relatives, friends, and paid mourners. Often those closely connected with the dead person have to bathe or undergo other rites of purification. The custom of wearing mourning probably arose as a way of distinguishing such people (see TABOO). Primitive people in mourning commonly reverse their usual customs; for instance, if they usually wear their hair long they cut it short, or the other way round. The Arapaho Indians unbraid their hair as a sign of mourning, and in Guiana mourners go naked. At our own military funerals rifles are carried reversed. We wear black, but the Chinese wear white. Some Pacific islanders (Melanesia) blacken their bodies, while the Dakota Indians whiten theirs. The Ainu of Japan wear their coats inside out.

Many and varied are the rites and ceremonies connected with death. When someone dies, strong emotions are aroused—grief, fear, and awe—and it is on such occasions that people express their feelings in RITUAL (q.v.). The form the ritual takes depends on the ancestral customs and magical and religious ideas of the particular people, but we can understand most of these rites if we bear in mind two beliefs which are very widespread. First, the dead person's spirit is liable to prowl about and harm the living; and secondly, the spirit has to make a journey to the land of the dead and has to be provided with what is needful on the way and at its destination.

The mode of disposing of the body is usually connected with the religious ideas of the people concerned. Stone Age men buried the corpse, many peoples cremate or burn it, the PARSEES (q.v.) of India expose it to the vultures on a tower;

Camera Press

THE FUNERAL OF WINSTON CHURCHILL, LONDON, 30 JANUARY, 1965
The coffin is being carried into St. Paul's Cathedral. Members of the family (*right*) wait to follow it

the Tibetans allow animals or birds to eat it, and some Siberian tribes place the coffin in a tree.

Strange as are many of the beliefs and customs connected with death, there is always the belief underlying them that death is not the end. The purpose of many death ceremonies is to enable the dead person to graduate to another stage of the community life. As there were ceremonies to receive him at his BIRTH (q.v.) and to give him full membership at his INITIATION (q.v.), so funeral rites usher him into the presence of the ancestral spirits with whom the lives of the members of the tribe are so closely bound up (*see* ANCESTOR WORSHIP). The faith in another life beyond the grave is shown, as we have seen, in the ancient customs of providing for the needs of the spirits and in the more modern folk-tales of how Death was tricked and kept a prisoner, being fettered (Greece), put into a bag or bottle or pouch (Italy), or kept up a tree (Germany). In many ways men have asserted their belief that Death, the great Enemy of Mankind, can be overcome. The highest form of this belief is the Christian 'blessed hope of everlasting life'.

DELPHIC ORACLE, *see* DIVINATION; TEMPLE.

DERVISHES. These are groups of friars belonging to the Muslim faith. ISLAM (q.v.) did not at first encourage monastic orders; but after some centuries there arose groups of mystical ascetics (*see* ASCETICISM) called *Sufis* (probably from *suf*, white wool, because of their costume which may have been copied from that of monks). These formed themselves into orders which were called Dervishes (Persian *darwish*, meaning poor). The number of them in recent years has greatly diminished. Some of them have rather curious self-torturing practices, others work themselves up to a state of religious ecstasy by rhythmical dances. These dancing dervishes undergo a severe training, which includes long fasts and the memorizing of the Koran (the Muslim Sacred Book). After their dances, which are circular and accompanied by flute-playing, the dervishes used to heal sick persons by first blowing on them and making passes over them, and then, after the sick had been wrapped in blankets, by walking on them. Faith-cures appeared to be effected in this way. One sect of dancing dervishes chant as they go round in a circle, at first slowly, and then faster, till they reach such a pitch of frenzy that they are said to be able to touch hot iron without feeling pain.

DEVIL, *see* SATAN.

DISSENTER, *see* BAPTIST; CONGREGATIONAL-IST; METHODIST.

DIVINATION. People everywhere are curious about the future—for example, whether they are likely to succeed in such future enterprises as their love affairs or business ventures. If we could look into the future and discover what was going to happen, we could plan our lives much more wisely. So strongly have people wanted to safeguard the future that they have concocted a great variety of ways of divining their best course of action. Also, when people are much afraid or in great anxiety, they clutch at any chance of finding a solution to their difficulties. Nearly everywhere it has been accepted as a fact that certain people, because of their special gifts, are able to read fortunes and foretell events. Such soothsayers, fortune-tellers, oracles, augurs, and diviners used to be consulted by rulers to discover how and when they would be successful in war, and on many occasions they altered history by their good or bad advice. Often, both amongst primitive people and more civilized nations, such as the Greeks, people considered to have these gifts received special training in order to develop them.

In ancient Rome there was a college of augury whose business it was to find whether the gods were in favour of, or against, proposed plans of action. The augur pitched his tent on a hill, asked the gods for a sign, and with head covered waited for the answer, which might consist of the appearance of birds or signs in the heavens, such as lightning flashes. Somewhat similar methods of augury are used by the natives of Borneo today. They sit in a shelter made of leaves and watch the sky. If they should see three hawks, one flying to the right, another to the left, and a third circling, this is a good omen. The magpie rhyme—

> One for sorrow, two for mirth,
> Three for a wedding, and four for a birth.

—comes from ancient augury. Beasts as well as birds are used in divination. Queen Boadicea once released a hare from amongst her clothes and drew a favourable omen from the way it ran away.

A very ancient means of divination was by inspecting the intestines of animals. The Babylonians examined the liver of a sacrificed sheep and drew conclusions from the markings on it. This custom was adopted by the Etruscans and Romans and is carried on nowadays in Uganda, Borneo, and Burma, where the liver of a fowl or pig is used. Divination was also practised in Rome and elsewhere by examining the shoulder-blades of animals. In Europe the breast-bone of a fowl was inspected. Our practice of breaking the wish-bone of a chicken after we have dined off it is derived from this kind of divination.

People who buy fortune-telling almanacs are supporters of ASTROLOGY (q.v.), which is a form of divination at least 5,000 years old. It supposes a close connexion between the movements of the stars and the fortunes of people. The false idea still survives that by 'reading the stars' we may tell what is going to happen amongst the nations, or that by noting the planets in the sky when a child is born we may discover his or her future. There is a widespread belief that the spirits of the dead may be conjured up to give information to the living (*see* SPIRITUALISM). We have a famous example in the visit of Saul to the woman at Endor who called up for him the spirit of Samuel (1 Sam. xxviii). Zulu witch-doctors pretend to call up the spirits of their dead ancestors and ask them questions.

The simplest types of divination, such as drawing lots, throwing objects, or shooting arrows,

Pitt Rivers Collection

A BANTU MEDICINE-MAN READING BONES

He shakes the bones in his hands and then flings them on the ground. He claims to be able to discover secret information from the way they fall

depend on the belief that more than mere chance is involved. In parts of Africa pebbles or nuts are shaken out of a horn, an answer being found according to whether the number is odd or even. Wizards in Lapland used to put a ring on a drum which had pictures painted on it, and then beat the drum so that the ring moved about, thinking that secret things could be discovered by noting upon which pictures the ring danced. Some of our games of chance probably arose from such methods of divination.

Although divination by most of these means is entirely a matter of chance, this is not often realized by the inquirers or even by the diviners themselves. The very fact that the interpretation of the omens is sometimes complicated makes people the more convinced that there must be something in it. Where people act as oracles the matter is not quite so simple. Such persons may use their own gifts of intuition or secret means of information to guide them in answering those who consult them. The most famous of all was the Delphic Oracle in Greece. At Delphi throughout many centuries a succession of prophetesses uttered oracles supposed to come from the god Apollo. They were consulted on all matters of importance and often gave very sound advice. The prophetess chewed laurel leaves and drank from a sacred stream, then seated herself on a tripod or stool and uttered prophecies during a kind of fit. Probably her mutterings were made to form sense by the priests and then announced to the inquirer. Often the answer to an awkward question was of the kind which can have two meanings, so that whatever happened the prophecy could be said to have come true.

There are a certain number of people who claim to have the power of 'second sight'—to be able to see into the future or to know what

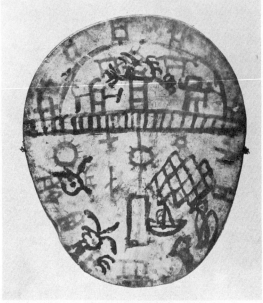

LAPP WIZARD'S DRUM
It is made of reindeer skin stretched on a wooden frame.
The painted patterns have magical meanings

is happening at a distance. We know of such 'seers' amongst the Mongolians, American Indians, Scots, and Gypsies, for example. It is not very uncommon for persons to become conscious of calamities befalling relatives many miles away. Some people develop in their minds images of distant or future things by gazing into a glass ball—crystal-gazing as it is called. These powers are by no means fully understood. Thought-transference between people definitely does occur, and may explain some instances of people being aware of events happening at a distance from them (*see* TELEPATHY, Vol. IV). Some people claim to be able to dream the future, and from ancient times dreams have been regarded as a means of knowing what is going to happen. Joseph interpreted the dreams of Pharaoh's butler and baker as well as those of Pharaoh himself (Gen. lx; lix), and Daniel was called on to interpret Nebuchadnezzar's dream (Dan. ii).

A special kind of divination was practised in the Middle Ages to discover evil-doers. The suspected person was made to undergo an ordeal in the belief that the result would show whether or not he was innocent. In Britain itself, for instance, women were ducked to find out if they were witches. If they sank they were regarded as innocent, but if they floated this was supposed to be certain evidence that they had been carrying on WITCHCRAFT (q.v.).

The motive inspiring many forms of divination was to get a decision about some important matter when, by ordinary reasoning on the facts available, a person could not be certain what to do. Religious and scientific ideas got mixed up with divination, but it is always most closely connected with MAGIC (q.v.). The desire to know about the future soon leads people to try to alter it, and so those who use divination often employ magic to gain their ends. There have always been, and still are, a great many people who, for payment, are ready to deceive others by pretending to be able to tell their fortunes or unfold the future.

DOMINICAN, *see* FRIAR.

DORIANS, *see* GREEK CIVILIZATION, Section 2*b*.

DRAGON. Of all the queer creatures which appear in MYTHOLOGY (q.v.) there is none more important and few more ancient than the dragon. Very many centuries ago this fabulous monster crawled and wriggled and flew its way all over Europe and Asia. Kings, emperors, and princes have proudly worn the dragon badge, and Roman soldiers followed the dragon standard into battle. Before the Norman Conquest the dragon was the chief English royal ensign in war. One legend relates how King Arthur's father, Uther Pendragon, saw a flaming dragon in the sky which foretold that he would become king. When the prediction was fulfilled and he came to the throne, he ordered two dragon standards to be made, one to be dedicated in Winchester Cathedral, the other to be borne into battle before him. During the reign of King Edward VII the dragon was included in the armorial bearings of the Prince of Wales. Not in England only, but all over Europe and beyond, the dragon has appeared on military standards. In China the dragon was the symbol of the Emperor, and in Japan there is a national dragon myth.

What is the dragon like? One detailed description by the Chinese writer, Wang Fu, who lived in the Han Dynasty (206 B.C.–A.D. 220), runs: 'His horns resemble those of a stag, his head that of a camel, his eyes those of a demon, his neck that of a snake, his belly that of a clam, his scales those of a carp, his claws those of an

A CHINESE DRAGON

Detail of the 'Nine Dragon Scroll', a Chinese painting of the Sung Dynasty, 13th century A.D.

eagle, his soles those of a tiger, his ears those of a cow.' The mixture of creatures in the dragon's make-up suggests that the monster was created by adding together bits of various animals. This is, indeed, what happened. One of the earliest pictures of a dragon appears on a Babylonian seal; it shows a serpent-like beast with horns and paws. This dragon is the goddess Tiamat, who is also depicted with wings (*see* BABYLONIAN MYTHS). She had the power to create monsters to help her in her fight against the god Marduk. But she was defeated, for he represented the life-giving spring sun, and she stood for dark confusion and chaos as well as for the ocean which the Babylonians thought of as existing in the beginning of things. The dragon also appears in the EGYPTIAN MYTHS (q.v.) of the battle between the gods Osiris and Set. Ever since those ancient days the dragon has been thought of as representing evil in the struggle which goes on in the world between the powers of good and evil. Thus in the book of Revelation (xii. 7) we read: 'There was a war in heaven: Michael and his angels fought against the dragon.'

Many legends tell how a wicked dragon was challenged by various heroes—Siegmund, Beowulf, Sigurd, Arthur, Tristram, and Lancelot—and, of course, St. George. The French Bishop Arculf, who lived in the 7th century, heard the story of St. George in the Middle East. When he was returning to France his ship was blown off its course and driven northwards; so he landed in Britain, came to Iona, and met Bishop Adamnan. He seems to have been the person who brought the story of St. George and the Dragon to Britain. At Beirut in Syria people still point out the well into which St. George threw the carcass of the monster. St. George became the patron saint of England. On one side of English golden sovereigns he was represented astride his horse and transfixing the dragon with his spear.

In Japan there are similar dragon legends. One of them describes how an eight-headed dragon came every year to eat a child, until of a family of eight there was only one left. The hero slays him, but not quite in fair fight, for he first makes the dragon drunk. The dragon of the book of Revelation (xii. 3–4) has one head less than this Japanese monster, and in the Bible story his tail knocks the stars out of heaven.

According to the mythology of the Greeks and Romans there were, however, some good dragons in Europe. But they became increasingly regarded as bad beasts, and the devil himself was depicted with claws, horns, and wings

ST. GEORGE AND THE DRAGON
Painting by Vittore Carpaccio (*c.* 1450–1522)

like a dragon. In China, on the other hand, though there are ancient records of horrible dragon monsters lurking in the rivers which had to be appeased by human sacrifices, the dragon has long been thought of mainly as the bringer of prosperity and good fortune. The mythological beast is always connected in some way with water, either in the rivers, sea, or clouds. The Chinese dragon is believed to be 'the heavenly bringer of the fertilizing rain' without which the crops would fail and people would starve. When the Chinese want rain they perform a dragon dance. These contrary notions about the dragon probably arose from its connexion with the thunderstorm. People thought of the thunderstorm as the source of prosperity, as with it comes the fertilizing rain which matters so much to the inhabitants of parched countries; but they also feared the thunderbolt and noticed how the lightning could shatter trees or strike people dead. Thus the dragon of the rain and thunder-cloud came to be considered in some places and at some times as the bringer of good and at other places and times as an evil power. The dragon is a mythical creature but it stands for a universal experience —the conflict between good and evil. This is one of the reasons why beliefs about it have been popular over a great part of the world.

See also FABULOUS CREATURES; FOLKLORE.

DRUIDS, *see* RELIGION, PREHISTORIC.

DRUZES (DRUSES), *see* SYRIANS.

DUTCH. The Netherlanders, as they officially call themselves, are a Germanic people, closely related in race and language to the people of north Germany. They are inhabitants of a country for which they have had to struggle and suffer more than most peoples of the world. This struggle has developed in them some very strong qualities of patriotism, self-reliance, and industry, and made them a frugal, thrifty, practical-minded people with a great capacity for attention to detail. Their love of precision was early evident in their achievements as printers and engravers and as mapmakers. Mercator and Ortelius, the first scientific mapmakers, were Dutch (*see* MAPS, Vol. IV), as were also the first hydrographic chartmakers, Wagenaer and Blaev. Dutch maps of their own country and of their East Indian Colonies are still excellent. They put a high value on education and scholarship: indeed ERASMUS and GROTIUS (qq.v. Vol. V) rank among the world's greatest scholars. Their passion for detail is shown in the work of Dutch artists, in the carved gables and fine brickwork of their architecture, in Delft tiles, and in the rich marquetry and patterned veneers which decorated their furniture. The Netherlands in early times included most of what we now call Belgium. At the beginning of the 16th century they became part of the great Hapsburg Empire, and there followed through the 16th and 17th centuries one of the most heroic struggles for liberty known in history. The great hero WILLIAM THE SILENT, Prince of Orange (q.v. Vol. V), from the time he was twenty-two led the Dutch in their fight for political freedom and for freedom to follow the Protestant teaching of CALVINISM (q.v.). In spite of disasters and persecutions under the INQUISITION (q.v.) and the ruthless Spanish Governor, the Duke of Alva, the Dutch people kept up the fight for some 80 years until, in 1648, their independence from Spain was finally established.

By the beginning of the 17th century the Dutch had become masters of the sea and the chief traders of the world. The Dutch East India Company explored and colonized the East. The trading towns (the most important being Amsterdam) became wealthy and powerful, and the burghers or chief citizens of each town set up their own local governments. This, too, was the period which produced the famous Dutch School of painters of whom the best known is REMBRANDT (q.v. Vol. V). It was also, however, a time of great rivalry with the English over trade and sea power, resulting in many naval battles between the two countries. During the 18th century the Dutch were involved in a succession of wars with France and England which ended in the setting up of a Dutch republic in close alliance with France. Napoleon for a short time made the Netherlands part of the French Empire; but on his overthrow, in which the Dutch played their part, the head of the House of Orange, another William, was made King of both Belgium and Holland. In 1831 these two countries split into the two kingdoms we know today.

Between 1943 and 1958 the former colonies either achieved independence—notably the Republic of Indonesia—or, like Surinam and the Netherlands Antilles, became responsible for their own domestic affairs and equal partners of the Netherlands within the Kingdom. During the 20th century the Netherlands has changed from a predominantly agricultural country to a heavily industrialized member of the European Common Market. This has brought a corresponding change in peoples' lives. Now only 8% of the population is engaged in agriculture compared with 42% in industry, and 24% in trade and transport. The Netherlands has the greatest population density in the world, and the population, now 13 millions, is increasing, mainly because the mortality rate is the lowest in the world. Moreover the population is unevenly distributed; nearly half the people live in three of the eleven provinces, and 65% live in towns.

The Dutch are meeting the increase in population by land reclamation; by stepping up agricultural production, and by industrialization.

K.L.M.

THE CHEESE MARKET AT ALKMAAR, HOLLAND

THE RIVER ZAAN, NEAR AMSTERDAM

Netherlands Tourist Office

They have always been skilful at improvising, inventing, and engineering. Shortage of stone led to a great brick industry: much of the English brickwork of the 17th century was designed by Dutchmen, and their own towns have beautiful brickwork. Nowhere has their ingenuity been more successful than on their land reclamation. Dunes and dykes have always been very important. Now, about half the country's land area consists of polders, that is, land surrounded by dykes and artificially drained, in these low-lying Netherlands. Since 1900 large schemes have been undertaken, aimed at reclaiming 2,600 km^2 by A.D. 2000. The Zuyder Zee works will be completed about 1980. The land is cultivated intensively, and dairy farming and horticulture, especially the growing of bulbs, are flourishing industries. Although the Zuyder polders were planned for agricultural use—and this is still their main use—they also provide land for villages, industrial sites, and recreational areas. The polder farmers have come from all parts of the country. The scientific approach is encouraged in farming and horticulture as much as in industry.

Since the Second World War home petroleum and natural gas have largely replaced coal. Petroleum is also imported and refined near Rotterdam, the largest port in the world. The majority of industrial workers are employed in the metal industry. Efficient consumer industries also employ many workers and keep the standard of living high.

The people of this constitutional monarchy are actively democratic, both in their political and in social life. They have an excellent system of schools and universities of world rank, and good social welfare provisions.

See also Vol. III: HOLLAND; INDEX, p. 143.
See also Vol. IV: GERMANIC LANGUAGES.
See also Vol. XII: DUTCH ART.

DWARFS. From very early times people have been interested in men and women so far below the normal height as to be considered dwarfs. Homer, in the Greek epic, the *Iliad*, tells of a race of PYGMIES (q.v.), living in the distant southern land to which the cranes fly in autumn, and other Greek writers mentioned battles which take place between the little men and the birds.

According to one of these writers, when Hercules had defeated a giant called Antaeus, he fell asleep somewhere in Africa and woke up to find an army of pygmies shooting tiny arrows into his arms and legs. The story reminds us of Gulliver's adventures in Lilliput, described centuries later by Dean Swift. The historian, Herodotus, heard of five men who were taken prisoner by dwarfs in the African desert and led to a town beside a great crocodile-infested river. This may have been the Niger, and the dwarfs members of one of the African pygmy tribes.

Among peoples of normal height dwarfs occasionally occur, usually owing to defects in the pituitary or thyroid gland. Because of their quaintness they used to be kept at kings' courts and in wealthy families. Of the Greek poet, Philetas of Cos, who was the teacher of one of the Egyptian kings, the story was told that he was so tiny that he had to wear shoes of lead to prevent his being blown away. The niece of the Roman Emperor Augustus had two dwarfs, each of whom was 71 cm in height. One of the most famous of English dwarfs was Jeffery Hudson (1619-82), who had an adventurous life. He claimed that between the ages of eight and thirty years he was only 46 cm in height, but he then started to grow and stopped when he was 1·14 m. When the Duke of Buckingham gave a dinner to Charles I and his queen, the dwarf, Hudson, stepped out of a cold pie to everyone's surprise, and was given as a present by the duke to the queen. He fought and won two duels, one with a turkey-cock and the other with a man. On one occasion he was taken prisoner by the Turks, but was ransomed and brought back to England. Queen Henrietta Maria had two other dwarfs, Richard Gibson and his wife Anne, whose combined height added to 2·18 m. They had nine children, five of whom grew up and were of normal height. Charles Stratton, known as 'General Tom Thumb', a famous American dwarf of the 19th century, was 78 cm high. He married another dwarf, Lavinia Warren, who was 5 cm taller. The dwarf Richebourg was only 58 cm high and lived to the age of ninety. In the siege of Paris a nurse carried him through the enemy lines, dressed as a baby, with important dispatches concealed in his clothes.

Dwarfs are frequently quite bright mentally, strong, active, and long-lived. The bodies of some are well proportioned, but others have rather large heads. Dwarfs occur more commonly than GIANTS (q.v.).

Some people think that the belief in ELVES and FAIRIES (qq.v.) arose from glimpses of pygmy people, but this is not very likely, for elves are believed in where no dwarf races ever lived.

See also FOLKLORE.

Vernacci

A DWARF AT THE COURT OF PHILIP IV OF SPAIN

Painting by Diego Velasquez (1599-1660) in the Prado, Madrid

TOM THUMB

E

EARTHWORKS AND HILL-FORTS. 1. Prehistoric man in Britain made earthworks for a great number of purposes: for defences; as boundaries between agricultural or political units of land; for surrounding a farm-yard or a burial-ground; or for making the walls of a fort. They were usually ditches dug in the ground with the soil piled up as banks alongside. In regions where the subsoil is rocky, stones were piled up into walls for the same purposes, and both earthwork and wall-making of this kind continued into the Middle Ages. We can still see a modern version of the same idea in the tank-traps and slit-trenches of warfare today.

2. EARTHWORK ENCLOSURES, usually called 'camps' and marked as such on the ordnance maps, are known to have been used for enclosing settlements and cattle-yards as early as the New Stone Age (about 2400 B.C.) in Sussex and Wessex. Small squarish enclosures for agricultural purposes were built in the late Bronze Age (about 800 B.C.) in the same regions, and a number of small miscellaneous earthworks with not very large ditches and banks surrounded farms and homesteads in the Iron Age (from about 300 B.C.). In a stony country these early agricultural settlements took the form of hut-circles and 'pounds' built of stone walling.

The most impressive 'camps' are the hill-forts which sometimes have enormous banks and ditches, often forming several lines of defence. One of the very largest is Maiden Castle in Dorset (*see* p. 99). Small hill-forts with single lines of earthworks were being built as early as about 350 B.C. in southern Britain; and in the following centuries most of the earthworks which are so noticeable on our hills today were being built or enlarged and re-fortified. They continued to be used, either as semi-permanent settlements or strong places of refuge, down to the Roman invasion of A.D. 43, when many of them are known to have become centres of military resistance. In Wales and Scotland forts built of earthwork or stone were used by the native tribesmen during the Roman occupation.

The banks of these hill-forts were more often than not strengthened and interlaced by timber-

Ashmolean Museum

THE WHITE HORSE AND UFFINGTON CASTLE, BERKSHIRE
The horse, which is cut out of the chalk hill-side, and the hill-fort are early Iron Age

G. M. Boumphrey

OFFA'S DYKE NEAR CRIGGION

Built by Offa, the King of Mercia, about A.D. 800 to keep back the Welsh. It stretched from the mouth of the river Dee to the mouth of the river Severn

work so that they made solid walls. At the entrances there were elaborate gateways which could be closed in time of danger. The only traces of gates now remaining, which can be detected by the excavator, however, are the post-sockets and stains indicating rotted timber. When the timber-work in stone-built forts was burnt, as often happened in a siege, the stone might melt together in slaggy lumps. Such fused ramparts are frequently found in Scotland where they are now called 'vitrified forts'. In Scotland and Northumberland there are tiny enclosures which could have served only a chieftain and his immediate dependants: these are really 'castles'.

3. BOUNDARY EARTHWORKS range from huge cross-country dykes, like that built in the late 8th century A.D. by Offa between England and Wales, to small local dykes marking out individual property or forming part of a defence system. The Roman Walls in north Britain are examples of cross-country defences, and indeed these walls may have suggested to the Britons the building of large-scale dykes against the Saxon invaders later on. Early dykes are as old as the late Bronze Age (about 800 B.C.) and mark out cattle-ranches or farms; others, such as those near Colchester and Chichester, belong to the defence system round the capital towns of the British princes in the half-century or so before the Roman Conquest.

There are other earthworks such as those built by the Romans—military camps of the early part of the Roman occupation have been found in many areas, but they are usually inconspicuous. Earthworks were built also in the Civil Wars—for example, those for the defence of Oxford; but little now remains of most of these temporary defences. From the Middle Ages onwards banks and ditches were often used to enclose deer-parks and for similar purposes.

A distinctive type of earthwork is the castle of the early Norman period—a high circular mound, known as a *motte*, on which originally stood a timber castle, and a large earthwork enclosure of bank and ditch attached to this (the *bailey*) in which wooden buildings for the retainers and horses, &c., of the owner of the castle were set up.

See also PREHISTORIC MAN; CELTIC CIVILIZATION.

EAST AFRICANS. In the 20th century independent governments have been established in all the countries of East Africa except Mozambique. The population of east Africa consists today of an overwhelming majority of indigenous peoples and a small number of foreign residents, such as Asians, Arabs, and Europeans. The indigenous peoples consist of small numbers of the older hunters (including Pygmies); a considerably larger proportion of

Nilotic, pastoral peoples; and a preponderance of Bantu-speaking peoples.

It has taken a long time to piece together the history of east African peoples, but now knowledge about them is growing so fast that ideas are constantly changing, and will probably continue to do so for some time. Written records, starting at A.D. 110 when a Greek traveller described his voyage down the Red Sea to Zanzibar, are at first sporadic and sketchy, but become ever more plentiful from the time Vasco da Gama sailed up the coast from the Cape of Good Hope in 1498. Arab chronicles, ancient geographies, observations of the early travellers, and missionary accounts have all given information, and the spoken traditions of the East African peoples themselves, as well as the discoveries of archaeologists, are now helping to fill in many of the large gaps left by written records.

The discovery of stone tools and human bones at East Rudolf on the shores of Lake Rudolf in Kenya shows that more than two million years ago early forms of man lived in this part of Africa (*see* EVOLUTION OF MAN). The first present-day men (*Homo sapiens sapiens*) who began to appear more than 30,000 years ago,

EAST AFRICA

were hunters and food-gatherers. Possibly the oldest surviving people today are the Hadzapi of Tanzania; the 'click' sounds in their language suggest a connection with the Central Bushmen

Camera Press

KENYANS STUDYING COFFEE PESTS AND PARASITES

of South Africa (*see* AFRICAN LANGUAGES, Vol. IV).

Later, large-scale migrations of pastoral peoples came south from the direction of Ethiopia and the Sudan. The migrations lasted well over a century, perhaps even for several centuries. A striking result is that the Iraqw, at the end of one mountainous migration route in Tanzania, speak a language more nearly related to a Cushitic tongue in Ethiopia than any intervening language. Today there are still various peoples, scattered throughout East Africa, who are descended from these early pastoral migrations. Among them are the MASAI (q.v.), and the LUO (*see* NILOTIC PEOPLES).

An equally large, or even larger, migration of agricultural, Bantu-speaking peoples came from the east, passing through gaps between the Great Lakes or using routes to the north and south. These movements overlapped with those of the pastoralists. The Bantu-speaking peoples are far more numerous than any other group in eastern Africa, and include several hundred distinctive peoples, such as the Kikuyu of Kenya, the Ganda of Uganda, and the Nyamwezi of Tanzania.

Foreign traders visited eastern Africa from the 3rd century B.C. onwards—Graeco-Roman expeditions at first, and Persian ships from the end of the 4th century. In later centuries, Chinese, Indonesian, and Indian traders played their part. But the most important traders have been the Arabs, who after earlier visits had, by the 7th century, established numerous settlements along the coast and off-shore islands. Since then, until the 1960s, Arabs have settled in ever-increasing numbers. In 1498 the Portuguese arrived and fought the Arabs for two centuries over control of the coast, with alternating success. The coastal trade of this period is important for many reasons, not the least being that it led to a common language, Kiswahili, which is now spoken, often as a second language, over a large portion of eastern Africa.

During this time, the peoples of the interior were in a state of flux: acquiring new land by conquest, moving in the face of population pressures, and intermixing with other peoples. However, in the 18th and 19th centuries, French British, and Germans became interested in Africa; and in the 19th century explorers such as Burton, Speke, Livingstone, and Stanley revealed the secrets of the unknown lands to the

J. Allan Cash

TEA PLUCKERS ON A KENYAN TEA PLANTATION

J. Allan Cash

UGANDA: READY FOR THE 'GIRAFFE DANCE'

Western world. It was but a short step from these events to the colonization of eastern Africa by European powers, completed by the turn of the century. Colonization brought in its wake Asian settlers from western India, who became successful traders and shopkeepers. An important consequence of colonization was the drawing of boundaries which divided ethnic groups, but established administrative areas. These often provide the boundaries of the new, independent African states.

See also AFRICANS.
See also Vol. III: ETHIOPIA; KENYA; SOMALIA; TANZANIA; UGANDA.

ECUADOR, PEOPLE OF. This South American equatorial country is a republic with a population of 6·5 million which, like Peru's, is almost equally divided between Indians and people of mixed blood. It formed the northern part of the INCA Empire (q.v.) before the Spaniards came, and its capital, Quito, is one of the oldest towns of South America. Half of the people live high up in the Andes valleys where the climate, although on the Equator, is cool all the year round. In their primitive and picturesque villages in the mountain valleys the Indians still speak their own native dialects and

Camera Press

MOUNTED POLICE IN QUITO

lead a life that has changed little since pre-Spanish times. Wrapped in their bright-coloured ponchos or blankets, they drive their llamas into market once a week to sell their goods and buy the necessities of life. But the three centuries of Spanish rule have left a deep mark on the country and many Spanish colonial ideas and customs still survive.

Ecuador was freed from Spain in 1822 by one of the lieutenants of SIMON BOLIVAR (q.v. Vol. V), the great liberator of Spanish America. It declared its independence of Colombia in 1830. Since then, there have been fierce struggles between supporters and opponents of the Roman Catholic Church, and more recently between the conservative uplands and the more progressive coast, with its port Guayaquil. A large oil-field has recently been found in the eastern jungles.

See also Vol. III: ECUADOR; INDEX, p. 139.

EGYPTIAN CIVILIZATION. It is possible to trace the beginnings of Egyptian civilization in the Nile valley right back to the Old Stone Age. By the end of the Ice Age an immense change had taken place in the climate of northern Africa. Great areas of forests and grass-lands, over which had roamed vast herds of game, had become stretches of desert, such as the Sahara, incapable of supporting much life. Therefore the great cleft of the Nile valley, where vegetation never failed, became a refuge for men and animals. Excavation at various points along the Nile valley has shown the existence of very early settlements and the beginnings of that river valley civilization which grew into the brilliant civilization of Egypt.

The history of Egypt falls into fairly clearly defined periods. The beginnings of the earliest, the pre-dynastic, period reach back into the Neolithic or New Stone Age, between 10,000 and 5000 B.C. The unification of Egypt into one kingdom and the beginning of the First Dynasty occurred about 3000 B.C., and the Old Kingdom lasted until about 2250 B.C. Then followed a hundred years of civil disorder before the Middle Kingdom began about 2150 B.C. This lasted until about 1750 B.C. when there followed another period of national disturbance together with a foreign invasion. These invaders were driven out in 1580 B.C., and the New Kingdom began, lasting until about 1050 B.C. The last ten dynasties of Egyptian history are known as the Late Period, and during this time Egypt was

4000	
3500	**PRE-DYNASTIC PERIOD** (STRETCHING BACK TO PERHAPS 5000 B.C. OR EVEN EARLIER)
3000	
	FIRST DYNASTIC PERIOD (DYN. 1–2)
2500	**OLD KINGDOM** (DYNASTIES 3–6)
2000	FIRST INTERMEDIATE PERIOD (DYN. 7–10)
	MIDDLE KINGDOM (DYNASTIES 11–12)
1500	SECOND INTERMEDIATE PERIOD (DYN. 13–17)
	NEW KINGDOM (DYNASTIES 18–20)
1000	
	LATE PERIOD (DYNASTIES 21–30)
500	
B.C.	GREECE
A.D.	
500	ROME
	MUSLIM CONQUEST
	THE EGYPTIAN DYNASTIES

down from the Abyssinian plateau and deposited on the rocky subsoil and the desert sand. The great characteristic of the Nile, which gave shape to so much of Egyptian religion and mythology, is the regularity of its floods. For the Egyptians this was the annual miracle of their river, and its cause was a mystery to them. We know now that the annual flooding of the Nile is caused by the winter rains in the regions of the great African lakes and by the melting snows on the high Abyssinian plateau. The flood, laden with rich earth, reaches the lower valley about 15 June, at a time when the whole land has been burnt black by the sun. It brings what the Egyptian Hymn to the Nile called 'water of renewal' and 'water of life'. From June to September the Nile rises and submerges the whole valley; then in the beginning of October it begins to fall, until by the end of November it returns to its normal level, leaving the land saturated with water and covered with a deep layer of rich black earth, ready for the ploughman and the sower. In the course of centuries the Egyptians learnt how to control and distribute the flow of water by dams and irrigation ditches; and during the Middle Kingdom Lake Moeris in the Fayyum was made into a large reservoir. An outstanding peculiarity of Egyptian political life was due to the Nile, for the Nile had created two Egypts, Upper and Lower Egypt, each of a very different nature and history. Upper Egypt, a long, narrow strip of fertile land stretching for some 500 miles on each bank of the river, and shut in by high cliffs of limestone, sandstone, and granite, was cut off from intercourse with the outside world, and this gave rise to that deep-rooted conservatism so characteristic of ancient Egyptian civilization. Lower Egypt, the land of the Delta with its 400 miles of Mediterranean coast, was open to all the influences which streamed in from the Mediterranean and Asia, and these gave rise to the inventiveness and resourcefulness which made Egypt the pioneer in so many arts and crafts. This dual character of the kingdom of Egypt is shown in many ways: the king wore a double crown—the two crowns of Upper and Lower Egypt combined into one; he was crowned in each of the capitals; most of the officials were duplicated, and all the great royal religious ceremonies were performed twice. In these ways we can see how profoundly the Nile influenced the character of Egyptian civilization.

dominated by Libyans, Ethiopians, and Persians. In 332 B.C. Alexander the Great conquered Egypt, which was then ruled first by the Greeks (see PTOLEMIES, Vol. V) and later by the Romans. The influence of ancient Egyptian civilization, however, remained throughout, and it was only after the fall of the Roman Empire when Egypt was conquered by the Arabs that the ancient culture died out. The civilization of modern Egypt is mainly Arab (see EGYPTIANS).

The two great factors which have dominated the shape and development of Egyptian civilization are, first, the river Nile, and second, the intense interest of the Egyptians in everything connected with death. The whole of Egyptian life revolves about the NILE (q.v. Vol. IV); it depends upon the Nile for its very existence. The old Greek historian, Herodotus, tells us that the priests of Egypt called their country 'the gift of the river', a description which is literally true, for the soil of Egypt consists of the fertile black mud which the Nile has brought

Griffith Institute

TUTANKHAMEN'S GOLDEN COFFIN

The mummy lay within three coffins and a sarcophagus in the Burial Chamber of the rock-cut tomb at Thebes. The sarcophagus is of quarzite, the two outer coffins of gilded wood. The third, which contained the mummy, is of solid gold and is decorated with symbols and hieroglyphics. The King holds the crook and flail, the insignia of Osiris, to show his divine origin. Middle of 14th century B.C.

But the second factor—the Egyptian's intense interest in death—had an even deeper influence upon the character and development of Egyptian civilization. It is not easy to say how this arose. It has been suggested that the discovery of the power of the dry desert sand to preserve from corruption the bodies buried in it gave the early inhabitants of Egypt the idea that by preserving the body from decay, life could be made to last for ever. But however the idea started, it is clear that the original purpose of embalming the body (mummification) was to preserve the life of the one person whose continued existence was essential to the well-being of the community, namely, the king, the Pharaoh. The myth of Osiris (*see* EGYPTIAN MYTHS) embodies this belief that the dead Pharaoh became Osiris; it gives the pattern of the funeral ritual for the dead king by which his body undergoes all the processes of mummification, is magically brought to life again and becomes the god Osiris, united with the sun-god, Re, in the Egyptian heaven, the land of the Blessed.

From this central belief and the practices connected with it all the main elements of Egyptian civilization developed. First, the desire to build splendid tombs for the kings led to the development of the extraordinary skill in masonry and architecture which the Egyptians had attained before the end of the Old Kingdom period. The PYRAMIDS (q.v. Vol. XII), the greatest witness to the skill of the Egyptian builders, were built in the time of the 4th Dynasty, about 2500 B.C. The pyramids were royal tombs, and probably developed from the simpler stone-built, flat-topped tombs of the 3rd Dynasty. The Great Pyramid, the most magnificent tomb in the world, was built by the 4th Dynasty Pharaoh Khufu, better known as Cheops, for his own last resting-place. It is 137 metres high and contains 2·4 million cubic metres of masonry. Herodotus says that it took ten years to quarry the stone and ten more years to build, and that 300,000 men were employed in the work.

Similarly, the desire to place portrait statues of the deceased and figures of servants in the tomb led to the development of sculpture in stone and wood, and the pictorial representation of those activities which the dead would enjoy in the next world gave great impetus to the arts of relief sculpture and painting. In the same way the need to provide the dead with adornment led to the employment of all the skill of the jewellers and goldsmiths which produced such exquisite jewellery as that discovered in TUTANKHAMEN's TOMB (q.v. Vol. XII). The requirements of the funeral rituals stimulated the making of various musical instruments and the development of the art of music with its sister art of dancing. The need for fine linen wrappings for the mummies developed the art of weaving to such a pitch that 'the fine linen of Egypt' was famous throughout western Asia and the seaports of the Mediterranean.

Another important element of Egyptian civilization, the art of writing, also grew from the same kind of religious activities. Like the Sumerian writing, the earliest writing in Egypt, of the pre-dynastic period, is 'pictographic', that is, picture-writing. The history of writing in Egypt followed more than one line of development. The picture-writing, known as HIEROGLYPHIC (q.v. Vol. IV), remained, with very little change, the type of writing used for sacred purposes and for inscriptions on monuments. But in the course of time the hieroglyphic writing was found too slow for ordinary use, so the scribes evolved a shortened form of it which was called 'hieratic', and by about the 3rd century B.C. a still simpler form called 'demotic' or 'the people's writing'. Long before these developments had taken place, however, the Egyptians had discovered the principle of the alphabet—the representation of each sound in the language by a single sign or letter. All the early forms of writing, like many oriental forms of writing today, were syllabic, that is, each sign represented a syllable. As the number of syllables in a language is very great, anyone who wished to write had to learn a great number of signs. The Egyptian sign-list as we now know it contains between 700 and 800 signs (at an early period of the development of Sumerian writing the sign-list contained more than 2,000 signs). So it is not surprising that writing remained largely in the hands of professional scribes. But the alphabet replaces this cumbrous system by a list of between twenty and thirty signs, and it is one of the most curious examples of the extreme conservatism of the Egyptians that they should have made this important discovery and yet made so little use of it (see WRITING, HISTORY OF, Vol. IV).

This is enough to show how much of Egyptian civilization had its origin in and was shaped by these two central facts, their remarkable river, and their unusual interest in death and the after

Griffith Institute

COLOSSAL STATUE OF RAMESES II IN THE TEMPLE OF LUXOR. 14TH CENTURY B.C.

life. But our picture of Egyptian civilization would be incomplete without some account of the way in which the country was governed, and of Egyptian literature.

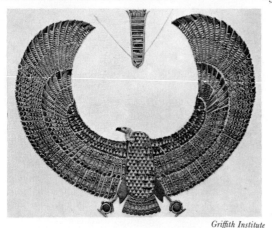

COLLAR FOUND ON THE MUMMY OF TUTANKHAMEN
It represents the hawk god Horus, holding the symbols of
eternal life. Gold inlaid with plaques of coloured glass

The political development of ancient Egypt may be divided roughly into four stages. First, there was the pre-dynastic period, when the country was divided into a number of small city-states, as they might be called, each with its own capital and without any central government. These small units gradually came together into the two kingdoms of Upper and Lower Egypt, and after years of struggle, of which we know little, the Delta was conquered by the Upper Egyptians, and Egypt united. During the first two dynasties the rule of the Pharaoh became absolute. During the Old Kingdom period the king was regarded as a god, who possessed the power of life and death over the whole of Egypt: his will was the only law. But in the early part of the Middle Kingdom a change took place, and the feudal lords, the chiefs of the states, reduced the power of the king to a shadow, somewhat as the English barons did in the time of King John. Then, in the middle of the 12th Dynasty, about 2000 B.C., the king was able to throw off the power of the feudal lords, and set up a government by a local system of sheriffs and royal officers throughout the land. This system lasted for over 300 years, and was gradually transformed into the bureaucratic system of the New Kingdom, whereby Egypt was ruled by a kind of civil service, a network of viziers, mayors, scribes, and priests. The priesthood was particularly powerful at this period because of its great wealth and the influence it had on the appointment of the Pharaoh.

Lastly, a word must be said about Egyptian literature and science. Besides the great collections of magical and ritual texts contained in the Pyramid Texts and the *Book of the Dead*, the Egyptians produced a large body of other literature dating from the period of the Old Kingdom. There are several collections of moral precepts and wise sayings, like the Hebrew book of Proverbs. Egypt, from very early times, was famous for its wisdom. A popular book, known as *The Admonitions of an Egyptian Sage*, was a kind of prophetic book, containing warnings to the king and a prophecy of better times. There is a great deal of love-poetry of a high order, and of religious hymns, of which the best known is King Akhnaten's great hymn of praise to Aten, the sun's disk. The earliest romantic literature comes from Egypt: the well-known *Tale of the Two Brothers* and the *Story of the Shipwrecked Sailor* being among the best examples. The Egyptians were a seafaring people, and some of their literature consists of works of travel: the *Story of Sinuhe*, belonging to the 12th Dynasty, and the *Journey of Unamon*, from the 20th Dynasty, are valuable accounts of travel and adventure in Canaan. Finally, we have a number of medical papyri coming down from the Old Kingdom, showing that the Egyptians had a good knowledge of anatomy and of the nature and cause of various diseases, though the treatment was largely magical.

This is only a brief picture of one of the greatest civilizations ever known.

See also ANCIENT CIVILIZATIONS.
See also Vol. XII: EGYPTIAN ART.

EGYPTIAN MYTHS. Myth was a very significant part of ancient Egyptian religion. Egyptian myths were closely connected with religious ritual, and are often alluded to in preserved ritual texts. But, in contrast with BABYLONIAN MYTHS (q.v.), few coherent narratives of Egyptian myths are preserved. So we rely heavily for our information on very late Egyptian sources (300 B.C.–A.D. 300) and on the writings of Greek and Roman authors. Egyptian religion was highly conservative, and earlier versions of myths were not discarded when later ones grew up. This means that we often cannot tell which elements belong together in a single version. The Egyptians themselves wrote commentaries on some of their important religious texts, and they frequently gave alternative interpretations to obscure passages, making them refer to different mythical characters or events.

Unlike many African peoples, the Egyptians were very much preoccupied with the creation of the world, and a number of their myths describe this. All the versions are variants of one basic scheme. In this the state of the cosmos before creation is depicted as a watery chaos, out of which the earth later emerged. The creator god brought himself into existence, and then created unaided a family of 'younger' gods. There were various means by which he was said to produce offspring without a female partner, and the Egyptians even had a notion of the creative power of the mind. The world before creation was described by being analysed into eight deities, four male and four female—who therefore existed before the creator god. They were personifications of negative qualities such as Absence, Darkness, and Endlessness. The creation of the earth was explained in different ways; it could be the same as the appearance of the creator god, or he could create the earth, or he might stand on the first solid ground when he created his family of gods. Other myths depicted the emergence of the god as a flower on the water, or as a bird perching on a reed; both of these images probably derive from the appearance of plants after the annual Nile flood. The first solid land was of great religious importance, and all Egyptian temples contained symbolic representations of it. Egyptian towns themselves were built on mounds within the Nile valley which flooded each year, so that Egyptians were very familiar with the sight of a small amount of land appearing amid water.

In the best known creation myth, which may have originated in the town of Heliopolis, the creator was the sun-god Re. The family of gods produced by him consisted of Shu and Tefenet, who represented air and moisture respectively; their children Geb and Nut, representing the earth and the sky; and their children Osiris, Isis, Seth, and Nephthys. Horus, the son of Osiris and Isis, was loosely associated with this group. Isis was the wife of Osiris, and Nephthys the wife of Seth. Seth murdered Osiris and was the enemy of Horus. Dead kings were identified with Osiris, who may have been considered to be the first king of Egypt, and living kings with Horus. This means that symbolically each king was killed by Seth, and in the role of Horus the new king avenged his father by defeating Seth.

Ashmolean Museum

HORUS

Seth symbolized the forces of disorder in the world, and was ultimately identified with chaos and the uncreated world, which was envisaged as surrounding the created world at all times and constantly threatening to engulf it. Thus each new king defeated the forces of disorder and chaos, and reunited the two lands of Upper and Lower Egypt: in a sense he performed the function of the creator of the world. However, this cosmological interpretation was not the only one possible. A folk story, for example, depicts the conflict of Horus and Seth as part legal battle, part semi-ceremonial contest for the inheritance of Osiris. In many types of religious text the legal aspect is the most prominent.

This crucial myth was elaborated endlessly, and Isis' part in it assumed great importance. Isis was the prime example of the faithful wife and loving mother; another side of her character was her guile and skill in magic. In her role of wife she reassembled Osiris' body, which had been dismembered by Seth, and then became pregnant by it. After the birth of Horus she reared him in the marshes of the Delta, hidden from Seth who was marauding over the country, and protected him from snake-bites and other such dangers. In the battle between Horus and Seth she aided Horus by magical means.

Relatively few major Egyptian myths deal with the organization of the world after creation, the creation of mankind, and so on. According to one tradition men were the tears of the sun-god, while in another the ram-headed god, Khnum, made men on a potter's wheel. Gods were held to have ruled on earth, and the sun-god Re retreated from the earth when he grew old; he was carried into the sky on Nut's back, and Nut changed herself into a cow. A number of episodes from the reigns of Shu and Geb are also known. Yet although agricultural rituals, for example, were common, we only know of the founding of agriculture by the gods from Greek authors. Many myths recount how particular deities came to have particular forms, like how Isis came to be represented sometimes with the head of a cow.

The characters in the following myth are familiar, but it may also serve as an example of a completely different type from the ones mentioned hitherto. The story recounts how the god Re had grown old and feeble towards the end of his reign on earth. His limbs shook, and he dribbled so that his spittle fell on the earth. Isis kneaded the spittle and the earth on to which it fell together and made a deadly snake, which she left in his path. The snake bit Re and he fainted. When he came to he cried out in unspeakable agony, and summoned all the gods who were masters of magic to help him. Isis came, with others, and asked Re about his misfortune. He told her, and then she asked him to tell her his true name, as he would live if it were pronounced. He told her one name after another, but his pain continued unabated. She then repeated that he must tell her his true name. So he sent everyone else away and told her the name (which is not given in the papyrus). Isis then pronounced a magic spell, and Re was cured. This means that she tricked him doubly, first by making the snake and then by saying that he would be cured if he pronounced his name, when this was only the condition on which she was willing to cure him. It can be seen that the behaviour of Egyptian gods in myths was no better than that of the Greek gods in GREEK MYTHS (q.v.), and Egyptian gods were not immortal, omnipotent, or omniscient.

We know very little about the sources and background to Egyptian myths, for many of them must have originated in prehistoric times. In the historical period (from about 2900 B.C.) it is evident that the central institution of Egyptian society was the kingship. The stabilizing role of the kingship was expressed in myth by saying that the king resolved the conflict of the two brothers (or uncle and nephew) Horus and Seth; but this myth, in a more abstract way, also unites a number of opposing pairs like the two halves of the country, Upper and Lower Egypt, or two different words for 'king', *nesut* and *biti*. (These words had a variety of associations, as well as meaning king of Upper and Lower Egypt respectively.) Apart from this central feature of society, a number of other factors influenced both the form and subject matter of Egyptian myths. The Nile and its flooding largely determined the basic pattern of creation myths, while the various versions of the Osiris myth probably reflect in part varying types of kingship structure in Egyptian society. Some highly typical elements in Egyptian religion appear to have had little influence on myths. Thus in visual art a large number of gods are represented as animals or in a mixed animal and human form —Horus, for example, is a falcon or has a human body and a falcon's head—yet in the most important myths gods are seldom described in such a form, and when they are, the forms are not always the ones we know from pictures.

The Egyptian religious texts which are a main source for our knowledge of Egyptian myths are vast in number, and they occur in a wide variety of contexts. The best-known category is funerary texts, which were placed with the dead in their tombs; royal texts include the Pyramid Texts, from the burial chambers of Old Kingdom pyramids, and a series of books describing the underworld and the sun's journey through it each night, from the royal tombs in the Valley of the Kings; the Coffin Texts and the Book of the Dead were buried with non-royal people. Apart from the underworld books, these are all loose collections of fairly short texts on a variety of subjects. Other important sources are allusions to myths in magical texts, and ritual texts on papyrus and in temples, especially from the first millennium B.C. Some of these late texts include coherent narratives of myths, and among them purely local versions, some of which do not belong to any of the main groups we know.

FOWLING IN THE MARSHES

Fragment of an Egyptian wall-painting, 1420–1375 B.C.

Major myths also differed in different parts of the country, and a local chief character was often substituted for the nationally known hero. Finally, a few myths were reworked as short stories.

As is common elsewhere in the world, the mass of Egyptian myths can be reduced to a relatively small number of basic motifs. These are repeated in endless variants, and are also found outside the realm of myths proper, for example in allegorical stories. So, whatever the names of the chief characters in myths, it is often possible to recognize that they conform to familiar basic patterns.

See also EGYPTIAN CIVILIZATION; MYTHOLOGY.

EGYPTIANS. The early history of the people of Egypt is outlined in EGYPTIAN CIVILIZATION (q.v.). Before the Arab conquest of Egypt in the 7th century and its subsequent conversion to Islam, the Pharaohs, Greeks and Romans ruled the country successively. Egypt encountered another conquest at the beginning of the 16th century by the Ottoman Turks, under Selim I, and they ruled for three centuries. In 1869 the Suez Canal (q.v. Vol. IV), which connects the Red Sea with the Mediterranean, was opened. In 1882 the British went into Egypt to restore order and to ensure the safety of the Suez Canal. Egypt became independent in 1922, but British troops stayed until after the Second World War. In 1952 a revolution led by army officers ended the monarchy. The Suez Canal was nationalized in 1956 which provoked short-lived military intervention by Britain, France, and Israel. Gamal Abdul Nasser, the most famous Arab leader of recent years, ruled the country from 1953 till his death in 1970, and Egypt achieved some economic and industrial development.

The Egyptian population is of mixed ancestry —ancient Egyptian, Arab, and Turkish. Their language is ARABIC (q.v. Vol. IV) and the majority of the people are Muslims, but there is also a Christian minority, members of the COPTIC CHURCH (q.v.). There are also a few Greeks and Armenians, and some Nubians who live mainly in Upper Egypt.

Egypt is essentially an agricultural country and livelihood depends upon the river NILE (q.v. Vol. III). Most of the population have

Paul Popper

AN EGYPTIAN VILLAGE

always lived near the banks of the Nile and on its delta. About three-quarters of them are *fellahin* (peasants); of the rest, some are townsmen, some nomadic people living in the western and eastern deserts. The Nile flow, which used to flood most of the country every summer, has now been controlled by one of the world's biggest engineering works, the High Dam at ASWAN (q.v. Vol. VIII); the water is held upstream during the flood season and is released during the dry periods into canals which branch off into irrigation ditches. Though wheat, barley, maize, and rice are grown, cotton is the principal export and the backbone of the economy. The recent introduction of industries (ginning, textiles, cement, petroleum products, tanning, leather, etc.) which cluster near main cities contributes to the economy.

An Egyptian village, set among palm-groves, looks much the same today as it must have looked in the time of the Pharaohs, although now electricity is being brought to most villages. There are many traditional feasts and occasional celebrations which do much to vary the monotony of village life. The *fellahin* live in mud-brick houses or huts. Each village is headed by an *Omda* who is a government employee dealing with village affairs. Men undertake agricultural work and women tend the cattle, fetch water, and perform other domestic duties. Village industry is simple and includes pottery and basketry.

Life in the cities is very different. CAIRO (q.v. Vol. III), the capital, is the biggest city in Africa, with more than four million inhabitants. The main cities are drawing people from villages to work in the growing industries. There are state-owned schools throughout the country but with a greater concentration in the cities. Two principal universities in Egypt—Cairo and Alexandria—attract students from other Arab countries but now many Egyptians come to western universities.

See also Vol. III: EGYPT; INDEX, p. 140.

EL DORADO, *see* INCA CIVILIZATION.

ELVES. A general name for imaginary small beings with partly human characteristics, which are supposed to inhabit mountains, old earthworks, and mines. The mountain dwarfs of Europe are little men, rather ugly and misshapen: some of them are metal-workers, but not iron-workers, because, like most supernatural beings, they do not like iron. Other elves are thought of as being of the goblin type, sometimes definitely harmful (such as the boggart and pooka), and often mischievous and capricious in their ways. Some are helpful, such as the brownie and kobbold which tidy up the house and look after the animals on the farm, but even these are easily offended, sometimes disappearing when food has been offered to them in a tactless way or a suit of clothes has been provided.

See also DWARFS; FAIRIES; FOLKLORE.

ELYSIUM, *see* HEAVEN.

ENGLISH, *see* BRITISH PEOPLES.

EPICUREAN, *see* Vol. V: EPICURUS.

ESKIMOS. These are people who live in the northeastern tip of Siberia, along the northern shores of North America, and round all but the northern and north-eastern shores of Greenland. Most groups live north of the treeline, where summers are short and winters long and severe. The race probably developed in Siberia in Neolithic times and spread east when Bering Strait was a land bridge. The total population is about 90,000, of whom almost half are Greenlanders of mixed Eskimo and Danish stock. Today the Eskimos are full citizens of the four countries they inhabit and participate in varying degrees in the local and national governments. Greenland, for instance, functions as a province of Denmark, and the Alaska Eskimos own land in the state and the mineral rights to it.

Eskimos vary a little from one region to another in physical type, language, folklore, and hunting and living patterns. In general they are of medium height and stocky build with long bodies, short limbs, and small hands and feet. They have long, narrow heads with broad, rather flat faces; dark eyes; straight, black hair; and sallow skins. The language spoken in Siberia is easily understood by a Greenlander, and there is a body of folklore common to all groups. The first men from temperate climates who discovered the Eskimos were astonished at their ability to live in what seemed a wholly hostile environment. From the natural resources of their world—snow, ice, stone, an occasional mineral deposit, and a few species of animal life—

AN ALASKAN ESKIMO ARROW STRAIGHTENER

It is made of bone with animal heads carved at either end and reindeer on the sides. The wooden arrow is placed in the hole and bent straight near a flame

they obtained the tools, food, clothing, and shelter to live contentedly. Eskimos are known to be among the most cheerful, adaptable, and ingenious of peoples.

Until recently Eskimos were a mobile people. They lived in small, independent hunting groups, each moving over a territory of several square kilometres. Many hunted seals and polar bears on the sea ice in winter and spring, moved inland to fish in lakes and rivers in summer, and intercepted the migrating caribou herds in early summer and autumn. Some stayed inland or on the coasts the year round. Others specialized in hunting the bowhead whale during its spring and autumn migrations. Still others hunted marine mammals in the broken ice and open water of summer. For these pursuits they developed such special tools as the *umiak*, a large, open skin boat, and the *kayak*, a one-man, enclosed skin boat. All groups had wooden, bone, or skin sledges, and nearly all had dogs to pull sledges and carry packs. Dogs were also used to smell out seals' breathing holes. The various groups met one another periodically to trade. It was thus that the inland people got blubber for their lamps and the coast dwellers got caribou skins for clothing, and this is how materials and implements native to one region came to be used in other places.

A traditional Eskimo's daily life demanded physical fitness, skill, and infinite patience. A hunter might have to wait for hours without moving beside a seal's breathing hole in a temperature 70° below freezing. Men did the hunting and some of the butchering and made the tools; women cared for the children, cooked, prepared skins, and sewed. Food was almost entirely fish and flesh eaten raw, frozen, or lightly boiled. A system of sharing food ensured that no family went hungrier than another in hard times. The people lived in skin tents in summer. A few lived in tents in winter, but most

ESKIMO CUTTING THROUGH ICE WITH A BONE HARPOON

built either igloos—low, domed houses of snow blocks with a window of fresh-water ice—or semi-underground houses of earth and stones roofed with turf over driftwood or whale bones. Most houses were heated and lighted with a stone lamp, which melted blubber and burned its oil with a wick, often moss. Over the lamp hung a stone cooking pot. Men, women, and children wore fur or leather trousers, boots, mitts, and anoraks. In winter most wore two caribou skin suits, the inner with the hair in and the outer with the hair out; in summer one thickness of sealskin sufficed. The tools were of stone, bone, ivory, horn, wood, native copper, and meteoritic iron. Some were carefully decorated, as was the clothing of some groups.

Eskimos recognized no authority but public opinion, yet quarrelling and theft were rare. They cherished their children and never punished them physically. In religious matters the Eskimos were guided by an elaborate system of Taboos (q.v.), and by shamans who, they believed, could deal with the multitude of good and bad spirits that peopled their world in bird and animal form. Nowadays all but the Siberian Eskimos are Christian; the old religion survives as superstition and folklore.

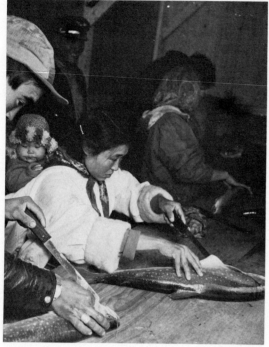

N.F.B. Canada
ESKIMO FAMILY CLEANING FISH

higher education is open to any able Eskimo. Some practise traditional crafts, some have become skilled workers, some have established local businesses, and others take wage employment when it is available. A few have left the north to settle in cities, but most Eskimos wish to combine the modern and the traditional in a way that will allow them to remain in their native places.

See also Vol. III: ALASKA, CANADA, GREENLAND.
See also Vol. XII: AMERICAN-INDIAN ART, PRIMITIVE ART.

ESTONIANS. Estonia became an independent republic, as did Latvia and Lithuania, in 1918 after the First World War; but in 1940 these republics were annexed by the U.S.S.R. Before this the Estonians had suffered six centuries of subjection, mainly under the Germans or Russians. In spite of this the people have retained strong national characteristics: they have preserved their language, customs, and way of dress, and they have a flourishing literature. Most of them are LUTHERANS (q.v.), but a minority belonged to the ORTHODOX EASTERN CHURCH (q.v.). The peasants are mainly Estonians, a people akin to the FINNS (q.v.), but the rest of the population, once known as Baltic Germans, are a mixed people. Russians make up about $2\frac{1}{2}\%$ of the population.

See also Vol. III: ESTONIA.

ETHIOPIANS. The inhabitants of Ethiopia (or Abyssinia as it used to be called) in northeast Africa, live in a country which has always been a land of mystery because of its inaccessibility. It consists for the most part of a high tableland surrounded by deep, thickly wooded gorges or by sheer desert cliffs and arid desert land. Communications are still poor in the rainy season, though road building and air-travel facilities are improving the situation.

Ethiopia is one of the most ancient kingdoms still in existence. The early kingdom of Ethiopia was probably closely connected with that of Egypt. There is also an old tradition that the kings of Ethiopia are descended from the Queen of Sheba and the Hebrew King Solomon. The Greek rulers of Egypt of the PTOLEMY DYNASTY (q.v. Vol. V), established colonies and brought Greek arts to Ethiopia in the 3rd century B.C. Judaism had long influenced the beliefs of the people, and in A.D. 330 Christianity was introduced and the first bishop of the COPTIC CHURCH

The Eskimo language, which is still spoken everywhere, is a complex one making use of a single word formed by piling up prefixes and suffixes where we would use a sentence. For instance, 'He wants to find someone to build him a large house' is 'Igdlorssualiortugssarsiumavoq'. In Greenland newspapers and books are printed in Eskimo using the Danish alphabet. The children everywhere are now taught in both Eskimo and the national language.

From the 17th century on, explorers, whalers, fur traders, and missionaries changed the Eskimos' lives by introducing tools, firearms, new goods, diseases, Christianity, and white men's customs. Since the Second World War, military and government officials, scientists, and industrialists have invaded the north, and as a result little is left of the old way of life. Nearly all Eskimos live in permanent settlements, where the governments have built them frame houses heated by paraffin stoves. They wear woven clothing and secure only some of their food by hunting. Because the economy of the north cannot now support the native population, they depend largely on government help. But education through at least primary school is universal, training in trades is being emphasized, and

(q.v.) consecrated. Many Ethiopians have followed Christianity ever since, though it has developed in its own way. In the 6th century the Ethiopian Empire was at its greatest, extending well into Arabia; but in the 7th century the Ethiopians retreated into their own inaccessible country before the increasing power of the Muslim Arabs, and they remained there, a little-known people until recent times. Towards the end of the 15th century the Portuguese sent an expedition to discover this reported Christian kingdom, whose monarch was known as PRESTER JOHN (q.v. Vol. V). In 1935 the attention of the world was focused on Ethiopia when the Italians, under Mussolini, attacked and occupied the country; but during the Second World War the British defeated the Italians, and in 1941 the Emperor, or Negus, was reinstated.

In Ethiopia there are many contrasts of race, language, religion, and tribal organization. The ruling people and main landowners are the Amhara people of the central plateau, who speak Amharic, one of the SEMITIC LANGUAGES (q.v. Vol. IV). The north is inhabited by the Tigreans whose two main languages, Tigre and Tigrinya, are also semitic. The predominant people in the south are the Gallas, traditionally a pagan nomadic tribe, who in the 16th century migrated in vast numbers into Ethiopia from what is now Somalia. They are not semitic people and their language, Galla, belongs to the Cushitic group. Now most of them are no longer nomadic but have largely integrated with the Amharas. Many Gallas occupy important positions, especially in the army. Many small groups exist, such as the Arab Muslim traders round the old walled city of Harar in the south-east, who speak Arabic; there are also numerous tribes of NILOTIC PEOPLES (q.v.) in the south-west and on the Sudan border, who contrast physically with the lighter-skinned, Arab-featured inhabitants of the central plateau.

Upon the high plateau the climate is pleasant and cool, and in many places the land is fertile. The people are mostly agriculturists. The landowners, proud people, expect the hard work to be done by peasants who are still treated much like slaves. The fields are tilled with primitive ploughs, but modernization of farming methods is under way.

On ceremonial occasions, such as weddings, Ethiopians eat raw meat with a hot red-pepper sauce called *wat*. With it they eat a bitter, grey, flat bread called *injera* and drink a heady honey-drink called *tej*. Village houses in the north are usually stone but in central Ethiopia they are often round mud-and-wattle huts with conical flat roofs. In the towns corrugated iron is much used for roofs. Amhara men traditionally wear white jodhpurs, long shirts to their knees, and *shammas*, or very long white scarves of a fine local cotton weave which they wind round their shoulders and whole body.

The religion, the Coptic branch of the Christian Church, has much pomp and ceremony, which enhances also the dignity of the Imperial Throne. A procession of priests, with their brilliantly-coloured umbrellas and silver or gold ornaments, or a royal procession when the Emperor is coming, is indeed a magnificent sight.

The traditional church schools are now supplemented by many modern government schools where Amharic is taught as the official language and English is used for secondary education.

The Ethiopian has always been wild and warlike, thinking more of his particular tribe than of the nation as a whole. The Emperor, until quite recent times, has often had little or no real

Camera Press

AN ETHIOPIAN FUNERAL

control over his country. Under the Emperor Haile Selassie, however, who is personally very much respected and revered by the majority of his people, some real central control and unity is beginning to grow. An attempt is being made to introduce many western innovations without destroying the traditional fabric of the country.

See also Vol. III: ETHIOPIA; INDEX, p. 140.

ETRUSCANS, *see* ROMAN CIVILIZATION.

EVOLUTION OF MAN. The theory of evolution, which is based on the careful study of the actual history of many forms of life, asserts that all living forms, plants, and animals, including Man, have developed from earlier and simpler forms by processes of change and selection, so far only partly understood. Up to the middle of the last century most people believed that plants, animals, and men were all created at the beginning of the world as described in the Book of Genesis; and the date was set down as 4004 B.C. During the 19th century facts were discovered which suggested a different theory of creation and a different time scale. These facts could be better explained by the theory that there had been a gradual succession of changes in the various forms of living creatures from the earliest living matter to the animals of the present day, and that of the many types produced by these changes, those which gave the best chances of survival were perpetuated, while others died out.

GEOLOGICAL EVIDENCE. The most striking evidence in support of the theory of evolution is found in the rocks. Geologists can trace the history of life in the world from its earliest beginnings by the fossils which have been preserved in layer after layer of the earth's crust. They tell us that at one time, millions of years ago, the crust would have been too hot for any animal to live, but that later it cooled down and crumpled up, the surface becoming separated into masses of land and vast sheets of water. Ever since those early times the world has been changing. Earth movements have raised up the sea-beds into mountain ranges and tilted the land under new seas. Rain and snow, wind and water, rivers and ice have been and still are at work on the surface (*see* EARTH, HISTORY OF, Vol. III). In the course of time and under great pressure, gravels, sands, and mud harden

into rocks, and the bits of plants and animals embedded in them are preserved as FOSSILS (q.v. Vol. III). From these fossils we can see that changes were slowly taking place in the forms of animals and plants and that, while some types of life become extinct, others survive.

GEOLOGICAL PERIODS. The earth is perhaps some 5,000 to 6,000 million years old. Of this immense time there has probably been life upon the earth for about 3,000 million years. Traces of man go back between a million and 3 million years. Man has left written record of his existence for only 6,000 years, a period which in a time-chart of the whole history of the earth would hardly show at all. In the very oldest rocks there are no certain fossil remains of living things. In the next stage fossils are found of early forms of plants, fishes, insects, and reptiles. The next stage, sometimes called the Age of Reptiles, shows traces of flowering plants, buds, early forms of mammals and the huge reptiles such as ichthyosaurs and dinosaurs (*see* PREHISTORIC ANIMALS, Vol. III). But as yet there is no direct ancestor for Man to be found. It is during the following Tertiary Age, or Age of the Mammals, that we find creatures that can be said to be of direct concern for the study of our own origins.

For convenience, Man, together with the Apes, Monkeys, and Lemurs is said to belong to one group—the Primates—distinguished by the possession of highly developed hands, eyes, and, above all, brains. This does not mean that Man is descended from his nearest living relatives, the existing species of ape, but only that apes and men are descended from common ancestral stocks now long extinct. This idea of descent from a common stock is often illustrated by a tree in which the trunk represents the ancestral line, the branches the different species which develop from it (*see* Vol. II, p. xvi).

The nearest ancestors of the primate group were the tree shrews, little creatures that spent their lives darting among the branches in pursuit of insects. The earliest-known primates, in which the brain is already well developed, are lemurs belonging to early tertiary times (Eocene) and species of tarsius, that nervous wistful-looking little animal with huge staring eyes; these in turn lead on to the most primitive of the monkeys, the marmoset. During the last two stages of the Tertiary Age (Miocene and Pliocene) a group of apes emerged that have features suggesting that they may be directly

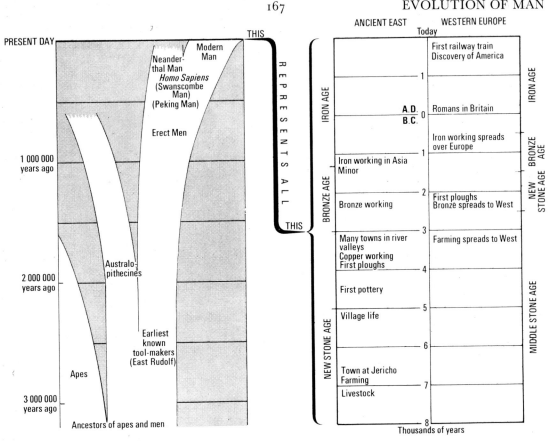

ancestral to man. The remains of these apes have been found in Africa and in India. In South and East Africa many finds have been made of primates with even more distinctly human features, particularly in their teeth and limbs. It is likely that these *Australopithecines* included toolmaking forms which were directly ancestral to early varieties of *Homo*. They were living either at the end of the Tertiary Age (Pliocene) or at the beginning of the period of the great ICE AGES (Pleistocene) (q.v. Vol. III).

With the great Ice Ages we reach the period when human species certainly appear and can be studied, not only from their fossil remains but also from their stone tools. These early men are described more fully in another section (*see* FOSSIL MAN); here we need only say that during the greater part of the Ice Ages two main types of human being seem to have developed side

by side: one of these was more ape-like and ended in the Neanderthal men; the second, which seems to have included the Swanscombe man, was already approaching very closely to modern man far back in the Ice Ages. By the last Ice Age the modern type was fully developed (hunters of this period could hardly have been distinguished from living races of today), while the old more primitive Neanderthal stock had disappeared.

This, then, is how during several million years the wonderful and still not perfectly understood processes of evolution have led from small insect-eating animals skipping among the tree-tops to ourselves, with our complicated civilizations, our scientists, artists and philosophers.

See also FOSSIL MAN; PREHISTORIC MAN.
See also Vol. II: EVOLUTION.
See also Vol. V: C. R. DARWIN; T. H. HUXLEY.

F

FABLES AND LEGENDS. Fables are stories in which an animal, tree, or some other object speaks and acts like a human being. They usually have a moral. Poets throughout the ages have used the FABLE (q.v. Vol. XII) as a literary form.

Legends were originally the stories read to monks and nuns at meals, and often told how the SAINTS (*see* INDEX, p. 113) had been tempted or attacked by evil spirits and had triumphed over them. In time the word 'legend' came to be used for any miracle-story, especially one connected with a particular place or person (*see* ARTHURIAN LEGEND).

FABULOUS CREATURES. In some of the myths connected with religious ritual, strange creatures such as DRAGONS (q.v.) are mentioned. Such monsters are sometimes symbolic figures representing the forces of nature which the ritual dramatized, and their shapes express this symbolic meaning. So, for example, the dragon's wings suggest its supposed connexion with the rain clouds. Animals have commonly been thought of as possessing special characteristic attributes —the fox is cunning, the lion strong and noble, and the lamb gentle. When the symbolic creature was intended to represent the attributes of more than one animal, it was made up of their parts. Thus the GRIFFIN (q.v.) is part lion and part eagle, the former signifying noble courage and the latter majesty. Sleipner, Odin's horse in NORSE MYTHS (q.v.) had eight feet to show that he was fleeter than an ordinary horse. Hydra, the many-headed snake, who was able to grow another head as quickly as one was cut off, represented an evil difficult to overcome.

Such creatures are to be found in the mythology of every nation and were often taken over from one by another. The Great Sphinx of Egypt stands guardian before one of the Pyramids. Its head is a portrait-statue of King Khafra, whose remains were preserved in the Pyramid, but its body is that of a lion. The Sphinx of Greek legend was represented with the head of a woman and wings on its lion body. She is said to have posed a riddle to her victims, devouring those who could not solve the riddle. The PHOENIX (q.v.) came originally into the West from Egypt. The Anglo-Saxon monster Grendel, a type wide-spread in Scandinavian folklore, was a huge giant-like creature who raided by night a king's hall where the warriors slept. He was finally destroyed by the hero Beowulf.

Other monsters owe their origin to travellers' tales. The few travellers who reached distant places came back with stories of the strange things they had seen, mixed up with the legends they had been told; it was said that the sciapod was a man with one leg, but with a foot so huge that he could lie down and use it to shield himself from the sun. Artists and writers interpreted their stories as best they could, and the results were often fantastic.

In the Middle Ages new meanings were given to the fabulous creatures. Instead of studying the natural history of animals, men tried to discover in their nature or supposed habits some religious significance or moral lesson. Books about animals, called 'Bestiaries', were written,

Alinari

OEDIPUS AND THE SPHINX

The Greek hero Oedipus answered the riddle of the Sphinx, and so rescued the city of Thebes. Painting from a Greek vase, 5th century B.C.

British Museum

MARINERS MISTAKING A WHALE FOR AN ISLAND
Illumination from a 13th-century Bestiary

in which real animals were mixed up with the traditional creatures of Greek, Roman, and other myths and legends. Animals were imagined to have human characteristics, and were used to illustrate religious doctrines. The UNICORN (q.v.) became a symbol for Christ, its single horn representing the Gospel of Truth.

Some stories were obviously simply exaggerated accounts of real animals. The whale was described in stories as being so huge that sailors mistook one for an island. They landed on its back and started to make a fire, and only discovered that they were on a sea monster when it reacted to the fire. The salamander is a kind of lizard, but a series of queer ideas became connected with it until people came to believe that this animal had supernatural powers. The Greek scholar, Aristotle, wrote that the salamander 'not only walks through fire, but puts it out in doing so'. People had believed in the fire-resisting powers of the salamander for centuries, and the idea arose that asbestos, which resists fire, was salamander skin. Later writers said that the salamander lived in the fire, or lived on fire. So the fable grew until the Elizabethan writer Nashe mixed it up with what Pliny, the Roman writer, had said of the basilisk. Nashe said that the salamander 'with his very sight blasteth the apples on the trees'. The idea of the basilisk arose from a Greek

translation of the Hebrew word for serpent. People, being uncertain what kind of creature it was, imagined strange things about it. Pliny said that its poison was so strong that it could break stones, and that if a man on horseback killed one with a spear, the venom would pass up the spear and kill both horse and rider. A basilisk could kill a man with its look—a form of the widespread belief in the evil eye (*see* WITCHCRAFT). A 13th-century scholar called Neckan stated that very aged cocks sometimes lay an egg which is hatched by a toad and from which emerges a basilisk. This supposed connexion between the basilisk and the cock may have arisen from the ancient notion that the basilisk dies when a cock crows. From the 14th century it was sometimes called the cockatrice and depicted with the head and wings of a cock and a serpent's tail.

With the growth of modern science, belief in fabulous creatures disappeared, but their symbolism remains; we still speak of sphinx-like or inscrutable behaviour; the lion still represents strength and nobility. Many of the fabulous creatures, such as dragons, griffins, and unicorns, survive in HERALDY (q.v. Vol. IV).

See also FABLES; MYTHOLOGY; MYTHOLOGICAL MONSTERS; SACRED ANIMALS.

FAIRIES

FAIRIES. Nowadays most people think of fairies as tiny, dainty beings in human form with insect-like wings. It was Shakespeare who made the idea popular. In *Romeo and Juliet* he described Queen Mab, the Queen of the Fairies, as:

> In shape no bigger than an agate-stone
> On the forefinger of an alderman,
> Drawn with a team of little atomies
> Athwart men's noses as they lie asleep.

It is quite unusual to find such diminutive fairies mentioned in ancient tales, but one of these exceptional stories of the 'Tom Thumb' type, composed about A.D. 1100, tells of fairies so small that the close-cropped grass reached above their thighs. As a rule fairies are said to be about the size of children, though some are as big as full-grown human beings.

'Fairy' is a term which includes elves, brownies, goblins, pixies, trolls, and banshees. In different places the 'little people' have different names. The brownie, for instance, is the house fairy; the banshee is a woman fairy connected with a particular family, who announces death with loud

AN ELF

Sketch drawn by a Welsh peasant to describe the creature
he had seen

wailing; the Irish leprechaun is a shoemaker fairy who knows where treasure is to be found.

In Europe people have believed that fairies are small people who dwell underground in ancient earthworks, inside the hills, or beneath the water of river, lake, or sea. They may live quite close to man's dwellings—sometimes they ask the housewife not to throw water out of the door as it goes down their chimneys! Their palaces are usually very grand but dim, as the sun, moon, and stars are absent. Here they live very like human beings, the women spinning, sewing, and weaving. They spend a great deal of time dancing and are excellent musicians. Their voices are sweet and soft; but in Scandinavia their singing is said to be mournful. People listening at the fairy hills hear the music and remember the tunes, for some folk-songs and lullabies are said to have been learned from the fairies. Births, weddings, and funerals occur. The fairies are divided into clans, with a king or queen over each, and sometimes the clans fight each other or come forth to join in the wars of human beings. They tend cattle and live on a milk diet. They may be clothed in green, but more usually they wear red caps or jackets. They are often said to have red hair. At night they come out and dance in the meadows—and folk may see the fairy-rings (really caused by a fungus) where they have been frolicking. In Ireland they disport themselves round clumps of rag-weed. Sometimes a human being is attracted into the dance, loses all sense of the passage of time, and is carried off to fairyland whence, if he partakes of fairy food, he can never escape.

It is very unwise to interfere with a fairy hill. In Ireland a farmer, who started ploughing a fairy hill, found that a cow died after the first

day's work, another after the second day, and yet another on the third—so he gave up. A Norse farmer managed affairs more astutely. He wished to cultivate a field where a troll lived, so he arranged with him that they should have, turn about, what grew above ground and what grew below. When it was the elf's turn to have what grew above ground the farmer grew carrots, and the next year, when it was his own turn the farmer grew corn. They remained good friends.

Solitary thorn bushes are connected with fairies, and it is believed that anyone who uproots or cuts a fairy thorn will suffer for it. This belief is connected with the world-wide belief in tree SPIRITS (q.v.).

It is at Midsummer Eve and Hallowe'en that 'the gentle folk' are most active. They swarm out of the fairy hills, and mortals are then in danger. In the Hebrides they say:

> Hallowe'en will come, will come,
> Witchcraft will be set agoing,
> Fairies will be at full speed,
> Running in every pass,
> Avoid the road, children, children.

At such times bold men may peep into the hills and see the hoards of fairy treasure, and the fairies may reveal secrets to people.

Some fairies help in the house and do good turns—though they leave if they are rewarded or the nature of their help is disclosed. An Irishman once said, 'If we knew how to be neighbourly to them, they would be friendly and neighbourly to us.' They dislike untidiness. 'Grant that the sweet fairies may nightly put money in your shoes and sweepe your house cleane' is an old-time good wish. Fairies are apt to be mischievous. There is a German fairy who delights in setting people quarrelling but is kind enough to remove all dangerous weapons from their reach. They steal children and leave horrid changelings in place of them. As they preferred boy babies, people tried to deceive them by dressing boys in girls' clothes. When cattle suffer from disease they are said to be 'elf-struck', and those which die suddenly are 'shot-a-dead' with a 'fairy-dart'. But when a child is born the fairies confer gifts on it. In spite of all, fairies are thought to do more good than harm. In some places in Ireland, where it is believed modern inventions and ideas have driven the fairies away, the people say: 'It was better for the country before they left.'

A KNIGHT VISITING A FAIRY CASTLE
Bodleian Library
Woodcut from Olaus Magnus, *Historia de Gentibus Septentrionalibus*, 1555

Fairies have very definite dislikes. Above all in common with WITCHES and DRAGONS (qq.v.), they hate iron. When forges were built in Germany they departed. A pin fixed in a child's dress or placed in a keyhole will keep them away. Two Highlanders one Hallowe'en mistook a fairy hill for a house, and as there were sounds of music they went in. One joined in the dance but his companion, being suspicious, stuck a needle into the door. He managed to escape, but when he passed that way a year later there was his friend still capering. When they dragged him out he was found to be nothing but skin and bones. A fairy once offered a man a pot of gold if he would marry her, but he refused. Fairies of all kinds may be driven away by books or other objects connected with Christianity. Priests have escaped from them by throwing a prayer-book at them. When people have attempted to baptize them by throwing water over them, they have vanished with screams. The sound of bells is enough to make them leave the countryside.

The actions and affections of fairies are rather unpredictable; some are friendly; others are malicious, while some, for no apparent reason, turn from kindness to spite. Though they have more than human powers, they often send for human help or try to marry human beings; yet they are often annoyed when people help them. The practice of calling them 'the gentle people',

'the gentry', or 'the good people' is an example of the widespread custom of giving a pleasant or kindly name to a spirit or power which you fear or feel cannot be relied on to be good-natured, in order to avoid offending it. The Arabs speak of the fairy spirits or 'jinns' as 'blessed ones', for they are liable to steal what they fancy or even to spirit away human beings if they are displeased. The mixed harmful-helpful character of fairies is connected with their belonging to the realm of MAGIC (q.v.), where the same spirit or power may either help or hurt.

There are similarities between fairies and the old Greek divinities and spirits of the woods and waters. Pan was a musician, and Dionysus frightened Greek sailors by transforming himself into various shapes—like Puck or Shakespeare's Ariel in *The Tempest*. The fairies' fear of anything connected with Christianity shows that they are associated with beliefs held before Christian times; and the German fairies' dislike of caraway seed, which was brought by the Romans, indicates that the fairy-faith goes back to before the Roman invasion of Germany.

Some people think that the belief in fairies is, at least in part, a recollection of some early, primitive, dwarf folk who sought refuge in the hills from invaders and lived in caves and underground dwellings. They say that this explains many ideas about them, as for example that they live in prehistoric earthworks, use flint arrow-heads ('elf-bolts'), steal children, and kidnap women to act as nurses. On the other hand, fairies are believed in where no dwarf people are known to have lived.

On the whole, it is most likely that the belief in fairies arose through fear of and respect for the spirits of ancestors. In many places, people have left food at night for the spirit of a dead person, just as they do for fairies. The belief that fairies steal the bodies or souls of mortals appears to be connected with widespread beliefs that the spirits of the dead sometimes drag away the living to the land of the dead. An old Scottish writer, one of the first to describe beliefs about fairies, says quite plainly that people believe that the souls of their forefathers live in the fairy hills, and we know that some of the earthworks in which the fairies dwell are, in fact, ancient tombs. In Scandinavia there is a belief in 'hill-people' who are partly elfish and partly human. They are said to be sad folk, and the belief in them may linger from the days when the first converts to Christianity thought that their heathen forefathers were doomed to wander, sighing, in the lower regions.

Whatever the explanation of the fairy faith may be, many people everywhere hold that in the woods, meadows, and mountains there are beings in some ways like themselves, seldom seen, but known by their activities.

See also FOLKLORE; SPELLS AND CHARMS.

FAIRY-TALES AND TRADITIONAL TALES.

In prehistoric times people told each other stories in their cave dwellings or round their camp fires. The story-teller's chief aim was to remember the traditional tales which he had been told and to pass them on intact to others. In this way many of mankind's earliest fireside stories have been handed down through the centuries to our own firesides.

Our old fairy-tales are full of ideas which are based on notions and customs still to be found amongst primitive people. These folk often believe that men can turn into animals and animals into men, that magicians can fly through the air, and that good fortune can come suddenly by magical means as it did to Aladdin when he rubbed the lamp. Such ideas are common in fairy-tales, partly because they are so old, and partly because ideas that appealed to our forefathers are also interesting to us and especially to children—though sometimes what they took

quite seriously we enjoy for amusement. Thus witches in fairy-tales only give us a pleasant creepy sensation, but two or three centuries ago they were considered really dangerous. We cannot, however, be sure because a story mentions some savage custom such as cannibalism—as in *Hansel and Gretel*—that it originated in the days of that practice, for the tale may have had old hearsay memories included in it. Some fairy-tales, such as those about some badly treated person like Cinderella who escaped from oppression, are stories which are likely to be popular amongst down-trodden people. Life becomes more bearable for them if they can delight in the mighty being outwitted or overthrown, even if only in a story.

Primitive people today still cling to the old oral tradition of story-telling, and are very particular that their tales should be told correctly. West African folk tell what are called 'Spider Stories', in which a spider, full of trickery, is the main character; but if a man makes a single slip in relating them, he is at once corrected. In Russia old story-tellers used to have contests in which they clasped hands and each recited long pieces of ancient poetry. The man whose memory failed first slackened his hold.

In islands off New Guinea the fairy-tales are 'owned' by particular people. Nobody has a

RUMPELSTILTSKIN

The little man stamped so hard in his fury that his leg stuck in the floor and he could not release it. Illustration from the earliest English edition of *Grimm's Fairy Tales*, 1823

British Museum

THE BABES IN THE WOOD
Woodcut illustrating a ballad, 1595

right to tell a tale but the owner, though he may give it to somebody else. In these islands three kinds of tales are told: (1) stories recounting imaginary happenings such as the adventures of a man and his two daughters who sail away to another island, are captured by an ogre, and manage to escape by cutting the ogre in two while he is asleep; (2) legends or traditional tales—for instance about huge fish, visits to the land of the dead, how queer rocks got their shape, historical tales of other times, hearsay stories about things and people around them; (3) myths, which were once connected with rites and customs, but have lasted on as stories long after the ritual has died. While the first kind of tale is told round the fire for amusement, and legends are related in ordinary conversation and at any time when people are inclined to listen to them, myths have great importance in the people's lives, as they form a background of ideas justifying and strengthening their religion, customs, and way of life (*see* MYTHOLOGY). The tales told in all countries may be roughly divided into these groups. Our nursery tales belong mainly to the first two kinds.

People's enjoyment of traditional tales led an Italian called Giovanni Straparola to collect and publish in 1550 the first European selection of fairy stories; it included *Puss in Boots*. A century later a Frenchman, Charles Perrault, collected together a number of stories such as *Cinderella* and *Little Red Riding Hood*. At the beginning of the 18th century the translation into French of *The Arabian Nights* made Europeans realize the wonders of Eastern story-telling, while in the 19th century the German brothers, Jacob and Wilhelm GRIMM (q.v. Vol. V), made what is perhaps the most famous collection of fairy stories. Nearly every book of nursery tales contains some of their stories, such as *Hansel and Gretel*, *Tom Thumb*, and *Rumpelstiltskin*.

Inspired, perhaps, by the charm of these traditional tales, authors such as Hans ANDERSEN and Lewis CARROLL (qq.v. Vol. V) wrote fairy-tales of their own invention, but delightful as these are to us, they do not hold the same scientific interest for the student of folklore as the tales handed down from long ago.

In studying fairy-tales, scholars collect as many versions as possible and compare them with each other. It may then be seen that details in a story as it is told in one part of the world are similar to details in the story as it is told somewhere else, and it becomes clear that somehow the story has been passed on from one place to the other. There are several hundred versions of the story of Cinderella. Here and there people have added to or subtracted something from the original story, but the main theme remains the same. We now know that while the earliest Cinderella tale was recorded in writing in Europe in 1558, it was written down in China 700 years earlier. As told in China, Indo-China, and Egypt the story is most like the Russian version. What we do not know is whether the Cinderella story first went from China to Europe or from Europe to China, or whether it was first told in Egypt or India and went both East and West. By studying fairy-tales scientifically we are able to solve problems of this kind and gain insight into how ideas and inventions spread in early times.

See also MYTHOLOGY; SAGAS; FOLKLORE; FABLES.

FATHER CHRISTMAS. Father Christmas is very old and has had many forms in his time. His remote ancestor was probably the god Odin, who rode about Northern Europe at midwinter, dispensing rewards and punishments.

Vatican, Rome

ST. NICHOLAS

The saint is throwing golden balls into the house of a poor family. Italian painting of the School of Gentile da Fabriano (*c.* 1370–*c.* 1428)

In Christian times, the god's place was taken by St. Nicholas (Santa Claus), a 4th-century Bishop of Myra and patron saint of children, who became the traditional gift-bringer because he once saved three girls from ruin by secretly dropping gold through their window. In Holland today Santa Claus comes on St. Nicholas's Eve (5 December), and there, as in Switzerland, Czechoslovakia, and Bavaria, he is dressed as a bishop. In England Father Christmas was not St. Nicholas but a personification of Christmas—a genial red-robed old man who appeared in many 16th-century masques, and in country Mumming-plays, and is hailed by name in one 500-year-old carol. He was not then a gift-bringer, but in the 19th century, when there was a great revival of Christmas festivities, he borrowed that attribute from St. Nicholas. He never quite forgot his ancient origin, however, and so today he still wears his scarlet robes and brings his gifts from the Far North in a sledge drawn by reindeer.

See also FOLKLORE.

FESTIVALS. In most religions, ancient and modern, particular times and seasons are set apart for the observance of rites or ceremonies, and these times are known as festivals. When the forces of nature were supposed to be directly controlled by supernatural powers, seed-time and harvest—spring and autumn—were the times when the most important festivals were held; and many of these ancient customs have gone on through the ages in some form or another, especially in country villages and towns. For example, on the Monday after 6 January (the Feast of the Epiphany), in some villages in Yorkshire, Lincolnshire, and elsewhere, plough boys may be seen with blackened faces, decorated with ribbons, and wearing masks and cowhides, going from house to house cracking whips, singing and dancing with swords in their hands, and occasionally dragging along a plough with them. These Plough Monday ceremonies were originally held for the purpose of drawing away evil spirits from the ground where the new crops were to be sown. Like so many seasonal rites, they often included the offering of a sacrifice, and the sword dance is a reminder of this.

In nearly all seasonal festivals the struggle between life and death was enacted in order to get rid of evil (famine, disease, and death) and secure good (food, health, and wealth). When supplies were scarce and so much depended on the weather, hunger and barrenness had to be driven away by performing rites of this kind at each and every point in the year whenever a fresh crisis arose. The first festival was Plough Monday, when the earth had been prepared for the sowing of the new crops. The next festival came at the beginning of spring and coincides with our Shrovetide. For this festival a man was chosen to represent the creative spirit of nature. In order that his life might be set free to make the ground fertile, this victim had to be killed, or to undergo a pretence ritual death. This is the origin of the old English custom at this season in which a Wild Man is dressed up in the bark of trees—bark being essential to the life of a tree—and is pursued by a crowd until he falls down. Underneath his clothes he carries bladders filled with blood which burst when he falls to the ground, giving the impression that his own life is poured out on the soil to give life to the newly sown crops. The next day a straw man is made to look like the Wild Man and thrown into a pool; this represents the drowning of winter, the season of death and decay.

In some places in England the struggle between life and death at the turn of the year takes the form of contests arranged on Shrove Tuesday between two sections of the town. Examples of survivals of this type of spring festival are to be found in the great tug-of-war at Ludlow and the Shrovetide football matches at Ashbourne, Chester-le-Street, and other places. The parish divides into two groups, Uptowners and Downtowners, and engages in a rough and tumble with a ball in an endeavour to throw it, or prevent its being thrown, into a river outside the town. The ball in this case represents winter, which one side (the good forces) is trying to drive away and the other (the evil forces) to retain.

These seasonal rites and customs reached their climax in the Annual Festival, which was usually held about Eastertide or in the autumn. This was the centre of all the religious activities of the year, and although the details were not the same everywhere, the underlying meaning of the ceremonies did not vary very much. As in the sacred drama, a divine hero was represented as fighting with an enemy. He was killed and was brought to life again; and his victory was celebrated by a procession and a ritual marriage, to ensure the fruitfulness of the earth during the

Victoria and Albert Museum
MAY FESTIVITIES
Illumination from an early 16th-century Flemish Book of Hours

forthcoming year and the increase of men and animals. In the course of the festival, which generally occupied about a week, the story of creation was often retold or re-enacted, in the belief that by repeating in word or act the things that were done at the beginning of the world, creative energy could be released to recreate nature. At the end of the season when the crops were safely reaped, festivals were again held.

In addition to festivals connected with the sowing, growing, and reaping of the crops and the changes of the seasons, there are those associated with the dead—in Europe these are usually held in the month of November. When the days were shortening as autumn passed into winter, and men's minds were turned towards death and decay, the departed were thought to return to their old homes and haunts and assemble round the fireside. Bonfires were lighted to renew the energy of the sun, lest it

ROGATION SUNDAY CEREMONY
The Rector blesses the fields at Hever, Kent

should burn itself out and leave the world without its light and warmth.

Death and fire festivals are usually held at All Hallows-tide on 1 November—a day which is still very closely connected with the Feast of All Souls (2 Nov.). Guy Fawkes Day customs (5 Nov.) are also a relic of the same rites, which were given a new meaning for political reasons in the reign of James I. Some of these November rites have been transferred to Midsummer Night's eve when, as Shakespeare reminds us, the other world is very active and the sun has also reached a critical moment in its course, being at the height of its power. Others have become associated with Christmas, the Winter Festival, since the sun was thought to be reborn on 25 December. That is why at Christmas the Yule log is burned, candles and lamps are lighted, ghost stories are told in a darkened room as we sit round the fire, and many similar customs are observed, all connected with fire and the dead. A gigantic sort of fair, known as the Saturnalia, used to be held in Rome at this

season: it included games, dances, the giving of presents, and such customs as the reversal of the position of servant and master, children and grown-ups. A mock king, originally representing Saturn, the god of the seed and sowing, was elected to preside over the revels. The merry side of Christmas has been largely derived from the Saturnalia—the deeper meaning being added when the Church took over the festival and made it the birthday of Christ.

This is, in fact, what happened to most of the ancient festivals when Europe adopted Christianity. Some of the old customs which could not be reconciled with Christianity were suppressed; but most of them, so long regarded as gleams of sunshine in the dull routine of everyday life, were retained, either as frolics and social festivities—such as the maypole dance, bonfires at midsummer or November, and the yule-log at Christmas—or transformed into Christian rites with new names and new meanings. It is interesting to notice that when an objectionable custom was suppressed, it tended to become a sort of 'underground movement' and to emerge, centuries later, in medieval witchcraft. The only sure way of destroying bad customs is to put something better in their place, and this is precisely what the Church did in most cases from the 4th century onwards. In the same way the Spring Festival became the chief feast in the Christian calendar, celebrated in honour of the death and resurrection of Christ, and illustrated by the earlier idea that the new life in nature broke forth from the grave of the earth at this season of the year. Similar festivals had been held at the end of March for this purpose in some of the secret mystery religions in the Roman Empire (*see* MITHRAISM). So, like Christmas, Easter was not a Christian innovation, but the development of all that had gone before with a new meaning.

Rogation-tide and Ascension Day also come from old festivals. Processions had long been held about the end of April to secure supernatural aid for the newly sown crops. The Church turned the occasion into a season of prayer for the blessing of God on the work of the farmers in the fields, and of thanksgiving for Christ's victorious return to heaven as the triumphant King from whom all blessings flow. Whitsuntide brought to an end the Spring Festival as the season of rebirth. On 15 August, when the fields were 'white to harvest', the Falling Asleep or Assumption of the Mother of God was celebrated at what was sometimes called the Feast of our Lady in Harvest. On this occasion some of the rites that had been held in connexion with the Great Mother of pagan times were changed into acts of devotion to the Blessed Virgin. The celebration of the feast of All Hallows, All Saints Day, on 1 November, marks the beginning of the month of the dead. In this way all the main festivals of the old pagan beliefs have been taken over, and reanimated and reinterpreted in the festivals of the CHRISTIAN YEAR (q.v.).

See also RITUAL; SACRIFICE.

FIJIANS, *see* PACIFIC ISLANDERS; MELANESIANS.

FILIPINOS, *see* INDONESIANS.

FINNS. Very little is known of the history of the Finns before the 12th century. Their language belongs, with Estonian and Hungarian, to the group of Finno-Ugrian peoples whose original home was probably in the lands between the Ural mountains and the River Volga. But racially, modern Finns seem to be related to the Nordic race, the Scandinavians, with some East Baltic racial elements. They show no physical signs of being related to the Mongols, nor are they originally related to the Germanic peoples or the Slavs.

The Finns, who live in the country which they themselves call Suomi, but which the Swedes called Finland, have gradually developed from a collection of tribes into a single people. The main influence in this development was Swedish rule which began in the 12th century and lasted 600 years. Swedish rule was not oppressive, and it brought the Finns in contact with Western civilization. In 1809 Sweden ceded Finland to Russia, and the Tsar of Russia became Grand Duke of Finland. The country, however, kept a great deal of freedom, continued to develop its own institutions, and had its own army and parliament (called Eduskunta) and its own currency. In 1917, following the Russian Revolution, the Finns declared their independence, which was recognized by Soviet Russia in 1920. In 1940 Finland was attacked and defeated by Russia, and this brought them into the Second

L. Hugh Newman

TIMBER FLOATING DOWN A FINNISH RIVER

Finnish Tourist Ass.

PORVOO, A SMALL TOWN IN FINLAND
The tall building on the left is the Cathedral

World War on the side of Germany. They lost some territory in consequence.

The Finns have intermixed with the SWEDES (q.v.) so much that there does not now appear to be much physical difference between them. The Finns generally have very fair skin, fair hair, and blue or grey eyes. Those living to the west and south-west (the majority of the population) are taller, and they have longer shaped heads than those from the east and north-east, where there is some mixture with the LAPPS (q.v.). Their character, often described as stolid and slightly melancholic, can well be attributed to the kind of country they live in. All around them there are the lonely, rocky, forest country, and the numerous and extensive lakes. In northern Finland, beginning slightly below the Arctic Circle, there are 51 days of uninterrupted night during the winter. On the other hand, in mid-summer there is constant daylight for 73 days.

Although Finland is the seventh largest European country (twice the size of England and Scotland), the population numbers only about 4,711,000 (1970 census), and was only a quarter the size 100 years ago. The Finns are, by ancient tradition, a nation of peasant proprietors. A system of state loans, introduced in 1927, enabled farmers to buy their land and to bring new land under cultivation. Agriculture was thereafter modernized and intensified. In 1969 the arable land was divided into nearly 300,000 farms; about a third contain less than 5 hectares of cultivated land; and over a half contain 5–20 hectares. Large estates are rare; there are fewer than 300 farms of more than 100 hectares.

In the rural districts the wooden houses are scattered and seldom close enough together to form streets. Each farm consists of separate wooden buildings which are often of a high architectural standard. The buildings are kept separate from each other, mainly as a safeguard against fire. The living-room is unusually large because the farmers have to be indoors a good deal during the long hours of darkness in winter. There is always a separate building for the steam-bath, which is one of the oldest Finnish institutions and a very healthy custom.

Livestock is the principal wealth of the farm, and half the arable land is used for growing animal fodder. The Finns export a good deal of butter, cheese, eggs, hides, and skins, but the most important exports are paper and timber. Much of the work is done by machinery. Like the Scandinavian peoples, the Finns have built up an efficient co-operative system, which handles a large part of the wholesale and retail trade and plays an important role in the life of the agricultural producer, and of the consumer, all over the country. A Finn (Väinö Tanner) was President of the International Co-operative Movement for many years.

The vast forests of pine, spruce, and birch are known as the 'green gold' of the Finns. Timber provides the farmer with building material, and the sale of timber forms an important part of his income. Timber and wood products constitute over one-third of the export trade of the country and the basis of her principal industries. Great efforts are now made to prevent the wasteful use of wood. For example, it used to be the main fuel, but now oil is the principal source of energy, for timber becomes more precious year by year.

Until the late 19th century 75 per cent of the population worked in farming and forestry. Now only 25 per cent do. Industries have developed fast since the 1860s, and have greatly affected peoples' lives. The Finns have shown themselves notable designers, especially in furniture, glass, and ceramics. Nearly half the Finns now live in the towns and cities, the majority of which lie along the coast. The standard of living, too, is rising rapidly and there is an efficient system of social security.

Finland is a republic with a parliament or Eduskunta of 200 members elected for a term of 3 years. The President is chosen by an Electoral College of 300 members, who are elected by a direct and secret vote, and he appoints the cabinet. The first President of independent Finland in 1919 was K. J. Stahlberg. From 1944 to 1946 Field-Marshal Mannerheim, who had led the Finns against Russia in 1917-18, in 1939, and again in 1941, was President. Finland in 1906 was the first European country to give women the vote. The Finns have a high standard of education: less than 1 per cent of the population are illiterate; there are six universities, and for a small country they publish a great many books. The 8 per cent Swedish-speaking minority cause language difficulties: indeed, in one district Swedish is the official language. Ninety-six per cent of the people of Finland belong to the LUTHERAN CHURCH (q.v.), and this is the state religion.

See also Vol. III: FINLAND; INDEX, p. 140.
See also Vol. IV: FINNISH AND ALLIED LANGUAGES.

FIRE WORSHIPPERS, *see* ZOROASTRIAN; PARSEE.

FLEMINGS, *see* BELGIANS.

FOLKLORE. Folklore is the branch of the study of man (Anthropology) which deals with local customs, tales, and traditions. Everybody is a store-house of folklore, though not everybody realizes it. Often, indeed, those who have never even heard the word folklore have the greatest store of it, for the people with least book education commonly cherish most firmly old ideas and superstitions which have been passed on by word of mouth for generations, and it is they who carry on faithfully the customs of their parents and grandparents. Everyone has heard stories of GHOSTS, WITCHES, FAIRIES, and GIANTS (qq.v.). We all know some proverbs and have heard some old songs. We are sure to have come across such ideas as, for example, that it is lucky to see a black cat and unlucky to see a single magpie. We keep certain seasons of the year as festivals, such as Christmas, and we are familiar with the special customs connected with weddings and funerals. It would be hard to find anybody who had not played games such as Ring-a-Ring-a-Roses or Blind Man's Buff. All such things are of interest to those who study folklore.

People who are studying folklore first of all try to collect accurate records of them, then see how these are connected with other ideas and customs of other places or times. By comparison with what is known of olden times or the folklore of other countries, they endeavour to discover how certain beliefs and practices came into being, and what purpose they serve now or used to serve in the past. Often we find that the beliefs which seem most peculiar and unreasonable, and the customs which appear least practical, are of the greatest interest and importance because they are commonly the oldest. Sometimes they were part of an ancient ritual or served a useful purpose when people's way of life was different from what it is now. So we not only learn about what people thought and did in the past but are better able to understand present customs. People often keep up customs when they have forgotten the original reason for them, and in course of time a fresh reason gets attached to the custom. Thus, when some joker ties an old shoe to the back of the taxi

MODEL OF A CHINESE WAR JUNK
The painted eye can be seen on the prow

there are definite methods of setting about it. We discover all we can about similar customs observed by people near or far; and we often learn a good deal by noting how these vary, and by comparing the customs of primitive peoples with the survivals of similar customs amongst more civilized folk. We also try to trace back details of the custom in which we are interested in old books and records of all kinds, especially in Greece, Egypt, and other early civilizations. In these records, which include sculptures and pictures as well as written descriptions, we may find information preserved from the time when people carried out the custom more completely or remembered more correctly its original meaning.

When we have collected all the knowledge possible by these two methods, we compare all the facts, and it often happens that we find that the two sets of facts taken together enable us to understand the significance of the custom. To give an example: if we ask a Chinese sailor why he paints an eye on the prow of his junk he will, perhaps, say, 'No have eye, no can see'. He has no useful information to give us, except that his forefathers did the same. But when we look around we note that eyes are painted on ships in other places, including India and islands in the Mediterranean. Greek records show that the eye appeared on Greek ships of 2,500 years ago. We eventually discover that eyes were first painted on ships in Ancient Egypt, where the sign of the god Horus was a falcon's eye. Thus it became plain that the long-forgotten reason for painting eyes on ships is because Horus, according to the myth, when on a voyage, stood on the prow of his ship looking out.

Another example of a widespread custom is the 'bull-roarer'. In Ireland boys still play with this toy, which is simply a lath of wood with notched edges, swung round on a string, thereby making a buzzing, booming noise. Old people there sometimes say it is unlucky if someone whirls a bull-roarer. To Australian natives who use it in their INITIATION CEREMONIES (q.v.), it is much more than a toy; it is sacred and its sound is believed to be the voice of their sky god. No woman must ever be allowed to see one. There are similar rules in New Guinea and West Africa. The bull-roarer was also used in ceremonies in Ancient Greece. Some American Indians use it in rain-making ceremonies, and in other tribes it must be made of wood from a tree which

taking the bride and bridegroom to the station for their honeymoon, he would say it was 'for luck', but actually a shoe is an old fertility symbol and has a place in the wedding customs of China and Palestine (*see* MARRIAGE CEREMONIES). In Ireland people explain the old custom of hunting the wren on St. Stephen's day by saying that, when James II and William III were fighting in Ireland, a wren, tapping on a drum, alarmed a sentinel of William's army, and so enabled his men to beat off a surprise attack. But this is only a comparatively recent explanation; the custom itself goes back to far earlier times. Men and boys take off their hats when a funeral passes 'in respect for the dead', as they say; but the present custom is really derived from the old practice of bowing to the cross which was carried at the head of a funeral procession.

If we are interested in some traditional custom and wish to find out its origin and meaning,

has been struck by lightning. Its use in many parts of the world almost certainly arose from the belief that, because the noise it made was somewhat like thunder, therefore it could cause rain to fall. A great anthropologist said of it, 'This insignificant toy is perhaps the most ancient, widely spread and sacred symbol in the world'.

The practice of hanging mistletoe in the house at Christmas is an example of a custom with an ancient origin. In Norse mythology mistletoe possessed magical powers, as is shown by the story of Balder who was slain with a twig of mistletoe. In places as far apart as Italy and Japan, to carry or eat some mistletoe was supposed to help a woman to have a child. According to an old tradition in Britain, mistletoe should not be used in the decoration of churches, because it is a plant connected with heathen ideas. Ancient writers tell how the Druids cut the mistletoe with a golden knife as part of their religious ritual. The mistletoe, growing so strangely on the sacred oak-tree, was thought to be a supernatural spirit with wonder-working powers.

Thus the study of folklore can reveal the original and earlier meanings of many customs and superstitions by comparing them with the practices of primitive folk and tracing them into the past. English people have a distaste for horse-flesh, which really is quite good to eat, because the horse was an animal sacred to the sun in northern Europe, and so its flesh was once taboo or forbidden. The Chinese do not drink cow's milk for a similar reason. The cow was once sacred amongst the Chinese as it still is in India. Even the custom which some people have of saying 'God bless you' when someone sneezes, reminds us of the time when people thought the breath was the soul, and if you sneezed you might lose your soul for good and all.

The science of folklore deals with myths,

British Museum

BULL-ROARER

From New Guinea

fairy-tales, legends and proverbs, as well as with customs and rites. Myths are not just imaginary tales which someone in the past has concocted. Often they have been originally a 'book of words' to ritual or a description of it. Fairy-tales contain many strange and ancient ideas. Local legends frequently preserve some historic fact in a veiled form. For instance, according to the legend, it had been intended to build Bisley church on a different site from that which it now occupies, but a supernatural power carried the material away every night. It has now been discovered that the place pointed out as the original site contains the remains of a Roman villa, and that materials from the villa, including an altar, were built into the church. So it is clear that the materials for the church were indeed carried away from another site, though not by any supernatural power. Thus the legend preserves some truth.

Nursery rhymes sometimes contain unexplained mysteries. The rhyme:

Snail, snail, put out your horn,
Or I'll kill your father and mother the morn,

has a version of one kind or another in England, Scotland, Germany, France, Italy, Romania, Russia, and China.

The folklore of games is full of interest. Many games originated as religious observances. Often they represented the struggle between summer and winter and were supposed to help the prosperity of the country-side and its inhabitants in various ways. In Morocco ball games are played with the idea of altering the weather. At Haxey in Lincolnshire, every Epiphany for 600 years, a ritual game has been played in which different gangs try to carry a kind of ball of sacking or leather into their particular village (*see* TRADITIONAL SPORTS AND CUSTOMS, Vol. IX).

The study of folklore reveals how closely

connected are the ways of thinking in different parts of the world, so that similar ideas, though with a different dress, are to be found among peoples widely separated from each other. Folklore studies throw light on many other aspects of man's life, such as religion, history, literature, and various arts and crafts.

See also MAGIC; MYTHOLOGY; FAIRIES.

FORTUNE TELLING, *see* DIVINATION.

FOSSIL MAN. In the article EVOLUTION OF MAN (q.v.) it is explained how fossils of extinct animals and plants come to be found in rocks. After being embedded in soft sands, clays, and similar substances in very remote times, they have slowly hardened into rocks over millions of years. Fossil remains, not only of many animals which are now extinct, but also of men, have been found in deposits which are comparatively recent when considered in relation to the many millions of years of the earth's existence, though they probably go back something like 600,000 years. These first men belong to types long vanished from the earth but who are the ancestors of the physical type known as Modern Man to which we, and all living men the whole world over, belong. These ancestral types of men are often very unlike Modern Man in details of bones, especially the skull and the brain-case. They show clear relationship with the higher apes which still survive, and even more with fossil apes now extinct, as might be expected if man and the apes have evolved from a common stem (*see* Chart, p. 166).

There are comparatively few of these early human fossils, considering that they cover a period of some 400,000 years at least. The colonies of earliest man must have been very small and widely scattered—spreading, in fact, all over the Old World from Britain to China. They are usually called after their place of finding (e.g. Peking Man or Neanderthal Man). In scientific language they are classified according to the international system of double names made up from Latin and Greek roots (e.g. *Homo erectus*, the Erect Man).

The earliest fossils of *H. erectus* come from east Asia, from the island of Java and from near Peking in China, and have strong resemblances to certain features in the skeletons of apes. The earliest fossil of Java Man is a child's skull dating from the first interval between the successive

great ICE AGES (q.v. Vol. III), perhaps about 570,000 years ago. Other human remains from Java belong to the same species of primitive man and to a slightly later period—the Second Ice Age. They all represent a type of being whose skull with a low forehead has very close similarities to the apes. His limbs, however, are not really strikingly different from those of Modern Man, so that he walked upright and did not shuffle, crouched up, as a large ape does.

Near Peking remains have been found in a cave-shelter of no less than forty skeletons usually known collectively as Peking Man. The most recent opinion among the experts is that these Peking men were really very closely related to those from Java—as closely as two races of Modern Man. All the remains of Peking Man (dating from between the second and third Ice Ages, about 300,000 years ago) show that there were considerable variations among this group of early men, though they all show the same ape-like characteristics in the skull and the modern type of limbs. A fact of enormous importance is that remains of hearths and fires and numbers of implements chipped out of quartz were found with the human bones in the cave. This means that Peking Man (and presumably his relatives in Java) had found a method of fire-making and could manufacture tools, and this represents a very important stage in the development of human control over nature.

From all this material we can form a picture of the Erect Man of Peking or Java as a man of rather short stature, with beetling brows, sloping forehead, powerful jaws with strong teeth, and heavy neck-muscles, but with limbs like those of Modern Man. His standard of intelligence was probably low, but he was definitely a man, not an animal. All the recent discoveries have emphasized this.

Some of the types of Erect man found in the Peking cave show similarities with the remains of a later type of fossil man whose remains have been found in Europe, in Israel, near Tashkent in Uzbekistan, Russia, and even in Java itself (though distinct from *H. erectus* of Java). The name given to this group of skull and other bones is Neanderthal Man (*Homo sapiens neanderthalensis*), from a place in Germany where one of the discoveries was made. This name, however, covers a wide range of variations, and the fossils range in time from perhaps as early as 200,000 to 35,000 years ago, the earlier being more like Peking Man than the later. Although they are later than the Java and Peking men, the Neanderthal people show a curious line of development in which the ape-like features did not die out but went on until the race became extinct, like a sort of dead end. We know a great deal about Neanderthal Man's competent flint-work. One man of this race was found to have been carefully and deliberately

rary with Peking Man, though later than Java Man. There was no need for archaeologists to invent a scientific name for Swanscombe Man, because he belonged to the same species as we do ourselves—*Homo sapiens sapiens*, the name used by archaeologists for Modern Man.

There are two other well-known finds of early men which are often mentioned in archaeological literature. The Mauer Jaw (belonging to Heidel-

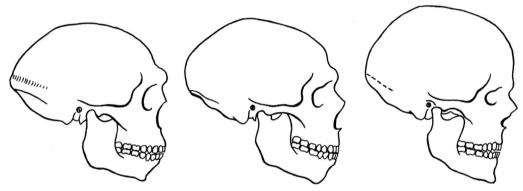

SKULLS OF (1) PEKING MAN, (2) NEANDERTHAL MAN (LA CHAPELLE), (3) HOMO SAPIENS SAPIENS (CRO-MAGNON)

The third skull, that of *Homo sapiens sapiens*, has much more room for the developed brain of modern man than have either of the others

buried in a grave dug in the earth of a cave floor. He was provided with flint implements and the bones from a joint of beef, which must surely mean that he was expected to make use of these offerings in some form of a future life. This burial may be attributed, like the majority of Neanderthal remains, to the beginning of the last Ice Age (about 75,000 years ago). Types of humans actually or nearly those of Modern Man were evolving at the same time as Neanderthal Man. These are our real ancestors who, by reason of their better brains, proved serious competitors to the more dull-witted Neanderthalers, and so survived when Neanderthal Man died out.

Thus from the general type of *Homo sapiens* there evolved on the one hand Neanderthal Man, and on the other hand the earliest representatives of *Homo sapiens sapiens*, Modern Man— our own direct ancestors. A very important discovery of the early *Homo sapiens* type of fossil man is from the gravel-pit in Kent, where a skull known as Swanscombe Man was discovered in a river gravel. He is associated with flint implements which date from the period between the second and third Ice Ages, perhaps about 200,000 years ago, and contempo-

berg Man) is a single lower jaw from Germany. He belongs to the same early group as Peking man. The second find, the so-called Piltdown Man, is really a fraud, and has been recently shown to be a fairly ancient skull of modern type and part of the lower jaw of a modern ape, assigned with other spurious relics to a hill-top gravel-pit in Sussex.

By the middle of the final Ice Age Modern Man (*Homo sapiens sapiens*) was the only surviving human species. The Neanderthal groups must have become extinct by this time (about 70,000 years ago), and the types of man hereafter peopling the globe differed no more among themselves than do Chinese and Negroes and Europeans of today.

See also PREHISTORIC MAN; ARCHAEOLOGY; EVOLUTION.

FRANCISCAN, *see* FRIAR.

FRANKS, *see* FRENCH.

FRENCH. When the Romans conquered the land we now know as France, most of the country was inhabited by a Celtic people whom they called the Gauls. Gaul remained part of the Roman Empire until the 5th century A.D.

when various Germanic peoples—the Goths, the Burgundians, and the Franks—invaded the country from the East, and of these the Franks eventually established their supremacy. During the 9th century the north of France was invaded by the Northmen, who by 911 had settled in what we know as Normandy. It can thus be seen that the modern French (like the English) are of mixed racial origin in which the Latin and the German elements prevail.

France is a rich and fertile land, but open to attack from land and sea, so that her history tells of almost constant war with her neighbours. Towards the end of the 8th century there arose a great leader, the Frankish king CHARLEMAGNE (q.v. Vol. V), who subdued the German tribes and conquered most of the western Roman Empire. He attempted to establish order and peace and to bring culture to western Europe. But because he left no powerful heir his empire fell to pieces after his death.

Until the last century France and England had been in constant rivalry. From the time of the Norman Conquest of England, the English kings were also barons of a part of France, and their claims on France increased, including even a claim to the throne itself. From 1337 to 1453, the period of the Hundred Years War, there was continuous warfare between the two countries. In 1429 JOAN OF ARC (q.v. Vol. V)

THE VINTAGE IN SOUTHERN FRANCE

E. O. Hoppé

started the campaign which finally drove the English out of all France, except for the town of Calais, which remained in English hands until the 16th century. During this period France was often split by civil war between king and powerful barons, and so was unable to stand strongly against outside enemies.

From the middle of the 15th century, however, the fortunes of France improved. By the time LOUIS XIV came to the throne in 1643, she was a rich, united, strong, and cultured land (q.v. Vol. V). The riches and the power were all in the hands of the king and great lords, and the court at Versailles was the most splendid in Europe. This too was the golden age of French literature—the age of the verse tragedies of CORNEILLE and RACINE, and the comedies of MOLIERE (qq.v. Vol. V) in which he shocked and delighted his audiences by his mockery of all that was foolish and hypocritical in the life of the day. At the same time LA FONTAINE (q.v. Vol. V) wrote his animal fables, which French children have learnt by heart ever since.

The 18th century—the age of reason—produced in France the great political philosophers, VOLTAIRE and ROUSSEAU (qq.v. Vol. V), and Montesquieu, whose ideas concerning individual liberty and social justice had a tremendous influence on the political thought of the time and undoubtedly prepared the way for the FRENCH REVOLUTION (q.v. Vol. X). When the Revolution came in 1789, its motto was 'Liberty, Equality, Fraternity'. The wealth and power of the Crown and aristocracy were swept away, the King and nobles were sent to the guillotine, and a republic was formed. The country, so much weakened by internal troubles, might well have fallen victim again to conquering neighbours, had not NAPOLEON (q.v. Vol. V) become her military leader and, in 1804, her Emperor. His wars brought poverty and suffering to the people of France, and finally also defeat, culminating in the Battle of Waterloo in 1815. But the systems of justice, administration, and education which he established or strengthened did much to make the next generation of Frenchmen sturdy and prosperous.

During the 17th and 18th centuries the rivalry with Britain continued—a competition in colonial expansion which resulted in struggles for supremacy in Canada, India, and elsewhere. During the 19th century and until the end of the Second World War, France's greatest

French Govt. Tourist Office

PARIS: A CAFÉ IN MONTMARTRE WHERE ARTISTS DISPLAY THEIR PICTURES

rival was Prussia and, later, Germany. In 1870 France was defeated and financially crippled in the Franco-Prussian War; by 1914 she had recovered and shared in the victory of the First World War. In 1940, during the Second World War, she was occupied by Germany and did not recover her freedom till 1945.

Though it is difficult to generalize about any people, one might say, perhaps, that the most outstanding characteristics of the French people are their realism, which sometimes tends to make them sceptical, their sense of logic, and their industry. By English standards they are vivacious and passionate—like all peoples with Latin blood—and they love gaiety. They are, too, a race of strong individuals, a fact which is apparent in their politics, where uniformity is often lacking.

The French are an intellectual people, and they are very proud of the lucidity of their language, a quality which it is the responsibility of the French Academy to preserve (*see* ACADEMIES, Vol. III). Frenchmen generally speak their language far more correctly than Englishmen speak English. The school children work ex-

tremely hard and reach a high standard in the French language and literature, foreign languages, history, mathematics, and philosophy. Public examinations are given much importance, and training for professions such as law, medicine, or teaching is long and severe. French education does not lay so much emphasis on training for leadership as English education; nor does it stress the need for the team spirit. Sport plays less part in the life both of the school and the nation. The average Frenchman is far more interested in literature and the arts than his English counterpart, and it is interesting to notice how much more space is given to these topics in French newspapers.

The French love of visual beauty is most apparent in the arts of painting and architecture. No European country has produced such notable masterpieces of art in every single period, from the Middle Ages to the present. But it is also apparent in such everyday aspects as the arrangement of cafés, shop-displays, and posters, and pre-eminently in the elegant women's clothes created by the couturiers.

The life of the peasant before the Revolution

J. Allan Cash

A BRETON LACE MAKER

is less important than cuisine. For breakfast they invariably have coffee and rolls or bread. Supper, in poorer homes at least, may be very simple—just a good soup and more bread—but at midday work stops for about two hours and everybody has the typical dinner which those who can afford it will repeat again in the evening. This meal begins with hors d'oeuvres or soup; then comes a vegetable, separately served, then a large piece of meat, usually steak, eaten with bread and a salad, and finally cheese, fruit, and coffee. Puddings, in the English sense, are rare, but *crême caramel* is usually available in restaurants. Almost everyone, even the children, drinks wine with meals, and in the innumerable cafés quantities of cheap spirits are drunk by the men. As a result alcoholism is a serious problem in France.

In the south, where the olive trees grow, housewives cook in oil, but elsewhere they use butter or lard. Regional dishes are manifold. The north coast excels in preparing sole, lobster, and shellfish. Snails and chickens are cooked in wine, especially in the wine districts of Bordeaux, Burgundy, and Champagne, while in the Alps *fondue*—Gruyère cheese melted in white wine—is a characteristic dish. The Massife Central has many local specialities such as sorrel soup, frog's legs, and a cherry tart called *clafoutis*; and farther south the cooking has the Mediterranean tang of garlic, saffron, and strong herbs. Egg-plant, fennel, globe artichokes, and sweet peppers are common vegetables, while all along the Mediterranean coast molluscs and crustacea, octopi, and squids are freely used in fish stews such as Bouillabaisse.

When the ordinary Frenchman is not at work, he often likes to sit in a café, or in summer at one of the little tables on the pavement outside, slowly sipping coffee or an aperitif and talking to a few friends. On Sundays and public holidays the villages and small towns often arrange fishing competitions. On great occasions the town band plays, and in the evening there are processions with lanterns and fireworks. *Le Quatorze*, 14 July (the date of the fall of the Bastille and a great national day) is the gayest of public holidays.

The religion of France is Roman Catholicism, but many Frenchmen take little share in the life of the Church. In the country, however, religious duties and ceremonies are much more conscientiously observed. This is especially true in Brittany, a part of the country which speaks

was one of ceaseless hard work with very little comfort or pleasure, and although things have gradually become better, these generations of hardship have left their mark on the national character. The countrymen in particular will work themselves, their families, and their servants unsparingly to wrest prosperity from the land. Their intense frugality tends to make them hoard money in the belief that it will give them security and power among their neighbours. This sometimes makes them avaricious. BALZAC (see Vol. V) and other French novelists have recognized this quality in their nation and it forms the theme of many novels. Fortunately the more attractive side of the same diligence is never far to seek in France, and we find many who take pleasure in hard work for its own sake, and who are most generous and kind.

One cannot be long in France without noticing how much importance is attached to family life, and how much the head of the family is respected. Children are expected to be obedient to their parents not only in small matters of everyday life, but in their choice of a profession and sometimes even in their choice of a husband or wife. The older people are proud of this tradition and try to preserve it.

The serious business of life for many French people is eating and drinking. To them comfort

its own language, and has kept its own costumes and customs more tenaciously than any other district of France.

See also Vol. III: FRANCE. See also INDEX, p. 140.
See also Vol. IV: FRENCH LANGUAGE.
See also Vol. XII: FRENCH ART; FRENCH LITERATURE.

FRIARS. In the 13th century there arose in the CHRISTIAN CHURCH (q.v.) several new religious orders whose members were known simply as 'brothers', or as 'friars'—a word derived from the Latin *frater*, meaning 'brother'. Unlike the MONK (q.v.), who was cloistered in his monastery, the friar was active in God's service outside the monastery. Friars were called into existence by the needs of the time, for this was a century of intellectual, religious, and social turmoil. The monks could not solve the world's problems, since they had chosen to retire from the world. Besides, although they were not allowed to possess anything as individuals, their orders could own property, and at times became quite wealthy, and this often led to religious laxity among their members. In southern France the people had given up the Christian Church in favour of beliefs known as the Albigensian Heresy. All over Europe the sick, the poor, and the outcast lived in utter misery, those suffering from the disease of leprosy being the most miserable of all. There was a widespread feeling of unrest, and the world seemed to have parted from its moorings and to be adrift, while the Church failed as its anchor.

The friars, who worked to remedy this situation, belonged to various religious orders, each with its own distinctive character. But all these orders had two things in common. First, they were resolved to live without income from landed property, and so, since they depended largely on alms from the people, they were all known as 'mendicant orders'. Secondly, they believed in going out among the people, to instruct the ignorant in the truths and practices of Christianity, and to exhort sinners to lead better lives. The three most important orders of medieval friars are the Dominicans, the Franciscans, and the Carmelites, of which the first two are more exactly called 'the Order of Preachers' (O.P.), and 'the Order of Friars Minor' (O.F.M.), or 'Little Brothers'.

St. DOMINIC (q.v. Vol. V) founded the Dominicans, after his duties as a priest had brought him into contact with the religious beliefs in southern France. He decided that the best way to re-establish the influence of the Church was for the priests to live as humbly as the poorest people, and to cultivate learning and eloquence in order to influence the people's beliefs. He was

| FRIARS: LEFT, DOMINICAN, AND RIGHT, FRANCISCAN

soon joined by a group of like-minded men, and in 1217 his order, which he had founded a decade earlier, was approved by the Pope. The Dominicans have always been first and foremost a learned preaching order, trying to bring back to the Church those who have strayed, and to win converts. So that they might concentrate on this task without the distraction of begging for their daily bread, the order was allowed after 1475 to own property. Famous 13th-century Dominican scholars were St. Albertus Magnus and St. Thomas AQUINAS (q.v. Vol. V).

The order of St. FRANCIS OF ASSISI (q.v. Vol. V) was quite different in origin from St. Dominic's, for St. Francis was neither a priest nor a scholar, but perhaps of all men he was the one who modelled himself most completely on Christ. Son of a rich merchant, he enjoyed a luxurious and dissolute youth. But he felt called to abandon everything he owned and devote his life to caring for the poorest and most wretched men, especially the lepers, and preaching to them the love and saving mercy of God. This he did, and owing to the power of his love and eloquence he was soon joined by a group of followers. In 1210 the Pope approved the first rule of this little group, though he realized that Francis' ideal of humility and self-sacrifice was so complete that it would be too difficult for many

THE CHURCH OF ST. FRANCIS AT ASSISI, BUILT 1228–53

aspirants. This unfortunately proved true. The order grew rapidly, and even in Francis' lifetime there were disputes about the strictness with which his rule of absolute poverty ought to be observed. After his death there was a kind of civil war within the order over this, and as a consequence there are now three main branches of Friars Minor: the Observants (or Brown Franciscans), the Coventuals (or Black Franciscans), and the Capuchins (so called from their 'capuche' or long pointed cowl).

Unlike the Dominicans and Franciscans, the Carmelites had no outstanding founder. Their order developed from a group of hermits who lived on Mt. Carmel in Palestine during the 12th century. In 1206 Albert the Blessed, Latin Patriarch of Jerusalem, united them and gave them a rule of life, and during the 13th century their order, which had now combined the teaching of theology with their earlier custom of contemplation, spread throughout Europe. Because of their white mantles they are also known as 'the White Friars'. In the 16th century a reform among them was initiated by the famous Spanish mystics, St. TERESA OF AVILA (q.v. Vol. V) and St. John of the Cross, which resulted in the founding of a distinct branch called 'the Discalced (barefoot) Carmelites'.

See also CHRISTIAN CHURCH.

FRIENDS, *see* QUAKERS.

FUNERAL CEREMONIES, *see* DEATH CEREMONIES.

G

GAELS, *see* IRISH; SCOTS.

GAULS, *see* FRENCH.

GAUTAMA, *see* BUDDHISM. *See also* Vol. V: GAUTAMA.

GERMANS. These are the largest group of people in central Europe. Their homeland lies between the Slav territories of Eastern Europe and those of the Latin nations, the French and the Italians, to the west and south. On the north it is bounded by the Baltic and North Seas and by Denmark.

The Germans, like other European groups, are of mixed racial origin. The early inhabitants of South Germany and Austria were of Alpine stock, and their descendants are smaller and darker than the Germans of the north. Along the Polish-Lithuanian borderlands considerable intermarriage has taken place through the centuries.

The most useful guide to German nationality is not race, but language. German is the native language of some hundred million people, over seven million of whom are Austrians. The Federal Republic of Germany (West Germany) has a population of 61·5 million and the German Democratic Republic (East Germany) of 17 million.

The earliest accounts we have of the Germanic, or Teutonic, peoples come from Roman times. Julius Caesar described their strength and bravery in battle, and the historian, Tacitus, praised the simplicity and honesty of their tribal customs. The Roman legionaries invaded the borders of their territory, establishing a military frontier along the Rhine and the Danube; but the tribes living beyond these rivers were never subjected to Roman rule.

From Roman days until relatively recent times there was no firmly united German nation. When the primitive tribal divisions disappeared they were succeeded by small kingdoms, principalities, bishoprics, and free cities, each with its own separate government. From 800 to 1806, Germany was more or less loosely united in the HOLY ROMAN EMPIRE (q.v.)—a federation of different states and communities which during its last 250 years stood under the presidency of the House of Austria. In the 16th century the German Protestant Movement led by Martin LUTHER (q.v. Vol. V) broke away from the Catholic Church. The German people were about evenly divided between the old and the new religions, and the Thirty Years War (1618–48) between Protestants and Catholics was conducted with great persecution and bitterness. Finally, North Germany became mostly Protestant while the south and west remained Roman Catholic—a distinction which is roughly true today.

Austrian supremacy was contested and finally obliterated by Prussia which, from the 17th century onwards, was served by an exceptionally able line of rulers. The most outstanding of them was FREDERICK THE GREAT (q.v. Vol. V) who established toleration of race and religion, a fair system of justice, and a good educational system. Prussia's great weakness was that all this was brought about by royal authority and not by the will of the people. In 1741 Prussia, under Frederick the Great, fought the first of a long series of wars which were eventually to establish her ascendancy in Europe.

The great Prussian Chancellor BISMARCK (q.v. Vol. V), finally achieved German unity after bringing Prussia triumphantly through three wars—against Denmark in 1864, Austria in 1866, and France in 1870–71. King William of Prussia was crowned first German Emperor at Versailles in 1871. Austria remained outside the new German Empire.

It helps to explain the emphasis which Germans have frequently put upon their national unity if we remember that this nationhood, which Englishmen or Frenchmen have taken for granted for centuries, was achieved in Germany only at the end of the 19th century.

In 1888 William II came to the throne. While Bismarck, after the foundation of the new German Reich, had been careful to avoid unnecessary foreign conflicts, William II had an unfortunate tendency to alienate other countries by demonstrations of German power. Thus Germany began to build a large battle fleet. Allegedly this was done to prevent Britain from attacking Germany, but in reality it only caused an increasing tension between the two countries.

The FIRST WORLD WAR (q.v. Vol. X) started in 1914 after the murder of the Austrian Archduke Franz Ferdinand by Serbian nationalists. This caused Austria to act against Serbia, which was supported by Russia. On account of the existing alliances, eventually all the great powers became involved. In 1918 Germany was defeated, stripped of her colonies, partially occupied, and ordered to pay huge reparations to the victorious Allies. In the hour of defeat the Germans revolted against the Imperial Government and set up a republic.

From 1918 to 1933 the Germans endeavoured to establish a parliamentary democracy. Unfortunately the Republic, inexperienced in this form of government, faced continual economic difficulties. These were partly caused by the reparations payments to the Allies and partly by the grave economic depression and unemployment, which in the 1930s affected most countries of the world.

In 1933 these conditions helped Adolf HITLER

J. Allan Cash

MUNICH: HOFBRÄUHAUS BEER GARDEN

(q.v. Vol. V), a native Austrian who had acquired German citizenship, and his National Socialists (Nazi Party) to come to power. He immediately introduced an anti-democratic programme, based on the philosophy of HEGEL (q.v. Vol. V). Determined and partly successful efforts were made to indoctrinate the whole population with the Nazi ideology of the absolute supremacy of the State and the Nordic 'master-race'. Political opponents and Jews, whom Hitler regarded as 'sub-human', were ruthlessly suppressed and put into concentration camps. During the SECOND WORLD WAR (q.v. Vol. X) in German-occupied Europe several million Jews were either systematically put to death or died of starvation (*see* JEWS).

Because of very strict surveillance by the Secret State Police (GESTAPO) and other Nazi organizations the political opposition to Hitler consisted only of loosely connected groups. Yet, after an unsuccessful attempt on Hitler's life in 1944 by Count Stauffenberg, a large conspiracy was revealed, and 5,000 people were hanged or shot by the Nazis.

In foreign policy Hitler's objective was to overthrow the peace settlement of 1918 and to establish a German domination over Europe, including Poland and large parts of Russia. In 1938 Austria and Czechoslovakia were annexed. In 1939 Germany attacked Poland, thus starting the Second World War. The war ended in 1945 with the total defeat of Germany.

From 1945 to 1949 Germany was divided into four occupation zones under Military Govern-

German Embassy

GERMAN APPRENTICES

ment. But in 1949 the Federal Republic was created, which combined the United States, British, and French zones of occupation; and the Russian zone of occupation became the Communist-dominated German Democratic Republic. BERLIN (q.v. Vol. III) was split between the two.

In the Federal Republic military government was gradually replaced by German authority. In 1954 the country acquired full sovereignty. The surprisingly quick recovery of the Federal Republic was helped by American Aid (q.v. Vol. X). Its main architects were Chancellor Adenauer, former Mayor of Cologne, whom Winston Churchill regarded as Germany's greatest statesman after Bismarck, and the Minister of Economics, Professor Erhard, whose social market economy relied on free enterprise and the efficiency of German labour.

Adenauer based his foreign policy on the alliance of the Western nations with the U.S.A. He advocated a united Europe, an idea which strongly appealed to the overwhelming majority of all Germans who were disillusioned with the effects of nationalism and afraid of Communist expansion. During Adenauer's Chancellorship (1949–1963) the Federal Republic was able to restore much of the reputation Germany had lost under Hitler. Relations with the Soviet bloc, including the Communist part of Germany (German Democratic Republic) remained strained, however. On account of this Chancellor Brandt, who came into office in 1969, introduced his 'Ostpolitik', which aims at achieving a détente between East and West. In 1970 the Federal Republic, in full agreement with her Western allies, concluded a Treaty with the Soviet Union, in which both powers renounced the use of force. The Federal Republic also aims at improving relations with the German Democratic Republic.

The character of the German people presents some curious contrasts. Traditionally this nation glorified war and delighted in military display, yet it distinguished itself in every art of peace. The great philosophers LEIBNIZ and KANT, the poets GOETHE and SCHILLER, the artists HOLBEIN and DÜRER, and the great composers BACH and BEETHOVEN (qq.v. Vol. V) were all Germans. German scientists have added greatly to our knowledge of the universe. KEPLER, the astronomer (see Vol. V), discovered the laws governing the movement of the planets. Gauss, the

B.E.A.

DUSSELDORF: TOWNHALL AND MARKET

mathematician, Haber, the chemist, and Hertz, the physicist (see WIRELESS TELEGRAPHY, Vol. IV) all opened new fields of research.

After two lost world wars and 12 years of totalitarian oppression under Hitler, the former German tendency towards nationalism and military glorification has been replaced by an overriding longing for peace. Foreigners travelling to Germany are often impressed by the tidiness and hospitality of their surroundings. Yet, just as in many other countries, the modern problems of materialism and an affluent society still await solution.

See also Vol. III: GERMANY; INDEX, p. 141.
See also Vol. IV: GERMANIC LANGUAGES.
See also Vol. XII: GERMAN ART; GERMAN LITERATURE.

GHANA, PEOPLE OF, *see* ASHANTI; WEST AFRICANS.

GHETTO. Members of the same race living in a foreign country tend to herd together, and to reside in the same locality. This is specially convenient if they happen to need the same kind of food, not easily obtainable elsewhere, or if they possess the same religious and social habits. They are bound together also by their language. Thus there is a block of streets in Marseilles entirely inhabited, not by French people, but by Arabs from North Africa; Soho in London is noted for its Italian quarter, and there is the

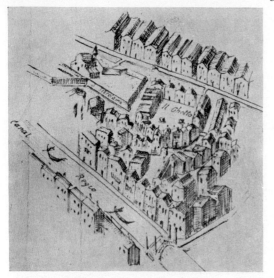

VENICE GHETTO IN THE 18TH CENTURY
The houses form a wall enclosing the ghetto and shutting it
off from the rest of the city

Irish Roman Catholic quarter in Liverpool and Chinatown in San Francisco. It is not surprising to find that so distinctive a people as the Jews have always tended to form separate communities wherever they live.

'Ghetto' is the name given to the area of a town inhabited by Jews. The word is short for *borghetto*, an Italian word meaning 'a little town'. So far as is known, it was not used until the year 1611, and then at first only in Italy; but later it was applied to any Jews' quarter in any city. The institution existed before the name, although the degree and object of living apart has varied according to time and place. It was at first a convenient arrangement freely accepted by the Jews, and later even a favour granted by well-meaning rulers who respected the claim of the Jews to seclusion. Thus one German bishop, who founded one of the first ghettos in Germany, did it, as he said, 'to enhance the town's renown'; and he had it surrounded with a wall 'to protect the Jews against the impertinence of the mob'. The same arrangement is said to have been made at Prague by a king of Bohemia, and the Jews were given keys so that they could lock the gates of the ghetto and live in security and peace. Elsewhere, in parts of England for example, the Jews lived where they pleased.

Right through history the Jews have been subjected to waves of persecution. They often became unpopular simply because of their money-lending activities. During the time of the Crusades hostility against them increased because they were said to be the 'descendants of the murderers of Christ'. For this reason the followers of Peter the Hermit ravaged the Jews' quarters in central Europe. The ghettos became objects of contempt and loathing, and were attacked and broken into. Jews were compelled to wear a distinguishing dress or badge, they suffered civil disabilities and loss of liberty, and were treated as outcasts from society. Many Jewish persecutions and massacres took place in the 13th and 14th centuries. After 1290 no Jews were officially allowed to live in England until the time of Cromwell, and there were similar expulsions of Jews from France in 1394, and from Spain in 1492. At the time of the Black Death the unpopularity of the Jews increased still further. Their better sanitary laws and their sober habits made them less liable to infection than their Gentile neighbours, who became jealous, and even accused them of causing the plague and of poisoning wells. Thousands of Jews were exterminated, especially by the fanatical order of flagellant friars. The one country which gave them a haven of retreat was Poland, and this is why the ghettos of eastern Europe have been so large.

During and after the First World War a great many of the Polish Jews moved into Germany, thereby greatly increasing the Jewish element in that country. The Germans feared and suspected the Jews because of their skill in commerce and finance, and the Nazi Government played on this fear as a means of arousing a national spirit based on racialism. There followed the Nazi anti-Jewish agitation and massacres. The Zionist movement has withdrawn many Jews from the eastern European ghettos to Palestine, which in 1948 became the independent state of ISRAEL (q.v. Vol. III). In Russia, under Soviet rule, the walls of the ghettos have fallen, and some liberty for travel and residence has been granted to Jews—a liberty granted them centuries ago in the English-speaking world.

See also JUDAISM; JEWS.

GHOSTS are the supposed appearances on earth of spirits of dead people. The belief in ghosts is very ancient, probably far older than the belief in Heaven and Hell. Many peoples

A GYPSY ENCAMPMENT

Painting by Vincent van Gogh, 1888

have believed that on one day of the year the dead come back to visit their old homes. In Europe this day is known as the Feast of All Souls. At all times of which we have knowledge certain people have claimed to possess special powers enabling them to see or communicate with spirits, and even to make these visible or audible to others. Thus in the Bible story Saul employed the witch of Endor to conjure up the ghost of Samuel before him, and, today, many believers in SPIRITUALISM (q.v.) use the services of 'mediums' who, they think, are able to put them in touch with the spirits of the dead. But the best-known type of ghost is that which appears uninvited, perhaps in some 'haunt' of its life-time, or on a certain anniversary, or at the time of its owner's death many miles away from the relative or close friend who perceives it.

Most people wish so strongly for life after death that they tend to accept eagerly and not too critically any evidence suggesting that their wish will be fulfilled. Also, people think that the possession of supernatural powers is a sign of superiority, and, indeed, many mediums find such powers can be very profitable. We may be inclined to think, therefore, that all ghostly apparitions are due either to imagination or deliberate fraud. But in recent years attempts have been made to explore ghostly phenomena by strict scientific methods, and the results so far achieved suggest that they can not be dismissed quite so lightly. Up to the present no ghost has been photographed or had its voice recorded under conditions strict enough to satisfy unbiased scientists of its genuineness. This suggests at least that the visions have no existence outside the minds of the observers. The reality of a ghost might be proved if it should impart to a living person some piece of information which could only have been known by the dead person. But an absolutely indisputable case of this has never been recorded, although some extraordinarily interesting cases have been investigated. The one possible exception lies in the class of death-bed apparitions—but here the person appearing in ghostly form is actually still alive, though perhaps at the very point of death, so that the explanation may rest in TELEPATHY (q.v. Vol. IV).

In 1889 a committee of the International Congress of Experimental Psychology undertook an inquiry, in the course of which some 17,000 people were asked if they had ever had any supernatural experience. Of these almost one in ten answered 'Yes', about two-thirds of them having 'seen something'. Three hundred and eighty-one people had seen the ghost of a human being—sixty-five of these having appeared within a few hours of the death of their owners. After making generous allowance for errors and exaggerations, the committee came to the conclusion that about one ghost out of every forty-three seen was a death-bed apparition, whereas the normal chance of the vision coinciding with the time of death would be only one in 19,000. As in no fully authenticated instance did the vision appear after death, the most probable explanation of such cases is to be found in 'telepathy', or the power of one brain or mind to communicate with another through some channel other than the usual sense organs. Telepathy is an easier subject to investigate under strict laboratory conditions than apparitions of the dead, which usually require seances in darkened rooms and various other paraphernalia making exact observation impossible. The proofs of the existence of telepathy are so numerous and unanswerable that they are now often accepted—as indeed they are by many eminent scientists who are far from being spiritualists or even, in many cases, convinced of human survival after death.

Telepathy, then, furnishes a satisfactory explanation of death-bed apparitions, being itself 'supernatural' only to the extent that science does not yet know a great deal about it. It may very possibly be at any rate partly the explanation for all ghosts which are not mere hallucinations in the mind of the beholder. If we sleep in a room which we think to be haunted, our imagination may conjure up the ghost in some form perceptible to our senses; if we sleep there not knowing its reputation, our brain may still receive by telepathy impressions from someone not so ignorant—and the result be the same. There are, however, instances less easy to explain by telepathy, as, for instance, of apparitions seen in lonely places or in empty houses when no one would be expected to be present to see them; but the possible ramifications of telepathy are so wide and so unexplored that it is wise to withhold judgement in such cases, even in that small proportion of them which seem to be unassailably authentic. Almost nothing is known of the nature of thought itself: it is accompanied by electric disturbances in the physical brain—it may or may not itself be electrical in origin. If it is, one brain may, under certain conditions, pick up waves of thought from another, as a wireless set picks up the sound of an electric lift or of a flash of lightning. It is not beyond possibility that in places where intense emotion has been experienced, as at the scene of a murder, some sort of static charge of thought-electricity may have been deposited, capable at times of influencing the minds of people visiting the place even years later. But these are mere speculations.

That people 'see' ghosts we need not doubt; that the ghosts have any existence outside the minds of living persons still remains unproved and, on the whole, unlikely. A whole host of so-called 'supernatural' phenomena, many of them undoubtedly genuine, await scientific investigation. We should resist the temptation to see proof of the return of the spirits of the dead in the mere occurrence of events which cannot at present be given a natural explanation. Whatever other views we may hold on the after-life, we are safe, so far as modern scientific knowledge can guide us, in believing that the dead do not return to this earth.

GIANTS. The myths of peoples all over the world tell of the doings of giants. In Greek mythology the Giants, like the Titans, were thought to be the offspring of Uranus (Heaven) and Ge (Earth). But while the Titans, who, though huge, were of perfect form, were always esteemed gods, the Giants, who were monstrously deformed in some way, were nearly always regarded as the barbarous enemies of gods and men. Among this monstrous brood of Heaven and Earth were the hundred-handed giants, Cottus, Briareos, and Gyes, who helped Zeus to defeat the Titans, and the one-eyed Cyclopes, the most famous of whom was Polyphemus, who so nearly killed Odysseus. Zeus and the gods defeated the Giants when they rebelled against them, and imprisoned them under volcanoes in various parts of Greece and Italy. One of them, Enceladus, was held down by Mount Etna and caused its volcanic eruptions.

The size of these legendary giants varies a great deal. Some of them are said to have been not a great deal taller than ordinary men, but others are thought of as gigantic beings with powers more like gods than men. Goliath, who was slain by David with a stone from his sling,

By courtesy of Brasenose College, Oxford
JOHN MIDDLETON, THE 'CHILDE OF HALE'
This giant, who lived from c. 1572 to 1633, was 2 m 82 cm tall

was 2 m 90 cm in height (1 Sam. xvii). People nearly always exaggerate when they tell of giants or dwarfs, making giants rather taller and dwarfs somewhat smaller than their actual height, so perhaps those who told the story of the fight between these two champions added something to Goliath's height. Once your enemy is defeated it is pleasant to think how powerful he was. In Scottish and Irish folklore giants are described as very mighty, but local heroes are nearly always able to vanquish them.

There is no evidence that men were ever much higher than they now are. The tallest men of whom we have definite records—two Dutchmen, Jan van Albert and Regardus Rijnhout, who visited London recently, and a Russian called Machnow, who came in 1905 —all measured about 2 m 80 cm. John Middleton, born about 1578, whose portrait is in

Brasenose College, Oxford, is said to have reached the same height. Ireland has produced a number of giants, including Cornelius Magrath (2 m 25 cm); Charles O'Brien (2 m 43 cm), whose skeleton may still be seen in the Royal College of Surgeons in London; and Patrick Cotter (2 m 45 cm), who died in 1802. Cotter used to go for walks at night in order to avoid attracting too much attention. One night, at Bath, a watchman was frightened nearly out of his wits when he saw this man reach up to a street lamp, lift off the cover, and light his pipe at it. A Russian girl, Elizabeth Lyska, who came to London in 1889 when she was twelve years old, was already 2 m 2 cm. The average height of a tribe in Patagonia in South America is 1 m 77-79 cm, though individuals may be several centimeters taller. But the early Spanish travellers who saw these people, reported that their own heads hardly reached the Patagonians' waists. This sort of exaggerated traveller's tale is the origin, no doubt, of many reputed giants.

Some real giants, like the giants of fairy-tales, are rather stupid. Growth is controlled by the pituitary gland under the base of the brain. If a child's pituitary secretes too much hormone, the child will grow unusually big; if too little, the child becomes a dwarf. The abnormality which causes growth may cause stupidity too.

People came to believe in giants, not only through exaggerated stories of unusually big men, but also because of things found in the countryside, which they supposed to be the work of giants. In many

A. C. K. Ware

GOG AND MAGOG
Statues of London's giants in the Guildhall

countries there are great stone monuments, such as circles of immense blocks of stone, built by people long forgotten. STONEHENGE (q.v.), which used to be called 'The Giants' Dance', is the most famous example in England. The people living in the neighbourhood of such monuments very often tell stories of how giants built them. It is also likely that people's experience of storms and earthquakes encouraged the belief that enormous giants caused these disturbances. Sometimes, when bones of some large animal have been dug up, people have jumped to the conclusion that they were human bones. Saint Augustine once saw on the seashore what he took to be a human tooth, a hundred times larger than any normal tooth. This he felt sure, was evidence of the existence of the giants mentioned in the Old Testament (Gen. vi. 4). Some large bones found in England were taken for giant's bones until the scientist, Sir Hans Sloane (one of the founders of the British Museum) examined them and proved them to belong to the backbone of a whale. Even natural objects, if they are large and odd looking, have been supposed to be the work of giants. Near Portrush, in the north of Ireland, there are numbers of five-sided and six-sided columns of volcanic rock, created by the cooling and cracking of a sheet of basalt. This strange place, called GIANT'S CAUSEWAY (q.v. Vol. III), was, according to legend, built by the Irish giant Finn MacCool, to bridge the channel between Ireland and Scotland. In England and Germany there are places where, according to the legends, two giants played games with each other, throwing bowls or a hammer several miles across a valley; and at Turton, in Lancashire, strange grooves in a rock are said to have been made by a giant's fingers when he used it as a plaything.

While some of these huge giants, connected with immense boulders and queer features in the landscape, are supposed to have been playful, others belonging to mythology are described as savage cannibals—like the one-eyed monster Polyphemus who captured Ulysses and his men. This belief in barbarous and wicked giants may be due to the natural idea that what is huge is likely to be dangerous. However these notions arose of monsters outwitted and defeated by men, we may be sure the stories were told, generation after generation, because it gave people a kind of gruesome pleasure to think of mighty beings who could yet be overcome by men. The tale of Jack the Giantkiller is an example of this type of story, and John Bunyan made good use of the idea when, in Part II of *Pilgrim's Progress*, he described Mr. Great-heart killing Giant Maul who had sought to prevent him from continuing with Christian's wife and family, on their pilgrimage to the Heavenly City.

Various cities have their own giants. Thus Gog and Magog are connected with London, and giants support the coat of arms of Lucerne. It is said that they owe their presence there to the fact that a doctor, who examined some animal bones which were discovered near Basle in 1577, decided that they belonged to a giant about 4 m 90 cm in height. In London giants used to walk in the Lord Mayor's Show. Like the giants which sometimes appear at pantomimes, they were disguised men walking on tall stilts. There is a record of such giants appearing in the May games in St. Martin's-in-the-Fields, London, in 1555.

See also FOLKLORE; FABULOUS CREATURES.

GOBLINS, *see* ELVES.

GOD. The word 'God' is used to describe any divine being who is given religious worship, whatever form or shape he may take, be it that of a man, an animal, a mysterious mountain, tree, or stone, or the One Supreme Creator and Ruler of all things. It is also used sometimes to mean a divine principle running through every-thing in the world. This shows that there are and have been many ways of thinking about the idea of God, and these have changed and developed as people's notions about things in general have altered. Thus, to people living under primitive conditions God seems to be the highest, wisest, and most powerful Person or Thing of which they can conceive, and so they make 'God' a great chief in the sky or some very wonderful animal or natural object. At the other end of the scale people who think of God as the ground and support of the entire universe realize that no bodily shape or form could adequately describe Him. Nevertheless, people have to try to form some picture or idea in their minds, whether it be concrete or abstract, to make the notion of God intelligible to them. Thus, for example, when the Greeks pictured a god called Atlas holding the pillars on which the universe rested, this was only a picturesque way of describing a very profound truth, namely, that God who is perfect and complete in Himself 'holds up', so to speak, everything that exists.

All these various ideas about God fall roughly into three main divisions which are commonly classified as follows: (*a*) polytheism, or the belief in more than one god; (*b*) monotheism, or the belief in only one God; (*c*) pantheism, or the belief that everything is God.

(*a*) POLYTHEISM. In many parts of the world, especially in the great ancient civilizations such as Egypt, Babylonia, Greece, and Rome, and among many primitive races it has been commonly supposed that there is a multitude of gods and spirits inhabiting natural and mysterious objects such as the sun, moon, and stars, running water, peculiar trees, stones, and animals, and sacred mountains. These may be either friendly or harmful to man, but, for good or ill, they are thought to be responsible for making things behave as they do. When the unseen powers show themselves in terrifying events and are thought to be the cause of misfortune, they are propitiated (*see* SACRIFICE). But often they are imagined to be bearers of good gifts and the authors of all that man needs for his well-being—food, children, rain, sunshine, &c. As such they are often looked upon as glorified mortals who live in the sky or on the top of a mountain under a Supreme Being or Powerful Chief. Thus in Scandinavia, Odin, the highest of the Norse gods, was regarded as the all-wise ruler of heaven and earth who lived in his palace in the sky. He was also the god of war and, therefore, he had his seat in the warrior's paradise, Valhalla (*see* HEAVEN). As the source of all life in the world, he had many different names and numerous wives and chilren. His queen, Frigga, was the mother of the mildest, best, and most cunning of all the gods, Balder the Beautiful. Balder apparently kept his soul safely stored away in the mistletoe, but when this secret was discovered, he was killed by a blow from a branch of this plant sacred to him. His death brought terrible misfortune on gods and men and was believed to hasten the day when the whole earth would be destroyed, because he was the god who gave life and prosperity to everything (*see* NORSE MYTHS).

In Greece the principal god was Zeus, a name that may originally have meant the 'sky'. He, too, was the source of all life and light, the god of thunder and lightning and of rain. All mountain-peaks were sacred to him, but his chief home was Mount Olympus in Thessaly, where he ruled over eight other gods as their overlord. There they feasted, drank, played music, and quarrelled with one another, just like the old warrior chieftains and princes on whom they were modelled. Therefore, Zeus and his companions (collectively called the Olympian gods) were gods made in the image and likeness of men (*see* GODS OF GREECE AND ROME).

In the religion of Ancient Rome Zeus had his counterpart in Jupiter, who was a personification of the sun and the sky. He controlled the weather, manifested his power in thunder, lightning, and rain, and came to earth in the form of a thunderbolt. Both Jupiter and Mars looked after the crops, especially the vine, but neither of them was so strongly associated with the fertility of vegetation as Osiris in Egypt. In no country has the cultivation of the soil seemed to be more miraculous and supernatural in its origins than on the banks of the Nile, where the life-giving waters annually turn desert into very fertile land. Egypt, in fact, has been described as 'the gift of the Nile', and the god believed to be responsible for all this was called Osiris. It is suggested that he was really the first man who discovered the secret of growing barley, or of cutting the canals through which the waters of the Nile were carried to the fields. Therefore, the Egyptians looked to him for sustenance on earth and, since he was also the judge of the

Ashmolean Museum
ZEUS PREPARING TO THROW A THUNDERBOLT
From a cast of a bronze statue, *c.* 470–460 B.C.

dead, for a joyful resurrection hereafter (*see* EGYPTIAN MYTHS).

In Egypt each district had its own special local god or gods; but when Upper and Lower Egypt became a single kingdom, the god of the capital of the kings—Heliopolis, near Cairo—rose to great importance and was worshipped all over the country. In this way the Sun-god, Re, worshipped at Heliopolis, became widely recognized as the creator of the universe and the source of all life. Around him were grouped eight other gods; and these nine deities of Heliopolis collectively made up the most important of the Egyptian assembly of gods. But in early times in Egypt there were also other gods who were thought by their respective worshippers to have created the world, such, for instance, as Ptah of Memphis. In the end, however, the worship of Osiris eclipsed that of the Heliopolitan Sun-god, Re. One of the Pharaohs, Akhnaten (about 1375 B.C.), attempted to bring Egypt to recognize one supreme and only creator and father of mankind—the Sun-god, Aten. When Akhnaten died, however, the power of Aten declined, and Egypt returned to her polytheistic beliefs in many gods.

(*b*) MONOTHEISM. In early times it was only

National Gallery

THE HOLY TRINITY WITH SAINTS
Painting by Pesellino (1422–57)

among the Jews, Muslims, and Christians that the entire universe was thought to be the creation of a single deity controlling all things in heaven and earth. In Persia, about the 7th century B.C., Zoroaster, or Zarathustra, taught that over and above all the good and evil spirits and gods, there was one supreme Creator of the universe, called Ahura Mazdah, the all-wise, all-powerful, and wholly good God. But soon after his death this idea was lost, and his followers divided up good and evil into two groups of gods, with their respective spiritual armies, fighting against each other. His attempt at monotheism was as temporary as that of Akhnaten in Egypt (*see* ZOROASTRIAN).

The great prophets in Israel declared that JEHOVAH (q.v.), the god of Israel, was the one and only God who has created the earth, and orders everything that happens in the world to His own ends and purposes, however long these may take to work out. They thought that Jehovah's chief interest was with His own nation, but, nevertheless, they believed that through the Jews all mankind was to come to a knowledge of Him and worship Him alone in His temple at Jerusalem. They believed that He was guiding the ups and downs of their history to this goal, and then at last they would fulfil the purpose for which He had chosen them and separated them from the rest of the nations of the earth (*see* JUDAISM).

From the Jews CHRISTIANITY (q.v.) took over the belief in the unity of God; but since Christians believed that Jesus was the human embodiment of God in the relation of Son to Father, and that the work He began was carried on on earth by the divine Spirit, Christian monotheism was rather different from that of Judaism or Zoroastrianism. God is one; but He was manifested in Christ, and is active in the world and in human beings in the Holy Spirit. This God is thought to be a Trinity, i.e. that He exists as 'three Persons' in one God. Moreover, He is thought of not only as a Ruler but also as the God of love, who not only rules His people with perfect wisdom and justice, but is eternally merciful towards them. This was a new conception.

A third form of monotheism arose in Arabia in the 7th century A.D., when Muhammad, the prophet of ISLAM (q.v.), proclaimed that there is no god but Allah, 'the strong' or 'mighty one'. As the Arabs were polytheists when Muhammad began his mission, he had to insist on the absolute unity of the one true God. So high and unique is Allah, he declared, that He is quite separate and apart from man, whose only duty is to submit to His commands. Nevertheless, the Arabs think that God is 'merciful' and 'compassionate', although man in His hands is like a pawn in a game of chess.

(*c*) PANTHEISM. In India, among followers of HINDUISM (q.v.), polytheism has moved in a different direction. In very early times a female vegetation goddess was worshipped, together with sacred trees, horned cattle, and snake-spirits, and a god of vegetation later known as Shiva. Then came the Aryan invaders from the north (*see* INDIAN ANCIENT CIVILIZATION), who brought with them a whole collection of nature gods not unlike those of the Vikings of Scandinavia. The greatest was Brahma, a rather remote god who was less popular than the fair-haired and bearded Indra. Indra rode into battle on a great chariot, wielding the thunderbolt as his weapon. He represented the energy dis-

Victoria and Albert Museum

SURYA, THE INDIAN SUN-GOD

He rides a chariot—the tiny horses can be seen at the base— and can be compared with Apollo, the Greek sun-god.

played in the thunderstorm, and was a god of the air, just as Agni was the god of fire, the hearth, and the altar. Then there was Varuna, representing the heavens that stretch across the sky. He became a universal monarch, king of gods and men, and established the heaven and the earth, made the sun to shine, kept the moon and the stars in their courses and gave to nature and mankind their law, which he upheld. As he was all-seeing, he guarded the moral order of right and wrong and, like Jehovah, he punished evil and rewarded good.

Later these gods were brought together and

conceived of as a single divine principle, controlling the whole of nature and man, so that the idea of God became that of an indwelling power that orders and animates all things—Brahma—so that everything is God (Brahma) and God is everything (*see* BUDDHISM). As Brahma comprehends all existence, so in every individual there is an invisible part, the 'self' or 'spirit', which is identical with the Great Self of the universe (Brahma). Thus God ceases to be regarded as a 'person' but is an impersonal principle pervading all things. In practice, however, most Hindus have continued to worship the earlier gods, such as Vishnu, the preserver, and Shiva the destroyer, of life, while Brahma has remained the remote Absolute, so great that He (or It) is beyond all understanding and yet is in everything.

See also RELIGION.

GODS OF GREECE AND ROME. 1. GREEK

GODS. These began by being merely forces of nature thought of by the Greeks as personal and divine, each having his own history and special ceremonies of worship (*see* GREEK MYTHS). By the time of Homer, about 750 B.C., the original connexion of the gods with the phenomena of nature had faded, and they were thought of in the shape of men and women with many of the needs, desires, and characteristics of mortals. The poems of HOMER (q.v. Vol. V) gave much more definite shape and uniformity to these ideas.

The gods and goddesses lived in a community on Mount Olympus and were ruled over by Zeus. They directed the affairs of men, but their power was limited: they did not, for instance, know everything, they could be in only one place at a time, and they needed food and sleep like mortals. They were also subject to the decrees of Fate, a power never clearly explained. They governed mankind according to their own inclinations, not according to any ideas of morality or standards of right or wrong (such ideas came gradually into Greek religion as Greek civilization developed). They quarrelled and interfered with each other; they were moved by jealousy and revenge as well as by pity and kindness. The justice of a cause did not influence them much. Humans, therefore, were compelled to conciliate them by prayers and offerings.

The chief of the gods of Olympus was Zeus, the god of the sky. He was the son of Cronos and Rhea (or Cybele) the great Earth Mother,

descended from the giant Titans. Zeus' sister Hera was his wife, the queen of heaven. His two brothers, Poseidon and Hades, ruled respectively the sea and the underworld. Poseidon lived in a golden palace in the depth of the sea. Bearing his mighty trident he drove over the sea in a chariot drawn by swift-footed steeds and around him frisked all the monsters of the deep. The underworld, the kingdom of Hades (or Pluto), was separated from the land of the living by the rivers Styx and Acheron. This land, also called Hades, was inhabited by the dead who were ferried across the Styx by Charon, the ferryman. Hades was grim but just and, unlike Satan, in no sense a personification of evil. He seized and took to the underworld to be his queen Persephone, the daughter of Demeter, the goddess of corn and agriculture.

National Museum, Athens

ATHENA

Relief of the 5th century B.C.

The myth of Persephone is one of those myths about the spring common to many religions. Persephone was destined to spend half the year with Hades in the underworld, but for the other half she might return to her mother. As she came back into the land of the living, the grass began to grow and the flowers to spring up at her feet; spring was returning to earth. In autumn, when she had to return to Hades, all growing things began to fade and die.

Athena, or Pallas Athene, the daughter of Zeus, was the goddess of wisdom, the patron of all towns, and Athens in particular, and of all town crafts. She is depicted as severely beautiful, clad in armour. Apollo was the god of medicine, poetry, and music, and especially of prophecy. At Delphi he had a shrine with a priestess whose replies to questions put to her by the Greeks were supposed to contain the answers of Apollo himself. This was the Delphic Oracle. Dionysus was the god of fertility, especially of the vine. Being a god of the earth, Dionysus, like Persephone, disappeared in the winter and returned or was reborn in the spring.

Aphrodite was the goddess of love, judged by the mortal prince of Troy, Paris, to be the most beautiful of the goddesses. She was the mother of the little winged god of love, Eros. Artemis was the goddess of hunting, and the patroness of all very young things. She was identified with the moon. Hebe was the handmaiden of the gods, pouring out nectar for all to drink. She was the spirit of perpetual youth. Hermes, the god of luck and wealth, was the gods' messenger and was responsible for conducting souls to Hades. He was also the god of roads. He had wings on his feet, a broad-brimmed hat, and a staff round which serpents were twisted.

The god Pan of flocks and shepherds, unlike the rest, was not entirely manlike in form, but had the legs and horns of a goat. He had the reputation for exciting sudden terror in the lonely wanderer in the forests—hence the word 'panic'. He invented the musical pipes, which he was said to have made from a reed into which a nymph, fleeing from his love, had been changed.

It is interesting that the Greeks' god of War, Ares, is comparatively unimportant and takes a much less prominent place than does his Roman counterpart, Mars.

2. ROMAN GODS. Roman religion began much as did the Greek, but the ideas in it developed

P. Hart

APOLLO

The central figure of the west pediment of the temple of Zeus at Olympia. Beside him are fragments of other figures from the same pediment. *c.* 460 B.C.

in a different way. The Greeks endowed their gods with real and individual personalities: the Romans, although they personified their gods, thought of them rather as abstract powers. In early times they did not make images of their gods, but represented them by symbols—a flintstone for Jupiter, a spear for Mars, and fire for Vesta, the goddess of the hearth. As well as the principal gods and goddesses the Romans had a great number of lesser gods, especially for the earth, fields, and woods, and for house and home. The Lares and Penates, the gods of the house and family, were important objects of worship. Every individual had his own protector, his Genius.

The religion of the Romans was gradually influenced and very much altered by the Greeks. The Romans introduced shrines for their gods and began to think of them as having human characteristics. Three gods—Jupiter (or Jove), the supreme god, Juno, the goddess of women, and Minerva, goddess of wisdom—were recognized by the state as supreme, and given a temple at the Capitol. The principal Greek gods were adopted by Rome and identified with native gods. They were as follows: Jupiter (Zeus), Juno (Hera), Neptune (Poseidon), Minerva (Athena), Mars (Ares), Venus (Aphrodite), Cupid (Eros), Diana (Artemis), Ceres (Demeter), Mercury (Hermes), Bacchus (Dionysus).

See also GREEK CIVILIZATION; ROMAN CIVILIZATION, Section 5. See also INDEX, pp. 117-122.

GOLDEN HORDE, *see* TARTARS.

GOTHS. The origin of this Germanic people is still a matter of uncertainty. They were first known of for certain in the 3rd century A.D., in the lands north of the lower Danube. They

THE GOTHIC INVASIONS

began to move westward, no doubt because of the attacks of the HUNS (q.v.), and they became the leading Germanic people of the 4th to 6th centuries A.D. They adopted a form of Christianity, called Arian, which the Roman Church refused to accept as true Christianity. Their history is closely connected with the history of the last period of the Roman Empire. They first appeared in the east of the Empire, and moved across it to the west, playing a considerable part in its final downfall. In 410 Alaric, king of the group called the Visigoths, made his third attack on Rome and finally captured the city. After this, the break-up of the Western Roman Empire was only a matter of time. All through their history, however, the Romans exercised great influence over the Goths, who showed an almost superstitious reverence for things Roman.

The Goths came into Europe in two main groups—the East or Ostrogoths, and West or Visigoths. After various migrations and a long and complicated history of wars and alliances with the Eastern and Western Roman Empires, the West Goths settled in Spain and southern

France, and the East Goths in Italy. At the end of the 5th century Theodoric (A.D. 455-526), King of the East Goths in Italy, had gained control of all Italy, both Gothic and Roman, although the Romans continued to be governed through their own ancient institutions. After Theodoric's death in 526, however, the Gothic rule in Italy ended, and the power of the East Goths vanished, leaving very little trace.

The West Gothic kingdom in Spain lasted much longer. The Goths became very much romanized, but their power outlived that of the Romans. The Visigoth kingdom in Spain lasted until A.D. 713, when their king Roderick was finally defeated by the Muslim Arabs, and the Goths only remained as scattered groups.

It is remarkable that a people who played such a part in history for nearly three centuries should have left so little trace behind them. They have never given an abiding name to any part of Europe, as did other early peoples such as the Franks, Angles, and Saxons. Their only legacy is a title, Gothic, applied to a style of art, especially architecture. Gothic Art does not mean the work of the Gothic people, but rather a style of art in the later Middle Ages which did not follow the classical style of the Greeks and Romans. In the Renaissance the word 'Gothic' was used as meaning 'barbaric', since anything which was not derived from Greece or Rome was thought of as barbarian and therefore inferior.

See also Vol. IV; GERMANIC LANGUAGES.

GREEK CHURCH, *see* ORTHODOX EASTERN CHURCH.

GREEK CIVILIZATION. 1. Greece has given so much to the glories of civilization, in art, science, literature, and philosophy, that only the briefest idea of her contribution can be given in an article of this length. The source of much of this richness is the city of ATHENS (q.v. Vol. III) where Greek civilization reached its summit. In consequence, this account will be more concerned with Athens than with any other city. But many other cities, among them Sparta, the age-long rival and foe of Athens, and Thebes, the home of Pindar, had also a share of the glory of Greece. To understand the character of Greek civilization we must know a little about the Greeks themselves and how Greece came into being.

2. HISTORY. The deepest roots of Greek

Peter Jones

THE ERECTHEUM ON THE ACROPOLIS, ATHENS

The Acropolis, rising steeply above the city was the ancient Athenian citadel. The Erectheum, built in the 5th century B.C.,
was a temple dedicated to Athena, Poseidon, and Erectheus. Through the Ionic columns of the peristyle can be seen other
5th-century ruins and the distant view across the Athenian Plain

civilization go back to Crete and Mycenae (*see* MINOAN and MYCENAEAN CIVILIZATIONS), but at present no one is certain where the various peoples who settled in the mainland of Greece originally came from. According to early Greek traditions, the first Greeks who invaded the mainland and drove out the pre-Greek inhabitants were called Pelasgians. They remained to form part of the original stock of the Athenian people and were at their most prosperous in the 13th and 12th centuries B.C. Apart from these early people, there were, according to Greek tradition, three main elements in Greece—the Achaeans, the Dorians, and the Ionians.

(*a*) *Achaeans*. It is now thought that there is some connexion between the Achaeans and the people known as HITTITES (q.v.) who dwelt in Asia Minor. The Achaeans also gained a foothold in Crete, and are mentioned in an Egyptian inscription of the 13th century B.C. as helping the Libyans to invade Egypt. The tradition of an Achaean expedition to the Hellespont is to be found in the story of Jason and the Argonauts. In the picture drawn by Homer of the various petty states of Greece and the Aegean, the Achaeans occupy by far the most important place.

(*b*) *Dorians*. The Dorian invasion of Greece was part of a great movement of peoples which took place during the 12th century B.C. and profoundly affected the whole of the ancient Near East. The Dorian invasion, coming from the north, drove the Achaeans into the more remote parts of Greece, and it ultimately spread as far as Crete, Rhodes, and even into the south-west corner of Asia Minor. The principal Dorian centres of classical Greece, however, were Sparta, Argos, Corinth, and Megara and their colonies, of which Syracuse, Tarentum, and Cyrene were among the most notable. In some states the invaders were absorbed in the conquered people; in others the conquerors retained a privileged position. Thus in Sparta the foundation of the State was the slave class, called 'helots', who were the property of the State; next came a class of freemen who had no political rights, but engaged in commerce and menial crafts which were forbidden to the upper class; the highest class were the pure-blooded descendants of the Dorian invaders, the true Spartans, whose business was to govern, to make war, and to train their minds and bodies to endurance and strength.

(*c*) *Ionians*. The origin of the Ionians is also obscure, but the name is very ancient. It occurs in a very early Egyptian inscription, and also in the Old Testament, and is the name by which the early Semites knew the Greeks. The Ionians appear to have migrated across the Aegean to the west coast of Asia Minor where they founded many prosperous settlements, the most important of which was Miletus. They mingled freely with the non-Greek peoples of Asia Minor, and because of this wider contact not only outstripped the cities of the mother country in wealth and culture, but developed a free and inquiring spirit which made them the pioneers of early Greek philosophy and science. They were conquered by the Persians but later played an important part in the great struggle for independence waged by the Greeks against the Persians under Athenian leadership. This struggle was followed by the most glorious period in the history of Athens, now recognized as the leader and champion of the Ionians.

Though these three peoples—the Achaeans, the Dorians, and the Ionians—differed in the dialects they spoke and in their ways of life, to outsiders (or 'barbarians' as the Greeks called them) the similarities were much more striking than the differences. For one thing almost all Greeks were organized in small, independent, cities, each with its own surrounding territory; though this was the cause of faction and later of serious political weakness, yet the Greek genius in its variety and individuality was closely bound up with the existence of the city-state. It was the mould in which that complex thing which we call Greek civilization was shaped; this we must now attempt to describe.

First, something must be said about what is the foundation of almost all civilizations—the art of writing. As early as the 8th century B.C. the Greeks had an alphabet which was directly derived from the early Phoenician script in use in Canaan and Syria in the 14th century B.C. So they were very early equipped with the most important tool of civilization, the alphabet, which was unknown to the scribes of Mesopotamia and unused by those of Egypt (*see* WRITING, HISTORY OF, Vol. IV). From the Greek alphabet all our Western alphabets are descended.

3. ART. The Dorian invasions in the 12th century B.C. brought to an end the Mycenaean Civilization and started a period which was from the point of view of arts and crafts a Dark Age. In the 8th century B.C. a revival began which led to the full flowering of Greek art, above all in Athens. The pottery of this transition period was decorated with a formal, geometrical type of design. But in the 7th and 6th centuries B.C. we can see how much the Greeks had developed a feeling for form and proportion from the fine Attic vases of that period with their vase paintings illustrating early Greek myths. In the following two centuries—the greatest period of GREEK ART (q.v. Vol. XII)—most of the well-known achievements of the Greeks were created—the Parthenon, for instance, and the work of the great sculptors such as Phidias and Praxiteles. The influence of Greek architecture is still seen in many of our public buildings.

4. POLITICAL THOUGHT. Great as were the achievements of the Greeks in the fields of architecture, sculpture, and painting, their greatest contribution to European civilization lies in the fields of political thought, philosophy, and literature, especially the drama. The Ionians, Achaeans, and Dorians, when they invaded Greece, were organized on a tribal basis. The poems of Homer give a picture of a number of petty states ruled over by a king, who was himself a vassal of a more powerful king. That was the relation of the Achaean chiefs to Agamemnon; they were entitled to sit in council with the king and share in the direction of affairs. In fact the king's control over his more powerful vassals was often far from firm. The Dorians retained their tribal system more unbroken than the rest of the Greeks. In Sparta, for instance, the most purely Dorian part of Greece, all political power was at first in the hands of a small military caste headed by two kings, equal in power. Later, the main power passed into the hands of five annually elected officials, called *ephors*, who managed all the affairs of Sparta except religion (*see* SPARTANS). On the other hand, from Athens sprang the idea of political freedom and that special form of government called democracy; and this is the most important development to consider.

The old Greek story about Midas, the Phrygian king whose touch turned everything into gold, illustrates the actual situation in the beginning of the 7th century B.C. The exploitation of the gold- and silver-mines of Phrygia and Lydia and the invention of a coinage led to the

British Museum

ATTIC VASE

The painting, in black and white, shows Achilles slaying the Amazon, Penthesilea. Late 6th century B.C.

growth of a new class, the merchant princes of Ionia and Greece, who were able by their wealth to seize political power and become what the Greeks called Tyrants. During the period of the Tyrants the tribal structure of society underwent a gradual change. The old aristocracy was based on the possession of land, and only those descended from one of the ancient tribes had the right to call themselves citizens of Athens. But the growth of these new commercial and manufacturing interests, and the consequent immigration into Attica of artisans and other workers, broke down and transformed the old exclusive tribal system. The Attic tribes were increased in number from four to ten, and Attica was divided into *demes* or parishes, each of which was a political unit with an elected chief called a *demarch*. Every male in the deme, except the slaves, had the right to vote as soon as he came of age. At the time of the first reform movement in 593 B.C. a Council of Four Hundred was set up, and this was later increased to five hundred, the members being elected by lot. In addition fifty members from each of the ten tribes acted in rotation, month by month, as a standing committee of the Council. The same method of election by lot was soon used for appointing the highest officers of state, the *archons*, but only holders of property could be elected as archons, so that the poorer classes were excluded. This, in short, was the political machine created by the Athenians, and the way in which it worked was called by Aristotle 'democracy'. It had two important defects: first, it excluded the lower classes from office and was really the outcome of a middle-class revolution; secondly, the working of the machine depended on the existence of a large body of slaves without any political rights at all. But the Athenian system of government, together with Aristotle's penetrating analysis of it, remains a permanent monument to the political genius of Athens (*see also* ARISTOTLE, SOLON, Vol. V).

5. PHILOSOPHY. Next, something must be said about what the Greeks accomplished in the field of philosophy and science. It was natural that the impulse to explore the meaning of the universe should come from the free and restless minds of the Ionian Greeks, and most of the early philosophers of the 7th and 6th centuries B.C. come either from the Ionian settlements in Asia Minor, or from the Greek colonies in Italy. The earliest of these was Thales of Miletus. His

answer to the question 'What is the universe?' was that all things were made of water. A hundred years later Heraclitus of Ephesus declared that fire was the basic element of the universe, and maintained that the particles which compose the universe are in perpetual motion. All these thinkers were occupied with the nature of the physical universe and so have been called the Physicists. In the west the most famous name was that of Pythagoras, who was associated with developments in mathematics and the theory of music. But the most vital figure of Greek philosophy was SOCRATES (q.v. Vol. V). He was born about 470 B.C. in Athens, and was put to death in 399 B.C. on the charge of impiety. Socrates wrote nothing himself, but his portrait has been drawn for us by his disciple, PLATO (q.v. Vol. V), in the *Dialogues*, and by another disciple, XENOPHON (q.v. Vol. V), in the *Memorabilia* and the *Symposium*. It is possible that much of the philosophy in the *Dialogues* which is attributed to Socrates is really Plato's. We know that Socrates was passionately interested, not in what the universe was made of, but in the nature of man—in such questions as 'What is justice?' or 'What is courage?' He tried to make people realize that they used many words without any knowledge of their meaning, and his method of teaching was by asking questions. This method is now known as the Socratic method, and was used by Plato in the *Dialogues* in his attempt to learn about and analyse the nature of reality. From these great Greek philosophers has grown the study of Moral Philosophy and Ethics, and Socrates is the first in a long line of great thinkers.

Plato was succeeded by his pupil ARISTOTLE (q.v. Vol. V), born at Stagira in Thrace in 385 B.C. He was intensely interested in collecting and analysing facts, whether about man and man's activities or about the natural world. A man of unparalleled industry, he brought order into wide

B. Ashmole

THEATRE AT EPIDAURUS
The audience sat on stone seats rising in a semicircle above the central space where the chorus danced and sang. On the right can be seen the ruins of the stage building with the low stage in front of it

areas of knowledge and invented the terminology and systems of classifications that made further advances possible. His contribution to the biological sciences was outstanding, and the study of his terms and logical methods still has an important place in philosophy. Other famous schools of philosophy sprang from the great Athenian thinkers at a time when the Greek cities had lost their effective independence to the successor kingdoms of ALEXANDER THE GREAT (q.v. Vol. V). Among these schools were the Epicurean School (*see* EPICURUS, Vol. V) and the great Stoic School which played an important part in Roman life. The names of Stoic philosophers are ZENO (q.v. Vol. V) and Chrysippus, and its central doctrine was the idea of living according to nature. The great Roman emperor MARCUS AURELIUS (q.v. Vol. V) was a follower of the Stoic philosophy.

6. DRAMA. Lastly, a word must be said about that most splendid and distinctive of all the achievements of Attic genius, the GREEK DRAMA (q.v. Vol. XII). It is through the drama that we get closest to the true spirit of ancient Greece, because the drama grew directly out of the great rituals which expressed Greek religious feeling at its deepest. In the drama we find expressed the triumphant surge of patriotic emotion after the repulse of Persia in the 5th century B.C.; there, too, we find all the stories of ancient GREEK MYTHOLOGY (q.v.) and tradition transmuted into splendid poetry; and in the brilliant and bitter satires of the comedies of Aristophanes we find reflected the passions and prejudices of contemporary political life in Athens, just as a hundred years later Menander mirrors the vagaries of social and domestic life. There were many dramatists in Athens in the heyday of the drama, but the three great names which will always be remembered are those of AESCHYLUS, SOPHOCLES, and EURIPIDES (qq.v. Vol. V).

See also ANCIENT CIVILIZATIONS.
See also Vol. IV: GREEK LANGUAGE.

GREEK HEROES.

GREEK MYTHS (q.v.) are full of stories of the heroic adventures of legendary heroes whose fortunes were often either helped or hindered by the participation of the gods in their affairs. These heroes were themselves sometimes descended from the gods, and came to be worshipped almost as gods.

Perhaps the greatest of the Greek heroes is Heracles (Hercules is the Roman version of his name). He typified the virtues of courage and

ATLAS BRINGING HERACLES THE GOLDEN APPLES

Heracles, helped by Athena, holds up the firmament for Atlas while he fetches the apples. Metope from the temple of Zeus at Olympia. *c.* 460 B.C.

endurance, and he was a symbol for strength. According to the legend, he strangled two serpents when still a child in his cradle. Heracles won immortality by performing the twelve labours set him by Eurystheus, King of Tiryns. These included cleaning within one day the Augean Stables of the accumulated filth of huge herds of cattle. This he achieved by diverting the river Alpheus, so that it flowed through the stables. Another labour was to catch the Erymanthian Boar alive, which he did by driving the boar into a snowfield, where it became so exhausted that he could catch it in a net. Hera, the wife of Zeus, always opposed Heracles, bringing disasters upon him, because he was reputed to be the son of Zeus by another mother.

In many of the legends the Greek heroes are engaged in overcoming some MYTHOLOGICAL MONSTER (q.v.) which is causing harm to mankind. Perseus, another son of Zeus, set out to fetch the head of Medusa, the Gorgon, who had the power of turning to stone all who looked on her. In this enterprise he had the help of the gods. Pluto gave him a helmet which made him invisible, Hermes gave him wings, and Athene provided him with a mirror which prevented his having to look directly at the Gorgon. With these aids he slew Medusa. On his way back he rescued Andromeda from a rock where she had been chained, and married her.

Anderson

JASON DELIVERED FROM THE DRAGON OF COLCHIS

The Golden Fleece can be seen on the tree behind the dragon.
This painting from an Attic Vase of *c.* 475 B.C. illustrates an
unusual version of the myth

Theseus, the Athenian, delivered his country
from the fearful yearly tribute to Crete of seven
youths and seven maidens to be sacrificed to
feed the monster, the Minotaur. Theseus found
his way through the labyrinth in which the
Minotaur lived, slew the monster, and, with the
help of Ariadne, daughter of the king of Crete,
found his way out again. Jason set forth with
some fifty of the chief heroes of Greece, the
Argonauts, in the ship *Argo* to recover the Golden
Fleece from the King of Colchis. To gain the
fleece he had to perform a number of apparently
impossible tasks, all of which he achieved with
the help of the magic arts of Medea, the king's
daughter.

The Greek heroes often behaved in a way
which seems dishonourable and mean according
to our ideas of heroic conduct. Theseus, after
receiving the help of Ariadne, deserted her,
leaving her heart-broken. Jason also deserted
Medea. The behaviour of the Trojan hero,
Aeneas, to Dido, Queen of Carthage, seems to
us heartless and contemptible.

Many of the legends of the Greek heroes
are connected with the war between the Greeks
and the Trojans (q.v.). Agamemnon was the
leader of the Greeks. He sacrificed his own
daughter, Iphigenia, to the goddess Artemis, to
bring good fortune to his fleet; and in the end
he was killed by his own wife, Clytemnestra, in

revenge. He had a great and disastrous quarrel
with Achilles, the hero of the Trojan wars.
Achilles had been plunged as a baby into the
river Styx by his mother and made invulner-
able, except for his heel by which she held him.
He slew the Trojan hero, Hector, and was
himself killed by being shot in the heel by Paris.
He was of a fierce and implacable temper—a
contrast to Hector who was noble in victory and
defeat and was represented as a man of human
affections by HOMER (q.v. Vol. V).

Odysseus (Ulysses in the Roman version) after
the Trojan wars was detained by the goddess
Calypso for seven years, and then started on the
long journey back to Greece and his faithful
wife, Penelope, during which so many misfortunes and adventures befell him.

Homer's epic poems are the source of our
knowledge of many of the Greek heroic legends
(*see* HOMERIC LITERATURE, Vol. XII). Many of
them formed the subjects of the great Greek
dramas. Some of the heroic characters may have
begun with real people, around whose name there
had collected many legendary tales until the
real person was lost in the legend.

See also INDEX, pp. 117-122.

GREEK MYTHS.

Until about a hundred
years ago Greek mythology was the only mythology of which European scholars had any considerable knowledge; and so until quite recently
all theories about mythology have been based
on Greek mythology. We now know a great
deal about other mythologies—Egyptian, Babylonian, Indian, Chinese, and Japanese, as well
as of those of lower cultures; and we find that
in all these the myths are, or were, closely connected with religion (*see* MYTHOLOGY). In
Greece, on the other hand, we find many myths
which seem to have no connexion with religion,
and many others which seem to be at variance
with the religious beliefs of the Greeks.

To take an example, we know that Zeus was
regarded by the Greeks as the king of the gods
and the ruler of the world, and was revered and
worshipped as such. Yet many stories were current which told of his making love to women on
earth, going about disguised as an animal, quarrelling with his wife, and behaving generally
in a manner quite unsuited to his divine character. Probably these stories have grown from
very early religious beliefs of which little is
known. Most of our ideas of Greek religion have

been derived from the more highly civilized Greeks, so that we tend to forget that even in the 5th century B.C. it retained many primitive features. And many of the myths date back to the period much earlier than the 5th century, when writing was first introduced. If writing had not been introduced when the best of the Greeks were still rather barbarous, these earlier elements might well have been lost.

It is probable that the Greeks originally had few myths of their own but borrowed freely from their neighbours, both civilized and savage, sometimes without adopting the religious beliefs with which these myths were associated. Such myths, or those which had lost their religious associations, could be used by philosophers or poets to point a moral or adorn a tale.

Thus, we may find in Greece three types of myths: firstly those connected with Greek religion as it is known to us; secondly, those connected with religious practices such as are found elsewhere but are not certainly known to have existed in Greece; and, thirdly, those which had no connexion with Greek religion.

As an example of the first we have the story of Iphigenia: when the Greek fleet was ready to sail for Troy, the goddess Artemis kept it from sailing by sending contrary winds. The Greeks consulted Calchas the seer, who said that the goddess must be appeased by the sacrifice of Agamemnon's daughter, Iphigenia. The girl was brought and was about to be sacrificed when the goddess snatched her away, and, according to one story, put a bear in her place. This was supposed to have happened at Brauron in Attica, and was obviously connected with the worship of Artemis there. A leading feature of this worship was a dance by girls in the character of bears. We may suppose that at one time it was the custom to sacrifice a girl of high rank, that later a bear was sacrificed instead, until finally they just danced a bear dance, and names familiar from Homer were put instead of those in the original myth.

Ashmolean Museum

THE JUDGEMENT OF PARIS
Attic Vase painting, early 4th century B.C.

An example of the second type of myth is a story in the *Odyssey*. Odysseus, when he wishes to talk to the spirits of the dead, has to dig a trench, kill a sheep, and let its blood run into the trench. The spirits come to drink the blood, and he then talks with them. The Greeks in historic times did not feed their dead with blood: either they must have borrowed this idea from their neighbours or it must have come from an old religious custom of the Greeks of which we have no record.

For the third we will take the judgement of Paris. The story tells how a golden apple, labelled 'for the Fairest', was thrown among the gods and goddesses when they were feasting. Three goddesses claimed it, and Zeus, being unwilling to decide between them told Hermes to take them to Paris, a Trojan prince, and tell him to award the apple. All three goddesses tried to bribe him, and he decided in favour of Aphrodite, who promised him the love of Helen, fairest of women. It is impossible to say how this story arose, but it is difficult to connect it with any religious cult.

This story draws attention to a remarkable feature of Greek religion and mythology, the important part played by goddesses. In historic Greece women played no part whatever in public affairs; yet the Athenians had a goddess, Athene, as protector of their city, and a myth tells how she reached this position by overcoming the god Poseidon. Other goddesses, such as Hera and Artemis, were very prominent both in myth and religion. It would seem either that the Greeks greatly changed their social customs after their religion had been formed and their myths recorded, or that they had taken these over from some other people, perhaps the Cretans, among whom women played a much greater part in public life.

In this, as in many other respects, Greek mythology offers many problems which have not been solved.

See also GREEK CIVILIZATION; GODS OF GREECE AND ROME. See also INDEX, pp. 117–122.

GREEKS. The Greeks today proudly claim that they are the descendants of the Ancient Greeks—people who have had more influence on Western civilization than any other race. How far this is true has been a matter of much dispute, but the modern Greek language is certainly a direct descendant of ancient Greek.

Although towards the end of the 2nd century B.C. the Romans conquered Greece, Greek culture remained supreme. In A.D. 330, when the Emperor Constantine finished building Constantinople (see ISTANBUL, Vol. III), the centre

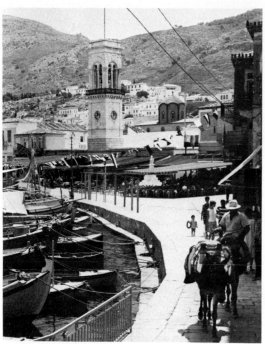

Camera Press

THE HARBOUR OF THE GREEK ISLAND, HYDRA

of the Greek world was gradually transferred from Athens to this new imperial city. During the Middle Ages Crusaders from western Europe tried to set up a feudal system in Greece, and even today their ruined castles may be seen. In 1453 the Ottoman Turks, after a long period of gradual conquest, captured Constantinople and spread over the whole Balkan Peninsula. In Greece, however, the ORTHODOX EASTERN CHURCH (q.v.) kept alive in the minds of the people their faith, language, and national consciousness. The Greek struggle for freedom from the Great Ottoman Empire in the early 19th century, in which the English poet Byron took part, received sympathy and help from all Europe: and in 1829, Greece again became an independent state. At first a Bavarian prince was made king, but in 1863 George I, son of the King of Denmark, became king and founded the dynasty to which the present King Constantine II belongs. In 1940, during the Second World War, the Greeks were attacked by Italy and later by Germany. Their fierce patriotism and love of freedom inspired them to resist in a spirit worthy of their Athenian and Spartan ancestors.

The Greeks today, like the Ancient Greeks, are passionately interested in political discussions. But, unfortunately, they do not find it easy to combine in stable and responsible political parties for the general good of their country, and in the last 100 years there have been periods of damaging political instability. In December 1944 the Communists, who had gained power and influence through the resistance movement against the Germans, attempted to seize the country. This resulted in savage civil wars which ended only in 1949 with the victory of the nationalist forces, who had been supported at first by British and later by American money and supplies. After 18 years of stable parliamentary government and considerable economic progress, the Army seized power in April 1967 because the officers feared the growing power of liberal political groups (which they claimed were Communist-influenced). King Constantine could not accept these changes and fled into exile in December 1967. In 1973 Mr. Papadopoulos, hitherto Regent, declared Greece a republic and himself its President. These changes were later ratified by referendum. Nevertheless, there seems little hope that this military leadership will restore democratic government and free elections.

The Greek people are very able merchants

and traders, and are to be found all over the world working preferably in small family businesses of their own. In their own country, they receive travellers with the most hospitable welcome and lively interest, especially in the more out-of-the-way villages.

In 1973 about half the population still live in the Greek countryside and islands. Although many have left the mountain villages to look for more rewarding work in Greek cities or abroad, the money they send home is often used to rebuild the simple stone houses typical of the countryside. Most villages now have electricity, a road to the outside world, and even television. Improved strains of seed and better stock have improved the peasant farmer's lot. The contrast is very marked with conditions obtaining before 1950—when mule tracks, subsistence farming, and malaria in the plains were normal. But other aspects of country life are less changed. As in Homer's day, the food is simple—a lamb or kid on feast-days, otherwise bread, yoghourt, cheese, honey, olive oil, grapes, olives, figs, and Greek wine which is mixed with resin. The peasant women sit outside and spin their wool from a distaff or weave material on a hand loom. And at festivals in some districts women still wear beautifully-embroidered traditional dresses.

ATHENS (q.v. Vol. III), as well as being the centre of government and higher education, dominates the commercial life of the nation and has the largest concentration of light industry. Greece had little industry before the First World War. But in 1922 after a disastrous war between Greece and Turkey, over a million descendants of Greek colonists in Asia Minor returned to Greece, and set up small factories and workshops, which stimulated the first real growth of small manufacturing industry. Since 1950, with the aid of American and west European capital, a number of very large industrial undertakings have been established outside the Athens area and in northern Greece. These include oil and aluminium refineries, shipyards, and chemical plants.

See also Vol. III: GREECE; INDEX, p. 142.

GRIFFIN. This fabulous creature, usually depicted with an eagle's head and the hind quarters of a lion, is one of the most famous of the various imaginary beasts which combine the nature and characteristics of two or more animals. A number of the four-footed creatures in

Italian State Railways

A GRIFFIN

Sculpture on the Palazzo dei Priorti, Perugia, Italy

ancient sculpture, such as are shown on the bas-relief carvings in Persia, were represented with the wings and beaks of eagles. These beasts represented to people who thought in pictures the idea of several kinds of power united in one being. Like the eagle, the griffin was connected with the sun. They were also said to guard gold-mines and hidden treasures. The griffin became popular as an heraldic emblem and appears on many coats of arms. The bird known as the griffin-vulture is named after the fabulous creature.

See also FABULOUS CREATURES.

GUATEMALA, PEOPLE OF, *see* CENTRAL AMERICANS.

GUIANAS, PEOPLES OF, *see* WEST INDIANS.

GURKHAS, *see* INDIAN HILL TRIBES, Section 3; INDIAN PEOPLES.

GYPSIES. The word Gypsy is a contraction of the word Egyptian which Gypsies were thought at first to be when they entered Western Europe in the 15th century. Nowadays the name Gypsy is applied to a large number of nomadic and sedentary groups of people who often call themselves Rom (meaning men), Romanies, Travellers, Cale (meaning Black), or some other name, rather than the often slightingly used word Gypsy.

The Gypsies are a distinct people with their own language (Romanes), their own customs, and their own laws. Since their language, like modern Hindustani, is a modern variant of ancient Sanscrit, it is believed that they are originally from India, whence they have migrated to all parts of the earth; there are still groups of Gypsies in India today. The first definite record of their entrance into Western Europe is in 1417, but it is certain that they were well established in the Balkans long before that date. They are first heard of in Great Britain at the end of the 15th century when James IV of Scotland added a Scottish Earldom to the Gypsy titles claimed by one John Faa. From then on they are mentioned frequently. Gradually towards the beginning of the 16th century the privileges some of them enjoyed by claiming to be 'kings' or 'queens' of the Gypsies began to wane. In country after country, not least in the England of Henry VIII and Elizabeth I, it was made a capital crime even to be a Gypsy.

Although it is no longer illegal to be a Gypsy, persecution of the Gypsies has not ended. During the Second World War, Eastern European Gypsies were exterminated in German concentration camps; in France they must register as Gypsies with the police when they enter a town; in Czechoslovakia the Gypsy children are not permitted to speak Romanes, even though they come to school speaking no other tongue. In Britain, until the 1968 Caravan Sites act, Gypsies were moved on by local authorities, which made it very difficult for them to earn a living in their traditional ways. Nowadays, primarily because of pressure from the Gypsy Council, their political organization in Britain, local councils are required to provide stopping places for Gypsies in their area, and pubs are no longer allowed to post their 'No Gypsies' signs.

The traditional occupations of Gypsy men in Britain are horse-dealing, peg-making, basket-making, and hawking. Modern occupations include dealing in scrap metal and antiques, tarmacadam, roofing, and seasonal agricultural labour. Women are traditionally fortune-tellers and hawkers, occupations which continue today along with seasonal agricultural labour. Most Gypsies can do more than one trade, and if a traditional trade dies out, they usually can turn to another with relative ease; but they prefer to turn to trades which allow them to travel and to be self-employed. Thus, when they resist entering jobs which require them to stay in one place and

to work under a non-gypsy employer, this gives them the reputation of being unwilling to work, settle down, and become ordinary members of society.

All over the world, Gypsy women are known as fortune-tellers, palm-readers, or predictors of the future, and some are so uncanny in their ability at character reading that many people feel they have some mystical power which others lack. Actually this ability to 'size up' a person is based more on knowledge transmitted from mother to daughter than on any special gift. Fortune-telling among the Gypsies is primarily a method of earning a living rather than reflection of Gypsy beliefs. Nevertheless, Gypsies often call upon their own religious beliefs to aid them in their profession. It is generally the women who have knowledge of religious beliefs and medicinal plants, and this gives them a considerable claim to mystical powers, even among their own people.

There are no Gypsy 'kings' or 'queens', titles which journalists love to pick up from Gypsies. Political authority rests primarily with the elders, both men and women, and the young are expected to obey them and show them respect. Adult men have a great deal of authority over their families, and enjoy considerable freedom from social restraints in comparison with their wives who are expected to lead stricter lives and uphold the morals of the community. Contrary to popular opinion, Gypsy women are very closely supervised by their parents and husbands and are expected to be chaste, clean, and moral. Gypsy women often work, but they are no longer the major bread-winners, for the men are taking over the roles of supporting the family.

Gypsies living in one or another country are often referred to as being of that country. There are French Gypsies, English Romanies, Irish travellers, American Romanies, and so on, but these designations do not refer to specific groups of Gypsies, only to the country they live in at present. Many Gypsies travel from one country to another and consider themselves to be Kalderash, Lowara, Churara, Sinte, Yenishe— to mention but a few of the diverse groups of Gypsies. In Britain, although the Gypsies are more isolated than in Europe or America, there are English Romanies, Welsh Romanies, Scottish and Irish Travellers. Each group of Gypsies speaks the language of the country as well as

J. Allan Cash

A GYPSY FAMILY CAMPING NEAR WEXFORD, IRELAND

their own language, which is usually a dialect of Romanes. In Britain, Anglo-Romany, for example, is spoken by most Gypsies, especially in situations when they wish Gorgios (non-gypsies) not to understand them. Anglo-Romany is so influenced by English that it has been referred to as a creole language and is unintelligible to speakers of inflected Romanes. However, all dialects of Romanes have borrowed vocabulary from other languages, and it is now difficult to designate one dialect as 'purer' than another.

Gypsies often have their own name or nickname used by family and Gypsy friends and another name which they use with non-gypsies. Some traditional Anglo-Romany surnames are: Burton, Cooper, Boswell, Stanley, Smith, Lovell, Wood, Faa, Gray, Young, Lee, and Buckland.

The Gypsies are a very proud and independent people. They prefer to marry only with each other, though they do not always do so, and they, like most people, consider their way of life superior to any other and resist any attempts to assimilate them to the local population. Generosity is considered one of their greatest virtues, but they do not often extend this to non-gypsies. They have strict standards of cleanliness, but these do not always conform to the standards of others, and many things which we consider clean they consider dirty, and vice versa. Thus conflict between Gypsies and non-gypsies is not uncommon, but it is based more on mutual misunderstanding and a divergence of aims in life than on anything else. (*See* Colour Plate opp. p. 192).

H

HARVEST FESTIVALS. Nearly all peoples who grow corn celebrate the end of harvest in some way. In many parts of Europe, particularly Scotland and Germany, it was the custom to attach great importance to the last sheaf. This was cut with special ceremony, carried home in triumph, and often, dressed as a woman, hung up in the room in which the harvest supper was held. Elsewhere it was widely believed that when the last of the corn was cut, its spirit went into some animal such as a cock or a hare. This animal was then killed and eaten as part of the harvest feast.

Among peoples who believe in divine kings or chiefs it is a common practice to offer some of the new crop at their tombs, to thank them for the harvest, and to pray for a good harvest next year.

In many parts of the world it is, or was, the custom to celebrate the feast of the dead at the end of the harvest. A feast of food and liquor is prepared and the spirits of the dead are invited to come and partake of it. Their way is made easy by leaving the windows open (as in France), by clearing the paths (as in Assam and California), or by providing them with miniature boats to travel in (as in Borneo). The houses are lit with lamps or torches. When the spirits are supposed to have eaten and drunk their fill— usually after three days—they are bidden to depart, and the living then fall to feasting.

A survival of some of these customs is found among Christian people. It is still usual to decorate the church for the Harvest Festival with choice specimens of all the crops, which are afterwards often given to the local hospital. In some places a sheaf of corn or miniature cornstack is, or was, placed in the church and left till the following harvest. In America the first harvest reaped by the Pilgrim Fathers in 1621 is still commemorated with a national holiday, Thanksgiving Day, held on the fourth Thursday in November. Turkeys eaten on this day are a reminder of the wild turkeys eaten at the first thanksgiving feast.

See also FESTIVALS.
See also Vol. VI: STRAW DOLLIES.

HEAVEN. This word when used in the plural means the sky where the sun, moon, and stars are to be seen: in the singular it is the name given to the abode of God and His angels, or the state in which He exists. Most peoples have thought of the earth as only part of a much larger scheme in which there are other worlds where the gods and spirits live, and from which come the souls of men (and sometimes of animals and other 'animated' objects) when they are born, and whither they will return after death. The Ancient Egyptians, for instance, believed that the sun, moon, and the sky were gods, and that, since these heavenly bodies were in the sky, all life came from and would eventually return to the sky. At first, however, they thought that only the Pharaoh was immortal and at his death he would return to the home of his father, the Sun-god, while everybody else continued to live on in a nondescript sort of way under the earth. But when Osiris, who ruled over the underworld, was raised to the sky, then it became possible for all whom Osiris declared to be 'true of heart and voice' (i.e. properly qualified) also to enjoy immortal life in the heavens. The necessary qualifications for heaven were mainly of a magical nature, though they did include good behaviour on earth (*see* EGYPTIAN MYTHS). In the neighbouring civilization in Mesopotamia, on the other hand, no one went to the sky. Good and bad, rich and poor, spent the next life without any distinction in a dreary underworld (*see* BABYLONIAN MYTHS).

The first gods of the Greeks, we are told by Plato, were the heavenly bodies, and their chief, Zeus, was the sky-god. They lived in great splendour where Mount Olympus towers up through the clouds into the mysterious heavens. In fact, in Greece there were some twenty or more mountains called Olympus, and probably they were regarded as all pointing to the heavenly home of the gods, who lived there like fighting chiefs, playing music, eating, drinking, and marrying, and conquering and deceiving one another in a very ungodlike manner (*see*

Alinari

PARNASSUS
A Renaissance artist's conception of the classical heaven. Painting by Raphael (1483–1520) in the Vatican, Rome

GODS OF GREECE AND ROME). But human beings did not go to Olympus after death. On the contrary, they were said to pass to a dismal underground region (Hades), rule by Pluto and his wife Persephone. There, all the souls of the dead, good and bad alike, mingled together as shades. Later, however, Hades was divided into two compartments. Good people all went to Elysium where they lived in great comfort, enjoying plenty of everything desirable, with no rain or violent storms but only cool refreshing showers from the west. The other division was Tartarus, the place of the wicked (*see* HELL). The Greek poets developed a great variety of ideas about the character of the next life. Some pictured Elysium as a highly delightful abode, either below ground, in mid-air, or in the centre of the earth, or as Isles of the Blest in the western sea, reached only by a few highly favoured individuals. Homer, on the other hand, painted a sombre picture of the state of departed souls—for instance, Achilles, though in Elysium, is made to envy the life of the poorest man on earth (*see* GREEK MYTHS).

About the 6th century B.C. a belief arose in Greece that ordinary people, as well as heroes, could go to heaven, if they were helped by elaborate rites—purifications, stately processions, hilarious dances, and solemn dramatic performances held in very strictly guarded secrecy. Those who passed through these stirring experiences felt that they had entered into communion with the god of the mysteries and so gained an assurance of a happy life beyond the grave as well as peace and security on earth. They had, as it were, died to live again—not really, but in a kind of make-believe or ceremonial manner.

In Scandinavia it was thought that those who fell in battle, instead of descending to the underworld, went to a special 'hall of the slain', or Valhalla, where they were honourably received by their god, Odin. At first the abode of Odin may have been in the hills, like that of Zeus in Greece, because the souls of dead warriors were often supposed to return from the mountains. But in the mythological poems of Iceland, called the *Edda*, Valhalla is represented as being in

DANTE'S VISION OF PARADISE

In the Divine Comedy Dante visits Hell and Purgatory, and then Paradise, where Beatrice, whom he loved on earth and who is now an angel, guides him. The drawing shows Beatrice and Dante talking with SS. Peter, James, and John whose souls, like those of the other blessed, are flames of light encircling the godhead. Drawing by Botticelli (1444-1510)

the sky, and brave warriors are said to have been taken there by the Valkyries—the divine maidens who were sent by Odin through the air during a battle to collect the slain. When they arrived there, they were entertained by Odin and served with wine by the Valkyries in the great hall which was decked with shields and coats of mail. From it they went out every day, through one of its 540 doors, to engage in combats with each other, and at night returned to feast, drink mead, and amuse themselves (*see* NORSE MYTHS).

Besides Valhalla we are also told in Teutonic mythology of a heroes' paradise on a glass mountain. Below the mountain there were beautiful meadows reached through a well, where the souls of the dead fluttered about like birds or butterflies, surrounded with elves. The ruler of the 'glittering plains' was Gudmund, a divinity who had banished from his country all weakness, old age, and death; only those, however, who had performed deeds of daring were allowed to enter it. Ordinary mortals presumably lived

under much less ideal conditions in and around their tombs. In fact, Heaven—in the sky, in one of the planets, on a mountain or a magic island —was nearly always a privileged abode reserved for rulers, warriors, or semi-divine heroes. Entrance to Heaven was generally accompanied by special funeral rites, such as cremation, so that the soul might get to the sky in the smoke of its own body: sometimes the corpse was sent to the Isles of the Blest in a canoe or boat attended by slaves (*see* DEATH CEREMONIES).

The ancient Hebrews, like the Babylonians, do not seem to have adopted these beliefs and practices so common in other civilizations. The word 'Heaven', in fact, is seldom mentioned in the Old Testament except as the place where God lives. The dead were thought to go to a dreary underworld called Sheol (translated into Greek as Hades), where kings and commoners dwelt in darkness, huddled together, eating the dust and cut off from their God. Only one or two heroes like Enoch and Elijah were translated to the sky and 'went up by a whirlwind into heaven' (Gen. v. 24, 2 Kings ii. 11), which was situated in the upper firmament, or roof of the world, supported by the mountains as pillars. But heaven was shut against ordinary mortals, who only brought disaster upon themselves when they tried to reach it by building a tower to the sky (Gen. xi. 4 ff.).

After their exile in Babylonia, however, when the Israelite people returned to Palestine and re-established themselves in and around Jerusalem, the Jews were no longer content to regard the grave as the end of all their hopes. Jehovah had restored them to their own land, and surely He would not forsake them in death. And so they came to believe that 'God will redeem my soul from the power of Sheol', 'for He shall receive me', as the Psalmist continually declared. They began to look forward to that great day when the Messiah should come, and the dead would be raised up to share in His just rule on a restored earth (Isa. xxvi. 19, Dan. xii. 2), (See JUDAISM.)

Although there is no mention in the Old Testament or in the early Christian writings of Paradise as a beautiful garden with wonderful trees and orchards like Eden, this is the picture that is drawn of the home of the righteous in some of the Jewish books. Sometimes it was said to be the final abode, sometimes only a temporary place where they stayed while they were waiting to pass to the many mansions in the sky after the Day of Judgement. In the New Testament Paradise is only mentioned three times, and in none of these is anything said about what it was like and what happened there. Heaven was the abode of God where the angels beheld the face of their heavenly Father (Matt. xviii. 10, Luke xxiv. 51), and whither Jesus Himself expected to return. There the angels rejoiced when a sinner repented, and there would be the scene of the final reward of the faithful on earth (Matt. v. 12, Luke vi. 13). St. Paul described it as 'a house not made with hands, eternal in the heavens', and regarded it as the final home of the righteous (2 Cor. v. 1 f.).

In these Christian Scriptures Heaven is thought of, not as the scene of endless banquets and amusements as in the ancient religion, nor as a place where everything is exactly as we should like it to be on earth. It is where God is, and there is joy, peace, goodness, beauty, and truth in all their fullness. The Kingdom of God, as understood and taught by Christ, could only be realized when and where human beings do the will of God and obey His commandments, whether it be on earth or anywhere else (see CHRISTIANITY).

The Heaven to which Muslims look forward is described rather simply and vividly in the Koran, the SACRED BOOK OF ISLAM (qq.v.), as a place of abundant pleasures for the senses. 'The pious shall be in gardens and pleasure, enjoying what their Lord has given them.' Heaven is a place where the pious shall have 'fruits such as they deem the best, and flesh of fowl as they desire'. A soul's claim to Heaven depends upon the will of Allah and the results of the great judgement day.

See also RELIGION; GOD.

HEBREW CIVILIZATION. The history of the people whom we call the Hebrews is mainly known to us from their own literature which is contained in the Old Testament (see BIBLE). In this important collection of ancient documents we have the HEBREW MYTHS (q.v.), sagas, laws, religious poetry, histories of the kings, and other materials, from which a picture can be drawn of the gradual growth of the political and religious life of this strange people who have exercised an influence upon the history of the world out of all proportion to their political importance. Indeed, their main contribution to human history was made after they had ceased to be of any political importance whatsoever. Besides the information gained from these Hebrew documents, we can learn a great deal which supplements and corrects what the Hebrews say of themselves, from records of Assyrian kings, from Egyptian inscriptions, and from correspondence between the rulers of various states of the Near East.

The Hebrews formed part of a series of migrations from Mesopotamia, which ultimately peopled the greater portion of the Near East with a large group of nations closely related in speech and custom. This group is called the Semitic group or family of nations. Its common bond is language, and it includes Hebrews, CANAANITES, SYRIANS, BABYLONIANS, ASSYRIANS, PHOENICIANS, ARABS (qq.v.), and a number of smaller peoples such as Moabites, Edomites, and Ammonites. All these peoples spoke languages which were very much alike. When, for example, David took refuge from Saul in the country of Moab, he found himself among a

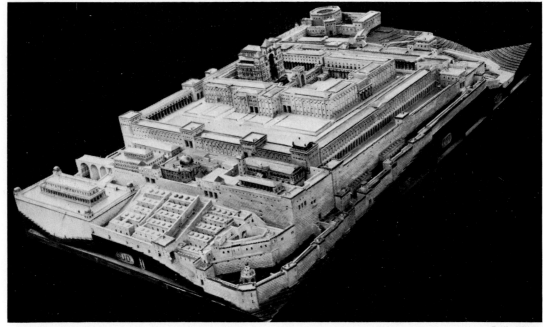

Berlin Museum

RECONSTRUCTION OF SOLOMON'S TEMPLE

people who spoke practically the same language as himself.

The Hebrews began to settle in Canaan about 1750 B.C. They did not enter the land as a united nation and at one definite period, but in different tribal groups, from different directions, and at different times. According to their own tradition, the earliest group, under the leadership of Abraham, came in from Mesopotamia and finally settled in the south of Canaan round about Hebron. Other groups of tribes continued to come in at intervals from the east and the south, and the settlement was probably complete about 1200 B.C. But the various tribal groups remained separate and independent, often fighting with one another, much as the Bedouin tribes of Arabia have done for many centuries. About 1000 B.C., however, the threat of Philistine conquest forced them to unite under an elected king, and they began to develop a national consciousness. Under Saul, DAVID, and SOLOMON (qq.v. Vol. V), the Hebrews became a state with some kind of political organization, ruled by a despotic monarchy, like the rest of the small kingdoms of Syria and Palestine. The united monarchy only lasted for about 100 years, and after the death of Solomon a split took place which divided the Hebrews into two unequal and independent kingdoms, the larger in the north being known as the kingdom of Israel, and the smaller kingdom in the south, named after its most important tribe, the kingdom of Judah. The northern kingdom came to an end in 721 B.C., when the Assyrian king Sargon took Samaria and carried away most of the northern Israelites to Mesopotamia, replacing them by settlers from other parts of the ASSYRIAN Empire (q.v.). The southern kingdom of Judah continued to exist for another 150 years, until Nebuchadnezzar II of Babylon took Jerusalem in 586 B.C. and carried away a large part of the population of Judah to Babylon. In 539 B.C. the Persian king, Cyrus, took Babylon and allowed the various deported peoples to return to their own countries. A small number of the exiles from Judah, henceforth known as JEWS (q.v.), returned to Judah. They rebuilt the Temple in Jerusalem, restored the ruined city, and, for the next 500 years, continued to exist, with a certain amount of self-government, as subjects of Persia, Greece, and Rome successively. Their political existence came to an end in A.D. 70, when, after a siege whose heroism and horror stirred the imagination of the ancient world, Jerusalem fell before the armies of the Roman, Titus. Since then the Jews have been a scattered people, maintaining their religion and distinctive way of life among nearly all the nations of the world.

Although this article is called 'Hebrew Civilization', there is in fact no such thing as a distinctively Hebrew civilization. It is possible that the kind of life lived by any BEDOUIN tribe (q.v.) today may give us some idea of how the Hebrews lived before they left their original home in Mesopotamia. But the earliest group of Hebrews to enter Canaan had already lived in Mesopotamia for at least one generation, in contact with the urban and agricultural civilization of that country. Hence it is misleading to think of the Hebrews as being still a simple nomad people when they entered Canaan. When a country has been invaded and conquered by a foreign people, archaeologists can often find evidence to show whether the invaders were of a higher or lower culture than the people they have conquered. For example, the excavation of such a site as Colchester shows a clear break between the levels of Roman and British civilization. So in Palestine excavations have shown that while a distinct decline in standards of culture can be detected in many cities, there was no absolute break in town life when the Hebrew invasion occurred.

Some of the earliest Hebrew legislation is found in what has been called 'The Book of the Cove-

nant', in Exodus xx–xxiii. Here we have a picture of the way of life of a settled agricultural people: there are laws relating to straying cattle, to the damage of corn-fields by fire or a neighbour's cattle, to damage done by a vicious bull; the three great festivals of the year are agricultural festivals; there is nothing to suggest a nomad way of life. Further, by comparing the early Hebrew laws with the far earlier Babylonian Code of Hammurabi, it is easy to see that the Hebrew law and custom was largely based upon early Mesopotamian law.

Again, excavation has shown that when the invading Hebrews occupied a Canaanite city, such as Beth-shan, they took over the temples which they found there, and adapted them to their own use. In the early 1940s there were found in the excavation of Samaria some pieces of carved ivory, known as the 'Samaria Ivories', which may have formed part of the decoration of furniture belonging to the time of King Ahab, and which were probably the work of Phoenician craftsmen. These have mythological scenes, religious symbols, and decorative designs strongly influenced by Egyptian art. King Solomon's temple is described as decorated with some of the same designs. These examples of borrowings in Hebrew law and craftsmen's designs go to suggest that Hebrew civilization was almost wholly derived from Babylon, Egypt, or Canaan.

British Museum

JEHU DOING OBEISANCE BEFORE SHALMANESER III (859–824 B.C.)
Part of an Assyrian relief showing the conquered Hebrews paying tribute

From representations on Assyrian and Egyptian monuments we can see that Hebrew dress and arrangement of the hair is the same as that of other inhabitants of Palestine or Syria. The patterns and material of Hebrew pottery are Canaanite. When King Solomon wanted an architect and master-craftsman for the building of his temple he had to send to Phoenicia to get one, and the general plan of domestic and public architecture was based on foreign models. The Hebrews even practised human sacrifice like their Canaanite neighbours. When Jeroboam, at the time of the split into two kingdoms, set up new sanctuaries for his northern kingdom, the Hebrew god was represented by bull-images, as was the common practice in agricultural religions in the Near East.

If, then, the civilization of the Hebrews was so lacking in originality and so indistinguishable from that of their neighbours, what was it that in the end made them so distinct from all the other small peoples of Canaan, and caused them to have such a profound and enduring influence upon the history of the world? The answer is not to be found in the material aspects of their civilization, but in the fact that one element, a non-material element, of their civilization developed in a way which has no parallel elsewhere. The class of sacred persons variously known as 'seers' or 'diviners', whose function it was to interpret omens and dreams and to perform certain important ritual ceremonies, was by no means peculiar to the Hebrews (*see* PRO-PHECY). But only among the Hebrews did it produce a succession of great religious figures whose utterances and writings have been preserved in the collection of Hebrew literature, and whom we know of as 'the Prophets'. As the result of a religious experience which is vividly described in their writings, these men arrived at a conception of God, and of the relation between man and God, which gradually transformed the old nature-religion, with its conception of a storm-god or a fertility-god who might be represented under the form of a bull-image, into a religion whose vital centre was the belief in one God who was a spiritual being, who could not be represented by any man-made image. Under their influence a code of conduct was developed with, as its standard, the character of the God whom their religious experience had revealed to them. History bears witness that, during the closing centuries of their existence as a nation,

there was a widespread recognition in the ancient world of the unique character of what the Jews called their *Torah*, that is their Law, especially their moral code; and in the century before and after Christ many Gentiles were attracted to the Jewish worship (*see* JUDAISM). But this process was suddenly interrupted by an event which, strangely enough, was the crowning achievement of what we may call Hebrew civilization—the birth of Christianity. Christianity in its beginnings was wholly Jewish; its central figure was a Jew, its earliest adherents were Jews, its conception of the Kingdom of God and of the Messiah were Jewish, and its moral standards were Jewish. Whatever opinions may be held about the truth of Christianity, it cannot be denied that it has played a very profound part in the growth of Western civilization, and in this fact lies the final judgement on the contribution of Hebrew civilization to the world.

See also ANCIENT CIVILIZATIONS; JUDAISM; CHRISTIANITY; Vol. IV: HEBREW LANGUAGE.

HEBREW MYTHS. Myth is a word which has, so to speak, come down in the world. Today, if we say that a statement is a myth, we mean that it is false and unworthy to be believed by intelligent people. Hence many people are unwilling to admit that there are myths in the Bible. But in the early stages of human history, myths were not only regarded as true, but they were an essential part of religion.

Long before the appearance of the Hebrews on the stage of history, the Sumerians and Egyptians on the banks of the Euphrates and Nile had learned the arts of agriculture and how to live together in cities. They had learned how to control their environment and make it serve their needs. In doing this they had found that they were surrounded by forces whose nature they did not understand. They did not know why the buried seed sprang up to new life, nor whether the miracle would be repeated the next year; what made the life-giving flood of the Nile come with such marvellous regularity, nor what caused the destructive and incalculable floods of the Tigris and Euphrates. So in an attempt to control these unknown forces surrounding them, the dwellers in Egypt and Mesopotamia had developed a system of RITUAL (q.v.), that is, a set of actions performed in a fixed way, at regular times, by authorized persons (priests). The ritual consisted of a

Alinari

THE CREATION OF MAN

Painting by Michelangelo (1475–1564) on the ceiling of the Sistine Chapel in the Vatican, Rome

dramatic representation of the acts which they believed had brought their civilization into being, in other words, the drama of creation. As the priests performed the drama, they chanted or sang the story of what they were acting, and this was the 'myth' or spoken part of the ritual. At the most important point of the great Babylonian New Year Festival the priests chanted a myth, known as the Epic of Creation, which told how the god Marduk had died and risen again, how he had conquered the chaos-dragon, Tiamat, and how he had separated the heavens from the earth, created the heavenly bodies, and finally made man out of clay and the blood of a god. All this was repeated every year in the spring, because they believed that the ritual, and the myth which was part of it, were necessary in order to keep creation going. In the earliest form of the creation-myth, which goes back to the SUMERIANS (q.v.), the creation is connected with the story of a great flood from which one man was saved in a specially constructed boat, built by the orders of a god, so that the 'seed of life' should be preserved. There are other early BABYLONIAN MYTHS (q.v.), all having some connexion with ritual. These myths with their ritual spread to those neighbouring countries which came under the influence of Babylonian civilization, and especially to Canaan and the Hebrews.

When the first Hebrew settlers came into Canaan they had already, according to their own tradition, lived for some time in Mesopotamia and come under the influence of BABYLONIAN CIVILIZATION (q.v.). In Canaan they found the same type of religion and civilization in altered forms. The Hebrew traditions of their origins were collected by the editors of the Old Testament in the 5th century B.C. and woven into the story which we have now in the first eleven chapters of the book of Genesis. This contains the creation-story, the stories of the garden of Eden, the Fall, Cain and Abel, the Flood, and the Tower of Babel. There are other fragments of myth scattered about the Old Testament, such as the myth of the slaying of the dragon in Ps. lxxiv. 12–14 and Isa. li. 9, and another form of the Paradise-myth in Ezek. xxviii. 11–19. It is clear that there is a close connexion between the stories in Gen. i–ii and the Sumerian and Babylonian myths of Creation and the Flood: for instance, the Hebrew word for the chaos of waters in Gen. i, 2 is *tehom*, and this corresponds to the Babylonian name of the chaos-dragon Tiamat. In the Babylonian myth the character corresponding to Noah sends out birds to find out how far the waters of the flood have gone down, just as Noah does in the Hebrew story; and there are many other striking parallels and resemblances. Hence it seems certain that the Hebrews drew their myths from the common stock of myths which formed a part of the religious ritual of the ancient Near East. Also, whereas we can see the Babylonian and Egyptian myths in their original setting as an essential part of the ritual to which they were attached, the Hebrew stories have been separated from the ritual and completely transformed by the influence of the religious ideas of later writers who gave the Old Testament its present form. In the minds of these writers the myths of Creation, Paradise, the Fall, and the Flood came to be thought of as history—the history of the Hebrew people, intended to teach them that everything that had happened from the beginning was a part of the plan of God for His people. By the 5th century B.C., when most of the books included in the Old Testament were taking their present form, the religious ritual of the Hebrews, as well as their idea of what God was like, had greatly changed, and so these stories became entirely separated from the ancient ritual to which they had originally belonged. But the sacred character of the stories was not lost. The story of the slaying of the dragon disappeared save as a picturesque image to be found in the poetry, but the other stories were retained and added to, so that they should convey religious and moral teaching; and these are the stories to be found in the familiar narrative of Genesis.

See also HEBREW CIVILIZATION; MYTHOLOGY.

HELL. The word comes from the name of the Scandinavian goddess of death, Hel, Queen of the Lower Regions.

In English the word Hell is usually used to mean either the place of torment of the wicked after death, or, as in the Apostles' Creed, the place of departed spirits, like the Greek Hades or the Hebrew Sheol. In the more primitive beliefs, however, the idea of rewards and punishments after death is not inspired by any ethical or religious consideration. The next life, it is thought, will be either better or worse than that on earth, but only in a material sense. That is to say, there will be more opportunities for exciting fighting, good hunting, excellent harvests, and perfect weather, or there will be none of these things, and life will be just a dreary, shadowy, ghost-like existence, as the Greeks and Hebrews pictured it (*see* HEAVEN). In neither case is the lot of the dead fixed by right or wrong conduct in the moral sense in which we understand these terms. It is all pre-arranged according to a general plan, every soul going to its appointed place either below ground, in the sky country, in the western paradise where the Sun sets, or to the Isles of the Blest. Virtues like bravery and conspicuous service to the community, or vices such as blasphemy and breaking the rules of society, often play an important part in the ultimate fate of the soul; but, generally speaking, it is not until people begin to understand the idea of a holy and righteous God, that right and wrong in the higher meaning of good and evil are made the test. The more primitive ideas are by no means confined to savages—we find them in all the great ancient civilizations, and many have survived in most countries to this day, even where higher beliefs prevail.

In Greece the abode that corresponds to hell was called Tartarus and was represented as a deep, sunless, underground region where those who rebelled against the gods were confined behind closed gates and afflicted by a variety of punishments. Sisyphus, for instance, was condemned to roll an immense stone up to the top of a hill. Whenever it reached the summit, it rolled down to the bottom, and so he had to begin his wearisome task all over again. Another

From W. Reizler, *Weissgrundige attische Lekythen*

HERMES LEADING A SOUL TO THE STYX

The Greeks believed that dead people were rowed over the River Styx by Charon on their journey from earth to Hades. From an Attic vase, *c.* 450 B.C., in the National Museum, Athens

THE LAST JUDGEMENT

The Souls are weighed in the balance by the archangel Michael. The saved climb the ladder of Heaven, while the damned
are cast down to everlasting torment. 12th-century painting in Chaldon Church, Surrey

notorious 'sinner', Tantalus, a son of Zeus who
had betrayed the secrets of the gods, had to
stand parched with thirst in a lake, the water
of which receded every time he tried to drink.
Over his head grew clusters of fruit, but always
just out of his reach. Another victim was Tityus
who was preyed on by vultures. In one branch
of Greek beliefs Tartarus was the name of the
place where those who had not been purified of
their sins on earth endured torments before they
were reborn into this world.

In Indian mythology those who did not perform the proper rites or disobeyed the commands
of the priests were hurled into a prison of great
darkness and sat among streams of blood chewing hair. According to the beliefs of HINDUISM
(q.v.) there are between twenty and thirty hells
which are reached after a terrible journey.
On arrival at one of these the wicked man is
plunged into a heated cauldron, or a lake of
blood or of stinking mud; or he may be driven
through a dense jungle full of plants with leaves
as sharp as knives; or he may have to walk over
a plain paved with iron spikes. After these tor-

tures have been endured for a time, the soul is
reborn in another body and given a chance to
do better and to reach heaven at last. To this
end some Hindus put their whole trust in a
divine saviour such as Vishnu, Krishna, or Shiva,
but others think that the process of reincarnation
(i.e. rebirth in a series of bodies) works according
to fixed laws based on the principle that what
a man sows in this life he reaps in the next.

In the Scriptures of BUDDHISM (q.v.) eight
hells are described. These are situated below
the earth, and there murderers, liars, persecu-
tors, infidels, and those who have killed their
parents or a religious teacher or certain animals
undergo grim punishments. Attached to each
great hell are sixteen lesser hells, some of which
are very hot, others intensely cold. As among
the Hindus, the punishments are thought to
come to an end when the soul has been purified,
though it may take several thousand years before
release is secured. And that is not the end:
peace at the last can only be secured when all
traces of earthly contacts and activities (*karma*)
have been removed through a series of lives.

In Persia ZOROASTRIANISM (q.v.) abandoned the idea of reincarnation in a series of different bodies. Those whose deeds were named as evil, when their actions had been weighed in the balances, were led away to the 'house of the Druj', where they were condemned to live in endless darkness surrounded with demons and wicked souls, and to eat loathsome and poisonous food until the resurrection. Then, after three days of further punishment in a restored body, there would come a great flood of molten metal which would purify even hell itself. So that, at the last, God (Ahura Mazdah) would reign supreme everywhere, and the Devil and all his works would be destroyed.

The Jews, who borrowed a great many of their later religious ideas from the Persians, when they gave up thinking of Sheol as the place where all the dead went (Heaven), gradually changed that gloomy underworld into a sort of 'waiting-room' for either the good Israelites before the final resurrection, or for both the righteous and the wicked. It was also sometimes called 'the pit' and was sometimes a prison-house with barred gates where evil kings and bad angels were sent for punishment. But when it came to be thought of as a place of torment, it came to mean the same as Gehenna, the name given to the Jewish hell. This place derived its name from the valley of Hinnom on the south-west of Jerusalem, where all the refuse of the city was burnt, and children were offered in sacrifice to the god Moloch (Jer. vii. 32, xxxii. 35). Such a spot would readily suggest the unhappy lot of those who because of their sins were cut off from God and were condemned to live in a fiery abyss where 'their worm dieth not and the fire is not quenched'.

This is the meaning attached to it in the New Testament, where Jesus Himself is said to have used the name Gehenna in this sense. But although He spoke of the wicked being consumed in everlasting fire, He was careful to explain that it was the *spiritual* consequences of wrongdoing that were experienced on the other side of the grave. Every man has before him the choice of two ways, the one leading to life in the Kingdom of God, the other to destruction in Gehenna. In the end, however, all evil, it was said, would be conquered and the devil and his angels would be consumed (Matt. xxv. 41; Rev. xx. 13 ff., xxi. 8). But even when the heavens and the new earth have been created, and the wicked have been cast into the lake of fire, there will still be evil-doers who will have to dwell outside the city of God (Rev. xxii. 15).

Islam borrowed most of these Jewish and Christian ideas. According to its teaching, when Jesus descends from heaven, the Anti-Christ will be destroyed, but unbelievers and demons will remain in hell for ever, tormented by huge serpents, fire, and boiling water. When their bodies have been burned up new ones will be created to suffer more torment. No one, however, will be eternally damned who believes in the prophet Muhammad; and as some think that in the end everybody will become Muslims, it should follow that eventually all will be saved. But the Koran teaches that those who go either to Paradise or to Hell will dwell for ever in whatever abode they reach.

If these beliefs seem today to be rather crude and materialistic, it has to be remembered that they are attempts to put into words and pictures, as in the parables in the Gospels, truths about the awful reality and far-reaching consequences of evil in a world which, nevertheless, has been created and is controlled by a good God who is just as well as loving. The evil as well as the good that men do lives after them, and if the one carries with it consequences in the eternal world, so must the other.

See also RELIGION; SATAN.

HELLENES. A term used by the Greeks to describe, not a Greek nation or state, but all Greek-speaking peoples, as opposed to non-Greek-speaking peoples whom they called 'barbarians'. The Greeks liked to think they were descended from a common ancestor called Hellen.

See also GREEK CIVILIZATION.

HINDUISM. This means the religion of Hind or India. Yet it is not by any means the only religion of this vast country. In 1961 there were 366 million Hindus in the Republic of India, 47 million Muslims, and far smaller numbers of Christians, SIKHS, JAINS, and PARSEES (qq.v.).

Although as a system of belief Hinduism is extremely tolerant, and will make room for almost any sort of religious idea or practice, it is also extremely national, especially of recent years, and does not normally make converts of foreigners. As we shall see, it has quite a distinct

VISHNU RECLINING ON THE SERPENT ANANTA, THE SYMBOL OF ETERNITY, WITH OTHER GODS WATCHING ABOVE
Sculptured panel

Museum of Fine Arts, Boston
THE HINDU GOD SHIVA, THE DESTROYER
Copper figure from South India

way of thinking about life, but when it seeks to spread this attitude outside India, it ceases to be Hinduism, and becomes something else, as, for example, BUDDHISM (q.v.), a religion which first grew up in the mind of a Hindu. Hinduism is indeed rather a form of civilization than a religion, as we understand the term in the West. To be a Hindu you must properly be a member of some CASTE (q.v.), and it is expected that Hindus will not live outside India except as visitors—strict Hindus of high caste will seldom cross the ocean. If some non-Hindu group of people in India or near its frontiers seeks to be included in Hinduism, it is said that this is only possible by the formation of an additional caste. Hinduism is not a state-controlled religion, and in this respect India is very different from China or Japan.

A Hindu accepts five main general ideas as the framework of his spiritual life.

(1) The Hindu's idea of the highest way of living is that of the holy ascetic (*see* ASCETICISM),

the hermit who is a vegetarian and lives a solitary life. Although it is recognized that during his life a man may become in turn a student, a householder, and the father of a family, sooner or later he is expected to pass on into the final stage of the hermit. There are many different sorts of 'holy' persons besides the *purohit*, or priest, who is in charge of a temple or shrine. There is the *guru*, who is a spiritual teacher and adviser, and who has one or more disciples. Then there is the *sādhu*, or wandering ascetic, who may be also a teacher; and the *bhagat*, or emotional devotee, who believes that he can achieve salvation by single-minded devotion to his god. Although their occupations may vary, they have in common the possession of a mental and bodily technique for putting and keeping themselves in a state of consciousness which not only claims to unite the soul with God, but also makes for calmness and good health. This technique is known as *yoga*, a word meaning much the same as our word 'yoke', and coming from the same root. Hindus do not believe in an essential difference between human souls and the divine soul. They believe that the sense of difference is the result of *maya*, or illusion, and all their philosophies and religious practices are aimed at destroying this illusion so that the individual can realize his unity with the divine.

(2) The Hindu does not believe, as most Europeans do, in the importance of historical events or historical accuracy. He does not much care whether a story is true, so long as it contains an inward and spiritual meaning. The reason for this is that he does not usually believe that God acts with a purpose in history, nor does he believe that a single human life could express any important purpose. Hence he is not interested in such things as the record of important events, or the biographies of great men, or keeping a National Portrait Gallery. He believes life to be due to the surplus and abundant energy of the Supreme Being, rather than to any plan on His part.

(3) At the same time Hinduism seems to allow beliefs or disbeliefs of almost any kind, so long as the framework of caste is preserved. Thus there are Hindus who are virtually atheists, others who are believers in many gods, and yet others who put their faith in a single god—one not entirely unlike the God of Christians, who comes from time to time and lives in human (or animal) form on earth. Almost all Hindus think

that there are a number of divine beings, gods and goddesses, such as Vishnu, Shiva, Kali, and so on, who are different aspects of the Supreme Being, known as Brahma, Himself beyond description, since He embraces and constitutes *everything that is*. Some Hindus might be called idolaters; others will have nothing to do with idols, though they generally acknowledge that the use of images is helpful to many people. Some are meditative philosophers; others sing emotional hymns. Some perform animal sacrifices; others believe in *ahimsā*, or harmlessness, which is a reverence for life so intense that it makes them even strain the liquids they drink to avoid killing any small organisms that may be floating in them. There is, in fact, among Hindus a toleration of opposites, and they seem able to accept contradictory ideas at one and the same time.

(4) Hindus usually believe that living things have a succession of lives, past and future—reincarnation. This claim of births and rebirths, called *samsara*, or 'migration', is governed by a law or principle called *karma*, or 'action'. Thus the result of virtuous deeds is to be re-born in a higher state, while the result of vicious action is to be re-born in some unpleasant state, as a worm, a moth, or a pig. It must not be supposed that Hindus like this idea of reincarnation. Far from it. The most earnest of them seek, and have ever sought, to escape from its dreary round into a condition of peace and of freedom from the passions which vex and disturb humanity, and to be swallowed up in the life of God. Yet even this does not satisfy all of them. One sage remarked, 'I like the taste of sugar, but I should not like to become sugar.' There are also Hindus who believe in a future life not unlike that expected by Christians, in which the soul will enjoy the presence of God and the fellowship of other human beings, without entirely losing its own self.

(5) Lastly, Hinduism teaches that, whatever Being lies behind and above this physical world, that Being is not concerned with morality—with questions of right and wrong, good and evil, and so on. A Hindu would not be likely to have written the Ten Commandments.

It is rather hard to describe what it is like to be a Hindu, in view of the great variety of beliefs and practices which Hindus acknowledge; but in the main there are two broad types.

The first type does not believe in any personal

Paul Popper

A *SĀDHU*, OR WANDERING ASCETIC, AND TWO BRAHMINS OUTSIDE A HINDU MONASTERY

God, whether one or many. 'We philosophers are above it', they would say. For simple people it may be useful to make acts of worship or devotion to such a Being, but for those who claim to have climbed from the lower to the higher knowledge this idea seems childish and even foolish. There is really one Existence and one only, and the soul is identical with it. About this Existence you can really say nothing, since it is beyond definition, and you yourself are part of it. Hindus call this idea of everything being part of a Single Substance *Advaita*, which means 'only one thing really exists, i.e. God, and we are all part of God'.

The second type of believer generally tries to live in a gracious personal relationship with one single deity, generally Vishnu or Shiva, though there are admitted to be many others. This means saying prayers, singing hymns, and offering sacrifices to one or other of these gods. The worshipper uses images and symbols freely, and often makes quite simple gifts such as rice or marigold flowers, or a kid or calf. Vishnu is a kindly god who protects and restores, but Shiva represents the ruthless force of tropical nature. Neither has the clear-cut personality of Jesus Christ or Muhammad. The cults associated with these divinities are called *marga*, or ways, and each cult has its own philosophy and its own social and ethical code. Followers of Shiva carry on the forehead, breast, and arms three parallel lines called the tripundram Ξ. Followers of Vishnu carry on the forehead a sort of V-shaped sign, ⍰.

Hindus, especially in southern India, have built a great number of large and richly carved temples, which are thought of as the earthly palaces of the gods, whose images are treated as though they were actually princes or nobles, having to be waked, washed, fed, amused, taken for drives, and presented with petitions. Besides the temples there are many outdoor shrines, some of them connected with lesser deities concerned with special human needs. Thus there is a goddess of small-pox. On one festival in the year, the *Ayudha puja*, everybody worships and makes offerings to the tools of his trade or profession. Thus a student may sacrifice to his books, his pen, or desk, or to the goddess of learning, and a mill-hand in Bombay may offer a kid to the machine which he minds. When it is remembered that Hindus believe that everything is part of God, it is easier to understand the reason for this practice, also found in other old religions. In the Old Testament (Habakkuk i. 15 and 16) there is an account of some people who sacrificed and burned incense to their fishing-net.

Hinduism changes as Indian society changes, and it has never been without its reform movements, some of which have introduced elements from Christianity and from Islam. As the caste system crumbles, the modern city dweller is more likely to pay attention to the teachings of his *guru*, or of his sect, than to the older beliefs associated with caste.

See also INDIAN PEOPLES.

HITTITES. The importance of the Hittites in the ancient history of the Near East has only come to light in the 20th century. They used to be thought of as one of the unimportant peoples driven out by the Hebrews when they conquered Canaan. But in 1888 there was discovered in Egypt the correspondence of the Pharaohs of the 14th century B.C. with various Asiatic powers. This correspondence, known as the Tell el-Amarna Letters, revealed that the Hittites at that period were a first-rate military

Mansell

HITTITE CHARIOTEERS AND BATTLE VICTIM
Bas-relief found in the Hittite city of Carchemish, 9th–8th century B.C.

power, standing on an equal footing with Egypt and Assyria. At the beginning of the century archaeologists excavated a site in northern Asia Minor called Boghaz-Koi, which proved to be the ancient capital of the Hittite kingdom. More than 10,000 tablets were found there, most of them written in a language not before known to scholars. After years of patient labour it was found that this language belonged to the INDO-EUROPEAN family of languages (q.v. Vol. IV), and had remarkable resemblances to Latin. The translation of these texts threw new light on the history, laws, and religion of the Hittites.

The Hittites appear to have used two different forms of writing, one a cuneiform script, rather like that used by the Babylonians, and the other a picture-writing or hieroglyphic script, like the writing of the Egyptians (*see* WRITING, HISTORY OF, Vol. IV). Why they should have used two such different forms of writing is not yet fully explained.

There are three distinct stages in the history

of the Hittites. First, before 2000 B.C., there were peoples called Luvians and Proto-Hittites, living in west and north-east Asia Minor. Then between 2000 and 1900 B.C., invaders came from the north-east and conquered the Proto-Hittites, made Boghaz-Koi their capital, and ruled Asia Minor and northern Syria until about 1200 B.C. It is their records which were discovered at Boghaz-Koi, and to them belongs the greatest period of Hittite supremacy. They had adopted at an earlier period a modified form of the Babylonian cuneiform writing, which became their official script, but they probably learnt the hieroglyphic script from the people they had conquered. Lastly, about 1200 B.C., they were themselves conquered probably by the Phrygians. It is to the period after this conquest that most of the hieroglyphic inscriptions belong.

The people whom the Egyptians and Assyrians knew as Hittites, and whose civilization is here described, were the second of these groups—those who dwelt in Asia Minor and north Syria between about 2000 and 1200 B.C.

At first the power of the king of the Hittites was limited by the existence of a council of nobles—a kind of feudal system rather like that which existed among one of the early groups of Greeks. But after a period of struggle between the king and the nobles, a struggle which is described in an early Hittite text, the kingship became more after the pattern of the kings in the ancient Near East. In the early period the bare title 'king' was always used, but after about 1600 B.C. the king was addressed by the title 'my Sun'. This shows that the position of the king was becoming much more elevated and powerful. The early feudal system also disappeared; instead, the king governed by means of local officials whom he could dismiss at will—a system also to be found in Egypt at much the same period. An interesting feature of Hittite civilization was the important place held by the queen, a position independent of the king and with a special religious significance. This is to be connected with the fact that a goddess, the Sun-goddess, and not a god, held the chief place among the Hittite deities—a state of things also to be found in Cretan religion, where the Mother Goddess was the centre of the worship (see MINOAN CIVILIZATION).

At the end of the 14th century B.C. the Hittite Empire was organized into a kind of federal state made up of a number of small conquered states. These had some part in the government, but the central Hittite kingdom had always the decisive voice. From the valuable documents found at Boghaz-Koi we have been able to learn a great deal about the foreign treaties of the time and we can see the beginnings of what might be called international law. Among these documents was a Hittite code of criminal and civil law. Compared with the codes of other Near East peoples, such as the Assyrians or Babylonians, the Hittite code was much more humane: it was quite without the more brutal forms of punishment used by their neighbours, and the death penalty was limited to certain capital offences and could only be inflicted on a freeman by sentence of the king's court.

Our knowledge of the religion of the Hittites has been gained partly from carvings and inscriptions found in certain ancient Hittite holy places, and partly from the many religious documents found at Boghaz-Koi. The names of the many Hittite gods and goddesses mostly came from the older Proto-Hittite period. A famous rock-carving called Yazili-kaya shows a gathering of the gods and goddesses of the Hittite Empire in two converging processions led by

A HITTITE GOD IN FULL ARMOUR

A HITTITE KING PRESENTING HIS SON TO THE GODS

Behind him are his younger children and the Queen. Sculptured relief from the King's Gate at Carchemish, *c.* 800 B.C.

the great weather-god Teshup and his consort Hepat. Various sacred animals appear in the group, such as the panther or lioness on which the Sun-goddess stands and the bull on which Teshup stands. The rock-carving is a good example of early Hittite sculpture, as are also the two stone lions guarding the gate of Boghaz-Koi. Among the contents of the religious documents relating to everyday affairs there are spells for protecting a person or a house against evil spirits, and rituals for the cure of diseases and promoting fertility.

Among the most interesting of Hittite literary remains are the historical documents. The Hittites had an entirely different idea of writing history from that of other ancient peoples. The records, for instance, of ten years of the reign of the Hittite king, Mursilis II, can be called real history, and illustrate the kind of royal chronicle of which we have later examples preserved in the Hebrew Books of Kings.

Hittite art is seen at its best in the stone carvings in deep relief, and in statues of gods supported on lions or sphinxes. They show the influence of Egypt and Mesopotamia in the choice of designs and mythological subjects; but the treatment shows a rough vigour which is peculiarly Hittite. Further excavation will no doubt throw fresh light on the civilization of this remarkable and important ancient people.

See also ANCIENT CIVILIZATIONS.

HOLY ROMAN EMPIRE. Europe in the Middle Ages was not divided into nations as it is now, but was split up into countless small provinces ruled by dukes, princes, and kings. Yet there was a sense of unity which knit Europe together. The members of each state were also members of Christendom and believed in the brotherhood of all Christians and in the authority of the Pope as head of the Church. The Pope's authority was real and binding, covering not only spiritual matters but some temporal ones as well.

The idea existed that there should be a temporal power corresponding to the spiritual authority of the Church, to which all the feudal lords would owe allegiance. The Roman Empire had been such a unifying power, and men still looked back on the greatness of the Roman Empire under which Christianity had developed. In A.D. 800 CHARLEMAGNE (q.v. Vol. V), who sought to revive the culture of ancient Rome and to unify the peoples he had conquered, was crowned Emperor of the Romans by the Pope in Rome. He was a great and powerful leader and had conquered most of what is now western Germany, Austria, France, Belgium, and Holland. But after his death there was no leader, until the German Otto 200 years later, with vision or power enough to give reality to an idea so unfamiliar to many of the peoples of Europe. Otto and the more powerful among his successors gave new importance to the Holy Roman Empire and its crown, but there were intervals in which the Empire was no more than an empty name. Nevertheless, although it was impossible to give real meaning to the Empire, the ideal of a single temporal power ruling Christendom as a counterpart to the spiritual rule of the Church persisted throughout the Middle Ages.

Unfortunately the theory of equal spiritual and temporal heads of Christendom—Popes and Emperors—co-operating for the good of all Christian people broke down in practice in the 11th century. Popes and Emperors quarrelled bitterly and even fought each other for supremacy. By the end of the 13th century they had ruined each other, and both institutions collapsed. The Emperors never recovered their strength, but during the Counter-Reformation of the 16th century the Popes made the Papacy the strong and influential institution that it still is today.

At the end of the 13th century Rudolph of Hapsburg, the ruler of Austria, became so strong that he was elected Emperor. From that time until its dissolution in 1806 the title was usually held by the Hapsburg family. In theory the title was not hereditary, the Emperors being chosen from among the rulers of German states by seven Electors—the Archbishops of Mainz, Cologne, and Trier, the King of Bohemia, the Duke of Saxony, the Margrave of Brandenburg, and the Count Palatine of the Rhine. But in practice the heads of the Hapsburg family were elected Holy Roman Emperors because they were the most powerful German princes.

The Emperors ruled with a Diet or parliament to which the member states belonged, but they only acknowledged its authority when it suited their convenience. As it depended on the various states for its army, it had little real power. Rather, the states used the Diet to further their own ends, and the electors often sold their votes to the highest bidder.

In the 17th century many states were developing into powerful nations over which the Emperor had no control, and the Empire lost entirely its original significance. By the 19th century it held authority only over the Hapsburg territories of the Austrian Empire, and in 1806 the title was finally abolished.

HOMO SAPIENS, *see* FOSSIL MAN.

HONDURAS, PEOPLES OF, *see* CENTRAL AMERICANS.

HOROSCOPE, *see* ASTROLOGY.

HOTTENTOTS. This was the name given by the Dutch to certain groups of natives whom they found in Cape Colony in the 17th century. These people speak mainly in words of one syllable, most of which, as in the Bushman language, begin with a click, which makes their speech sound jerky and staccato. The Hottentots once occupied the greater part of Cape Colony and, although many have been driven out, a number of tribes still survive in South-West Africa. Not only in language but in appearance the Hottentots are somewhat like the BUSHMEN (q.v.). They have slightly narrower faces, are taller in stature, and have a more yellowish skin, but they have the same 'peppercorn hair', growing in little tight spiral tufts. The main difference between them is that, while the Bushmen were always hunters and collectors in the mountains and gorges, the Hottentots occupied the plains and kept cattle and sheep —and this influenced their way of life, their food, their clothes, their huts, and their fate. For while the frontiersmen relentlessly shot down the hunting Bushmen, like any other animals that attacked their cattle, they encouraged the Hottentots who were useful to them as herders, and therefore more of them survived. Their clothing originally consisted of garments of skin, the men wearing a loin-cloth, the women aprons, while a kaross, or sheepskin cloak, kept them warm in winter. Nowadays most Hottentots wear European garments. Their social organization is also more complex than that of the Bushmen. They are divided into a number of groups or clans—the head of the senior clan being chief of the group. Marriage is marked by the exchange of cattle between the families of the couple, and a special feast is held. There are also elaborate ceremonies for BIRTH, INITIATION, and MARRIAGE (q.v.), though some of the original initiation ceremonies for boys, which were concerned with hunting, are no longer held. The Hottentots still rely mainly for their living on their cattle, sheep, and goats, and these are dependent on pastures and water. But they cannot always find pasture, and water is often scarcer than grass. So the group cannot long remain in one place but must be always ready

Mansell Collection

HOTTENTOT WOMEN AND CHILDREN PLAYING A GAME

diameter. These are then bent over and tied at the top to make a skeleton framework which is strengthened by intertwining rods and sticks, as in making a basket. Then they thread reeds into mats by means of bark string, and tie these mats on to the cross-sticks of the hut to make an excellent covering. If it rains the reeds swell and make a waterproof roof; in hot sunshine they shrink and let in the air. In cold weather a lining of skins makes the inside warm and snug. The main entrance is away from the direction of the wind and is covered by a mat which will roll up or let down. A hollow in the centre of the floor is the fire-place, and round this are the mats or skins on which the family sleep. When they move on, they merely have to untie and roll up the mats, pull up the poles, tie them up with ox-hide thongs, and pack the bundles on the backs of the oxen, who plod off with them to the next camping-ground. The whole encampment is surrounded by a fence of thorn bushes.

The material culture of the Hottentots is more sophisticated than that of the Bushmen, and they know how to smelt iron. They make vessels of wood and bags of skin for water containers.

Music and dancing—religious and non-religious, or a mixture of both in pantomime—play a large part in their lives. They have a musical bow, and they also form orchestras of reed pipes which are conducted by a bandmaster.

Their religion has been very much influenced by missionaries, and little is known of their original beliefs. But they worshipped the moon as well as certain mythological heroes, some of whom were especially prayed to for rain.

See also AFRICANS; SOUTHERN AFRICANS.

to move, wandering from pasture to pasture and from water-hole to water-hole. Milk is their chief food, which they drink sour and store in skin bags. They do not kill their animals for food except on special occasions such as feasts, births, or marriages. They obtain some meat by hunting and snaring wild game, by fishing, or by catching lizards and mice. Vegetable food is obtained from wild plants, roots, fruits, and grasses. In recent times, with the restrictions on hunting, these wandering groups are obliged to supplement their food-supply by growing crops such as wheat, maize, millet, and beans, and in consequence they are beginning to lead a more settled life.

The Hottentots' huts are exactly suited to their wandering way of life—made of materials ready to hand, easy to set up, take down, and transport, yet strong enough to resist a storm. A number of light poles—twenty to sixty, according to the size of the hut required—are collected and planted in a circle some 3-5 yards in

HUGUENOTS were French Protestants who followed the reforming movement of CALVINISM (q.v.) in the 16th and 17th centuries. In the latter half of the 16th century there were no fewer than eight minor civil wars (known as the French Wars of Religion) between the Huguenots and the Catholics, and a terrible massacre of Huguenots took place in Paris on the eve of St. Bartholomew in 1572. However, this strife was ended in 1598 when, by the Edict of Nantes, King Henry of Navarre gave full liberty to the Huguenots to worship as they pleased. Nearly a hundred years later, in 1685, the edict was revoked by Louis XIV, and Huguenots for a time were forbidden to worship in public places. As a result many thousands fled abroad and took refuge in England and other countries, which benefited from the Huguenots' skill in craftsmanship and trade.

HUNGARIANS. A review of the distracted history of the Hungarians is necessary for any understanding of this proud, romantic, passionate people. The origin of the Hungarians, or rather the Magyars as they call themselves, is not known for certain. Their language is akin to that of the Finns, the Estonians, and the Lapps, and it is therefore probable that the Magyars came from north-east Europe, though many scholars believe that all these northern peoples came originally from the Ural mountains (*see* Finnish and Allied Languages, Vol. IV).

When they raided central Europe and finally settled in Hungary in 896, the Magyars were nomadic horsemen, very different in origin and language from their Slav neighbours. For a hundred years the land they held depended on their success in battle, until at last in 997

Hungarian Embassy
THE FOLK ART OF HUNGARY
Decorating the cultural centre of the Kalocsa district

Stephen I, a great statesman and soldier and the most famous figure in Hungarian history, became their king. He established his authority over the warlike tribes, welded them into a nation, completed their conversion to Christianity, and invited settlers from the west to teach them the arts of peace. Thus Hungary became a member of the European family of nations, and under King Matthias in the 15th century was noted as a centre of Renaissance learning.

In 1526 the Turks conquered most of Hungary, settling in the rich central plains, and remaining there as masters for about 150 years. The western part of the country accepted monarchs from the Hapsburg family, who also ruled in Austria and Bohemia. At the end of the 17th century the Turks were driven out, and the whole of Hungary came under their dominion. This brought much friction, since the Magyars always resented any attempt to rule them from the Hapsburg capital of Vienna, especially as it meant a threat to their language and institutions. In 1848 they rebelled under the leadership of Kossuth, but were defeated. In 1867, however, after a campaign of passive resistance, they regained full self-government. The peaceful half-century which followed saw a new prosperity and cultural advance. Then came the First World War, in which Austria-Hungary fought on the side of Germany. After its defeat the boundaries of Central Europe were completely redrawn. Hungary became independent, but lost two-thirds of her territory. During the Second World War she again allied with Germany, largely in the vain hope of recovering this land, but at the end of it Russian troops overran the country amid scenes of terrible destruction.

In 1949 the Soviet Government helped local Communists to establish a revolutionary regime. Its rule was cruel, harsh, and arbitrary. Discontent erupted in 1956, when a popular uprising was only crushed by the Soviet Army. Consequently 200,000 Hungarians fled abroad. Since then, Hungary has remained an obedient satellite of Russia, but the life of her people has gradually become easier, and some of the scars of her history are healing.

The Hungarians are a musical people, and the greatest contribution they have made to European life has been through their music. Hungarian folk-tunes and Hungarian dances such as the Czardas have influenced Haydn, Beethoven, Schubert, and Brahms. Liszt and

Bartók (q.v. Vol. V) were famous Hungarian composers.

In the past there was a great contrast in Hungary between the lives of the nobles and of the peasants. The nobles used to own most of the land, and on all state occasions wore their magnificent historic costumes of velvet and brocade with the 'slung jacket' and the jewelled sword. Now their great estates have been broken up, and class distinctions are obliterated. Although there are many kinds of industry in modern Hungary, half the population still works on the land. Stock-rearers and horse-breeders, who have lived for generations on the Great Hungarian Plain, are practically a community of their own. They lead very simple, isolated lives, except when they round up their horses, cattle, or sheep, and drive them to the big stock-fairs. Until recent days they wore a special most picturesque costume—wide-skirted trousers, leather aprons, and felt hats with broad brims. They are spectacular horsemen, and are very skilled with the lasso, which they use to catch and bring in animals from the herds on the plains. Old methods of stock-breeding are being replaced by modern ones, however, and the picturesque cowboy is disappearing.

Gypsy encampments are a common feature of Hungary. The gypsies have great musical gifts, so that, in spite of their vagabond, thieving ways of life, they are welcome with their violins and guitars at village festivals and at cafés in Budapest, and their wild music and dancing form part of every festivity (*see* GYPSIES). Budapest (Buda on the west bank of the Danube and Pest on the east) is one of the most spectacular capitals in Europe. Despite its stormy history, it has a tradition of gaiety, and its inhabitants pride themselves on their friendliness towards visitors. On hot summer evenings many of the population still sit out or stroll beside the wide river, while the lights sparkle on the water and the old castle of Buda on the far side glows like a stage set.

See also Vol. III: HUNGARY; BUDAPEST.
See also INDEX, p. 143.

HUNS. These were a nomad people once scattered widely in Asia in the steppe country, north of the Caspian Sea. They were probably akin to the Mongols and the Turks, and were short in stature with black hair, yellow skins, broad noses, and small, deep-set eyes. In the 4th century A.D. they began to move westward across the Danube into Europe, spreading panic before them. They rode small, swift, tireless horses and made surprise attacks with such ferocity that no one could withstand them. Their wild, ferocious appearance, and the cruelty with which they enslaved or exterminated the peoples they overran filled Europe with terror.

They later settled north of the Danube in the lands which are now Austria and Hungary, and dominated the peoples for a wide area around them. In the 5th century, under their ruthless leader ATTILA (q.v. Vol. V), they reached the height of their power, their dominions stretching from the river Rhine to the Urals and the Caucasus. Attila attacked the territories of the Roman Empire, and for a time it looked as though he would overrun all Europe; but in A.D. 451 he was defeated by a combination of the Romans, Goths, and Franks in a very bloody battle on the plain of Châlons, south-east of Paris. The next year, however, Attila struck south and advanced on Rome, destroying everything on the way. Rome was not sacked, partly because Attila's armies were stricken with pestilence, and partly because the Pope, Leo I, went out to make a personal appeal to him and bought him off with large sums of money.

Soon after Attila's death in A.D. 453 the Hunnish Empire destroyed itself by internal quarrels and fell to pieces. The main body of the Huns moved back to the Urals, where they remained as a nuisance to the Byzantine Empire for some seventy years.

The present Hungarians have no connexion with the Huns, in spite of their name: they are the Magyar people who came into Europe at a later date, after the Huns had disappeared. The word 'Hun' as applied to Germans has no reference to their racial descent.

I

IBERIANS, *see* SPANIARDS.

ICELANDERS, *see* Vol. III: ICELAND.

INCA CIVILIZATION. When the Spaniards conquered Peru in 1533, they found a vast Inca empire extending from Ecuador in the north to about the middle of Chile in the south, a distance of over 3,200 km. It also included a considerable part of the highlands of Bolivia and Argentina, but to the eastward it stopped short at the tropical forests of the Amazon basin. These Incas (so-called after their king, the 'Inca') were a highland folk, having their capital at Cuzco, 3,360 metres above sea-level. Their empire followed roughly the lines of the Andes mountain range, but included the narrow strip of lowland on the Pacific coast.

The Incas were originally an unimportant small tribe, of whom the first traces are found in Cuzco about the 12th century A.D. In 1438, when the ruling Inca was old, they narrowly escaped utter defeat by the neighbouring Chanca, but one of the Inca's sons, Pachacuti, assumed command and won a resounding victory. By contrast with the short campaigns usual in Andean warfare, the Incas embarked on a sustained series of conquests. They started in their native highlands, went on to subdue the great Chimú state on the coast, and then conquered and organized the rest of their Empire, all in about 90 years. We know much more about the Incas than about earlier peoples, since we have the help of Spanish writers who described what they saw.

The Inca state was very highly organized, and dominated by one supreme ruler, the Inca, and the members of his royal clan. The Inca himself was worshipped as the divine representative of the Sun, and lived in magnificent state.

The ordinary people lived a simple, industrious life; they were provided with the necessities of life, but had very little liberty and owned no property. All their work was regulated and controlled by state officials, and a fixed amount of all that they produced was allotted to the Inca and to the Sun for the maintenance of the priesthood and the temples. Writing was not known, and no form of money was in use; yet accurate accounts were kept by means of elaborately knotted and coloured strings called *quipus*. Even to this day Indian shepherds in the Andes use knotted strings to keep a tally of their flocks.

The Incas showed great skill in the construction without machinery of roads, aqueducts, and reservoirs, suspension bridges, and other public works. Two main roads ran from north to south, one through the mountains and the other along the coast. In some places they were paved or raised on causeways, in others hewn out of the solid rock: their excellence excited the admiration of the Spanish conquerors of South America. The Incas also showed great ingenuity in the vast system of terraces which they built with much labour along the steep slopes of the valleys for the cultivation of their crops, and which are still in use. For solidity of construction the walls of their fortresses and temples equal anything ever achieved elsewhere. With extraordinary skill they handled huge blocks of hard stone, such as granite, weighing many tons,

Bennet Greig

WALLS AT MACHU PICCHU, NEAR CUZCO IN THE ANDES

The blocks of stone are accurately cut and fitted together without the use of mortar

British Museum

WATER BOTTLES
They were carried on the back by means of a cord passing
through the handles and round the forehead

cutting them into irregular shapes with many angles, and then fitting them accurately together like the pieces of a jig-saw puzzle. These walls are practically indestructible, and have resisted the shocks of earthquakes for centuries. Many of them still form the foundations of Spanish buildings in Cuzco today. The Incas knew the art of casting bronze, but the chisels which they made from this alloy were not hard enough to cut the tough rock used in some of their buildings, and these must have been shaped with stone tools. The roofing, which has long perished, was constructed of timber and thatch, for the principles of the arch and the vault were unknown.

The Incas had little interest in stone sculpture, although miniature alpacas, used in fertility ceremonies, and decorated stone bowls show that they were competent carvers. Their pottery was well made in a limited number of standard shapes. Of these the most characteristic are a liquid container, the aryballus (*see* picture), and a plate with a solid bird-head handle on the rim, balanced by a vestigial tail, both of which are found, sometimes made in local wares in slightly modified forms, wherever the Empire reached. Decoration is mostly geometrical, in black, white, and red, but a very typical design (*see* picture) represents a stylized plant, and many vessels are powdered with miniature life forms such as butterflies. Like all Peruvian peoples, they were skilled weavers, although few highland examples have been preserved. Cloth was very important to them, and the finest sorts, particularly tapestries, were reserved for the Inca himself.

If we try to assess the position of the Incas in the scale of civilization, we notice that they had failed to make a number of important discoveries known to the Old World, such as writing, money, wheeled transport, and the smelting of iron. They also retained some cruel and barbarous practices, including occasional human sacrifice. On the other hand, their skill and refinement in many of the arts and crafts, as well as their remarkable social organization and engineering achievements, were such as to arouse our admiration. Among the useful contributions which they have made to humanity one might specially mention the potato, and the coca plant from which cocaine is obtained.

The conquest of the Inca Empire in 1533 by less than 200 Spaniards led by PIZARRO (q.v. Vol. V) was an astonishing feat of arms. The Spaniards captured and put to death the Inca himself; and the people, who had believed their ruler to be divine, lost heart and gave up resistance. And so Peru became a Spanish colony. But although the old civilization was destroyed, the Indians, speaking their own languages, survive as the chief element of the population, and in spite of European influence

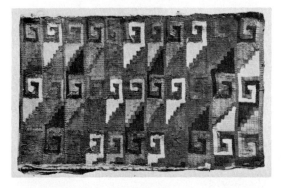

TAPESTRY STRIP WOVEN IN FOUR COLOURS, COAST STYLE

British Museum

COLOURED CLOTH, INCA STYLE

Bennet Greig

RUINS OF THE FORTRESS TOWN AT MACHU PICCHU, NEAR CUZCO IN THE ANDES
Note the stone terracing on the precipitous mountain slopes

retain many native beliefs and customs, especially in the remoter highland regions. Women can still be seen spinning by hand on the way to market, and men cultivating the ground with the old type of digging-stick; dehydrated potato (chuño) is still prepared in the ancient way; the llama carries its load along the rough mountain paths. But the glory of ancient Peru has departed never to return (*see also* AMERICAN INDIANS, CENTRAL AND SOUTH).

The motives of the Spanish conquerors were

various. Love of adventure and fame, and the desire to convert the Indians to Christianity played their part. But one of the main incentives was certainly the quest for gold. *El Dorado*, which means 'The gilded one', was originally the name given to a Colombian chief, who covered his body with gold dust at his installation ceremony. But later, in the 18th century, the name was used for various imaginary places in the far interior of South America which were believed to contain fabulous riches, and many ill-fated expeditions have set out in the hope of discovering 'the Inca gold'.

See also ANCIENT CIVILIZATIONS; PERU, ANCIENT.
See also Vol. IV: AMERICAN-INDIAN LANGUAGES.

INDIAN CIVILIZATIONS. 1. INDUS. The existence of the earliest known pre-Aryan civilization of the Indian sub-continent was only brought to light between 1920 and 1930, when excavations at the site of Mohenjo-Daro in Sind and Harappa in the Punjab (both in what is now Pakistan) revealed cities going back to a date between 3000 and 2500 B.C. Like the ancient civilizations of Mesopotamia and Egypt, these very early peoples developed their civilizations in river valleys, especially in the valley of the INDUS (q.v. Vol. III); but recent excavations have also revealed a series of cities further east and south in the Indian sub-continent. They may have been at some time connected with SUMERIANS (q.v.): indeed some of the finds in their cities show resemblances to the finds at Ur.

The ruins excavated show that these ancient cities had wide streets, with an elaborate drainage system and substantial buildings of burnt brick. Houses were of more than one storey, and had flat roofs, and baths and latrines on the upper as well as on the ground floor. Kitchens had serving-hatches; drains were built into the thickness of the wall and led into covered sewers running down the centre of the streets. The houses had narrow, steep stairs of brick to the upper floors, and nothing in the plan of them suggests that women were secluded, as later was sometimes the case in this part of the world. Large pottery jars were used, as they still are in that region, for storage, and it appears that wooden chests, beds, and seats were also used, since fragments of carved legs and bone or shell fasteners have survived. Houses had their own wells, and there were public as well as private baths. Indeed, frequent bathing seems to have been an important feature of the life of the ancient inhabitants.

For tools and weapons, copper and bronze were used—copper for fish-hooks and copper-headed arrows, bronze for razors and for mirrors. Flint blades were, however, commonly used for knives. Pottery was made on the wheel, and some of it, particularly candlesticks, has a most modern appearance. The painting on it is generally in black pigment on a polished red surface, designs being predominantly geometric but sometimes more naturalistic with animal figures. They kept domestic animals—dogs, sheep, goats, fowls, and cattle which were used to draw vehicles. They used the plough and grew wheat and barley as well as lentils and oilseeds. They were renowned for their beautiful stone beads and seals. Women wore short, scanty petticoats,

RUINS AT MOHENJO-DARO OF AN ANCIENT PRE-ARYAN CITY, THE BUILDING IN THE CENTRE WAS A BATH
From *Mohenjo-daro and the Indus Civilization*, edited by Sir John Marshall

and men a cloth worn over the left shoulder and under the right arm. Their clothes were made of cotton and possibly also of other materials, such as linen or wool. They had ornaments made of gold, electrum, silver, copper, bronze, shell, and semi-precious stones, such as jade, cornelian, and lapis-lazuli.

The religion of these early people seems to have been a fertility cult—that is, its main purpose was to encourage increase, especially of crops. Certain animals, such as the bull, the goat, the snake, and the crocodile, were held sacred, and perhaps also the fig-tree or *pipal*, which Hindus still hold sacred. They worshipped a god rather like the god Shiva of modern Hinduism, and a mother goddess. It is also probable that their ritual required regular and plentiful bathing.

This civilization seems to have come to an end somewhere about 1500 B.C., after a phase of decline. At some time during this period the Indus state must have been invaded by strangers from the Persian plateau; there is clear evidence of a massacre at Mohenjo-Daro. These invaders may have been impelled by pressure of the main Aryan advance behind them. They were probably not of the same physical type as the Aryans who invaded the Punjab about 1500 B.C.

2. ARYAN. This term really refers to language only, not to race. The Aryan invaders who came about 1500 B.C. are most important as they brought with them a branch of the Indo-European languages, which has since profoundly affected all the languages with which it has come into contact, and which has formed the basis of most of those spoken in India today, except in the south. In race these Aryan invaders were probably an offshoot of the peoples who, besides migrating north-westwards and populating northern Europe, invaded Mesopotamia and Asia Minor to the south-west and gave rise to such peoples as the Philistines and the Dorian invaders of Greece (*see* ARYAN).

It was their possession of the horse and the bronze and, later, iron sword which ensured the Aryans their conquests; but the bow also was an important weapon, being used probably from a chariot. Their mode of life was primarily pastoral, great value being set upon herds of cattle. They also kept sheep, pigs, and dogs. Agriculture by means of the plough was also practised, possibly with irrigation. They made garments from skins and from sheep's wool. They sacrificed cattle, sheep, and goats to the gods and also slaughtered them for feasts. Milk and grain were important foods, and intoxicating drink was brewed from grain. Chariot-racing, gambling, dancing, and music were popular as recreations.

The religion of these Aryans was a form of NATURE WORSHIP (q.v.) in which the great natural phenomena, such as the sky, earth, dawn, the sun, fire, and thunder, were thought of as deities in human form, and worshipped as such. There were minor deities such as water-nymphs, the titans who opposed the gods, and demons who were evil and destructive. There were a great many popular stories, songs, and poems about these gods and godlings. The gods were worshipped in the hymns now collected together and known as the *Rig-Veda*, in the latest book of which there is a tendency to change over from simple nature worship to the kind of philosophy found in later Indian religions (*see* SACRED BOOKS, 2). In the later HINDUISM (q.v.) Rig-Vedic features were supplanted, and even the god Indra was reduced to a mere door-keeper in the house of the god Shiva, one of the chief gods of Hinduism.

The Aryan society was divided into four classes: the nobles, who were the rulers and leaders in war, the priests, the common people, and the serf or slave class. These social divisions became greatly modified, largely no doubt as a result of mixture with the earlier inhabitants and absorption of their ideas. From this developed the CASTE system (q.v.), which became a characteristic feature of Hindu society. Of their history for 10 centuries nothing certain is known. Traditions survive of wars, leagues, battles, and a grand all-India fight that lasted 18 days. During these centuries the priesthood became more powerful, and the Brahmins, originally kings' servants, became king-makers, and laid the foundation of their supremacy, social political, and intellectual, which has dominated Hinduism until recently. Between 1000 B.C. and 750 B.C. the restless Aryan tribes in the north of India settled down and developed into static kingdoms. Around this time new cities begin to appear, surrounded by great brick ramparts and wide moats, and these cities often remained as regional capitals well into the historic period. This was a time of great intellectual development.

PILLAR SET UP BY THE EMPEROR ASOKA (273–232 B.C.) AT
LAURIYA-MANDANGARH

It is nearly 10 m high, and made of polished sandstone

With the dawn of history in the 6th century
B.C. this priestly power was challenged in the
east by the rise of BUDDHISM (q.v.) and the rise,
or more probably the resurgence, of JAINISM
(q.v.), the founder of Buddhism and the champion of Jainism both being of noble lineage. In
the west, 'India' (which at that time meant no
more than the Indus valley) became a province
of Persia and continued so for nearly two centuries. Then a Greek army under ALEXANDER
THE GREAT (q.v. Vol. V), having overthrown
the Persian Empire, marched into India to
claim it as their own (327–325 B.C.). Alexander
advanced across the Punjab until his troops
refused to go farther, and he had to withdraw.

3. BUDDHIST AND HINDU INDIA. Within a few
years of Alexander's death an Empire known
as the Mauryan arose which drove the Greeks
from the Indus valley, and brought most of the
Indian sub-continent under one rule. This Empire lasted at its height for about ninety years,
under three great rulers, the best known of

whom is ASOKA (q.v. Vol. V). Its founder,
Chandragupta, managed his enormous Empire
with autocratic power, but his organization was
highly efficient. He built up a strong army consisting of four parts: elephants, chariots, cavalry,
and infantry. He built a magnificent royal city
which stretched nine miles along the Son river
to a depth of two miles. It was defended by a
massive timber palisade, strengthened by 570
towers and surrounded by a deep moat, filled
from the river. There were sixty-four great gates.
The royal palace was also built mainly of timber,
with gilded pillars and fine stone sculptures. The
king himself appeared in public carried in a
golden palanquin or mounted on an elephant
with gorgeous trappings. He wore fine muslin
embroidered with purple and gold.

Asoka must have been as efficient and strong
a ruler as his predecessors, since he held together his great Empire. But he is known to us
for his preaching of peace and gentleness, courtesy to the aged, the poor, the servant, and the
slave. Horrified by the suffering caused by the
major war of his reign, he accepted Buddhism and
devoted the rest of his life to spreading its doctrines. He set up inscribed and carved pillars
in places associated with events in Buddha's life,
and along the pilgrim roads which led to them.
He carved sermons on rocks, and sent missionaries to countries beyond his Empire, to the
independent Tamil kings of south India, to
Sri Lanka, and to the kingdoms of the Greeks.
Till Asoka's conversion Buddhism was little
more than a sect of Hinduism: he made it a
state religion. But his peace plans failed, as
peace plans so often do, and not long after his
death in 232 B.C. his Empire collapsed, and the
sub-continent was divided into smaller, often
warring, kingdoms.

Some 600 years later, in the 4th century A.D.,
another great Hindu Empire, the Gupta Empire, arose in north India, and reached its
climax in the 5th century. This period is often
called the Golden Age of the Hindu Renaissance. The greatest Empire since the days of
Asoka was united and governed with efficiency,
and yet without the ruthlessness of the Emperor
Chandragupta. During this period, religious
ideas developed and changed without persecution. This was the golden age of Sanskrit literature and music. The scientific ideas of Greece
had influenced Indian thought, and mathematics and astronomy were studied. Many of

ENTRANCE TO A CAVE TEMPLE AT AJANTA

There are 29 caves at Ajanta: some are Buddhist temples and others monasteries. They are elaborately decorated with sculpture and paintings which date from the 3rd-6th centuries A.D. This is a 6th-century example

the large buildings of the Gupta age have been destroyed by later conquerors; but enough remains to show that their architecture, sculpture, and metal-work were outstanding, as also were their paintings in the Ajanta and other cave monasteries and temples. The great intellectual vitality of this period resulted in the exchange of ideas with other lands, both east and west, particularly with China, Persia, and Rome.

4. MUSLIM INDIA. The Mogul Empire. Towards the end of the 5th and throughout the 6th century the Gupta Empire suffered continuous attacks from hordes of HUNS, and then TURKS (qq.v.). During the 7th century there was a short revival of power in North India under the strong Emperor Harsha, but after his death the Empire broke up. The first invasion of India by Muslims took place in A.D. 712 when Sind was occupied by the Arabs. After a respite of nearly three centuries came a long period of further attacks by Muslim tribes of AFGANS, MONGOLS, and TARTARS (qq.v.). India endured frequent warfare while kingdoms rose and fell; the Muslim power increased until in the 16th century the first of the great Mogul Emperors, Babur, established himself, and founded an Empire which lasted, though in a weakened state, until the 18th century.

The greatest of the Mogul Emperors was AKBAR (q.v. Vol. V), who reigned from 1556 to 1605. He built up a great Empire embracing all northern and central India, which he ruled with justice and efficiency. During the reign of his grandson, Shah Jahan, some of the most magnificent of the Mogul building was carried out. The Imperial palace at Delhi and the famous TAJ MAHAL at Agra (q.v. Vol. XII) are among the most splendid of India's monuments.

During the 16th century began the first European trade settlements in India. The Portuguese came first, and then the Dutch and the English, and later the Danes and the French. They settled along the coast of India, forming companies to trade with the Indians and to send merchandise to Europe. In 1600 the EAST INDIA COMPANY (q.v. Vol. VII) was formed. From that time on, the European powers, and in particular France and Britain, took more and more part in Indian politics, until the French were driven out, and Britain came to rule India. In 1947 India regained its independence.

See also ANCIENT CIVILIZATIONS, INDIAN PEOPLES.
See also Vol. XII: INDIAN ART; INDIAN LITERATURE.

INDIAN PEOPLES. To write of the peoples of the sub-continent of India is rather like writing about the peoples of Europe, except that the differences of race, language, and religion, as well as of living conditions are even greater. Moreover, Indian civilization is much older than that of Europe. In the valley of the Indus, in what is now Pakistan, there was an advanced civilization before 2500 B.C., when most of Europe was still primitive (see INDIAN CIVILIZATIONS). In the sub-continent today there are to be found cultured and educated people as advanced as any in the world; others have never progressed beyond the most primitive stages (see INDIANS, HILL TRIBES).

The history of the Indian sub-continent from the 18th century up to 1947 was one of increasing British influence and conquest followed by the assertion of Indian independence. The EAST INDIA COMPANY (q.v. Vol. VII) traded with the Mogul Empire for 150 years before the time of CLIVE and HASTINGS (qq.v. Vol. V), whose victories over Indian princes and French trade rivals first established the British power or *raj* in Bengal and elsewhere. Successive Governors-General extended it by war and treaty-making until, with the annexation of the Punjab (1849), the whole sub-continent had been brought under control either as provinces of 'British India' or as native states whose princes were subordinate to Britain. In 1857, however, the MUTINY (q.v. Vol. X) broke out among the sepoys or native soldiers, who formed nine-tenths of the Company's army, and was helped by local rebellions. After order was restored, the Company was abolished; India became first a Crown possession, and in 1876 an Empire again, with Victoria instead of the Mogul as Kaisar-i-Hind. The growth of irrigation, famine relief and prevention, railways, and public education marked the work of British officials. George V at his lavish Coronation Durbar in 1911 announced the building of an all-Indian capital at New Delhi, but generally the country remained economically poor and backward.

These conditions did not satisfy educated Indians, who in 1885 had founded a National Congress to claim self-government. Their demands gained popular support in 1905, when Indian feeling was offended by the partition of Bengal. Britain granted instalments of self-rule in 1909 and 1921; but growing discontent had helped to create a mass following for GANDHI

Paul Popper

BATHING GHATS, BENARES

The waterfront is lined with *ghats* (steps) where Hindu pilgrims wash and drink the muddy water of the sacred Ganges

(q.v. Vol. V) and his claim to complete independence. This was not conceded, but under the Government of India Act of 1935 a parliamentary system was set up in the provinces, and control of the central government (except its foreign and defence policies) offered if India formed a FEDERATION (q.v. Vol. X). The effect of the Second World War, when India was exposed to Japanese attack, was to bring independence nearer (*see* INDIA, GOVERNMENT OF, Vol. X).

In 1947, when British rule in the Indian subcontinent ceased, a separate Muslim state, PAKISTAN (q.v. Vol. III), was established in the east and west, and the remaining area became the State (now Republic) of India. This division left a large minority of Muslims in India and a smaller minority of Hindus in Pakistan and, in spite of mass migrations, there are still considerable minorities in each country. At the time of partition there were many Indian states ruled by their own princes, some large, such as Mysore and Hyderabad, others only a few square

kilometres in area, but these have now all joined either India or Pakistan (*see* PAKISTANIS). The Union of India consists of eighteen States and twelve Territories.

The 1971 census of the Union of India enumerated a total of 845 languages or dialects spoken in India, but 91% of the population speak one or other of the 14 major languages specified in the Indian Constitution. These languages belong in the main to two language families. The one, Indo-European (to which European languages also belong), is spoken by about three-quarters of the population in northern India; the other Dravidian, is spoken by the remaining quarter in the four states in south India—Andhra Pradesh, Mysore, Madras, and Kerala.

The population of the Union of India in 1971 was 547 millions, more than that of the rest of the Commonwealth put together, and greater than any of any other country in the world, except China. The distribution of this vast population varies according to rainfall and physical

H. D. Keilor

INDIANS PREPARING A PADDY FIELD BEFORE PLANTING OUT RICE
SEEDLINGS

conditions from 2,150 people to the square kilometre in some parts to only 150 to the square kilometre in the desert regions.

The two main religions of India are HINDUISM and ISLAM (qq.v.). In 1961 there were 366 million Hindus, 46 million Muslims, as well as nearly 8 million SIKHS (q.v.), about 2 million JAINS (q.v.), some 100,000 PARSEES, and about 11 million Christians. BUDDHISM (q.v.), which was founded in India, has spread east, and to Sri Lanka in the south, and has now only a relatively small following (about 200,000) in the land of its origin. There are also about 19 million aboriginal tribes who are neither Muslim nor Hindu but follow primitive beliefs.

Since 1947 India has built up an impressive industrial base, but the country remains a land of villages (*see* INDIANS, VILLAGE LIFE). Agriculture is the most important industry: the chief crops grown are cotton, wheat, jute, rice, sugar, millet, tea, coffee, and tobacco according to differences in climate and soil. In the last 30 years, however, there has been a marked move to the towns, partly because of the pressure of population on the soil, but also because of improved services of transport, lighting, water, and amusements, and the better chances of employment in the rapidly expanding industries which produce the wide range of goods characteristic of an industrial society. This increase in the urban population, and the spread of education, have had a marked effect in breaking

down the barriers of CASTE (q.v.), which has hitherto been the basis of the Hindu social structure. Indeed, under the Indian Constitution of 1950 caste has been officially abolished.

Despite the great strides India's industrial development has taken, agriculture still remains the way of life of most Indians. A great deal of the country's agricultural, as well as industrial, development depends upon her efforts to increase irrigation, for drought is one of the chief causes of hardship among Indian peasants. The well-watered plain of the River GANGES (q.v. Vol. III), with its heavy monsoon rainfall, is one of the most densely populated parts of the country. It is here that people speak Hindi, the language nearest akin to the Sanskrit of Hindu Scriptures. The Ganges plain might, indeed, be called the Holy Land of Hinduism, for the river is accounted sacred and Benares (or Varanasi), on its northern bank, is a holy place to which all devout Hindus try to make a pilgrimage.

Farther west, in the Punjab, conditions were harder until modern irrigation works brought new life to the fields. This part of the country is the homeland of the SIKHS (q.v.), who once ruled over it and still play an important part in the Indian army.

To the south lies peninsular India, or the Deccan plateau. Here the main rivers flow eastwards from the high Western Ghats. Population is densest near the coasts, the interior for the

Tea Bureau

INDIAN WOMEN PLUCKING TEA IN SOUTH INDIA

most part being thinly populated. From the west coast there has been an age-long sea trade with the West to which it owes its settlements of Abyssinians, Jews, Portuguese, half-Arab Muslims (Moplahs) of Malabar, and others. There is, for instance, a community of over a million 'Syrian' Christians who claim that their church was founded by the Apostle St. Thomas. Muslim rule extended as far south as Mysore in the days of Hyder Ali and Tipu Sultan, but their numbers and influence have always been less in the peninsula than in northern India. An overwhelming majority of the people are, of course, Hindus, including the Marathas in the northwest of the region. At one time the Maratha armies overran almost the whole of India. Perhaps the shrewdest and most enterprising of the Dravidian-speaking Indians are the Tamilians. They have not only played an important part in the development of Hinduism but have emigrated to most countries in South-east Asia as well as to Guinea, Natal, and even as far as Fiji, and these countries owe much to their intelligence and industry.

See also Vol. III: INDIA; Vol. IV: INDIAN LANGUAGES.

INDIANS, HILL TRIBES. 1. These peoples are interesting for several reasons. Those of the Indian Borderlands are influenced by the civilizations of adjacent countries: Persia and Islam on the north-west, Tibet and Buddhism on the north, and Burma and south-east Asia on the north-east. The central and southern hills preserve some of the most primitive elements in all Asia. Population is sparse, for the peaks and glaciers of the Himalayas, and the rocks and jungles, wild beasts and malaria elsewhere, make cultivation difficult or impossible and limit the food-supply. Further, on account of the difficulties of access from the plains, and from valley to valley in the hills, the people are split up into small isolated communities, and there is a bewildering multiplicity of dialects and customs.

2. NORTH-WEST AND NORTHERN TIBETAN BORDER. The peaks and glaciers of the Himalayas between the bend of the upper Indus in the west and the Brahmaputra in the east are a stiff barrier between India and Tibet. Yet Tibetan races, language, and religion are found on the Indian side of the frontier, in the far north of Kashmir, in Nepal, and in the Buddhist states of Sikhim and Bhutan. Most of the people are Mongolian, but Indians from the Plains long

ago invaded the hills, married hill women, established many little principalities, and remodelled society on the lines of Indian CASTE (q.v.). None of these little chieftaincies now survive; in the 18th century many of them were absorbed by the Gurkhas and formed into the independent kingdom of Nepal, and others by the Sikhs in Kashmir. The composite character of Himalayan society has resulted in a multitude of languages and dialects. In Nepal, where tribal distinctions are still alive, there are at least a score. From two of the Nepal tribes come the Gurkhas, some of the best soldiers in the world; and another tribe, the Sherpas, have become famous because of the part they have played in the conquest of EVEREST (q.v. Vol. III).

3. NORTH-EASTERN BURMESE BORDER. Except in the Hindu areas of Manipur, the hill tribes of North-east India have more in common with Burmese and Tibetans than with other Indians. They are for the most part Mongolian both in physical type and language, and in customs they are in some ways like the hillsmen and islanders of south-east Asia. The best-known group are the Nagas; but even among the Nagas customs differ from tribe to tribe. Their villages, usually large and perched on the crest of a mountain ridge, are stockaded for defence. The approaches to a village bristle with short bamboo spikes, so sharp that they can pierce a leather boot. All the Naga tribes share a tradition of fighting and hunting, which formerly included ceremonial head-hunting, but the rapid spread of education and new political, social, and economic opportunities are radically changing tribal society.

Where traditional ways survive, boys at about the age of 10 leave home and live together in a club-house where they learn to be good tribesmen. In some villages girls too are trained in the same way (see INITIATION CEREMONIES). For the most part their methods of cultivation are simple—they cut and burn a tract of jungle and sow seed in the ashes. But most tribes now terrace their fields and irrigate the crops. Most tribes love dancing and have extremely picturesque dancing costumes.

4. CENTRAL AND SOUTH INDIAN HILL TRIBES. These tribes are very different from the frontier tribes: they are much darker, and some of them still follow a very primitive way of life—they are mere food-gathering jungle folk clad in aprons of leaves. In south India the tribes are few in numbers; some of them have customs similar to

BHIL HILLMEN WITH THEIR BOWS

Paul Popper

They are also courageous hunters, but they do not decapitate their neighbours. The best known, Santols, Orauns, and Mundas, have migrated in tens of thousands to the tea plantations of Bengal and Assam or wherever jungle needs to be cleared.

Farther south are the tribes called Khonds, who were notorious for their custom of human sacrifice. They believed that the bodies of human victims were needed to fertilize their fields. They kidnapped their victims, fattened them, and then hacked them to pieces so that they might bury the bits in fields. About a century ago they were persuaded that the bodies of buffaloes would do instead of men. 'Hook-swinging', once widespread throughout south India, is undoubtedly a relic of the old custom of human sacrifice; the practice is now prohibited, and puppets are swung from the hooks instead of men.

See also Vol. IV: INDIAN LANGUAGES.

those of the more primitive of the Malayan tribes—such as their methods of fire-making, of building houses in trees, and of chipping the front teeth (*see* MALAYSIA, PEOPLES OF).

The biggest tribal communities are in the fever-stricken hills of central India, from the borders of Gujarat in the west to Bengal. The western group include a number of distinct tribes known generally as Bhil. They vary greatly in their degree of development. They have little sense of community and have lost their tribal languages, speaking instead dialects of the languages of their Hindu neighbours. In some Hindu states where Bhils are numerous there was an old custom that the Bhils should publicly recognize a new rajah (king or ruler) by marking his brow with blood from a tribesman's thumb or toe. The Bhils perform elaborate death ceremonies, that traditionally lasted for 12 days and involved great feasts.

Tribes of the eastern group have a stronger sense of tribal solidarity, and their languages, Dravidian and Munda (an ancient south-east Asian language), still thrive. These eastern peoples, like North-east tribes, are keen dancers. They train their boys in club-houses, and their traditional agriculture is by jungle-burning.

INDIANS, VILLAGE LIFE. The majority of the INDIAN PEOPLES (q.v.) live in villages and are occupied in some way upon the land. The villages vary a good deal in different parts of India: in the Peninsula, for instance, on the west coast the houses are scattered, while in the Deccan they were often crammed inside a small fort for defence against marauders, and again, in parts of the east they are neatly arranged in streets. The houses themselves also differ according to the climate of the area and the building materials available. In areas of heavy rainfall the houses have sloping roofs; in dry areas the roofs are flat. In some parts wood is available for building; in others stone. Mud is used everywhere—either as plaster or made into burnt or sun-dried bricks.

Although conditions vary, the life of the villagers is much the same all over India. A Tamil village in the south may be taken as an example.

The Tamil word for our word 'build' means

'tie', and indeed their houses are tied together. The simplest house is a circular one-roomed hut of bamboos, tied together with string and thatched with grass, straw, or palm-leaves. Rectangular houses, however, can be divided into several rooms and added to when necessary, and the better houses in a Tamil village have several rooms opening onto interior verandas surrounding a small, square courtyard. There is also usually a veranda on the street side. The houses are sometimes tiled, but generally thatched, and are almost always of one story only. The floors are of beaten earth, and there is very little and very simple furniture. The household equipment consists of vessels of earthenware or brass, a grain-bin or two, and perhaps a chest. Chairs, tables, bedsteads, forks, and spoons are rare, for Tamils prefer to sit and sleep on the floor and to eat with fingers.

The villages are largely self-supporting: each village has its own potters, blacksmiths, carpenters, tanners, barbers, washermen, herdsmen, and fishermen. Particular kinds of jobs belong to particular families. Under the CASTE system (q.v.) no one was allowed to do a job which did not belong to his family, and even though caste barriers are breaking down, people still tend to follow their traditional family occupations.

Wages are usually paid in grain instead of money. The peasant cultivators, the largest section of the community, have, therefore, to grow enough food to feed their own families and their field labourers, and also to have enough to sell so that they can pay for their rent, taxes, and other expenses. In most villages there is a money-lender, who is also a grain merchant and perhaps a shopkeeper too. A weekly open-air market is held at some convenient centre to serve a number of villages. There the villagers can buy the few things they do not produce— salt, for instance, and cloth.

In southern villages, where the climate is always warm, people wear little clothing. A man wears a white cotton loin-cloth, a girl

J. Allan Cash

INDIAN VILLAGERS LOAD THE BRICKS THEY HAVE MADE ON TO DONKEYS

Pitt Rivers Collection

WOMEN HUSKING RICE

Paul Popper

A VILLAGE WEAVER IN RAJPUTANA

He works on a primitive loom in the road outside his hut

wears a long piece of bright-coloured cloth, part of which she winds round her waist to hang below the knee, the rest goes across her breast, over her left shoulder, and tucks in behind.

The principal food is rice in the wetter parts or millet in the dryer, except in north-west India where wheat is grown. In the Tamil country it rains heavily from October to December, and after that for 6 months there is hardly any rain at all, and the rivers run nearly dry. Storing water and irrigation are therefore very important matters, since without water the rice will not grow. They dam the rivers and make artificial lakes called tanks, from which run channels to take the water to the fields. They also raise water from wells by various devices, the commonest being a sort of see-saw. There is a long rod and bucket at one end of the see-saw and a weight at the other; a man stands in the centre and raises or lowers the bucket in or out of the well by shifting his weight from one side to the other.

Although modern tractors are increasingly seen in the countryside, the Indians still plough with oxen and light wooden ploughs. They thresh the rice by driving a row of half a dozen bullocks tied together by the neck round the threshing-floor till all the grain is trodden out. They winnow the grain by shaking it gently in a basket shaped like a dust-pan; the heavy grain falls to their feet while the chaff is carried away by the wind. The Indian bull or *zebu* is different from an English bull, his horns point backwards, a flap of skin hangs loosely from his neck and chest, and there is a convenient lump over his shoulder which prevents the yoke from slipping along his neck. Bulls and cows are sacred and must not be killed: in consequence old and useless animals go on eating up the precious fodder needed for young and useful beasts. The buffalo is not sacred. It produces a rich milk and is a very useful draught animal.

Some of the games of an Indian village, such as hop-scotch, prisoner's base, and leap-frog, are very ancient and found among many peoples, including ourselves. Indians also play a kind of backgammon, using the ground marked out as a board, bits of stone or pot for 'men', and split beans shaken in the hand for dice. They do not dance but are very fond of their own music, which is now often enjoyed in the Western world. Bargaining and gossiping in the weekly market, domestic celebrations, such as weddings, and the regular rotation of religious festivals are their main form of entertainment.

Each village is like a little municipality with a council of elders and officers. The headman is a magistrate and he collects the taxes; the accountant keeps a register of all the land, the extent and owner of each field, the tax to be paid, and other details. The strength of the village is its unity—every member must do his best for the welfare of the whole. For instance, in the rainy season, if the tank dam starts leaking, every man, woman, and child must help to prevent a breach which would ruin the year's crops and bring starvation.

See also Vol. III: INDIA; Vol. IV: INDIAN LANGUAGES.

INDOCHINESE, *see* CAMBODIANS, LAOTIANS, VIETNAMESE.

INDONESIANS. This term has come into use in recent decades to signify all the peoples who inhabit the archipelago now known as Indonesia. The string of islands stretches over 4,800 kilometres, from the northern tip of Sumatra in the west to Irian Barat (former Dutch New Guinea) in the east. A great number of languages are represented, and a variety of cultures, but the people have a common origin far back in time on the Asian mainland. Today the majority of the population is still engaged in agriculture, but many others are employed in mining, transport, commercial plantations, and a small manufacturing sector.

The population in 1971 was nearly 120 million. At one extreme, there are a few thousands who still live by hunting and gathering in mountain and jungle, while rather more practise shifting cultivation (a skilful agricultural technique involving regular rotation of fields and crops over wide geographical expanses). At the other extreme, the Indonesians in the modern sector run almost the whole gamut from clerks and construction labourers to atomic scientists and pop musicians of international repute. Many big commercial plantations, such as those cultivating rubber, and many extractive enterprises, such as those mining bauxite and petroleum, are owned and directed by foreigners, despite vigorous efforts to nationalize them during President Sukarno's period (1945–65). In such enterprises Indonesians find it hard to climb to the highest positions, but this will change with time.

Camera Press
JAVA: FISH-FARMING IN FLOODED PADDY FIELDS
They put in young fish to grow amongst the rice seedlings

The overwhelming mass of the population is still agricultural, and an unusually high percentage are engaged in fishing. Methods in both vary greatly from island to island, but there is sufficient in common to justify some generalization. 'Wet' rice cultivation in flooded paddy fields, if not now the most common technique, is still very typical. Its practice and requirements over the centuries have given rise to many words and phrases in local speech and have affected local crafts. Not only have the Indonesians put under the plough all available flat lands, but they have shown great ingenuity in pushing remarkable terraced rice fields up the sides of mountains. The sporadic eruptions of volcanoes, especially in Java, keep the soil fertile.

Because of the complex irrigation systems, and the occasional need, as at harvest time, to work as a village unit, community feeling is strong. Ritual feasting to mark this solidarity is a feature of village life. Until recently, the typical village was also fairly democratic, in a way sometimes described as 'shared poverty'. But the villages are breaking up on a class basis, with a few rich landlords, many peasants, and a fast-growing class of landless labourers. This development will greatly affect the future.

Already the urban sector is growing very much more rapidly than industry, as poor peasants are driven off the land and into the cities in search of work. Fish supplies the bulk of protein in the rice-based Indonesian diet. Most of the fishing is from rivers and coasts rather than from the deep sea. This industry is capable of development.

Housing and clothing vary as widely as do the occupations and natural surroundings of the Indonesian peoples. The cities have modern skyscrapers and luxury hotels as well as stolid old Dutch villas and local feudal palaces—and horrific slums largely of corrugated iron. In the rural areas, the building varies geographically: in some villages the houses are built on stilts (for example, in Sumatra); in others they are in clusters on the ground (as in Java). In most villages every spare inch seems pressed into use for growing flowers and vegetables or nurturing livestock, especially chickens and fish.

The ankle-length sarong of printed cloth is the characteristic garment of both men and women almost throughout the archipelago. Men wear it with a short jacket, women with a jacket, scarf, or blouse. But today many city dwellers wear European dress. One of the best-known products of Indonesia is batik, a waxed dyed cloth from which the sarongs are made. The crafts of batik work, silver-working, wood-

carving, and cane-work with rattan palms have survived, though other handicrafts vanished during the colonial period. The two or three per cent of the population who are of Chinese origin dress, work, and live much as they do throughout the rest of south-east Asia and Hong Kong.

When the Western powers first arrived in the East Indies in the 16th century, in pursuit of the coveted spices to be found in eastern Indonesia, they found an already developed civilization and culture. There were universities founded hundreds of years before by scholars from China and India and well-known over south-east Asia. Merchants from the archipelago already had excellent sea-going ships and sound navigational techniques which enabled them to sail round to West Africa. One of the greatest temples in the world had been erected at Borobudur in Java in honour of the Buddha.

The trading reputation of the East Indies caught the attention of Muslim merchants soon after the foundation of BUDDHISM (q.v.), and there were Islamic colonies by the time Marco Polo went there in the 13th century. But the coming of the Europeans greatly accelerated the spread of ISLAM (q.v.), which was seen as an almost nationalist protest against the Western intruders. Today, the great majority of Indonesians are at least Muslims in name, though Hinduism, marking the earlier Indian influence,

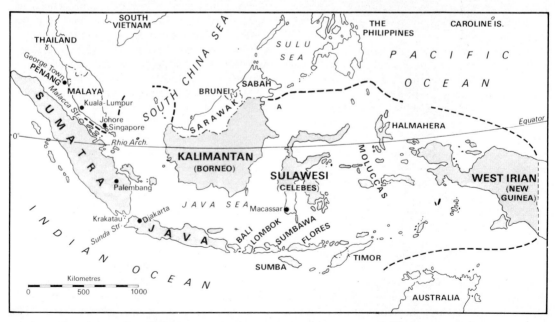

INDONESIA: THE DOTTED LINE SHOWS THE EXTENT OF INDONESIA

Mrs. T. Muir

A VILLAGE LAW COURT IN JAVA
The chief sits in the centre of the village square while the defendant pleads his case

lingers on in Bali. The Javanese were the last to be converted to Islam (since their kingdoms were more often land-based than those of the other islands whose traditions were mercantile), and even today they are less orthodox.

After some strife among the European powers, Holland gradually asserted her authority over the entire archipelago. From the 19th century on, Indonesia, then known as the Netherlands East Indies, became a vast source of produce and profit for Holland. The colonial régime was harsh and insensitive, and there were constant rebellions which were put down by military force. In the 20th century a nationalist movement uniting the different islands and joining urban, western-educated intellectuals with the peasant masses came into being.

In 1942, Japan occupied the archipelago, and during their brief stay many young men learned to handle firearms. The Dutch tried to return after the defeat of Japan, but the nationalist forces were by then too strong for them. In 1945, Sukarno, the leader of the movement, declared independence. This was conceded by the Dutch, after a ferocious war, in 1949.

Since then, there have been many ups and downs. Sukarno himself was overthrown in 1965–66 by a group of generals who have subsequently reversed the former President's policies of evicting foreign influence by inviting back British, American, Japanese, and Dutch businesses to help the Indonesians to build up their industries and trade.

See also Vol. III: East Indies; Philippines: Index, p. 144; Vol. IV: Indonesian Languages.

INITIATION CEREMONIES. It is a very widespread custom amongst peoples of varying grades of civilization to make young people undergo initiation ceremonies by which they become full members of the community. The age at which they undergo the rites varies a great deal, but it is usually only after initiation that young men and women are allowed to marry. Initiation rites are also performed for adults when joining secret societies or when moving

British Museum

IVORY MASKS WORN AT INITIATION CEREMONIES

These small masks represent the old life of the initiate which ends when he begins his new life. Zaïre

from one age-group to another. Witches and witch-doctors are initiated into the mysteries of WITCHCRAFT (q.v.) by other sorcerers.

There are usually three stages in initiation ceremonies, though they may not always be definitely marked off from one another: seclusion from most of the other members of the community, especially from the other sex: preparatory ceremonies by which the boy or girl qualifies for admission into the community; and acceptance by, or graduation into, the community. These ceremonies may last for several months. All through many of them there is also the idea of education—of teaching those who are being initiated the rules and customs of the tribe or group.

The suggestion that a person is being reborn to another kind of life underlies the ritual celebrated at initiation, as well as at BIRTH, MARRIAGE, and DEATH (qq.v.). The original purpose of such rites was not only to celebrate the change from one kind of life to another, but also to bring about the new life. In order to understand this one must remember that primitive people think that acting what you want to happen is a way of magically making it happen (see MAGIC).

How strong was this idea of rebirth will be seen if we consider a few of the rites which form part of initiation ceremonies. Among some Australian natives a scene of death and rising from the dead was enacted. The boys were placed beside a grave in which a man was concealed as if dead. A procession of men then approached, chanting invocations, and suddenly the apparently dead man jumped up. During the initiation as witch-doctors the boys of an African tribe, the Azande, are actually partly buried, as in a grave, and then jump out, feeling rather dizzy and out of breath.

In some tribes boys to be initiated are put into what is supposed to be a magic sleep: when they awaken in the morning they are regarded as having become men. The idea of entering a new life is sometimes emphasized by giving a new name at the initiation. The main initiation ground of a North Transvaal tribe is called 'the place where things are forgotten', and the Indian boys of Virginia were given a medicine which was believed to blot out all memory of the past. It is not unusual for boys after initiation to pretend to have forgotten their early life and how to do the simplest things, even how to talk.

In some communities of Eskimos, the magician, when initiating someone into the mysteries, pretends to kill him; his soul is believed to fly off and find out the secrets of the earth and sky while he lies still on the ground. Then he is 'revived' and becomes a magician in his turn. Before a man becomes a Benedictine monk he is laid on the ground, covered with a sheet, and the service of the burial of the dead is performed. This idea of rebirth is expressed in the New Testament: (1 Pet. ii. 24) 'that we, being dead unto sin, should live unto righteousness'. The words are quoted in the Church of England baptismal service. At confirmation in the Roman Catholic Church the candidate is given a new name to mark his or her new life.

Hindus emphasize the idea that at initiation a boy undergoes spiritual rebirth—becomes one of the 'twice-born', as they say. The ceremony in which a young Hindu is 'girded with the sacred thread' is a most important occasion. When he is 8 years old, musicians play at the house, which has been specially cleaned and in which an altar facing the east has been erected. He is anointed and his head is shaved, leaving only a topknot. His mother takes him on her lap to feed him and for the last time eats from the same plate with him. At the 'lucky' moment the priests and guests throw red rice over him, and the priest puts the sacred thread over his left shoulder and below his right arm. On the fifth day after this ceremony he goes in his best clothes to the temple to worship.

As with marriage ceremonies, it is probable that many initiation ceremonies are derived from a very ancient ritual in which the king at

Pitt Rivers Collection

AN AUSTRALIAN INITIATION CEREMONY

The initiates crawl through the legs of the men in the central group. Kakadu tribe, N. Australia

his coronation or enthronement was thought to die and be reborn as a god. Thus, at initiation, an Indian boy is anointed like the king of England at his coronation, and the Indian's sacred thread corresponds to the girdle which the Dean of Westminster places around the king. The Indian boy receives a yellow cloth to wear, shoes, and a staff; the king is vested in a robe of cloth of gold and given spurs, sceptre, and a rod. The boy takes his seat on a stool, the king on his throne.

There is the notion that people are centres of magical power at the times when they change their status in the community, and that at such times the powers of evil are particularly active. Therefore those to be initiated are secluded and isolated. As initiation is a time of education there are practical advantages in isolating the candidates. The responsibilities, duties, arts and crafts of men and women are so different that the instruction in adult life is different for boys and girls, as also is the sex instruction. Girls during initiation may be taught basket-making and cooking, and lads cattle-herding or hunting technique, as well as being instructed in the traditions and marriage customs of the tribe.

In many East African tribes there is a series of initiations at different ages. Amongst the Didinga, for instance, there are initiations at the ages of 8, 13, 18, and 28—and others later on.

After the ceremony at the age of 8, a boy may carry a spear and is trained to use it. He is taught dances and songs, good manners, and the duty of obedience to his elders. At 13 he is instructed in rain ceremonies, shown how to hunt, and taught the use of herbs as medicine. At 18 he begins his period of about 10 years' service as a warrior of the tribe. During these initiations a youth gains a wider outlook by mixing with others of different clans. The system serves somewhat the same purpose as our junior and senior schools, universities, and military service.

During the period of initiation boys and girls often have to undergo various frightening, painful, or otherwise unpleasant ordeals to impress them with the importance of the occasion and give them the opportunity to show that they can undergo hardship manfully and are fit to be full members of the community. They may have to submit to circumcision, tattooing, or ear-piercing. Candidates, both boys and girls, may have to fast, eat nasty or dirty food, keep silence, and observe various TABOOS (q.v.) and rites of purification. Boys are told that they must now behave with dignity as men and no longer in a childish manner. Various customs are often reversed during initiation. In a North Transvaal tribe the boys wear their loin-cloths the wrong way round; some Australian tribesmen tell the candidates the opposite of what they mean; and some initiates are made to walk backwards and turn their plates upside-down.

In many ways initiations serve useful purposes. Amongst the Australian blacks each lad is given, 'by one of the elders, advice so kindly, fatherly, and impressive, as often to soften the heart, and draw tears from the youth'. An Indian in North Carolina told a European that initiation meant the same to them as it did for Europeans to send their children to school 'to be taught good breeding and letters'. When Basuto boys are initiated they are told: 'Be men, fear theft, fear adultery, honour your father and mother, obey your chiefs.'

We can understand the part that initiation plays amongst primitive people only when we remember that they have no schools, and no way of writing down or recording their customs and laws. The traditions of the tribe must be passed on from old to young, by word of mouth and example, and with care and solemnity, or what knowledge and organization the tribes-people possess would be lost and they would perish. Therefore they make every effort to impress the new generation with their duty to be loyal to tribal traditions and to carry on its religious practices, its code of conduct, and its way of life.

INQUISITION.

INQUISITION. Literally, 'inquisition' means 'investigation', but the word has come to be applied almost exclusively to the special organization in the Roman Catholic Church for searching out heresy.

From an early date the Church was troubled by men who formed their own ideas about the Christian religion, instead of accepting the doctrines of the Church. Such men are called heretics. The Church believed that it had a duty to discover heretics and bring them back to correct doctrine. There were three reasons for this belief: firstly, it was thought that if a man died believing false doctrine, his soul went to hell; secondly, like illness, heresy was apt to spread, endangering souls and the unity of the Church; thirdly, the ordinary people often killed heretics, with the result that their souls went to hell without the Church having had a chance to save them. Sometimes, too, the common people, because they were not sufficiently educated to identify heresy, killed innocent men and women.

For many centuries it was part of the duty of

AN *AUTO DE FÉ*   *Vernacci*

Victims about to be burnt at the stake, while others, with ropes round their necks, await their turn. Painting by P. Berruguete in the Prado, Madrid

each bishop to search out and punish heresy. But in the 12th century heresy became so common, particularly in the south of France, that the Popes had to take special steps against it. In 1233 Pope Gregory IX sent Dominicans (or Preaching FRIARS (q.v.)) to deal with heresy in France, and this is usually taken as the foundation of the Inquisition.

In 1478 the Pope authorized the rulers of Spain to establish a more effective Inquisition to deal with the religious troubles of their country. This is the origin of the Spanish Inquisition which, owing to its efficiency and zeal and to its reputation for cruelty, is the most famous section of the Inquisition.

The Spanish Inquisition was as much a department of the Spanish government as an institution of the Church in Spain. Its organization extended to every part of the kingdom and was controlled by an Inquisitor-General appointed by the king, who allowed the Pope no say in its proceedings. All the property of its victims was confiscated and most of it went to the royal exchequer.

The Spanish Inquisition's reputation for cruelty rests on three things: the extent to which its procedure was designed to strike terror into the accused and hinder his defence; the use of torture on the accused and on witnesses; and the severity of the penalties, particularly burning at the stake. While this reputation for cruelty is undoubtedly deserved, certain facts which explain the Spanish Inquisition are often overlooked. The Spanish people were fanatically hostile to foreigners and heretics, so the Inquisition was immensely popular and the *autos de fé* (Acts of Faith) at which its punishments were publicly carried out were great national festivals. Torture was a normal part of all criminal investigations in every country of the mainland of Europe until the 18th century. The inquisitors believed that they were carrying out a duty imposed on them by God, to save the soul of the accused by persuading him to admit and give up his errors. Only those who refused to give up their errors, or returned to them after giving them up, or who had deliberately converted others to their errors, were burned.

So successful was the Spanish Inquisition that in 1542 the Pope established a new Holy Office in Rome, modelled on the Spanish organization, to protect the Church against the Protestant reformers. With the decrease in religious fanaticism and the beginnings of humanitarianism in the 18th century, the Inquisition became much less active and torture was no longer used. The Spanish Inquisition was abolished in 1820. In 1968 the Holy Office was reorganized and named the Congregation for the Doctrine of the Faith, and concerns itself with the protection of faith and morals.

See also ROMAN CATHOLIC CHURCH.

IONIANS, *see* GREEK CIVILIZATION, Section 2 C.

IRANIANS, *see* PERSIANS.

IRAQIS. Mesopotamia, through which run the great rivers the Tigris and Euphrates, was the home of one of the earliest civilizations of the world—the SUMERIAN (q.v.), which flourished over 6,000 years ago. This was followed by the civilization of the BABYLONIANS and the ASSYRIANS (qq.v.). From about 1700 B.C., however, a series of invasions began which subjected the country to foreign domination—Egyptian, Persian, Mongol, and Turkish—until in 1921 Iraq became a kingdom. In 1958 the king was murdered, and a republic was set up.

The people of modern Iraq number over nine million. Of these the majority are ARABS (q.v.), inhabiting the great plains of the Tigris and Euphrates and the surrounding deserts. The other large element consists of Kurds, over two million of whom live in the northern mountains and the rolling plains at their foot.

The Iraqis live across routes which have been used for centuries by armies and traders passing between Europe and Asia, and their blood contains many strains. But they have refused, usually for religious reasons, to mix with some of the new-comers, so that Iraq contains many small pockets of minorities who are relics of its history. Turcomans, still speaking a form of Turkish, live near Mosul; Assyrian Christians inhabit prosperous villages—almost small towns—round Kirkuk; Persian communities live in holy cities near the Euphrates, and in the north-west are Yezidis, a nature-worshipping people descended from very early invaders.

Religion has played a large part in Iraqi life. Much as a Christian country may contain Protestants and Catholics, so Iraqi Muslims are

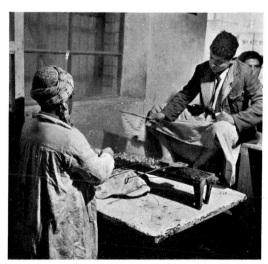

Petroleum Information Bureau

COOKING KEBAB—MEAT ON SKEWERS—IN KIRKUK, IRAQ

Petroleum Information Bureau

A METAL WORKER IN KIRKUK, IRAQ

divided into two denominations, Sunnis and Shias (*see* ISLAM). Iraq's Turkish masters of the last few centuries were Sunnis, so that Sunnis were favoured and formed the ruling class; but the Shias are more numerous and, with the spread of universal education, have made their mark in all professions and in the armed forces. The army has come to play an increasing part in politics and provides a road to advancement for children from humbler families.

In the big towns all Arabs and Kurds wear western dress. In the countryside and the desert the Arab's normal dress is a long cotton shirt buttoned to the throat, and, in winter, a cloak without seam of brown camel-hair or wool called an *aba*. If he is rich, he has its edge embroidered with a gold thread. On his head he wears a cotton cloth with a circlet of rope to hold it down; the ends of the cloth are useful for tying over his mouth in sandstorms. His house is usually made of baked mud, and has to be rebuilt—a job seen to by the whole family—about once in six years. The Kurd, being a mountaineer, lives in a stone house strong enough to stand up to the weight of winter snow; he wears baggy trousers and a huge turban, which he winds as jauntily as the Scotsman slings his plaid.

From ancient times, the inhabitants of Iraq have depended on agriculture and stockbreeding, but under Turkish rule even this re-source dwindled through neglect and lack of outlets for its produce, until the population, once perhaps twenty million, fell in 1900 to two million only.

But today this poverty is reduced, thanks to a new resource—OIL (q.v. Vol. VII). The Iraqis had always known that oil was there. It seeps to the surface near Kirkuk, where it burns like an eternal bonfire. They had long used it in their lamps, and to caulk their boats. But its possibilities for sale in large quantities and for powering modern industry were realized only lately. Since its 'discovery' for these purposes in 1927 the Iraqis have started to draw a large income from it, which they are using to arm and modernize their country.

In particular, the Iraq Government is spending the oil money on making better use of the rivers so as to restore the country's ancient fertility. Till a few years ago, the Tigris and Euphrates used regularly to flood the country. Today, thanks to the oil money, both floods can be stored for use in summer when the rivers are low. New roads, new schools, new bridges, new tractors, and new factories powered by oil or natural gas have also been built.

Nevertheless, many country districts are still poor; there is a great gap between the lot of the rich townsmen and that of the peasants, on whom little has been spent. The revolutionaries of 1958 hoped to better them, but political quarrels at home and abroad held up their plans. So Iraq still counts chiefly on oil for prosperity; luckily it has huge reserves in the ground.

See also Vol. III: IRAQ; INDEX, p. 144.

IRISH. The population of Ireland has been formed by successive waves of invaders. Early in the Christian era the whole island was conquered by a Celtic-speaking people, who imposed their language, their religion, and their social institutions on the earlier inhabitants. The Ireland to which ST. PATRICK (q.v. Vol. V) brought Christianity in the 5th century, though split up into many small states, had a common culture. In the 6th, 7th, and 8th centuries, Ireland was renowned throughout Europe for its piety, its learning, its literature, and its ILLUMINATED MANUSCRIPTS (q.v. Vol. XII), of which the 8th-century Book of Kells is the most splendid example. But this golden age was shattered by the Norse invasions of the 9th and 10th centuries. As so often happened in their history, the Irish

AN ARAB WITH HIS CAMEL

Water-colour by J. F. Lewis, 1858

J. Allan Cash

HARVESTING TURF TO FUEL A POWER STATION

licism became the badge of the defeated majority, Protestantism that of a new English colony that included the ruling and land-owning minority.

In the 17th century this new colony was strengthened by the settlement in Ulster of tough and resourceful small farmers and manufacturers from Scotland and England. They made Ulster the most prosperous part of Ireland, while remaining distinct from the Irish around them. When, in 1641 and 1688, the Irish tried to throw off the conquest, the Ulster colony played an all-important part in maintaining English rule and Protestant supremacy.

In spite of this, the Presbyterians, who formed the great majority of the Ulster Protestants, were treated as inferior citizens; only the land-owning Protestants of the Established Church enjoyed full political power. This was especially resented by middle-class Protestants of Belfast, who in the later 18th century took the lead in demanding equal civil rights for all and the removal of English restrictions on Irish trade. Important reforms were then achieved. But the more radical Protestants believed that the great evils of Irish life could be cured only by a union of Catholics and Protestants pledged to obtain a democratic constitution. The Society of United Irishmen was formed with this object in 1791. After vain attempts by legal means, the United Irishmen took up arms in 1798, and lost disastrously. To bind Ireland more securely to England the British government abolished the Dublin parliament and incorporated Ireland in a United Kingdom of Great Britain and Ireland (1800). But the spirit of revolt was not quenched.

After 1800 Ireland's people were divided between those who sought to maintain the union with Britain and those who demanded independence. Broadly the division corresponded to that between Protestants and Catholics, for the Protestants of Ulster abandoned the idea of union with the Catholics. Belfast grew rapidly into a flourishing centre of industry (especially linen and shipbuilding), closely attached to industrial Britain. The old antagonism between Presbyterians and Churchmen died out, and they made common cause against the Catholics, as they had done in the 17th century. The Catholics, under the leadership of a great Irishman, Daniel O'CONNELL, learned how to organize in defence of their rights. In their successful struggle for Catholic emancipation the foundations of the

were prevented from making a united effort against the invaders by divisions among themselves; but they showed immense power of local resistance. Though the Norsemen became permanent settlers, they were confined to the towns that they founded on the coast—chiefly Dublin, Wexford, Waterford, and Limerick.

In the 12th century more formidable invaders arrived, the Anglo-Normans, who established themselves in Dublin and its neighbourhood and planted feudal lordships widespread over the island. The Anglo-Normans set up a centralized system of government, including a parliament, on the English model, introduced the English language and common law, and reorganized the Church. But they were never able to subdue the whole island. Outside the Dublin area Gaelic lordships maintained their independence, and it was not till the 16th century that the whole of Ireland was made subject to the English crown. Even this Tudor conquest was incomplete, for the Tudors failed to impose Protestantism on either the Gaelic Irish or the Old English colony. These victims of a common oppression eventually merged. Catho-

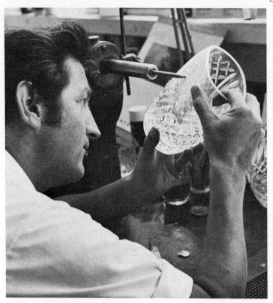

J. Allan Cash

CUTTING GLASS AT WATERFORD GLASSWORKS

modern Irish nation were laid—a nation over-whelmingly Catholic, which none the less cherished the United Irish ideal and found some of its most gifted leaders, most notably Thomas Davis and Charles Stewart PARNELL, among Protestants (qq.v. Vol. V).

The mass of Catholics were poverty-stricken peasants, depending vitally on their potato crop and holding their small farms at the will of alien landlords. Yet their numbers steadily increased until the great famine of 1845-7. This catastrophe, caused by the repeated failure of the potato harvest, removed nearly one-quarter of the population through death or emigration. The broad stream of emigration continued for over half a century, building up in the U.S.A. and Britain an Irish population larger than that of the mother country, which today is only about 4 millions. The famine also had disastrous effects on the traditional culture of the Irish. It hastened the decline of the Irish language, which was then spoken throughout most of the western half of Ireland, but by the end of the century survived only in a remote western fringe. Indirectly, however, the famine, by reducing the population, prepared the way for improved conditions of life for the peasantry; and soon the Irish who had emigrated began to send money home to support both their relatives and the national cause.

In the 1880s, under the inspiration of Michael Davitt, son of an evicted peasant from Mayo, the Catholic peasantry organized in a great movement of moral-force resistance to the landlords. This 'land war' induced the British Liberal leader, GLADSTONE (q.v. Vol. V), to reform the land system, so that under his successors Irish tenants were enabled to buy out the landlords and to own their own farms. This, the greatest social change since the famine, has made life immeasurably better for the whole farming population, Protestant as well as Catholic. There is still rural poverty and primitive farming, but the old 'monster misery' of the Irish country-side has gone.

This and other great reforms were due not only to the efforts of the Irish themselves but also to a growing realization among British people of the justice of Irish claims, including the claim to self-government. A great many British people followed Gladstone in his courageous attempt to carry through parliament the Home-Rule Bill demanded by Parnell and the Irish members. But Britain as well as Ireland was divided over this question, and Gladstone's Home-Rule Bills were defeated. In the end Ireland won independence not through parliamentary means but through rebellion, in 1916; and the independence finally gained in 1921 applied only to twenty-six counties. The other six counties, in north-east Ulster, remained part of the United Kingdom, but with a government and parliament of its own for local affairs. This partitioning of Ireland has ever since been a cause of bitterness among Irishmen and between Ireland and Great Britain. In the twenty-six counties (since 1949 the Republic of Ireland), the small minority of Protestants (about 6%) is an accepted part of the nation; but in the six counties called Northern Ireland there is a strong Catholic minority (about 33%) which seeks reunion with the rest of Ireland. The Republic claims the whole island as the national territory; but the unionists of the north-east insist that Northern Ireland must remain permanently attached to Britain.

These divisions are in a sense based on religion, but in a deeper sense on history and cultural tradition. Thus the Irish government has endeavoured, but with small success, to revive as the mother tongue of Ireland the IRISH LANGUAGE (q.v. Vol. IV) which, to Ulster unionists, is as foreign as Norse. Belfast has much more in common with the industrial cities of Scotland

and northern England than with Dublin. Northern Ireland has a higher standard of living and of social services, a higher marriage-rate, and a lower birth-rate, than the Republic. Yet there is much in common between all sections of Irishmen. The majority on both sides of the border are small farmers, and though farming is more profitable in the north-east, there is a highly progressive element among the farmers of the Republic. Most Irish families have relatives in Britain or America, and there is continual movement between both parts of Ireland and Britain. Yet Ireland is essentially conservative: religion is everywhere taken seriously, the family group is of immense importance, and ancient folkways survive. The wealth of traditional music that Ireland has inherited from its Gaelic past is no less cherished in the Protestant north than in the Catholic south.

In recent years economic growth and social welfare advanced in both north and south. Both committed themselves to entry into the European Economic Community in January 1973 and therefore to full economic co-operation with each other. On the other hand Northern Ireland was brought to the verge of civil war by renewed conflict, after 1968, between the Catholic minority and the Protestant majority. What began as a peaceful agitation for civil rights by moderate Catholics became a bloody sectarian struggle, dominated by the violence of extremists, aiming at forcibly re-unifying the whole island. The British government sent an army to Northern Ireland in 1969, and assumed direct responsibility for its government in 1972. The Republic, too, became deeply involved both because of its traditional claims over the whole island and because the guerillas (the Irish Republican Army) used its territory as a base for their operations against government and society in the north. But most people in the Republic, while sympathizing with the minority in the north, do not approve of a violent re-unification of Ireland, and society in the Republic is not split as in Northern Ireland. The government of the Republic gradually hardened its attitude to the I.R.A. and worked in close accord with the moderate leaders of the minority in Northern Ireland for a peaceful settlement. In this it had a common interest with the British government.

The efforts of the 4 years (1968–72) to unify Ireland by violence only intensified Irish division, which itself was both the result and the continuing cause of violence. Yet the overwhelming mass of Ireland's population, both north and south, want peace, on a basis of goodwill and justice.

See also Celtic Civilization; Fairies.
See also Vol. III: Ireland; Dublin; Belfast; Shannon.
See also Index, p. 144.
See also Vol. V: Joyce; Synge; Yeats.
See also Vol. VI: Famine.

ISLAM. 1. Islam, also called Muhammadanism, is the youngest of the great world religions. It was founded in Arabia in the 7th century by Muhammad, the Prophet (q.v. Vol. V), and its followers are called Muslims. There are at present about 365 million Muslims, including the great majority of the Arab, Iranian, and Turkic peoples. In the Arabic-speaking Near East, including Egypt and the Sudan, there are 47 millions, of whom about 12 million are to be found in Arabia proper. In 1970 there were about 20 million in North Africa, 14 million in Nigeria, 15 million in Iran, 12 million in Afghanistan, 21 million in Turkey, and another 21 million in parts of the U.S.S.R. It is estimated that in Pakistan and India there are not less than 106 million; and in Indonesia, Malaya, and the rest of southeastern Asia, including the Philippines, they number 75 million. In the United States there are hardly more than 10,000 Muslims (not including the so-called 'Black Muslims') while Latin America has at least 150,000.

2. Beliefs and Practices. Islam is based on a series of revelations to Muhammad, which are collected in the Koran, the sacred book of the Muslims (see Sacred Books). Muslims believe the Koran is the very words of Allah (God), and as Allah's speech it is eternal and uncreated. Muslims are strict monotheists. To them, Allah is the sole creator who is beyond compare. He creates all substances, qualities, and happenings in the universe. Nothing can happen except by His will and decree. He also decides what is good and what is bad. He cannot be questioned about what He does. However, orthodox Islam has always insisted on the responsibility of man for his fate.

Allah's mercy is a recurrent theme of the Koran. Muslims believe that Allah in His mercy sent a succession of prophets with a message addressed to their peoples or to mankind is general; the first was Adam, others were Abraham, Moses, David, and Jesus, and the last and greatest was Muhammad. As signs of their mission,

Allah's messengers performed miracles—overriding breaches of the usual course of events. The only miracle that Muhammad claimed was the Koran. Other miracles, including his ascent to heaven, were attributed to him later.

The end of the world—to be preceded by fearful signs—the resurrection of the dead, the day of judgement, Paradise, and Hell are often described in the Koran. Unbelievers will remain in Hell for ever; believing sinners will be punished in Hell but will eventually be admitted to Paradise.

The word Islam means submission—submission to Allah, and to Muhammad, His Prophet—not in the sense of fatalism, but in loyalty and obedience, political as well as religious. Islam is not a church, for it has no clergy, ministry, ecclesiastical hierarchy, or religious head. Neither does it have sacraments or liturgy in the usual meaning of the terms.

The MOSQUE (q.v. Vol. XII) is a place in which the ritual prayer can be performed in common, not a consecrated building. The only essentials in a mosque are an enclosure with a sort of pulpit or stage in the middle for the leader or preacher, and a niche in one wall to mark the direction of Mecca. Any Muslim may lead prayers, although every mosque has a prayer-leader, called an *imam*. All questions concerning religious matters are settled by the scholars of the community (the *ulema*), and each scholar's opinion carries weight according to his standing among his colleagues and the public. If the leading scholars disagree, there is no higher authority to appeal to, and their differences of opinion can be solved only in the course of time. The *ulema* are the spokesmen on all religious matters and are deeply respected. Muslims do not see the need for priests. Each individual must himself listen to the commands of Allah as expressed in the Koran. At the same time Islam fosters the brotherhood and solidarity of the community.

The teachings of Muhammad did not form a complete system of doctrine, and law and dogma were worked out in detail by the scholars during the three centuries (7th to 9th century A.D.) after his death. This official doctrine of Islam rests on three fundamentals: the Koran, *sunna* (example of the Prophet), and *ijma'* (consensus on agreement of the community).

Muhammad's way of life, or *sunna*, is equal to the Koran in importance, so that, for the Muslim, there can be no contradiction between it and the Koran. The *sunna* is documented by the so-called 'traditions', which are statements on the Prophet's sayings and acts, transmitted by his followers over the years, and collected in a number of works.

'My community will never agree on an error', is a saying traditionally attributed to Muhammad, and it expresses concisely the third fundamental doctrine of Islam—the *ijma'* or consensus. This has been defined as the agreed opinions of the scholars of any one generation. It forms the sole basis of a number of important rules and institutions. Consensus, too, recognizes the legitimacy of alternative interpretations of the Koran and *sunna*, so that differing schools of opinion may coexist peacefully. Thus, Islam is tolerant of anyone who has made the essential profession of faith.

Islam as a whole takes a positive view of life; it encourages marriage, trade, and the enjoyment and display of worldly goods. There are five essential religious duties commanded by Allah; the profession of faith that there is no god but Allah and Muhammad is his prophet; prayer and fasting; paying alms-tax, a regular form of charity including contributions to the 'holy war'; and the pilgrimage to Mecca. (The pilgrimage was retained by Muhammad from former Arab rites, but purged of pagan elements.)

The ritual prayer, which the worshipper must perform five times every day at stated times, facing the sanctuary in Mecca (the Kaaba), consists of certain positions and movements (standing, bowing, prostrating himself, sitting), and the recital of Arabic formulae that include passages from the Koran. The midday ritual prayer on Fridays, which includes a short sermon in Arabic, is arranged somewhat differently from the others and, unlike them, must be performed in common with other worshippers. Fasting, or abstinence from all food, drink, stimulants, and intercourse, is observed during the ninth month of the Islamic lunar year, Ramadan, from dawn to sunset. The alms-tax, an annual graduated property-tax payable to Islamic states, has in general fallen into abeyance throughout most of the Islamic world. Only those who can are obliged to make a pilgrimage to Mecca to participate in ceremonies from the 8th to the 13th day of the 12th month.

Next in importance to these religious duties come the practical religious laws that deal with

J. Allan Cash

THE GREAT MOSQUE AT MECCA; PILGRIMS SURROUND THE SACRED KABBAH

such matters as marriage, divorce, inheritance, and legacies. The Koran permits Muslim men to marry more than one wife, four being the maximum, but in practice most Muslim have only one wife, sometimes for economic reasons. Dietary laws order ritual slaughter and ban pork and alcohol. Gambling and lending money for interest are forbidden. Muslims are also forbidden to represent humans or animals in their art (*see* ISLAMIC ART, Vol. XII).

3. REFORMING MOVEMENTS. Very early in the history of Islam the movement split over the question of succession to the leadership. The larger section, called Sunnites, preferred to elect their caliph leader from the Prophet's tribe, the Quraish; the smaller section, the Shiites, now mostly to be found in Persia (Iran) and Pakistan, would accept only Muhammad's cousin and son-in-law, Ali, and his descendants

as leaders. Thus, this schism was political and did not concern any question of religious law or dogma. The split remains, although there is no recognized caliph for either group today.

In Islam there are numerous religious orders that grew out of an early ascetic movement called 'Sufism'. Although a few of these religious orders still adhere to asceticism and withdrawal from the world, most of the members continue to live in society. Each order usually has its own patron saint, as well as special rituals and celebrations which only the initiated can understand and benefit from. These religious orders, however, have been on the wane in the central parts of the Islamic world since the last century (*see also* DERVISHES).

4. HISTORY. Muhammad's original aim was to bring to the Arabs of his time essentially the same message that had been brought by the

Biblical prophets to their peoples, namely, monotheism or the belief in one God. He very soon became involved in wars against pagan Mecca which he succeeded in conquering shortly before his death. The wars against Mecca expanded into the wars of political conquest which his followers waged, starting immediately after his death and continuing throughout the Middle Ages and beyond. There were three main waves of Muslim expansion: the first, from the death of Muhammad in 632 to about 750, covered Iran, Iraq, Armenia, Syria, Palestine, Egypt, North Africa, Sicily, and Spain; its main agents were the ARABS (q.v.). The second wave, between about 1000 and 1500, added northern India, Afghanistan, parts of central Asia, Anatolia, the Balkan Peninsula, and the Sudan; and the main agents were the Turks (see OTTOMAN EMPIRE) together with some Iranians who had themselves been converted to Islam. Constantinople, the centre of the Byzantine Empire, fell to the Muslim Turks in 1453. During this period, however, Sicily and Spain were reconquered by the Christians. In the third great movement, which partly overlapped its predecessor, Islamic advance was commercial rather than military. Since the 17th century, Islam has advanced, not by war, but by means of the trader whose beliefs appealed to many whom he met. There has never been any organized missionary activity as in Christianity, yet Islam has reached Malaya, Indonesia, and Africa, and is still making converts, especially in Africa. Islam's appeal seems to lie in the simplicity of its creed, the practical character of its ethics, the feeling of solidarity and superiority it inspires in its followers and the higher degree of civilization it represents in many regions.

Behind most of the Islamic expansion before the 16th century was the concept of the 'holy war' against unbelievers, the only kind of warfare Islam recognizes. Its aim was not so much the forcible conversion of unbelievers outside Arabia, but their subjection to the supremacy of Islam. Jews, Christians, Zoroastrians, and Hindus, so long as they peaceably accepted the government of the Muslims and paid their tribute-taxes, were allowed to preserve their religion, their laws, and their lands under the protection of the Islamic state. The Muslim conquerors were keenly interested in learning, and they absorbed much of the cultures of the various countries they overran. They made important contributions in the fields of science, mathematics, and philosophy, and though many of their innovations—such as the zero in mathematics, and the mariners' compass—were possibly taken from other oriental cultures, much of their work was a basis for the subsequent advances made in Western thought during the RENAISSANCE (q.v.).

Islam is still a political force, as the formation of the Islamic Republic of Pakistan in 1956 shows. As a religion, Islam has, like other religions, been affected by 20th-century ideas, and there are movements for modernizing the faith. One of these movements is Wahhabism, which started in the 18th century and found its political expression in the State of Saudi Arabia. It also influenced other parts of the Islamic world, particularly Egypt, Pakistan, and India. Wahhabism preaches going back in all details to the exact teaching of the past. In Turkey Islam is no longer the state religion, and under the impact of western ideas many Turks have tended toward pure secularism. This secularism has left sincere Muslims in Turkey free to concentrate on those aspects of historical Islam which may be called religious in the essential meaning of the term, whereas in the other more or less westernized Islamic countries there has been more emphasis on harmonizing the traditional idea of Islam, as a social system and a way of life, with modern ideas and conditions, while paying less attention to formulating the Islamic faith in contemporary terms.

ISRAELI, see JEWS. See also Index, p. 145.

ISRAELITES, see HEBREW CIVILIZATION.

ITALIANS. In order to understand modern Italy it is important to remember her long and troublous history. The Italian nation as we know it today only started a united existence in 1870. Before that the country was composed of several different states governed independently, often by foreigners and often at war with each other. Italian history is therefore very complicated, for every great Italian city has its own distinct history. This has led to a tendency among the inhabitants to think of themselves first as Romans, Venetians, Florentines, Neapolitans, or whatever they may be, and only secondly as Italians, and thus it is not easy for them to understand and attain that kind of national unity which has been a birthright for centuries.

Differences of racial origin have produced differences in character among Italians which also hinder national unity. Italians claim that they are the most mixed people in Europe, for during their history wave after wave of invaders have visited or settled in the country. Generally speaking the northern Italians are more Germanic and the southern more Latin in origin, and the differences between them are very marked. As a whole, the northerners are more practical, industrious, progressive, and efficient than the southerners, who, living in a hotter climate and on poorer soil, find it more difficult to come to terms with life.

Although it is dangerous to generalize, there are certain characteristics which are common to most Italians. They are great lovers of beauty and intensely proud of their ancient civilization, their art, and their music, especially opera. On the whole they are content with simple pleasures, are gay and talkative, passionate and quarrelsome, and extremely sensitive to any slight. They love to gather in the streets, make a noise, and talk for hours. Until recently Italian girls led a secluded life in the home and were not allowed out unless escorted by a member of the family. Now they are much more emancipated and go to the universities and take up professions. But women doctors or lawyers are still comparatively rare in Italy. Italian women do not play games very much, but the men are particularly good at any sport which demands speed and ingenuity. Italians are clever engineers and mechanics—the pioneer of wireless, MARCONI (q.v. Vol. V), was an Italian. They are not militaristic, though Mussolini tried to make them so. They have little respect for law, for they are a race of individualists who wish to be left alone to manage their private affairs in their own way.

Italy has been inhabited since the Old Stone Age, and the remains of settlements of all periods since then have been discovered by archaeologists. The Etruscans, early settlers who probably came from Asia Minor, were not only great architects, but sculptors, painters, and craftsmen (q.v. ETRUSCAN ART, Vol. XII), and their influence is to be seen, after more than 2,000 years, in the small industries and crafts of central Italy. Colonies of Greeks settled on the coasts of southern Italy, and some of the most

J. Allan Cash

ROME: THE SPANISH STEPS AND FLOWER MARKET

beautiful of the Greek temples are to be found at Paestum, south of Naples, at Agrigento, and near Palermo in Sicily. The establishment of the Roman Empire brought fresh incursions of foreigners. Rome itself attracted scholars, merchants, and adventurers from all over the known world, and these strains mingled with the original inhabitants (*see* ROMAN CIVILIZATION).

After the fall of the Roman Empire successions of invaders, particularly from the north, came either to plunder and depart or, like the Lombards, to settle down and establish kingdoms in what is now known as the Plain of Lombardy. In Sicily and the south there were invasions of Saracens in the 9th century and of Normans in the 11th, and these occupations, as well as that of the Spaniards in later times, have left their mark, especially upon the Sicilians— a people distinct from their neighbours in many ways. In A.D. 800 the HOLY ROMAN EMPIRE (q.v.) was founded—the Emperor to be head of the temporal world as the Pope was head of the spiritual. In the late Middle Ages a great rivalry grew up between the Holy Roman Emperor and the Pope. The Pope was not only head of the Western Church but was also ruler of certain Italian states called the Papal States. Some of

Italian State Tourist Office
VENICE: RIO DI PALAZZO DUCALE

the great Italian families supported the Emperor and some the Pope, and there was continual warfare between them.

Most of the city-states were governed by despots who were often tyrannical in their treatment of the people and who did not hesitate to assassinate those who threatened their positions. In the Republics of Florence and Venice there were constant intrigue and murder amongst the great families who controlled the states. But these wealthy families, such as the MEDICI (q.v. Vol. V) in Florence, the Visconti in Milan, and the Este in Ferrara, encouraged learning and the arts, and fostered an individualism which allowed genius to develop freely. In the 14th century the poet DANTE and the painter GIOTTO (qq.v. Vol. V) foreshadowed the RENAISSANCE (q.v.) of the 15th and 16th centuries. The 15th century was one of the most brilliant periods of artistic achievement, and Florence was the chief centre of activity. Stimulated by the revival of classical learning, poets, painters, architects, sculptors, and scientists were developing new ideas, exploring new countries, and devising new forms of expression. The genius of these men was not confined to one subject but ranged over many. LEONARDO DA VINCI was a scientist as well as a painter and sculptor, and MICHEL-ANGELO (qq.v. Vol. V) was a sculptor, painter, architect, and poet. The wealth of the Papal

Court in Rome drew artists from all over Italy for such great works as the building of St. Peter's. Milan, the most important commercial city, also attracted artists though it did not produce many noteworthy ones of its own. The Venetian State, the greatest of the maritime states, drew its wealth from its trade with the East. There is an Eastern richness in Venetian architecture and painting, which reached its greatest height in the 16th century with the painter TITIAN (q.v. Vol. V).

In the 16th century and for the following three centuries Italy was ravaged by the invading armies of France, Spain, and Austria, and most of her cities came under the power of one foreign conqueror after another. The Reformation in northern Europe had reduced the power of the Popes, and there was no one with sufficient power to unite the country against the invaders.

After the Napoleonic wars in the 19th century a movement for a united Italy, inspired largely by the idealist MAZZINI (q.v. Vol. V), began to take shape. The King of Sardinia, Victor Emmanuel, of the House of Savoy, became its leader, and after a series of wars, revolutions, and much clever diplomacy, in which the brilliant statesman CAVOUR and the romantic soldier GARIBALDI (qq.v. Vol. V) played important parts, Italy was finally united in 1870 with Victor Emmanuel as the first king and Rome as capital.

After the First World War political unrest and bad social conditions allowed MUSSOLINI (q.v. Vol. V) to establish himself as the dictator of a Fascist régime. Although he brought efficient organization into Italy and inspired the Italians with a sense of unity and pride in their country, he misled them into a policy of military aggression. With dreams of a second Roman Empire he became more and more militaristic, finally involving Italy in the Second World War on the side of Germany, with disastrous results both to himself and his country.

In 1946 the country decided by plebiscite to become a Republic. With a democratically elected Parliament, the Italians achieved considerable economic advance and some degree of political stability. One of the strongest unifying forces in the country is the ROMAN CATHOLIC CHURCH (q.v.) to which most Italians belong.

Italy has a population of over 54 millions (1971), of whom some 25 per cent are employed on the land and some 40 per cent in industry.

J. Allan Cash

SARDINIA: WASHING WOOL IN THE RIVER FLUMENE

The industrial quarters in the large cities in the north, such as Turin with the Fiat motor works, are much like those in other countries. Farming conditions vary from the big dairy farms in Piedmont in the north-west to tiny patches of land on the mountain-sides of central and southern Italy. Since the war there has been a big movement of workers from the land into industry, and from the impoverished South to the large industrial towns of the North, where the influx of Southern workers has created considerable housing problems. Strong efforts have been made to establish more industries in the South and to improve farming conditions there, but many Southerners also go to Germany, Switzerland, or France to find work.

Education is free and compulsory—nearly all the children go to the same State schools, though there are a few boarding-schools run by the teaching orders of the Roman Catholic Church. The people still cling to their local dialects, which are almost different languages, especially in the country districts.

The popular holidays are the saints' days of each town or village. The day begins with Mass, then in the country there is a fair with stalls and side-shows, and people sit about all day and most of the night eating and drinking in the restaurants and cafés. Each district prides itself on its cooking and local delicacies, but the most popular dishes are *pasta*, that is, macaroni or spaghetti, and *minestrone*, a soup of vegetables and meat stock, both eaten with grated cheese. Practically every Italian midday meal begins with an enormous plate of *pasta*, with either gravy or tomato sauce poured over it. Everyone—even the small children—drinks the local wine with meals; coffee is a popular drink, but tea is an expensive luxury. Olive oil is used a great deal for cooking, especially in the south.

See also Vol. III: ITALY. See also INDEX, p. 145.
See also Vol. IV: ITALIAN LANGUAGE.
See also Vol. XII: ITALIAN ART; ITALIAN LITERATURE.

J

JAINS belong to a relatively small religious community in the Republic of India, numbering in 1961 just over two million members, as compared with 366 million Hindus, 47 million Muslims and 11 million Christians.

Jainism began rather earlier than BUDDHISM (q.v.) but in the same period of Indian religious history, and apparently for much the same reason; and the two movements to some extent resemble one another. The founder, properly called Vardhamana, but by his disciples Mahavira (the great hero), was, like Gautama (Buddha), the son of a nobleman of princely

rank, and was born somewhere about 599 B.C. When he was twenty-eight his parents died, and he became entirely devoted to the quest for spiritual enlightenment. Like Gautama, he began by joining an already-existing order of ascetics (*see* ASCETICISM); but at this point the likeness ceases. Guatama lost confidence in the extreme forms of the ascetic life, and pursued what he called 'the Middle Way'. Vardhamana sought even more severe forms of discipline. He gave up clothes entirely and taught that to 'fast unto death' was meritorious. Vardhamana taught that there was an infinite number of souls which inhabited the material universe in different forms according to their degree of merit. Stones, vegetables, insects, as well as human beings are the temporary dwellings of souls. It is for this reason that Jains have great respect for all life forms.

The Jains are divided into two groups, the *Digambara*, 'the Space-clad', and the *Svetambara*, 'the White-clad'. The former are found in the Deccan, and the latter in Gujarat. The different names referred to the differences between the monks and nuns of the two divisions. The Digambara go naked, and the Svetambara wear white cloaks. These distinctions do not apply to

A JAIN TEMPLE AT AHMADABAD, BOMBAY, INDIA

the laity, nor are there other marked differences in doctrine between the two sections.

Jain monks and nuns wear masks, like surgeons, to stop them from breathing in tiny insects, and they sweep the ground in front of them as they walk to prevent them from treading on ants and the like.

Although the laity is less strict, all Jains are strictly vegetarian, shield their lamps, and take their last meal of the day before sunset to avoid killing insects which would be attracted by flame at night.

Yet extreme asceticism and kindness to animals are not the most important doctrines of the Jain religion. Both Vardhamana and Gautama gave up the idea of a personal God—a God who was in any real way like a more exalted kind of human person. At this stage of religious thought in India some thinkers had come to give up the belief in this kind of God. In place of this Vardhamana taught that the Universe was eternal and made up of six substances, space, time, units of matter, laws of merit (of which there seem to have been two), and souls. The goal of life, and also its final stage, is a sort of Paradise called Jiva, in which those souls which have gained enough merit to win release, live happily for evermore. The word 'Jain' means a conqueror or one who lives victoriously.

Vardhamana's disciples seem in one sense to be more truly atheists than the Buddhists, whose idea of the Universe takes the place of God. But in recent years a famous Jain preacher has publicly denied that they are atheists, and says that they believe in a Supreme Spirit, whom they call Paramatman. If this is true, it means that the Jains have been misunderstood for many years. But it may also mean that the Jains are themselves altering their faith and changing its balance.

Jain temples are clean and beautiful, with much white marble and bright colours. Their chief features are statues of Jain saints, who are numerous. Jains believe in a succession of spiritual leaders called Jinas or Tirthankaras, who have all been members of the warrior caste (*see* CASTE). Every fully professed Jain monk or nun has to take five vows—not to kill, not to lie, to take nothing that is not given, to abstain from all sex-experience, and to take no pleasure in any material thing.

Perhaps the best work which the Jains do is to maintain hospitals for animals, and they make a practice of collecting and rearing young animals which have been discarded by their owners. The worship in the temples consists partly of acts of silent meditation, partly of simple offerings of flowers, incense, and lights in front of the images of the Jinas, accompanied by the singing of hymns.

See also INDIAN PEOPLES.

JAPANESE. Among the earliest inhabitants of Japan were the Ainus, called the 'hairy Ainus' because they were hairy-chested, long-bearded men. Less than 20,000 of them now survive in the bleak, mountainous island of Hokkaido, the most northerly part of Japan.

Over many ages northern Mongolians from China and southern Malay peoples, as well as some from South Sea islands, had spread to Japan. The race formed from a mixture of these peoples was already present at the same time as the Ainus, whom they gradually drove to the north. Typically, the Japanese have small bones, sallow skin, and dark, straight hair.

Civilization came late to Japan, as compared with China, and then came with great suddenness. In the 7th century A.D., when CHINESE CIVILIZATION (q.v.) was at its height under the T'ang Dynasty, the Japanese were so much impressed that they adopted for themselves all its main features. The Japanese had no writing, so they borrowed the Chinese characters and used them for their language. They studied the classics of Confucius and the scriptures of Buddhism; they refashioned their whole system of government, their social habits, rules of behaviour, and even their style of dress in imitation of the Chinese. About a thousand years later, in the 19th century, they took over Western civilization in the same wholesale way and, with great rapidity, made themselves comparable to Western nations in modern science, especially military science.

In spite of this tendency to borrow new ideas wholesale, however, the Japanese were for many years, and especially in the 20th century, taught to see themselves as a master race, sons of the Sun, born of the Gods, with their own rules of right and wrong, and appointed by the gods to discipline the world, if necessary by force. It was this spirit, combined with fanatical loyalty to an Emperor whom they thought of as semi-divine, which made them so formidable a foe when they set out in 1940 to conquer the Far East.

AN AINU FAMILY

Paul Popper

to shut out completely the outside world, especially the West. Foreigners were expelled, Christians massacred, no ships were allowed to sail to or from foreign ports, and returning Japanese were beheaded. For 250 years, from the time of Queen Elizabeth I to the time of Queen Victoria, the Japanese people lived in almost complete isolation.

This artificial state of affairs was brought to an end by force from the European nations, starting with an American naval expedition under Commodore Perry in 1853. From then on the Japanese reversed their policy and borrowed all they could from the Western World. The last Shogun resigned, and the Samurai were abolished. The Emperor became the head of a parliamentary system of government. But, although superficially Westernized, the Japanese still retained their old belief in the master race. The vast increase in population made room for expansion essential, and the Japanese began to cast greedy eyes on the territory of their neighbours, especially China. In 1932 they invaded the Chinese province of Manchuria, thus starting a policy of military expansion which culminated in their attempt in 1940 to master the whole Far East. After their defeat in the Second World War the Emperor publicly resigned any claim to being divine, and a more constitutional form of government was set up. From that time on Japan, the victim of atomic bombing, has often denounced war and has devoted her vast energies to rebuilding her cities and her economy.

By the end of the 12th century the central government under the emperor was gradually losing control, and court nobles struggled for power. As a result, the country became divided into military clans, practically independent and always fighting one another. The clan-chieftains, called *Daimyos*, like the great barons in England at the time of the Wars of the Roses, commanded hosts of armed retainers, called *Samurai*. The Samurai were bound in loyalty to their chief by the strictest code of honour, but were utterly ruthless and contemptuous in their treatment of the wretched peasant serfs. At the beginning of the 17th century, however, one clan, the Tokugawa, made themselves masters over the rest and established a firm rule under which Japan remained at peace for over 250 years. The position of the Emperor during this time was very strange. He became a mere puppet, kept like a bird in a golden cage, the centre of a brilliant court, worshipped almost as a God by his people, but with no political power. All authority lay with the Shoguns, the heads of the clan.

The Shoguns at the end of the 16th century grew disturbed at the influence in Japan of the increasing number of European merchants coming to trade, and also of the Catholic missionaries who were converting the people to Christianity. The Shoguns wished to preserve the old feudal state of affairs and to keep the people submissive, and so they decided

The American occupation of Japan in 1945 had a considerable influence on Japanese ways of living. American manners were increasingly adopted and Western foods including bread, meat, and dairy products were added to the traditional Japanese diet of rice, fish, and vegetables. Food is still served in sets of little bowls and eaten with chopsticks. Green tea is drunk at meals, and all through the day. Coffee and Western 'black tea' are also popular.

In more remote country districts there is less change. The country houses are built for the most part of wood, on platforms raised above the ground, with walls that can be pushed back to let in the light and air or to convert several small rooms into one large one. There is little furniture: the people sit on padded mats on the floor, using low tables for their meals. Bedding is kept in a cupboard and spread on the floor at night. But the traditional charcoal braziers have given way to oil or gas heaters, though country people still wear padded clothing in the harsh winter.

I.S.E.I., Tokyo

A JAPANESE FAMILY AT HOME

Most Japanese now wear European dress. When men come home after work they sometimes change into the national kimono. Elderly women often wear the kimono at home, but most women wear it only for formal occasions—weddings, funerals, festivals, or parties. The formal kimono is very beautiful, usually of rich silk crepe, worn with an *obi*—a wide stiffened belt of patterned brocade.

Japan is now a highly industrialized country with some of the largest modern cities in the world. Industry is well organized with active trade unions; and though the people work for what seem to Europeans long hours and low wages, conditions of work and welfare services are good. Three-fifths of Japanese production, however, still comes from small industries employing fewer than 100 men, and much of that is family work done at home.

The Japanese year is marked by many festivals which are the public holidays. First, there are the great New Year festivals lasting a week. March 3 is the feast-day of girls, at which the family dolls are set out—tiny figures of the old emperors and empresses and their courtiers, beautifully dressed. In May is the boys' festival with more dolls—this time figures of famous warriors in armour. Huge cotton fish are flown like flags from the roofs: the boys' fish is the carp because it swims upstream against difficulties as a boy should do. In July is the feast of the dead, when offerings of food are carried to graveyards, and tiny, frail boats, carrying a cargo of food and a light, are launched on lakes and rivers (*see* ANCESTOR WORSHIP). The different flowers—plum, peach, iris, and wistaria—have each their own festival: in cherry-blossom time the whole country goes on holiday. Every temple has its festival days with praying, acting, and holiday-making. In summer people go on pilgrimages to famous shrines on the mountains and beside lakes. The theatre is also very popular: the Japanese will sit for hours watching their own immensely long classical plays as well as translations of Shakespeare's plays. Professional wrestlers will collect large audiences; and recently young Japanese have taken up what they call 'foreign-style' games and sports.

The Japanese as a whole are a highly literate, cheerful, busy, courteous, and good-tempered people: the women in particular are patient, hard-working, and long-suffering. But for generations they were taught to consider the individual of no importance compared with the country or the family. Marriages were traditionally arranged by the family, and the bride might never have met her husband until the wedding day, when she would return with him to become a member of his father's family. Nowadays, however, young people prefer to make their own choice, and then to set up house for themselves. Again, the Japanese were taught

I.S.E.I., Tokyo

TEA CEREMONY
The Japanese girl is wearing a kimono and *obi*

to believe what their rulers told them and to obey them. Their religions, BUDDHISM and SHINTO (qq.v.), encouraged this attitude—the former to think little of the importance of this life, and the latter to glory in the greatness of their country. The Japanese way of life has greatly changed, but old customs may still affect their thinking.

See also Vol. III: JAPAN. See also INDEX, p. 146.
See also Vol. IV: JAPANESE LANGUAGE.
See also Vol. XII: JAPANESE ART; JAPANESE LITERATURE.

JAPANESE RELIGION, *see* SHINTOISM.

JAVANESE, *see* INDONESIANS.

JEHOVAH. This is really a mis-spelling in English letters of the Hebrew name for God. Hebrew is frequently written with consonants only and without the markings or 'points' which indicate the vowels. Thus the Hebrew name for God is written יהוה or, as near as we can give it in English block lettering, YHVH or YHWH. The vowel-pointing is usually judged to give a form varying from YAHOH or YAHU to YAHWEH.

Some think that YAHU or YAHOH is the oldest, and that it may have been the name for an ancient wind-god of the early Semites (Arabic, *hawah*, to blow). But the Bible story in Exod. iii seems to show that by the time it was written YHWH had become connected with the Hebrew verb, HVH, 'to be', and that YAHWEH properly means 'He Who is', or, as we might render it, 'The Supreme or Self-Existent Being'. This Name was held so sacred that the Hebrews, from motives of reverence, would not say it if they could help it, but substituted another word ĂDONAI, or Lord. This word had different vowel-points, and JEHOVAH is the result of trying to write YHWH or YHVH with the vowels of ĂDONAI. 'Jehovah' is not used earlier than the Protestant Reformation (1520).

See also JUDAISM; GOD.

JESUIT, *see* Vol. V: LOYOLA, IGNATIUS.

JESUS OF NAZARETH, often referred to as 'the Founder of Christianity' but more correctly described by St. Paul as its 'Foundation', lived and worked in Palestine during the reigns of the Roman Emperors AUGUSTUS (q.v. Vol. V) and Tiberius. Almost all that we know about his life comes from the New Testament, and what little there is of historical worth from other sources serves to confirm the New Testament account. Our information is nearly all concerned with the short period of two or three years which we call the Ministry. The Gospels of Matthew and Luke supply a few particulars about Jesus's birth and infancy, and Luke has a single story of a visit to Jerusalem when he was about 12 years old.

According to Matthew's account, the birth of Jesus took place while Herod the Great was still alive, that is, before the spring of 4 B.C. The family home of Joseph and Mary seems certainly to have been at Nazareth in Galilee, but both Matthew and Luke agree in making Bethlehem the birthplace. According to Luke the birth took place at the time of a census of the population ordered by the Emperor Augustus; but unfortunately we know too little about these registrations to say whether such a census was held before 4 B.C. and, if so, when. Matthew's narrative indicates that Jesus was born between the years 8 and 4 B.C. More than that we cannot say.

It was widely held in the early Church that

Jesus was a descendant of King DAVID (q.v. Vol. V). Both Matthew and Luke give genealogies which make Joseph the last link in the chain connecting him with David. In the first three Gospels he is occasionally addressed as 'Son of David'; but this does not necessarily mean that the speakers knew his ancestry. More probably, since it was believed that the Messiah would be a descendant of David, this form of address meant simply that the speakers thought of him as the Messiah. To others, who did not think of him in this way, he was 'Jesus the son of Joseph from Nazareth'.

Matthew and Luke agree in reporting that Jesus was not the son of Joseph in the ordinary sense, but that he was miraculously conceived by his mother through the agency of the Holy Spirit, without any human father. But if Joseph was not in the strict sense Jesus's father, then Jesus's descent from David, which is traced through Joseph, can be maintained only in the legal sense that Jesus was Joseph's adopted son. The question of the parentage of Jesus could be settled only by the personal testimony of Joseph and Mary; therefore, our acceptance of the account of the miraculous conception of Jesus must depend on whether we believe it to go back to Joseph and Mary and to be a truthful report of what they truthfully told to people whom they trusted.

We learn from the Gospels that Joseph was a carpenter; and tradition, which there seems no good reason to doubt, suggests that Jesus was trained also as a carpenter, and that after Joseph's death he continued the work of the carpenter's shop in order to support the family. Mark tells us that he had four brothers, one of whom, James, later played a large part in the life of the early Church in Jerusalem. There were also sisters. It seems reasonable to conclude that these brothers and sisters were the younger children of Joseph and Mary. The story of the family visit to Jerusalem for the Passover shows us that Joseph was still alive when Jesus was 12. At the beginning of the Ministry some 20 years later it would seem that Mary was a widow.

Though we have no direct information about the years preceding the Ministry, it is possible to make a few inferences from the records of the Ministry itself. It can be inferred from what the Gospels tell us that Jesus had had some schooling; and there is ample evidence that he knew the Jewish Scriptures intimately. Indeed, he showed such mastery of them that he was frequently addressed as 'Rabbi', 'Teacher', even by those who were opposed to his teaching. He was able to express his thoughts in either poetry or prose; and in prose he was adept in the method of teaching by parables. Those who heard him teaching were impressed by the authority with which he spoke; and it is clear that he was able to evoke great loyalty and devotion from his followers.

Life in Palestine in the first half of the first century was dominated on the political side by the Roman Empire, of which Palestine was a colony. On the religious side it was dominated by the elaborate ritual in the Temple at Jerusalem and even more powerfully by the Jewish Scriptures (see BIBLE, section 2), which were read in the Synagogue services and expounded by the scribes. The Law, defined in the Scriptures, was rigidly kept by the Pharisees and Sadducees, and accepted broadly by the mass of the people as the standard of belief and behaviour. The Jewish people, believing that they were God's chosen people and had a great future, bitterly resented the Roman domination, and open revolt against Rome was at any moment likely to flare up. For the devout and patriotic Jew in Palestine the political rulers, whether the Roman-appointed Princes of the family of Herod, or the Roman governors, or even the Emperor himself, were all usurpers and oppressors. The only rightful ruler of Israel was the legitimate heir of the royal line of David, the Lord's Anointed or Messiah. The Jews were taught that in the Scriptures God had promised that this King would come and would save God's people. And so the Jews were constantly on the look-out for the coming of the King and were ready to serve him with hand and heart whenever he should appear. An eager expectation such as this by the mass of the people could be, and was, only too easily exploited by fanatics and ambitious adventurers; and in the end it led to great disasters for the Jewish nation.

Not all the Jews in Palestine shared this hope of a Messiah. Many of those in positions of wealth and power realized only too well that the coming of the rightful king would undoubtedly lessen their authority, if not bring it to an end. The princes of the family of Herod, in particular Herod Antipas, the ruler of Galilee and Trans-Jordan, would be certain to lose their positions, as would also the leading members of the Temple priesthood. The Roman officials would obviously oppose with all their force any move for Jewish independence.

Complicated as was this political position, it was not the whole story. Some of those who looked for a Messiah dwelt upon those parts of the scriptures, in particular Isaiah xl–lv, which suggested that a glorious political future was not the true destiny of the Jewish nation, but rather that the Chosen People were to be God's servants, to carry the knowledge of him and his ways to the other nations, and to do this by service and self-sacrifice rather than by political power. It is unlikely that this ideal had much hold on the masses in Palestine, but it will have been in the minds of some thoughtful Jews.

About A.D. 28, in the Jordan valley in Southern Palestine, there appeared a man who, though disclaiming to be the expected Messiah himself, declared that he had come to prepare the way for the Messiah by preparing a people fit to receive him. John the Baptist called his countrymen to prepare to be God's people by repenting and to accept baptism as a sign of a new start. Jesus came under the influence of John's teaching, and when he received baptism by John he underwent an experience, during which he became aware that God had chosen him to fulfil the divine purpose for Israel and mankind.

After this there followed a period during which Jesus reflected on his call and the ways in which he could fulfil God's will. Matthew and Luke describe in the pictorial story of the temptation how Jesus rejected various methods of bringing about the new Kingdom of God—methods which would merely have made yet another kingdom of the world, depending for its success not on God but on economic and political expedients. During this time he came to see clearly that the Kingdom of God must mean the absolute supremacy of God, with no other purpose and no other will but God's; that to bring about this Kingdom, God's people, Israel, must fully and frankly accept this idea; and that he himself must be dedicated completely to God's purpose, as presented in the Old Testament. In the Book of Daniel (vii. 13) God's Kingdom is represented by a human figure, the Son of Man, to emphasize the contrast with the political empires of the world based on ferocity and cunning. In Isaiah xl–lv the figure of the Servant of the Lord puts the emphasis on the divine way of self-giving rather than self-assertion. In his teaching Jesus both stressed and added to these pictures by his knowledge of God as Father, with a boundless care for all his children.

With these beliefs in his mind it was inevitable that Jesus should think of his work as one of service in the deepest and widest sense. It is not without good reason that we call it his Ministry —a word derived from a Latin word meaning 'to serve'. He proclaimed that the Kingdom of God was already present and active, and that he possessed divine powers, not to force or enslave men, but to set them free from the forces that degraded and destroyed them, and to enable them to live lives worthy of children of God. And so Jesus started on a period of great activity, teaching, and healing, and this soon aroused intense interest and curiosity and drew great crowds to hear him. Where men were interested and sympathetic Jesus looked for disciples and helpers; and so he gathered round him a band of supporters, from whom he chose twelve as his personal companions and assistants. These men, known as the Twelve or the Apostles, were to learn his ways by living with him and later were to be sent out to enlarge the scope of his Ministry.

But when we remember that the mass of the Jewish people had set their hopes on the restoration of Israel to political greatness under a king of the family of David, we can understand the opposition that Jesus's conception of the Kingdom was likely to meet. The Gospels show how frequently Jesus was pressed to become a national political leader, and how swiftly he lost popularity when it became clear that he would not do so. At the same time those who feared any such revolutionary movement regarded him with suspicion and dislike, and all the more for his absolute refusal to compromise where the Ministry was concerned. If the way the scribes interpreted the Jewish Law got in the way of his Ministry, so much the worse for the scribes. If long-established practices in the temple interfered with its use as a place of worship for all men, so much the worse for those practices. If the claims of any human authority conflicted with the will of God, so much the worse for those claims. No considerations of personal popularity or tactful compromise entered in.

Mark, whose Gospel is the earliest, describes Jesus's Ministry as falling into three main stages. During the first stage, in Galilee, which lasted we know not how long, but ended about

THE NATIVITY

Painting by Sandro Botticelli (1444–1510)

AN EARLY PORTRAIT OF JESUS

This 2nd-century painting from a catacomb in Rome may preserve the likeness of Jesus. From a copy by Thomas Heaphy (1813-73)

a year before the Crucifixion, Jesus's influence and popularity grew rapidly, culminating with some people's wish to take him by force and make him king. In the second period Jesus spent much of the time outside Galilee in neighbouring territories such as Tyre and Sidon. During this period the twelve apostles were gradually making up their minds who he was, and finally Peter acclaimed him as the Christ the expected Messiah. Jesus now spoke much more plainly to them about the nature of his Ministry and about the final utmost self-sacrifice which would be needed to fulfil it. During the third period Jesus made a journey to southern Palestine and was active in Trans-Jordan, Judaea, and Jerusalem itself. To this period belong the triumphal entry and the cleansing of the Temple. The anger which his teaching was arousing among the religious leaders was becoming acute, and this period ended in his arrest, trial, and Crucifixion. How long this third period lasted is not known; but astronomical calculations suggest that the date of the Crucifixion was either 7 April A.D. 30 or 3 April A.D. 33.

In the closing stages of the Ministry Jesus might have won much more popular support had he sought it. But he would never compromise for the sake of winning support, nor would he renounce any of the claims he had made for the Kingdom of God, however much these claims antagonized those powerful enemies who wished to preserve the existing conditions in Palestine. These enemies were constantly on the look-out for opportunities to discredit him or prove him the enemy of the people. They tried to trick him into making damaging admissions or claims which would bring him up against the Roman authorities.

The opportunity for which his enemies were waiting came in the end through the treachery of one of the twelve, Judas Iscariot. It was the Passover season, and Jesus and his disciples were in Jerusalem for the festival. They had an evening meal together—whether actually the Passover meal or not we cannot be sure—and on this occasion the things said and done by Jesus made an indelible impression on those who were present. Looking back on it afterwards they understood that here they had been brought face to face with the deepest meaning of the service and sacrifice of their Master; and so out of this last supper came the Lord's Supper, the Eucharist, the most sacred rite of the Christian Church.

When the supper was over all, except Judas who had slipped out during the meal, went to a garden called Gethsemane. It was here that the Temple police, guided by Judas, came upon them, and after a brief struggle, arrested Jesus. The disciples escaped and the police took Jesus to the city to the High Priest. From there he was taken before the Roman Governor, Pontius Pilate, and according to Luke also before Herod. Pilate knew very well that Jesus deserved no punishment, but the Jewish religious leaders had so stirred up the passions of the mob that Pilate feared an uproar if he released Jesus. So, in the hopes of avoiding a serious disturbance, he found him guilty of claiming to be 'king of the Jews' and condemned him to death by crucifixion. The sentence was carried out the same day, and late that afternoon the body of Jesus was buried by friends in a rock tomb, and a great stone rolled to the mouth of the tomb. It was a Friday.

Early on the following Sunday things began to happen. In the first place various people visited the tomb early in the morning and found it empty, except for the grave-clothes. They were told by an angel or angels that Jesus had risen from the dead. Then the disciples and others of Jesus's friends had experiences in which they met someone whom they recognized as Jesus alive and active. The earliest record of such appearances is given by St. PAUL (q.v. Vol. V) in his first letter to the Corinthians, xv, and Paul himself claimed a similar experience. These appearances express or imply the promise that even when Jesus was no longer visibly present he would still be with his followers in spirit and power. Finally, in Luke and the Acts we have accounts of Jesus's Ascension.

As a result of the experiences during the weeks after the Crucifixion, the disciples, who had been utterly dispirited and disillusioned by the apparent failure and end of Jesus's Ministry, took heart again, convinced that the living Jesus himself was continuing his work in the world and that they must continue as his associates and helpers. They now had no doubt whatsoever that the Ministry of Jesus was destined to be as wide as the world and to continue as long as human history. In that conviction they went out on their ministries, and in that conviction successive generations of Christians have continued until now.

See also CHRISTIANITY, CHRISTIAN CHURCH, SACRAMENTS, JUDAISM.

JEWS (from 'Judah'). The Jews are the descendants of the southern branch of the Israelite tribes who settled in Palestine, probably in the 15th century B.C. (see HEBREW CIVILIZATION). In the year A.D. 70 they were utterly defeated after a revolt against the Romans, and their capital Jerusalem was destroyed. Their political hopes being crushed, the Jews reorganized their lives in a new fashion under intellectual leaders or Rabbis whom they recognized henceforth as their supreme authority in all things, much as other people recognize their government. They began to study their traditional lore based on the Bible with an ever-increasing passion. The Talmud—the edition (about A.D. 500) of the Jewish law and the discussions based on it—is one of the most remarkable productions of the human mind, and includes, in what seems a rather haphazard and confusing form, every conceivable human interest. This great work afterwards formed the main subject of Jewish studies in every land,

and made it possible for a Jew to carry about with him, as it were, in all the lands of his exile, the very atmosphere of the ideal Jewish life of long ago. It was this, together with his burning religious conviction, that enabled the Jew to preserve his individuality during so many centuries.

A great deal of the intellectual activity of the Talmudic period took place in Mesopotamia (Iraq), where the descendants of the Jews, deported from Palestine by Nebuchadnezzar hundreds of years before, still survived and maintained an active intellectual life.

The Jews, taken prisoner by the Romans in increasing numbers every time they revolted against the harsh Roman rule in Palestine, were scattered as slaves throughout the Roman Empire, until in the end, only a tiny handful remained in Palestine. But the Jews, though scattered, were held together by their common faith, their common literature, and their common hope of a restoration to their Promised Land, and never surrendered their individuality. Minorities who refuse to be absorbed may well be a difficulty in a country and are often disliked. Moreover, in the Middle Ages people actually thought that the Jews of their own day were responsible for the crucifixion of Jesus many centuries before, and were inclined to forget that Jesus himself was a Jew, as were most of his early followers. Therefore a period of Jewish persecution began: they were forced to live in a separate quarter of the town, later known as the GHETTO (q.v.); they had to wear a disfiguring badge to mark them off from other people; they were not allowed to own land, to practise handicrafts, or to be physicians; they were compelled to earn their living as pawnbrokers and moneylenders, and if they became rich at these callings they were hated all the more. All manner of incredible charges were made against them, for example, fanatics often accused them of the 'ritual murder' of Christian boys at Passovertide. From time to time they were attacked by mobs, and appalling massacres took place: e.g. in the Rhineland in the period of the Crusades, when it was actually believed by the ignorant that the murderer of a Jew was secure of a place in Paradise; or in England in 1189-90, when an exceptionally terrible onslaught took place in York; or all over Germany at frequent intervals. Conditions in the Muslim countries were not quite as bad, for the indignities were not enforced quite so systematically.

Camera Press

TEL AVIV: THE JAFFA MARKET

In spite of persecution, many Jews were able to continue their high standard of intellectual achievement. In every place where they lived they had not only their synagogue but also their House of Study. They collaborated as far as they could in the intellectual life of their neighbours. They did great work in medicine, science, and philosophy, especially where conditions were more favourable, as they were in Spain during the period of Muslim influence. Some of the important names of this period, such as those of Rashi, the learned French Biblical commentator (1040–1105), Moses Maimonides, the greatest of Jewish philosophers (1135–1204), and Judah haLevi, the sweetest singer of Zion (1186–1241), are among the most famous in Jewish history: all are scholars and artists rather than soldiers or men of action.

The medieval persecutions culminated in the total expulsion of the Jews from country after country—from England in 1290, from France in 1306, from Spain in 1492, and so on. By the close of the Middle Ages no Jews were left in western Europe, except in parts of Germany and Italy where the number of independent states

made concerted action impossible and some Jews managed to exist but under degrading circumstances. The great mass of the Jews lived in the East—in the hospitable Turkish Empire then at the height of its power, and in Poland, where the kings had realized how valuable the Jews were for economic life and had therefore encouraged their immigration. The great majority of Jews at the beginning of the 20th century were still living in eastern Europe.

At the close of the 16th century and during the 17th there was more toleration of the Jews in the West, especially in the rising seaports of the Atlantic, where people were beginning to be more interested in developing trade than in religious prejudices. Thus, Amsterdam and Hamburg became great Jewish centres, while the Jews were readmitted to England largely through the broad-mindedness and keen practical sense of Oliver Cromwell. With the triumph of liberalism in the 19th century, the Jews received emancipation everywhere in central and western Europe. In Tsarist Russia, however, which had by now absorbed the greater part of Poland with its huge Jewish population, there took place after 1881 an appalling number of massacres of Jews ('pogroms' they were called) which drove hundreds and thousands of Jews out of the country. The vast proportion of them went to America where there are now more Jews than in any other country of the world. A certain number also went to Germany, England, and the Commonwealth countries.

In every country the Jews took advantage of the new opportunities that emancipation brought them. It is enough to mention people such as Albert EINSTEIN, the scientist, Paul Ehrlich, a very great physician, or persons of Jewish birth but professing Christianity, such as Felix MENDELSSOHN, the musician, or Benjamin DISRAELI, the English statesman (qq.v. Vol. V). While some countries valued the contribution which the Jews could make, the Germans became jealous of it and considered it a national menace. Towards the end of the 19th century there started in Germany and elsewhere a new anti-Jewish movement, based on what they called 'racial' grounds and termed therefore 'anti-Semitism'. From 1933 onwards the Nazi party in Germany used the anti-Semitic movement as a means of rousing German national emotions, and the Jews were useful scapegoats for all Germany's difficulties. This persecution

Camera Press

FARMING ON DESERT LAND NEAR THE DEAD SEA

Kalyah settlement workers cover plants, growing in chemically treated volcanic rock, with thin sheets of plastic

caused a terrible amount of misery in central Europe where Jews were thrust out of their positions, incredibly maltreated, and forced to leave the countries where their ancestors had lived for centuries. During the Second World War this persecution developed into a homicidal mania on the part of the Germans, who attempted to exterminate the Jews in all the countries Germany occupied. There were on the Continent (outside Russia) in 1939 something like 7,200,000 Jews. By 1945 about 5,700,000 had perished; only some 1,500,000, or one in five, remained; in many countries nine persons out of ten had disappeared. It was the most brutal tragedy that had ever happened to any people throughout the course of human history.

Only one thing kept up the Jewish morale in this terrible time. Throughout their history the Jews had preserved, together with their faith, the hope of being restored one day to the land of their fathers, Palestine. When anti-Semitism began to sweep Europe at the end of the 19th century, a Viennese Jew named Theodore Herzl had launched the Zionist movement, with the object of making a Jewish national home in Palestine. The British Government expressed sympathy with this in 1917 (the 'Balfour Declaration') and in 1920 was assigned the 'mandate' for administering Palestine under the League of Nations. Thousands of Jews were admitted into Palestine and in 1948 an independent republic, ISRAEL (q.v. Vol. III), was set up. The Israelis have improved methods of cultivation, developed industries, founded a Hebrew university, and established all-Jewish towns. Jews throughout the world take pride in this achievement.

There are now only about 12 million Jews. Almost half of them live in the United States, and $2\frac{1}{2}$ million in Israel. The remainder are distributed over every continent.

See also Vol. III: ISRAEL; INDEX, p. 145.
See also JUDAISM, HEBREW CIVILIZATION.
See also Vol. IV: HEBREW LANGUAGE.

JORDANIANS, *see* INDEX, p. 146.

JUDAISM. 1. HISTORY. Judaism, the religion of the Jews, is one of the oldest living religions, and one of the smallest. The Jews were originally a nomadic people of the Middle East and, ethnologically, belong to the Semitic-speaking group. According to the Hebrew Scriptures, known to Christians as the Old Testament, the Jews owe their foundation as a people to Abraham, who was the first man to preach the idea of monotheism—that is, that there is only one all-powerful God. Later they received, through Moses, the revelation of God that began with the Ten Commandments, which were to be the constitution of a 'kingdom of priests and a holy people'. Moses' teachings were concerned not only with religious beliefs but also with moral and ethical matters, and their fundamental purpose was to help men to carry out God's will in their daily lives. Eventually, the teachings of God to Moses were written down in the Five Books of Moses, known by the Jews as the *Torah* (Teaching), namely, Genesis, Exodus, Leviticus, Numbers, and Deuteronomy.

Moses also warned the Jews that their future history would depend on how they lived and behaved, saying that if they obeyed God's commandments they would live happily in the land He had promised them, but if they disobeyed Him, they would be driven out of their land. Under the kings Saul, DAVID, and SOLOMON (qq.v. Vol. V), the prophets in the tradition of Moses conveyed God's will to the king and the people. Again they proclaimed that the destiny of the people depended on its social morality, and they warned them that God might use the pagan nations to punish Israel for its backsliding.

These prophecies proved accurate, for in 586 B.C. Jerusalem was razed to the ground by the Chaldeans, and the Temple of Solomon was destroyed. Though taken into exile in Babylon, the Jews remained faithful to their belief in one God who ruled all men, and they took heart in the message of a new prophet whose writings are included in the Book of Isaiah (x–xvi). This prophet told them that God would remember his promises, punish the other nations for the sin of worshipping idols, and lead the Israelites back to their land. A new form of worship through prayer only, and without sacrifice, was carried on during the exile in the Jews' meeting

Camera Press

THE WAILING WALL, JERUSALEM
This historic wall is built on the site of Solomon's Temple

Camera Press

THE ANCIENT ITALIAN SYNAGOGUE, TRANSFERRED TO
JERUSALEM

places that later came to be called 'synagogues' (the Greek word for 'meeting places'). When Babylon was conquered by the Persians under CYRUS (q.v. Vol. V), those who wished were permitted to return to their homeland. By 538 B.C. many Jews had gone back and by 520 B.C. the Temple was rebuilt.

During this period, the Jews began to convert pagans to their monotheism, thus indicating that their faith and community were open to all. In time, however, new enemies arose to conquer their land, namely, ALEXANDER THE GREAT (q.v. Vol. V), in 330 B.C., who was followed by the Romans in 63 B.C. As a result, many Jews began to emigrate, settling in such places as Alexandria, Egypt, and the cities of Asia Minor and of the Italian peninsula. The Second Temple was destroyed after the Jews in Israel had revolted against Rome, between 66 and 73 A.D., but their religion survived for they had come to see that God could be worshipped through prayer and through their way of life in any place. Thus, many Jewish communities, other than those in Israel and Babylon, developed throughout the Mediterranean world, and spread gradually into western Europe and beyond.

The Jews were now led, by their wise men or rabbis (meaning 'masters'), to an even greater loyalty to the *Torah* and its daily commands. During the next five centuries the various rabbis' interpretations of the Hebrew Scriptures came to be accepted by most Jews all over the world. These teachings were written down in the Talmud, which consists of two parts: the *Mishnah* (repetition of the traditions), compiled by Rabbi Judah the Prince at the beginning of the 3rd century A.D.; and the Gemara (learning and discussion of the *Mishnah*), which was written down by Rav Ashi, a Babylonian teacher, in the 5th century A.D. In this way, Judaism came to revolve around the teachings of the *Torah* and the Talmud, and the scattered communities accordingly centred on the synagogue, the school house, and the religious and social life of their own group. Living under their own laws, they governed themselves in all matters that the state permitted, and although they spoke the language of their adopted countries, they also preserved a knowledge of Hebrew, and observed their own calendar.

The Jews continued to maintain their religious unity, with many local variations, until the beginning of the 19th century, when the rest of the world began, after centuries of intolerance and persecution, to grant them political and economic freedom, and in some places, social freedom as well. In the West, many Jews began to reinterpret some of the ancient beliefs, and reform religious practices, rendering them more compatible with an advancing world. These Jews called themselves 'liberal', or 'reform'. In America, a more moderate reform group is known as 'conservative'. The third, or 'orthodox' group, remained loyal to the ancient form of Judaism.

2. BELIEFS AND PRACTICES. The basic beliefs common to all the branches of the religion today may be summarized as follows: (1) There is one, living God, who rules the world through law and love; (2) Man is created in the divine image, endowed with moral freedom, and is held responsible for the overcoming of evil and the search for moral ends; (3) God reveals himself not only through creation, but also through revelation to Moses, the prophets, and the later sages of Israel; (4) The Jews have been chosen to bear witness to the unity of God in the face of every form of paganism and materialism, and to seek the establishment of God's rule based on the principles of justice, truth, and peace; (5) Jews ought to express their faith through the home, the synagogue, and through the education of their children. Orthodox, and some Conservative Jews also believe in the resur-

Israel Tourist Office

THE RAM'S HORN, USHERING IN THE HOLIDAYS

rection of the dead, and a last judgement, and most religious Jews believe that God rewards goodness and punishes evil.

The modern Jew fulfils many practical commandments. The first is the commandment of circumcision, which, performed on the eighth day after birth, symbolizes the consecration of the male children of Abraham to the God of Abraham, and it is observed by all. Second is the *bar mitzvah*, which marks the acceptance of a boy into the community as a responsible person. It is celebrated at the age of 13, when the boy is called to the reading of the *Torah* during synagogue services. Among Reform congregations, girls are similarly called. Some congregations hold a confirmation service as well at the age of 15 or 16. Marriage constitutes the third major commandment, which, with the founding of a family, is considered a sacred obligation. The final religious occasion is, of course, the funeral rite. Burial prayers emphasize the righteousness of God's judgement, a belief in the immortality of the soul, the hope for a judgement day and a righteous judge, and the resurrection of the dead. Believers are expected to pray in the synagogue not only on the Sabbath (Saturday) but also daily. Prayers are also said at home before and after eating.

There is public prayer on the special holidays throughout the year, which begin and end at sundown. The Sabbath begins on Friday night with a benediction of bread and wine before the evening meal. The rule against work on the Sabbath (Saturday) is strictly kept, and there

are services in the synagogues marked by special prayers, readings from the sacred books, and explanations by the rabbi of their application to present-day life.

The Jewish New Year begins in September with *Rosh Hashanah*, the Day of Judgement. The following 'Ten Days of Penitence' conclude with *Yom Kippur*, the Day of Atonement, observed with fasting and prayers of confession and contrition. The *shofar* (ram's horn) is sounded during morning service during the month before New Year and the Ten Days, and just before sundown on the Day of Atonement.

Five days later, the Feast of Tabernacles begins, marking harvest time. The other annual festivals are *Pesah* (Passover), the spring festival in April and Pentecost, the autumn festival, 50 days after the Passover.

As historical festivals, each has a special meaning, for example, Passover commemorates the exodus from Egypt, and then unleavened bread is eaten, such as the ancestors prepared in their haste to escape Egyptian slavery.

Laws about food, based on Biblical commandments, are an important part of traditional Judaism. Jews may not eat some meats, especially pork, and certain types of fish, and there are rules on the method of slaughter. The eating of dairy products after meat is also prohibited. These laws are intended to consecrate the act of eating. Food which conforms to them is called kosher, which means 'suitable'. Traditional Jews wear a special prayer shawl adorned with fringes at the four corners, and also a skullcap when they pray, and some keep their heads covered at all times, a custom symbolizing humility. Some Orthodox adherents do not shave.

The Jews did not accept JESUS (q.v. Vol. V) as Christ, the Messiah. To Christians, Jesus is the Son of God and a divine being; to Jews, the Scriptural prophecies do not indicate that the Messiah was to be divine, and they cannot, in their strict monotheism, conceive of another personage on a level with God. The traditionalist Jews still await the Messiah.

The restoration of the land of Israel to the Jews, within the past half-century, has now enabled them to create a society based on the teachings of their faith.

See also HEBREW CIVILIZATION; JEWS.
See also Vol. III: ISRAEL, JERUSALEM.

K

KENYA, PEOPLES OF, *see* East Africans.

KNIGHTS OF THE ROUND TABLE, *see* Arthurian Legend.

KNIGHTS, ORDERS OF. The romantic idea of knights fighting for their faith against the powers of evil was a common one in the medieval world. The Arthurian Legend (q.v.) consisted mostly of stories of such knights. When in 1096 the call came to free the holy places in Palestine from the infidel Turk and to protect pilgrims from molestation, the response was enthusiastic. Some of the Crusaders wanted not only to fight for Christianity but to dedicate themselves to its service for the whole of their lives in the same way as the monks did. They formed themselves into Military Orders, following the same rule of poverty, charity, and obedience as the monks practised, but pledged also to fight the Saracens and protect pilgrims. The Orders of Knights Templar and Knights Hospitaller were founded at the beginning of the century, and the Order of Teutonic Knights in 1190.

1. Knights Templar. The First Crusade succeeded in recovering Jerusalem and parts of the coast of Syria and Palestine from the Turks; and many of the knights from Europe seized land and settled there. But the Saracens still continued to harass pilgrims on their way to Palestine. Nine knights therefore formed themselves into a brotherhood to defend the pilgrims, calling themselves 'poor fellow soldiers of Christ Jesus', and setting themselves to follow the monastic rule. Later they were called Knights Templar because they established their headquarters in a house near Solomon's Temple in Jerusalem. The appeal of the Order was strong to adventurous knights, who joined in great numbers, while kings and wealthy people gave money and lands. The knights wore white tunics with a red cross.

The Templars built strongholds from which to defend the Holy Land and fought valiantly against the Saracens, often with great losses. But much of the crusading effort was spoilt by bad organization and quarrels between those who should have been uniting against the Turk. At one time the rivalry between the Knights Templar and the Knights Hospitaller grew so bitter that open fighting broke out, and most of the Templars in Palestine were killed.

The Knights Templar also established houses in many parts of Europe where they accumulated great wealth and lived for the most part in idleness. In England their headquarters was the Temple Church in London. This and other churches which they built were round, in

Crown copyright

THE TEMPLE CHURCH OF ST. MARY'S, LONDON

The round church was built in the 12th century and the chancel on the right was added later

imitation of the Church of the Holy Sepulchre in Jerusalem.

In the 13th century, when Palestine was lost, the Templars established themselves in Cyprus. Their wealth and possessions aroused envy and hatred, and they were accused, quite falsely, of

A KNIGHT TEMPLAR IN MILITARY UNIFORM, AND A KNIGHT HOSPITALLER IN CIVILIAN COSTUME

idolatry, heresy, and immorality. The Pope was persuaded to suppress them, and horrible tortures were inflicted on them to make them confess their guilt. A few remained in Spain where they continued for some time to fight the Moors. The order was finally suppressed in 1312.

2. KNIGHTS HOSPITALLER. As early as 1023 a 'hospital', dedicated to St. John the Baptist, was founded in Jerusalem to help poor and sick pilgrims. The medieval meaning of the word 'hospital' was a place of refuge for the needy, not only for the sick. In the next century the Hospital of St. John was organized into a military order on the same lines and for the same purpose as the Knights Templar. Their uniform was a black tunic with a white eight-pointed cross on it. In the 13th century when the crusading spirit was weakening, crusaders returning to Europe sold their lands to the knights, so that the Hospitallers grew as wealthy as the Templars. When Palestine was retaken by the Turks, the Hospitallers went with the Templars to Cyprus; but instead of suffering the same fate, they conquered the island of Rhodes and remained there, known as the Knights of Rhodes, for 200 years. They built strong fortresses and kept the Turks at bay until 1522 when at last the island fell. The knights retreated to Malta where they became known as the Knights of Malta. Again they withstood the attacks of the Turks with magnificent valour in many battles, notably Lepanto in 1571. The order declined in the 17th and 18th centuries. It is now a very small organization, devoted to maintaining hospitals. The modern organization, the St. John Ambulance Brigade, adopted the badge of the Knights Hospitaller.

3. TEUTONIC KNIGHTS. In 1128 some German merchants founded a 'hospital' in Jerusalem which survived until the city fell sixty years later. During the Third Crusade, in 1190, the hospital was revived by German knights who formed themselves into a military order. Their uniform was a white tunic with a black cross. This Order also became strong and wealthy. When crusading came to an end, they turned their attention to the heathen in east Prussia. Under pretence of spreading Christianity, they attacked the Lithuanians and Russians, seizing their lands and treating the people with great cruelty and barbarism. In 1525 the Grand Master, Albert of Brandenburg, converted their possessions into a duchy for himself, and the Order came to an end.

See also CRUSADES.

KORAN, *see* SACRED BOOKS, Section 8; ISLAM.

KURDS, *see* IRAQIS; SYRIANS; TURKS.

L

LAKE DWELLINGS. After the last Ice Age the retreating glaciers left behind them a landscape with a multitude of small lakes occupying depressions in the clay which they had laid down. These lakes, with their rich resources of fish, water-birds, and plants, provided a valuable part of the diet of the Middle Stone Age hunters, 8000–3000 B.C. Some of the small camp-sites for one or two families in which these people lived have been excavated, such as the one at Star Carr in Yorkshire. The waterlogged conditions have preserved their bone fishing-spears, mattocks of elk-antler, and tiny arrow-heads set in resin.

At first the incoming farmers of the New Stone Age (4000–2000 B.C.) avoided such areas, where hunting groups still survived. In some parts of Europe little use was made of such areas until much later; but in Switzerland from 3000 B.C. onwards the farmers built their villages on wooden platforms on the reed-swamps which surrounded them. The clay soils were not good for growing crops, but there was plentiful grazing on the hills in summer, and in winter the villagers could feed the animals from fodder collected from the lakeside. Such a village consisted of a dozen or so two- or three-roomed rectangular houses, each with its own hearth and oven, and a larger 'village hall'. This pattern of settlement continued in the Bronze Age (2000–800 B.C.), though individual villages often had to be moved on account of floods. Because the lakes were slowly filling up, as sediment and dead vegetation formed peat at the edges, the oldest sites are found on the edges of the depressions and more recent ones nearer to the centre as they followed the shrinking shore-line. Some of these lakes have disappeared entirely, and the whole depression is now farm-land, but in steep-sided lakes like Lake Con-stance or Lake Zurich the remains of villages are still under water and are sometimes exposed in dry summers.

These 'lake villages' give archaeologists a chance to find remains of many kinds of perishable material which are not preserved on drier sites. These include woodwork, baskets, cloth, bone, horn and antler tools, fishnets and their floats, and even food remains of bread and fruit. Cow-stalls preserved with heaps of fodder and manure have been found on one site. The wooden piles allow botanists to count the tree-rings and say how long it was before the houses were rebuilt. We can even reconstruct the patterns used in textiles over 4,000 years ago. Stone axes still remain in their wooden hafts, and wooden bowls are found as well as pottery forms.

In the later Bronze Age a new motive entered into the use of lakeside sites—defence. In the Federsee—a lake in south Germany near the Swiss border—the remains of a fortified village have been excavated on what was a small island that could be reached only by boat. This was surrounded by a palisade, and when first built around 1000 B.C. consisted of forty square houses

A LAKE DWELLING
Based on a New Stone Age village in Switzerland

round an open space; two or three centuries later these were replaced by nine big houses with their barns and storehouses. This site is called the *Wasserburg* or 'water-fort'. In Switzerland and adjacent areas the farmers of the Iron Age seem to have had a different pattern of settlement, and did not use lakeside sites like those described here.

Lake villages of the New Stone Age and Bronze Age are most common in the areas around the Alps—Switzerland, Austria, south Germany, north Italy, and north-west Yugoslavia. In other areas they are not such a common feature, though lakes were still visited for hunting and fishing, and apparently for ritual purposes—in Denmark and Holland wooden wheels and pottery vessels have been found thrown in as offerings.

In Britain there seems to have been a greater use of marsh areas during the late Bronze and Iron Ages, when more attractive areas had already been settled. In Ireland there are many lakeside sites from this period called *crannogs*, while in southern England the most famous are the Somerset sites of Meare and Glastonbury. The latter was excavated in the early years of this century, and revealed a village of up to twenty round huts in half a dozen clusters representing family groupings, each with its own granary, stables, and workshops, and parking space for chariots and carts. This was sited just on the edge of the lake, with access on the landward side and a landing-stage for canoes on the other.

The economy of the village was based on providing summer pasture in the marshes for sheep which spent the winter on the drier limestone hills nearby. These were the basis of a household woollen industry, and many objects such as spindle-whorls, loom-weights, and weaving combs were found. Wheat and beans were grown in summer, and winter barley. The peat preserved many everyday objects such as wooden bowls, a ladder, cartwheels, tubs, and the handles of iron tools such as billhooks for cutting reeds. Villages with a similar character survived in Ireland down to medieval times.

See also PREHISTORIC MAN.

LAMAISM, *see* TIBETANS.

LAOTIANS. The kingdom of Laos is a vast area along the middle reaches of the Mekong river, sparsely inhabited by perhaps three million people. Some of these belong to minority tribes, but the majority are Laotian; they are related to other people of Laotian stock who live in Thailand. The country, though it has an administrative capital at Vietiane, is not highly centralized. The king normally resides in the more ancient capital of Luang Prabang, farther up the Mekong. Certain areas in the North are virtually controlled by the Communists, and the country has been seriously disrupted by warfare and heavy bombing during the years 1964-72. Previously it was a peaceful back-water, whose

rulers wished simply for good relations with their more powerful neighbours, Vietnam and Thailand.

From 1893 until 1954, the country was ruled by the French as part of Indochina. Before that it had consisted of a number of almost completely separate principalities, which occasionally became involved in wars with the Thai and the Vietnamese, but were usually content to pay tribute to one or the other in return for being left alone. The Laotians are Buddhists, and much of their life centres round the Buddhist temples found in most of the villages. They grow irrigated rice, and their economy is not much affected by world markets.

See also Vol. III: LAOS; INDEX, p. 147.

LAPPS. These are people who live within the Arctic Circle in what is marked in most maps as Lapland, but which actually is territory divided among Norway, Sweden, Finland, and the Soviet Union. The Lapps call themselves *Sämen*, which means people of the marshes.

Their early history is a mystery. They may have come originally from the Ural Mountains or the Volga. They speak a Finno-Ugrian language, and believe that they were the first people who lived so far north. Originally they lived farther to the south-east, but they withdrew northwards when the FINNS (q.v.) and the Scandinavians penetrated these areas.

Today there are about 32,000 Lapps of whom over 21,000 live in Norway, 7,700 in Sweden, 2,600 in Finland, and about 1,700 in the Kola Peninsula in Russia. Because of intermarriage with Norwegians and Finns over the centuries, not all Lapps have the characteristic physical features of their race—short stature, broad head, and predominantly dark skin, hair, and eyes. Today only a few thousand Lapps, mainly in Sweden, still follow the traditional occupation of reindeer-herding. Most of the Norwegian Lapps are fishermen, and most of the Swedish Lapps are farmers or work in forests. The Russian Lapps herd reindeer in winter, and move to the coast to fish in summer.

Of the reindeer herders some are mountain or nomad peoples, and others forest peoples. The mountain Lapps have the larger herds and follow them regularly every year into the mountains. The herdsman has to withstand the snow, the dark autumn and winter months, and the fact that the domesticated reindeer is not a

Norwegian Embassy

A LAPP WITH A REINDEER

faithful animal like the horse. The forest Lapps have to guard those reindeer which remain in the valleys grazing among the low-lying forests and swamps. They worry lest the mountain reindeer pass through their grazing-grounds on the way to the mountains, for unlike the forest reindeer, the mountain reindeer tear up roots and thus ruin pasture lands. Another difficulty is the pest-fly or gad-fly which the Lapps call *Kurbma*.

The early Lapps gathered into bands called *sida* to follow, trap, and care for the migratory reindeer more easily. Nowadays, the older tribal organization has disappeared and has been supplanted by the laws and organization of the countries within which the bands migrate or where the settled Lapps live. The bonds between relatives remain very strong and important.

All Lapps are now Christians, though it took missionaries a long time to find many of the groups of wandering Lapps. Strong Puritan influences have practically destroyed the old Lapp culture—their dances, feasts, games and songs, legends, and art. The Russian Lapps belong to the Orthodox Eastern Church, but they are said to have retained some of their old beliefs.

The Lapp language is related mainly to the FINNISH (q.v. Vol. IV) and Estonian, but there are about fifty dialects, so that Lapps from one region often cannot understand those from another region. The Lapps have full rights of citizenship in the various countries in which they live. A modern electric railway which runs from Lulea in Sweden across Lapland to Narvik in Norway has broken down a good deal of their former isolation, and so has the building of a highway through North Norway to the Russian frontier.

It is doubtful whether the Lapps, considering their small number and their increasing contact with modern life, will remain as a separate people much longer. The more northern Lapps, who carry on extensive reindeer herding, have a summer and a winter residence. They build little turf huts or sometimes occupy small wooden dwellings for part of the year. Tents are still used among some of the more nomadic Lapps. The southern Lapps, on the other hand, often retain one residence all year around, keeping only a few reindeer in nearby pastures for milk and meat. These Lapps, particularly, utilize the products of the country in which they live.

LATVIANS. The small Baltic state of Latvia includes the old province of Livonia which in the 13th century belonged to the Teutonic Knights (*see* KNIGHTS, ORDERS OF). The Knights defended their territory from all their neighbours until the middle of the 16th century. By 1721, after a long struggle, the country became part of Russia and remained so until, in 1918, an independent republic was formed out of Livonia and three other provinces. In 1940 Latvia and the two other Baltic states, Estonia and Lithuania, became part of the U.S.S.R.

The original Livonians (people akin to the Finns) have almost entirely died out. Latvia (or Lettland) is now inhabited mostly by Letts with considerable groups of Russians, Jews, Germans, Poles, LITHUANIANS, and ESTONIANS (qq.v.). They are mostly foresters and farmers, particularly dairy farmers. In 1920 the large estates were all broken up and divided among the peasants. Riga, the capital, is an important Baltic port connected by railway to Leningrad, Moscow, Warsaw, and Berlin. It is ice-bound, however, most of the winter.

See also Vol. III: LATVIA.

LEBANESE, *see* Vol. III: LEBANON. *See also* INDEX, p. 147.

LETTS, *see* LATVIANS.

LITHUANIANS. In the 13th century a Lithuanian prince called Ringold gathered together into one nation the scattered tribes of Lithuanians in the lands north of Poland. After a century or more of fighting, especially with the Teutonic Knights (*see* KNIGHTS, ORDERS OF), their prince, Jagiello, married the heiress of Poland. From that time Lithuania was ruled by grand-dukes appointed by the Poles until, in 1569, it was incorporated into Poland. When Poland fell under the power of Russia, Lithuania also became Russian. A strong spirit of nationalism developed, and in 1918, after the First World War, Lithuania became an independent republic. In 1940 the republic became part of the U.S.S.R.

The Lithuanians are generally fair and blue-eyed, with good features and fine physique. They are mostly farmers and foresters. The great forests, marshes, and lakes which cover much of their country have played their part in forming the national character. Although most Lithuanians are Christians, the peasants still cling to ancient heathen customs—religious ceremonies carried on in the forests and including the veneration of great oak-trees. In times of dangers they have relied upon the forests and marshes for protection. National folklore and

songs are full of the peacefulness and melancholy loneliness of the vast forests, and their literature draws its inspiration from the country rather than the town.

See also Vol. III: LITHUANIA.
See also Vol. IV: SLAVONIC LANGUAGES.

LOGIC. This is the study of the various ways in which a statement may follow from another statement. For example, the statement that 'all whales are vertebrates' follows from the statement that 'all whales are mammals and all mammals are vertebrates'. Logic examines the ways in which one statement may follow from another, and distinguishes the cases where a statement really follows from those where it only seems to follow. The first are called 'valid' inferences; the last are called 'invalid' inferences. Thus logic studies and tries to classify the various kinds of validity and invalidity. Valid inference is called deduction.

ARISTOTLE (q.v. Vol. V) was the founder of logic. He discovered that the way to find the general forms of valid inference is to use letters to stand for a whole range of different things. For example, by letting W, M, and V stand for Whales, Mammals, and Vertebrates, the above argument about whales can be shortened to 'All W are V, because all W are M and all M are V.' We then discover that, whatever other words we substitute for W, M, and V (e.g. men, human, sinful) the inference still remains valid. 'If all W are M and all M are V, then all W are V', no matter what these letters stand for. Aristotle was the first to realize this general necessary truth about the relations between statements. He also realized others, including this one: 'If all W are M and no M are V, then no W are V.' He also discovered many falsehoods of this kind; for example, he knew that it is false that 'If no W are M and all M are V, then no W are V'.

If we use a single letter to stand for a whole statement, we can quickly write a great many necessary truths about the relations of statements to each other. For example, let the letter P stand for 'the shop is open'. Then the following are necessary truths. (1) If P, then P. (2) Either P or not P. (3) Not both P and not P. Now let us add a second statement: Let Q stand for 'it is Sunday'. Then the following is a necessary truth. (4) If either P or Q and not P, then Q. (If either the shop is open or it is

Sunday and the shop is *not* open, then it is Sunday). Each of these four deductions is a necessary truth, no matter what statements we take the letters *P* and *Q* to stand for. Once we have grasped the idea of letting a single letter represent a whole statement, many more such necessary truths can be discovered.

The subject-matter of logic, or formal logic, as it is sometimes called, overlaps with that of mathematics. The kind of inference which Aristotle first started to classify can be thought of as dealing with classes or sets of things (the set of whales, the set of mammals), and it also deals with relations. These ideas also form part of the subject-matter of mathematics. In the 20th century, some of the most important work in exploring the connexions between mathematics and logic was done by Bertrand Russell.

Apart from the logic of 'deduction', or the necessary relations between statements, logic is sometimes held to cover 'induction', the relation between evidence and conclusions, in our discoveries about the world. For example, 'all swans are white' is made probable by 'all the swans I have seen or heard of are white', although it does not follow necessarily from it. Inductive logic was particularly studied by Francis BACON and John Stuart MILL (qq.v. Vol. V), and has led to the systematic study of scientific method. Like deductive logic, it has connexions with mathematics, in that it is concerned with the theory of probability.

LUTHERAN. This large section of the Christian Church looks back for its origin to the very beginning of the Protestant Reformation in Europe. Martin LUTHER (q.v. Vol. V) was Professor of Theology at the small German University of Wittenberg. An abuse had grown up in the Church of allowing people to pay a sum of money to gain absolution and cancel punishment for sin. This cancelling of penance was called an 'indulgence'. To a man of Luther's deep religious experience the idea of the Church selling the forgiveness of sin was abhorrent, so in 1517 he made a public protest against the whole system. He expected to raise a keen theological argument; the result was far greater —a revolution which cut off most of northern Europe from the control of the Papacy, and the formation of a Church which now claims the pastoral care of some 70 million people.

The heart of Luther's teaching was the subject of Christian salvation. The medieval Church had come to look at the matter mostly from the point of view of discipline: those who were obedient to the doctrines of the Church were sure of salvation. Luther, like St. Paul, St. Augustine, and all the greatest teachers, went deeper. He regarded salvation as a change in the relationship between man and God. The Church taught that man is saved from sin by a gradual process guided by the discipline of the Church: man is saved by the grace of God through the sacraments; man's part is to make use of the grace to benefit by it. Luther, on the other hand, taught that man is saved from the wrath of God caused by his sin and taken back as a son again, not by a gradual process but by an immediate sudden accession of God's graciousness. Man has no part in it, except to have faith in that which God does. This is the main Lutheran teaching—justification by faith alone—and is the basis of much Protestant doctrine. This doctrine was set out in a creed called the Augsburg Confession in 1530.

The modern Lutheran Church is most active in northern Germany, Scandinavia, Iceland, and parts of America, especially the Middle West, where European Lutherans have settled. Lutheran missions have planted churches in many parts of Africa and Asia. There is a good deal of variety in church organization. In Germany the Church, reorganized after it was freed from Nazi interference, is now called the Evangelical Church and is independent of the State. In Denmark, Norway, and Sweden it is the national State Church, including most of the population in its membership. In Sweden the Church has preserved the succession of bishops from pre-Reformation times. In the United States Lutheran groups of different European origins tended to remain separate for many years.

There is also much variety in the form of service. Luther made the sermon the central feature; he also encouraged congregational singing of hymns, many of which he composed himself. In many German and Danish churches Holy Communion is a special service rarely held, whereas in the wooden village churches in Norway, Communion with much medieval ritual crowns Sunday morning's worship. The most elaborate form of Lutheran service is to be found in the Church of Sweden.

See also CHRISTIAN CHURCH.

M

MAGI, *see* Zoroastrian.

MAGIC. This is a word which many people use without knowing definitely what they mean by it. 'It worked like magic', they say. Most of us do not take magic seriously, but to a great number of people all over the world it is a very serious matter. Even amongst educated people there are some who believe in magic more than they would like to admit: they carry mascots about with them and believe in certain days or things as 'lucky'. When a professor at an American university once asked how many students carried any object supposed to have magic-working powers, nearly half of the class admitted that they did. Belief in magic does not easily die out, and therefore amongst primitive people it is naturally very much alive. It is important for all who have to work among such people to understand their ideas about magic.

In order to get a better idea of what magic is, let us imagine ourselves watching a witch-doctor making magic in one of the South Pacific islands. He is trying to bring about the death of another man. First he spies on his proposed victim, getting to know his habits. When he is away from his hut the witch-doctor creeps in and finds some object belonging to his victim, such as a hair from his head. He puts the hair into a tube made of a section of bamboo, and in order to keep it warm he places it under his arm-pit. Having returned to his own hut he makes a fire of sticks, selected because the sap in them blackens when they are cut, just as blood from a wound darkens as it coagulates. He lays the bamboo with the hair in it on the fire and says:

> Eagle and Hawk. Ye both, here is your prey. Seize it with sharp claws. Rend his body and tear it in pieces.

Again and again he repeats the spell, while his assistant turns the packet on the fire. All this time the witch-doctor acts as if he were the victim of his own magic, writhing as if in terrible agony and uttering groans and loud shouts. He cries for help and pleads for sympathy. At last he collapses, pretends to draw his final breath, and lies down as if dead.

As this illustration shows, a man working evil magic may try to secure something connected with his victim—hair, clippings from his nails, or even dust from a footprint—because to possess such things is believed to give the magician power over the person he wishes to injure. Secondly, we note that here, as in practically all cases of magic-making, the operator has a definite aim and object, something good or bad which he is intent on bringing to pass. He may be called in to cure a man or to kill him, but his magic is always for a precise purpose. Thus magic is often used to change the weather. If rain does not fall at the proper season the crops may fail, so rain-makers beat drums or perform other ceremonies to bring rain. The people know very well that they must cultivate their gardens or fields if the crops are to prosper, but they believe that magical ceremonies are also necessary. Since no one dares to leave out these ceremonies, the people never have any proof that they are useless, and they prefer to be on the safe side. If rain happens to fall after rain-magic has been made, then it seems that the magic has been effective; and as the rain-making goes on for months if necessary, there is usually rain sooner or later. The victim of evil magic does sometimes die because he is so completely scared. So we need not be surprised that those who believe in magic are not easily persuaded that it is useless.

The sorcerer on the South Pacific island whom we have been describing recites various words expressing his hatred, and such words used in this way make a spell. The spell or charm is a very important part of magic—few magical ceremonies are performed without the use of spells. The sorcerer says what he wants to happen, though not always aloud; but there are occasions when the spell is made up of meaningless words or syllables, for makers of magic sometimes feel that the magic will be more powerful if it is mysterious even to themselves (*see* Spells and Charms).

Not only does the magician say what he wants

The pole is nearly 40 feet high, and is cut from a single tree trunk. It formerly stood in front of the Chief's hut in a village in Queen Charlotte Island, British Columbia. The figures are totemic animals or mythical figures representing traditional stories of the Chief's ancestors. He sits at the top, wearing his ceremonial hat. Beneath him is a bear holding a frog. Lower down is another bear killing a hunter. At the bottom is a raven

A NORTH-AMERICAN INDIAN TOTEM POLE

to happen, but often he also acts it. In so doing he causes it to occur—so he believes. In the
South Seas a rain-maker paints his body black
and white because white clouds become black
when rain is coming. He thinks if he paints himself in the colours of a cloud it will help to bring
rain. The rain-maker usually beats a drum to
imitate thunder, for he knows that rain accom-
panies thunder and thinks that if he makes
thunder there is likely to be rain. People in
some places jump as high as they can, believing
that thus they assist the crops to grow tall. A
Zulu in love with a girl will chew a piece of
wood to soften her hard heart. In many parts
of the world there is the belief that you can
injure your enemy by making a figure of him
and ill-treating it. A Malay mixes his enemy's
nail-parings or hair into a figure of wax and
scorches it over a lamp every night for seven
nights saying,

It is not wax that I am scorching,
It is the liver, heart, and spleen of So-and-so that I scorch.

In Scotland pins are stuck into a clay model,
and a spell said which begins, 'As you waste
away, may she waste away; as this wounds you,
may it wound her.'

Also very widespread is a belief in the 'evil
eye'. It is supposed that by magical means a
person, envious or jealous of another or for some
other reason wishing him ill, can bewitch or
magically injure him by looking at him. This
belief is thousands of years old. It is fear of the
evil eye which makes some ignorant people
frightened of the camera—they see its glass eye
pointing at them and run away or cover their
faces. About fifty years ago, when a Somerset
woman's pig became sick, she assumed that it
had been 'overlooked' and sent for a white witch
to cure it. The witch ordered a sheep's heart to
be stuck full of pins and roasted over the fire
while a group of people chanted this incantation:

It is not this heart I mean to burn
But the person's heart I wish to turn,
Wishing them neither rest nor peace
Till they are dead and gone.

Iron in many parts of the world is believed to
have power to counteract magic. This is why
horseshoes are supposed to be 'lucky'.

Amongst many peoples there are individual
sorcerers or groups of witch-doctors who are

Smithsonian Institute

A NORTH AMERICAN INDIAN MEDICINE MAN
He holds medicine pipes and has foxes' tails tied to his heels.
Painting by George Catlin, *c.* 1830

regarded as being the great experts in magic.
The tribesmen go to these magicians to get them
to foretell future events (*see* DIVINATION) or to
perform magic on their behalf. But it is usually
recognized that ordinary people may perform
magic or witchcraft without being 'professionals',
and in some tribes anybody may be suspected
of casting spells, though no one would own up
to being a witch. Even at the present day in the
Scottish Highlands and Islands there are spells
and charms which anybody might use, but only
a comparatively small number of people are
believed to have 'second-sight' and other such
mysterious powers.

A person who believes in magic is not necessarily stupid. He argues, as we do, that when
something happens, or some action or ceremony
is performed, certain things follow, but he makes
the mistake of thinking that, because things are
connected in his thought, therefore they must
be connected in actual fact. He hears the wind
whistling as it blows his boat along and realizes
that wind and whistling go together, but he then
jumps to the conclusion, or more usually believes it when he is told, that if he whistles like
the wind he can get it to blow. He hears a bird
call, and then rain begins to fall. He accepts

J. Allan Cash

A WITCHCRAFT STALL, KANO, NIGERIA

the explanation that it was the bird's call which made the rain fall, and thinks, 'If I make a sound like the bird it will bring rain'.

How is it that the magic-maker does not realize that magic does not work? We must remember that, according to his ideas, magic may be opposed by more powerful magic. If the sorcerer is not able to kill or cure a man—whichever he wishes to do—he may conclude that it is because he is up against a greater sorcerer. Also it is often difficult to decide between success and failure; and, still more significant, successes are nearly always remembered after failures have been forgotten.

Belief in magic often occurs mixed with religious ideas, but there is one great difference between magic and religion as these are commonly understood. In performing magic a person tries to control events by what he does and says. He does not humble himself in reverence towards a divine being, praying the god or gods to do this or prevent that. His magic is often meant to work his will contrary to the well-being of someone in the community. He acts as one who has skill in an art and performs his magic as if, by his skill, he could force what he desires to happen. He believes that his magic has power in itself to do what he wants, unless he performs it incorrectly or it is baffled by greater magic. In religion a person does not trust in himself and his own powers in this way, but

relies on higher and greater powers to aid him. We must remember, however, that primitive people do not see clearly the difference between magic and religion. Indeed, even in England there are people who do not realize that their beliefs about mascots and lucky charms do not fit in with their religion.

Witch-doctors and sorcerers may sometimes practise their art in groups, yet there is always something secret about magic-making. There are such groups in one tribe in the southern Sudan—the Azande; they will allow other people to learn and perform their dances, but they will allow only those who are, or are learning to be, witch-doctors to know their lore about plants and the medicines, poisons, and magic preparations which can be made from them. The secrets of the magic art are passed on privately or revealed in the INITIATION ceremonies (q.v.) of the witch-doctors. While the tendency in magic is towards secrecy, the tendency in religion is towards publicity. People, of course, have their personal prayers and religious experience; also some religious ceremonies are only for those who have qualified by a special rite or a series of rites; but as a rule, in religion, people seek the good of everybody and are glad when the whole community joins in, and this is particularly true of primitive people. At their festivals all rejoice together. Religion gives a feeling of unity to the group taking part and thus helps to weld the community together. The effect of magic is often to make people suspicious of one another and to create bad feeling within the community.

See also FOLKLORE.

MAGYARS, *see* HUNGARIANS.

MAHRATTAS, *see* INDIAN PEOPLES.

MALAYSIA, PEOPLES OF. Many different kinds of people live in Malaysia. In the western part of the country, that is in the Malay Peninsula in the south-eastern corner of continental Asia, slightly over half of the inhabitants are Malays, who are Muslims; rather over one third are Chinese; and the remainder are largely descendants of Indian immigrants, mostly Hindu but including some Christians. In addition there are some 40,000 aborigines of various tribes; a few thousand Europeans, Australians and Americans; several thousand Eurasians (the descendants of mixed marriages of Europeans and

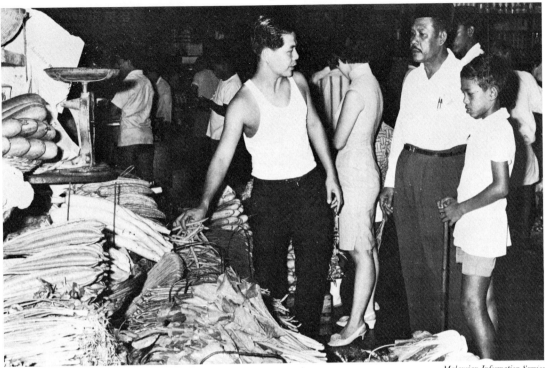

Malaysian Information Service

BARGAINING IN A MALAYAN MARKET

Asians); and other minority groups. In the two Borneo States of Sabah and Sarawak, which are together known as East Malaysia, the population is just as diverse, with many Chinese in the towns, Malays and other Muslim peoples living on or near the coast, and Christian and pagan tribes in the rural areas in the interior. West Malaysia with some 10 million people, has about 86 per cent of the country's population and East Malaysia only 14 per cent, although the latter is much bigger in area than the former.

The Malay peasant ploughs his rice fields with a buffalo-drawn plough and attends the village mosque on Fridays; he has little in common with the hard-working Chinese shop-keeper or artisan, who may speak a little Malay and English but usually converses in one or other of the Chinese dialects, and who eats pork which is regarded by Muslims as unclean. And both the Malay and the Chinese tend to ignore the Hindu rubber-estate worker, who speaks Tamil and lives with other Indians in the estate village. In the Borneo states, too, there is a wide cultural and language difference between the large immigrant Chinese communities and the native peoples. The Ibans and Land Dayaks of

Sarawak, the Dusuns and Muruts of Sabah, the Sakais and Semangs of West Malaysia all have their own languages and way of life, and, among those who call themselves Malay, there is great variety in dialect and customs.

The racial and cultural complexity of Malaysia is largely explained by the accidents of history and by geography. The original inhabitants of West Malaysia, of whom the present Sakais and Semangs are the descendants, were pushed back into the hilly interior of the country by Malays who began to settle on the coasts and up the rivers of the peninsula many hundreds of years ago. The strategic position of West Malaysia on the sea route from the Indian Ocean to the China Sea attracted a few Chinese and Indian traders, particularly to the once-important port of Malacca. From Europe came the Portuguese, the Dutch, and the British in turn: the Portuguese captured Malacca from its Malay ruler in 1511; the Dutch ousted the Portuguese in 1640; and the British replaced the Dutch in the early 19th century; the British started to penetrate the Malay peninsula by acquiring the island of Penang from the Sultan of Kedah.

The development of tin-mining and also of

Malaysian Information Service

SARAWAK: CENSUS-TAKING IN A LONG HOUSE

rubber plantations and the building of railways and roads in the latter half of the 19th century led to large-scale immigrations from South China and South India, which continued into the 20th century. These immigrations led to the present position in which most Chinese and Indians are engaged in commercial agriculture, mining, small-scale industry, commerce, transport, and the professions, whereas most Malays still continue to depend largely on peasant agriculture, particularly rice-farming and rubber. Today, however, more and more Malays are moving to the towns and finding employment in civilian jobs, in government service, and in the armed forces and the police. The population has grown so rapidly in recent years that there is now a serious unemployment problem among young men of all races in the towns.

In the Borneo states plantation agriculture and mining industries have not been developed on the same scale as in West Malaysia. There is, however, a very valuable timber-exporting industry in Sabah, and a large variety of agricultural products are produced in Sarawak. Despite the lower level of economic development, Chinese immigrants have entered Borneo in considerable numbers in the past, and many of the Malays and other Muslims who inhabit the coastal areas of the two states have migrated there from Indonesia.

The Malays are politically dominant in Malaysia, as one would expect in a democratic country in view of their numbers. The constitution places on the Paramount Ruler, himself a Malay, the responsibility for safeguarding the special position of the Malays and other native communities of Malaysia. They enjoy certain advantages over other communities in obtaining employment in the government service, in the award of scholarships, and in the grant of permits and licences to engage in some forms of business activity. Tracts of land are reserved for them for agricultural and residential use. Children of all races in West Malaysia entering primary school now receive their education in Malay as the main language of instruction, though it will be some years before English ceases to be used in secondary school and university education. The special position of the Malays and other native peoples has not, however, given them as high an average standard of living as the Chinese, who control most of the small and many of the large business concerns in Malaysia and are rather clannish over their choice of employees.

Malaysia is a healthy and rich country by Asian standards. There is, however, a racial difference in health as in living standards. For example, about fifty Malay babies out of every 1,000 born alive die in the first year of life, whereas the Chinese figure is about thirty infant deaths. One reason for the better health of the Chinese as compared with the Malays is that a much bigger proportion of Chinese live in the towns, where medical attention and hospital services can be obtained more easily and quickly than in the rural areas.

Nation-building in a newly independent country such as Malaysia is made difficult by the fact that for many people loyalty to Malaysia tends to take second place to loyalty to one's own community. The Government is trying very hard to create a sense of national unity, but the fact remains that at present it is difficult enough at times to prevent tensions between different communities.

See also Vol. III: MALAYSIA; INDEX, p. 148.
See also Vol. IV: INDONESIAN LANGUAGES.

MALTESE. The people of Malta occupy an archipelago which has had an eventful history for many thousands of years, mainly because of its key position in the middle of the Mediterranean. The nearest land is Sicily, 100 km away to the north; the Libyan coast is over 320 km to the south.

The history of this highly individual people goes back to prehistoric times: the neolithic sites of Malta and Gozo (two of the three inhabited islands in the archipelago), especially the rock-cut hypogeum or underground burial chamber at Hal Saflieni, are among the most interesting in Europe. Malta was colonized in the 5th century B.C. by the PHOENICIANS (q.v.) from their colony at Carthage, near modern Tunis, and later by the ROMANS (q.v.). St. Paul is said to have been wrecked on the shores of the bay now called after him, and to have converted Publius, the Roman governor of Malta, to Christianity. After the break-up of the Roman Empire, Malta was occupied for some 200 years by the ARABS (q.v.). It then became a Norman stronghold, and later was in the power of the Aragonese and Castilians of Spain. From 1530 to 1798 it was ruled by the famous international crusading order of the Knights of St. John of Jerusalem (*see* KNIGHTS, ORDERS OF)—whose eight-pointed emblem we now call the Maltese cross. This wealthy and splendour-loving group of men built massive fortifications and magnificent palaces or 'auberges', some of which still survive. After they had successfully resisted the attacks of the Turks in the 16th century, their Grand

Malta Tourist Board

A STREET IN MEDIEVAL MDINA, MALTA

Master, La Valette, built the present capital, Valetta, named after him. In 1798 Malta was taken by the French under Napoleon, who broke up the power of the Knights. In 1814, with the consent of the Maltese, the island became a British colony; and it achieved prominence during the Second World War when, as a strategic British base, it came under intense attack and siege by the Axis powers. German bombers had only to fly from Sicily, whereas the nearest Allied base was 1,600 km away. Between June 1940 and June 1942 the island endured over 2,500 air-raids, mostly by day, and shelters tunnelled in the rock saved many lives from bombing. There had to be severe food rationing; but civilian morale held firm, and on 15 April 1942 the George Cross 'For Gallantry' was awarded to the whole Maltese people—the first time a British decoration has been won collectively by a community.

After the war the island remained a British base, and the naval dockyard continued to be the largest single employer of labour. In 1964 Malta became an independent nation within the Commonwealth. In recent years its importance as a base has declined, leading to unemployment problems and the necessity for British financial aid.

The Maltese are a cheerful, friendly people who have made the most of their limited natural resources. The islands are so rocky that most of the soil has had to be imported, but terrace farming produces good-quality potatoes and some figs and grapes. Stone-masonry is an important craft: the local limestone, which is easily worked by hand when freshly quarried but hardens on exposure, has always been the staple building material. The keeping of goats has virtually died out since the discovery that goats' milk carried the organism responsible for undulant fever ('Malta fever').

The Maltese language is essentially a dialect of Arabic, with Italian vocabulary additions: it is the only SEMITIC LANGUAGE (q.v. Vol. IV) written in the Roman alphabet. Italian was for a time the official language of the church and the courts, until replaced by Maltese in 1934; and there was much Italian influence up to the time of the Second World War, especially among the upper classes. Women on the whole have so far played a much smaller part in public affairs and the professions than men. The Maltese have been universally and devoutly Roman Catholic for many centuries, and the church hierarchy has tended until recently to dominate political as well as cultural life. This influence also is on the wane, as shown by the support won in the 1955 and subsequent elections by Mr. Dom Mintoff's anticlerical Labour Party. Under his leadership the Maltese have been engaged in the uphill struggle towards economic independence.

See also Vol. III: MALTA.

MAN, EVOLUTION OF, *see* EVOLUTION.

MANCHUS, *see* CHINESE PEOPLES.

MAORIS. The Maoris are a POLYNESIAN people (q.v.) who migrated between the 12th and 14th centuries A.D. from the small tropical islands of Tahiti and Raratonga to New Zealand. Their skill in sailing their double canoes more than 3,000 km across the Pacific Ocean was matched by their enterprise in adapting themselves to life in a new and harsher land.

In New Zealand frosts are usual in winter, so the Maoris fashioned with their stone tools planks and posts from the great forest trees and built a more solid type of house than they had known in their tropical islands, with closed sides and a porch opening towards the sunny north. They carved intricate designs on the massive posts and broad planks and decorated the inside of their homes with painted patterns and reedwork. The women learned to prepare the silky fibre of the native flax and from it wove garments and cloaks which they adorned with dyed designs. They cultivated the kumara and taro plants that they had brought from the tropics, but they made use of the native fern-root, too. They farmed and fished and snared birds in summer and autumn and preserved their foods for winter use. So successful were they in their new life that when Captain COOK (q.v. Vol. V) visited New Zealand in 1769 he found a numerous and vigorous people of fine appearance, proud and warlike in temper, but friendly and hospitable too. Most of them had light brown or olive skins and features that resembled those of Europeans; but some had darker skins and flatter noses, which showed that they came in part from Melanesian stock.

Throughout their history the Maoris have shown their readiness to make use of new ideas. After Cook, came sailors, traders, and missionaries, who brought them new iron tools, new methods of agriculture, and new religious creeds. Unhappily the Europeans also introduced alcohol and fire-arms into New Zealand, and woollen blankets, which soaked up the rain instead of

High Commissioner for New Zealand

MAORI GIRLS, WEARING TRADITIONAL DRESS, COOK VEGETABLES IN A HOT SPRING

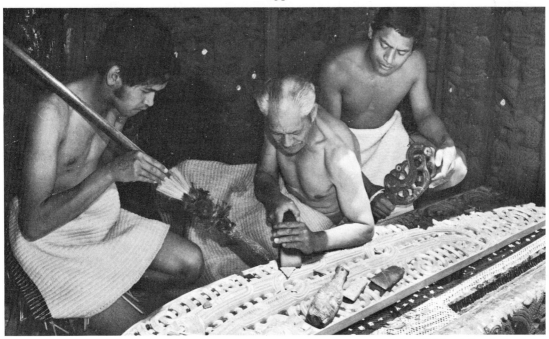

A MASTER MAORI WOODCARVER AND HIS PUPILS
They are wearing traditional costume

being waterproof like the flax cloaks the Maoris had formerly woven for themselves. Drink and damp clothing and European diseases, against which they had not built up an immunity, impaired their health. Yet, by and large, the Maoris profited from their early contact with Europeans, and by 1850 the great plains of Waikato were golden with grain and rich with cattle, and neat Maori houses stood in well-cared-for orchards and gardens.

Tragically, this prosperity was a source of envy to certain British settlers, who coveted the Maoris' rich farmlands. Between 1856 and 1870 wars over land sales, and Government confiscation of their land after these wars, brought the Maori people to a degree of despair and wretchedness never before known in their history. Yet their courage did not entirely desert them. Towards the end of the 19th century a group of young Maori leaders urged better conditions of health and housing upon their tribes, encouraged education and better farming methods, and sought some settlement of the vexed problem of land. Soon after 1900 the Maoris were increasing in numbers and beginning to prosper again.

Today they are a young and vigorous race, numbering about 235,000, of whom nearly half are under 15 and only a quarter over 30. They have full rights as citizens and are respected by their fellow white New Zealanders for their courage as fighting soldiers in the two World Wars, for their lively and often brilliant performance in games such as football, tennis, and basket-ball, and for their considerable artistic gifts. Today there are Maori or part Maori musicians, novelists, poets, painters, and sculptors.

The great majority of the Maori people live in the North Island, where in certain northern districts they outnumber the New Zealanders of European descent. But over the country as a whole, the 'Pakeha' (the name Maoris gave to the European section of the population) outnumber the Maori by about eleven to one. Nowadays, however, more and more NEW ZEALANDERS (q.v.), Maori and Pakeha alike, think of themselves as belonging to one nation. 'We are one people' is today's slogan among leaders of both races.

There is still not enough land in New Zealand for the Maoris, and in recent years an increasing number of young people have migrated from the country to the big cities such as Auckland and

Wellington, where they work in factories, shops, and offices, or become school-teachers, nurses, and Civil Servants. Yet even in city life they preserve their ancient virtues. They may not always speak their native language, but the Maori tradition of hospitality is not forgotten (in the old days even a hungry enemy was fed). Nor have they lost their tribal discipline of working together for the good of all. Best of all, they still think that men and women—relations, friends, and even enemies—are more important than money or worldly success.

Unfortunately, largely because the Maori population is increasing faster than that of the Pakeha, who still has his eyes on the remnants of the Maori tribal lands, there is today some friction in rural areas, and discrimination against Maoris who come to the cities for work. To counter this, young Maori leaders ask that lands be returned to Maori use and communal forms of agriculture revived. They claim that recent laws affecting Maori land make their loss more inevitable, and they want the Maori to have more effective control of his own affairs and the future of his race. These young leaders see the Pakeha policy-makers as biased against much that Maori people most value. Increasing inter-marriage is bound some day to ease these tensions, but until then the problems call for the understanding and goodwill of both races.

See also POLYNESIANS; NEW ZEALANDERS.
See also Vol. III: NEW ZEALAND.

MARRIAGE CEREMONIES. The marriage of individuals in a community affects the lives of many others in various ways, so both primitive and more civilized peoples, both in the past and present, have always made regulations and cere-monies in connexion with marriage. When a man and a woman marry, their position in society changes, each of them becomes 'related', as we say, in a new way to other people, and the question of the status of their children arises. Amongst most peoples there are strict rules as to whom a person can marry. In many primitive tribes, such as the AUSTRALIAN ABORIGINES (q.v.), men and women must marry someone outside their section of the clan. Civilized peoples, too, have their rules of this kind. At the back of the Church of England Prayer Book there is a long list of those 'forbidden in Scripture and our laws to marry together'. These regulations are part of the system of rights and duties among kinsfolk on which so much in primitive society depends, and they are backed up with all the force of religious authority.

Amongst a great many peoples marriage is a religious rite or is attended by religious observ-ances. It is very natural that the joining together of a man and woman to bring up a family should be regarded as an occasion for ceremonial when blessings are sought. Bride and bridegroom are making a momentous change in their way of life, so people do all in their power by prayers, religious ceremonies, and magical practices, to enlist the aid of good against the forces of evil.

As law, tradition, and religion regulate the conditions of marriage to a large extent, it is not surprising to find that 'arranged' marriages are the rule in many parts of the world. The Japanese, for example, employ a 'go-between' as match-maker. In Persia and many other countries the match is brought about by the parents and friends. Wedding preliminaries often take a good deal of time, and the cere-monies connected with marriage may cover a period of weeks or months; indeed, the com-bined betrothal and wedding ceremonies may be spread over a number of years. Often various devices are used to try to discover a lucky date for a wedding. There were such practices amongst the Greeks and Romans, and even now astrologers are often consulted before a Chinese wedding is arranged. The exchange of gifts is one of the most widespread marriage customs. Amongst many peoples a girl is very useful to a family or clan because of the work she does, so she is not given up without some return. Usually it is the man or his family who gives the presents, but amongst more cultured societies the bride or her family also send gifts, though generally less valuable ones. The bride-price in cattle of an African girl may be of great value. In many societies the bride is expected to bring a dowry with her—her contribution to their joint estab-lishment.

Although there are innumerable differences in the details of marriage ceremonial, yet many marriage rites have main features which are similar to those occurring in the coronations of kings and queens. This marriage ritual is in fact derived from extremely ancient coronation cere-monies. In these rites the kings and queens were thought to represent the gods of heaven and earth respectively. Often present-day wedding

The Times

THE MARRIAGE OF QUEEN ELIZABETH II (THEN PRINCESS ELIZABETH) IN WESTMINSTER ABBEY, 20 NOVEMBER 1947

ceremonies include customs which remind us of these ideas. In ancient Greece bride and bridegroom were crowned; in Rome they wore wreaths; in Yugoslavia at the present day crowns are placed on their heads, and so also in Russia, where the wedding is called 'the matrimonial coronation'. In an ancient Indian ceremony the bridegroom used to say to the bride, 'I am the heaven, you are the earth; let us unite and have children'. In Malaya, even amongst the poorer people, bride and bridegroom are called 'sovereigns of a day'. At the coronation of the king a ring is placed on his finger, just as the bridegroom in the wedding service places a ring on the bride's finger. An ancient Roman wedding included the giving of presents and a ring, the joining of hands, veiling, crowning with flowers, prayers, and partaking of a sacrificial cake. The Christian wedding service follows much the same pattern.

In general, wedding ceremonials are designed to achieve these main ends: (*a*) The transition from one family or condition of life to another.

(*b*) The banishing or subduing of evil influences. (*c*) The stressing of the idea of fertility. (*d*) The stressing of the unity of the married couple. These ends are achieved in many different ways, some of which we will describe.

(*a*) MARKING A TRANSITION. It used to be the custom in Scotland when the bride left her home to throw an old shoe after her to signify that her father no longer had a legal right over her. Amongst the INCAS OF PERU (q.v.) the bridegroom placed a sandal on the bride's right foot as a sign that he accepted her as his wife. Shoes play a part in many wedding ceremonies, usually representing that the wife must be submissive to her husband, although they may have an older meaning as fertility symbols. The custom of lifting the bride over the threshold of her new home, which is observed in England, Algeria, Palestine, Java, and China, is probably a way of marking the change from one home to another, though it is sometimes explained as a means of preventing the bride from stumbling on the

Paul Popper

A WEDDING IN MALAYA

The bride and bridegroom, in their ceremonial dress, have
to sit still for hours or their luck is broken

doorstep, which would be unlucky. Amongst
various peoples, such as the tribe of the Amaxosa
in South Africa, a mock fight is staged at a
wedding, apparently symbolizing the resistance
of the bride's family to the carrying off of one of
its members. A Chinese bride marks her coming
to her husband's house by worshipping at his
ancestral shrine. At English weddings the bride's
father or some relative is present to 'give her
away'—thus marking the transition from one
family to another.

(b) BANISHING EVIL. Before the Chinese bridal
sedan-chair leaves the house, it is searched for
evil spirits by women who use lighted spills of
red paper—red being the Chinese lucky colour
and therefore also the colour of the bride's costume. Then they go over it again with a mirror,
for they believe that if an evil spirit catches sight
of himself in a looking-glass he gets such a fright
that he hurries away. At some African and
Indian weddings arrows are discharged to trans-
fix any evil spirits which may be about. In
Palestine and elsewhere guns are fired with the
same idea, and a similar custom was observed

in the north of England until recently, though
the old significance of it had been forgotten. An
English bride sometimes carries a horseshoe of
silver paper. Horseshoes are considered lucky
because they are made of iron, which is believed
to have the power of driving away evil spirits.
The bride's veil was originally a means of inter-
cepting evil influences such as the 'evil eye' (*see*
MAGIC). One of the most widespread practices
before a marriage is for the parties to undergo
ritual purification by taking ceremonial baths or
exposing themselves to incense. When a Matabele bride arrives at the bridegroom's house she
pours water over him as a ceremonial purification.

(c) FERTILITY. In Ireland oatmeal used to be
scattered on the bride, and in the north of England she was sprinkled with bits of cake; in
Greece she was showered with nuts and figs and
in Minorca with almonds. An old Spanish song
referred to the pelting of the bride in these words:
'All down the street the ears of corn are flying.'
In Persia the officiating priest sprinkles the
couple with rice during the wedding service.
Our custom of throwing confetti at weddings is
a recent change from the older practice of casting rice. At Jewish weddings the guests used to
shout 'Increase and multiply' as they threw corn
over the bride and groom. In north China the
third day after the wedding, a mother of a
thriving family empties a vase containing rice
and millet into the laps of the bride and bridegroom. In the Slav nations a boy is placed in
the bride's lap. All these customs signify the
desire that the marriage should be fruitful, and
the idea underlying them is to make it so by
sympathetic magic.

(d) UNITY. In south Celebes the bride and
groom are sewn together by their clothes and
one garment is put over them to show that they
are united. During the Persian marriage ceremony a symbolic knot is tied. Part of our marriage ritual is the joining of hands, and the
exhortation in the service quotes from St. Paul
the meaning of such rites—'They two shall be
one.'

In modern marriage emphasis is increasingly
laid on wedded life as a state in which husband
and wife share rights and duties. Christian marriage involves a solemn pledge of lifelong faith-
fulness, which will make it possible to provide
children with the best chance of continuous
loving care. True love in marriage involves a

spiritual relationship, and the essentials for a happy marriage are mutual physical attraction and the sharing of similar ideals.

See also FOLKLORE.

MARTYR, *see* SAINT.

MASAI. All speakers of the East African language *Maa* may be called Masai; but it is only one distinctive group of about 115,000 purely pastoral Maa-speaking people who strictly refer to themselves as 'IlMaasai', the Masai. The rest, although also pastoral to a large degree, are called IlOikop. The Masai inhabit a stretch of country which starts at Lake Baringo in west-central Kenya and ends in central Tanzania. They are tall, slender people with long limbs.

The purely pastoral Masai value cattle highly and abhor all forms of agriculture. Indeed, they disdain breaking earth even to provide the wells necessary to water their cattle, and rely on other peoples for such services. Through trade with neighbouring peoples, they obtain agricultural products to supplement the staple diet of milk, blood, and meat, which they get from their own livestock.

Masai are polygamous: that is to say a man may marry more than one wife. Each wife builds her own hut—a low structure made of bent saplings plastered with a mixture of mud and cattle-dung—which she occupies with her unmarried children. There may consequently be several huts in the family of one married man; and these, together with the huts of other families, are enclosed in a single brushwood fence which also protects the cattle at night. Each married man, however, has his own 'cattle-gate' into the enclosure as a sign of his economic independence and status.

Men in Masai society are divided into a series of age-grades: boyhood, warriorhood, elderhood, and ancient elderhood. They move through these various stages of life in groups, or 'age-sets', whose members are bound to help each other. Boys are recruited to an age-set after circumcision in adolescence. The recruiting period is common throughout the Masai society and lasts from 7–8 years; then there is a gap of about 5 years before the next recruiting period, so members of an age-set may not be precisely the same age or from the same locality. A whole age-set moves up to the next age-grade together, much as a class moves up to the next form. Women are not admitted to these sets as members, but tend to identify themselves with the set who were in the warrior grade when they danced with them as maidens.

On entering the warrior (*moran*) grade, young men used to live in special villages known as *manyata*, and were expected to defend the

British Museum

MASAI WARRIORS
Their decorated shields are made of coloured hide

territory and carry out organized cattle raids. They also received, and still do, an education in tribal affairs and social integration. The point at which warriors are allowed to marry is a significant stage in their promotion to elderhood.

The elders wield political authority, and decide such matters as when age-sets should move up a grade, or when cattle raids should take place. Ritual authority is wielded by experts called *oloiboni*, who see that the elders' decisions have divine approval.

Warriors are noted for braided hair coloured with red ochre, and ceremonial head-dresses of feathers or lion mane; women often wear heavy metal ornaments (up to 6 kg.) on arms and legs.

See also AFRICANS; EAST AFRICANS.
See also Vol. IV: AFRICAN LANGUAGES.

MATABELE, *see* RHODESIANS; SOUTHERN AFRICANS.

MAYA CIVILIZATION. The highest civilization in North and Central America before the coming of the Europeans was developed by the Maya people in the tropical lowland forests and mountains of Guatemala, Honduras, Belize, and the south east of Mexico. These people had a very great influence upon the culture of their neighbours, especially in Mexico (*see* MEXICAN ANCIENT CIVILIZATION).

Maya history may be divided into four main periods. These are known as the 'Archaic' or 'Formative', lasting from about 900 B.C. to A.D. 250; the 'Classic' from A.D. 250–900; the 'Mexican' from A.D. 900–1200; and finally the Mayapan 'empire', leading to independent chieftainships which lasted until the Spanish conquest in the early 16th century.

In the Formative period Maya and the contemporary Mexican civilizations resembled each other; maize was cultivated as a staple food, pottery and textiles were manufactured, and temples began to be built on pyramids. The earliest developments occurred in the highlands of Guatemala, but they soon began also in the wooded lowlands of Peten and Yucatán and seem to have been essentially indigenous.

It was during the Classic period that Maya civilization reached its highest level in art, architecture, and mathematical science, and developed an elaborate form of hieroglyphic writing. During these six centuries they built many large 'cities' with fine stone buildings, some of which, though overgrown and damaged by tropical vegetation, can still be seen in a fair state of preservation. At a few of the more important sites the forest has now been cleared away, and many of the buildings have been thoroughly restored. The result is extremely impressive. A typical Maya 'city' consisted of a spacious ceremonial centre court enclosed by platforms. On some of these platforms stood palaces which were probably occupied by the rulers and priests. The temples on pyramidal mounds were built of well-dressed stone plastered over and were approached by steep and lofty stairways. Inside they contained a few narrow rooms, and were surmounted by high roof-crests to give them strength. These were richly decorated with sculptured or stucco figures, generally of gods, priests, and worshippers. There were also other strange symbolic figures among which the most usual were iguanas and jaguars, representing the gods of the earth, sky, and underworld.

British Museum

SCULPTURED STONE PILLAR OR 'STELA'
The figure is wearing ceremonial costume. At the sides are hieroglyphic inscriptions. Classic Period: Copan, Honduras.

Another characteristic feature of the Maya cities was the massive stone pillar or 'stela', generally rectangular and entirely covered with sculptured figures and hieroglyphic inscriptions. The tallest of these single-stone pillars is nearly 13 metres high. Many of them have colossal figures in ceremonial dress carved in relief on one or two sides. But the most interesting thing about them is their inscriptions. These record the dates on which they were set up and certain astronomical calculations. At present only part of these writings in stone can be deciphered. The Maya had invented a kind of picture writing in which many of the symbols stood for the days and months of the year, and others for numbers. For numbering they also used a system of bars and dots—a bar standing for 5 and a dot for 1. Instead of decimals they used a system of counting by twenties, and were thus able to make advanced mathematical calculations. Their knowledge of astronomy was also so good that they had worked out a calendar with leap year corrections almost as accurate as our own Gregorian calendar. They knew the movements of the planets and were able to predict eclipses. In fact, in astronomical and mathematical science they were far ahead of any of the other American Indian civilizations and of many of the ancient civilizations of the Old World. They had many religious books or 'codices' written on lengths of folded paper, but unfortunately all except three of these were destroyed in the 16th century by the Spaniards as works of the devil.

The life of the Maya people was dominated by religious ceremonial, and most of their more permanent buildings were connected with it. (The houses or huts of the ordinary people were built of timber and thatch and have perished.) They worshipped a large number of different gods, among which were the SKY-GOD (q.v.), regarded as the Creator, the gods of the earth, the moon, rain, maize, and death. There were many religious festivals, accompanied by the music of drums, flutes, trumpets, rattles, and conch-shells, at which animal sacrifices and gifts of crops were offered to the gods. The gods were also offered human blood collected by piercing the tongue or ears, but human sacrifices seem to have been rare at this period, though they became more common later.

The various city states were probably not united under a single ruler although they were

British Museum

SCULPTURED STONE LINTEL

The standing figure is a priest, and beside him is a worshipper making a blood-sacrifice by drawing a cord with thorns through his tongue. Classic Period: Menché (Yaxchilan) Chiapas

closely associated. They must certainly have organized their labour effectively to have been able to construct such large buildings and to clear the dense forest for agriculture, which was their principal occupation. When we remember that they had no metal tools, no draught animals, and no wheeled transport, it is all the more astonishing that they should have achieved so much.

Their food consisted mainly of maize, which they ground and baked into bread and cakes. But they also grew beans, squash, manioc, and other food plants, and they made a chocolate drink from the cacao bean. They domesticated turkeys and bees, hunted deer, dogs, and wild pig, and fished from canoes. They grew tobacco and smoked it in pipes. They were masters of the art of flaking and polishing stone tools, and their tools were as fine as any in the neolithic age of the Old World (*see* PREHISTORIC TOOLS AND WEAPONS). They made beautiful pottery without

British Museum

STONE TEMPLE, CHICHÉN ITZA, YUCATAN (MEXICAN PERIOD)
It is dedicated to Quetzalcoatl, the god of life and crafts. It has now been restored

the potter's wheel, and many of their jars, bowls, and dishes were richly decorated with paintings or incised figures and designs. The costumes carved on the stone figures show that they had reached a considerable degree of skill in weaving, featherwork, and embroidery. We get a vivid idea of their appearance from some beautiful mural paintings at Bonampak in Chiapas. They made various small ornaments, such as pendants and beads, cut skilfully from jade and other hard stones, and in the Mexican period they worked gold and copper ornaments. Altogether Maya art must be given a high place. Even though it is sometimes over-elaborate, and its symbolic character often makes it difficult to understand, the sculpture shows great dignity and the paintings and reliefs a strong sense of design. The technical skill of the Maya in dealing with difficult materials with such simple tools is admirable.

During the 10th century A.D. the old ceremonial centres were abandoned and fell into decay. Strong Mexican influence now reached Yucatan with the invasion of the warlike Toltecs from Tula, who imposed their rule and introduced their own forms of religion and art, including the cult of Quetzalcoatl, the god of the feathered serpent. The decoration of buildings became more formal with geometric patterns;

the use of columns in architecture appears for the first time. They built larger courts for the ball game, the finest of which is still to be seen at the Toltec capital of Chichén Itza in Yucatan. The ball game was a semi-religious game played with a large solid rubber ball; one of the chief objects was to knock the ball through stone rings fixed high up on the sides of the court. A simplified form of this game is still played in parts of Mexico today, but it dates from the Olmec period of the 9th century B.C.

After A.D. 1200 this Mexican influence declined. The centre of power shifted to the city of Mayapan, and there was some revival of the older Maya pattern of life. This peaceful interlude was soon broken by the rise of petty chieftains, whose warlike rivalry prevented any return to the past glories, and Maya civilization finally perished with the Spanish conquest of Guatemala in 1525 and of Yucatan in 1541.

See also ANCIENT CIVILIZATIONS.
See also Vol. IV: AMERICAN-INDIAN LANGUAGES.

MEDES, *see* PERSIAN ANCIENT CIVILIZATION.

MEGALITHS (MEGALITHIC MONUMENTS). This name, (the Greek for 'large stone'), is given to constructions of large blocks of stone—usually unshaped—which are found in many parts of the world, and date from many different periods. In Europe, however, they are characteristic of the New Stone Age period especially (beginning around 3500 B.C. in Britain), though they were also built in later prehistoric times. The technique was used mainly to construct burial monuments (*see* BARROWS AND CAIRNS), and later ceremonial centres (*see* AVEBURY and STONEHENGE).

Some of the stones used are of enormous size; the largest stone at Stonehenge is over nine metres long, while a fallen 'standing stone' from Brittany was almost twenty metres long. Some capstones weighing up to 100 tonnes are perched on the top of other, standing, stones (*see* illustration). In cases like this the monument was probably free-standing. However, large stones were often used to form chambers, sometimes in conjunction with dry-stone walling, and this chamber was then covered with earth. These chambers were then used for communal burial, as a family vault which could be periodically re-opened.

It used to be thought that the megalithic monuments of New Stone Age Europe, which are most common in Spain, France, Britain, Scandinavia and north Germany, were the result of the spread of a cult from the Mediterranean along the western Atlantic seaboard. This is no longer believed, since new techniques of dating have shown that megalithic tombs in Brittany, for instance, are older than any possible Mediterranean prototypes. Instead, they must be seen as part of the beliefs and customs of the first farming

G. M. Boumphrey

LEGANNANNY DOLMEN, COUNTY DOWN, N. IRELAND

groups in these areas. Part of the reason for their existence probably lies in the need to clear agricultural land of obstructions; this probably suggested the idea of building in large stones. The communal burial in passage graves, which often had a forecourt in front of them where rituals were carried out, may indicate that the beliefs of these peoples included some kind of ANCESTOR WORSHIP (q.v.).

In the British Isles the use of megaliths is naturally confined to areas where large rocks and boulders are plentiful; elsewhere long earthen mounds (long barrows), sometimes with a wooden chamber, took their place. It is possible to distinguish regional groupings in the areas where megaliths are common. The area around the river Severn including the Cotswolds, for instance, has large numbers of complex tombs with side-chambers, similar to ones in France on the lower Loire. North-west England and western Scotland, however, have more in common with northern Ireland. These tombs in particular are often decorated with spiral motifs laboriously pecked into the rock.

In the later part of the New Stone Age, towards the beginning of the Bronze Age, these large communal tombs were replaced by individual burials under round barrows. At the same time (around 2000 B.C.) we find large stones being set in circles at tribal ceremonial centres. The most elaborate of these is Stonehenge, but simpler settings of stones are found in many parts of the country. The custom of using large stones survived longest in the form of single standing stones, which were erected down to medieval times.

See also PREHISTORIC MAN; BARROWS AND CAIRNS.

MELANESIANS. This name applies to the dark-skinned native inhabitants of many of the western PACIFIC ISLANDS (q.v. Vol. III; *see also* OCEANS, Map). As might be expected, there are many local differences in physical appearance and way of life between the inhabitants of different islands and island groups scattered over so wide an expanse of ocean. The following account gives a general picture which has to ignore many of these differences.

Racially the Melanesians are a part of the great negroid stock. Their ancestors many generations ago reached the islands by migrating from south-east Asia. They have frizzy or curly hair, dark chocolate or black skins, and though they vary in height, they are generally rather short—about an

Haddon Library, Cambridge

INTERIOR OF A HUT IN SANTA CATALINA, SOLOMON ISLANDS

hayricks. The houses are scattered about among palms and fruit-trees. Villages in many parts of Melanesia each have a large, finely made building which serves as a club-house for the men. The timbers of these buildings are elaborately carved to represent spirits and creatures who figure in the local religious beliefs.

Close by the village in the jungle are small garden plots where the people grow their crops of taro, yams, sweet potatoes, and sugar-cane. The land is seldom owned by one man or family, but generally by the whole village or by the local clan, though the use of the land is shared out between individual men and families. The men do the heaviest work in chopping down and clearing the jungle ready for planting, and the women folk generally do all the planting, hoeing, and weeding. Relatives and neighbours help one another. A man can always count on the support of his kinsmen in cultivating his plot and gathering and storing the harvest, and he in his turn must assist each of them. A newly married young man wishing to build a house can obtain help from his kinsmen and neighbours in preparing and erecting the timbers for the frame and in putting on the thatch covering; the women among his relatives meantime busy themselves in cooking a feast for the workers.

In some ways family life in a Melanesian village is not so different from our own. The family generally live together in one house; though where there are European plantations the grown-up sons often leave home to go to work as labourers and to earn money with which to buy European goods. Where Christianity has not forbidden it a wealthy man may have more than one wife.

Throughout Melanesia society is organized in clans, which vary very greatly in numbers. These clans are social groups whose members trace their relationship to one another through either the male or the female line. Members of a clan tracing its descent through the male line (patrilineal) belong to the same clan as their brothers and sisters, father, father's brothers and sisters, father's father, and so on. Members, however, of a clan tracing descent through the female line (matrilineal) belong to the same clan as their mothers, mother's brothers and sisters, and so on. It is a general rule that a member of a clan must marry someone of some other clan than his own. In some Melanesian societies a man is free to choose a wife from any clan except his own; but

average of 1 m 58 cm. The shape of their heads also varies: most are long-headed, though in some islands many broad-headed types are met with. Their noses are generally very broad.

Before Europeans persuaded them to dress in cheap cotton fabrics, most Melanesians went almost naked. The men wore kilts or loin-cloths made from a kind of cloth prepared from the bark of a tree; the women wore skirts made of grass—frequently half a dozen skirts at a time. The old forms of dress are still worn in the Solomon Islands, the New Hebrides, and the Bismarck archipelago.

Melanesians live in villages varying from a few dozen to one or two hundred inhabitants. On many of the larger islands we can distinguish between the 'salt-water people' and the 'bush people'. The 'salt-water people' are expert fishers and canoe-men who live in coastal villages and depend on their fishing for a livelihood. The 'bush people' live in inland villages and specialize in gardening. At regular intervals they come down to the coast and barter vegetables for fish with the 'salt-water people'. The coastal villages are often larger and more permanent than those of the inland people, who frequently move their villages in order to cultivate fresh land, a method called 'shifting cultivation'. They build small rectangular houses made of a framework of poles covered on the walls and roof with palm-leaf thatch. Consequently a village looks rather like a group of

in Fiji it is customary for a man to ask for a daughter of one of his mother's brothers as wife. This system of marriage of first cousins is known as cross-cousin marriage.

Marriage between members of different clans is looked on as a link between the respective clans. Throughout most of Melanesia the custom of 'bride-wealth' was in force, though European influence has caused it to disappear in some parts. A young man intending to marry seeks the support of members of his own clan in accumulating valuables to be presented to the members of the girl's clan. Wealth in Melanesia takes the form of pigs (especially boars with long curving tusks —the longer the more valuable), the teeth of many other animals, and strings of shell beads and other kinds of shell 'money'. Large quantities of food are also produced for the wedding-feast. This system of bride-wealth is not thought of as purchase money for the wife, but as a proof that the young man's clan approve his choice (otherwise his kinsmen would not help him in collecting the bride-wealth); it is also a stimulus to work hard to save the necessary wealth; above all it is a ceremonial which binds together the clans concerned.

In many parts of Melanesia clans have also a religious aspect: all members of a clan are held to be descended from some mythical supernatural ancestor who today is thought to dwell in the body of some species of bird or animal from which the clan takes its name. This animal is sacred and must not be killed or eaten by the clan members; thus, all members of the Eagle clan are forbidden to eat eagles (see TOTEMISM). In some areas each clan has an hereditary priest whose duty it is to make sacrifices to the spirits of the clan ancestors. The animals in which the spirits dwell, the priests who commune with these spirits, and other exceptional people and things are said to have a supernatural power known in many Melanesian languages as *mana*. Success in love-making, in gardening, fishing, or trading is held to show that a man has mana. All these vital activities are also assisted by the performance of appropriate magical spells (see MAGIC).

Clans also have political functions. In some parts of Melanesia political decisions and the maintenance of law and order rest with the hereditary chief of the clan. In others a council of old men rule the clan. In Fiji and locally in the other main island groups several clans are bound together under one chief to form a tribe. The tribe lays claim to a definite territory over which in old days it frequently went to war.

Haddon Library, Cambridge

NATIVE HUT ON THE SHORE OF MALAITA, SOLOMON ISLANDS

CANNIBALISM (q.v.) used to accompany warfare in Fiji and some other parts of Melanesia. It apparently began as a religious rite but was later indulged in just to gratify a taste for human flesh. In the Solomon Islands whole districts were terrorized by raiding bands of head-hunters. The belief in mana was the basis for head-hunting: if a man killed an enemy and collected his head, he believed that the mana of his enemy was added to his own mana.

See also ANCESTOR WORSHIP; ANIMISM; NEW GUINEA PEOPLES.

See also Vol. IV: OCEANIC LANGUAGES.

See also Vol. XII: OCEANIC ART.

MERMAIDS. These are fabulous beings, half-woman and half-fish, believed to live in the sea, rivers, or lakes. People have always imagined often as being weird, elusive, and tricky, and bringers of misfortune. Some FAIRIES (q.v.) are believed to live in palaces at the bottom of the sea. In Greek mythology the naiads were connected with brooks and fountains, and the nereids were sea-nymphs. The kelpie is a spiteful Scottish water-fairy; the nixie lives in German streams; and the rusalka is a Russian sprite somewhat like a mermaid.

The name 'mermaid' is derived from *mere*, a sea or lake. The usual idea of a mermaid is a very beautiful woman with the tail of a fish instead of legs, but on the Continent mermaids are sometimes depicted with two tails. The notion of a being partly fish and partly human is very ancient. The Babylonian god Oannes, the Phoenician god Dagon, and the Greek Nereus had tails like fish. However, our mermaids did not origi-

ST. NICHOLAS PROTECTING A SHIP IN A STORM

Ashmolean Museum

The mermaid, which has almost caused the destruction of the ship, is seen swimming away at the approach of the saint. Painting by Bicci di Lorenzo (1373–1452)

strange beings to exist in unexplored places, such as mountain peaks and deep waters. The belief in such beings is not surprising, for some of the natural animals of the waters are very strange. Moreover, water is both beautiful and treacherous. A calm pool can swallow up a man who cannot swim, and a stormy sea is much to be feared. Whirlpools, currents, and tides are difficult to understand. So the imaginary beings which live in the water are thought of, sometimes, as being beautiful and helpful, but more nally have tails. People's imagination added them in later times. The mermaids and mermen which, according to the Chinese, inhabit the southern seas, are also without tails. They are white-skinned and spend their time weaving. When they weep their tears become pearls. The idea of mysterious and lovely water-women, only partly human, who lure men to destruction, is also many centuries old. Ulysses had to be tied to the mast of his ship so that he might not be enchanted by the sweet singing of the sirens; and the Lorelei, a maiden who, forsaken by her lover, was turned into a siren, is said to sit on a rock in the Rhine and to drive men who see her out of their wits.

Dealings with a mermaid or merman usually lead to trouble. Legend relates that when a man marries a mermaid they may live together for years, but sooner or later he breaks some promise and she leaves him and returns to the water. In one form of this story he promises not to inquire what she does on Saturdays, but at length his curiosity gets the better of him, and he finds his wife in a bath with her tail clearly visible. This story is closely connected with a very widespread type of tale in which a seal or a swan lays aside her sealskin or feather cloak, marries the man who steals it, and escapes later. Other stories tell of how a mermaid marries a man and lures him to live with her in the sea. After many years he manages to return. In some cases mermaids fore-tell the future, give marvellous powers to human beings, or punish people who do them harm. There is a Norse tradition that mermaids have no souls.

Occasionally, so legend relates, women are transformed into mermaids. In north Ireland a tale is told of Liban, who swam the sea for 300 years, together with her lap-dog which was trans-formed into an otter. Having attracted the atten-tion of men by her singing, which was like the chanting of angels, she announced that she would come ashore at a certain place in a year's time. So she was baptized and honoured as a saint. In the case of at least one mermaid story, we know that it was people's imagination which turned a woman into a mermaid. A monk recorded that in 1403, a wild woman came through a dyke into a lake in Holland and was taught to spin. A later writer argued that she could not have been a woman because she could live in the sea, nor was she a fish for she could spin—so she must have been a mermaid. The story of this 'mermaid' was repeated for centuries.

Probably glimpses of sea-animals have helped to keep alive the belief in mermaids. Seals are inquisitive, and when one of them hears strange sounds, such as men in a boat talking, it may thrust its round head above the surface and gaze around. In a mist or a poor light, people seeing such beasts might easily imagine mermaids were watching them.

See also FOLKLORE.

MESOLITHIC AGE, *see* PREHISTORIC MAN.

MESOPOTAMIAN CIVILIZATION, *see* SUMERIAN; BABYLONIAN; ASSYRIAN.

METAPHYSICS, *see* PHILOSOPHY.

METHODIST. A methodist is a member of a denomination which began within the CHURCH OF ENGLAND (q.v.) in the 18th century and gradually became separate. The Methodist Church has now about 600,000 members in the British Isles, and 13·7 millions in North America. Throughout the world the membership is just over 18 millions.

Methodism began with John WESLEY (1703-91) (q.v. Vol. V). As he described it himself: 'In November 1729 four young gentlemen at Oxford began to spend some evenings a week reading, chiefly the Greek Testament.' Other young men joined them, and the nickname 'Methodist' was given to them because of the regular and metho-dical way in which their religion led them to conduct their lives. These early followers of Wesley did not wish to break from the English Church, but only to lead people to take their religion more earnestly. They began to preach, often in the fields and market-places, and to organize their many converts into societies under local leaders who carried on after the preacher had passed elsewhere. These local groups held their own meetings for inspiration and discipline in their new religious life, but continued to use the Sacraments and Sunday worship of the parish church. In many places the meetings of the 'Society' counted for more with its members than Church services.

The break with the Church of England came in 1784. Wesley was sending a group of preachers to look after the Methodists in America. The Bishop of London refused to ordain them, and therefore Wesley, who was a priest, ordained them himself. In the Church of England only bishops can ordain priests, so in doing this Wesley broke with episcopal church order.

Methodist worship is rather like that of other Free Churches, but their set services, including their Communion service (generally held once a month), are almost the same as those of the English Prayer Book. Methodists claim to hold the Apostolic Faith of the Creed and the doctrine of the Protestant Reformation, with special em-phasis on two doctrines—first, that a man not only needs to be saved but to have a sense of salvation in his heart; secondly, that salvation should result in a life of victory over sin. They particularly emphasize that the Gospel is for all men, and therefore they have been pioneers in the modern missionary movement since 1786, when they started work among the slaves in the West Indies. The Methodist Missionary Society was founded in 1813, and it and the Church Missionary Society are the two biggest British Missionary Societies. Its American counterpart is bigger still.

The organization of Methodism is close-knit and efficient, and it has a strong sense of solidarity. Instead of being organized on the parish system, the basis is the 'circuit', a group of churches. The circuit is served by a team of several ministers, who are reinforced by local preachers and class leaders. A group of circuits forms a 'district' under a chairman who, in America, is called a bishop. The districts form the nation-wide Church, which has an annual Conference and an annually elected President. The World Methodist Conference dates from 1881 and takes place every ten years.

See also CHRISTIAN CHURCH; REFORMATION.

MEXICAN ANCIENT CIVILIZATION.

America is spoken of as the New World, and its existence was not really known to the Old World until the discoveries of Columbus in the 15th century. But the beginnings of civilization had been growing among the American Indians for hundreds of years before this, especially in the centre of the continent, with particular centres of culture in Mexico and Peru (see PERU, ANCIENT CIVILIZATION). The earliest traces of American Indian culture are not as old as those in Mesopotamia or Egypt, but they go back at least two thousand years before Christ. In some ways these ancient Indian civilizations reached heights worthy of comparison with the early civilizations of the Old World —in their stone-carving and modelling, their building, their hand-made pottery and weaving, and in their social organization. But right up to the time of the arrival of the Europeans they were without some inventions known for centuries in the East—the most

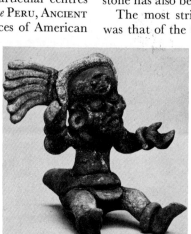

British Museum
PAINTED TERRA-COTTA WHISTLE FIGURINE
The mouthpiece of the whistle projects at the back

obvious of these being the use of iron and the wheel. When the Spanish conquerors Pizarro and Cortes led their small forces against the INCAS (q.v.) in Peru and the AZTECS (q.v.) in Mexico, the possession of firearms and horses gave the Spaniards overwhelming advantages.

The earliest-known culture in Mexico is called the 'Archaic' or 'Formative'. It was very widespread, extending, though not quite continuously, from Mexico through Central America to Panama and beyond. We cannot date its first beginnings at all precisely, but these Archaic people had clearly outgrown the stage of wandering hunters and had settled down to grow maize and other food-plants before 2000 B.C. Much of our knowledge of them is derived from the little terra-cotta figures which they made. These were rather crude, with the features modelled from clay pellets stuck on to the head; but they have plenty of character and give us a good idea of the dress and ornaments of the time: for instance, they show that the art of weaving cloth was already known. These little figures, some of which seem to represent fertility gods, are often found buried at a great depth, and are always underneath the remains of later cultures (*see* ARCHAEOLOGY). A great many ancient undisturbed graves, sealed off long ago from the upper strata by a flow of lava, have been excavated, revealing skeletons and objects of stone and pottery lying as they were originally placed. A large oval altar-crowned pyramid built of clay bricks faced with stone has also been uncovered near Mexico City.

The most striking of the Formative cultures was that of the Olmec, which flourished on the Gulf Coast. Recent excavations at San Lorenzo Tenochtitlán have shown that Olmec culture begins before 1400 B.C. and continues until at least 800 B.C., probably for several centuries more. Around 800 B.C. Olmec influence becomes apparent in the earliest lowland Maya settlements to the east in Petén. At San Lorenzo and the other major ceremonial site, La Venta, many massive stone sculptures have been found, including heads larger than a man.

The Formative period of Mexican civilization had for

H. J. Braunholtz

SUNK COURTYARD AND FACADE OF PALACE II AT MILTA, NEAR OAXACA

The walls both inside and outside are adorned with stone mosaic patterns in relief, originally coloured. Zapotec culture 15th century A.D. (Restored)

the most part come to an end by A.D. 200. The cultures which followed it were all to a greater or less degree in contact with the Maya area, whose people developed the most advanced civilization to be found in middle America (*see* MAYA CIVILIZATION).

In southern Mexico an important centre grew up at Monte Alban, a long mountain ridge, near the modern town of Oaxaca, where the Zapotec Indians lived. The remains of massive temple pyramids and other buildings have been excavated and restored on the flat top of Monte Alban. A great many walled chamber tombs have been found there, containing urns modelled in the shape of figures in ceremonial dress, much fine pottery, alabaster vases, gold ornaments, jade amulets, and other precious objects. The gold work with delicate filigree is particularly beautiful. The insides of the tombs were often painted in bright colours with religious and mythological scenes. Another famous Zapotec site not far away is Mitla, 'the place of the dead', where chiefs were buried in cruciform tombs. The most remarkable monument is a large stone temple or palace, unusually well preserved, containing

many groups of rooms and open paved courts. The walls were decorated with stone mosaics in geometric patterns, while the outer surfaces were painted red and adorned with frescoes of religious ceremonies.

This Zapotec culture lasted for over a thousand years. Its later phases were influenced by the Mixtec people, whose sacred picture books show exceptional skill (*see* Colour Plate opposite p. 448). These were much like the books of the Aztec people, who conquered them at the end of the 15th century. Zapotec and Mixtec Indians survive in large numbers in Mexico today, speaking their own language and still preserving many features of their ancient art.

On the south-east coast of Mexico, in the state of Vera Cruz, other Indians called Totonacs had developed their own distinctive culture. The Totonacs were particularly skilful at making painted pottery. They also made finely modelled heads with a peculiar smiling expression, elaborately carved stone objects shaped like yokes and apparently used in burials, and large paddle-shaped stone slabs carved in relief with animal or human figures. They built large pyramidal temples rising in a series of terraces and faced with rows of niches like windows built of stone. Stone columns inscribed with hiero-glyphs have also been found.

Perhaps the most remarkable of the early Mexican cultures was that which grew out of the 'Formative' in the Valley of Mexico and is known as 'Classic Teotihuacan'. Its great religious centre was at Teotihuacan (about 48 km north-east of Mexico City), which flourished from about A.D. 200 to 900. Its builders evolved many elements of the civilization which was taken over later by the Toltecs and Aztecs. At the height of their power their influence extended to southern Mexico and to the Maya in Guatemala.

They are best known for the enormous pyramids which they erected as bases for their temples. The so-called 'Pyramid of the Sun' was about 213 metres square at its base and rose to a height of over 60 metres, with four great terraces connected by stairways. It was built of clay bricks (adobes) and rubble faced with stone and plaster, and it was surrounded by the priests' houses. The temples which stood on the flat tops of these pyramids were not built of stone like those of the Maya and no traces of them remain.

Teotihuacan must have been a most imposing sight. It covered an area of over 18 km². Altars, shrines, and monastic buildings stood on either side of a broad straight road, which ran for some 3 km through the city. At one end was the Pyramid of the Moon, only slightly smaller than that of the Sun. But the most interesting building is the temple dedicated to Quetzalcoatl, god of learning and the arts, or possibly to Tlaloc, the rain-god. The terraced front of the pyramid and the stairway were adorned with splendid stone sculptures and reliefs painted blue, white, and red, and portraying the god's emblem, a feathered serpent, rain-god masks, and other symbolic objects. The feathered serpent, or serpent-bird, appears later in Toltec and Maya temples, as does the figure of the popular rain-god with his trunk-like nose (*see* MAYA CIVILIZATION).

Like most of the Central American Indians, these people were expert potters and decorated their vases beautifully in various styles of painting

British Museum

ANCIENT MEXICAN RITUAL AXE IN HUMAN FORM

It is made of greenstone and is about 28 cm. high. Olmec culture

and engraving. They also made, for religious purposes, great numbers of small terracotta figures with admirably modelled features. They were very skilful at flaking a kind of natural volcanic glass called obsidian which they used for tools and weapons. They cultivated most of the known domesticated plants of Mexico, including maize, beans, and chili peppers. Cotton was grown for spinning and weaving cloth. The men wore robes and breeches and sandals of plaited fibre; the women dressed in sleeveless blouses and skirts as they still do today. Details of costume can be seen in the fresco paintings which have survived in some of the buildings. Like many other Indian tribes, both ancient and modern, they made use of steam baths as aids to health and cleanliness.

Teotihuacan was overthrown in the 7th century A.D. Later a warlike people called Toltecs invaded the Valley of Mexico from the north, and founded a new capital at Tula. They also worshipped the god Quetzelcoatl, and introduced new features in their architecture, such as columns. They were the first Mexicans to practise metalwork in gold, copper, and bronze. At the end of the 10th century their power was shaken by religious and civil strife, and many of them migrated to Yucatán, where they introduced their special style of art at Chichén Itzá and other Maya centres. The power of Tula declined in the face of fresh invasions in the early 13th century, which culminated in that of the AZTECS (q.v.). Though the Aztec Indians were a somewhat primitive tribe of wandering hunters when they arrived, they soon established their power in the valley of Mexico, settled down, and absorbed the older culture of their Toltec neighbours.

See also ANCIENT CIVILIZATIONS.
See also Vol. IV: AMERICAN-INDIAN LANGUAGES.

MEXICANS. Mexico is the most northerly country of Latin America—just south of the United States. But it is misleading to think of it as Latin, for Mexico is largely an Indian country. The majority of the Mexican people are of mixed Indian and European blood; about a third are pure Indian; and only comparatively few are

Hugo Brehme

PYRAMID OF THE SUN, ON WHICH A TEMPLE FORMERLY STOOD, AT TEOTIHUACAN

About 213 metres square at the base and 60 metres high. Teotihuacan culture. (Restored)

TEMPLE OF QUETZALCOATL OR TLALOC AT TEOTIHUACAN

The carved and painted stone panels represent feathered serpents, masks, shells, and other emblems. Teotihuacan culture

white. The present population is around fifty million, and is growing very fast. There will be seventy three million Mexicans by 1980. It was the home of the only advanced Indian civilizations in North America before the Europeans came (*see* MEXICAN, ANCIENT, and AZTEC CIVILIZATIONS), and today Mexico is more and more remembering its Indian traditions.

But the three centuries during which Mexico was part of the Spanish Empire have left a deep impression. Indeed, Mexico has a certain resemblance to Spain. Like Spain, it consists largely of barren plateau and has great mineral wealth. It is like Spain in its stormy and passionate history, and in the courtesy, poverty, and idealism of its people, though Mexico is four times the size of Spain. But there is one great difference. Like France and Russia, but unlike Spain, Mexico is the country of a revolution. To understand this it is necessary to know the outline of its history.

The modern history of Mexico began when CORTES (q.v. Vol. V) landed on the shores of the Gulf in 1519 and burnt his ships so that there should be no retreat for him and his 500 Spaniards. By 1521 they had conquered the Aztec Empire and taken possession of its capital, which is now Mexico City. Thus Mexico became part of the Spanish Empire, and was given the name of New Spain. The Spaniards tried to convert the Mexicans to Christianity, but they were even more eager to gain the wealth of the Mexican silver- and gold-mines. Much of the land was divided up into large estates, and the Indians were set to work. Very soon the Church became powerful, owning great properties.

Mexico was ruled from Spain for exactly 300 years, from 1521 to 1821. The Spanish colonists, as elsewhere in Spanish America, revolted against Spain when Spain was conquered by Napoleon; but in Mexico the movement for independence soon became something deeper, a revolt by the Indian peasants against the Spaniards. This, however, was not successful, and when Mexican independence was finally gained in 1821, it simply meant that the Spanish colonists had won freedom for themselves alone, and that the Indians had changed their masters.

The history of Mexico since its independence is one of the most dramatic of modern times. It is full of exciting episodes, romantic figures, and tragic failures. In the 19th century the country was reduced in size, and slowly gained in unity. Its frontier with the United States on the north was vague and undefined. In 1845 Texas, which had been part of Mexico, revolted and joined the United States, and in the war which followed (1846-8) the United States defeated Mexico and annexed all the country north of the Rio Grande together with California. In this way Mexico lost more than half its territory.

Foreign war was followed by civil war. At the same time as the great American Civil War (1861-5), another civil war was raging in Mexico (1858-67) in which the French took part in the hope of winning a colonial empire for themselves. The hero of the American War was Abraham Lincoln; the hero of the Mexican War was Benito Juarez (1806-72). He was an Indian who became president of Mexico, and the greatest statesman Mexico has had. He has often been compared with Lincoln for his honesty and his belief in democracy; and like Lincoln he saved his country, driving out the French and restoring peace.

Civil war was followed by dictatorship. Five years after the death of Juarez, one of his lieutenants, Porfirio Diaz, seized power and ruled Mexico with an iron hand from 1877 to 1911. He developed the wealth of the country, but did little for the welfare of its people. Then came the revolution. It began in 1910, and all the governments since then have continued its work, in a

J. Allan Cash

MEXICAN FATHER AND SON

J. Allan Cash

THE MARKET AT TLACOLULA, NEAR OAXACA, MEXICO

long, slow effort to reorganize the country. The three chief objects of the revolution have been to reduce the power of the Church, to divide up the great estates and give the land to the peasants, and to develop the wealth of the country for the benefit of the Mexican people and not of foreigners. Like every revolution, it has brought new struggles and new sufferings, and has committed many mistakes and crimes. But it has given a new hope to the Mexican people, and especially to the Indians. For the first time they have a government which they feel is concerned with their welfare. For all its ugly and disturbing features, the Mexican Revolution is one of the most important events that has happened in Latin America since the winning of independence from Spain.

The revolution is interesting because in some ways it is an attempt to modernize Mexico, but in other ways it is a harking back to the Indian traditions which existed before the white man came. In the main thoroughfare of Mexico City there is an imposing monument to the last of the Aztec emperors, but in all Mexico there is no statue of Cortes to be found. This shows how the Mexicans look at their past. And indeed, in spite of independence and the revolution, life has changed little for the Mexican peasant since Aztec days. He wears the same brightly coloured

square blanket; he eats the same 'national dish' of red, brown, or black beans; he drinks the same 'national drink' of *pulque*. He has the same festivals, though these have now become the Christian holidays; he uses the same simple tools; he tills the same fields. The Aztecs used knives made of obsidian, a glassy volcanic stone. The Mexican peasant today sometimes uses razor-blades made of the same material.

The full name of the country is the United States of Mexico. It consists of twenty-eight states, and has a constitution modelled on that of the United States of America. The language of the country is Spanish, but many Indians speak only their own various tribal tongues (*see* AMERICAN INDIAN LANGUAGES, Vol. IV); Mexico is rich in popular arts and crafts, in folksongs and folkstories. The peasant expresses himself in beautiful potteries, tapestries, woodcarvings, and leatherwork. The chief art of Spanish colonial times was architecture, which filled the cities of Mexico with splendid churches. But since the revolution the supreme art has been painting. The two most famous Mexican painters are Rivera and Orozco; their frescoes are found on the walls of buildings all over Mexico; and they rank among the greatest of living artists.

See also MEXICAN ANCIENT CIVILIZATION.

See also Vol. III: MEXICO; INDEX, p. 149.

MICRONESIANS. These people, as their name implies, live in the 'small' islands north of the Equator in the western Pacific Ocean. The Micronesian Islands include the Caroline, Mariana, Marshall, and Gilbert Islands (*see* PACIFIC ISLANDS, Vol. III). Most of these are low coral atolls providing a poor living from the coconuts and other trees growing on the sandy soil, and from the fish which abound in the lagoons. A few of the larger volcanic islands of the Carolines and Marianas offer greater scope.

The Micronesians are brown-skinned like the POLYNESIANS (q.v.), but show signs of mixture with other races. Some have frizzy hair like MELANESIANS (q.v.); others, in the west, are more like MALAYS (q.v.), and their language is a mixture of Malayan and Polynesian. It is believed that the Polynesian voyagers, passing through the islands on their way eastwards many centuries ago, left some groups behind them, and that other peoples from Indonesia, the Philippines, and perhaps New Guinea moved in behind and mixed with the survivors. In 1668 the

Marianas were settled by the Spaniards, who introduced Western ideas and customs. The rest continued a primitive way of life till the Japanese mandatory government began to develop the islands in 1920. Ever since, they have resisted Japanese attempts to change them, but inevitably, especially during the Second World War, much of their old way of life has disappeared. More of it remains in the Gilbert Islands which are under British rule.

Before the Japanese and others changed their way of life, the people of the Micronesian Islands lived in scattered groups along the coasts of the coral atolls, or in more regular villages in some of the bigger islands. On two of the Caroline islands they built stone causeways, jetties, and sea-walls, as well as large ceremonial club-houses in which the young unmarried men slept, and where visitors could be lodged and important village meetings held. In two places the traces of larger towns with canals running through them have been found, which probably belonged to the ancestors of the present people. The buildings of these towns were simple structures made of rough, natural, six-sided blocks of basalt found nearby.

The island people for the most part grew yams, taro, sweet potatoes, and coconuts; they kept a few pigs and chickens and caught all sorts of fish. They lived in simple wooden huts with mat screens for walls and palm-leaf thatch for roofing. They used tools made of stone or the ground-down shells of the giant clam. Their weapons were slings and spears and, especially in the Gilbert Islands, weapons edged with sharks' teeth; their armour consisted of thick coconut-fibre matting. They, and some Melanesians, were the only Pacific peoples who knew the art of weaving on simple breast looms with strips of pandanus fibre; but they did not spin. The women wore grass skirts and the men loin-cloths. They had necklaces, belts, ear-rings, and combs made of wood and shell. Other works of art are spoons made of turtle-bone and beautiful wooden bowls inlaid with white shell to be found in one Caroline island.

The Micronesians excelled as sailors and navigators. They built single sailing-canoes with an outrigger float on one side—probably the fastest craft in the Pacific. They used to hold a yearly

Pitt Rivers Collection

A VILLAGE BESIDE THE LAGOON, BUTARITARI, GILBERT ISLANDS

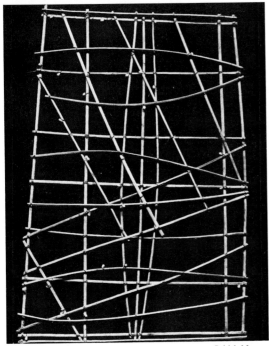

British Museum

A NAVIGATIONAL CHART USED BY MARSHALL ISLANDERS

Small shells represent islands and curved sticks the swells set up by intersecting currents. By following the ripples caused by the swells the islanders can find their way when out of sight of land

canoe race round the island of Babelthuap, the winner of which was held in great honour. In the Gilbert Islands today native regattas are common, and there are elaborate rules of etiquette to be observed when sailing. In the Marshall Islands they made charts on strips of bamboos with shells to show the position of the islands, and curved strips of bamboo to indicate the swells and ripples caused by the meeting of ocean currents. In the Gilbert Islands they navigated by the stars.

The islanders had several kinds of currency (money). In the island of Truk, for example, small cakes made of powdered Turmeric root known as *taik* had an exchange value—an axe-blade cost ten pieces of taik, for instance. In the Marshalls strings of black and white shell-beads were used. The most extraordinary money was that of the island of Yap. It consisted of large stone disks, some as much as 2·5 m across.

Micronesian society was, and largely still is, divided into many classes. The clan relationship with its obligations spread over many villages and islands, so that a man visiting a strange island could be sure of obtaining hospitality from members of his own clan. A man had to seek a wife from some other clan than his own.

See also Vol. IV: OCEANIC LANGUAGES.

MIGRATION OF PEOPLES. Mankind has wandered over the earth since the beginning of time. At first, the wandering of peoples was prompted by the need to satisfy hunger and thirst, and to find shelter. Man was still in many ways close to the animal world and so the migrations were widespread, continuous, and unplanned. That is how the earth gradually became peopled, and why we find evidence of prehistoric cultures all over the world (*see* PREHISTORIC MAN). As the more favourable parts of the world filled up and man learnt how to grow food rather than hunt it, migration had less point and therefore became less general. In the course of time, the original motives became obscured by others more complex, and the physical and geographical factors that had determined the migratory routes became overshadowed by political and commercial considerations.

We know a good deal from the Bible records about the wanderings of the ancient HEBREW people (q.v.) during the course of their migrations from the Arabian steppes to their new home in Palestine. And they were only one of many Semitic tribes in that part of Asia who were moving through the countries of the Near East. The migration of people from Ancient Greece or Phoenicia to other parts of the Mediterranean area was more of a colonizing venture than an aimless wandering. The pressure of population in a small infertile country induced many Greeks to seek their livelihood by commerce. The settlements that were founded on the coast of Asia Minor, in Sicily, Spain, and North Africa were as much trading posts as colonies.

Another type of migration in classical times was that of military movements of armies as empires rose and fell. ALEXANDER THE GREAT (q.v. Vol. V) led one of the greatest military migrations in history, and with his soldiers went a knowledge of Greek civilization. The legions of Rome reached the four corners of the then known world, and laid the foundations of western European culture.

From the 4th to the 7th centuries A.D. successions of barbarian hordes swept at intervals from the East into Europe, breaking through the defences of the Roman Empire, and finally settling in the lands they conquered. The reason which made these peoples—HUNS, GOTHS, VANDALS, MAGYARS, and TARTARS (qq.v.)—leave their eastern homes is not certain. It is probable that a gradual change in climatic conditions made life precarious on the marginal grasslands of central Asia, whilst the attraction of better land and a superior way of life to the west and south helped to set them on the move.

In the 9th and 10th centuries the remarkable sea-migrations of the Vikings (*see* NORWEGIANS) peopled Iceland and Greenland and affected events in Britain, France, and even the Mediterranean countries, and it is now widely believed that America was originally discovered by these Norsemen. In time, though, all these peoples were absorbed into the populations they assailed or overthrew.

In Asia, also, there were periodic mass movements of people, the reasons for which are not always easy to tell. China throughout her history has been subject to periodic inflows of foreign conquerors—the MONGOLS (q.v.), for instance, who were akin to the Huns who came to Europe, and the Manchus (*see* CHINESE CIVILIZATION). Similar movements have taken place in India and Sri Lanka. One of the most remarkable of all was the astounding migration of POLYNESIANS (q.v.) from Asia which probably took place at the beginning of the Christian Era. These people travelled enormous distances in long, light craft, each carrying up to 100 people, with only the stars to steer by, and settled in the islands of the Pacific including, in course of time, New Zealand.

One of the other most remarkable migrations, about which practically nothing is known for certain, is the great movement of people of a Mongolian type from Asia across the Behring Straits into North America, and from there right through the American continents. These were the ancestors of the people we now call the AMERICAN INDIANS (q.v.). This must have happened thousands of years ago, shortly after the Ice Age.

When America was rediscovered by Europeans in the 15th century, another period of migration began. During the following 200 years many Spanish, Portuguese, Dutch, English, and French sought their fortunes in the Americas. The motives were mixed: greed for gold, lust for power, genuine missionary zeal, and a desire to find a new route to Asia. But these ventures had

as their aim exploration and exploitation rather than permanent settlement. The first colonies that were founded were based on slave labour. It was not until the 17th century that the New England settlements were founded by English Puritans, driven from their country by religious persecution. Emigration to these settlements was steady but did not reach great proportions until the 19th century. Between 1820 and 1914 approximately sixty million Europeans emigrated to the Americas, South Africa, and Australasia. More than 60% of them went to the U.S.A. Before 1880 the majority of these emigrants came from Britain, Germany, and Scandinavia, where the economic and social effects of the Industrial Revolution and the increase in population had brought about social distress and unrest. But the great majority of 19th-century emigrants went voluntarily, not as forced labour or as fugitives from persecution. These people saw in the open spaces of the New World the hope of a better life.

Of the twenty million people that entered the U.S.A. after 1880 the majority came from Italy, Poland, and Russia. By 1921 the U.S.A. had introduced restrictions on immigration and since then the flow of peoples to the Americas and elsewhere has been strictly controlled and limited. The entrance of Orientals into the U.S.A. and also into Australia has been especially restricted, since, in recent times, the need for emigration has been felt chiefly amongst the overpopulated countries of the Far East.

After 1933 began the emigration of thousands of political refugees from the Fascist-controlled countries of Europe. The JEWS (q.v.) formed the majority of the refugees. Their migrations during the centuries have generally been the result of persecution. 'The Wandering Jew' is a historical fact.

After the Second World War the number of immigrants into Britain from Commonwealth countries expanded very rapidly. They were attracted, particularly from the West Indies and Pakistan, by the opportunities for advancement in Britain, where there was a shortage of manpower. By two acts of Parliament (1962, 1968) further IMMIGRATION (q.v. Vol. X) was restricted.

Apart from migrations between countries, there are also migrations that take place within a single country, as for example, the northward movement of the AMERICAN NEGRO (q.v.) from the south of the U.S.A. in search of a better job and a higher standard of living. This can be paralleled by the drift of the rural population in Britain to the towns, and the migration of people from the Scottish Highlands to the industrial areas farther south.

From this brief survey it is obvious that human migrations are due to a variety of causes and are of several kinds; but all migrations lead to a mingling of peoples and cultures and so contribute to the civilization of mankind. Perhaps there is something fundamental in man's nature that makes him at heart a wanderer, always ready to believe in something better somewhere else. There are still some large areas of the world relatively unsettled, notably the great expanses of Canada with their riches still unexploited.

See also RACES AND PEOPLES; POPULATION.

MINOAN CIVILIZATION is the civilization which flourished in Crete for some 1,500 years, from about 3000 to about 1350 B.C. The legends of Greece told how there had once been a Golden Age of splendour and prosperity connected with the name of King Minos. That the legends were based on historical events has been proved by Sir Arthur Evans's excavations of Minoan remains on the island of Crete. The two chief centres of this civilization were KNOSSOS (Cnossus) (q.v. Vol. XII) on the north side of the island, and Phaestus on the south side. Our knowledge of Minoan civilization rests at present largely on the evidence of excavation and not on written documents. Recently, one of the various systems of writing used in Crete has been deciphered and found to be an early form of the Greek language, but the earlier scripts are still not understood.

The history of this brilliant island civilization falls into three main periods which, for convenience of classification, archaeologists have labelled Early, Middle, and Late Minoan. It is possible that the first impulse to the development of civilization in Crete came from Egypt, which was also at this time in the early stages of her civilization. In fact a number of ivory seals have been found of which the material could only have come from Africa, and the designs resemble those on Egyptian seals of about the same time.

The first or Early stage of Minoan civilization covered the period from about 3000 to 2000 B.C. The people of this period lived in small rectangular houses gathered into villages. They made gracefully designed pottery, decorated with geometrical designs scratched on a polished surface.

Ashmolean Museum

THE SNAKE GODDESS

From a facsimile of the faience statuette found at Knossos

They also made beautiful polished stone vases, like those made in Egypt at an earlier period. In the graves of this period have been discovered bronze daggers, axes, knives, pincers, and other implements showing a high degree of skill in craftsmanship; also gold armlets, diadems, pendants, and crystal, amethyst, and agate beads. The centre for this culture was the Mesara plain, near Phaestus. The number of small towns on the east coast and on the adjoining islands points to a very active foreign trade.

The Middle Minoan period began about 2000 B.C. or a little later, coinciding with one of the greatest periods in Egyptian history, and ended about 1600 B.C. The cities Knossos and Phaestus, with their magnificent palaces, were evidently two of the great centres of power in Crete, but there were other palace centres at Mallia, on the north coast, and Zakro, on the east. In this period the Cretans developed an elaborate system of picture-writing much like

Ashmolean Museum

THE BULL SPORT
Copy of a fresco in the Palace of Knossos

the Egyptian hieroglyphs, which developed, as did the Egyptian, into a more practical and less cumbersome form of picture-writing. There was certainly a vigorous trade going on between Crete and Egypt during this period. The Egyptian inscriptions frequently mention a people called the Keftiu (probably their name for the Cretans), and there are pictures showing Keftiu or Cretan messengers bringing presents of vases and blocks of metal to the Egyptian king.

The walls of the Cretan palaces were decorated with coloured frescoes, the brilliant colours and natural freshness of which are characteristic of Minoan art at its best. In this period the potter's wheel was introduced, and geometric decoration gives place to a style of decoration based on floral motives and polychrome patterns of curved lines. In addition to this advance in pottery, the metalwork and fine gem-cutting show a high degree of artistic skill.

The Middle Minoan period ended with a general destruction, possibly brought about by earthquake shocks. Whatever the cause, the revival was rapid, and the two great palaces at Knossos and Phaestus were rebuilt almost at once. The last period of the palaces, lasting from about 1600 to about 1350 B.C., ushered in an age

of greater splendour and prosperity than Crete had yet known. This too is the period in which we have for the first time written tablets which can be read as Greek. So far they have only been found at Knossos, and it now seems likely that Crete was at this time under the dominion of mainland Greece, where the MYCENAEAN CIVILIZATION (q.v.), which was truly Greek, was flourishing. Hitherto it has been supposed that the Cretans gained control of the mainland, but it is now clear that the reverse is true, at least in Knossos. The tablets record the treasures and stores of the palace, as well as ration accounts for palace servants. Unfortunately no literature in the form of poetry or letters has been preserved.

The civilization of the Late Minoan period shows no sharp break with the preceding period, but the palaces and houses were rebuilt on a larger and more luxurious scale. The palace frescoes give a vivid picture of various aspects of Minoan life: particularly interesting are the pictures of the bull-games which may be the origin of the Spanish and Mexican bull-fights. On the frescoes may be seen the figures of the athletes, young women as well as young men, engaging in this exciting sport: they are shown awaiting the bull's charge, grasping the bull's horns, and somersaulting over his head. The representations are full of life and naturalness, a characteristic of all Minoan art. The Minoan artists were very fond of depicting scenes from nature: cows and goats suckling their young, a monkey hunting lizards among the rocks and flowers, and very fine and delicate representations of marine life. No art of the ancient world can show anything approaching the freedom and joyousness of feeling, and the sureness of execution of these artists—in both frescoes and crafts such as seal-cutting and jeweller's work. From the frescoes we learn what the dress of the Minoans was like. The women's dress was very elaborate; a full, flounced skirt, a short-sleeved blouse or bodice, cut very low in front to show the breasts, and the whole surmounted by a high conical hat; the hair was worn long and flowing on the shoulders. This seems to have been the ceremonial dress for processions and court occasions. It is also the dress of the Snake Goddess, who is represented in statuettes as grasping snakes in both hands, while a snake is coiled round her high ceremonial hat. The ordinary dress of the men consisted merely of a short kilt, but they wore elaborate robes for court occasions.

The principal deities of Cretan worship were goddesses. The Mother Goddess is frequently represented standing on a mountain, attended by lionesses and young male priests. The Snake Goddess was evidently much worshipped, and many of her shrines have been found in the palaces. The bull was an object of worship: bull's horns, the symbol of the bull cult, are found everywhere—on altars and decorating the walls. The myth of the Minotaur bears witness to the bull's importance. The myth tells how the monster, with a bull's head and man's body, was concealed by King Minos in the Labyrinth and fed once in nine years with seven boys and seven girls from Athens. The legend of the Labyrinth may have arisen from a memory of the winding passages of the palaces of Knossos and Phaestus.

About 1500 B.C. the palaces were destroyed by the eruption of the island of Thera. Knossos passed into Mycenaean control and was itself destroyed about 1350 B.C. Now that we know that Knossos was Mycenaean, it may be that the destruction of the palace powers was due to a revolt of Cretans against their overlords and not, as was formerly thought, an invasion from the mainland. In later years Crete remembered more vividly than most of the Greek world her Minoan

traditions, and with the finds in the island we can see the continuity from the civilizations of the great Bronze Age palaces through to Classical Greece.

See also ANCIENT CIVILIZATIONS.

MIRACLE. If by miracle is meant a marvellous event due to the exercise of supernatural power, then to the primitive mind almost any remarkable happening may be and generally is miraculous. The savage, in fact, has no word for 'nature' or 'natural'. He thinks that everything that arrests his attention or requires an explanation is the work of supernatural forces—spirits or gods from 'the other world' (*see* RELIGION). Since he explains in this way nearly every mysterious and inexplicable object or occurrence he thinks that the whole universe is filled with influences and actions beyond the understanding and control of men, and therefore miraculous. Thus, simple folk are so surrounded with what seems to them marvellous and unaccountable that they see supernatural agencies at work all around them.

This, in fact, is how the natural order and the course of human history have been interpreted everywhere until recent times. Modern science has taught us that the universe is governed by fixed laws which always act in the same way under the same conditions. Thus, for example, in the Bible, especially in the Old Testament, many events which we should explain in terms of natural laws, such as thunderstorms, volcanic eruptions, healing by auto-suggestion, &c., are represented as miraculous acts of divine intervention. The same is true of all the other ancient civilizations where the gods were thought to be responsible for everything out of the ordinary that happened in the world. The Jews, however, differed from their neighbours in placing the main emphasis on God's direction of the history of their nation as a whole to predestined ends. For instance, the miracle that stands out above all others in their traditions is the deliverance from Egypt, because it was a turning-point in the fortunes of the nation. This they thought was the Lord's doing and it was marvellous in their eyes.

Human beings have gradually come to know that natural processes follow orderly laws. As far as they have discovered natural law they have learnt to control nature and have therefore changed the whole face of the earth since they first appeared upon the scene. This human stage

THE MIRACULOUS DRAUGHT OF FISHES

By gracious permission of H.M. the Queen

Cartoon by Raphael (1483–1520) for a tapestry

of development has been reached by a process of evolution from the most primitive stage of life to the human beings of the 20th century. At each higher stage new powers are revealed which produce results that are perfectly 'natural' at that level but would be regarded as supernatural and miraculous at the lower levels. If a piece of rock could think, it would doubtless look upon the power of growth in the trees as a miracle. The tree similarly would look upon the power of primitive man to run and throw as miraculous; and primitive man in his turn naturally thinks of the modern inventions of the motor-car, the aeroplane, or telephone as miracles. It is not surprising therefore that human beings should still explain in much the same way situations and achievements which are still outside their normal range of knowledge and experience. Many extra-

ordinary events, therefore, that used to be called miracles we now know to be perfectly natural happenings because we understand the natural law which caused them.

Sometimes stories of miracles which have grown up round a sacred place have in fact developed from very slight origins, but have been encouraged because they gave the sacred place greater importance in the eyes of the worshippers. In other cases the great actions of famous people have, after their death, been exaggerated and recounted as miracles. It was, for instance, thought that a saint, holy man, or hero must have had miraculous powers: even as late as the time of the Stuarts our own kings were thought to be able to cure certain diseases by touching those suffering from them. Then there are traditions of extraordinary happenings which, at the time when they occurred, seemed to be so unusual and arresting that they could not be explained except as supernatural events, and have been handed down the ages as such by subsequent generations. The story of the crossing of the Red Sea, when the Israelites fled from Pharaoh, may be quoted as a familiar example of this type of miraculous tradition. Today volcanoes in eruption, avalanches, typhoons, severe droughts, and the appearance of comets have ceased to be explained as miraculous happenings because we understand the underlying causes. Nevertheless, there are still times when, to many quite intelligent people, it seems that forces from another world intervene to restore the balance of our own world. For example, hundreds of sick people every year in modern Europe make a long and difficult journey to Lourdes in the Pyrenees in the hope and belief of receiving miraculous cures of their complaints.

Whether or not miracles do really happen, those who believe they do, if they are intelligent folk, do not think of them as arbitrary acts of an all-powerful God who plays fast and loose with His creations according to His whims and fancies like a despotic king. If He is the Creator of the universe He must control the forces of nature and guide the fortunes of the world in the way in which He wills. But having made and set in motion the laws and processes of nature He must, as it were, play the game according to the rules He has drawn up. Otherwise everything would be in a state of chaos and confusion. So He could not be continually interfering in the orderly course of events. But, on the other hand, since man is able to use the forces of nature for his own purposes, it must be possible also for the divine mind and will behind the universe to make use of them.

MISSIONARY. From the days of the Apostles (a Greek word meaning Missionary) the Church has had the commission to 'preach the Gospel (good news) to every creature'. Every period of revived zeal in the history of the Church has been accompanied by a return to this, the Church's central charge. The main missionary activities of the Church are described in the articles on the various branches of the Christian Church. The other great world religion which takes part in missionary activity is ISLAM (q.v.).

Besides the work of spreading the Gospel, missionaries have often been instrumental in enlightening primitive peoples, and bringing new life and vigour to some ancient civilizations. Mistakes are inevitable in all great enterprises, but taken as a whole, missionaries have played a leading part in spreading literacy, raising the standard of life, enriching culture, reforming society, combating disease, and contributing to international and inter-racial understanding and goodwill. On the whole, the missionary works for the good of the people and upholds the importance of the individual person, whatever his race or colour. This was an attitude of mind often entirely lacking among the conquerors and traders.

From the 4th century onwards translations of the Bible have been the means, again and again, of giving illiterate languages a script (see TRANSLATIONS, Vol. XII, Section 2). Modern medicine was first introduced to most parts of Asia and Africa chiefly by missionaries. All over the world those suffering from leprosy have depended for help almost entirely on mission homes and settlements (*see* Father DAMIEN, Vol. V). Wherever missionaries have gone, schools and colleges have been established. Such men as Alexander Duff in India and Timothy Richard in China did much to determine government educational policy. In China there were fourteen universities founded by Protestant Churches. In Africa a very large proportion of the population are educated in mission schools.

In the 16th century during the time of Spanish and Portuguese imperialism in South America, it was such missionaries as LAS CASAS in Spanish America who opposed the exploitation of the natives. In the 19th century missionaries such as DAVID LIVINGSTONE (qq.v. Vol. V) played a large part in exposing and finally abolishing the slave-trade in Africa and the West Indies. Today missionaries are combating the evils of the colour bar in Africa and facing the problems of advancing industrialization in the East.

See also CHRISTIAN CHURCH.

MITHRAISM. Mithras was a god of the ancient Persians representing the light of the day and bright heaven. He was retained in the Persian religion of ZOROASTRIANISM (q.v.), where he was one of the lesser gods surrounding Ahura Mazda, the Great God and 'Lord of Wisdom'. Later, Mithras was apparently worshipped as a sun-god who overcomes the demons of darkness; and by the 4th century B.C. he seems to have become a god of purity, moral goodness, and wisdom— a warrior-god always fighting against the powers

Musées Nationaux

MITHRAS SLAYING THE BULL

Relief from an altar from the Capitol, Rome, now in the Louvre

ascent of the human soul to God. The bull, it is believed, was therefore not thought of as evil but as a noble beast from whose blood came life. In this idea of sacrifice for mankind Mithraism had something in common with Christianity, though the conception took a much cruder form.

Not a great deal is known with any certainty about the beliefs and practices of Mithraism. It appears that a candidate, before being admitted to the secret mysteries, had to undergo a series of trials of increasing difficulty. Those initiated as soldiers of Mithras had continually to undergo periods of fasting and penance considered essential for the purification of the soul.

MONGOLS. In the remote past the Central Asian country of Mongolia received many migrants from the west, and its population is of very mixed descent. In the Middle Ages successive war-bands of Mongols swept westwards, and came to dominate large parts of Europe and Asia. The warriors of defeated tribes often took service under the new rulers. GENGHIS KHAN (q.v. Vol. V), led the Mongols in the 12th century to conquer all the neighbouring countries. For longer or shorter periods they held dominion over China, India, Persia, and Russia.

The Mongols were overthrown by their Chinese subjects in the 14th century, and in the 17th century both China and Mongolia were successively conquered by the Manchus, a people akin to the Tungus tribes of Manchuria. To break up old tribal allegiances, the Manchus created feudal 'banner' territories, whose hereditary princes had to be approved by the Manchu court before they took up office. But the Manchus brought under much more complete subjection the region called Inner Mongolia, south of the Gobi Desert. From the end of the 19th century, Chinese farmers pushed their way into this region, displacing the Mongols who were rapidly becoming outnumbered. In 1928 the Chinese divided up Inner Mongolia and incorporated the sections into three Chinese frontier provinces. Ten years later the Japanese created a self-governing state under Prince Teh, a descendant of Genghis Khan.

Outer Mongolia, on the north side of the Gobi Desert, never so closely controlled by China, broke away from China in 1911 shortly before the Manchu Dynasty came to an end. They allied themselves with their northern neighbours, the Russians, in the vain hope that Russia would support their ambition to unite all Mongol tribes

of evil on behalf of mankind. His followers became 'soldiers of Mithras'; they had to take part in the struggle and obey commandments demanding purity, loyalty, and fraternity among comrades.

Mithraism spread into the Roman provinces in the 1st century B.C. and became a popular cult with the Roman army—the warrior-god appealing to the soldier's mind. With the Roman legions it spread all over the Roman Empire even as far as Britain: remains of Mithraic cave temples have been found at York and on Hadrian's Wall in Northumberland, and in 1954 a Mithraic temple was discovered during excavation in the City of London. Mithraism was encouraged by some of the Roman emperors and flourished in Rome during the 2nd to 4th centuries A.D. Indeed, the Emperor Constantine, before finally adopting Christianity, is said to have leaned towards Mithraism. In A.D. 378, however, the Mithraic mysteries were prohibited in Rome, and the holy cave there destroyed.

Mithras was always worshipped in a cave—either natural or artificial. The figures of Mithras found in these caves show him as a young man in Persian dress in the act of stabbing a bull with a dagger. This represented a perpetual mystic sacrifice which Mithras was conceived as performing on behalf of mankind, and through which he achieved the triumph of good over evil and the

Urgunge Onon

NOMAD MONGOLIAN HERDSMEN CAMP IN YURTS

into one state. Since 1924 Outer Mongolia is a separate state, the Mongolian People's Republic, with its capital at Ulan Batôr Khoto (Red Hero Town). It has been a member of the United Nations since 1961, and is firmly allied to Soviet Russia, trading mainly with the countries of the Soviet bloc. Britain supplies some of the textile machinery and receives camel-hair and cashmere wool.

The change of the Mongol people from the earlier warrior race to a comparatively peaceful people is often attributed to the Yellow Religion, the Lamaist form of BUDDHISM (q.v.) from Tibet. But a much more important factor was that the Manchu rulers who subjugated the Mongols took a large share of power and revenue from the hereditary Mongol princes and gave it to the Buddhist Church. The Manchus also prevented Mongols from reaching a position of power within the Buddhist Church; for example no descendant of Genghis Khan could become a priest. But a great part of the male population—as many as 60% in the last century—became lamas (priests).

As they were exempted from military service there were fewer men available for the army.

In 1924, when the Mongolian People's Republic was established, the government, confronted with the social, political, and economic power of the Church, was determined to break it. There had long been bitter criticism of the monasteries within Mongolia, and of the influence of the Dalai and Panchen Lamas from outside (rather like the criticism of monasteries and papal influence in pre-Reformation England). Now the government levied a special tax on all lamas of military age, prohibited the monasteries from taking men under the age of 18, and in 1936 forbade the two eldest sons of a family to become lamas. Russian aid helped to improve the country's economic position and to change the traditional way of life in many ways. This rather sudden change from an archaic to a 20th century way of life brought with it some hardships.

The Mongols are a nomad people, and their very large territory is thinly populated. The Mongolian People's Republic now has about 1,300,000 inhabitants (of whom 1·8% are Russian) compared with an estimated 647,000 in 1928. The rise is largely due to new public health measures, particularly against venereal disease and tuberculosis. The former Inner Mongolia, now the Inner Mongolian Autonomous Area of Chinese People's Republic, has about 2 million Mongols, and about ten times as many Chinese. In 1962–64 there was a detailed re-survey of the Sino-Mongolian frontier, with a written agreement between China and the Mongolian People's Republic. Since then there have been no frontier disputes.

Cattle- and sheep-breeding have been the chief means of livelihood of the Mongols for centuries. Their essential needs have been provided by the by-products of the herds, mainly of the sheep. Wool is used to make felt to cover the yurts— round Mongol tents; wool and sheep skins make their clothes; and cattle and sheep dung is burnt as fuel. Their main food is meat and dairy products, and their foreign trade depends on livestock, wool, hides, and hair.

The government plan is to change this nomadic pastoral economy into an 'agricultural industrial economy'. Only about half the people are now engaged in agricultural and pastoral work, and they are organized in co-operatives. For the most part, each family lives within the co-operative centre, in a small house built of log, stone, or brick; and they also have a felt tent where they live when they do their turn of herding duties.

The rest of the population are engaged in service and manufacturing industries, in mining, and in transport. There are major coal mines near Ulan Batôr and Darkhan, oil in the Gobi Desert, some gold mines, and surveying goes on for copper, phosphorites, tin, and fluorite.

Transport, too, has been modernized. Mongolian Airlines operate an internal service, linking with the Moscow and Peking services at Irkutsk. The main railway is the Trans-Siberian Railway which goes through Ulan Batôr, on the way from Moscow to Peking. Roads have been built and road transport motorized. But the hardy Mongolian pony has not lost its traditional importance, and every co-operative and encampment has its herd; even in wild unfenced pastures, the ponies are early domesticated and trained always to return to the same watering-place. Women are as hardy and as much at home on horseback as men. The Mongolians are as notable for their hospitality and their sense of humour as for their prowess at horsemanship and wrestling.

See also Vol. III: MONGOLIA; INDEX, p. 150.
See also Vol. IV: TURKISH AND ALLIED LANGUAGES.

MONK ('one who is alone'). Christianity is not the only religion which has inspired people to leave the ordinary ways of the world for a life of prayer and self-imposed hardship. For instance, Hinduism, Buddhism, and Taoism have their holy men and monks. This article, however, is concerned with the monks and nuns of the CHRISTIAN CHURCH (q.v.).

Very early in the history of the Church men began to move away from the wickedness and luxury of the world to seek God in the solitary desert. They were called hermits (Greek for 'men of the desert'). The best known of them, St. Anthony, became a hermit in the Egyptian desert in A.D. 285.

St. Pachomius was one of the first to gather these hermits together into a community in A.D. 318. His community settled on an island in the lower Nile, where they worked hard on the land, with fastings and regular times for prayer. Before long a sister colony for nuns was set up. In A.D. 370 St. Basil, Bishop of Caesarea, gave a pattern for monastic life, called the Rule of St. Basil. This rule is still used for monasteries of the Eastern Church. He gave good reasons for the advantages of a community over a solitary life, and he fixed the canonical hours (times for corporate prayers). These are Prime (first hour, 6 a.m.), Tierce (third hour, 9 a.m.), Sext (sixth hour, noon), Nones (ninth hour, 3 p.m.), Vespers (evening, sunset), Nocturn (midnight), Lauds (praise, dawn). Later there was added an eighth hour, Compline, to follow Vespers.

In the 4th century the monastic movement began to spread into western Europe. In 527 ST. BENEDICT (q.v. Vol. V), from his monastery at Monte Cassino in Italy, drew up the Rule of St. Benedict which has been the pattern of Western monastic life ever since. He made the typical Roman contribution of order and discipline. He added to the rules of poverty and chastity the rule of obedience—the community must obey the Abbot (father), the head of the Monastery. The life that he established was strict, but it was well balanced. The periods of worship, the canonical hours, together took a little over two hours. Four to six hours were given to manual work in field or kitchen. Three hours were fixed as a minimum for study: 'a cloister without books', he wrote, 'is

H. D. Keilor

THE RUINS OF FOUNTAIN ABBEY, YORKSHIRE
It was founded in the 12th century by Cistercian monks

a fort without an armoury.' No one undertook this disciplined life without a year's trial, after which the 'novice' took his vows which bound him for life.

In the 10th century the great Orders of Monasteries began. The first order, the Cluniacs, grew from the great monastery at Cluny in south-east France, founded in 909. Soon it had many houses or branches in different countries, all of whom were controlled by the Abbot of Cluny, the head of the whole order and a powerful figure in medieval Europe. The order of Cistercians, founded about 1098, modified this extreme centralization: the abbots of the different houses met yearly at a council presided over by the Abbot of Cîteaux, but each house kept a considerable measure of independence.

In the later Middle Ages religious orders arose whose main purpose was active work in the world rather than retreat from the world. The Military Orders of the 12th century—the Templars, Hos-pitallers, and Teutonic Knights—were founded to take part in the Crusades (*see* KNIGHTS, ORDERS OF). The FRIARS (q.v.) of the 13th century were preaching and teaching orders, playing an active part in the lives of the people.

The contribution of the monasteries to medieval life was great. They developed in the West just as the Roman Empire was going to pieces. They provided refuges for learning and civilization when Europe was suffering from a wave of barbarism. Such books as survived were kept and copied in the monastery libraries and scriptoria (writing-rooms). The building and beautifying of monastic churches and cloisters gave encouragement to architects, painters, and sculptors (*see* MONASTIC ARCHITECTURE, Vol. XII). Monks were the main historians and poets. They kept alive the ideal of the dignity of labour and they cleared forests and drained fens. The monks provided the hostelries of the Middle Ages and relief to the surrounding poor. The monasteries were the hospitals and schools. Monks were also the medieval missionaries, not only in the West but right across Asia.

Under the rule of poverty no monk was allowed to possess property or money. Rich men and women who became monks and nuns gave their money to the monasteries. In addition wealthy patrons, bishops, kings, and princes endowed monasteries with wealth and land. In this way the abbots became very rich and powerful land-owners, often controlling and farming large estates and taking considerable part in the poli-tical affairs of the country. In England by the 16th century there were about 600 monasteries owning at least one quarter of the country.

Inevitably dangers accompanied this wealth and power of the monasteries, and luxurious living sometimes took the place of the rule of poverty. People no longer respected the monks and nuns for their lives of self-sacrifice; instead they envied their wealth. In England the RE-FORMATION (q.v.) hastened action against the monasteries: in 1536 the monasteries were offic-ially dissolved, and many of them were ran-sacked and destroyed.

On the Continent at this time a revival of reli-gious community life began which culminated with the founding of the Society of Jesus (the Jesuits) by the Spaniard, Ignatius LOYOLA (q.v. Vol. V). This society began among students of the University of Paris. It was organized on mili-tary lines with Loyola as General, and it sought service in dangerous places. The Jesuits are not monks, but members of the first of the 'religious organizations'. They were dispensed from the monastic obligation of chanting the divine office and so had more time to work in the ministry. Their ruthless zeal sometimes made them dis-liked; but their work as missionaries and in edu-cation has been extremely effective and far-reaching.

In the following centuries many new 'religious congregations' were founded in the Catholic Church, whose members are now active primarily in missionary and educational work. Some of the better known are the Passionists, Redemptorists, Salesians, and Christian Brothers. Also, the Church of England has returned to the idea of monastic life, and there are some Anglican Orders both of monks and nuns.

See also ASCETICISM; FRIAR.

MONOTHEISM, *see* GOD, Section (*b*).

MONTENEGRINS, *see* YUGOSLAVS.

MOORS. The word 'Moor' is derived from *Mauri*, the name given by the Romans to the inhabitants of the region of north-west Africa known as Mauritania (*see* INDEX, p. 149). This region was conquered by the ARABS (q.v.) in the 7th century A.D., and they called the inhabitants Berbers (from *barbar*, to speak indistinctly). How-ever, most Berbers became Muslim and learned to speak ARABIC (q.v. Vol. IV). The Moors are considered to be physically and culturally an intermixture of Arabs and Berbers.

The Moorish people also once lived in Spain. In the 8th century Spain was a Gothic kingdom (*see* GOTHS). A ruler of the extreme south, called Julian, invited the Moorish Arabs to help him in a rebellion against the Gothic king, Roderic. Their leader, Tariq, captured Gibraltar and gave it his name Jebel Tariq (Mountain of Tariq), and overran the whole of southern Spain. The Moors pushed into south-western France and captured Bordeaux in 732, but they were defeated in a battle at Poitiers and were finally ejected from France at the end of the century. The Moors in Spain fought so much among themselves that the Christians in the north were able to avoid being conquered, but they were too disunited them-selves to drive the Moors out.

Moorish Spain became a renowned cultural centre; to Cordoba came men from the Muslim world, as well as Christians from France and Italy, to study arts, astronomy, geography, chem-istry, and natural history. The ideas of chivalry and the love of poetry and music spread from there northward, chiefly by means of the trouba-dors of Provence. Many of the beautiful build-ings of the Moors are still to be seen in southern Spain and North Africa. The Moors' most flou-rishing period was the 10th century, after which came a gradual decline during which the SPAN-IARDS (q.v.) regained southern Spain. GRANADA (q.v. Vol. III) continued as a Moorish centre until its surrender in 1492. In order to avoid expulsion, many of the Moors adopted Christian-ity nominally and were henceforth known as 'Moriscos'. But the Moors were finally expelled from Spain in the years 1609-14.

The majority of the present-day Moors, who number nearly one million, live in the Republic of Mauretania and are mainly pastoral nomads. They also practise some agriculture and trade. Most of their country is barren, and mountainous

Moroccan Tourist Office

A MOROCCAN TRADITIONAL DANCE

and agricultural centres and oases are few. They are divided into many tribes, each of which consists of a number of sections and sub-sections. The sections of a tribe are headed by chiefs who form a council, and each tribe has its own code of law which may be modified by the tribal council.

There are four classes of people among the Moors: the free people who are the rulers; the slaves who work on the land and carry out domestic services; the artisans; and the hunters. While there is a tendency among some of these nomads to adopt a semi-sedentary way of life, the majority have retained their nomadic existence and regard agriculture as a degrading occupation.

See also Vol. XII: MOORISH ART.
See also ARABS; ISLAM; SPANIARDS.

MORAVIAN CHURCH. This community, which calls itself *Unitas Fratrum* (the Unity of Brethren), was founded in the late 14th century by John Huss of Bohemia, and its members are sometimes called Hussites. Huss was a forerunner of Protestant reformers in the medieval Church (*see* REFORMATION). He was much influenced by the English pre-Reformation reformer, John WYCLIFFE (q.v. Vol. V); and like Wycliffe he wanted to reform people's beliefs by turning their minds back to the teaching of the Bible. Huss was condemned as a heretic and was burnt to death in 1415. His followers were persecuted, but they struggled on with varying fortunes in Bohemia and Moravia (now parts of Czechoslovakia). In the year 1722, when they were being severely persecuted, a party of refugees found welcome in Germany on the estate of Count von Zinzendorf, a pious LUTHERAN (q.v.); and there they founded a settlement which they called *Herrnhut* (Lord's Watch). This was the beginning of the revival of the Moravian Church.

The Moravian Church today is a small one. There are about 3,000 members in the British Isles, about 21,000 on the mainland of Europe—chiefly in Germany and Denmark—and nearly 60,000 in America. In proportion to its size, however, its missionary work is tremendous; as many as 229,000 people have been baptized in its mission-fields in North India, South Africa, Alaska, Labrador, the West Indies, and Central and South America.

See also CHRISTIAN CHURCH.

MORMONS. The Mormon Church is officially called the Church of Jesus Christ of Latter-Day Saints. It was founded in 1830 in western New York State, by Joseph Smith, then 24 years old. He offered as proof of his divine calling the *Book of Mormon*. He said this was a translation from an ancient record of American history, engraved on gold plates. An angel called Mormoni had helped him find the spot where the plates were buried, and had taken them back after the translation was made. Joseph Smith soon won a devoted following, but wherever the Mormons went they were persecuted. From western New York they moved in turn to Ohio, Missouri, and Illinois, where the young prophet was murdered by a mob in 1844.

Eventually, under the leadership of Brigham Young, a true colonizing genius, they emigrated westwards to Utah and founded Salt Lake City. Here they established themselves as a well-organized and self-reliant community within the jurisdiction of the United States. For a time the Mormon Church allowed worthy men to have more than one wife, but today polygamy is a thing of the past, and all Mormons conform with current marriage laws in America.

Members of the Mormon Church profess belief in the Trinity as three separate and distinct persons, and in a universal resurrection of all mankind through Christ. They look forward to the second coming of Christ and His personal reign on earth. A voluntary missionary system is carried on mostly by young men and women who go to all parts of the world. This work is performed at their own expense, the Church having no paid ministry. While most young Latter-Day Saints aspire to be considered worthy to perform such service, it is not compulsory. This Church has grown from 6 members in 1830 to 3,091,000 members today in 7,077 congregations throughout the world, of whom over 2 million are in the United States, most of them in Utah, Southern California, and Idaho.

See also CHRISTIAN CHURCH.

MOZAMBIQUE, PEOPLES OF, *see* EAST AFRICANS.

MUHAMMADAN, *see* ISLAM.

MUSES. Greek goddesses of learning and the arts, especially poetry and music. They were thought of as nymphs whose favourite haunts were certain springs, near which temples and statues were erected in their honour. Apollo, the god of music and poetry, was their leader, and they shared with him knowledge of the past, present, and future.

The Muses were generally supposed to be nine sisters—the daughters of Zeus and the goddess Mnemosyne (Memory). Calliope, the Muse of epic song, was the noblest of them, and she was depicted carrying a tablet and pencil. Clio, the Muse of history, carried a scroll; Euterpe, the Muse of lyric song, carried a flute; Thalia, the Muse of comedy is shown with a comic mask, wreath, and shepherd's staff; Melpomene, the Muse of tragedy, had a tragic mask and wreath; Terpsichore, the Muse of dancing, carried a lyre; Erato, the Muse of love poetry, had a smaller lyre; Polyhymnia, the Muse of sacred songs, is usually veiled and pensive; Urania, the Muse of astronomy, possesses a celestial globe.

Greek and Roman writers often begin their work with a call to the Muses, and there are allusions to them in works of many later poets, especially those influenced by classical ideas. The word 'museum' originally meant a place dedicated to the works of the Muses.

MUSLIM, *see* ISLAM.

MYCENAEAN CIVILIZATION, called after the great city of Mycenae on the mainland of Greece, is important because it represents the first great civilization in Greek lands, which is truly Greek. It is the ancestor of the classical civilization which is more familiar to us. Its flourishing period was from about 1600 to 1200 B.C. It was not until the writing on the clay tablets found in the Mycenaean palaces was finally deciphered that it was proved that the Mycenaeans were Greeks, speaking a Greek language. The Greeks first entered the Aegean area around 2000 B.C. They soon came into contact with the brilliant MINOAN CIVILIZATION (q.v.) of the island of Crete and were greatly influenced by it, although they eventually dominated at least part of Crete.

Our knowledge of early Mycenaean civilization has been gained from the excavation of a remarkable group of tombs in Mycenae called the 'Shaft-Graves'. This form of grave consisted of a sloping or perpendicular shaft cut in the rock, leading to a burial chamber. These were evidently the burial-places of kings and members of the royal family. The objects found there are of great richness and show that the Mycenaeans had reached a high degree of artistic skill. Gold is very conspicuous in the two richest graves: the bodies had gold masks, gold diadems and breast plates, gold bracelets and signet-rings. Buried with them were long swords, richly decorated with gold, and large numbers of gold and silver cups. One of these was a libation-cup, that is, a cup for pouring ritual drink-offerings, upon which was embossed an interesting scene depicting the repulse of a pirate-raid on some Mycenaean strong-

Ashmolean Museum
GOLD CUP DECORATED WITH LIONS IN COURSE
From a facsimile

hold. There were amber and amethyst beads, alabaster vases, great copper cauldrons, ostrich-eggs mounted for use as libation-vessels, and an inlaid gaming-board. Among the most beautiful objects are the bronze daggers inlaid with gold, depicting hunting-scenes, which include spirited lion-hunts. The vividness and naturalness of these works of art is much like that of the late Minoan art.

The graves were enclosed in a circle just inside the fortress wall at Mycenae. Recently another grave circle has been found just outside the wall. It is rather earlier, but the graves contain similar fine golden objects.

By about 1400 B.C. the Shaft-Grave kings were succeeded by a succession of kings who were buried in tombs called *tholos* graves—buildings of great blocks of stone surmounted by domes built like beehives and covered with earth. The people of this period made better pottery than the earlier Mycenaeans; the decoration is more luxuriant and unrestrained. Two famous gold-embossed cups found in a tholos tomb at Vaphio depict the capture and taming of wild bulls, and are so much like the best Minoan work that they have been thought to be the work of a Cretan master craftsman. The Mycenaean masons and builders of this period were very skilled in the handling of stone blocks, some of which were of great size—a remarkable achievement for work-men with no iron tools, iron being as yet un-known in Greece. The huge tomb known as the Treasury of Atreus is a famous example of this skill in the use of immense blocks of masonry. It was built for a king of Mycenae when Mycenaean civilization was at its height. With its magnificent decoration in gold, bronze, and ivory, it is a monument to the power and splendour of the kings of Mycenae in the 14th century B.C. Other great tombs of the same period, and almost as splendid, have been discovered at other Myce-naean sites in Greece.

The Mycenaean rulers were heirs to the trade relations established by the Minoans, and once they had gained control of Crete they largely dis-placed the Minoans in the markets of the East, and in Egypt. Mycenaean objects have been found in Spain and Sicily; and there were Myce-naean colonies on the coasts of what are now Turkey and Syria. One form of pottery specially characteristic of the Mycenaeans is the 'stirrup' vase, apparently used for the export of oil, and this is found everywhere in the Mediterranean

Mansell

THE LION GATE, MYCENAE

One of the strongly fortified entrances to the Mycenaean Citadel, c. 1300 B.C.

area among the civilizations of the Mycenaean period.

The religion of the Mycenaeans, like their art, was very much the same as that of the Minoans. The principal deity was the Mother Goddess, as in Crete, and her symbol, the double-axe, is fre-quently found in excavations. The Mycenaeans were more warlike than the Cretans, and they developed armour, richly decorated with gold, not to be found in Crete. The Greek poet Homer in his *Iliad* and *Odyssey* recounted events which took place in Mycenaean times and sometimes described objects which excavation in Myce-naean palaces have now made familiar to us—in particular, the helmets made of boars' tusks sewn on to leather.

In the 12th century B.C. there was a general movement of peoples in the Ancient Near East which caused many changes in political power. Greece, at this time, was invaded by the Dorian peoples; and it was possibly this invasion which brought to an end the Mycenaean civilization. The Mycenaeans themselves at this time were marauding overseas, and the Trojan War may be the memory of a joint raid on the coast of Asia Minor. After the fall of the Mycenaean palaces the civilization of Greece lapses into some obscurity, but continuity is still clear until the 9th century B.C. when renewed contact with the East reawakened Greece and led to the brilliant civilization of classical Athens.

See also ANCIENT CIVILIZATIONS; GREEK CIVILIZATION.

MYSTICISM. The word 'mystic' comes from the Greek, and meant originally someone or something connected with the 'mysteries'. The *mustēs* was one who had been made a member by a ceremony of a secret religious fellowship or 'mystery', which possessed some private religious knowledge. But in time the word 'mystic' changed its meaning, and it has gradually come to mean anyone who, in his private life, is very closely and immediately united with a supernatural being. For example, a Christian becomes in mystical union, as it were, 'one with God'.

It is possible to reach this feeling of union in different ways and by different methods. By one method which takes a great deal of self-sacrifice to practise, the mystic tries to become detached from the world around, and to treat it as unreal or unprofitable compared with God, who is the only completely real and satisfying Object in the whole universe. By another method the mystic tries to see God in and behind everything in nature, so that nature leads on to God, or explains God through signs.

Mystics of different religions are aiming at different goals. Some mystics, as for example Hindu mystics, think that the right aim is to see everything, including themselves, as part of God, with the object of ceasing to be individuals, and becoming simply part of God. Christian mystics always distinguish carefully between God and human beings. They say, as St. Paul says: 'I live, yet not I, but Christ liveth in me.' They draw near to God through Christ, and because of their union with Christ they find themselves acting in daily life as Christ would act himself if he were in their place (as indeed they believe he is). This may make the Christian mystic very practical, and he may be fully engaged in a constructive life. The two greatest Christian mystic writers, ST. TERESA OF AVILA (q.v. Vol. V) and St. John of the Cross were also active workers in the Carmelite order.

A great many mystics, however, are people so full of the sense of God's presence that they want to dwell on it the whole time. Anything except thinking about God, speaking to or watching God at work seems to them a waste of time and

National Gallery

ST. FRANCIS RECEIVING THE STIGMATA
The Saint attained such close mystical union with Christ that his body bore the marks of the Passion. Painting by Sassetta (1392–1450)

energy. These people are called contemplatives. There are not many of them in the Anglo-Saxon world of today, but in India they are common.

All mystics, it is probably true to say, believe that the visible world is not the whole world, but that it is like a veil hiding us from another but invisible world, which is as real as, or more real than, the world we see. The difference between mystics at this point seems to be that some of them love nature, and find God through nature, while others think of nature as unreal and unsatisfying, and not worth troubling about except to escape from: some mystics also find it hard to think of God as a Person at all, and prefer to use some other word, like 'the Absolute', or 'the Godhead', or 'the Self-Existent'.

Mystics generally find that their sense of the unseen needs training. The methods used by mystics of some religions may seem rather strange. They include such physical devices as breathing in a certain slow fashion, or taking a special drug (as among Indians in New Mexico), or gazing at a red flower, or sitting in a special position, or saying a particular word a number of times. But these devices are only steps on the way, and as soon as the mind and body are quieted, then the real meditation begins.

The methods of Christian mystics are all simple and straightforward compared with these others, with nothing extravagant about them—their chief object being to bring about union with Christ by using the imagination to picture scenes in his life or sayings uttered by him. Yet it is improbable that any mechanical technique will bring about by itself a mystic vision. Perhaps God gives and withholds such visions as and when He pleases, for the flash of insight which some people have spoken of is not something that we can command when we choose.

Mystics have their own special troubles. Sometimes they come to feel that nothing is of any value, and that God has completely deserted them or does not exist. This 'dark night of the soul' often distresses people very much, especially if they have not been forewarned to expect it. For those, however, who can endure it with patience, there follows the period of peace and brightness when they have won through to the sense of God's presence.

See also RELIGION.

MYTHOLOGICAL MONSTERS. Mythology,
especially NORSE and GREEK MYTHS (qq.v.), contains accounts of a great variety of monsters, both in human and animal shape. They were not so popular with the Romans. These monsters are of three main types: (*a*) humans, either of exaggerated size or possessing some extraordinary feature; (*b*) monsters, half human and half animal; (*c*) animal monsters often combining the shapes of two or more animals.

(*a*) HUMAN MONSTERS. The most common and widely spread are the GIANTS (q.v.). Some of these were merely huge in size, like the Titans, Tityus of Hades, and the Norse giants, for example, Ymir. Others had some extraordinary characteristic, for example the Hundred-handed Giants, or the one-eyed Cyclopes. Other human monsters included Argus, the herdsman, who had eyes all over his body. When Hermes killed him his eyes were transferred to the feathers of the peacock's

MEDUSA, THE GORGON WHOSE LOOK TURNED PEOPLE TO STONE AND WHO WAS SLAIN BY PERSEUS

Painting from a Greek vase

tail. The Gorgons were female monsters with serpents in their hair and round their waists. They had hideous faces, and their gaze had the power to turn to stone anyone on whom it fell.

(*b*) HALF-HUMAN, HALF-ANIMAL MONSTERS. There were a great many of these in Greek mythology. The Sphinx was a winged woman with a lion's body. Sphinxes were also to be found in Egypt and probably originated in Mesopotamia. The Satyrs were goat-footed, and had horns and tails; the Centaurs were human as far as the waist

British Museum

A CENTAUR FIGHTING A LAPITH

Metope from the Parthenon, Athens

with the body and legs of a horse; the Minotaur had a human body and the head of a bull. (There was a Phoenician god, Baal-Moloch, who took this form.) Of sea monsters the best known are the Tritons and Scylla. The Tritons were sons of Poseidon, lord of the sea. They had human bodies and fishes' tails like MERMAIDS (q.v.). Scylla, according to Homer, lived in a sea cave in the Straits of Messina, and had twelve feet and six heads on six long necks, each with three rows of teeth. According to Virgil, the Roman poet, Scylla was less fearsome, possessing a woman's body and a dolphin's head, with a girdle of dogs' heads. In the Greek myth Scylla seized and devoured sailors passing up the Straits. The sailors, in endeavouring to escape her, fell into the whirlpools of Charybdis. The Sirens and the Harpies had women's heads and the bodies of birds, a common form of fabulous monster in many parts of the world. The Sirens lured men to destruction by the attraction of their song. The Harpies, or snatchers, may have been connected with the idea that the souls of the dead were snatched away from the living.

(c) ANIMAL MONSTERS. The most widespread of these were DRAGONS and GRIFFINS (qq.v.). Cerberus, the watchdog of Hades, had three heads and hair composed of snakes. The terrible monster, the Chimaera, had the head of a lion, the body of a goat, and a dragon's tail. It was finally destroyed by the hero, Bellerophon, who rode to attack it on Pegasus, the flying horse. The Greek sea-gods had a horse with a fish-like tail: the Norse God, Odin, rode a horse, Sleipner, which had eight legs to carry him swiftly over the world. Serpents are common, one of the most remarkable being the huge earth serpent, Jormungand, of Norse mythology, who lay curled round the whole world.

The myths, particularly of Greece, are rich with stories of these monsters, most of whom were harmful to mankind, and had to be fought and overcome by the heroes.

See also FABULOUS CREATURES; GREEK HEROES; GREEK MYTHS; NORSE MYTHS.

MYTHOLOGY. The word 'myth' has come to be used for any fable or invented story, especially for an obviously untrue or improbable story. Its proper meaning is very different. The word is derived from the Greek word *muthos*, which means word or speech, and is akin to our word 'mouth'. Properly speaking, a myth is the spoken part of a religious or magical rite: a rite consists of two parts—the things done and the things said—and it is the latter which form the myth.

In very early times, it seems, people came to think that they could get what they wanted by pretending that they had got it: that they could cause rain by pouring out water, wind by blowing or waving fans, sunshine by lighting fires, and could kill animals or enemies at a distance by pointing weapons in their direction, or drawing pictures of them with weapons sticking into them. Many primitive peoples still perform such rites today. Later on they went further and came to believe that nothing that they wanted to happen would happen unless they first acted its happening. They thought, for example, that the sun would not keep on its course unless they rolled a burning wheel along, and that the corn would not grow unless they first planted and carefully tended a little seed in a pot. In time they came to think that it was not enough merely to do such things, if they were to be quite sure that all would go well, they must do them in a special way, the way that, as they supposed, had always brought success. So that everyone should know what was being done, and should be sure that everything was being done in the proper way, they made up songs which told how they were setting the sun on his course, or causing the crops to grow. In these songs the people who took the various parts were given names, and in course of time it came to be believed that these names were those of heroes of the past who had been the first to grow corn, or perform the rites. These songs were the first myths.

Later still it came to be believed that it was not enough to act what you wanted, you must also act the destruction of what you did not want. Finally a complex ritual arose, in which pretence was made first of destroying the old world, with all its deaths, diseases, and failures, and then of creating a new and perfect world. In one of its forms there was a human sacrifice of a victim who represented the bad old world, followed by the coronation of a king and queen who by their joyful union would bring about a time of happiness and plenty. The persons who were candidates for the throne had to go through a number of tests to prove their fitness for their important task. Perhaps the reason why, in many myths, the hero and heroine have so many dangers and difficulties to overcome, and are always successful, is that the myths tell only of the chosen couple. The un-

SONNENAUFGANG

THE RISING SUN AND SETTING MOON

Helios, the sun-god, rises in his chariot from the waves into which the setting stars are diving. Eos, the dawn, is chasing
Kephalos, while the moon-goddess retires on horseback. Greek vase, 5th century B.C., in the British Museum

successful drop out of the myths, as they dropped out of the running. In any case, as time went on, the tests became largely a matter of form; but the myths went on speaking of them as if they were real. Similarly, though the king and queen had to perform many ritual acts, the myths did not describe what they actually did, but what they were supposed to be doing. The king put on a golden crown, and, mounting a chariot, drove men dressed as demons before him; but the myth told how the sun was driving away the demons of darkness. The king waved a glittering sceptre while drums were beaten; but the myth told how the lord of the sky was thundering, and would cause rain to fall. The king roared through a lion mask, and the myth told how his enemies fell before him as the other animals before the king of beasts. The queen represented the earth; she pretended to sleep until the king embraced her, and the myth told how the earth sprang to life with the kiss of the sun. Or she was the moon, alone in her white robe till rescued by the sun from the powers of darkness. There were many such rites, which took different forms in different places; but the ideas were always the same.

Traces of these rites survive among ourselves. We have the King and Queen of the May, and they have their myths in such stories as those of Robin Hood and Maid Marian. Robin Hood is the god or king of the spring. In his suit of green he fights the old demons who keep happiness from the people.

We must realize that the people who spoke

these myths had no idea of being romantic or poetical. They were priests saying what, according to their beliefs, was necessary to make their people prosperous. They spoke in verse because verse is easier than prose to remember and repeat. It was only when the myths had lost their connexion with the rites that people turned them into romantic or moral tales. We must also realize that though we may be fairly sure that myths arose in the manner outlined above, we cannot be sure of the actual steps in their growth, because the few myths which have been known to arise in modern times have merely followed the lines of the old myths, and these arose long before there was anyone who could write them down. But though our ideas about these myths and rites are based on careful study of ancient times, this study is fairly recent.

In former times myths were studied as if they existed entirely on their own, and very different views were held as to how they arose. According to one of these views, myth is a kind of history, the kind of history which was told by people who cannot read or write. It was supposed that these people told and retold the stories of how their ancestors had won battles, or moved from one country to another, and that to make them simpler and easier to remember they spoke of tribes as if they were single men. One objection to this view is that most myths are nothing like real history. A well-known Greek myth, for example, tells how Zeus took the form of a bull and carried off Europa. Nobody can suppose that anything

Anderson

THE RAPE OF EUROPA
Roman fresco from Pompeii. Museo Nationale, Naples

like that really happened in Greek history. It can, however, be explained as the account of marriage ritual in which the king wore the horns of a bull, the emblem of strength, and the priests sang of how the mighty bull has come to wed the queen. There are many pictures of early kings partly disguised as bulls. Another objection to the view that myths are a kind of history is that people who cannot read generally forget everything about the past that has not something to do with the present. We do the same ourselves unless we write it down. We may remember most of what has happened in our own lifetime (though we forget a great deal of that), but we know what happened before only if we have looked it up in a book. We may remember a few odd bits of what our parents told us; but that will not take us very far back unless our parents happen to be readers of history. Many people in this country do not know what their grandfather's Christian name was or where he lived, and they do not care. We are taught in school to take an interest in the past; but savages have no interest in the past for its own sake, they take an interest in their myths because, as has been explained, in their view these myths

belong to the present even though they may speak of an imaginary past.

Another view of myth once widely held is the opposite of that just mentioned. It is that there is no truth in myths at all. According to this view, early man looked about him and, seeing the wonders of the heavens, of the changing seasons, and of birth, growth, and death, felt he must explain them. He knew nothing of science, however, and so his explanations took the form of fanciful stories, such as that the dawn was a fair maiden pursued by the sun, who was a man in a chariot. The chief objection to this view is that early man, if we may judge him by modern savages, was probably not in the least interested in the wonders of nature, and felt no urge to explain them. He took them all as a matter of course, just as most of us do when our curiosity is not aroused by what we read or learn. Some early men did take an interest in nature, but it was a purely practical one, as they thought they could make it work as they wanted. Another objection is that the sun is not in the least like a man, for instance, or the dawn like a maiden; and nobody would think they were, unless he had seen people pretending to be the sun or the dawn, or had been told that the sun and the dawn were really people. It has often been supposed by those who do not know savages, that savages naturally think of stars, animals, and trees as if they were human beings; but those who have studied savages have never found a savage who thinks in the least like that.

Yet another view of myths which has been suggested is that they are the result of day-dreams. It has been supposed that all over the world people have had the same sort of day-dreams, in which they pictured themselves as heroes and heroines, and that these have led to the same sort of myths. People nowadays draw the matter of their day-dreams largely from novels and fairy-tales; but in the days when there were no books, people must have confined themselves to their own experiences, and it is most unlikely that they would have made up their day-dreams out of things they could not possibly have seen, such as enchanted castles, fire-breathing dragons, talking animals, and two-headed giants. Yet such things are found in many myths. Nor are myths everywhere the same. The Romans and Greeks were closely related in race and language; yet the Greeks had many myths and the Romans very few. Are we to suppose that the Greeks went in for day-dreaming but the Romans did not? The fact is that the Greeks, living close to Asia, took over many Asiatic rites and myths.

We see then that myths are not untrue, in the sense of having no connexion with fact, nor are they true, as history is true, in the sense of being accounts of things that happened once only. They are true as things that happen on the stage are true. It is not true that there was a real boy called Peter Pan who really flew in through a window; yet it is true that Peter Pan did, and does, fly in through a window.

It is in this sense that myths may be said to be true; and it is for this reason that while the facts of history are forgotten, myths are remembered because they have been spoken and acted again and again.

See also Ritual; Babylonian Myths; Egyptian Myths; Greek Myths; Hebrew Myths; Norse Myths.

N

NAGAS, *see* INDIANS, HILL TRIBES, Section 3.

NATURE WORSHIP. Until people come to understand how the laws of nature work, they tend to think of everything that is strange and mysterious as being due to supernatural causes and therefore as sacred. A peculiar mountain, rock, or tree, an unusual animal or plant, a bubbling stream, a great cataract, a dangerous crossing of a river, or a devastating storm, may all be looked upon as belonging to the 'other world' (*see* RELIGION) and so not to be carelessly approached (*see* TABOO). The natives of the Melanesian islands of the Pacific Ocean use the word *mana* to describe the power which shows

Pitt Rivers Museum

RAINMAKER'S DANCE IN UGANDA

The woman on the left is the witch doctor making rain. She sprinkles the others with water from a gourd. The drummer is seated behind the drum in the centre

itself in the unfamiliar, powerful, and puzzling, whether it be in a person, event, or thing; and this term is now sometimes used to describe the attitude of mind lying behind the worship of nature in its simplest form.

Worship means the approaching with reverence, veneration, and awe that which has sacredness or supernatural power, and this generally finds expression in a ritual act or ceremony of some kind (*see* RITUAL). Thus in Greek Legend the Trojans regarded their sacred river, the Skamandros, as containing supernatural power, and so they threw live bulls and horses into it as an offering, very much as Jacob anointed with oil the sacred stone at Bethel (Gen. xxviii. 18). Later, when they had come to think of the river as the home of a spiritual being with an independent life of its own, they built altars on the banks for the sacrifice of bulls, because they believed that the god or spirit of the river would leave the stream to partake of the offering in the holy place on the shore (*see* SPIRITS).

Probably it was not until man became aware of himself as a living being that he thought of nature also as having a spirit or soul. But once he arrived at this idea he peopled with a multitude of spirits certain trees and flowers, rocks and mountains, streams and rivers, wind and storm, and every cloud and heavenly body which seemed to be alive, active, and, as he believed, able to do things like himself. Rivers and clouds moved, trees and plants grew, thunder rolled, lightning flashed, mountains quaked, rain fell, the sun and moon gave light, and stars twinkled. Moreover, he himself was so dependent upon nature for his food, shelter, and general wellbeing that he regarded it as a sort of Providence and therefore as an object of worship. He thought that by sharing in food sacramentally with nature and its spirits and gods, he shared in its providence and so would enjoy in greater abundance the fruits of the earth.

But nature is not always kindly and generous with its gifts. It can be hostile and unfriendly and produce famine, blight, and pestilence. Therefore people feared and tried to propitiate it (*see* SACRIFICE) so that its destructive powers might be avoided and rendered harmless. Thus the worship of nature has two aspects; on the one side it seeks to maintain favourable relations with the mysterious forces and supernatural powers controlling nature, on the other side it endeavours to appease their wrath when they are angry and spiteful. There is also a third element in it. Not only do human beings depend upon nature for their food and protection, but in primitive society it is believed that if the gods and spirits in nature are to do their good work properly and not become weak and resentful, they in their turn must be given sustenance by man. The sun, for instance, must be strengthened and its energy renewed by the sacrifice of human

NEGRILLOS, *see* PYGMIES.

NEGRITOES, *see* ANDAMAN ISLANDERS.

NEGRO AFRICANS, *see* AFRICANS; ASHANTI; BUSHMEN; CENTRAL AFRICANS; EAST AFRICANS; HOTTENTOTS; MASAI; NILOTIC PEOPLES; PYGMIES; WEST AFRICANS; ZULU.

NEGRO AMERICANS, *see* AMERICAN NEGROES.

Le premier jour de la grande FÊTE du SOLEIL, L'YNCAS lui presente un Vase plein de Liqueur, et l'invite a boire.

Mansell

INCAS CELEBRATE THE FESTIVAL OF THE SUN

or animal victims, or by the burning of fires at the turn of the year (*see* FESTIVALS). In the same way rain is made to fall, storms are driven away, and the fruitfulness of the earth is increased by rites performed by man in the belief that the gods and spirits of nature, like human beings, need to be nourished in order that they can do their work properly and efficiently and thus benefit mankind.

See also ANIMISM; RELIGION.

NESTORIAN CHURCH. A branch of the Christian Church sometimes known as the East Syrian Church. Nestorians prefer, however, to call their church the Church of the East. There are now only about 60,000 members, spread over Iraq, Syria, Persia, Russia, and America. The Nestorian Church has never gained the protection of any state but has always consisted of minority groups, scattered through the countries of central and western Asia.

It is called Nestorian because it has retained some theological ideas derived from the teaching of Nestorius, a Patriarch of Constantinople. Nestorius was condemned at the general Church Council of Ephesus in A.D. 431 for heresy. He taught that it was blasphemous to call the Virgin Mary 'Mother of God', not because he doubted Christ's divinity, but because he believed it essential to keep separate His divine and human natures.

At this time the Roman and Persian Empires were at enmity, and the rejection by the Church of the Roman Empire of Nestorius' teaching made it all the more welcome in the Persian Empire. The Nestorians, therefore, split off from Rome and were ruled by their own Patriarch, or 'Catholicos', from Seleucia in Persia. Church language, instead of being Greek or Latin, was Syriac, as it still is. For some time they spread widely in the East. The Syrian Christians of south India date from about A.D. 300. In 635 a Persian bishop reached Ch'ang-An in China where the Nestorian Tablet, a carved granite slab set up in 781 and bearing their history, is still to be seen. In the 8th century a Nestorian bishop of Tibet was appointed. By the 9th century there were twenty-five Nestorian bishops scattered over Asia. At one time it even looked as though the Mongol emperor, Kublai Khan, might adopt Christianity; in the 13th century, however, the Mongols chose ISLAM (q.v.). From then on the Nestorian Church has declined.

See also CHRISTIAN CHURCH.

NEW GUINEA PEOPLES. 1. PRIMITIVE NEW GUINEA. The aborigines of New Guinea include the largest number of little known primitive peoples of modern times.

New Guinea geography varies sharply, but even so the diversity of the peoples of the island is amazing. Some 500 distinct languages are spoken, as well as many different dialects. There is a great variety of racial types.

The races of New Guinea have sometimes been called 'Oceanic Negroids' because of such traits as the typical dark skin, woolly hair, and wide-flaring nostrils. These traits may well be the result of mixture with an early Negrito population. There is an extremely wide range of skin colour, a single local population sometimes having both light-skinned and dark-skinned individuals. People also vary greatly in height.

At least three distinct racial types have

Camera Press

BIRD OF PARADISE PLUMES FOR DECORATION

settled or concentrated unequally in different parts of the land. The first waves of people probably reached New Guinea over land bridges which may once have connected it to mainland Asia. The two earliest races appear to have been Negritos and Australoids. The next waves were of MELANESIANS (q.v.), who may have first started entering the region by the beginning of the Christian era.

The Melanesian peoples and the Melanesian languages are concentrated largely along sections of the northern and eastern coasts and adjacent off-shore islands. By way of distinction, the peoples of the interior and of much of the southern coast are sometimes lumped together as 'Papuans', and the term is applied to the non-Melanesian languages of New Guinea as well. It is not yet known whether all the non-Melanesian or 'Papuan' languages of New Guinea are related. In any event, 'Papuan' peoples are both racially and linguistically more diverse than the Melanesians. The Melanesian languages are related to Malayan, Indonesian, and Polynesian languages, but no outside connection is as yet clear for any 'Papuan' languages (*see* OCEANIC LANGUAGES; PAPUAN LANGUAGES, Vol. IV).

The island has been one of the principal gateways for peoples migrating from Asia to the Pacific. The techniques of cultivation and many of the basic crops of New Guinea appear to have come with the Melanesians. Some depend for food primarily upon sago, the starchy pith of the sago palm (*see* PALM TREES, Vol. VI). The crops they cultivate include yams, taro roots, bananas, and breadfruit, and also sweet potatoes which may have been introduced more recently from the New World, and are now the basic foodstuff in the highlands. They grow bamboo and casuarina trees for building materials, and in lowland and coastal areas, coconut trees. They grow tobacco almost everywhere, and some betel, the leaves of which they chew.

In some coastal places and up rivers, fishing is intensively developed and is the main source of protein. Meat is generally scarce and is mainly pork; the pig is the only pre-European domestic animal besides dogs and fowls. Almost everywhere pigs are eaten not only for their food value, but to mark ceremonial occasions.

The natives of New Guinea are often called men of the Stone Age. Few had discovered metal and, except perhaps the most westerly peoples of the island, none knew how to use it to make tools. They made their cutting tools out of ground stone or materials such as bamboo. But in cultivating vegetables many peoples of New Guinea are very much more skilled and experienced than other peoples of the Stone Age.

The way of life of the New Guinea peoples varies a great deal in the different parts of the island. Throughout the island, however, individual dwellings are typically small and made of perishable materials. Pile dwellings are common, and the houses are either clustered in villages or are widely scattered, each arrangement being characteristic of a particular area. Everywhere there are large club houses for the men, some of which are impressive in size and design, particularly those in the Sepik River area and on the Papuan Gulf. The coastal and river valley peoples use various types of canoes. For costume, the men usually wear a girdle of some sort, made

Camera Press

COOKING A PIG IN A NEW GUINEA ISLAND

of bark or similar material; and the women wear petticoats of grass, bark, shredded palm, or some such material.

Their commonest musical instrument is the drum, which has a characteristic long 'hour-glass' shape, open at the bottom end. In some areas there are also wooden slitgongs. Reed or bamboo flutes are widespread, often being the sacred property of a young man after his INITIATION (q.v.). So are bull-roarers—long, thin blades of bamboo or wood whirled on a cord, to make a buzzing sound.

The family is everywhere important, but clans and other related groups are prominent in rituals of initiation, marriage, death, and blood revenge. Giving and receiving is a very important part of these New Guinea rituals. The giving of food, brides, pigs, and other favours constitutes a serious obligation that the receiver must eventually pay. Usually, it is the father's family that is the important side of the family, but the emphasis in some areas is on the mother's family, particularly in the east. New Guinea political units are small and highly localized; a single community is often the largest effective unit. Its alliances with other communities are quite limited and often short-lasting. Native New Guinea political systems generally lack strong, highly centralized leadership.

We do not as yet know a great deal about New Guinea religions. What may loosely be described as a 'cult of the dead' or ANCESTOR WORSHIP (q.v.) is widespread. Death by sorcery, and divining methods for identifying the sorcerer, are probably universal beliefs. CANNIBALISM (q.v.), which has been widespread in New Guinea, was often, like blood revenge, connected with religious belief.

2. MODERN NEW GUINEA. Present-day New Guinea, though among the least developed large areas of the world, is changing rapidly. Australian and Dutch colonial rule have had important effects; they have brought a uniform standard of law and order, with police, law, and the orderly administration of justice instead of a system of revenge. They have weakened the former local-ism of the people in the areas where they have been longest influential. European control has helped to establish and spread common lan-guages. Officials, the missionaries, and others use Police Motu in Papua, Melanesian Pidgin in the Territory of New Guinea, and Malay in former Netherlands New Guinea. The building of

missions and the establishment of schools have spread Western ideas and beliefs, and such techniques as reading, writing, carpentry, mechanics, medicine, commercial practices, and agriculture. Private traders and missionaries have taught the people to use money, and there are now readily available imported steel tools and cheap trade goods. A system of contract labour for work on private plantations, docks, ships, shops, government buildings, and roads has helped to develop the idea of wages and regular employment outside the village. A future native middle or upper class has been started with the training of clerks, skilled technicians, medical personnel, and small entrepreneurs in copra, gold, coffee, and trading. Western medi-cine has sharply reduced the incidence of certain diseases, all but eliminating yaws, a chronic contagious disease, and setting in motion trends that will result in decreasing the death rate.

These effects are most obvious in or near towns or government and mission stations, while life in remoter places outwardly has much of its aboriginal character. Even in such places, how-ever, the old life is in ferment. The effects of European contact are sometimes strange. One of the results of government and mission contact is a belief known as the 'cargo cult', a belief in the imminent arrival of a quantity of goods, coupled with the expectation that a radical change in the lot of the natives will bridge the gulf between their life and that of Europeans.

The native peoples of New Guinea have as yet produced no large-scale nationalistic move-ment such as has occurred in many parts of Africa. However, common law, common lan-guage, and a common sense of purpose and identification, even common grievances, have already united people in much larger groups than formerly. Men of the type who will eventually lead movements towards self-government have already appeared in both the Australian and former Dutch administrative centres. The Aus-tralian government in recent years has taken notable steps to increase native responsibility and self-administration, particularly in the form of 'tribal councils' and the Territorial Legislative Council which meets at Port Moresby. In the western half of the island the Dutch had developed similar programmes, and it remains to be seen in what form and degree the Indonesians, who succeeded them in May, 1963, will now carry forth these measures.

See also Vol. III: EAST INDIES.

NEW STONE AGE, *see* PREHISTORIC MAN.

NEW ZEALANDERS. Europeans first came to New Zealand in 1642 when Tasman, the Dutchman, discovered it; but no landing was made until James COOK (q.v. Vol. V) visited the country more than 100 years later. Even then little was known about New Zealand. Early in the 19th century, however, large numbers of whalers and sealskin and flax-traders began to establish themselves there. Escaped convicts from Australia also took refuge there. This kind of colonization was naturally without law and order, and it was not till 1840 that the British Government rather reluctantly took over control, partly to prevent the French from making a settlement. The treaty of Waitangi was signed with the Maori chiefs, and in this the rights of the Maoris to their land were fully recognized.

Missionaries led by the Rev. Samuel MARSDEN (q.v. Vol. V) came to New Zealand with the early traders, and they played a very important part in the early development of the country.

The history of New Zealand since 1840 has been the history of the development side by side of two races—the whites (or *pakeha* as the Maoris call them) and the MAORIS (q.v.). There were wars between them from 1843 to 1870. These were mainly over the question of land, for the whites wanted to buy and some Maoris wanted to sell in defiance of their tribal law by which all land is communally owned and not individually owned. The war of 1860 went on for nearly ten years, by which time both Maoris and whites were exhausted. Since then the two races have lived together in peace, and the original distrust has died away. The Maoris are now progressing vigorously, and their numbers are increasing. They live mainly in the North Island, and there are very few in the South.

The Maoris themselves originally came to New Zealand between the 12th and 14th centuries. Before then it is thought that New Zealand was inhabited by some aboriginal people called the Morioris who were either killed off or driven out by the Maoris. Some of them fled to island groups near New Zealand, especially the Chatham Islands, where they existed until quite recently.

The High Commission for New Zealand

A SHEEP FARM IN TARANAKI, NORTH ISLAND, NEW ZEALAND
In the background is Mount Egmont

The total population of New Zealand in 1971 was about 3 millions, of whom 233,000 were Maoris. The white New Zealanders are nearly all of British stock—and are the least mixed of all the Dominion peoples.

The way of life in New Zealand is very much governed by its climate and situation. Its climate is ideal for stock-farming and fodder-growing: its isolated position, very far from the rest of the civilized world except Australia, and its small, mainly agricultural community, make it peculiarly suitable for social experiments which can be carried out without fear of outside interference. At first the country was ruled, like most other countries, by the big landowners, but at the end of the 19th century power was transferred to the people by peaceful election, and since then government policy has tended towards the welfare state. Today New Zealand has a highly developed social legislation—old-age pensions, unemployment benefits, medical, health, and dental services, and their road, rail, and air communications are developing in spite of the difficult shape of the country.

New Zealand is a free Dominion, linked to Britain under the Statute of Westminster of 1931. It has an elected House of Representatives on the English parliamentary pattern, with majority government and a Prime Minister. The Sovereign is represented in New Zealand by a Governor-General.

Though many New Zealanders have close connexions with England, they have a social and a farming tradition peculiarly their own. They have developed a system of co-operative production among farmers, somewhat like that in Denmark, different from the systems of co-operative buying as carried out by the Co-operative Stores to be found in Britain and other countries. Though about half the population now live in the four big towns, they are mainly a country people. This is natural in a land where nearly everyone has to do with farming directly or indirectly. To an outsider there is a sameness about them, though South and North Islanders would hotly deny this. They have the same speech and the same stocky build. There are no great extremes of wealth and poverty, and an Englishman would be struck by the fact that there are almost no slums. The only group which is a little apart from the others is the 'squatocracy' or holders of huge sheep runs, who are, in some cases, the descendants of the original land-holders. New Zealanders are a healthy, practical, and cheerful race, very well off for the material things of this world, especially food, which is excellent and cheap. A country with so small a population cannot support the range of artistic life—concerts, ballet, theatre—that is found in Europe. But there are excellent libraries and the New Zealanders are great readers. Radio programmes carry more classical music than in Great Britain and there is a National Orchestra. Although there are few professional acting companies in the country, there are flourishing amateur societies. The cinemas and television show many programmes from the rest of the world. Their picture galleries have good collections of reproductions and modern paintings. Most New Zealanders live in wooden houses, brightly painted, with corrugated iron or shingle roofs; nearly all are supplied with electricity. Their manners are informal and friendly and they are kind and hospitable, but their outlook is perhaps a little parochial because they are far away from the centre of things. They follow the same religions as in England, the largest Church being that of the Church of England with over half a million members.

Primary education is free, secular, and compulsory between the ages of seven and fifteen years. Most children go to state schools, but there are some private schools. There are also many excellent secondary and technical schools, both state and private. Maori children are included in the general state school system, but there are also native village schools for their primary education in areas where there are many Maoris. The existing universities are Otago, Canterbury, Auckland, Victoria, Massey, and Waikato; another is planned for Albany.

New Zealand is a sportsman's paradise. There are excellent opportunities for shooting, yachting, mountain climbing, ski-ing, fishing, golf, and tennis. Everyone is especially keen on racing and there are many racecourses, while rugby football is almost a religion. New Zealand is also a gardener's paradise, and flowers which have to be grown with great pains under glass in Great Britain flourish out of doors there. New Zealand will also one day be a paradise for the tourist, and places such as Rotorua, where there are famous GEYSERS (q.v. Vol. III) and hot springs, are already well known to the outside world.

New Zealand is a young country, only at the

beginning of its history; but, in spite of its small population, great areas of land have been farmed, towns, roads, and communications built, and an advanced social system set up. What traditions it has are those of the rule of law, of personal freedom and justice, and of democratic government. It will develop these in its own way in the future.

See also Vol. III: NEW ZEALAND.
See also INDEX, p. 150.

NICARAGUANS, *see* CENTRAL AMERICANS.

NILOTIC PEOPLES. This group of African peoples inhabit the flat country watered by the Blue and White Nile in north-east Africa. They include the Shilluk and Dinka of the Southern Sudan, the Nuer of the Southern Sudan and Ethiopia, and the Anuak of Ethiopia as well as various Luo peoples stretching from the Southern Sudan, through Uganda and Kenya, into Tanzania. All these peoples practise agriculture, fishing and hunting, and are in general remarkable for their high regard for cattle, although some of them are losing this tradition. The languages they speak are all related, belonging to the Nilotic group of AFRICAN LANGUAGES (q.v. Vol. VI). The various peoples themselves consider that they sprang from a common stock. Many Nilotic peoples choose their chiefs from leading families, but the Shilluk have a hereditary king, and the Anuak have several.

As an example of the upper Nile peoples, let us take the Nuer. They are tall, slender, long-limbed people who inhabit a flat country watered by the Nile and its tributaries. Their deep attachment to cattle is evident in the way rules governing kinship ties are often stated in terms of cattle. Moreover, men are frequently addressed by names describing their favourite oxen; women take names from oxen and from the cows which they milk; and even small boys call one another by ox-names when playing together in the pastures. At night the cattle are driven into byres, or large thorn enclosures where fires are kept smouldering as a protection against mosquitoes.

During the rainy season from May to December, when the rivers overflow their banks and flood most of the lowlands, the Nuer live in settlements situated on higher ground or on low ridges. According to the lie of the land, houses are either close to one another, or strung out along a ridge for a considerable distance. The houses

Camera Press
A DINKA CARRYING WATER IN CALABASHES

are round, with thatched conical roofs and with walls constructed in the manner of wattle and daub. During this season the Nuer grow corn and millet.

In the dry season, from December to May, young men and women leave the settlements and take the herds to pasture near the rivers. There they make temporary shelters and huts for themselves out of millet stalks, or grass plastered with dung. They fish the shallows and the pools left by receding floods, and occasionally hunt wild game.

See also AFRICANS.
See also Vol. III: SUDAN; NILE.

NONCONFORMIST, *see* CONGREGATIONALIST; BAPTIST; METHODIST; QUAKERS.

NORMANS, *see* FRENCH.

NORSE MYTHS. Our knowledge of Norse mythology comes from more or less obscure allusions in poems of various dates, the later ones at any rate having been written under Christian influence. It is impossible to get from them a clear idea of what the pagan Norsemen really believed. This is not surprising when we remember that myths were originally accounts of religious rites, and that these rites had mostly,

YGGDRASIL, THE TREE OF LIFE

Drawing by Sir E. Burne-Jones from William Morris's *The Story of Sigurd the Volsung*, Kelmscott Press, 1898

if not entirely, ceased to be performed before the poems about them were written down.

In the beginning, according to Norse mythology, was the Yawning Gap which had on one side of it the world of cold and on the other the world of heat. In this gap lived the first being in human form, the giant Ymir. He drank the milk of the cow Audumla. This cow licked the salt rock, and as she licked it there gradually emerged a being called Buri. Whom he married does not appear; but his son Bor married a giantess and had three sons, Odin, Veli, and Ve. These three slew Ymir, and his body filled the gap, and his blood overflowed, causing a great flood which drowned all the giants except one, Bergelmir, who with his wife took refuge in a cunningly made boat.

Space was now void and drear. The new gods did not like this state of things; so, in accordance with the will of Allfather who dwelt somewhere in the abyss, they began to create. They made the world of Ymir's body, the sky out of his skull, the trees out of his hair, and so on.

The chief feature of the world was the ash-tree Yggdrasil. Its boughs stretched to heaven and overshadowed Valhalla, the hall of heroes. Its three roots reached down to Hel, to the land of the giants and to Midgard, the home of men. On its branches browsed various animals including the goat Heidrun from which flowed the mead which the dead heroes drank.

According to another version Midgard was in the centre of the world, and above and in the midst of it stood Asgard, the home of the gods. Round it was the sea, and round that was curled the huge earth serpent, Jormungand. Outside was the land of the giants, and from there to Asgard stretched the Rainbow Bridge at the end of which stood Heimdal, the watchman of the gods. The sound of his horn could be heard over the world, and it was his duty to give warning should the giants attempt to invade Asgard.

At first there were no people in the world; but one day the gods Odin, Veli, and Ve, when taking a walk, found two lifeless bodies whom they endowed with life. These became Ash and Alder, the first man and woman and the ancestors of all mankind.

Somewhere to the south of the world was the land of heat, where Surtur of the flaming sword reigned over the sons of Muspel. These were among the chief enemies of the gods.

On the highest point of Asgard stood the throne of Odin or Woden, father of gods and men. As he sat on his throne he was visited by his two ravens, Hugin and Munin, who brought him news of all that was going on in the world. But he was already possessed of all knowledge of the past, present, and future. This knowledge he had gained by pledging one of his eyes for the right to drink from the well of Mimir, underneath the world: he is therefore always represented as one-eyed. At times he left his throne to go about and direct the affairs of men. He went barefoot, with a long cloak, and a wide hat or hood over his eye. Sometimes he went on foot, sometimes on his horse, Sleipnir, which with its eight legs carried him at lightning speed. At times, with a train of horsemen and hounds, he went hunting through the air—in parts of northern Europe the peasants are said still to believe that they see Odin's wild hunt in the storm. 'Wednesday' is originally 'Woden's day'.

According to one version, Mimir had his head cut off, but his head continued to prophesy, and from it Odin learnt the runes and the Norse alphabet which were some of the sources of his power. He knew runic songs that would give victory in battle, quicken the tempest, and win the love of women. He often went among the giants in disguise and engaged in various kinds of contest with them; but though he sometimes got into difficulties, he always emerged victorious.

Beneath Odin's throne the other gods lived in twelve palaces. The largest palace—540 storeys high—seems to have been that of Thor, the son of Odin by Mother Earth. Thor, also called Thunar, was the god of thunder. His hammer, Miolnir, not only caused thunder but also fixed landmarks, sanctified marriages, and consecrated the funeral-pile. Thor was thought of as upholder of all laws and proper customs, and was more widely worshipped, perhaps, even than Odin. We can judge of his popularity among our ancestors from the number of names that begin with Thor-, Thur-, or Thir-, for men took their god's name as part of their personal name. 'Thursday' is originally 'Thor's day'.

Many stories are told of Thor's adventures and contests with the giants. Once they stole his hammer and demanded the goddess Freya as the price of its return. Thor disguised himself as the goddess and got his hammer back.

Freya, when she is the wife of Odin, is also called Frigg. At other times she is a separate goddess, the sister of Frey and the goddess of spring and love. In her gorgeous palace Frigg sat spinning on her golden distaff and her spinning-wheel. She bestowed her silken thread on the most worthy housewives. She was the goddess of marriage; and among the Germans her day, Friday, was regarded as fittest for a wedding. But in the Norse myths Freya appeared rather as the goddess of spring and of the earth, and as such wore Brisingamen, the necklace of stars, jewels, or spring flowers which shone as brightly as the sun. She had a falcon dress which she sometimes lent to the other gods.

Another of the palaces was occupied by Bragi, the god of poetry, and his wife Iduna. She had charge of the apples of immortal youth, one of which she gave daily to the gods for breakfast. Once she was captured by the giants, and until she was recovered the gods got daily older and greyer.

Baldur dwelt in the palace of Wide Outlook in which no evil could be done. He was the god of everything that is young, bright, and fair, and was beloved by all the gods except the jealous Loki. One night he dreamed that he must go down to Hel. The gods were much disturbed, and it was decided that his mother Frigg should make everything swear not to harm him. The gods then amused themselves by shooting arrows and throwing spears at him, and these did him no harm. But Loki found out that Frigg had left out the mistletoe, so he made a dart of it and put it into the hand of the blind god Hodur. Hodur aimed it at Baldur and killed him. His body was burnt on his ship with his faithful wife Nanna and went down to Hel, there to await Ragnarok and the renewal of the world.

Of the other gods not mentioned as having palaces the most important and the bravest is Tyr or Tiu, the god of war. He had only one hand as he lost the other in a fight with the Fenris wolf. 'Tuesday' is originally 'Tiu's day'.

Loki is the most mysterious of the gods. He is both the cunning adviser of the gods and their bitter enemy. It must be remembered that all these stories are myths—that is, stories connected with the rites—and that the rites are repeated at regular intervals. There is, therefore, a sense in which all these incidents happened in the past and another sense in which they will all happen in the future. Loki's dual character is due, at least in part, to his being the god of fire which both helps and hurts mankind. He often travelled about with Odin and Thor, sharing in their adventures, sometimes helping them and sometimes playing tricks on them. After the death of Baldur, however, the gods decided to make an end of him, and after a long chase caught him in the disguise of a salmon. He was chained to a rock, with an adder fastened above him in such a way that its poison dripped on to his face. His wife caught the poison in a bowl; but whenever she had to empty the bowl the poison fell upon him, causing him such agony that he shook the earth to its foundations. This was said to be the cause of earthquakes. By his wife, Sigyn, Loki had two sons, one of whom was changed into a wolf and devoured the other. By the giantess, Angurboda, he had three children, Hel queen of the underworld, the Earth Serpent, and the fierce Fenris wolf.

One of the palaces in Asgard was Gladsheim, the home of the glad, in which was Valhalla, the hall of the heroes. It was roofed with spearshafts and thatched with shields, and the benches were strewn with chainmail. The Valkyries, the maidens who chose the slain, rode about the battlefields in splendid armour on white horses and brought to Valhalla those who had died bravely. The heroes spent their days in fighting and their evenings in feasting, waiting for the great day of Ragnarok and the renewal of the world.

At last came a terrible winter which lasted for three years. All the trees and plants perished, men died of cold and hunger, and the world was full of treachery and bloodshed. Two huge wolves swallowed the sun and moon, and a great earthquake shook the earth so that all chains were broken. Loki and the Fenris wolf were set free. They were joined by Surtur with his flaming sword, by his followers, the sons of Muspel, and by all the giants and monsters. Heimdal, the watchman, sounded his horn; the gods and heroes assembled, and the last battle began. The heroes and the giants slaughtered each other. Odin was killed by the Fenris wolf, Thor slew the Earth Serpent but was killed by its poisonous breath. All the gods and monsters perished except Surtur, who grew till he reached the heavens, and then with his flaming brand plunged the whole world into a sea of fire. When the fire went out everything was dark and dead. Eventually a new earth appeared and was warmed by a new sun; so that the trees and flowers grew again. The gods assembled and built a new golden palace where they dwelt in love and peace. From out of a wood came a youth and maiden, Lif and Lifthrasir, whom Allfather had miraculously preserved. They came into a world full of fruits and crops which no human hand had tended. There they lived happily and became the ancestors of the new race of men.

See also MYTHOLOGY.

NORWEGIANS. Typical Norwegians are tall, fair-haired, blue-eyed members of the Nordic race. Farming engages about 30 per cent of the population, which is nearly 4 million, and like their Viking ancestors many of the men are half-farmers, half-sailors. The mercantile fleet ranks fourth in the world, and a greater proportion of Norway's population are merchant seamen than of any other nation's. Fish and fish products make up one-third of the country's exports. Industry now absorbs more people than farming, and hydro-electric power is used in the processing of raw materials, wood being one of the most important, and in the electro-chemical and electro-metallurgical industries.

Norwegians have always been bold explorers. From about A.D. 800 the Vikings launched their 'long ships' in the early spring and late summer and sailed away to raid and loot their neighbours. Their raids grew more frequent and bolder, and they reached farther and farther afield—as far as Spain, Morocco, and the Balearic Islands. In one year they sailed up the river Rhône in south France, and the next year they captured Pisa in north Italy. One of the boldest of them, Eric the Red, discovered the island of Greenland. In the year 1000 his son, Leif ERICSSON (q.v. Vol. V), with a band of followers sailed across the Atlantic in the small open Viking ships without compass to steer by and with no maps or fresh food, and reached a land they called Vinland, which was almost certainly part of North America. In 911 a Viking founded the Dukedom of Normandy, and it was his descendant, William of Normandy, with his 'Northmen' or Normans who finally conquered England in 1066.

Meanwhile, in Norway itself a united kingdom was established, which at one time ruled part of Scotland, Iceland, Greenland, and the Faeroes. It began to decline in 1319, and in 1397 Norway became a junior partner in a union with Denmark. In the resettlement of Europe after the Napoleonic wars the Danish-Norwegian kingdom was broken up, and Norway shared a king and a foreign policy with Sweden. This union lasted till 1905 when the two countries became independent kingdoms.

The Norwegians are intensely democratic: even before the 19th century there were few large landowners, and incomes were far more equal than in England. All education is free, from the elementary schools to the universities; and everyone is taught English for two years. The languages of all three Scandinavian peoples—the Norwegians, Swedes, and Danes—are so much alike that they can understand each other, though the spelling, grammar, and pronunciation differ (see GERMANIC LANGUAGES, Vol. IV).

Since one-quarter of Norway is covered with forests, everything possible is made of wood. In the south the painted wooden farm-houses have slate roofs, while in the north there are log houses with turf roofs. In the summer when the cows, sheep, and goats are sent to the high pastures, the elder boys and girls, or perhaps the

Royal Norwegian Embassy

NORWEGIANS SKI-TOURING IN THE MOUNTAINS OF RONDANE

farmer's wife with her small children, are sent with them. There the small log cabins with their low blue-painted doors look rather like the illustrations to a fairy story.

A third of the population lives in towns such as OSLO (q.v. Vol. III), the Hanseatic town of Bergen, and the cathedral city of Trondheim. In the north, especially in the Lofoten Islands and at Tromsö and Hammerfest, there is great activity from May to July, when the sun never sinks below the horizon, for these are the chief centres of the whaling fleets and the big cod fisheries. The narrow streets of the towns are thronged with bronzed seamen of many nations, and the smell of cod-liver oil fills the air.

In much of Norway outdoor work is impossible in the snow-bound winter, so the women are busy with their looms and embroideries, and the men, unless they are working in the saw- or paper-mills, make and mend the farm implements or fishing nets, or do beautiful wood-carving. All Norwegians, even the very little children, can ski and skate, and when everywhere is thick in snow, ski-ing and sleighing are the natural ways of getting about. Even Norwegian townsmen never lose touch with the land; they return as often as they can to the farms, travelling great distances in winter on their skis to spend week-ends with their families.

See also LAPPS.
See also Vol. III: NORWAY.
See also INDEX, p. 151.

NUER, *see* NILOTIC PEOPLES.

NUN, *see* MONK.

O

OLD STONE AGE, *see* PREHISTORIC MAN.

ORTHODOX EASTERN CHURCH. This branch of the Christian Church consists of ten self-governing churches: these are the ancient churches of Constantinople, Alexandria, Antioch, and Jerusalem, and the later ones of Russia, Serbia, Roumania, Bulgaria, Greece, and Cyprus. There are also 2·5 million 'Orthodox' Christians in North America, and smaller groups in several lands of western Europe.

The Early Church was organized under five Patriarchs (Father-Rulers), the bishops of Constantinople, Alexandria, Antioch, Jerusalem, and Rome. When the Roman Empire accepted Christianity, the Roman Patriarch became particularly important and tried to assert authority over the others. With the split of the Roman Empire into West and East and the development of the Eastern or BYZANTINE EMPIRE (q.v.) with its headquarters at Constantinople, the Roman Patriarchate became even more separate from the four eastern ones. The Roman Church used Latin as its official language; the others retained Greek—which is why the Eastern Church is often referred to as the Greek Church. The separation into two distinct churches came gradually and was completed tragically in 1204 when the Fourth Crusade was turned against Constantinople.

The Arab invasion of Egypt, Palestine, and Syria in the 7th century and the Turkish invasions in the 15th century reduced the old Patriarchates to minority communities in the midst of Muslim countries. In the meantime the Russian Orthodox Church had grown up, and in 1589 the Bishop of Moscow was declared a fifth Patriarch to take the place of Rome. Russia became the centre of the Eastern Church and remained so until the Revolution of 1917. Two further Patriarchs were later added, those of Serbia and Roumania. Since 1830, when Greece won her freedom from Turkey, the Greek Church has expanded and is now the most important centre of Orthodox Eastern Christianity.

The word Orthodox means right teaching. The Church claims to hold the faith as revealed by Christ to the Apostles, as found in the Holy Scriptures and as set forth by the early Fathers. The two Fathers of the Church in whom they put most trust are St. Basil (d. 379), whose Rule fixed the way of life for eastern MONKS (q.v.), and St. John Chrysostom ('Golden-mouthed'; d. 407), the great preacher and bishop of Constantinople. The four Patriarchs are the ancient heads of the Church, and of these the Patriarch of Constantinople has the title 'Ecumenical Patriarch' (Universal Father); but he holds no such position as the Pope does in the Roman Church. Except for the bishops, often chosen from among the monks, the clergy

GREEK MONKS IN A MONASTERY ON MOUNT ATHOS

S.C.R.

THE PATRIARCH OF MOSCOW BLESSING THE CONGREGATION AT THE ASSUMPTION CATHEDRAL, MOSCOW

may marry. Both monks and clergy have beards. Their churches are often rich and beautiful and contain many icons—paintings or mosaics of the saints which are held in great honour. The chief service is the Eucharist, or Holy Communion, a beautiful service celebrated with much ritual. There is no organ, but the choral singing is generally magnificent. The congregation is much less formal than in an English church: people move about, kneel to pray or stand to watch, as they think fit. There is little emphasis on preaching.

See also CHRISTIAN CHURCH.

OTTOMANS, *see* TURKS.

OXFORD MOVEMENT, *see* CHURCH OF ENGLAND. *See also* Vol. V: NEWMAN.

P

PACIFIC ISLANDERS. The islands of the Pacific, varying from tiny coral atolls to large islands like New Guinea, almost of continental size, were found by Magellan and later explorers to be inhabited by three main groups of peoples —MELANESIANS, MICRONESIANS, and POLYNESIANS (qq.v.) (*see* Vol. III, Map, p. 323).

While there were local differences, the islanders had many things in common. They all lived a stone-age life—that is, they had not discovered the use of metals, and used mainly stone for their tools and weapons. They were all dependent on fishing and gardening for a livelihood, and on canoes for transport.

Civilization has come to some extent to almost all, except to certain tribes in the interior of New Guinea and to some of the larger islands of the New Hebrides.

PAKISTANIS. The composite State of Pakistan, created in 1947 out of the westernmost and easternmost 'wings' of the Indian subcontinent, disintegrated in 1971. The western wing alone, now, is known as Pakistan: the eastern wing is Bangladesh. The reason for their having formed a single state in 1947 was that both are Muslim-majority areas, whereas in the Indian Republic the bulk of the population is Hindu. However, the two areas of the then Pakistan were separated by nearly 2,000 kilometres of Indian territory and inhabited by peoples of very different race and language. These were major factors in bringing about the breakaway of Bangladesh (*see* BENGALI).

Pakistan consists of four provinces: Punjab; Sind; the Frontier Province; and Baluchistan. Into the last two, various former minor princely States and specially administered tribal or border regions have recently been merged. United Nations estimates of 1969 suggest that

Camera Press

IRRIGATION FROM INDUS BASIN PROJECT

Pakistan's population is over 57 million, of whom 97 per cent are probably Muslims. The most important races inhabiting the country are the Jat, the Rajput, the Pathan, the Sindhi, the Baluch, and the Brahui. The Sindhis, Rajputs, and Jats descend from the indigenous Hindu inhabitants of the basin of the Indus and adjoining areas and were converted to ISLAM (q.v.) in widely varying periods. The Baloch, Brahui, and Pathan embraced Islam relatively early, while living outside the Indian sub-continent. The majority of all these people are still either cultivators, graziers, or shepherds, but since 1947 many have moved to industrial work in towns.

Camera Press

CAMEL DANCING EXHIBITION, LAHORE

Substantially the richest part of Pakistan is the Punjab. The land east of the Jhelum river is largely flat and richly fertile, being well-watered by tributaries of the INDUS (q.v. Vol. III) and a splendid system of irrigation-canals. The Jats, Muslim Rajputs, and other peoples of the Punjab plains are mostly peasant proprietors. West of the Jhelum, however, is a largish tract of Punjab consisting of much broken, rocky country known as the Salt Range, inhabited by hardy people such as the Awans.

The Pakistanis are mostly farmers, growing mainly rice, wheat, sugar cane, maize, and tobacco. Nearly 60 per cent of the labour force works on the land. The biggest city, Karachi, is also the chief port and occupies an important position on international air routes.

See also Vol. III: PAKISTAN; INDEX, p. 151.

PALAEOLITHIC MAN, *see* PREHISTORIC MAN.

PANAMA, PEOPLES OF, *see* CENTRAL AMERICANS.

PANTHEISM, *see* GOD, Section (C).

PAPUANS, *see* MELANESIANS; NEW GUINEA PEOPLES.

PARAGUAYANS. Although Asuncion, the capital of Paraguay, is one of the oldest South American cities, founded by the Spanish invaders in the early 16th century, Paraguay is one of the most isolated republics in South America. A large proportion of the people cannot read or write, and though the government is making strenuous efforts to combat the illiteracy, many of the children in the scattered rural areas have no opportunity to attend school. Progress is made more difficult by the fact that the old Indian language, Guarani, is still widely spoken, and the newspapers often carry part of the news in Spanish, and the rest in Guarani. The mixture of virile Guarani blood with that of the Spanish colonists has produced in the Paraguayan a remarkably patriotic fighting spirit. Early in its history of independence from Spain the little republic was at war at one and the same time with Argentina, Brazil, and Uruguay. The president at that time, Francisco Solano Lopez, though a thoroughgoing dictator, was a great leader of men. So fierce was the fighting that, at the close of the war, there were very few men left

Camera Press

A PARAGUAYAN VILLAGE MARKET

alive. The Paraguayans still love to gather in the starlight, after the day's work is done, and, to the accompaniment of the guitar, an instrument well suited to these old-time patriotic airs, sing the old songs of the Lopez war. Paraguay also lost many men in her victorious war with Bolivia, the Chaco War of 1932–35.

The Paraguayans are a hard-working, happy people, and contented, in spite of a very low standard of living. The women and children do much of the field work. Two meals a day, eaten at midday and at sundown, are the custom of the country, with a drink of maté in the early morning and another after the siesta rest in the heat of the day. Yerba maté, or Paraguayan tea, is a mixture of crushed dried leaves with a proportion of stalk from the yerba plant. A cow's horn, or a gourd, is partially filled with yerba maté, and boiling water is poured on it. A silver tube with a filter at the lower end, called a *bombilla*, is inserted into the brew which is sucked up, piping hot. More boiling water is then poured on, and the next person takes a draw, and so on until all have drunk. It is a point of etiquette that the host always takes the first drink to show his visitors that there is no poison in the maté, a relic of the old days when such suspicion was often well founded.

The Paraguayans are great meat eaters: they will tell you that if there is no meat it is not a meal. The ration of meat issued to the cowboys is 2 kilos a day (roughly 4½ lb.). When a cow is killed, much of the meat is dried in long strips called *charqui*, which needs soaking and long boiling before it is fit for the table. The Paraguayans are fine horsemen, and take great care of their horses. A Paraguayan has to be in serious financial need before he will sell his horse. In times of prosperity the bridles and saddles are often ornamented with silver.

On the Chaco side of the river Paraguay there are still Indians living their old tribal life of hunting; but these are now rapidly coming into contact with the mainstream of Paraguayan life.

See also AMERICAN INDIANS, CENTRAL AND SOUTH.
See also Vol. III: PARAGUAY; INDEX, p. 152.
See also Vol. IV: AMERICAN-INDIAN LANGUAGES.

PARSEE. This is the name of an Indian religious community, the members of which are descendants, at least in spirit if not entirely by kinship, of Persian followers of ZOROASTER (q.v.), who are said to have fled into exile from their native land 1,200 years ago, in order to escape from its Muslim invaders. It has also been said that they came to India mainly for trade reasons; but this cannot be proved. For whatever reason, they landed not far from Bombay: and in 1971 there were about 111,000 in India as well as smaller settlements in other places such as Colombo, and about 200 in London. In Persia itself there are still about 10,000 Zoroastrians, mostly in either Yezd or Kirman. They are said to be fairer and rather different in build from the Parsees in India, who call them Iranis. Till about the end of the 18th century the leaders of the Persian Zoroastrians were regarded as a kind of central authority, to whom reference could be made by those in India concerning problems of religious procedure.

Parsee priests, who are usually the sons of priests, are not very highly educated and are often content merely to memorize texts from the ancient Zoroastrian sacred books without understanding them. Their concern is mainly with the ceremonies of their faith, the chief of which is connected with fire-worship, a cult common to many religions. The connexion between a

fire and the sun is fairly obvious, and reverence for fire is akin to reverence for the sun, which Parsees also observe. But educated Parsees will declare that the reverence for angels, fire, and sun are only symbolic ways of approaching the one Wise Lord.

Religious Parsees visit the fire-temple almost daily, and on four days of the month the attendance is very large. As soon as the worshipper gets to the temple, he washes and repeats a short prayer which he was taught when as a child he was vested with the sacred thread or girdle. (Hindus also have a similar initiation ceremony.) After that he goes barefoot through an outer and an inner hall, till he comes to the sanctuary where the Fire is burning. Here he stands on the threshold (for only the priest goes into the sanctuary), and hands to the priest a piece of sandalwood to burn, and some money. The priest brings him ashes from the sacred urn in a ladle, and with these he anoints his forehead and eyelashes. After some prayer he retires backwards to where he took off his shoes and then goes home. Apart from two or three set prayers the worshipper may pray in his own words.

The Parsee disposal of the dead by exposure to vultures has grown up since the time of Zarathustra, the founder of Zoroastrianism. It is derived from a belief that the cause of death is the work of a malignant spirit which has somehow to be prevented from harming the survivors. The quickest and most effective way of getting rid of a corpse is either to burn it or to let birds of carrion devour it. Since the Parsees hold fire to be sacred, they cannot use it for such a purpose as cremation, and they are left with the alternatives of either burial, which they reject, or the *dakshma* or Tower of Silence. This is a round, open, brick or stone structure placed on rising ground, with a floor inside, sloping down to the middle and divided into three sections, for men, women, and children. A special class of professional corpse-bearers—who have to live apart from other people and are not allowed inside a fire-temple—carry the body to the *dakshma*. When it has been laid down, a furrow is drawn round it with a piece of metal, and two priests, having their mouths covered with a cotton cloth, making them look rather like surgeons in an operating theatre, recite a sacred text. Then the body is left, and in half an hour it is stripped to a skeleton by the vultures. As soon as the bones are dry, they are raked into a central well, where

THE DEATH OF MAJNUN ON THE GRAVE OF LAYLA

Persian miniature from the Nizami MS., a book of five poems written in 1495 for the Sultan of Samarkand.
One poem tells how Layla is prevented by her father from marrying her lover Majnun. He remains faithful
to her, and at Layla's death he also dies, heart-broken, on her grave

they gradually crumble away. There are only sixty places where there are enough Parsees to make it possible to maintain a *dakshma*; but Parsees only very reluctantly resort to burial, while hardly any have dared to advocate cremation.

Parsees are a highly educated, rich, charitable, well-behaved, and industrious body of people. But their birth-rate is shrinking; and since the 18th century they have been a closed community, opposed to the making and admitting of converts. Probably this is partly from fear that needy individuals may pretend to become Parsees in order to benefit by the large endowments which exist for the relief of their poor. It has in fact been declared illegal by an Indian court of law to initiate any foreigner as a Parsee.

See also ZOROASTRIAN.

PARTHIANS, *see* PERSIAN ANCIENT CIVILIZATION.

PATHANS, *see* PAKISTANI.

PERSIAN ANCIENT CIVILIZATION. In the last 20 years archaeological excavations have thrown considerable light on the prehistoric settlements of Persia from about 9000 B.C. onwards, but much still remains to be discovered about the Iranians who gave their name to the country. These people, connected with the Indo-Aryans who migrated into North India, invaded Persia from the east in the second millenium B.C. and slowly moved westwards. By the 10th and 9th centuries B.C. the best known of the Iranian tribes, the Medes and Persians, had established their authority in west Persia where they came into conflict with the Assyrians.

The Iranians, and in particular the Persians, excelled as administrators. The Medes had already created a powerful state; but when it was taken over by the Persians, under CYRUS (q.v. Vol. V) in 550 B.C., the Persian Empire reached dimensions never before attained by any empire. When it reached its height under DARIUS and XERXES (qq.v. Vol. V) it stretched from Greece to India, from Russian Turkestan to Upper Egypt. The Persians no doubt learnt a good deal about empire-building from the ASSYRIANS (q.v.); but instead of massacres they brought peace to their subjects, and religious freedom and cultural independence in the place of repression and slavery. They encouraged trade, instituted a postal service, and, like the Romans in later times, built a network of good roads. With their administration they introduced the art of writing into even the remotest provinces. They did what they could to bring together the different cultures of their subject nations (Babylonians, Syrians, Egyptians, Lydians, &c.) into a unified and living whole, without destroying the individuality of the separate groups. Yet even the consummate statesmanship of the Persians was unable to keep together this great empire for much longer than two centuries. In a moment of weakness it fell an easy prey to ALEXANDER the Great (q.v. Vol. V), who continued the unifying work of the Persians, but added the elements of Greek clear-sightedness and adventurousness.

Soon after Alexander's death the grand Persian Empire was broken up. The Greeks continued to rule in Afghanistan, but were expelled from Persia by the Parthians. Persia, therefore, did not remain under Greek influence as did most of the countries of the Near and Middle East. Although weakened within, it was just able to maintain its political and cultural identity even against the Roman Empire, at a time when no one seemed strong enough to resist the march of the Roman legions.

At the beginning of the third century A.D. there was a great renaissance of Persian power. The movement began again in the province of Persis, the ancient home of Cyrus and Darius. The Parthians had been bad administrators, and the power had become divided among many small potentates, who warred against each other and thought only of their private interest. Their Persian successors, a family of rulers called the Sassanids, created a strong state which became a leading world power from the 3rd to the 7th centuries A.D. The Sassanids regarded themselves as the rightful heirs to the ancient Persian Empire, that state of Cyrus and Darius, and imitated its administration with great success. Neither before nor after did Persia attain so high a level of civilization. The irrigation systems, on which all agriculture depends in Persia, were kept in good order; social measures of tax alleviation and land assessment were introduced; commerce and industry flourished in the cities, several of which boasted more than a million inhabitants; traders went out to China, India, Arabia, and Byzantium. The law courts could be relied on to give justice irrespective of the person; books were translated from Greek

Roger-Viollet

THE RUINS OF PERSEPOLIS, BUILT BY DARIUS THE GREAT (521–485 B.C.)

and Sanskrit, and were widely read by the large section of the population who had been through the schools; there was a good university for the study of medicine; Greek philosophers, expelled by the Christians of Byzantium, found a refuge in Persia, where a learned man was allowed to have an opinion of his own.

Unfortunately, the strength of the Sassanian state was sapped by the unending wars in which its rulers indulged. Much defensive warfare had to be carried on against the raids of nomad tribes from Turkestan; but the senseless and destructive battles, lasting for some four centuries against the BYZANTINE EMPIRE (q.v.), in which neither side was strong enough to gain a decisive victory, brought no permanent advantage to Persia. By the 7th century both the Byzantine Empire and the Persians were so exhausted that they fell victims to the Muslim Arabs, who, fired by the message of Islam, carried everything before them. The Arabs, whom the Persians should have been able to defeat without difficulty, crushed the mighty Persian state in the course of a few years. For a long time Persian culture became merged in the comprehensive Islamic civilization (*see* ISLAM).

The importance of Persia in the general history of civilization lies, not so much in its original creations, as in the fact that it carried eastern civilization to the west and western civilization to the east. It was due mainly to the Iranians that the links between China and India on the one hand and Europe on the other were never broken, and that progress in cultural development was in many ways uniform and sustained for the whole of the Eurasian world. In literature they produced nothing of real importance. Later, however, especially from the 10th century onwards, Persian poetry is particularly fine. The famous Persian miniaturists drew their inspiration from the painting of Sassanian times, especially from the admirable illuminated manuscripts. Throughout the ages the Persians have been celebrated for their skill in the weaving of tapestries and rugs. In architecture, as in other aspects of civilization, the

British Museum

A SASSANIAN KING HUNTING STAGS
4th-century silver dish

Persians derived most of their ideas from else-where but carried them out with great magnificence. Contemporary inscriptions tell us that workmen were brought from all over the Empire by Darius to build palaces at Susa and Persepolis, where their own local styles of working influenced the development of Persian art and architecture of this period.

The most original contribution of Ancient Persia was in the field of religion. Through the teachings of ZOROASTER (q.v.) the Persians came at an early date to believe in a single benevolent God; later, to explain the presence of evil in the world, they evolved a dualistic system of a good God and an evil God, always at war against each other, with man at liberty to choose which God he would join.

See also ANCIENT CIVILIZATIONS.
See also Vol. XII: PERSIAN ART; PERSIAN LITERATURE.

PERSIANS. The modern state of Iran takes its name from the Aryans, who were early arrivals in the country. The people are called Iranians or Persians, a name that derives from Persis, a province of southern Iran. The language of Persis, or Pars, was Parsi (Persian) and the Persian language of today is still called Farsi.

In modern Iran the term 'Persian' includes not just the descendants of those ancient Aryans, but all those people who have Persian nationality, whether they are of Arab, Turkish, or Mongol origin. Since the country has always been a cross-roads of various conquests, the modern Persians reflect many diverse origins. In the south are Arabs, some descending from the Arab occupation of Persia in the 7th century. In the north-east are Turkomen, and in the north-west other groups of Turkish origin whose families possibly arrived during the 11th and 12th centuries. To the west live the Kurds, kinfolk to tribes in Iraq and Turkey. In the east are Afghans and Mongols, dating from Genghis Khan's occupation in the 13th century and Tamburlaine's in the 14th and 15th centuries. So today the Persians are a combination of the many fascinating peoples that inhabit Iran.

Most Persians are Muslims (*see* ISLAM). This religion arrived in Persia with the Arab invasions of the 7th century A.D. The previous religion Zoroastrianism was practically completely stamped-out and today only a few ZOROASTRIAN (q.v.) families survive in the town of Yazd. They make up an even smaller proportion of the total Persian population than do the Armenian Christians. The Muslims of Iran are Shiites. In this they differ from the people of most other Muslim states, who are

Camera Press

TEHRAN; MODERN AND TRADITIONAL MINGLE

Camera Press

NORTH IRAN: VILLAGE WOMAN BAKING BREAD

Sunnites. (This split in Islam, which developed very early, is explained in the article ISLAM.) The schism has been the main cause of much fighting and antagonism between the Persians and the peoples of other (Sunnite) Muslim states.

About 3 million Persians are still tribal, and many of these are nomads. They live in black goat-hair tents and move from spring pastures in the mountains to winter pastures in the plains and valleys. The livelihood for these tribes is based on sheep and goat herding with some agriculture. It is a way of life that is gradually ending as more pressure is put on these wanderers to settle in the modern state.

Because of Iran's great economic wealth in oil, copper, ores, and other resources, towns have been growing fast. The capital city TEHRAN (q.v. Vol. III) now has a population of over 3 million out of a total population in the country of 23 million. Although oil provides the major resource for the Persian economy, other industries

are just as important in providing work and income for the people. The most famous of these is the carpet weaving which is done throughout the country in towns, villages, and tents. The skill of the workmanship and the beauty of the finished product has rightly given the carpets an important place in the heritage of the Persians. Today the large, world-renowned carpets made on vertical looms in towns such as Isfahan, Mashad, Tabriz, and Kerman are mainly woven by boys; but other famous carpets, such as the Turkoman rugs, are made by the women of the tribes in their tents, on horizontal looms.

The Persian political organization is headed by a strong monarchy. Mohammed Riza Shah Pahlavi succeeded his father Riza Shah, who founded the dynasty in 1925, and it marked a new era of development and change for the Persians. The tendency now is to modernize industry and at the same time to relax rigid religious laws. The Shah has a Parliament (Majlis) with two Houses to guide his policy. He also has a local structure of fourteen Provinces (Ostans) and Governor-Generals (Ostandars) to guide local policy. Recently, extensive social reforms have been enforced. These include land reforms; education reforms establishing village education and female education; medical reforms; and the provision of services in all areas of the country for developing knowledge of modern techniques in building, sanitation, family planning, and agriculture.

See also Vol. III: Iran; Index, p. 144.

PERU, ANCIENT. When the Spaniards came to Peru in the 16th century, they found a well-developed civilization already established by the Inca people (*see* Inca Civilization). But the Incas were comparatively late-comers in the history of South America. Our knowledge of earlier civilizations in Peru comes from archaeological evidence.

Man first began to live in South America between 10,000 and 20,000 years ago: radiocarbon dates from southern Chile show that he was there by 9000 B.C., and it now seems likely that there may have been men in the Peruvian Andes nearly 20,000 years ago, in the Ayacucho region. Certainly by 9500 B.C. hunters had come to live over most of the highlands. At first they hunted big game animals, but about 7000 B.C., as big game vanished, they had to change to hunting small game. They supplemented their diet with plants which they collected. In some parts of South America this hunting and gathering way of life continued for thousands of years (*see* American Indians, South).

On the coast of Peru by 5000 B.C. men came each year to fish and collect shellfish. At first they lived in temporary settlements, but by 4000 B.C. they were permanently settled there. The coast consists of a desert crossed by forty small rivers, each of which creates an oasis. In these well-watered spots the inhabitants began to cultivate plants. By 2500 B.C. they were growing maize, beans, manioc, squash, cotton, avocado, peanut, chili pepper, and guava.

These settlers made no pottery. The first pottery in Peru did not appear until after 2000 B.C.

Between 2500 and 1800 B.C. some of them— as at the Huaca Prieta site on the coast—were making complex decorated textiles and carving gourds. During this period, too, monumental architecture was built at sites such as Playa Culebras, which has artificial terraces faced with basalt blocks, and Chuquitanta, where a large building has been excavated, which is thought to have been a temple.

Temples were also built in the highlands soon after 2000 B.C. At Kotosh on the upper Huallaga, a tributary of the Amazon running through the Andes at 6,000 feet, a series of temples built one above the other have been excavated. The archaeologists had to dig down through 13 metres of layers. Towards the bottom they found the 'Temple of the Crossed Hands', so-called from a mud-brick relief on its walls, and above it the slightly later 'Temple of the Little Niches'. No pottery was found with either temple, and both of them, together with one still earlier, were built before 1800 B.C. By radiocarbon methods the temple above has dates ranging from 1800 B.C. to 1150 B.C.

On another tributary of the Amazon, northwest of Kotosh, is the larger and later temple-complex of Chavín de Huantár, dated from 900–200 B.C. The Chavín site consists of a number of stone-built platforms of different dates, riddled with underground galleries containing strange sculptures. The art is dominated by fantastic man-like creatures with feline fangs and rows of serpent heads. The influence of this art is found over much of the coast of Peru and restricted areas of the highlands.

During the following period various different local styles of art and ceramics appeared and developed in their own way. The most notable of these is the Mochica, based on the Moche valley of the north coast, where the city of Trujillo now stands. Mochica pottery includes portrait vases and others depicting warriors and scenes from daily life.

In such regions where art traditions were growing up, the first Peruvian cities also arose. They had strong rulers and a rigid class-structure. One of the classes was that of the art-workers, who each specialized in his own particular art or craft and, as in Renaissance Europe, had a patron.

Nazca, on the south coast, was another place where art tradition appeared, as it did in Mochica. Nazca produced pottery painted in many brilliant colours ('polychrome'). The people were, we know, organized enough to work together, for they made huge designs on the desert surface by clearing away stones which were lying on the ground. The designs

British Museum

MOCHICA VASE

It represents a water-bird sitting on
its nest among reeds with fishes below

British Museum

NAZCA VASE

The coloured design represents a demon
figure with a border of heads below

British Museum

MOCHICA POTTERY PORTRAIT HEAD

they made in this simple, laborious way include
huge spiders, monkeys, and other animals, and
also straight lines running for long distances.
Some of these lines undoubtedly marked out
cultivation plots, but some of the others may
have been of astronomical significance. The
animal designs could not have been seen from
the ground, but only 'in the mind's eye', like
a maze.

One of these regional styles later spread
throughout southern Peru. This happened between A.D. 600 and 1000, the period that
archaeologists call the 'Middle Horizon'. This
influential style was centred on Tiahuanaco
near Lake Titicaca and seems to be associated
too with the 'city' of Huari, also in the southern
highlands. It is at this period that a political
organization called the 'state' began to emerge
in Peru. It controlled not only food resources

British Museum

WOVEN FABRIC: NAZCA STYLE

With a design of birds in several colours

and other products, but also the movement and
location of populations over a wide area: the
stage was being set for the emergence of the
Inca empire.

On the coast between A.D. 1000 and the Inca
conquest of 1476 one such state was that of the
Chimu, based on the city of Chan Chan near
the modern town of Trujillo, and only a few
kilometres from the capital of the Mochica of a
thousand years before. Chan Chan is one of the
largest native sites in all America, covering 28
square kilometres. Its core consists of a number
of huge walled enclosures, each divided intern-
ally into many small courts. Each of these may
have acted in turn as the palace of a Chimu
king, and when he died a new palace may
have been built for his successor, the old one
being maintained as a memorial. The Chimu
were masters of gold and silver work, but most of
the treasures buried with the Chimu nobles
have been looted since the Spaniards conquered Peru.

Other such states existed at the same time,
notably that based on Cajamarquilla near
modern Lima, and that based on Cuzco in the
highlands. The lords of Cuzco were the Inca,
and they gradually conquered all of present
Peru together with southern Ecuador and
northern Chile in the course of less than a
century. They built enduring monuments in
stone, still to be seen at Cuzco, Machu Picchu,
Huanaco Viejo and other sites, and ruled the
largest empire known in the New World (*see*
INCA CIVILIZATION).

PERUVIANS. The Indian people of Peru have a very ancient history, dating back to before the birth of Christ (*see* PERU, ANCIENT CIVILIZATION). Later followed the civilization of the INCA people (q.v.), who, before the arrival of the Spaniards, had developed an elaborate and efficient form of government under their emperor, the Inca. They cultivated the fertile land, building a wonderful system of terraces up the foothills of the Andes Mountains. They built roads and organized their society so that unemployment and poverty were unknown. This was the civilization existing in Peru when the Spaniards under PIZARRO (q.v. Vol. V) invaded and conquered the country in 1531.

The Spaniards were lured on by greed for gold and the rumours of *El Dorado*, the Man of Gold; and indeed they found much gold and other riches, as well as an intelligent Indian population whom they forced to work for them. In consequence, with an idle aristocracy of Spaniards and an Indian population in a state of serfdom, the colony developed quickly, in contrast to the slower, sounder, more democratic methods of the CHILEANS and ARGENTINES (qq.v.). In 1821 Peru liberated itself from Spain and set up an independent republic. Indians and Europeans have intermarried, so that the population is divided almost equally between pure Indians on the one hand and whites and people of mixed blood on the other—some 14 million in all.

The republic of Peru divides itself into three natural regions. In the coastal strip live the majority of those of mostly European descent. The climate here is temperate because of a cold ocean current. Most of the principal towns, including Lima the capital, are built in this strip.

In the highlands of the Andes live the Indians and the *cholos* (people of mixed blood who speak Spanish). They are rather backward as a result of their isolated position and the poverty of much of the country. The Indians of the high-

Camera Press

A PERUVIAN SAVES HIS CAFÉ EQUIPMENT WHEN THE AMAZON RIVER RISES

lands are mainly of the Quechua and Aymara tribes, descendants of the Incas (*see* INCA CIVILIZATION). Indians and *cholos* from the highlands have migrated to the coast in large numbers where they work on the sugar plantations and in the fishing industry: Peru has the largest fishing fleet in the world.

On the eastern side of the Andes, down in the Amazon jungle, live many wild tribes of Indians, still little touched by modern civilization. These Indians still live by hunting and fishing, with little attempt at agriculture, and they are often hostile to travellers. They still speak their old tribal languages, most of which have never been written down. Some tribes still follow the custom of the Inca ruling classes, piercing holes in the lobes of the children's ears and stretching the holes so that, in time, quite large disks of wood can be inserted. Other tribes possess the curious art of treating the head of their slain enemies by a secret process so that they shrink and are preserved. These shrivelled heads can be found in curio shops near the coast.

Means of transport are still primitive over large parts of Peru. There are few railways, except in the coastal region, and many of the villages are only reached by mountain tracks, transport being provided by pack-animals— mules, donkeys, and the tough, sure-footed llamas—or by Indian porters. But the truck and the aeroplane are making rapid changes.

See also AMERICAN INDIANS, CENTRAL AND SOUTH.
See also Vol. III: PERU.
See also INDEX, p. 152.
See also Vol. IV: AMERICAN-INDIAN LANGUAGES.

PHARAOHS, *see* EGYPTIAN CIVILIZATION.

PHILISTINES. The Philistines were a Mediterranean people who invaded the south-west corner of Palestine and settled there in the 13th century B.C. In fact, the name Palestine is simply another form of the word Philistine. The Philistines formed a highly civilized and warlike nation, and proceeded to harry the Hebrews, who were finding it difficult to unite into a nation. In spite of the Hebrew legend of the young David's victory over the Philistine hero, Goliath, the Philistines defeated King Saul and routed his army. But a few years later, when David became king, he succeeded in beating back the Philistines and ruling over a united Hebrew kingdom.

Because the Philistines were the traditional enemies of The Chosen People, the word 'Philistine' has come to denote an enemy or an outsider. Early in the 19th century German students derisively called a man not at a university 'a Philistine'. Hence the word is now used contemptuously to denote an uncultured, worldly person.

See also HEBREW CIVILIZATION.
See also Vol. V: DAVID.

PHILOSOPHY. Originally a Greek word meaning love of wisdom. Among the ancient Greeks there were a number of great philosophers of whom PLATO (428–347 B.C.) and ARISTOTLE (385–322 B.C.) (qq.v. Vol. V) were pre-eminent. Among the Greeks and in the Middle Ages philosophy included the study of many subjects that are now included in science, and even in Victorian times science was often called natural philosophy. But from its beginning philosophy was largely concerned with questions with which science does not deal; and it is this kind of question that interests philosophers today.

These questions spring from the impulse that comes to most thoughtful persons at some time to inquire into beliefs that are ordinarily taken for granted. There are a great many beliefs which we use in our everyday life and accept without question. For example, we believe that some actions are right and others wrong, that democracy, or government by the people, is a good thing, that each of us is free to choose his own course of behaviour. When habitual ideas of this kind are criticized or challenged, then we are led to think about them. Now when we begin to think carefully about these customary beliefs, we find that we are obliged to ask ourselves what the general ideas underlying these beliefs mean. Let us take the first example mentioned above. We use every day the word 'right', and many words that are equivalent to it, such as decent, proper, fitting. We say 'it is right to be honest' or 'a man ought to do his job well'. What precisely is the meaning of 'right' and 'ought'? When we try to give an answer to the question, we are entering upon the work of philosophy. We may come to the conclusion that 'right' means obeying our conscience; or we may decide that it means helping to make ourselves and other people happy; or we may decide on some other definition of this familiar word.

The fact that different people give different accounts of the idea is a reason for pursuing the question further, in order to find out which account is nearer the truth. Now books on philosophy show us that a great deal of careful thinking is required in order to reach a satisfactory description of such an idea as 'right'. They examine numerous accounts that have been given by different thinkers at different times, and in considering these accounts they work methodically towards a deeper understanding of the idea. The branch of philosophy that deals with ideas such as 'right', 'good', 'duty' is called Moral Philosophy or Ethics, from the Greek word meaning moral.

Philosophers, in a similar way, inquire carefully into the meaning of ideas that are used, often carelessly, in political discussions. Examples of such ideas are democracy, the State, liberty, and 'rights' (in the sense of the right to property, or the right to free speech). This branch of philosophy is known as Political Theory.

In all these inquiries into the meaning of ideas there is an important point that must be made quite clear. When philosophers consider ideas—such as right, good, liberty, and so on—they are not trying to advise people what they ought to do, or how they can become better persons, or what political party they should vote for. Advice of this kind must be sought for from persons with practical experience of life. Of course a philosopher may also have considerable experience, and be able to give good advice about practical problems. But when he is making philosophical inquiries into the meaning of ideas such as goodness or duty, he is trying only to understand and truly describe these ideas: his aim is to think about them clearly, not to make himself or others better men. Nevertheless, the knowledge that he has gathered about the ideas that are used in our ordinary beliefs is bound to affect practical life. When we have made a critical inquiry into our beliefs, we are less likely to be led away by false theories, and we shall have a deeper understanding of the principles that should guide our actions.

Let us glance at a quite different field of philosophy. Among the most obvious of our everyday beliefs are beliefs about the world of things that we see around us—furniture, houses, trees, clouds. We believe that the chairs and table, the curtains, and the carpet in our room are really there before us just as we see them, and we believe that another person coming into the room sees the same things as we do. Few of us ever dream of questioning these beliefs until we read a book on philosophy. Philosophers show that these common-sense beliefs about the world of things that surrounds us are not as obvious or certain as they seem. A careful reading of any good introduction to philosophy, such as Bertrand Russell's *Problems of Philosophy*, will make clear what difficulties there are. The critical inquiry into common-sense beliefs about the world that we see and hear and touch, found in such books, shows that it is extremely difficult to give good reasons for beliefs that we usually suppose to be beyond dispute.

The critical methods of philosophy are applied to many other fields, for example to science, to art, and to religion. Science takes many ideas for granted in order to carry on its work. It assumes, for instance, that what we have discovered about the universe so far will apply to the universe in the future as well, even though we have no experience of the future. Philosophers try to make clear what scientists are doing when they formulate a general law, and on what kinds of evidence a law such as the law of gravity is based. They are not concerned to call in question any particular law of nature, but to ask what a law of nature, in general, is. They may also ask what we mean, in general, by 'cause' and 'effect', by 'time' or by 'necessity'.

Philosophical questions about science try to start further back than the scientist himself will start, so that we may understand ideas that science uses. One of these ideas is that of knowledge, or science, itself. Since the time of DESCARTES (q.v. Vol. V) whose work *Metaphysical Meditations* was published in France in 1641, philosophers have concerned themselves with the question of what counts as knowledge, and what, if anything, we can be said to know for certain. This part of philosophy is called Theory of Knowledge, or Epistemology.

Philosophers also practise the science of LOGIC (q.v.) which studies the rules by which we may validly pass from one concept to another in arguments, whatever the subject matter. Logic is usually related to mathematics and shares with it the notions of classes, functions, derivation, and proof. Many other subjects are examined by philosophers. They ask what the nature of the mind is, and how it is related to the body.

They inquire into the meaning of beauty. They consider the kind of knowledge that is contained in the study of history.

This, then, is one side of the work of philosophy—a cool and thorough inquiry into the convictions and beliefs that we usually accept without question, in order to reach a clearer and more precise understanding of the meaning of these beliefs and of our reasons for holding them. This is obviously an important task; it helps to free ideas from vagueness and confusion, and brings a deeper understanding of the universe.

There is another great task that is undertaken by philosophy. Men have a profound impulse to connect the different sides of their experience together, to see the world as a whole. Human beings have many different interests. They are concerned with their families and friends, and with their daily work; they are interested in art and literature and history; they seek truth in science, and they respond to the call of religion. Men who think seriously about life feel a desire to see the relation between all these different interests. They desire to reach a coherent and unified way of looking at experience; they want to know whether the universe has a plan and, if so, what it is. Some philosophers try to meet these desires. They try to show how the material, the moral, and the spiritual aspects of the universe are systematically related to one another. The great constructive philosophers describe what each of the main interests, science, art, religion, and others, contributes to our knowledge of the system of reality. In making these very wide inquiries these philosophers show how methods and ideas that are useful in special fields cannot be applied to other fields or to the universe as a whole without confusion. Some scientists, for example, have thought that science was the only kind of truth, and they have tried to interpret the moral and religious sides of the universe in the same way as they describe the material sides.

In the history of philosophy there have been many attempts to carry out this great task of surveying the plan of the universe in its varied aspects. The names of the philosophers AQUINAS (1225-74), SPINOZA (1632-77), KANT (1724-1804), and HEGEL (1770-1831) (qq.v. Vol. V) may be mentioned. No one can study these great structures of thought without gaining deeper insight into the wonderful complexity and grandeur of the universe. This aspect of the work of philosophy is often called Metaphysics. The Greek word *meta* means 'after', and the term metaphysics is derived from the fact that Aristotle's work on philosophy was arranged by early editors to follow after his lectures on physics.

Anyone who wishes to pursue philosophy should begin on those sides in which he is interested. It is necessary when studying philosophy to read slowly and critically, taking instances of one's own to illustrate the arguments. It is no use disguising the fact that philosophy calls for considerable mental effort. But the effort is supremely worth making, even though the result may not be a specific set of answers to questions, nor something which will long remain uncriticized. For philosophical thought progresses by criticism, by dialogue, and by conversation.

The individual contributions of the great philosophers are described in the biographies of these men in Vol. V. To those already mentioned we might add ST. AUGUSTINE, HUME, and KARL MARX (qq.v. Vol. V).

PHOENICIAN CIVILIZATION. This ancient civilization of city-states developed in the narrow strip of coast along the eastern shore of the Mediterranean, stretching from Mt. Carmel northwards to the River Orontes. This strip was also known in the 14th century B.C. as Canaan. The most important of the city-states were Tyre, Sidon, Byblos (Gebal), and Ugarit (Ras-Shamra) excavated in 1929. Their inhabitants were called Phoenicians from a Greek word meaning 'red', which may have been suggested by the famous Phoenician factories of red dyestuffs. These cities were prosperous trading centres in the 14th century B.C., and by the 9th century their inhabitants had founded colonies on the north coast of Africa, the most famous of which was the Tyrian colony of Carthage.

The people of these cities spoke a SEMITIC LANGUAGE (q.v. Vol. IV), closely resembling Hebrew; but the population of the sea-coast was by no means all Semite, since many other peoples had settled along the coast at various periods. Our knowledge of Phoenician civilization was, until recently, mainly drawn from north-Semitic inscriptions, from the Old Testament (where there is a vivid description of the wealth and glory of Tyre), and from the Greek

Editions 'Tel'

GOLD DISH FROM RAS-SHAMRA (UGARIT)
First half of the 14th century B.C.

writers, such as Herodotus, and Philo of Byblos. But the discovery of the Tell el-Amarna Letters in Egypt in 1887 and texts and objects from the excavation of the site of Ugarit by French archaeologists, which began in 1929, threw a great deal of light on the religion, politics, and art of the cities of Phoenicia in the 15th and 16th centuries.

The people of the city-states of Phoenicia were seafarers, and were much influenced by their contacts with the other Mediterranean countries. Egyptian inscriptions, as well as many objects of Egyptian workmanship, have been found in cities like Byblos and Ugarit. In Ugarit masonry tombs have been found built in a style reminiscent of Mycenaean and Cretan architecture; and amongst small finds are objects of ivory and gold, carved or embossed with mythological and hunting scenes in a strongly Mycenaean style. The trade of Tyre, Sidon, and Arvad was mainly with Egypt and the Aegean; but Ugarit, owing to its special position, was not only a centre of the Mediterranean trade, but was the meeting-place of important trade-routes from Asia Minor, Cappadocia, Assyria, and northern Syria. Until its destruction by the sea-peoples in the 13th century B.C., it was probably one of the most important and prosperous cities of Phoenicia.

The Phoenicians were the first people to make use of an alphabetic mode of writing instead of the cumbrous systems of writing used in Egypt and Mesopotamia (*see* WRITING, HISTORY OF, Vol. IV). The early Egyptians had discovered the alphabetic principle but, owing to their intense conservatism, had not made use of it; but in Phoenicia two experiments in alphabetic writing were made, possibly about the same time, one of which survived to become the parent of all the Western alphabets. In the excavations at Ugarit there was discovered a large number of tablets written in a different kind of writing from any found before. The writing made use of twenty-nine signs, and therefore was obviously alphabetic; and the language proved to be a Semitic dialect, not unlike Hebrew. But, when Ugarit fell in the 13th century B.C., this form of alphabetic writing, of which rare examples have been found outside Ugarit, seems to have come to an end. The second alphabetic experiment, probably almost as early as the Ugarit alphabet, is generally known as the Phoenician script. An example of this script—the famous Moabite Stone, containing an inscription of a king of Moab in the 9th century B.C.—had long been known to scholars. But primitive examples of the script have since been found written on pottery in Canaanite cities as early as the 13th century B.C. Therefore it seems that alphabetic writing, one of the most important of all human inventions, may be credited to one of the vigorous merchant-cities of the Phoenician coast. It was carried by traders to Greece, and thus became the ancestor of all the Western alphabets.

The excavations at Ugarit showed that there existed in that city, in about the 15th century B.C., an elaborate religious organization in which the king played a central part, as in Egypt and Mesopotamia. There were temples, an organized priesthood, sacrifices, great seasonal rituals connected with harvest and vintage, and an extensive mythology. The names of some of the gods occur in the Old Testament: there is the high god, El; his wife, Asherat-yam (that is, Ashcrat-of-the-sea); his son, Baal, whose sacred animal is the bull. Baal was worshipped also at Tyre under the name Hadad, and in Syria. There are a number of lesser gods, among whom is the craftsman god Hiyan, a parallel to the Greek Hephaestus and the Roman Vulcan. Among the myths recorded is that of the conflict between two lesser gods, Aliyan and Mot, which is not unlike the Egyptian myth of Osiris and Seth.

Editions 'Tel'

BAAL

Bronze figure from Ras-Shamra (Ugarit), 14th cent. B.C.

Aliyan is slain, descends into the underworld, and returns in the spring. This is the familiar pattern of the dying and rising god, so widespread in the ancient Near East. Another of the myths tells of the fight between Baal and the dragon, who has the same name as the mythical Hebrew sea-monster, Leviathan.

We have already said that the civilization of the Phoenician cities was based on sea-going trade. In the vivid description of the wealth of Tyre in the Old Testament (Ezekiel, xxvi–xxviii), written about the time of Nebuchadnezzar's siege of Tyre, which lasted for thirteen years, 585–572 B.C., there is a catalogue of the places with which Tyre traded, and of the varied merchandise in which she trafficked. The account gives the sources of her shipbuilding materials: fir-trees for the deck-planks from the Amanus, cedars for the masts from Lebanon, and oak for the oars from Bashan. Linen for the sails came from Egypt, while her seamen were drawn from many sources. She is represented as trading with

Tarshish in Spain, with the Ionians of Asia Minor, with Armenia and the Caucasus, with Arabia, with the Red Sea ports, and India. The goods in which she trafficked were precious metals and precious stones, purple embroidered woven stuffs, wheat, spices, wine, wool from Miletus, and iron from Asia Minor. No doubt she largely imported raw materials and exported finished articles. It is a picture of great wealth and prosperity—a prosperity shared by the other cities of the Phoenician coast as well as Tyre.

During the early period of Phoenician history the government of each city-state was in the hands of a king and council of nobles. Ezekiel's description of the king of Tyre shows that the king was regarded as a divine person, perhaps as the result of Egyptian influence. But later on, at the time of the Punic wars, we know that Carthage was governed, not by a king, but by an oligarchy, whose members were called *suffetes*— a Semitic word meaning 'judges'.

The Phoenicians were the most daring sailors and explorers of the ancient world. They were the first to venture beyond the Pillars of Hercules (Straits of Gibraltar) in search of precious metals, and Herodotus tells us that when Pharaoh Necho (about 620 B.C.) sent a ship to sail round Africa, he manned her with Phoenicians.

See also ANCIENT CIVILIZATIONS.

PHOENIX. A phoenix was a mythological bird, which was said to be born from the ashes of its parent. The Greek historian Herodotus, who visited Egypt about 459 B.C., gives the earliest account of it. He confesses that he never saw one and did not believe the story, but refers to pictures of the phoenix in which it was like an eagle, but with red and gold plumage. He said that, according to the Egyptians, it appeared out of Arabia once in every 500 years, carrying the dead body of the father-bird in a ball of myrrh to the temple of the Sun. Actually it was to an egret or heron that the Egyptians gave the titles 'the soul of the sun' and 'the heart of the renewed sun'; so either Herodotus or his informants seem to have been mistaken or to have strayed away from the original idea. The egret has beautiful glistening white plumes radiating from its breast, which may have suggested the rays of the sun, and the purple heron's plumage is tinged like sunset clouds. One or other of these birds, being connected with the worship of the sun which 'dies' at sunset and

PHOENIX
Engraving from Arnold Freitag, *Mythologia Ethica*, 1579

rises again next day, may have given rise to the fable of the phoenix. The story was retold in an old collection of animal stories, called the *Physiologus*. According to this book, the phoenix lives on air for 500 years, and then, carrying spices, flies to the temple of the Sun and is burnt to death on the altar. A tiny worm appears in the ashes, and by the next day a young phoenix has grown up; by the day after that it is fully fledged, salutes the priest, and flies away. Another version records how the bird makes a nest of spices, which is set on fire by the sun's heat. The phoenix dies, fanning the flames with its own wings. Because of these stories the phoenix became a symbol of rebirth to new life, and was regarded as the king of birds. It was believed that there was never more than one phoenix alive in the world, and it was said to be surpassingly beautiful.

There is a Chinese mythological bird, which is commonly known as the Chinese phoenix but should be called the 'love pheasant'. It is a very frequent emblem in Chinese art. According to Chinese ideas, the love pheasant appears now and then in the course of centuries to indicate that a happy state of affairs will presently occur. The descriptions and pictures suggest that, like the DRAGON (q.v.), it grew up in people's minds by a process of adding together the characteristics of a variety of different creatures.

See also FABULOUS CREATURES; FOLKLORE.

PILGRIMAGES. Anyone who has read Chaucer's *Canterbury Tales* will know about the journey of a group of people to Canterbury to visit the tomb of Thomas à Becket. But the idea of such journeys is much older than Christianity, and occurs all over the world. The actual word 'pilgrim' comes from the Latin *peregrinus*, which means 'a stranger' or 'wanderer'. We may not think of ordinary churchgoing as a pilgrimage: in any case it is usually a very short one. But it certainly does mean breaking off one's ordinary occupation and leaving one's home to go, perhaps as a family or with a friend, to a place called 'holy'—that is set apart—in order to make contact in it with what is sacred and to feel in touch with the Power of the Universe, by whatever name we may call that Power. Another common kind of pilgrimage is that of people to cemeteries where their kinsfolk are buried. This may seem a purely human affair, but even there the idea of the sacred enters in. The cemetery is 'consecrated ground'—the old Anglo-Saxons called the churchyard 'God's acre'.

A pilgrimage, then, is a movement of people to a sacred spot where they are able to make at least temporary contact with the supernatural world. People expect to benefit by making a pilgrimage—whether bodily, by cure of sickness, or spiritually, by forgiveness of sins, or by inspiration from seeing or touching some object which recalls to them a wonderful work of God. Not unnaturally pilgrimages came to be associated with holy days, which were holidays when all ordinary work stopped. Social life came to centre round pilgrimages to distant holy places. There is a real gain, a true refreshment in the interruption of ordinary life by such a break, in which perhaps one comes to live in fellowship with other folk who are bent on a journey to the same spot. Of course some pilgrimages are made in solitude.

Sometimes the holy place is made by nature, such as the great River GANGES in India, or Mount FUJIYAMA (qq.v. Vol. III) in Japan, or the Mount of Transfiguration in the New Testament. Sometimes, however, it is connected with a great historical event, or a human life in which the working of the Deity seems visible—such, for example, as the group of places in India associated with the earthly life of the good king Rama, who is believed to have been an incarnation of the god Vishnu; or, in Arabia, the two cities of Mecca and Medina, so closely linked with the deeds of the great religious leader Muhammad; or, in China, one of the four specially sacred shrines connected with Buddhist

British Museum

THE EARL OF WARWICK STARTING ON A PILGRIMAGE

15th-century drawing (MS. Cotton Julius E. iv. 205)

Land, owning the ships in which the pilgrims travelled from Venice, and providing hostels for them (*see* KNIGHTS, ORDER OF).

But not every one could afford to visit the Holy Land, and after its capture by the Turks, it was for a time quite cut off from the West, until the crusaders restored communication (*see* CRUSADES). Places in the West, where famous Christians were buried, also became places of pilgrimage—the most important being Rome, where the tombs of the Apostles, Peter and Paul, were reputed to be. Throughout the Middle Ages thousands of pilgrims visited Rome every year, not only to visit the tombs of the Apostles, but to be blessed by the Pope and to obtain pardon for sins.

The body of the Apostle St. James was believed to have been buried at a town in Spain, Compostella (Sant Jago Apostola), and his shrine became even more popular than Rome for English pilgrims, who used to sail thither from Winchelsea in Sussex. Frenchmen favoured the shrine of St. Martin at Tours. There were other shrines all over Europe and more than sixty in England alone, visited by people who could not afford long journeys. The shrine of St. Thomas of Canterbury was visited by foreigners as well as by English—the road from Southampton to Canterbury is still called the Pilgrims' Way. Other roads called Pilgrims' Way in other parts of England showed the routes to other shrines—to Glastonbury in Somerset, for example, and Walsingham in Norfolk. Maps were drawn specially to show the pilgrims' routes, and guide-books written telling pilgrims what they must do, and what lesser shrines to visit on their way. Not everyone went willingly: some were ordered to do so as reparation for an offence. Sometimes they were ordered to walk barefoot and be scourged or wear chains. Even kings might be sent in this manner. Henry II, for example, went to Canterbury, and Henry VIII, before his break with the Pope, went to Walsingham. But it was often possible to pay a money fine instead of making the actual journey.

Pilgrimages played a very important part in European medieval life. People from all parts travelled great distances together. Many spoke Latin, and this common language and their common purpose gave them a sense of the fellowship of all Christian people, which was stronger than any feeling of separate nationality. Chaucer

saints; and for Christians, the Holy Land of Palestine with Jerusalem as its centre; or, in England, the place where some famous Christian lived and died or was martyred. Jews at the time of Christ were expected to make a journey to Jerusalem once a year, even if they lived outside Palestine: Jerusalem is still their Holy City.

Christian pilgrimages to the Holy Sepulchre began in the 3rd or 4th century; and Helena, the mother of the Emperor Constantine, was one of the first to make the pilgrimage. The Romans had built a pagan temple over the Holy Sepulchre; but Constantine had this removed and erected a church in its place. We learn a great deal about these early pilgrimages from a diary kept by a lady from southern Gaul, called Etheria, who went to Palestine somewhere about A.D. 534 and who visited, besides Jerusalem. Sinai, Horeb (the burial-place of Job), and the brook Cherith (the place where Elijah was fed by ravens). Later on, the Knights of St. John of Jerusalem organized pilgrimages to the Holy

expresses something of this in his *Canterbury Tales*. It is true that his pilgrims are all English; but though they are drawn from almost every walk of life, they live together and travel as equals. Each one is called upon to tell his or her story to enliven the journey, and the variety and jollity of the stories show clearly that, besides the religious purpose of the pilgrimage, it was considered a delightful holiday—indeed to some of Chaucer's characters this was plainly the more important aspect.

Pilgrimages were, incidentally, a means of spreading new ideas and of fostering trade. Travellers would bring home with them books and works of art, such as paintings, ivory carvings, and silk hangings, and from these, native authors and artists would get new inspiration.

Pilgrims were supposed to wear grey cowls down to their ankles and broad-brimmed hats, and only to carry a staff, a sack for money, and a gourd for water. (Chaucer's pilgrims did not dress in this way, if we may believe his description.) They organized themselves under a master who made all arrangements. Coming home, they wore an emblem to show which shrine they had visited. They lodged in hospices built specially for them along the route. These could charge no fees, but the rich pilgrims made gifts to them.

The travellers also gave large sums of money to the shrines and churches, which, in consequence, became very rich. The shrines themselves were decorated with gold and jewels, sculpture and paintings, and the churches often had to be enlarged to make room for the procession of visitors round the shrine. At Canterbury, the place where the choir had to be widened for this purpose can clearly be seen. The monks and priests realized how profitable it was to possess a shrine, and in some cases they bought, or even forcibly removed, relics from another place—

either the bones of a saint or a reputed piece of the Cross from the Holy Land—and set it up in their church, claiming that it had miraculous powers.

The English shrines were destroyed at the time of the Reformation, and pilgrimages were no longer allowed. They have, however, revived somewhat in recent years, and people once again go to such places as Lindisfarne, the spiritual home of St. Cuthbert, to St. Albans, to Edward the Confessor's chapel at Westminster Abbey, and in recent times to Little Gidding in Huntingdonshire, the former home of the saintly Nicholas Ferrar, who lived in the reign of Charles I, and built there a specially beautiful little church for his household to worship in.

For Roman Catholics Rome remained the chief place of pilgrimage until the 19th century, though a good many went to Chartres, to the shrine of the 'black Virgin'. Since 1850 one or two new places have become very popular, especially Lourdes on the French slope of the Pyrenees, where a little girl, Bernadette, is said to have had visions of the Virgin. It is now visited every year by thousands of invalids, because of the reputed healing quality of a spring

Pictorial Press

THE GROTTO AT LOURDES WHERE THE VIRGIN IS SAID TO HAVE APPEARED TO A SHEPHERD GIRL, BERNADETTE

The walls are hung with crutches left by pilgrims who have been cured which flows from the ground close to the grotto where the visions were seen.

PILGRIM FATHERS, *see* CONGREGATIONALIST.

POLES. Several Slav races first emerged into the light of history between A.D. 800 and 1000, and settled in central Europe. The Poles were one of these. The earliest Polish State, which came into being about A.D. 960, stretched from the Vistula to the Oder. Its capital was at Gniezno, near Poznan, in the extreme west, and the Archbishop of Gniezno is still regarded as the Primate of Poland. At the beginning of the 12th century Poland's western frontier lay even farther west than the line made after the Second World War in April 1946.

Though all the western Slavs, including the Poles, were frequently fighting the Germans to resist their eastward expansion, Christianity came to them through German bishops. The Poles became Christians about A.D. 970 under their first historic king, who married a Christian Czech princess. In spite of their fear of German aggression, the Polish kings remained faithful to the Roman Church, and all through its history of nearly a thousand years, until recent times, Poland has been in sympathy with the ideas and ways of life of western Europe.

Late in the 11th century Cracow became the royal capital. During the second half of the 12th century and the 13th century Poland was divided and weak; but from that date onward it grew steadily in extent and wealth. In 1386 the Queen of Poland married Ladislas Jagiello, the Grand Duke of Lithuania, who, with his whole people, became Christian. Lithuania was at this time a vigorous militarist state which had conquered several of the larger but weaker eastern Slav states. The union of Lithuania and Poland was a strong protection against the danger of being overwhelmed by the advance of German rule along the Baltic coast. Under the Jagiellonian kings (1386–1572), some of whom were outstanding statesmen, Poland, at the height of her power and prosperity, shared in the great intellectual movement of the RENAISSANCE (q.v.). Unfortunately, the Jagiellonian kings were followed by a weak and inferior ruler at a time when Russia and Prussia were rapidly gaining strength, and Poland became even further weakened by wars with Sweden. In spite of this, it was a Polish army, under King

John SOBIESKI (q.v. Vol. V) in 1683, which triumphantly came to the rescue of Vienna, the capital of Austria, and thereby saved south-central Europe from being overrun by the Turks.

In 1772, when the First Partition of Poland took place, and Russia, Prussia, and Austria seized vast tracts of her territory, Poland had hardly any effective government at all. This was the lowest point in her history. By two further partitions in 1793 and 1795, her three great neighbours put an end for the time being to Poland's independent existence. From 1795 to 1918 Polish history is confined to the efforts of the Polish people to secure, sometimes by armed revolt and sometimes by collaboration, conditions of existence which would make it possible for them to preserve their national individuality. At the end of the First World War an independent Polish State was re-created; but this was attacked by both Germany and Russia in the Second World War. After the war Poland emerged as a People's Republic, with four-fifths of her former territory.

In no race is the spirit of national solidarity stronger than among the Poles. All the efforts of their oppressors to destroy their national individuality only resulted in uniting them far more than before. Their national consciousness became wider and deeper until, by 1900, it had permeated all classes of the population and all districts inhabited by Poles, except Silesia and Mazuria (East Prussia). The fact that most Poles are members of the Roman Catholic Church may have been a unifying factor, although some belong to Protestant Churches, and some to the Orthodox Eastern Church. The possession of a language with hardly any dialect differences no doubt contributed to the growth of national solidarity. Any Pole from Wilno in the far north-east feels at one with any Pole from Cracow, because both of them speak the same language, no matter what their social class. Even in Silesia, which Poland lost in the 14th century and only partially recovered in 1921, the vast majority of the working-class population has always spoken Polish at home, even if forced to learn German at school and to speak it with German foremen in mines and factories. The ruined castles, which still exist in many places in Silesia, have always been called, even by the Germans, 'Piast castles', after the Polish dynasty of the early Middle Ages, under whom they were originally erected.

Poland has been predominantly an agricul-

Camera Press

AT A POLISH CHILDREN'S HOSPITAL, THE TRADITIONAL LAJKONIK FESTIVAL
The children enjoy the performance as British children would a Punch and Judy show

tural country: even the working classes of the towns are only separated from the peasantry by one or two generations. Indeed, during the economic crisis of the early thirties, many of the factory workers, who lost their employment, found refuge with farmer relations and thus survived the bad years without great hardship. In Poland everything which has to do with the land is respected. A great Polish poet, Wyspianski, in his most famous play, *The Wedding*, first acted in 1901, extolled the dignity of the farmer's life in verses of extraordinary fire. This universal love of the country and of country life has helped to strengthen the spirit of national solidarity, and has also fostered the individualism which is the most marked and perhaps the most valuable feature of the Polish character. All attempts to suppress and bully Poles in the past have proved useless. Although not militarists, they are proud to serve in their country's army. That they make first-class soldiers was well known to all who fought by their side in the Second World War. The Poles are still a people

not easily dominated by another power.

Post-war Poland faced many difficulties in repairing the damage of war years, adjusting to the communist way of life, and building up industry. Less than half the Poles now work on the land. COLLECTIVE FARMING (q.v. Vol. VI) was imposed for a period, but since 1956, when the Russians gave the Polish Communist Government more power to make its own decisions, this policy has been reversed and most farmers now own their land. Although Poland lost its valuable oil-fields after the war, it gained the rich coal-fields of Silesia. The Poles have nationalized and greatly increased their heavy industry, producing and exporting steel, machinery, locomotives, and ships.

They are a romantic and musical people. Among the many world-famous Poles have been the scientists COPERNICUS and Marie CURIE, the musicians CHOPIN and PADEREWSKI, and the novelist Joseph CONRAD (qq.v. Vol. V).

See also Vol. III: POLAND; INDEX, p. 112.
See also Vol. IV: SLAVONIC LANGUAGES.

POLYNESIANS (people of the many islands). These are the people of the eastern Pacific islands within the triangle bounded by Hawaii in the north, New Zealand in the south, and Easter Island in the east (*see* PACIFIC ISLANDS, Vol. III). They are a tall, brown-skinned race of seamen, who might be called the Vikings of the Pacific. At some unknown date, perhaps about the beginning of the Christian era, they sailed into the Pacific in long out-rigger canoes, generally one canoe at a time, from their forgotten homeland known as 'Hawaiiki'. Some authorities think they came from India—indeed traces of ancient Polynesian writing found in Easter Island, but at present undeciphered, are thought by some experts to be connected with northern India.

What is known of their history before the arrival of the Europeans towards the end of the 18th century has been learnt from the Polynesian chiefs. Family pride directed that the young members should learn by heart their family tree, even as far back as twenty generations or more, and also the principal exploits of their more important ancestors. From these records in the memories of the chiefs we learn of the discovery of many islands, of romantic voyages over long distances in search of wives or to wreak vengeance on enemies. One New Zealand legend of the MAORIS (q.v.) suggests that they went as far south as the Antarctic ice, and there is also a possibility that they reached the west coast of South America. It is indeed true that they cultivated the sweet potato, a plant which originated in America. The well-known Norwegian explorer, Thor Heyerdahl, who made a voyage from Callao in Peru to the Tuamotu islands in the *Kontiki*, a replica of an ancient Peruvian raft, believes that some Polynesians came from America. Though this view has been much criticized, Heyerdahl has persisted in his researches and proved that Peruvians reached the Galapagos Islands. Further discoveries may have been made by his excavations in Easter Island.

When the Europeans arrived, the Polynesians had not discovered metals: they still depended on stone tools for cutting down trees, making planks, and hollowing out canoes, and on sharks' teeth for finer carving. When the early explorers showed them iron, they were quick to see its value, even before they understood its nature. They were known to steal ships from the Europeans for the sake of the nails in them; but then they planted the nails in the ground hoping to grow more nails. Their principal weapons of war were clubs and spears. They used slings and sling-stones; but, though they possessed bows and arrows, they only used them for sport.

The Polynesians, like another Pacific people, the MICRONESIANS (q.v.), depended for their food largely on a combination of gardening and fishing. They grew yams, taro, and sweet potatoes, and also bread-fruit, coconuts, and bananas. They also grew pepper root from which they made a drink called *Kava* which, especially in western Polynesia, was drunk with great ceremony often accompanied with an exchange of gifts. CANNIBALISM (q.v.) was not unknown, especially in the Marquesas Islands, where there was continual fighting for the possession of the narrow valleys in these rocky islands.

Their houses varied a good deal from island to island. They were sometimes square and sometimes round, but nearly always were supported on stout poles with matting for walls and a palm-leaf thatched roof. In New Zealand, where timber was plentiful and the climate colder, the greater part of the house was built of elaborately carved planking, and the eaves came down almost to the ground. Their clothing was mostly of bark cloth made from the inner bark of a special tree, beaten out and painted with various designs. For important occasions the chiefs of Hawaii wore the most gorgeous cloaks of red and yellow birds' feathers sown on to a coconut fibre net foundation. In New Zealand the chiefs wore cloaks of flax made by a sort of basketwork. The Polynesians, unlike the Micronesians, had not learnt the art of weaving. But they had a rich sense of art. As well as the finely painted and printed designs on the bark cloth, their wood carving was developed and elaborate.

British Museum

WOODEN NECK ORNAMENT FROM EASTER ISLAND

The little figures carved round the edge are in the Easter Island script. It is not proper writing, for each symbol represents an idea, not a sound. Nobody can read them today

British Museum

WOODEN FIGURE OF THE HAWAIIAN GOD KUKAILIMUKU

Some people have seen a resemblance to classical antiquity, but the crested helmet is probably of native origin

They made strange images to represent their gods. Stone carvings were to be found in many islands, but most commonly in Easter Island, where large ancestral figures were carved out of the volcanic stone with stone chisels. In New Zealand, particularly, the pillars and lintels of their houses, as well as the prows and sterns of their canoes, were beautifully carved wood, in geometrical patterns.

The priests were a powerful body, exercising their influence by imposing TABOOS (q.v.). The Polynesians worshipped many chief or high gods, among whom were Tane, a creator god, Tangaroa, the god of fishing, and Oro, the god of war. As well, they worshipped many lesser deities—spirits of natural forces, such as Pele, the goddess of fire (the volcano goddess in Hawaii), and spirits of trees and other natural objects, and also family gods. Sacrifices, including human sacrifice, were made to these gods.

The people of the Polynesian islands are, and always have been, a cheerful, friendly people, fond of music, singing, dancing, and athletic pursuits. They possessed flutes, blown with the nose instead of the mouth, wooden gongs, and bamboo cylinders with which they beat time on the ground. Among their games and sports was surf-riding on flat boards, and they were excellent swimmers.

With the coming of the Europeans their numbers declined sharply; but now, especially in New Zealand, they appear to be increasing again. They are all now nominally Christians and in most places wear European clothes. In Hawaii they are intermarrying with Europeans and other Pacific peoples so much that soon no pure-blooded Hawaiians will remain. The only independent native kingdom now surviving in the Pacific is the kingdom of Tonga, a British Protectorate. The kingdoms of Hawaii and Tahiti belong respectively to the U.S.A. and France.

See also Vol. IV: OCEANIC LANGUAGE.
See also Vol. XII: OCEANIC ART.

POLYTHEISM, *see* GOD, Section (*a*).

POPE, *see* ROMAN CATHOLIC CHURCH.

POPULATION. In 1970 there were estimated to be about 3,660 million people in the world of whom 70 per cent lived in the relatively under-developed, low-income countries and about 30 per cent in the relatively developed, high-income countries. As the accompanying map indicates, they are unequally distributed over the earth's surface, much of which consists of water, frozen waste, desert, or tropical forest, so that only about one-fifth of it is habitable. The proportion living in urban areas also varies widely from one country to another, ranging from 63 per cent of the total population of Australia to 10 per cent or less for countries such as India, Nigeria, or Burma.

It is only since the Second World War that most of the less developed countries have taken regular population censuses, and these counts reveal that world population is now increasing at an unprecedented and accelerating rate. In 1800 it was 1,000 million people; by 1930, over 2,000 million and by 1960, over 3,000 million. The United Nations Population Division has estimated that, if present trends in birth and death rates continue, it will be over 7,000 million by the end of the 20th century with about 5,400 millions in the less developed countries. The

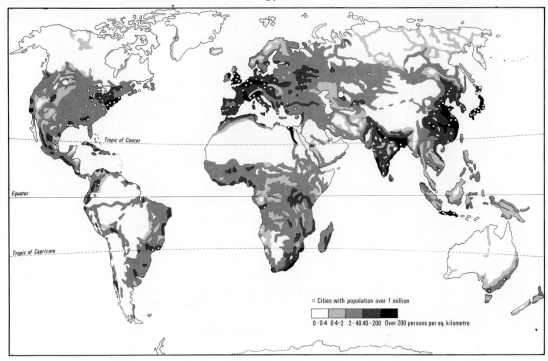

DISTRIBUTION OF POPULATION THROUGHOUT THE WORLD

world population explosion is thus gathering momentum fastest in the countries which, because they are so poor, are least capable of supporting an increased population.

The extra mouths can be fed by bringing new lands under cultivation or by applying more productive farming techniques. Most of today's less developed countries are located in tropical regions in which infertile soils and unfavourable climatic conditions have combined to keep agricultural yields low. Recently, however, agricultural research has greatly increased crop yields in some of these areas. New strains of staple crop seed have been developed which, when grown on irrigated land in association with ample fertilizers and pesticides, permit very high yields. For example, the new wheat varieties planted in Mexico have yielded a fourfold increase in output per acre, and new rice strains have made Japan and the Philippines virtually self-supporting in staple foods.

Easier and quicker communications have also made it possible for the world to support an increasing population by permitting countries which are rich in fertile land resources to supply cheap food to countries which have the resources

to specialize in mining, manufacturing, or commercial activities. Britain nowadays grows only enough food to feed about half her 60 million people: the rest is imported from all over the world in exchange for a variety of manufactured goods. As agricultural research enables the less developed countries to increase their crop yields, they will find it possible to support an increasing population with a diminishing agricultural labour force: but unless they can employ the displaced agricultural labourers in industry and sell their surplus crops or manufactures on world markets, they will be faced with a worsening unemployment problem and a stagnant or falling standard of living.

The continued growth of world population depends on the rate at which birth rates rise and death rates fall. In the 19th century populations grew fastest in Europe and the countries to which European emigrants went, such as the U.S.A., Australia, and Canada. The rise in population in European countries was largely due to a gradual fall in death rates as a result of rising standards of living, improvements in sanitation, and medical discoveries. Birth rates tended to fall as the standards of living rose in western countries, thus partially offsetting the effect of falling death rates and producing only a moderate rate of population increase. In England and Wales, for example, the birth rate reached a peak of over 35 per 1,000 of the population in the 1870s and then fell continuously to under 15 per 1,000 in the 1930s.

In today's less developed countries the increasing rate of medical progress in the 20th century has produced a very rapid fall in death rates, particularly in the infant death rate since the Second World War. This in turn has permitted a larger number of women to survive to childbearing ages in the 1960s and early 1970s. The birth rates in these countries now are generally much higher than they were in 19th-century Europe and have recently been rising where the age of marriage has been falling. There is already evidence that the more affluent and better educated sections of the less developed countries are experiencing a fall in birth rates as their incomes rise, just as happened in 19th-century Europe. But for most of today's low-income countries the recent fall in death rates and the increasing numbers surviving to childbearing ages is likely to keep the birth rate rising in the immediate future.

World population growth has been intensified in recent decades by the fact that even in the high-income countries of Europe, Australasia, and North America the birth rate rose in the 1940s and 1950s mainly as a result of a fall in the age of marriage. In England and Wales, for example, the birth rate which had fallen to under 15 per 1,000 in the 1930s rose again to 18 per 1,000 in the postwar 'baby boom'.

Short of catastrophic disasters the world's population can be expected to continue to grow at an accelerating rate into the 21st century. The problems are urgent for the less developed countries where incomes and productivity are so low that an increase in population poses a direct threat to existing standards of living. They are less urgent but nevertheless serious for the developed countries where overcrowding and congestion threaten the quality of life. Clearly some form of family limitation will be necessary if the world's population is not to outgrow its living space.

See also Vol. VI: AGRICULTURAL HISTORY, RESEARCH IN AGRICULTURE.
See also Vol. X: INTERNATIONAL CO-OPERATION.
See also INDEX, pp. 132–160.

PORTUGUESE. That part of the Iberian Peninsula which is now Portugal was inhabited for at least 2000 years before Christ. But the Portuguese language and civilization derive primarily from the Romans who occupied the country for five centuries, till A.D. 420. There were later occupations by the Suevi, from north of the Rhine, in the 5th century; by the Visigoths from the east in the 6th century; and by the MOORS (q.v.) and the Berbers from North Africa in the 8th century. During the Moorish domination, which ended in 1243, the Portuguese Jewish community was rich and celebrated for its learning.

In the 10th century Portugal was part of the Spanish kingdom of Leon, but the Counts of Portugal gained independence and Portugal became a kingdom in the 12th century. Successive kings fought the Spaniards, expelled the Moors, and consolidated the kingdom, which reached its peak in the 15th and 16th centuries. Inspired by HENRY THE NAVIGATOR, great Portuguese seamen led world exploration. In the 15th and 16th centuries the Kings of Portugal sent many expeditions to find new trade routes and unknown countries. Among the leaders of these expeditions were the Portuguese explorers Bartolomeu Diaz and Vasco DA GAMA (q.v. Vol. V) (the first man to sail from western Europe round South Africa) and the Italian navigator, Americo Vespucci (after whom America is named). The Portuguese Empire was the greatest European empire in the 16th century. Brazil was first colonized by Portuguese, and is still a Portuguese-speaking country (*see* BRAZILIANS).

There are just over nine million Portuguese in Portugal. About three-fifths of them are engaged in agriculture, cultivating especially vineyards, orange groves, fields of wheat and maize, and the cork-producing evergreen oaks. Many more live north of the river Tagus than south of it, since the northern provinces are broken up into small holdings, while in the south there are large estates. The Portuguese are also great fishermen, and the innumerable fishing villages along the coast of Portugal are scenes of busy and colourful life. The fishing-boats are double-ended, like Arab dhows, with bright-coloured lateen sails.

Each region has its own character, which is well illustrated in the pottery. Estremoz produces red and brown pottery; the region of Estre-

J. *Allan Cash*

THE MAIN STREET IN OBIDOS, PORTUGAL

madura produces green and brown and buff; while in Tras os Montes and Beira Alta, farther north, the pottery is black; and in the west, from Coimbra to Caldas da Rainha, there is cream-glazed work with floral designs.

The Portuguese are a colourful, cheerful people, delighting in pilgrimages to Catholic shrines (*romarias*), in *festas*, and market days. Wine is sometimes still carried in carts drawn by long-horned oxen with elaborately carved and painted yokes. Bull-fighting is a traditional sport, but differs from Spanish bull-fighting in that the bull is not killed at the end, and the bull's horns are sheathed.

See also Vol. III: PORTUGAL; INDEX, p. 153.
See also Vol. IV: SPANISH AND PORTUGUESE LANGUAGES.

PRAYER BOOK. The service book of the Church of England is generally known as the Prayer Book. Its full name is 'The book of common prayer, and administration of the sacraments, and other rites and ceremonies of the Church, after the use of the Church of England'. As this title shows, the contents are in three parts:

1. The Common Prayer, i.e. the daily services of Morning and Evening Prayer.
2. The Sacraments, i.e. Holy Communion and Baptism, along with Confirmation, Matrimony, and (added to the book in 1550) Ordination.
3. Other rites and ceremonies, i.e. Burial of the Dead, Thanksgiving of Women after Childbirth, &c.

The book was first issued under Edward VI in 1549, a few years after the Church of England had broken with Rome. Archbishop CRANMER (q.v. Vol. V), a master of glorious English, was responsible for most of it. It was founded on the medieval church services; but these were simplified, and many things which were regarded as superstitious by Protestants were left out. The medieval Church had five books of services—the Breviary (containing the eight daily services which made a round of worship day and night), the Missal (the Mass book), the Manual (the priest's service book), the Pontifical (the bishop's service book), and the Processional (made up of anthems, &c). The Edward VI Prayer Book reduced these to one book, and this was in the language of the people instead of in Latin. The preface to the new book said: 'The curates shall need none other books for their public service, but this book and the Bible.' In this book the eight daily services were reduced to two—Matins (Morning Service) and Evensong. This new Prayer Book was to be used, not only by priests, but by the congregation of the ordinary parish church. Based on the experience of worship through many centuries, it was adapted to meet the demands of the new day. Whereas in the eight services of the Breviary all the psalms were gone through every week, the two daily services of the new Prayer Book took a month to go through the psalter. The Edward VI Prayer Book established a unified form of service for the first time in England. The preface says: 'Heretofore there hath been great diversity . . . some following Salisbury use, some Hereford use, and some the use of Bangor, some of York, some of Lincoln; now from henceforth all the whole Realm shall have but one use.'

The first book was revised in 1552 and as the result of Calvinist influence made more definitely Protestant. Under ELIZABETH (q.v.) the third Prayer Book was issued in 1559. Not many changes were made except that vestments and ornaments of the altar, which the more Protestant book had displaced, were now ordered to be retained, and an offensive prayer for deliverance from the 'Bishop of Rome and all his detestable enormities' was left out. The 1662 book, which differs very little from the 1559, is in use today.

In 1927 the Prayer Book was revised again, bringing it back more nearly to the original Edward VI book. This new Prayer Book was rejected by Parliament but, in fact, some churches do now use the revised form, especially for the Holy Communion Service.

See also CHURCH OF ENGLAND.

PREHISTORIC MAN (WESTERN EUROPE). The human species first evolved outside Europe, in the tropics of Africa and Asia (*see* EVOLUTION OF MAN). There is evidence that the human stock had already diverged from the ancestors of present-day apes by 15 million years ago (the Miocene period, three-quarters of the way through the Age of Mammals). Not until about two million years ago, however, do we find creatures that actually make recognizable tools.

This last two million years were very unusual ones geologically, because of the great changes in climate which we call the ICE AGE (q.v. Vol. III). Before this, a tropical climate and vegetation reached as far north as the British Isles, and even present-day arctic regions had a temperate climate. What happened in the Ice Age was that a polar ice-cap formed, and successively expanded and contracted several times. At periods of maximum cold, parts of Britain were covered by ice in the way that Greenland is today. Glaciers also grew in mountainous areas such as the Alps or the Pyrenees. Such cold periods were interspersed with warmer ones when the climate was similar to the present day. We are probably now in a temporary warm period before the next ice advance (in about 10,000 years time!).

The earliest recognizable tools are simple flakes and choppers (*see* PREHISTORIC TOOLS AND WEAPONS); this simple phase of tool-making is largely confined to Africa. Around 500,000 years ago the *hand-axe* was added to the tool-kit, and for the first time man spread up into Europe. It was only possible for him to exist there in the warmer (interglacial) periods, and with the onset of a cold (glacial) period he was forced to retreat southwards or to perish. Much of his food at this stage must have come from gathering wild nuts and fruits, but he was also an accomplished hunter and could tackle elephant and wild boar.

It was a big step forward when man first learned to live in Europe during cold periods, in the extensive tundra areas on the margins of the ice-sheets. The men of this period required special aids to living, such as tents and skin clothing, and where there were caves they lived in them. Among the stone tools which men used in Europe from 70,000 years ago until 10,000 years ago (when the climate began to get warmer) are large numbers of tools for scraping skins to make clothes. Men in these colder areas must have eaten a much higher percentage of meat, especially reindeer, as there was little else to eat.

An important change occurred in the last glacial phase, around 30,000 years ago, when man finally evolved to his fully modern form. His command of speech probably improved. (Though we do not fully understand this, it is likely that in the earliest times language was not as complex as our own speech). From this time onwards, too, we find for the first time evidence of art, personal ornaments, and indications of small-scale trade between different groups.

The stone tools from the earlier warm periods in Europe come mainly from river-gravels, which are exposed in quarrying. The famous skull of a hand-axe maker from Swanscombe, Kent, came from a gravel-pit. The last cold phase (70,000–10,000 years ago) on the other hand, is best represented from finds in caves. Especially in south-west France where population was fairly dense, many caves were decorated with paintings and engravings of the animals which were hunted—reindeer, mammoth, horse, deer, and bison (see PREHISTORIC ART, Vol. XII).

The warm phase which we live in today (called the *post-glacial*) began about 10,000 years ago. The ice retreated, and the area of treeless tundra moved northwards. Once again forests began to cover Europe, and the great reindeer herds were replaced by smaller herds of red deer, along with elk, wild cattle and pigs. The first trees to arrive were those which spread easily, such as birch, and only later came oak, elm, and lime, with beech last of all. Man no longer had to live in caves; instead he camped by lakes and marshes where the animals came to drink and where there were plentiful fish and water-birds. Such camps sometimes came to be preserved in the peat and are found during peat-digging. The most famous is Starr Carr in Yorkshire.

For all this time—by far the greatest part of his two million years—man had lived by hunting local animals and collecting plants, and although he had spread from Africa to Europe and Asia, and beyond that to the Americas and Australia, population levels had remained low and social organization had probably not risen above the level of the simple band. The biggest change in the postglacial period (and one of the major turning points in prehistory) was the beginning of farming—the growing of grain crops and the domesticating of livestock.

Cereals such as wheat and barley are native to the highland areas of the Near East. The store of food in the large seeds allows the plant to survive in the severe dry climate of these upland regions with their sharp seasonal changes. Men found in these seeds a convenient supply of food, and when they first came to live in these remote places they collected them. At the beginning of the postglacial period, men were able to settle in new areas, and they took small supplies of cereals and planted them near the new settlements. From such small beginnings, the cultivation of cereals spread from group to group over most of the Near East, and finally to Europe. Instead of following animals such as gazelle and collecting small quantities of seeds on the way, men centred their lives on the fields of crops, and kept livestock such as sheep close to the settlements for most of the year.

This pattern of life first spread to south-east Europe around 6000 B.C. but only reached the British Isles by 3500 B.C. The first farmers cleared small fields in the forests which by that time covered much of the landscape. The use of cereals allowed larger numbers of people to live together in villages for the first time rather than camps, for agriculture could support a denser population than hunting and gathering. The population however was still small, only a fraction of what it was in medieval times, for instance.

In southern Europe, men built villages of mud brick; but further north they used more timber, and where stone was easily available they built stone houses. They still used flint and other stones to make tools—arrowheads for hunting and effective polished axes for tree-cutting. Cattle, sheep, and pigs were the main domesticated animals. The horse was not domesticated and the cattle were not used as draught animals. Indeed, ploughs and carts were not invented for another 1000 years. Agriculture was carried out with the hoe. It is probable that small tracts of forest were cleared and used for a short time, before the village moved on, and the process began again. This kind of farming, known as 'forest fallow' or 'slash and burn', is still carried on in parts of Africa today.

PREHISTORIC MEGALITHS AT CARNAC, BRITTANY
These avenues of standing stones may commemorate victories, the accession of kings, or they may mark boundaries

Each village would have been largely self-supporting, apart from supplies of good stone which were traded over considerable distances. A famous quarry, the products of which were traded all over Britain, was the one at Langdale in the Lake District. Pottery, too, was traded over shorter distances, for instance from Cornwall to Wiltshire. Seasonal fairs were occasions for gatherings of villages; sites like Windmill Hill in Wiltshire acted as tribal religious centres.

Some of the most obvious traces of these people in the British Isles are the remains of their tombs, constructed of huge mounds of earth and great boulders (*see* MEGALITHS). Later farmers wishing to use the land have destroyed many of them, but large numbers still survive in western Britain, especially on the chalk downlands where the soil became steadily worse for farming after its tree-cover had been removed and erosion set in. These tombs show that collective burial was practised, and that the stone-built chambers were periodically re-opened for further burials. Each tomb probably belonged to one family or lineage. As a medium-sized tomb would have taken a hundred men more than a year to make, it is fascinating to speculate as to whether these were the burials of chiefs and their families, or whether most families had their own monumental tomb.

Major changes began to occur some time around 2000 B.C. Population was growing, and the farmers began to take poorer land into cultivation. The effects of earlier agriculture, too, began to show in erosion and soil exhaustion. Society also was changing; the large communal tombs began to be replaced by individual burials under smaller, round mounds, and the men buried in them were often accompanied by a symbolic stone 'battle-axe' with a bored shaft-hole. There seems to have been more movement and contact between the scattered geographical groups. This is shown both in the very widespread occurrence of distinctive pottery forms, such as the highly-decorated 'bell-beaker', and the increasing occurrence of traded objects and materials. Britain had particularly close contacts with the Rhineland; a fragment of an imported grinding-stone, which must have come from this area, has been found on one site in Wiltshire.

Important among the materials traded at this time are the first metal objects, usually small daggers. The early ones are of copper, though later this was mixed with tin to produce bronze. Knowledge of metal-working must have spread from central Europe, where it was known earlier but at first was used mainly to make objects for display. Several new axe-factories and quarries were opened up at this period to meet the continuing need for hard stone.

During the second millennium the use of bronze continued to grow, especially for weapons. Daggers lengthened into swords, and metal 'battle-axes' replaced stone ones. Increasingly there is evidence of fighting equipment and fortification, though probably this was concerned with small-scale cattle-raiding rather than more organized warfare. The burial-mounds show that there were now chiefs who distinguished themselves by their finery and weapons; some graves, like the famous Bush Barrow in Wiltshire, contain gold ornaments as well as a ceremonial mace and dagger. The bulk of the population, however, must have lived much as their ancestors had done. One common-place feature which did change was clothing. Earlier garments were fastened with buttons, and were probably made of leather or skin; now metal pins began to be used, implying the use of loosely woven cloth. Large herds of sheep must for the first time have become a common feature of the landscape.

By about 1000 B.C., metal had become common enough to be the main material for working tools, and a more organized system of distribution brought this to the working population and not just to the chiefs. Often objects are found in hoards containing finished tools, scrap metal, and smelted copper ingots. Gradually, however, a new metal came into use for tools and weapons—iron.

Some of the most striking monuments of this period are the hill-forts of earth or stone that survive in many parts of Britain. Besides these there was a multitude of small farmsteads with circular farmhouses and outhouses, granaries, and storage-pits. Some of the field-systems of these settlements still survive, showing the layout of arable land and stock-enclosures. Farmers now practised intensive ROTATION OF CROPS (q.v. Vol. VI), using hardier types of cereal such as spelt, a type of wheat. They herded sheep on a large scale, moving the flocks from upland hill-forts to lowland pastures. The site of Glastonbury (see LAKE DWELLINGS), preserved

Name of period	Main changes in the technique of living and of tool-making	Beginning dates BC
Iron Age	Use of iron for tools and weapons; horses for riding and draught; increased trade; small coins; small towns as well as villages.	1,000
Bronze Age	First use of metal for tools and weapons; wheeled vehicles; widespread trade; gold and amber ornaments.	2,000
Neolithic (New Stone Age)	Farming, stockbreeding, villages, corn-growing; polished stone axes for forest clearing; mining for flint, trading in stones for axes; tools of stone, bone, wood; pottery; weaving.	3,500
Mesolithic (Middle Stone Age)	Hunting and food-gathering communities, partly nomadic; boats, sledges, skis; stone tools, some axes for chopping; perhaps some pottery, bone harpoons; fish-nets.	10,000
Palaeolithic (Old Stone Age)	*Upper*: Small hunting communities; throwing-sticks and bows and arrows; summer huts and winter houses or cave-shelters; fine flint-work.	30,000
	Middle: Flint tools, first evidence of deliberate burials.	115,000
	Lower: First use of chipped stone tools; wooden spears; use of fire; very nomadic units of hunters.	2,000,000

SUMMARY CHART

Archaeologists label the different periods by the materials used for tools: Stone, Bronze, and Iron. The very long Stone Age is subdivided.

in peat, gives a good impression of the activities of these lowland settlements with their weaving industry, with bone carding-combs and iron knives, sickles, and bill-hooks.

The early woollen industry, along with cattle-hides and grain, formed the basis of longer-distance trade which developed even before the arrival of the Romans. The fine metalwork produced by specialist craftsmen reflects the power of the chiefs who profited from this. Some of these products were even exported to the continent from larger settlements which, at the time of Julius Caesar's exploratory voyage in 55 B.C., were really native towns. We know from Caesar's accounts and later records that Britain was split up among native tribes and kingdoms, and indeed the Romans kept this framework of regional groupings based on major centres for the administrative system that they imposed on the province.

See also LAKE-DWELLINGS; PREHISTORIC POTTERY; PRE-HISTORIC TOOLS AND WEAPONS; RELIGION, PREHISTORIC.

See also Vol. VI: AGRICULTURAL HISTORY.

See also Vol. XII: PREHISTORIC ART.

PREHISTORIC POTTERY.

As long as Man was a hunter and collector of wild plant foods, wandering from camping-place to camping-place, he had few possessions. A hunter must travel light. When he moves camp he carries his weapons, both for defence and to help him to get food on the way. His wife carries the baby and everything else. So when the homes of the earliest men are found, there is little in the way of furnishings, only a few stones, perhaps some bones, and the ashes of the hearth. But when men had learned how to grow grain and had tamed animals for food and for milking, they could store provisions and make a settled home: then containers and cooking-vessels became more useful and necessary. Gourds and skins in scooped-out wooden tubs and baskets were all used, but none of these could be put in the fire for cooking, and it was the invention of pottery that solved this problem. In many parts of the world people plaster a basket with clay to make it watertight, and pottery may have developed from this. Suppose that the basket was accidentally burnt in the fire. It would be destroyed,

while the clay lining, hardened in the fire, would be left in the shape of a bowl. Such an accident may have given a man, or more probably a woman (for women are usually the primitive potters, basket-makers, and cooks) the idea of moulding clay into useful shapes and baking it into hard pottery, capable of being placed over the fire—an invention which would enormously increase the possibilities of cooking.

To make good pottery is not a simple process. The clay has to be carefully collected, freed from stone and grit, mixed to the proper consistency by the addition of sand, charcoal, ground up shells, or bits of broken pots, and moistened with water. Then it must be worked up in the hands to the proper shape and baked in the fire. Sometimes the clay is made into a sort of pancake and moulded over a gourd, basket, or another pot; sometimes the clay is drawn out into thin, sausage-like lengths and coiled into a spiral, the surface being then polished smooth. Both methods have been used in many parts of the world, and both methods appear to have been used in early days.

Primitive pots were fired in an open hearth; but it was discovered that the clay burnt black where it was covered with ashes, and red where there was an open flame. Some control of colouring was therefore possible, even under very simple conditions of firing, and with the introduction of a closed oven or kiln for pot baking, the colour of the surface could be kept constant. The earliest pots were moulded by hand; but later the potter's wheel was invented, and pottery-making became a specialized man's

Ashmolean Museum

PREDYNASTIC EGYPTIAN POT

British Museum

LATE NEOLITHIC BOWL FROM MORTLAKE, SURREY

Ashmolean Museum

BRONZE AGE BEAKER FROM SUTTON COURTENAY, BERKS

craft as much as that of the blacksmith.

The earliest agricultural villages in the Near East did not use pottery (hence they are called 'aceramic' Neolithic). Crude vessels of fired clay have been found in Turkey on a site of about 7000 B.C. These are thick and unfinished, without decoration. By 6000 B.C. in the same area fully finished pottery was being produced, and shortly afterwards elaborate vessels with a polished surface and painted decoration. Even earlier pottery is known from Japan, where it must have been invented independently. Early pottery was usually round-bottomed, the most useful shape on an uneven surface. Although pots break easily, the fragments can be as in-destructible as stone; so potsherds often survive on prehistoric sites, and their study can illustrate a good deal about the way of life of the people who made them—their migrations, their trade routes, their food, drink, and cooking—as well as revealing their artistic sense and sometimes their ideas of religion and a future life.

The simplest patterns were impressions made with the finger-tips or finger-nails. It was also found that effective strokes and dots could be made with a piece of stick or bone, and that these could be executed with endless variations of lines and zigzags, as in the Beaker pottery of western Europe, or with graceful curves, as in the New Stone Age ware of the Danube region. Especially in eastern Europe we find 'corded ware', so called because the clay, while still wet and soft, was im-pressed with patterns made with a cord or twisted thong, and other pots were evidently marked with the bone of a small bird. Beautiful painted pottery was being made in early New Stone Age times in Egypt and eastern Asia, but little painted pottery is found in western Europe before the introduction of copper, and none at all in Britain.

Pottery can be used for dating in the same way as stone tools are used—in fact, in Britain, several of the early groups of people are named from different types of pottery (such as the Beaker Folk of the Early Bronze Age).

The earliest pottery in Britain was introduced about 3500 B.C. by New Stone Age colonists from France, and consists of plain bag-shaped round-based pots. Wares connected with the east European cord-ornamented pottery were also made from about this date. Immigrants and traders during the Bronze and Iron Ages brought with them new ideas of pottery-making from their continental homelands, and it is these changing styles in pots that form the basis of much of our archaeological classification.

See also PREHISTORIC MAN.

PREHISTORIC TOOLS AND WEAPONS.
Early Man had two great advantages which have given him dominion over the beasts of the field—brains and hands. No animal as small as Man has so large and complex a brain, and few other animals stand naturally on their hind legs, with their fore-limbs free from the work of feet. With his brains Man could make discoveries and inventions: with his hands he could make tools. Discoveries must have come first. Even apes, whose hands come nearest to Man's in dexterity, are said to pick up a stone or stick to threaten an enemy and, when trained, they can learn various handy tricks; but it is doubtful if they can invent anything new for themselves. Moreover, apes are still dependent on their hands for support; while Man gave up walking on all-fours at an early age, leaving his hands free for touching, handling, and experimenting. With his hands he could pick up and hold or throw sticks and stones which he could use in his daily hunt for food. He could dig up edible roots or tubers, hammer and pound up tough roots or stems, crack nuts or shellfish, break limpets off rocks, and in many other ways increase his supply of food—so im-portant in his struggle for existence. With sticks and stones he could also defend himself against enemies or wild animals and, with well-directed shots, stun or kill animals and birds.

He soon discovered that a pointed stick would do more damage than a blunt one, and that a sharp stone was more useful than a round one. It was a great landmark in human development when he found that some stones, particularly flint, could be chipped by means of another stone so as to make a cutting edge. With a sharpened stone Man could lop off branches to build a roof for his shelter; he could dig holes in the ground for store-houses, or to make his hut larger and warmer; he could hollow out tree-trunks for a dug-out canoe; he could cut up and scrape hides for clothing. He could defend him-self from enemies, attack and kill even large and fierce animals, carve up their joints, scrape their bones for meat, and break the bones for marrow. Sharpened sticks and worked bones were pro-bably used too; but most of these have perished long ago, and as a rule only stones remain as records of the handicraft of Man. These earliest

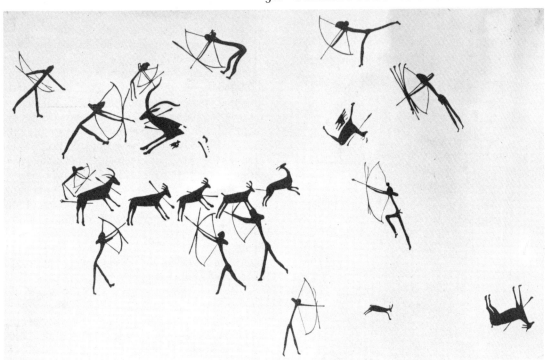

PREHISTORIC PAINTING FROM A CAVE IN VALENCIA, SPAIN

tools, a rounded stone for a hammer and a sharpened one for an axe, are the remote ancestors of all our present hammers, axes, adzes, chisels, knives, saws, planes, and other treasures of our tool-boxes and workshops.

The earliest tools or weapons—and they doubtless served as both—must have been of the simplest kind, so simple that it is impossible to decide with certainty if they have been shaped by Man or accidentally fractured by nature.

When once Man had started experimenting in chipping stone tools, it might be expected that he would provide himself with a varied outfit; but for thousands of years he seems to have continued making much the same tools in much the same ways. Among the most important of these are the so-called 'hand-axes' of the Early Stone Age, over 500,000 years old. To make these, the craftsman took either a lump of flint or a flint flake and chipped it at one end into a tool, shaped rather like a flattened pear. Such 'hand-axes' are found in Europe, Asia, and Africa; they vary locally because of the variety of rock, but they are much alike in general outline, though not all of the same age. Other peoples in Europe and Asia in this period made

tools of different shapes out of heavy flakes that they chipped off a lump of flint.

We can trace a slow evolution in the craft of making flint tools: they became gradually smaller, lighter, and more carefully trimmed, and were worked all round instead of only at one end. They could be fixed in short handles and used as knives, or in longer ones and used as spear-heads. It is not known what the handles were like, nor how they were attached to the blades, but they were probably of wood or bone, lashed on with strips of hide.

Man's progress in handicraft was very slow, and even during the middle Old Stone Age, 150,000 years or more ago, he only made a small range of tools or weapons. He had 'points' serving, doubtless, for knives or spear-heads, small hand-axes, scrapers for scraping hides and trimming spear-shafts, and sharp flint flakes used as awls, probably for boring holes in skins to be sewn together. Late Old Stone Age Man, some 70,000 years B.C., made more use of thinnish, flat, flint flakes, sharpened along the sides or at the ends. Some of these were serviceable knives, some were tools for engraving. Towards the end of the Old Stone Age special tools, both in stone

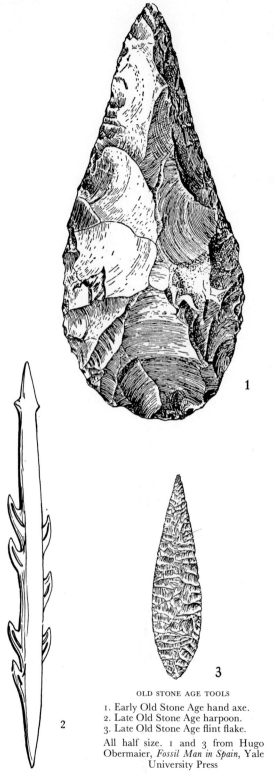

and bone, were made for special purposes. There is no doubt about the harpoons of reindeer antler or deer antler for fishing, nor about the bone needles with eyes threaded with sinews for stitching skins. Somewhere about this time men invented bows and arrows. They had already invented spear-throwers to increase the range of their weapons, and we can learn how they used them by seeing how the Australians or Eskimos use them today. The invention of the bow increased the range still farther. Among the rock-paintings of eastern Spain there are pictures of men shooting, and wooden arrow-shafts have been found in north Germany. Some of the arrows are pointed at the end, some are shaped to hold arrow-heads of flint. Similar flint arrow-heads were used down to historic times; when their origin was forgotten, they were called 'elf-darts' and treasured as charms.

After about 5000 B.C. great progress was made. The people of the New Stone Age still used stone as their principal material; but new discoveries in farming and a more stable way of life called for new tools. Flint flakes were still used for knives, scrapers, awls and borers, spears and arrow-heads, and numbers of sharp little flints were fixed in a row for a sickle. The typical New Stone Age axes, instead of being chipped, were ground and polished to give a smooth surface and regular blade, and mounted in a hole in a wooden handle. Experiments have shown that a polished axe cuts down trees more quickly and easily than a chipped one. Sometimes a socket of stag antler was fitted in between the axe-head and the handle to prevent the wood splitting. Later, when methods of boring stones were invented, the wooden handle was fitted into the holed stone, instead of fitting the stone into the hole in the handle. Axes like these were the weapons of the hands of warriors of northern Europe in the Bronze Age.

When copper and bronze were discovered, and men discovered the possibilities of the new materials for tool-making, they began by imitating the stone forms in metal, and so the first bronze axes were solid. But as the craftsmen grew more skilful, they made improvements, and successive stages in methods of hafting can be recognized. First they hammered up the sides of the blades to grip the handles; later they curved the edges round into a socket; finally socketed axe-heads with loops for attachment were cast in moulds. The steel axe of today has ancestors

OLD STONE AGE TOOLS

1. Early Old Stone Age hand axe.
2. Late Old Stone Age harpoon.
3. Late Old Stone Age flint flake.

All half size. 1 and 3 from Hugo Obermaier, *Fossil Man in Spain*, Yale University Press

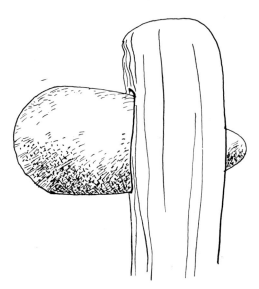

NEW STONE AGE AXE. Half size

in copper in the ancient civilizations of the East, and its wooden handle differs little from that made by prehistoric Man.

Bronze took the place of stone for axes, chisels, and spear-heads; but arrow-heads of flint were still used, even in the Iron Age, perhaps because arrows are so often lost, and metal was scarcer than flint. Flint knives and daggers were imitated in copper and bronze, but the new weapons soon showed little likeness to their earlier ancestors—there were no stone models for the rapiers and swords with which our forefathers fought their battles in the Late Bronze Age.

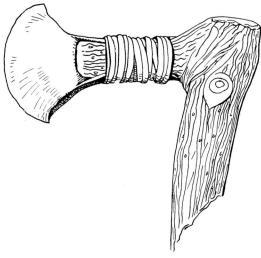

BRONZE AXE. Half size

The change from bronze to iron was a gradual one during the last centuries B.C., introducing us to historic times and to the tools and weapons which we use today. But we have not altogether emerged from the Stone Age as long as we still use stone pestles and mortars for pounding, or mill-stones for grinding our daily bread.

See also PREHISTORIC MAN.

PRESBYTERIANS, *see* CALVINIST.

PRIEST. A priest is an agent of god, who offers sacrifice to the god or performs other religious actions on behalf of the people whom he represents. He differs from a medicine-man or magician because he does not claim to act for himself by his own control of supernatural powers (*see* MAGIC). He has to be set apart for his office by the gods or spirits whom he serves.

The office, which is given him by a solemn act of consecration or ordination, used often to be confined to members of a royal or priestly line. In Egypt, for instance, the Pharaoh was the high priest, because he was the son and incarnation on earth of the chief gods who ruled over the country and controlled the course of nature. In Mesopotamia, too, the Babylonian king was the high priest. But although the monarchs in both these countries spent most of their time performing ceremonies for the benefit of their people, they could not be in more than one place at once. Therefore they had to appoint others to act as priests on their behalf in the temple services. In carrying out these duties priests also acted on behalf of the gods, of whom the kings were the earthly representatives, and, in so doing, they frequently acted as though they were the gods. In religious rites, for instance, they dressed as Osiris and Horus and Marduk, and behaved exactly as if they were gods. It was these priests who had to decide whether it would be lucky to do a particular thing on a given day, and to act as intermediaries between the gods and the people in the offering of SACRIFICES (q.v.), explaining omens and oracles, and performing rites of purification and penitence when the gods were angry and spiteful. The priests were also seers or soothsayers (*see* PROPHECY), who foretold what was going to happen by such methods as inspecting the liver and gall-bladder of an animal slain as a victim at the altar.

In Israel, before the exile in Babylon, the priests were usually royal officials, and the king

SAMARITAN PRIESTS WITH THEIR SACRED BOOK, THE TORAH

as the anointed of God offered sacrifices (1 Kings ix. 25; 2 Kings xvi. 12) and on occasions dressed and behaved as a priest (cf. 2 Sam. vi. 14) while his sons served in the priesthood. After the Israelites returned from exile to Jerusalem in 523 B.C. and began to re-establish their customs, beliefs, and institutions, the high priest took the place of the king in religious ceremonies, and the priesthood became quite separate and distinct from the royal family.

The priesthood, in consequence, became a very powerful body of men in the land. The priesthood is said to have started with Aaron, the brother of Moses, and the Levites to have been especially set apart to produce men suitable for the service of the sanctuary. In early days it was not necessary, though desirable, for a priest to be a Levite. In course of time, however, anyone who was attached to a shrine was treated as a Levite. But there were also other priestly families—the Zadokites and the Aaronites. Besides these priests engaged in the service of the Temple, there were the seers and in later Judaism the rabbis, doctors of the sacred Law, and teachers, who drew up very elaborate and complicated rules governing the way Jews were to live and behave among themselves and in relation to Gentiles. But they were lawyers rather than priests (see JUDAISM).

The Jewish priesthood was, in a sense, continued in the CHRISTIAN CHURCH (q.v.) when the worship of the Temple was transferred to the central act of Christian worship—the service at first called the Breaking of the Bread and later known as Holy Communion, the Eucharist, or the Mass. When this service was regarded as a sacrifice, the man who made the offering on behalf of Christ, the eternal High Priest in heaven (Heb. v. 5 ff., vii. 22 ff.), was spoken of as a priest and set apart for this purpose by a solemn act of ordination. This has been the custom in the Catholic Church all down the ages. At the Reformation in the 16th century, however, in many Protestant Churches the ancient line of bishops, priests, and deacons was brought to an end, and in its place a new order of ministers was established. Their chief work lay in preaching the Gospel, acting as shepherds of their flocks, and ministering to a congregation, rather than in acting as attendants at the altar.

The priesthoods of other religions, such as HINDUISM, BUDDHISM, and SHINTO (qq.v.), are described in those articles. In ISLAM (q.v.) there is no priesthood and no sacrificial worship.

PROPHECY. Prophet is a Greek word which meant a person who uttered or interpreted an

British Museum

HER-HERU, THE FIRST EGYPTIAN PRIEST-KING, AND QUEEN NETCHEMET PRAYING TO OSIRIS

Painting from the *Book of the Dead*, 21st Dynasty (*c.* 1050 B.C.)

oracle. Therefore, at first, prophecy was concerned with foretelling events, and the methods used for finding out what was going to happen often included the prophet working himself (or herself) into a state of frenzy by wild dancing and strange music, in order that he might become 'possessed' by the god who made the revelation. In this condition of ecstasy or delirium he proclaimed the god's mind and will about things that were happening in the present or going to take place in the future. Sometimes, however, oracles were consulted by crystal-gazing, casting lots, and other such devices used in DIVINATION (q.v.), and the prophet then became a seer, like Samuel in the Old Testament.

The Hebrew word, *Nabi*, translated 'prophet' in the Greek version of the Bible, means a person endowed with second sight (i.e. a seer), who was consulted on all sorts of matters. But it also means a member of one of the wandering bands called 'sons of the prophets', who had their headquarters at such sacred centres as Gilgal, Bethel, Ramah, and Jericho. These people roamed about the country preceded by players on the harp, tambourine, flute, or zither. They worked themselves up into a frenzy by the help of the music, and so great was the state of religious excitement which they created that the people who stood by also became infected and themselves 'prophesied', being filled with the divine spirit. We read of an experience of this kind in the book of Samuel, when Saul at the time of his anointing went among the prophets (I Sam. x. I–II). These prophets often practised divination and soothsaying, as well as their wilder methods, to obtain knowledge from heaven which ordinary people could not get.

In the 8th century B.C., however, a new movement arose in Palestine, in which a higher type of prophecy made its appearance. It was then that men like Amos, Hosea, and Isaiah declared the will and purpose of God in great pronouncements which they claimed to have received as a special revelation given to them by Jehovah, without the use of the magical methods adopted by the earlier seers, soothsayers, and dancers. They felt themselves moved by the spirit of God to deliver a message which very often was quite different from the beliefs, customs, and ideas of their own day. Indeed, it was usually an unpopular cry they uttered; but what they said was so original and spoken with such urgency that it sounded like a message straight from God.

So they generally began with the words, 'Thus saith Jehovah'. Often the prophets attacked the priesthood of Israel because their sacrificial worship had got mixed up with the pagan cults of Palestine and those of Egypt, Babylonia, and Phoenicia; and they refused to associate themselves with their predecessors, the local seers and soothsayers. Their first and chief pronouncement was that God was holy and righteous and demanded of His people right living based on justice, goodness, forbearance, mercy, and love. They also declared that He was a jealous God and would not tolerate the worship of any other divine being, great or small. Whether at this time they really believed that there was only one God of all the earth is not quite clear. But by the end of the period of the captivity in Babylon, the writer of Isaiah xl–lv taught in no unmeasured terms, as did the priest-prophet Ezekiel, that there is but one Creator and Sustainer of all things beside whom all the 'gods' are mere idols. They also taught that each individual was of value in the sight of God and personally responsible to Him for the way he used his life; and that the Jewish nation as a whole was a holy people, chosen by God because, through them, God was working out His purposes for the world.

These were new ideas of religion which the prophets declared to be the direct word of God. When the Jews returned from their exile in Babylon, the prophets had done their work, and while their influence was very strongly felt in the restored kingdom, the Hebrew prophets had no real successors in Judaism from the end of the 6th century B.C. But, while the period of the prophets was short-lived and unique in the religious history of the nation, and indeed of the world, it had far-reaching consequences. In Persia ZOROASTER (q.v.) also started to preach the idea of only One God, and early in the 7th century A.D., MUHAMMAD (q.v. Vol. V), inspired by a vision, became the great prophet of ISLAM (q.v.) and proclaimed the supreme majesty of Allah.

See also RELIGION; JUDAISM.

PROTESTANT, *see* CHRISTIAN CHURCH; REFORMATION.

PRUSSIAN, *see* GERMANS.

PUNJABS, *see* INDIAN PEOPLES.

PURITANS, *see* CONGREGATIONALIST.

PYGMIES (Negrillos). These people live in the thick, damp, forests of the Congo basin of Central Africa, in an area about 5 degrees north and south of the equator. This region of huge trees and massed undergrowth, where the temperature is seldom below 27° C, is still largely unexplored, and many of the Pygmies have never seen a white man. The African Pygmies are sometimes known as Negrillos, the word Negrito being used for pygmy peoples found in south-east Asia (*see* ANDAMAN ISLANDERS). They are very small—about 1 m 32 cm to 1 m 45 cm in height—with chocolate-coloured skins, black curly hair, broad noses, and wide mouths. Their bodies are often covered with fine downy hair. They wear practically no clothes—the men may have a strip of deer skin as a belt, and the women add branches of leaves tucked into the belt.

The Pygmies are a very shy and timid people, and very little is known about their social organization or their language. It seems that they speak Bantu dialects, often of neighbouring agricultural peoples, but sometimes of Bantu peoples in a far-away area (*see* AFRICAN LANGUAGES, Vol. IV).

They live in small bands. As they are continually on the move after game, they have no permanent settlements, but build themselves temporary huts. These are made of branches bent over in a semicircle and interwoven with twigs and leaves. A cluster of them is scarcely noticeable in the gloom of the tropical forest. They surround them with traps and pitfalls, with poisoned spikes set to catch game.

The Pygmies live by hunting and food-gathering. They collect fruits, roots, and nuts, and trap small animals. For large animals they use bows with poisoned arrows, and show great skill in tracking down wounded animals until the poison takes effect and the animal drops down. They are clever at climbing trees to collect honey. Some of the honey and game they trade for agricultural products, such as maize, with their Bantu neighbours. The game is put down at a

Mansell

PYGMIES SMOKING BESIDE THEIR HUT

convenient place, and the Pygmies hide in the neighbouring 'bush'. The Bantu come forward and put down the foodstuffs they have to offer in exchange and go away again. If the Pygmies are satisfied, they take away the foodstuffs and leave the game; if not satisfied, they may either take away their game or wait until more is offered. In this way trading takes place, though the two parties do not meet.

Their religious beliefs include belief in a supreme god under whom are good and bad spirits, and in ghosts and ancestral spirits. They worship the supreme god, and make offerings to the spirits and ghosts who are believed to be able to control the fortunes of the living.

A few Pygmies will work for traders, trappers, or travellers; some have been trained in mission schools where they prove quick-witted; but most seem to prefer their free life in the depths of the forest.

See also AFRICANS.
See also Vol. III: CONGO RIVER.

PYRAMIDS, *see* EGYPTIAN CIVILIZATION.
See also Vol. XII: PYRAMIDS.

Q

QUAKERS. The Society of Friends, the correct name for Quakers, is a group of Christians who base their religion on the belief that God speaks directly to the heart of every man. Quakers believe that all men and women, whatever be their race, class, or religion, are children of God, and as such have been given a measure of inner light, the Light of Christ, which, if they follow it, will give them a growing knowledge of God. They believe that it is man's duty not only to follow this divine element in himself, but to respond to it in others—therefore to help those in need and not to use violence or take human life. Right relationships between man and man come from the root idea of the relation between God and man: hence the Quakers' tolerance of other religions, belief in the basic equality of men, refusal to take part in war, and devotion to humanitarian work.

Friends believe that the Church is the whole family of those who seek to follow the Light of Christ. The Society of Friends, therefore, has no dogmatic creed, no set form of service or separated priesthood, and no specially consecrated building. In worship they gather together in a Meeting House in silent waiting upon the Spirit of God, and if anyone present feels moved by the Spirit of God to speak or pray aloud, he or she may do so. In the 17th century some Friends were so moved by religious emotions in their meetings that they would tremble and quake—and from this arose their nickname Quaker.

GEORGE FOX (q.v. Vol. V) founded the Society of Friends in the 17th century. At the time the Church was very intolerant: even the Dissenters, who had broken away from the Church, built up rules and dogmas and persecuted those who would not follow them. So whether the Dissenters or the Church were in power, the Quakers were still persecuted. In spite of this George Fox went about the country preaching and converting people. He was often imprisoned, beaten, and stoned, and meetings were broken up by soldiers. When the law had no other case against them, they imprisoned Quakers for refusing to take the Oath of Allegiance to the king. The Quakers had no wish to be disloyal to the king, but to take an oath was against their conscience, because they thought that to do so was disobeying Christ's teaching: 'Swear not at all, let your yea be yea and your nay nay.'

Many Quakers decided to go to America where the Puritans, the Pilgrim Fathers, had already settled. But in America they found that the Puritans were as anxious as the Church of England to make everyone conform to their rules. At last, William PENN (q.v. Vol. V), a friend and follower of Fox, decided to found a Quaker state. He was granted by Charles II a large area of America, north of Virginia, and started a settlement of Quakers there. The new state was called Pennsylvania. Penn became the first Governor and organized it according to Quaker ideals. Every member of the state, whether Quaker or not, was allowed to worship as he wished. Even people who were not Christians were tolerated—an idea which in those days was most unusual. Instead of turning the American Indians out of their land by force, as most of the colonizers had done, the Quakers bought their land from them, lived on good terms with them, and converted many of them to their faith. Thousands of Quakers settled in Pennsylvania, and today there are 120,000 in North America compared with 21,000 in Great Britain and 54,000 in the rest of the world.

It was common in the 17th century for friends and relations to call each other 'Thou', just as many people in Europe still do. The Quakers continued the use of 'Thou' to emphasize that all men were brothers. The simple grey dress of the women also proclaimed their sense of equality. They did not object to inequality of wealth, and they encouraged hard work and thrift; but they expected people to spend their money for the good of others. In consequence they built up a tradition of philanthropy which they still carry on. In America not only did they help the Red Indians, but they were among the first to defend the Negro slaves and to work for the relief of poverty and sickness. Elizabeth FRY (q.v. Vol. V) visited prisons and not only taught

A QUAKER MEETING
Aquatint from R. J. Ackermann, *Microcosm of London*, 1809

and helped the prisoners, but played a very important part in bringing about prison reform. In industry Quakers, realizing that employers had a responsibility towards their workers, built houses and pleasant factories for them and organized social welfare, long before this was an accepted idea.

Although Quakers will not take part in a war, they have always helped the victims of war, regarding equally both friend and enemy. They sent help to Europe during the war of 1870, though England was not concerned in the fighting. During the 1914–18 war they organized relief both for the soldiers and those who had suffered or had lost their homes through the fighting. During that war, conscription was introduced, and many Quakers were sent to prison as conscientious objectors. In the Second World War a man's right to refuse to fight on conscientious grounds was better recognized. The Quakers, however, though pacifist, were not passive: they played a useful and sometimes dangerous part by sending relief to many parts of the world where there was fighting or where there were refugees in distress.

The organization of the Society is democratic. Each district has a monthly business meeting open to all members, and this meeting appoints officials who are called elders. The Monthly Meeting admits new members, arranges for marriages and burials, and organizes help for those in trouble. There is a Quarterly Meeting responsible for a wider area, and the Yearly Meeting which deals with matters requiring a united decision of Friends throughout the country. The Irish and American Quakers have a separate organization, as do those in other European countries. Each kind of business meeting appoints a Clerk who is like a Chairman. These officials have no authority over the rest. No vote is taken at the meeting—each member can speak freely, the common purpose being to find the right decision by the leading of the divine spirit. At the end of the meeting the Clerk sums up the general decision. This is called the consensus or 'sense of the meeting'. If there is a definite difference of opinion, the question is brought up again at the next meeting.

The meeting houses are simple rooms. Quakers still meet to wait upon the Spirit of God in silence; but in some places they now also have more formal services with hymns and a set address. The headquarters of the Society in England is at Friends House in London, where religious and educational work at home and abroad, as well as the Friends' Relief Service, is organized.

R

RABBI, *see* Jews; Priests.

RACES AND PEOPLES. It is generally accepted that the 3,000 million or so inhabitants of the world today are derived from one ancestral type; and yet there are so many differences in appearance that it is difficult for us to recognize all the peoples of the world as our distant cousins. The typical Anglo-Saxon Englishman is tall, fair-skinned, with fair, wavy hair, and blue eyes; the typical African has short, black, woolly hair, black skin, and black eyes; the typical Chinese is smaller and slimmer, with yellow skin, long, straight, black hair, and slanting, black eyes. But variations in man are not more remarkable than contrasts between cart-horse, race-horse, and Shetland pony, all derived from the prehistoric horse; and far less remarkable than the very widely varying descendants of the ancestral dog. Horses and dogs can be classified in separate breeds, distinguished by certain physical characters handed down from generation to generation. Similarly, mankind can be classified and divided up into a number of breeds or 'races'.

A 'race' means a group of mankind genetically distinguishable by characters which are handed down from parents to children, so long as no mixture with other types takes place. But as men do not remain fixed in one place and tend to interbreed with other groups, so there arise variable mixtures. The individuals that make up a people, such as the British or Indians or Chinese, vary a great deal among themselves in physical appearance, as the result of inter-breeding between several distinctive groups.

In Britain we can see marked contrasts in the people we meet every day. While some are tall and fair, with flaxen hair and blue eyes, some are small and dark with dark complexions; some have red hair, some have black; their eyes may be of any tint from blue, grey, or green to dark brown. But they all have one feature in common: their hair is described as 'wavy', which means that it is neither as straight and lank as the Chinese or American Indian, nor as woolly and frizzy as the Negro or the Melanesian. In fact, the character of the hair, which is little affected by climate or way of life and is inherited unchanged when there is no mixture, is often taken as one of the chief features in distinguishing the main racial types of man.

Another feature which breeds true is less easily noticed—the proportions of the head. If looked at from above, people's heads vary between nearly round (*brachycephalic*, or 'broad-headed') and long and narrow (*dolichocephalic* or 'long-headed'). 'Roundheads' are rare in Britain, but are in the majority in central Europe.

The third feature, the colour of the skin, is the most obvious, but it is difficult to measure and is, moreover, affected to some extent by climate and even seasons. There are the broad distinctions, as mentioned above, of 'white' Europeans, yellow Mongols, and black Africans; but there are also 'black-skinned' Indians, as well as the Australian 'black-fellows', who are very different from Negroes as well as from each other. The colour of the hair and eyes, which at once attracts our attention at home, is of secondary importance outside Europe, for only in Europe, or lands which Europe has colonized or influenced, are fair hair and light eyes found among the population.

There are several less important differences of race. One of these is stature. People may be tall or short, though height is often affected by food, climate, or other environmental as well as hereditary conditions. But there are groups of people, such as some North American Indians, the Sudanese, or the Scots, averaging 1 m 72 cm to 1 m 77 cm, who are among the tallest in the world; while there are districts in Japan where the average is only 1 m 57 cm, and the Andamanese and the African Pygmies are not much over 1 m 22 cm high.

There are other characters that are regularly inherited, such as the shape of the nose, which may be narrow, prominent, large and long, as commonly seen in Europe and especially among the Jews; or it may be broad and flat as among the Negroes. The eyes may be level and widely open, or narrow and slanting. The forehead

Dr. P. Wolff

1. NORDIC (German)

Paul Popper

2. ALPINE (Swiss)

Paul Popper

3. MEDITERRANEAN (Italian)

Pitt Rivers Collection

4. NEGRO (Zulu)

5. MONGOL

U.S. Information Service

6. AMERICAN INDIAN

Haddon Library

7. MELANESIAN

High Commissioner for N.Z.

8. POLYNESIAN (Maori)

Haddon Library

9. AUSTRALIAN ABORIGINE

RACIAL TYPES

and jaws may be in a straight line, as with most Europeans, or there may be a retreating forehead and protruding jaws, as among the Australian aborigines.

Different combinations of these main race features—hair, head-form, and skin colour, together with stature, and details of noses, eyes, or jaws—are characteristics of a number of different people of the world today. But as intermarriage has been going on from the earliest times, we cannot expect to find any clear-cut boundaries or completely uniform groups. Domesticated horses and dogs have developed, with the aid of Man, into sharply distinct breeds, but Man himself is everywhere something of a mongrel. If there is any pure race—that is a people which is uniform and distinctive in its physical characteristics—still existing in the world, it is only in some remote and isolated region.

Over all the rest of the world we can recognize that certain racial types form the majority of the population, and these, which it is usual to call 'races', are distributed in the following way:

1. EUROPE. Most of the peoples of Europe are a mixture of several races, but all belong to the 'wavy-haired' group, as their hair is neither short and woolly like the Negro nor stiffly straight like the Mongol. In the north and west, the people generally have long and narrow heads, often fair hair and blue eyes (as nowhere else in the world), and tallish stature; there is a belt of rounder-headed, shorter, and less fair people stretching from Persia in the east, across central Europe, as far as western France. Darker-skinned people, with dark hair and eyes, and rather longer and narrower heads, moderate stature, and slender build, border the Mediterranean. These three racial types are called Nordic, Alpine, and Mediterranean; but it is difficult to find any considerable part of the mainland of Europe in which the population is not a mixture or blend of two or more. The various peoples of Europe are described in separate articles.

2. ASIA. Asia is the home of the Mongolian race, which stretches right across the continent, north and east of Persia and the Himalayas, and has spread east (Eskimo and American Indian), south-east (into the Pacific Islands), and west (European Lapps). Its main characters are long, straight, black hair, rounded heads (usually), yellowish or brownish skin, short stature, flat noses, and slanting eyes. In south-east Asia, the Pacific, and also in America, the Mongolian type

was probably mixed in remote times with other strains. In south-west Asia and to the south of the Himalayas the people are wavy-haired like ourselves, though with darker skins, hair, and eyes, and are akin to the Mediterraneans. There are small groups of other types here and there. The brown-skinned, wavy-haired Vedda of Ceylon, and the Sakai of Malaya, have some features like those of the Australian aborigines, and the Pygmies, such as the Andamanese and the Semang, have black skins and woolly hair like the Negroes (*see* ANDAMAN ISLANDERS; INDIAN PEOPLES; LAPPS; MALAYS; MONGOLS; VEDDA).

3. AFRICA. Africa, north of the Sahara, has been largely influenced by colonizations of Mediterranean types; but Africa, south of the Sahara, is the home of the Negro race who have short, woolly, black hair, long heads, black skins, and very dark eyes. Broad, flat noses and thick lips are common in West Africa and parts of the Congo, but are less marked to the east and south where there has been mixture with other types. The Pygmies of the Congo and the Bushmen and Hottentots of South Africa differ from each other a good deal, and are usually regarded as distinctive local variants of the Negro race (*see* BUSHMEN; HOTTENTOTS; AFRICANS; PYGMIES).

4. AMERICA. America, both North and South, is believed to have been peopled by early migrations from East Asia in which the Mongolian race predominated. The Eskimos still show many Mongolian features, such as slanting eyes and straight hair; although their heads are high and narrow. The American Indians of today, however, show many differences from their Asiatic cousins. Although their hair is long, straight, and black, and their skins are yellowish-brown, often with a coppery tinge (the reason for their nickname 'Redskins'), the tall stature and hawk-like nose of many American Indians are distinctly non-Mongolian characteristics. Their head-forms are also very variable (*see* AMERICAN INDIANS, CENTRAL AND SOUTH; AMERICAN INDIANS, NORTH; ESKIMOS).

5. AUSTRALIA. The AUSTRALIAN ABORIGINES belong to a dark-skinned, wavy-haired group, sometimes called the Pre-Dravidian or Australoid, which includes some jungle tribes of India, the Sakai of Malaya, and the VEDDA of Ceylon (qq.v.). They have long narrow heads, and their broad noses, slanting foreheads, and overhanging brow-ridges show some likeness to

Neanderthal Man (*see* Fossil Man).

6. Oceania. The natives of the islands of south-east Asia and the Pacific may be broadly divided into three main groups: Melanesians in the larger islands to the west; Polynesians in the smaller islands to the east and in New Zealand; and Indonesians in the south (qq.v.). The Papuans of New Guinea have frizzy black hair, long heads, and dark skins, like the Africans. But while the Africans have smooth rounded foreheads, those of the Papuans slant back with prominent brow-ridges, more like those of the Australian native. The Melanesians are more mixed and more variable. Polynesians and Indonesians are still more mixed. They have straight or wavy black hair, roundish heads, and light-brown skins. Many Polynesians look very much like Mediterranean people. In the more northern isolated islands, often distinguished as Micronesia, Mongolian features are common— as a result, it is thought, of mixture with the Chinese and Malays, who have been voyaging from island to island throughout the Pacific for many centuries.

RATIONALISM is a way of thinking which assumes that truth should be sought by reason and reason alone. Put in this way, the statement seems obviously true—for what thinker would admit that the conclusions he had come to were the result of anything but reason? The difficulty is to define clearly what we mean by reason.

Rationalism is a movement which, from its beginnings in the 16th and 17th centuries, has had an anti-religious twist. For when men began to claim that reason had the right to examine every experience and belief, it was religion that objected most strongly to any such examination. For instance, the Church held that the doctrines of the Trinity and the Incarnation could not possibly be discovered by reason alone—they were revealed by God, and it was therefore impious to question them. Rationalists were similarly denied the right to free inquiry when they turned to the Reformed Churches; for though the authority of the Church had been to some extent discarded, the authority of the Bible had been put in its place, which meant that no statement to be found in the Bible, whether relating to history, natural science, or morals, could be questioned.

The 16th and 17th centuries saw the rise of modern science. The new method of examina-tion, hypothesis, and experiment was opening out a field of knowledge which seemed marvellous and unending. The complexities of earth and sky were apparently being unravelled and explained by the operation of a few simple laws. Little wonder that men, who had begun to see the fruitful results of following reason wherever it led, were not content merely to accept religious doctrines because Christians thought it irreverent to examine them. Consequently rationalism, in itself a wholesome and legitimate method of inquiry, turned largely into an attack on religion. The theory was developed that primitive man lived originally in ignorance and fear. Knowing scarcely anything of the world around him, he supposed its operations to be due to mysterious beings whom he called gods and demons. Then clever men began to exploit their fellows by forming priesthoods, purely for their own interest, and by demanding the performance of rites to propitiate the gods. Thus religions arose. But now, said the rationalists, the age-long darkness was being dispelled. Little by little the mystery of things was being unveiled, and soon men would be able to penetrate all the secrets of nature, and the need for religion would disappear.

Not all rationalists held this crude system of ideas in its entirety. Some, like Voltaire (1694-1778) (q.v. Vol. V), although he attacked religious doctrines and practices with bitter sarcasm, retained a belief in God—but a God so far off and inactive that he seemed to count for nothing in human life. In England there was a measure of toleration unknown on the Continent. Indeed, English thinkers have never been tempted by the extreme forms of rationalism, for example David Hume (1711-76) (q.v. Vol. V), who was perhaps the most thorough-going sceptical philosopher there has ever been, called into question not only the basis of our belief in God, but also of our belief in reason itself, and argued that we had no good reason for believing anything at all, either about the world of science or of morality. He therefore concluded that we rely more on habits of thought and customary ideas than strict reason, in living our lives.

But rationalism and scepticism, the refusal to accept what we are told just because we are told it, are very closely linked. And the effect the rationalists and sceptics had is shown by the preface to Bishop Butler's *Analogy of Religion*,

THE ROAD TO RUIN
Caricature of Bradlaugh leading his followers over a precipice. The popular view of Bradlaugh's rationalism

published in 1736, which was an answer to current criticisms of religion. He writes that it was now 'taken for granted, by many persons, that Christianity is not so much as a subject for inquiry, but that it is now at length discovered to be fictitious'. Therefore, the bishop continues, men 'set it up as a principal subject of mirth and ridicule'. The works of these writers appealed chiefly to educated people; but the works of THOMAS PAINE (1737–1809) (q.v. Vol. V) were written so as to be understood by the common man. In *The Age of Reason* Paine fiercely assailed the Bible stories and the Christian plan of salvation based upon them. In the 19th century, two lives of Jesus were published, each describing Him as a purely human person. The first, by a German philosopher, David Strauss, described Jesus as a figure around whom mythical stories, derived from Jewish history, had gathered. The second, by a Frenchman, Ernest Renan, is an account of a purely human life, written with great poetic and sentimental charm.

All these works were, in varying ways, rationalistic, and they aimed at destroying the traditional Christian belief. Other rationalists, such as Charles Bradlaugh (1833–91), sought to establish the right of the individual to believe what he

liked. In Bradlaugh's day atheists were bitterly attacked; but, largely through his efforts, laws were passed giving equal rights to all men, whatever their beliefs.

The world wars and the development of scientific thought have done considerable damage to the rationalistic notion of man's inevitable progress to perfection by his own reason. Both the theories of DARWIN and those of FREUD (qq.v. Vol. V) cast doubt on the notion that man is a wholly rational creature, far above the other animals by his power of reasoning. For if we have gradually evolved from non-rational animals, and if, in our present state of evolution, much of our behaviour and thought is determined by unconscious and non-rational wishes, we cannot hope to isolate reason as the sole means of solving our problems. Nevertheless rationalism had, and still has, a service to perform. A Christian would say that it was no more irrational to believe in God than to be deeply moved by a scene of beauty or by music and poetry, or to love one's neighbour as oneself, or to give up one's life for another. The Christian holds that reason should be used as far as human reason will go, and always with the recognition that there is some truth which can only be reached by the heart and the soul, not by the mind alone. Christians hold that this is a perfectly rational point of view. However, just as in a home where, although the indispensable and unchangeable things are love and loyal companionship, there is often an undue attachment to certain externals—long-used articles of furniture, for instance, which might well be replaced; so religion is apt to confuse its externals—sacred books and ministers, customs, and rites—with the faith of which these are the expressions. All these externals are open to examination by reason: and religious people should feel no resentment when they are so examined. But where the rationalist differs from the Christian most fundamentally is in holding that religion, which springs from the inevitable attempts of man to grasp the meaning of his life, can be eradicated from the human heart.

RED INDIANS, *see* AMERICAN INDIANS, NORTH.

REFORMATION. The religious movement in northern Europe in the 16th and 17th centuries, when many Christians broke away from the Catholic Church and the Protestant Churches were founded, is known as the Reformation. During the Middle Ages the Church, with its centre at Rome, had been the single religious authority throughout Western Christendom. There had been attempts to reform the Church by such men as WYCLIFFE (q.v. Vol. V); while others like John Huss (*see* MORAVIAN CHURCH) had broken away from its authority; but their influence had been comparatively small and local. In the 16th century conditions were changed. The medieval attitude of respect for authority was giving away to an individualism and belief in man's right to think for himself. The growth of nationalism was replacing the earlier idea of a unified Christendom, and the Papacy no longer had the support of the kings and princes. The RENAISSANCE (q.v.) brought with it a new spirit of inquiry which led to the exploration, not only of new lands and sciences, but of philosophy and religion. Humanist scholars studied the Bible in its original texts: ERASMUS (q.v. Vol. V) not only made a new translation of the Greek New Testament into Latin, the common language of scholars, but commented on the text, pointing out where the practice of the Church differed from the original teaching of Jesus and St. Paul.

Men also protested at the abuses which had grown up in the Church. The Popes had become worldly, and their luxurious courts were maintained by money, extracted from rich and poor all over Europe, which should have been used for the Church. The most flagrant abuses were, first, the sales of indulgences, whereby men could buy absolution from sin and safe-conduct to Paradise, and, secondly, the sale of benefices, whereby priests and bishops could buy appointments or benefices.

At first, those who protested against these abuses sought only to reform the Church, and had no wish to break away from it. But those who depended for wealth and position on the continuation of the abuses, resisted the attempts at reform, so that determined reformers, like LUTHER in Germany and CALVIN in Switzerland (qq.v. Vol. V), had to choose between the authority of the Pope and that of the Bible. They chose the latter, and their teaching soon brought them thousands of followers. The rulers encouraged the reformers, or Protestants, because they were anxious to escape the temporal authority of the Church, and many coveted the riches of the bishoprics and monasteries.

In England the authority of the Pope rather than the doctrine of the Church was disputed. Medieval feudalism had been replaced by a national state, and the king claimed the right to be head of the state in spiritual matters as well as temporal (*see* CHURCH OF ENGLAND). In the Latin countries of Europe—France, Spain, and Portugal, Italy, and the southern Netherlands (now Belgium)—Protestantism made much less headway. After the middle of the 16th century there was a great reform movement within the Roman Catholic Church, known as the Counter-Reformation, which revitalized the Church, and ended the spread of Protestantism. This led to a century of religious wars in France (*see* HUGUENOTS) and Germany, which ended in deadlock in 1648.

The modern Ecumenical movement towards Christian unity drew together Protestant sects in the World Council of Churches (1948). Since the Second Vatican Council in the 1960s, the Council has gained a degree of co-operation from the Roman Catholic Church.

See also CHRISTIAN CHURCH.

REINCARNATION, *see* HINDUISM (4).

RELIGION. This is a very difficult term to define because it covers such a variety of customs, beliefs, and ideas, that no single definition would explain all of them. But, broadly speaking, whatever else it may be, it certainly springs from the belief that over and above the present world in which we live and move and have our being there is another order of existence of some kind which influences life on earth and its inhabitants. This very general statement needs to be filled in with many descriptive details to explain the different aspects of religion, but it provides a starting-point for a survey of this large and complex subject.

Thus it is better to avoid any reference to God or gods or 'belief in spiritual beings' in our definition, because, before the human mind was capable of forming ideas of individual spirits or gods, there can be little doubt it reacted in a religious manner to a sense of awe and mystery and wonder in the presence of strange and peculiar happenings, such as an earthquake or volcano in eruption, a mighty storm with thunder and lightning, or indeed to any event or object that appeared to be 'extraordinary' and inexplicable. Primitive man, like Jacob at Bethel, when he was confronted with some mysterious and awe-inspiring occurrence, was conscious, as is many a modern person today, of a stirring within him which found expression in the cry, 'How dreadful is this place'. And without forming any particular theories about it he was aware that 'the other world' had somehow burst into 'this world'. Therefore it was 'the house of God' and the 'gate of heaven'; but the word 'god' is hardly likely to have had any meaning more clearly defined than that of something sacred or set apart from the ordinary and commonplace and belonging essentially to 'the other' order of being.

This type of experience, very prominent among primitive folk, is found among all people at all times. It is the way the mind or spirit of man works everywhere and at all times, when the sense of wonder and awe is aroused by some beautiful scene or striking event in nature, by music, art, or any act of worship in the right setting. From it comes a realization of our personal needs and of our inability to provide for them without aid from 'outside' ourselves, that is, from the 'other' world. This belief is most easily expressed in terms of concrete beings; hence the idea of spirits and gods and all the beliefs that have grown up around them (see MYTHOLOGY). Furthermore, if man is to be

brought into relation with and get help from this source of strength, he must think of some ways and means of obtaining it. Consequently, his beliefs find expression in sacred actions or rites which enable him to establish beneficial relations with (a) the other world, (b) the universe, and (c) human society, This, in fact, is the principal purpose of religion in all states of culture from the lowest to the highest. Let us, therefore, very briefly examine these three relationships.

1. MAN'S RELATION WITH THE OTHER WORLD. This is twofold. First, there is his own personal life and its needs from the cradle to the grave. Secondly, there are the wider relations in which the human race as a whole, or a particular group of human beings, is involved. As regards the first, as soon as a baby is born it has to be translated, as it were, from the other world into a family on earth, since most people have believed that the soul is either a special creation or a new birth from some earlier existence (see BIRTH CEREMONIES). But having been given his proper place and status in the family, he still remains a 'child of God', as we should say and, therefore, his spiritual needs have to be satisfied by the prescribed rites described in the article on RITUAL (q.v.). Some of these are purely personal, concerned with the private needs of the individual. Others have a wider meaning, inasmuch as every child born into a family is also a member of society as a larger whole (i.e. the tribe or the nation). Thus, when he reaches adolescence, he is usually initiated into the adult fellowship of his social group or secret society, or becomes a 'confirmed' member of his church (see INITIATION CEREMONIES). To this end he undergoes a mystical experience which brings him into very close touch with the other world, and this contact has to be maintained for the rest of his life by the regular use of the prescribed rites, ceremonies, sacramental signs, acts of worship, and prayers. These, of course, vary according to the state of culture in which a person lives. They may be very crude and materialistic, or they may be highly mystical and spiritual, but the underlying purpose is much the same in each and every case, namely, to bring man into relation with the other world in order thereby to gain strength and power to live well in this life and the next.

2. THE UNIVERSE AND THE OTHER WORLD. But human life is lived on earth and governed by natural laws, which, according to the religious view of the universe, are under the control of the

THE MASS OF ST. GILES

Painting by the Master of St. Giles (15th century)

higher powers. For the religious man, therefore, these mysterious forces have to be approached with reverence and humility, since it behoves him to walk humbly before his God. The magician, on the other hand, unlike the priest and worshipper, relies mainly on his own supernatural powers to bring about the results he desires. Instead of seeking the help of the gods by prayer and sacrifice to do for him what he cannot do for himself, the medicine-man or worker of magic imitates the processes he is trying to control in the belief that, by so doing, he will produce the desired effects. Thus, a rain-maker does not pray to the rain-gods to send down water from above. His business is to make the rain and, therefore, he stages a dramatic performance with the actions and noises suggesting a storm (*see* MAGIC). Although a magical rite of this kind is not a religious exercise in the proper sense of the word religion, it is in some ways rather like it, so that in practice magic and religion frequently overlap.

Thus, for example, when Israel is said to have prevailed in a battle against the Amalekites so long as Moses stood on a hill with uplifted hands holding the rod of God (Exod. xvii. 9 ff.), it is not easy to be sure whether this was an act of religion or magic. The attitude of holding up the hands is that of prayer, but from the account it seems that it was the mechanical action of raising and lowering the arms that produced success and failure in the battle below, and that would be magic. Or, again, in Tibet, the Buddhists fix strips of paper containing prayers on a cylinder which is made to revolve, in the belief that by constant repetition the prayers will be answered. These examples show how readily the two ways of trying to get the help of the other world overlap. Magic, however, is really foolish because, while it is not unreasonable to believe that if God made the universe He should control its laws and operations in accordance with His divine will and purposes (since without Him it could not at any moment exist), for man himself to try to do this by his own supernatural powers is futile. That is why civilized communities of today have given up magic in favour of the control of nature by the scientific method.

3. SOCIETY AND THE OTHER WORLD. Besides the individual needs of man and the affairs of the universe, people have thought that human society itself is divinely guided and ordered. Thus among primitive people the laws, customs, and social organization are believed to have been ordained by the ancestors and heroes of the tribe in a Golden Age long ago, before these had left the earth and retired to the outer world. Therefore anyone who breaks the laws brings punishment from heaven upon himself and disaster on the community. Among the strictest rules are those regulating marriage, so that to marry a person belonging to a group akin to your own is a dreadful crime, second only to that of shedding the blood of a kinsman, because it is a breach of the right ordering of society laid down by the ancestors, totems, or gods, who control all things on earth as well as in heaven. According to CONFUCIUS (q.v. Vol. V), the Chinese sage, the most important of all social duties is that which everyone owes to his parents, and from it he derives all other virtues. Above everything else this is the will of Heaven.

When all law and government are thought to be of divine origin, it becomes difficult to change established customs and to bring about reforms when they are badly needed. Nevertheless, the belief does give a definite standard of right conduct, and holds society together. It has been by following tribal customs and obeying the laws of society, in fact, that man has developed a moral standard. The precepts have not always been good, but they have seemed to be right for those who have been bound by them, and so they have become for them a standard of value—and morality begins with judgements of this kind about right and wrong. In this way human beings have been brought together into communities, and have learnt to be concerned with the welfare of others.

The purpose of religion has been to provide a standard above that of this world for the right way of thinking and acting, both as individuals and as members of a group. Thus Moses, through a special divine revelation, welded Israel into a nation; and more recently ISLAM (q.v.), by a similar revelation, has become a widely dispersed yet unified civilization. Both Jews and Muslims are held together because their lives are ordered by divine command. When the Roman Empire began to fall to pieces, it was the CHRISTIAN CHURCH (q.v.) which took its place as the unifying centre of a new and higher order of society. And today many people are looking to religion to supply the spiritual foundations on which the world may be rebuilt.

See also GOD; SATAN; AGNOSTIC.

RELIGION, PREHISTORIC. The first evidence of man's spiritual life appears some 50,000 years ago at the Neanderthal stage of human evolution, during the last cold phase of the Ice Age. Deliberate burials, accompanied by goat or bear skulls, have been found in a few instances; while one skeleton from Iraq had apparently been covered with flowers. From 20,000 B.C. onwards small naked female figurines are found, and also at this time the first representations of animals painted on the walls of caves or rock-faces. These were sometimes in almost inaccessible places and are often associated with traces of ritual: the animals no doubt featured in the myths of the hunting peoples who drew them, and the female figurines symbolize fertility and the pleasures of sex.

Man the hunter was succeeded by man the farmer, and already in the earliest-known farming villages there is always one building, larger than the rest, set aside as a shrine. Each household, however, still had its own figurines and small cult objects. In western Europe groups of people performed their rituals around large collective tombs of huge stones (megaliths). Also in this period, and continuing into the Bronze Age, groups of villages gathered at sacred spots for seasonal fairs, where trade and

THE GREAT MOTHER
This figure probably represents the goddess of a prehistoric fertility cult

religion went together.

In the Iron Age we first have direct accounts by classical authors of the beliefs of the tribes to the north. Thus Caesar writes of the existence of human sacrifices among the Germans, and describes the Celtic priestly caste, the Druids. In the long-established urban societies of the Near East, religion in the Bronze and Iron Ages had a very different character. Here the temples were often centres of secular power also, and temple stores were the basis of the economy. Indeed, it is the archives and accounts of these temples which are the first use of writing, and mark the beginning of historic times (*see* ANCIENT CIVILIZATIONS).

See also PREHISTORIC MAN.

RENAISSANCE. 1. This is the name given to the civilization which began in Italy in the 14th century, reached its height in the 15th, and spread to the rest of Europe in the 16th and 17th centuries. The word means 'rebirth' and refers to the rediscovery of the ancient civilizations of Greece and Rome, which was one of the characteristic happenings of the Renaissance. But, in fact, that was only one of the things discovered at that time, for it was a great period of discovery of all kinds—of new worlds, new scientific laws, new kinds of art, and, above all, new strengths and possibilities in man himself. It would be better to define the word Renaissance as 'new birth', and even that would not be quite correct, since the Renaissance grew naturally out of the Middle Ages and was not a sudden occurrence.

The Renaissance is the beginning of the modern world. It was then that people began to think as we think today, and the foundations were laid on which our philosophy and our knowledge of the universe and of science are built. The nations of Europe came into being, and with them national languages and literatures. The forms of literature and art which were invented then are still in use today, and the political, economic, and religious ideas which govern our lives were first formulated then.

In the early Middle Ages, when life was precarious and unsettled, man had lost faith in his own ability and judgement, and relied on the teaching of the Fathers of the Church and of the classical authors, in so far as they survived. It follows that the civilization of the Middle Ages is based on tradition, to which every new discovery and development was referred. Later,

Alinari

STATUE OF GATTEMELATA AT PADUA

Bronze statue by Donatello (1383–1466). This figure of a Condottiere or General is one of the earliest Renaissance statues. The arrogant pose, the truthful portraiture, and the Roman costume all express the humanistic outlook. It is also a technical achievement, being the first full-size equestrian portrait to be cast since Roman times

men's ideas grew beyond this rigid tradition, and, at the beginning of the Renaissance, it was finally overthrown. There followed a period of immense activity and brilliance. Never before nor since have there been so many men of genius or men with such universal talents. Never have men dared so much and achieved such great results. It was in Italy, which had not been so fully immersed in the ideas and traditions of the Middle Ages as had the people of northern Europe, that the Renaissance first flowered. The first scholars, explorers, scientists, and artists were all Italians, though other countries soon followed their lead.

2. THE NEW LEARNING. During the Middle Ages the works of some of the Greek and Roman writers and philosophers had been read. This happened particularly in the time of the Emperor CHARLEMAGNE (q.v. Vol. V) at the end of the 8th century, when he tried to revive the culture of the Romans by encouraging the copying of their books and works of art. But few of these manuscripts continued to be read, and by the end of the Middle Ages much of classical literature was unknown.

The first scholars of the Renaissance, such as PETRARCH (q.v. Vol. V), found in Latin writings an outlook much the same as their own. Therefore they began to search for manuscripts which had lain buried in the libraries of monasteries for hundreds of years, to study and copy them and to make them widely known. All educated people could read Latin because it was the common language of the Church and of scholars throughout Europe, but very few could read Greek. In the 15th century some Greek scholars came to Italy and taught the Italians Greek, and when the Turks captured Constantinople in 1453, more came as refugees bringing manuscripts with them.

The scholars, or humanists as they were called, found in the ancient writings authority for their new ideas. Most fundamental of these was a belief in the power and dignity of man, which led to a new interest in the physical world. This was very different from medieval philosophy, which emphasized that man was insignificant with no power of his own apart from God, and that therefore this life was unimportant, except as a preparation for the next. The humanists believed that these new ideas were reconcilable with Christian belief; and the Church, too, encouraged the new learning. But when scholars such as Colet and ERASMUS (q.v. Vol. V) turned their trained minds to studying the New Testament in Greek, they discovered how far the Church had departed from the teaching expressed in Christ's actual words, and the revelation led to the REFORMATION (q.v.).

Though the belief in Latin as the only language of scholars died hard, interest in the new learning spread so much that soon there was a demand for books in the national languages. The timely invention of PRINTING (q.v. Vol. IV) in the 15th century made it possible to make books far more quickly and cheaply than before. The fact that many more people could now afford to buy books encouraged many more people to learn to read. Happily some of the greatest writers of all time were alive to write for this new reading public. Ariosto and Tasso wrote in Italian. CERVANTES wrote *Don Quixote* in Spanish. RONSARD, RABELAIS, and MONTAIGNE wrote in French; while in England, even those who could not read, could listen to CRANMER's fine collects and prayers in church and to the rolling blank verse of MARLOWE and SHAKESPEARE in the theatre (qq.v. Vol. V).

3. THE AGE OF DISCOVERY. The new life of the Renaissance not only stimulated scholarship, but also influenced the practical affairs of life. The new sense of man's strength and power, as well as the growth of trade and wealth, made men look beyond the Old World of Europe and the Near East to the unexplored countries of south and east. The urge to explore was stimulated by the vast profits gained by Venice and Genoa from their monopoly of the goods brought to Europe from India and the Far East by the old overland trade routes. After the fall of Constantinople, new routes to the east which would by-pass Turkish lands were needed. The European nations with an Atlantic seaboard tried to find them. Prince HENRY THE NAVIGATOR encouraged exploration, and Bartholomew Diaz found his way southwards round Africa. COLUMBUS and, later, many others sailed westwards to reach the east, and discovered the New World of America (qq.v. Vol. V). Later, English explorers tried to reach the east by sailing round the north of Europe. But they did not get farther than north Russia (*see* EXPLORATION, Vol. IV). These explorers were followed, as explorers nearly always are, by traders and missionaries who took Christianity to the heathen but also brought back treasures to their patrons.

THE SCHOOL OF ATHENS

Alinari

Painting by Raphael (1483–1520) in the *Stanza della Segnatura* in the Vatican, Rome. This painting is a tribute to classical learning; Plato and Aristotle are discoursing in the centre while around are groups of classical scholars

4. SCIENCE. The reborn spirit of inquiry was not confined to geography, but extended to all the sciences. When the Polish astronomer COPERNICUS, about 1500, argued that the sun was the centre round which the planets and Earth revolved, the way was pointed to many new astronomical discoveries. About a hundred years after Copernicus the German KEPLER, after observing and studying the orbit of Mars, established the laws which govern the movements of the planets; and the Italian GALILEO (qq.v. Vol. V) was able to show with his telescope the truth of the theory Copernicus had arrived at.

Biology, chemistry, and physics were all studied with equal fervour. Plants and animals were collected, described, and grouped. Nothing was too large or too small to escape man's curiosity. In spite of his disapproval of the Church, VESALIUS (q.v. Vol. V) dissected the human body and by his discoveries revolutionized the theory of MEDICINE and the practice of

SURGERY (qq.v. Vol. XI). Francis BACON (q.v. Vol. V) by his rejection of Aristotelian principles, and by his invention of inductive LOGIC (q.v. Vol. I), established modern scientific method, and paved the way to the founding of the Royal Society.

5. ART AND MUSIC. Not only humanists and scientists but composers and artists were stimulated to make bold experiments. In music the OPERA and the ORATORIO were invented, and a whole range of secular music, including madrigals and instrumental music, became popular (qq.v. Vol. XII).

The first great artists of the period, BRUNELLESCHI the architect, DONATELLO the sculptor, and MASACCIO the painter (qq.v. Vol. V), laid the foundations of Renaissance art. Human character was studied in portraits, figures were made more life-like by the study of anatomy, and settings more real by the use of perspective. Classical buildings suggested new forms for architecture. Art was of the greatest importance because it expressed the glory of man and his achievements, even when the subjects were religious. The great artists, ALBERTI, LEONARDO, and MICHELANGELO (qq.v. Vol. V) were not only architects, sculptors, and painters, but poets and scientists as well. In other countries the same spirit grew, though it was more limited than in Italy. In Flanders painters concentrated on the detailed representation of men and things, and the German HOLBEIN brought a similar interest to England. It was not until the 16th and 17th centuries that the full meaning of the Italian Renaissance was realized in northern Europe, when INIGO JONES brought classical architecture to England and RUBEN's painting in Flanders was based on his study of the Italian painters. DÜRER carried the spirit of the Renaissance to Germany, and Francis I of France brought Italian artists to his court at Fontainebleau (qq.v. Vol. V).

The achievements of this wonderful age seem to bear out the proud assertion of Alberti, 'Men can do all things if they will'.

RHODESIANS. There are about 4·9 million Africans, 234,000 Europeans, and 25,000 Asiatics in Rhodesia. The history of Rhodesia before the Europeans arrived is part of the history of the Bantu-speaking regions (see AFRICANS; SOUTHERN AFRICANS). The kingdom of Zimbabwe was, between the 11th and 15th centuries, the home of the Shona peoples. The Adebele (Matabele) settled in the southern part of the country. Conflict between the groups made the European conquest of the country easy.

Boer trekkers (Dutch pioneers) from the Transvaal and Scottish missionaries were the first Europeans to travel and settle in the country north of the Limpopo river. Some of these missionaries were also explorers—Moffat and LIVINGSTONE were the best known of them. Other explorers in the period after 1850, were STANLEY, Burton, and the great hunter Selous.

But it was not until Cecil RHODES (qq.v. Vol. V) used the money he had made at the Kimberley diamond-mines to develop this country that there was any settled European occupation. In 1889 he founded the British South Africa Company (or the Chartered Company) to develop the country between the Limpopo and the Zambesi and even farther north. This country was later called Rhodesia in his honour and 'Founder's Day' is its chief public holiday.

Lobengula, chief of the Matabele, gave Rhodes and his followers the right to prospect for minerals in his country, and most of the first men who went north from the Cape did so in the hope of finding 'New Witwatersrand', or goldfields. In 1890 Rhodes's friend, Jameson, took Mashonaland, where the town Salisbury was established, and in 1891 British prospectors gained permission to look for gold in Barotseland, north of the Zambesi.

They soon found gold, but only in small quantities. The proud Matabele, like the ZULU (q.v.) before them, began to regret the white man's presence, and in 1893 and again in 1896 tried to drive them out. Rhodes then went unarmed into the Matabele territory and persuaded the chiefs to make a permanent peace.

For the first 30 years or so Rhodesia was governed by the Chartered Company. In 1923 Rhodesia (then Southern Rhodesia) became a self-governing colony with its own elected parliament. In 1953 Southern Rhodesia, Northern Rhodesia, and Nyasaland together became the Federation of Rhodesia and Nyasaland. The Federation made possible some large achievements, such as the building of the KARIBA DAM (q.v. Vol. VIII). But the Africans in all three countries sought independence of European control, and in 1963 the Federation was dissolved. Its territories became three independent members of the Commonwealth, MALAWI (former Nyasaland), ZAMBIA (former Northern Rhodesia), and RHODESIA (qq.v. Vol. III).

Rhodesia went back to being a self-governing British colony. The white Rhodesians formed a united political front, led by Ian Smith, and were soon demanding complete independence. The British government did not want Rhodesia to become independent unless Africans were granted equal rights. The United Nations and many Commonwealth governments supported the African cause. Nevertheless, Rhodesia made a unilateral declaration of independence (U.D.I.) in 1965, which Britain did not accept.

The United Nations Security Council called upon all nations to stop trading with Rhodesia. In 1966 and again in 1968 talks were held between Britain and Rhodesia, with no success. In 1970 the Smith régime declared Rhodesia a 'republic'. Britain declared this illegal. In 1971 Britain again offered to negotiate but only if the basis proposed for independence was acceptable to the people of Rhodesia as a whole.

Camera Press

RHODESIANS BREWING MAIZE BEER NEAR THEIR HOMES

Africans particularly resent the Land Tenure Act (1970) which gives the same amounts of land for a European Area and for an African area, although Africans outnumber Europeans by twenty to one.

The most important food crop in Rhodesia is maize (corn), the staple food of the Africans. Tobacco is the most valuable export crop. Other crops include millet, wheat, ground-nuts, cotton, and sugar beet. Dairy-farming is important.

The most valuable minerals are asbestos, gold, and copper; chrome and coal are also mined. Since U.D.I. Rhodesians have increased their manufacturing industries quickly, to compensate for their loss of imports. Most of the Africans still exist by subsistence farming. In 1970 only 725,000 of them worked for wages, over a third of them on the land. Practically all the manual labour in mines and on farms is done by Africans, the white man being the owner, manager, or foreman. White Rhodesians run the civil services.

All educational services are under one ministry, but there are separate African and non-African primary schools. The University of Rhodesia at Salisbury has a thousand students, of whom some 360 are African.

Africans are working for majority rule in Rhodesia, but their leaders have been imprisoned for long periods. There are three African political parties struggling for the liberation of their country, and though they are divided on many things, they agree that they do not wish to be called Rhodesia. To Africans of all parties, their land, ancient before Rhode's schemes, is known as Zimbabwe.

See also Vol. III: RHODESIA.

RIG-VEDA, *see* SACRED BOOKS, Section 2.

RITUAL. This is a way in which a religious observance, such as a baptism, wedding, or funeral, is carried out according to a prescribed order. The ritual of a wedding, for instance, includes the words spoken and the actions performed by the priest or minister and his assistants, together with the singing of the choir (if there is one), the responses of the congregation, the acts of the bride and bridegroom—such as the joining of hands, the giving and receiving of the ring, and in some countries eating from the same dish, and similar customs suggesting the idea of uniting two people together—and the bestowal of a blessing upon the union. Without some kind of ritual religious observances could not be carried on at all, since the whole routine and method of holding a service is, in the broadest sense, a ritual. The rite may be long and complicated, as in the coronation of a king or the singing of the solemn High Mass on Easter Day in the great cathedral of St. Peter's at Rome; or it may be very short and simple, as at Evensong in a village church. But whether the things done and said are elaborate or simple, the performance of them is a ritual.

In primitive society people find it easier to 'dance out their religion' than to talk about it, and so their rites consist mainly of actions. Since everywhere simple folk more readily express the things that affect them most deeply in actions than in words, they tend to rehearse their experiences, hopes, and fears in a sort of pantomime, in the belief that by so doing they influence what actually happens. They are not interested in the problems that perplex philosophers and profound thinkers, such as what are the causes that lie behind the universe and the way things behave in this world. They are quite content to seek and find a religious satisfaction for their emotions in the performance of rites which represent, by signs and actions, their inmost desires and wishes. And this applies to ordinary people all the world over and at all times.

Thus, for example, in Greece the common folk were not in the least attracted by the reasoning and speculations of Plato and Aristotle, and they had not much use for the stories of the gods related by Homer, except as good tales. What really thrilled and gripped them were the sacred dramatic performances, or mystery plays, held in secret, amid signs and circumstances calculated to produce an intense sense of wonder and awe, in which mysterious lights, sounds, objects, and processions played an important part. This ritual re-enacted the ancient myths of famous heroes, such as Demeter and Persephone, Dionysus, or Attis and Cybele (*see* GREEK MYTHOLOGY), who passed through death to a new and fuller life, in order that those who beheld these sacred sights and took part in the rites might themselves undergo a similar experience—namely, be reborn as new creatures.

It was, in fact, in rites of this nature that the drama began. We go to the theatre to be entertained; the Greeks and other ancient people went for religious reasons—to obtain blessings on the

Haddon Library, Cambridge

THE DANCE OF THE ELAND BULL

A Bushman tribal dance. The dancers pretend to stalk the prey while women sing and clap their hands

DIONYSUS RITUAL

At the rites held in honour of Dionysus, the god of wine, women danced themselves into a frenzy round the effigy of the god.
From an Attic vase painting, 5th century B.C.

country and renewal of their own spiritual life, such as we seek in the sacraments in church. The word 'drama' means 'the thing done' or 'performed', and originally the action was in honour of a divine being, like Dionysus the hero of one of the Greek mystery cults, or secret societies. In much the same way, in the Middle Ages, the mystery plays were part of church ritual, like the greatest of all sacred dramas, the Mass. These medieval plays, indeed, grew out of the words spoken and the actions performed at the altar in the church service, until gradually they became separate performances. But they never lost their ritual character. In Greek drama, comedy was the ritual of life directed to making the crops grow, while tragedy was the ritual of death and decay in nature and in human existence. Together comedy and tragedy told the story in a ritual manner of life emerging from the grave. This same theme is found again in the mumming plays, and it lies behind Christian ritual in its most important and characteristic forms.

In this mystery type of ritual the general pattern is the same. A divine hero is born and, when he grows up, he fights an adversary, is himself killed or wounded, but is restored to life, often to fight again, this time victoriously. A sacred marriage follows with a triumphal procession in which the hero-king, dressed as God, with a train of lesser gods, is the chief figure. The details vary, but the outline and purpose are the same everywhere. Under the ritual form of the dying and rising god, supernatural power is set free to meet every kind of human need in this world and the next—birth, marriage, and death, sowing and reaping of crops, and, in the higher religions, the corresponding needs of the immortal spirit of man in its passage from life through death to new life. At every turn life is needing a fresh outpouring of life, natural and supernatural (see SACRIFICE). It is this which ritual supplies. Therefore, an annual festival has been held from time immemorial, either in the spring or autumn, to secure by ritual, wealth, prosperity, and health throughout the coming year. But man has never been completely satisfied to labour only for the good things of this life. In the higher religions, therefore, while the general ritual pattern remains the same, it has been used to meet the needs of the spirit rather than those of the body. Ritual has, therefore, been used from the earliest times up to the present day to minister to the religious wants and cravings of human beings in their various stages of development.

See also RELIGION; FESTIVALS; MYTHOLOGY.

ROMAN CATHOLIC CHURCH.
Members of this Church call themselves simply 'Catholics', and claim to belong to the whole Church, not to a sect which has broken away from it. (Other Christians deny that breaking from the Pope prevents them, also, from belonging to the Catholic Church.) There are about 550 million Roman Catholics, about half the total number of nominal Christians.

The official head of the Church is the Pope—Bishop of Rome and originally one of the five Patriarchs of the Early Church before the split between East and West (see ORTHODOX EASTERN CHURCH). The Pope is believed to be 'infallible' —which means that, when as Christ's Vicar (Representative) on earth he defines a doctrine, he can make no mistake. There are altogether 2169 dioceses of the Roman Catholic Church, each ruled by a bishop who is usually nominated by the Pope himself. The Pope and the bishops form a single college, considered to be the successors of St. Peter and the other Apostles. The clergy are required to remain celibate (unmarried). The Pope is elected by the Cardinals, who usually choose one of their own number. Cardinal means 'chief': they were originally the chief bishops, priests, and deacons in the diocese around Rome. About one-third of the Cardinals are Italians. There are about 126 Cardinals, only some of whom reside in Rome; they help direct the affairs of the Church throughout the world. Usually the senior Archbishop of a country is also a Cardinal.

Since 1968, ten committees, called Congregations, assist the Pope in the government of the Roman Catholic Church; each Congregation has a Prefect or President, who is always a Cardinal. The Congregation for the Doctrine of the Faith, which used to be known until 1968 as the Congregation of the Holy Office, is responsible for matters of doctrine and morals. Before 1908 it was known as the Congregation of the INQUISITION (q.v.), set up in 1542 by Pope Paul III. (This Roman Inquisition should be distinguished from the various national inquisitions such as the notorious Spanish Inquisition.) The Congregation for Bishops deals with defining the boundaries of dioceses and appointing bishops, except that, in those areas where there are Eastern Churches in communion with Rome, this is directed by the Congregation for the Eastern Churches; and in missionary areas, by the Congregation for the Propagation of the Faith. There is also a Council for the Public Business of the Church, which coordinates the activity of the Congregations and conducts business with civil governments; and there are two Secretariats, one for the Union of Christians and one for non-believers. The Congregation of the Index, which used to censor all books and list all those thought to be dangerous to faith or morals, no longer exists, and the Index itself has been abolished.

The Roman Catholic Church holds that Christ instituted seven SACRAMENTS (q.v.) by which God's grace comes to its members through the redeeming work of Christ in his Passion and Death on the cross and his Resurrection. The central service is the Mass or Holy Eucharist, in which the Church unites itself with Christ in his offering to the Father and renews itself in communion with Christ its Head. The services were until recently mainly in Latin, but are now generally in the local languages. As well as the old Latin translation of the Bible, the Vulgate (see TRANSLATIONS, Vol. XII, Section 2), the Roman Catholic Church now makes use of the many modern translations from the original languages of the Bible. The Church plays a central part in the lives of its members, although Church discipline and organization are no longer as strong and centralized as they used to be.

The unity of the Church in the West was not seriously challenged in the Middle Ages. From the 16th century onwards, following the REFORMATION (q.v.), northern Europe became mainly Protestant. The Reformation was followed by the Counter-Reformation, in which the Roman Church reformed itself and gathered together its forces to resist attack and to spread Christianity farther afield. The Council of Trent (1545–63) reformed many of the abuses which had helped to cause the Reformation, and stated more precisely than before what were the doctrines of Roman Catholicism. In 1540 the Society of Jesus (Jesuits) was founded, and this powerful and zealous organization played an important

POPE JOHN XXIII BEING CARRIED INTO ST. PETER'S, ROME

The procession of 10,000 persons, including 2,500 Vatican Council Fathers, files across St. Peter's Square, Vatican City

part in attacking Protestantism in Europe and, above all, in carrying Christianity along the newly discovered routes across the world (*see* IGNATIUS LOYOLA, Vol. V).

From A.D. 756 the Pope was not only head of the Church, but also ruler of a part of Italy called the Papal States. When, however, the various states of Italy became united into one kingdom in 1870, this temporal power of the Pope came to an end. In 1929 the Vatican Palace became the Vatican City, a sovereign independent state of 109 acres: this meant that the Head of a universal Church was independent of the political control of any one state.

In the past, particularly in the 18th century, the Roman Catholic Church has been thought of as the enemy of political and intellectual freedom. This was because of its close alliance with those monarchies which seemed most likely to preserve the state of society in which the Church had been an unquestioned power. Since the

Second Vatican Council (1962–65), summoned by the lovable Pope John XXIII and brought to an end under his successor Paul IV, the Church has embarked on far-reaching reforms in an attempt to adapt itself to modern needs, and is still undergoing profound transformations.

See also CHRISTIAN CHURCH.

ROMAN CIVILIZATION. 1. Our own civilization, before the Industrial Revolution and the advance of scientific knowledge, was largely the product of ideas about art, literature, law, religion, and philosophy that came to us through the Middle Ages and Renaissance from the Roman Empire. Hence the more we know of this the better we understand the origins of our own civilization. But the Roman Empire itself was a mixture of earlier civilizations. Rome absorbed all the civilized states that had existed earlier around the Mediterranean, including Greece, Carthage, and Palestine. She protected their ideas and handed them on. Thus a great part of Roman civilization simply consisted of Greek art, literature, and philosophy, with the addition, rather later, of the Christian religion. What Rome herself contributed was mainly the art of politics and GOVERNMENT (q.v. Vol. X). The history of her Republic, with its long struggle between the forces of freedom and dictatorship, became part of the European tradition, and had a real effect on the education of liberal and revolutionary leaders up to the 19th century. The history of the Roman Empire revealed a wonderful skill in the management of conquered peoples. From the constitution of the Republic many modern republics, including the United States of America, have taken basic ideas such as the veto, the block vote, and the rigid division of powers between independent ministers and assemblies (*see* REPUBLIC, Vol. X). So the first thing to know about Rome is something of her history. Her Latin literature, too, though less original, became the immediate model of early European poetry, drama, and prose, and her architecture lived again in the classical style that dominated Europe from the Italian palaces of the Renaissance to the banks and town halls of the 19th century.

2. ORIGINS AND EXPANSION. In the 5th century B.C., when Greek civilization was in its mid-course, the Romans were the local leaders of an obscure league of rather primitive peasant communities dwelling in the Flat Land, or Latium, of the lower Tiber valley, and in the surrounding foothills. These 'Thirty Peoples', as they were called, all spoke Latin. Rome gradually absorbed into a single 'city-state' other neighbouring folks dwelling in the western lowlands southwards as far as Naples, and thus she became the largest 'city-state' known in ancient times.

But the conquest of the whole Italian peninsula was a more difficult and lengthy task. To the north in Tuscany dwelt the Etruscans, a far more civilized people than the Romans (*see* ETRUSCAN ART, Vol. XII); while in the Appennines and eastward to the Adriatic lived tough and simple peoples such as the Samnites. In the far north numerous and warlike Celts inhabited the plains of the river Po; while in the far south along the coast there were Greek colonies with an Hellenic civilization, which came to be known as Magna Graecia. It was not until 280 B.C. that the Romans had brought these

people largely under their control, and formed them into a powerful league of free 'allies'. Their loyalty was immediately tested—and seldom found wanting—by the invasion of the Greek king, Pyrrhus, and again some 60 years later by the far more terrible invasion of the Carthaginian general, HANNIBAL (q.v. Vol. V). Hannibal came close to destroying the Roman people and the freedom of Italy. But the high courage of the Roman leaders, such as Fabius the Delayer and Scipio the Thunderbolt of War, and the loyalty of the Italian fighting men, remained unbroken by frightful defeats at the Trasimene Lake and at Cannae. The Romans won in the end, carried the war into Spain and Africa, and founded in 202 B.C. the first small overseas dominions of an empire.

During the next half-century the strong Greek kings of the east, Philip V of Macedonia and Antiochus, ruler of Asia Minor and Syria, intrigued with Rome's enemies and drew Rome into a series of wars, which by 146 B.C. made her the supreme power of the entire Mediterranean. It was left to the generals of the late Republic and early Empire, Pompey the Great in Asia and Spain, Julius Caesar in Gaul, and Augustus and Tiberius in the Alps and the Balkans, to bring all the world from the Rhine and Danube to the Euphrates and the Sahara under the direct rule of Rome. Only Britain was left to be conquered by the Emperor Claudius in A.D. 43 (*see* Map, INDEX, p. 52).

3. INTERNAL GOVERNMENT. By about 133 B.C. the wars of conquest were beginning to affect the internal life of Rome and Italy. The free Italian 'allies', who provided two-thirds of the Roman armies but benefited little from the long wars, were angry at the way in which the government of Rome treated them as inferiors and interfered with their own affairs. There was a great rebellion, known as the Social War, in 90–89 B.C. Though Rome won the battles, she wisely gave equality of rights to the allies by making them all citizens of the Roman State. For the first time in history a great national state was created, in which nearly a million men had political equality and freedom before the law, and were governed by a republican form of government which they could control by votes.

The second effect of the wars was, unfortunately, the gradual destruction of this republican government. Rome had for centuries been ruled by annually elected governors, the consuls, who acted as generals, judges, and as heads of the administration. They were advised and often controlled by a council of elder statesmen, the Senate, which decided most questions of policy. Laws were passed, and the consuls elected, by assemblies of the citizens at Rome. But in fact the common folk in the assemblies had very limited power. They voted in groups chosen according to wealth or place of residence, and each group had a single block-vote. But the mass of poor folk had fewer block-votes than the rich, and consequently they had little influence over elections. Moreover, only wealthy men could become governors and senators. The masses had rather more power in the assembly that passed laws, for there they elected leaders of their own, called tribunes. In the early Republic these tribunes championed the rights of the masses or Plebs against the aristocracy or Patricians, and won the right for any 'plebeian' to be elected to the highest magistracies, and for their assembly to pass laws. Tribunes also had the right of veto, a Roman invention, by which they could forbid any action of an official at Rome which was against the interest of the citizens. But by 150 B.C. many plebeian families had grown wealthy and powerful, and formed a new aristocracy which shared the government with the patricians, exploited the Empire of Rome for its own profit, and oppressed the common people, especially the peasants. These 'nobles' tried to check the rising power of a new middle-class of business men who threatened their interests. The latter joined hands with the masses against the tyranny of the upper classes, and looked once more to tribunes to oppose the Senate. Most famous of these tribunes were the brothers Tiberius and Gaius Gracchus, who carried laws to improve the lot of the common people and to limit the power of the nobles (133-123 B.C.). This conflict between the Senate and the tribunes resulted in street riots and violence, which had never before been known in Roman politics; but most of the great tribunes were killed and by about 90 B.C. the Senate had gained the upper hand.

In the first century B.C. the nobles began to quarrel amongst themselves and so weaken the authority of the Senate. There was so much profit and influence to be gained by those who held the great military commands of the Empire that the leaders began to appeal to their armies for support against one another, and also to intrigue with tribunes against the Senate, in bids for power. The quarrels of the great generals Marius and Sulla, POMPEY the Great, and JULIUS CAESAR, led to a period of civil war which in fact broke the power of both Senate and people alike. Supremacy at Rome passed into the hands first of Julius Caesar, the Dictator, then of MARK ANTONY, and finally of Octavian who, by the victory of Actium in 31 B.C., became the sole master of the Roman world and, with the title of AUGUSTUS, ruled for over 40 years (qq.v. Vol. V). Augustus created a new form of government out of the ruins of the Republic, in which the power of the dictator was thinly disguised by the pretence of restoring the Senate as the Council of State, and the consuls and proconsuls as governors of Italy and some provinces. In fact, the Senate did what it was told to do by the Emperor, who controlled the armies and the largest provinces.

4. ART, LITERATURE, AND THOUGHT. When Rome became the capital of the known world she had no writers, artists, or thinkers. Greek teachers flooded to Rome, and Romans began to write Latin histories, plays, and poems on Greek models. Though the metres and the pattern of their epic and lyrical poems were adapted from Greek writers, the Italian character and outlook made itself felt. Roman poets wrote intimately about personal feelings, private life, and the countryside, and broke out into ironical or savage satire about human weakness in a way that was new. Though they borrowed stories of gods and heroes from the Greeks, they had a native liking for patriotic sagas; many Latin poems are about early Roman history, and the great epics have a religious feeling about the universe that suggests Shelley and Wordsworth. Roman plays about the love-stories of young men and histories about wars and politics follow a formal Greek pattern, except for Caesar, who reports his own *Gallic Wars* in simple language, and Tacitus, who wrote like a novelist about the wickedness of men and society. In the art of the spoken word, which counted for much in public life, the Romans notably CICERO (q.v. Vol. V), transformed Greek oratory into something more serious and magnificent. They invented the letter as a form of literature and wrote humane essays about goodness and happiness with less logic and more charm than the Greek philosophers. But the sharpest Roman minds preferred law to philosophy, and their

Italian State Tourist Office

THE RUINS OF THE ROMAN FORUM

The Forum was the centre of Roman life where public meetings were held and business transacted

clearest thinking is to be found, free from Greek influence, in the writings of the lawyers.

In sculpture and painting the Romans were closer to the Greek than in their literature, and much 'Roman' work from Italy was done by Greek craftsmen. But in architecture they transformed Greek technique by developing the use of the ARCH and VAULT (q.v. Vol. XII), and by exploiting a new and stronger kind of concrete. This produced a new style altogether, which we can see in the great bridges, aqueducts, amphitheatres, and public baths which still survive in many parts of Europe and North Africa.

5. ROMAN RELIGION. The common people believed in a throng of lesser spirits, each with power over a particular human activity; they also paid respect to the ghosts of dead kinsmen and the guardian-spirits of the living. But the safety of the State was thought to depend on the goodwill of certain great gods, such as Jupiter, Juno, and Minerva, who were placated by public feasts and ceremonies. The chief priest (*pontifex maximus*) became responsible for

carrying out the state religion, and he was assisted by various sacred persons to whom certain duties were assigned. The flamens attended to the sacrifices and cult of the various gods; the augurs took the auspices (*see* DIVINATION), while priestesses called the Vestal Virgins kept the sacred fire continually burning. Neither the great nor the lesser gods satisfied the Romans as a faith, and in time new religions from the east attracted men away from the old pagan customs to more spiritual beliefs. Judaism, Christianity, and, among soldiers, MITHRAISM (q.v.) competed for men's souls, and after a long period of persecution, Christianity eventually became under Constantine (A.D. 324) an official religion of the Empire.

6. THE EMPIRE. The Romans had several devices for winning, and holding for centuries, the support of the peoples they conquered. Either they left them free to manage the affairs of their cities or tribes by their own customs, lightly controlled by Roman governors, or they encouraged them to adopt the customs and

Levy et Neurdein, Paris

THE PONT DU GARD, NEAR NÎMES, FRANCE

The ruins of a Roman aqueduct, built at the end of the 1st
cent. B.C. or early 1st cent. A.D.

language of Rome and in time to receive the
privilege of Roman citizenship, so that their
leaders could become officials, senators, and
governors in the service of Rome. St. Paul, for
example, a man of Tarsus in Cilicia, was proud
to be both a Jew and a Roman citizen, and the
Emperors Trajan and Hadrian were senators
from Spain.

The vast empire was knit together by secure
communications. Fleets kept the seas safe for
shipping, and a network of fine ROMAN ROADS
(q.v. Vol. IV), built to move troops swiftly from
one war-front to another, made trade and private
travel easy. A postal service brought the emperor news from the provinces, and helped him
to plan their defence against the attacks of barbarians by controlling the thirty Roman legions
stationed along the outer frontiers—the rivers
Rhine, Danube, and Euphrates, and the Sahara
Desert. Thus protected, civilization prospered
in the many cities of the Empire, while Roman
law developed continually to meet their needs,
and common languages spread over the Empire,
Latin in the west, Greek in the east.

The remains of country 'villas' in the English
countryside, and of splendid palaces, theatres,
stadiums, and other town buildings in southern
Europe, still show the reality of that civilization
from which our own sprang. It was mainly a
town civilization, and rather materialistic.
Wealth, fashion, comforts, and amusements—

drama, bathing, and GLADIATORIAL GAMES (q.v.
Vol. IX)—counted for much. The pleasures of
the town were cheap or free. But the big local
families kept the masses well under control. For
the first time Europe saw the rise of a large
and wealthy middle-class scattered through
hundreds of cities, and with values not very
different from those of more modern times.
Although radical views in politics were not
tolerated, there was much toleration in matters
of conduct and belief; so long as no nuisance
was created, as by the Christians, a man might
have his private religion—though he must pay
nominal worship to the State gods. There was
great respect for individual rights and personalities. The Roman law gave every man a fair
trial, though penalties for crimes were much
more severe for the poor than for the wealthy.

7. DECLINE OF ROME. The hey-day of the
Empire gave way after A.D. 235 to 50 years of
civil war and barbarian invasions, with rival
generals trying to seize power. Towards the end
of the century DIOCLETIAN restored order and by
A.D. 323 CONSTANTINE (qq.v. Vol. V) had become absolute monarch of both the western and
eastern Empire. In the east he established a
second capital at Constantinople—formerly
Byzantium. In the next 100 years, however, the
attacks of the barbarians increased, and Rome
was thrice sacked by Goths, Huns, and Vandals
until, in A.D. 476, the western Empire finally
collapsed. In the east the BYZANTINE EMPIRE
(q.v.), Greek in civilization and Christian in
religion, held the southern Balkans and Asia
Minor for the next six centuries.

See also Vol. III: ROME.
See also Vol. IV: LATIN LANGUAGE.
See also Vol. X: GOVERNMENT; LAW, HISTORY OF.
See also Vol. XII: LATIN LITERATURE; ROMAN ART.
See also INDEX, p. 52 (Roman Empire); pp. 117-122
(Roman Mythology).

RUMANIANS. The people of eastern Europe
are for the most part Slavs; but the Rumanians
are Latin people, a fact of which they are very
proud. The Dacians, a Thracian tribe living
between the Carpathian mountains and the
Danube, were conquered by the Roman Emperor
Trajan in A.D. 106. Roman colonists followed,
and the country became the Roman province
of Dacia. The name Rumania or Romania
means land of the Romani or Romans. After the
Roman Empire gave up its lands north of the
Danube in A.D. 271, there followed a series of

migrations by GOTHS, TARTARS, HUNS (qq.v.), Slavs, and Magyars (*see* HUNGARIANS), all of whom left their mark on the Dacian people. The Rumanian language is a Romance language, though it bears many traces of the languages spoken by the peoples who passed through and settled in neighbouring lands.

In the 15th century the Turkish conquest of eastern Europe brought the people of Dacia under Turkish rule. It was nearly 400 years before they again became free, and during that time the country, lying as it does between Turkey and eastern Europe, was the battleground for wars between the Ottoman Empire and its rivals, Poland, Russia, and the Hapsburg Monarchy. The Danubian Principalities, as they were called, of Moldavia and Wallachia became partly independent in 1829. Between 1859 and 1866 they were united, first under Alexandru Cuza and later under Prince Charles of Hohenzollern-Sigmaringen who was crowned King of Rumania in 1881 when the country's independence was finally proclaimed.

The Rumanians took part in the First World War on the side of the Allies. Although they were defeated, the territory and population of Rumania was doubled by the peace treaty at the expense of Russia, Austria, and Hungary. These new provinces included many people who were not Rumanian by race or language: Germans, Hungarians, Bulgarians, Ukranians, and Russians were handed over to Rumania by the victorious Allies as part of the land they lived on. While most Rumanians belong to the ORTHODOX EASTERN CHURCH (q.v.), many of the new peoples of Rumania, particularly the Germans and the Hungarians, were either Roman Catholics or Protestants. This same settlement left nearly a million Rumanians outside the borders of their own country, in Russia, Yugoslavia, Bulgaria, and Greece. Rumania has also a large Jewish population.

The Seond World War saw Rumania again fighting, but this time on the side of the Germans. She was defeated and, in consequence, lost some of the territory gained in 1918.

The country now fell under the influence of the Soviet Union. The Rumanian Communist Party grew in power, and in 1947 Rumania became a 'People's Republic' ruled by the Communist Party. The new government introduced dramatic changes in the political, social, and economic life of the country and its people.

Rumanian Embassy

A RUMANIAN MASTER POTTER

Since 1964 the Rumanian government has been less dependent on the Soviet Union and has developed closer relations with other countries in Europe, the Middle East, and Asia.

In the past the great majority of Rumanians were peasants who lived and worked in the countryside. Their dress, which can still be seen today on ceremonial occasions, was very colourful and often decorated with gay, embroidered designs. Before the First World War the gap between the few rich and the many poor was very great. After the war the great landed estates were broken up and the land divided among the peasants. But an increase in the population and the hardship of a general depression in trade caused widespread poverty and misery before the Second World War. Since the Second World War a great effort has been made to improve the methods of farming, to set up modern industries —using Rumania's rich oil and mineral resources, and to provide better education. The standard of living of the poor has risen, and many peasants have left the countryside to take jobs in the factories in the many growing cities.

See also Vol. III: RUMANIA; INDEX, p. 153.
See also Vol. IV: ROMANCE LANGUAGES.

RUSSIANS. The people of the U.S.S.R.—the Union of Soviet Socialist Republics (q.v. Vol.

III)—are usually referred to as the Russians. In fact, the Russians and the closely related Slav peoples, the Ukrainians and the Bielorussians, are only three of some 160 peoples that live in the U.S.S.R. In the course of centuries they have lived side by side with the Mongolian peoples of the north-east (*see* SIBERIAN PEOPLES) and with the Turkic-Tartar peoples of Central Asia (*see* SOVIET CENTRAL ASIAN PEOPLES). This mingling continues today as people come west from the remote areas of the north and east for education. In 1970, however, these Slav peoples made up 74% of the population of the U.S.S.R., their republics, the R.S.F.S.R. (q.v. Vol. III), occupying almost three-quarters of the land. Russian is the official language of the Union. It is with the Russians proper that this article deals.

The Russians, Ukrainians, and Bielorussians are descended from a Slav people who originally came from the Carpathians and settled in about the 7th century in the middle and upper reaches of the river Dnieper. From ancient times peoples from Central Asia had moved over these plains leaving burial mounds, *kurgans*, as traces of their civilization. The Slavs, as they moved eastward, encountered the Scythians, a warlike people who were great horsemen, a characteristic of the peoples of the Russian steppes. The Scythians, however, had been much influenced by the civilization of Byzantium and China, with whom they traded, and they had built up simple but distinctive civilizations of their own. The Slavs, or Rus, as they came to be called (the word Russia does not appear until the 17th century), had to contend with ever fresh invasions of nomadic tribes from Asia, and to defend themselves against these peoples they built fortified towns along the Dnieper, which in course of time became centres of principalities. The invading tribes, however, were also traders, and the history of the first principalities of Rus is a mixture of fighting and trade; and the settled communities and growing cities often paid tribute to nomadic overlords. Tradition says that in the 9th century three of these cities invited three Varangian princes from Scandinavia to come to rule them and defend them from nomad invaders; and, indeed, whether invited or not, it is true that Scandinavian adventurers such as Rurik, ruler of Novgorod, did become their rulers and military defenders.

Christianity came to Russia from the BYZAN-TINE EMPIRE (q.v.), with which the Russians did a good deal of trade. The richness and beauty of the ceremonial in the ORTHODOX EASTERN CHURCH (q.v.) appealed to the Russian love of colour and drama. In the 10th century the Russian princess, Olga, was converted to Christianity, and by the end of the century her grandson, Vladimir, accepted Christianity as practised by the Orthodox Eastern Church for himself and his people. In the 11th century many beautiful cathedrals were built in KIEV and NOVGOROD (qq.v. Vol. III). When Constantinople and the Byzantine Empire were later overrun by the Turks, Russia became the centre of Orthodox worship.

The early Russian principality, Kievan Rus, left a great cultural heritage; to it belong the *Ancient Chronicle*, the *Kievan Chronicle*, the first collection of laws called *Russkaia Pravda*, and the epic *Slovo o Polku Igorieve* which tells the story of the struggle of Prince Igor against the Polovtsi. Borodin's opera *Prince Igor*, which contains the famous Polovtsian dances, is based on this.

During the 12th century invaders across the plains succeeded in driving the Slav peoples of Kievan Rus both westwards and also to the north-east, where the forest afforded more protection. In the 13th century the TARTARS (q.v.) of the Golden Horde overran the Russian plain and remained powerful till the middle of the 15th century. Their purpose in conquest was not to settle, but to secure wealth. This eventually caused their downfall because later they allowed the Russian princes, in particular the Prince of Moscow, to collect tribute for them, and thus to become sufficiently rich and powerful to be able to regain their independence. In 1380 Prince Dimitri Donskoi defeated the Tartars at Kulikovo. In the 15th century Moscow, under Ivan III, grew so strong that she conquered several neighbouring principalities and gained independence from the Tartars. In the 16th century Ivan IV, Ivan the Terrible, proclaimed himself Tsar of all the Russias. Moscow (q.v. Vol. III) was in a central position in the new kingdom. Merchants came to its markets from Western Europe, from Greece, from China, from Central Asia, and from India.

The next three and a half centuries were periods of expansion, of pushing outward from the Moscow state, and pushing back the Asian tribal leaders to the south and east, while bringing together the Slav lands in the south-west. Settled colonization was slow because of raids of Tartars and other nomads; but at each advance a series of frontier posts was built, and towards the end of the 19th century Russia was established in Central Asia, in the Caucasus, and in Transcaucasia. In the south-west during the 17th century Russia and Poland disputed with each other for control over the Ukraine, the lands of the lower Dnieper, and those of the lower Don, where Slavs had resettled; but in 1655 the Ukrainians finally accepted Moscow's protection. The power of the Moscow Tsars grew with expansion, and they became more and more autocratic. The Romanov family ruled Russia from 1613 to the revolution of 1917. PETER THE GREAT (q.v. Vol. V) wanted to bring west European culture to Russia and also to increase Western trade through the Baltic sea. For this end he visited Western Europe, working himself as a boat-builder in Holland. In 1703 he built St. Petersburg (now LENINGRAD) (q.v. Vol. III) and made it his capital. CATHERINE THE GREAT (1762–96) (q.v. Vol. V) continued this policy, and in her reign the whole of the Ukraine became part of Russia, and ports were opened on the Black Sea.

The Russian empire of the 19th century differed from contemporary states of Western Europe in several ways: the Tsar remained an absolute ruler; there was a very small 'middle class' and a small, though brilliant, class of professionals and intellectuals; the gap between the well-being and culture of the land-owning class and the peasants was very wide indeed, for the peasants were serfs tied to the land until 1861, and they lived in great poverty. Towards the end of the century industry grew rapidly, and the social evils which marked the Industrial Revolution a hundred years earlier in the West hit Russia. It was far more difficult for reformers in Russia than in Western Europe to carry through reforms by legal means, because under Tsardom reforms could come only from the Tsar. In consequence, reformers tended to become revolutionaries. Alexander II, besides abolishing serfdom in 1861, started to reform the systems of justice and administration, but he was assassinated by revolutionaries in 1881, and a period of reactionary government set in. Reform parties were divided between moderates who hoped to persuade the Tsar, Nicholas II, to bring about reforms, and extreme revolutionaries who

John Massey Stewart

GORKI PARK, MOSCOW

Chess is a national passion in Russia

thought that the whole system should be destroyed, some of whom developed their ideas from those of German Communists, notably KARL MARX (q.v. Vol. V). These were the Bolsheviks, led by LENIN and TROTSKY (qq.v. Vol. V). Reforms might have been carried through without serious violence and bloodshed had not Russia been involved in two disastrous wars, one against Japan in 1905 and one with the Allies against Germany in 1914–17. The hardships which this brought on the people were increased by the inefficient government of the Tsar. Both the Tsar and the German-born Tsarina were influenced by a vicious faith-healer, Rasputin. Even the murder of the hated Rasputin did not save the situation, and in March 1917 revolution broke out. The Tsar abdicated, but he and his young family were brutally murdered. In November 1917 Lenin became head of the revolutionary government of the Bolsheviks, and in March 1918 the Russians made peace with Germany. Civil war between the Bolsheviks and the monarchists and moderate parties raged until 1921, bringing famine and terrible suffering.

From 1921 to 1928 the Bolshevik (or Communist) government built up the Red Army and police force, and restored industry and agriculture. From 1928 STALIN (q.v. Vol. V), Lenin's successor, introduced the first of a series of five-year plans for industry and agriculture under tight state control. The Communists set up a union of sixteen soviet socialist republics, held together by centralized control from Moscow (which again became the capital). The central authority was backed by a police force with special powers; and an extremely thoroughly planned economy, enforced by the Communist Party, was worked out. This has put industrial development above all else, and has demanded from the people the acceptance of a low standard of living. The Soviet Union withstood the German attack of 1941 with incredible fortitude and, in spite of great losses and devastation, shared the allied victory. Four western republics (Estonia, Latvia, Lithuania, and Moldavia) were added to the Soviet Union.

The climate of northern and central Russia with its long severe winters and short dry summers, and the centuries of hardship suffered under serfdom, have given the people of Russia great physical endurance and the ability to bear suffering. These qualities have been tested to the utmost since the Revolution. Much self-sacrifice and good humour have been needed to rebuild a country after the devastation of two world wars, and to educate what was largely a pastoral and agricultural people in modern and often highly industrial ways of life. Much has been achieved; old industries have been expanded and modernized; new industries have been developed, and large new industrial regions created. Dams and canals have been built, and machinery for large-scale agriculture has been introduced. Illiteracy has almost entirely been stamped out, and there have been great developments in secondary and technical education, and in health services.

To do all this, the Russians have had to forgo many of the ordinary comforts of life familiar in Europe. Houses, clothes, household equipment are still scarce and uninteresting; though under Khruschev, who succeeded Stalin, life became much more comfortable. Food is rather dull and heavy. Working conditions are near to those in the rest of Europe. Large numbers of teenagers and students both work in a job and continue their studies—the employing authorities have to give them time off to prepare and take their examinations. Most married women work full-time, so pre-school groups and nurseries are numerous. Russia has entered the space age; Soviet cosmonaut, Yuri Gagarin, was the first man to orbit the earth.

Throughout their history Russians of all classes have shown a great love of their own country, its actual land, rivers, and trees. The idea of Rus—the Russian land—came several hundred years before that of a Russian nation. They love, too, music and colour; many Russian composers, for example TCHAIKOVSKY (q.v. Vol. V) among the classic, and Prokofiev among the modern, have used native folk melodies in their major compositions. It has been said that Russians are natural socialists—many of the great novels in Russian literature deal with social problems rather than with individuals; in theatres, the leading actor in one play is likely to have a small part in the next; and in ballet great attention is paid to the *corps de ballet*.

Russians and their way of life have been only imperfectly understood by the peoples of Western Europe. Russian novelists, however, such as DOSTOEVSKY and TURGENEV (qq.v. Vol. V), have left memorable studies of Russian characters, and many other Russian writers have given vivid pictures of periods of Russian history. PUSHKIN, for example, in *The Captain's Daughter* has described life in a frontier post in the 18th century; Lermontov in *A Hero of our Times* has depicted frontier life in the Caucasus plain of the 19th century, and TOLSTOY (q.v. Vol. V) in *The Cossacks* that of the Caucasian frontier in the middle of the 19th century. Russian writers today still possess this power of describing vividly Russian contemporary life.

See also Vol. III: U.S.S.R.; INDEX, p. 159.
See also Vol. X: COMMUNISM; RUSSIAN CONSTITUTION.
See also Vol. XII: RUSSIAN ART; RUSSIAN LITERATURE.

S

SACRAMENT. An outward and visible sign of an inward and spiritual grace. The word today is used of certain ceremonies of the Church, through which God gives His grace to man.

By the 12th century in the Western Church the ceremonies called sacraments had been fixed at seven: Baptism, Confirmation, Eucharist, Penance, Extreme Unction, Ordination, and Matrimony. The Eastern Church had a similar list. At the Reformation the Protestants were determined that only those sacraments 'ordained by Christ Himself', i.e. those with definite New Testament authority, should be accepted. They found only two, Baptism and the Lord's Supper. Though the Roman Catholic and Orthodox Eastern Churches still hold on to the seven sacraments, they, too, regard these two as of paramount importance.

1. BAPTISM. Washing as a sign of spiritual purification is common in many religions, and was prominent in JUDAISM (q.v.), especially when a Gentile was converted. Just before the ministry of Jesus, John the Baptist called Jews themselves to repent and be baptized, as a sign of a new start in life. It was not enough to have been born into the Chosen People: they must be reborn, and baptism was the sign of this rebirth. Jesus took over this custom, and His disciples baptized those who believed (John iv. 2). Jesus added the idea that the new life, which began at baptism, was made possible by the coming of God's Spirit (Acts xix. 2–5). Baptism is the ceremony whereby a new member joins the Christian Church. The denomination called BAPTISTS (q.v.) oppose infant baptism.

2. EUCHARIST. This is also called the Lord's Supper, the Holy Communion, the Mass. The evening on which Jesus was betrayed He ate a meal with His disciples, told them of His coming death, and blessed and broke bread and gave it to them saying, 'This is my Body', and offered them the cup of wine saying, 'This is my Blood'. He told His disciples to repeat this action in remembrance of Him. This meal ever since has been the central act of Christian worship. Many ideas are included in it: repeating Christ's action when He gave Himself for men; Christ's special presence; and men's communion with Him through receiving the bread and wine.

The idea of a fellowship meal to mark special occasions is found in many religions, the best known being the Jewish Passover. Christ came to fulfil, not to destroy, the Law and the prophets, and He brought to completion the ancient idea of SACRIFICE (q.v.).

3. CONFIRMATION. This is the sacrament through which a Christian is strengthened by receiving anew the power of the Holy Spirit, and by accepting personally the vows made on his behalf at his Baptism. In the West the outward and visible sign of this establishment of grace is the laying on of hands by the bishop. The ceremony takes place when the child is thought to be old enough to take his own vows. In the Eastern Churches confirmation follows immediately on Baptism. Oil, consecrated by a bishop, is used to 'seal' with the sign of the cross the brow, eyes, nose, mouth, and ears, as the sign that the Holy Spirit comes to the aid of all man's natural powers.

In most branches of the Church no Christian may receive Holy Communion until he has been confirmed.

4. PENANCE. Confession to a priest was advised in the early Middle Ages, as an aid to true repentance; later it became the rule, especially before communion. The priest fixes his penance —some act which will be a sign of repentance and, as far as can be, a putting right of the wrong done. Then he pronounces absolution.

5. EXTREME UNCTION. In the Eastern Orthodox Church this is the ceremony of anointing the sick with holy oil as a means of healing, and has come from a Hebrew custom. In the West it had, rather, the idea of forgiveness for the sins of the various senses (eyes, ears, lips, &c., which are anointed) in preparation for death; but Roman Catholics too now prefer to see this ceremony as a sacrament of healing.

6. ORDINATION. From the time of the Apostles, those who were to rule the local churches were appointed with the laying on of hands, the sign of a special gift of the Spirit for a special work.

In all episcopal Churches a bishop ordains deacons, priests, and also new bishops.

7. MATRIMONY. Christian marriage, as set forth in the New Testament, and always in the services of the Church, is marriage to one partner for life. 'Those whom God hath joined together let no man put asunder.' The outward and visible sign of this unity is the giving and receiving of a ring: the inward and spiritual grace is the sanctifying of married life by the power of the Holy Spirit.

See also CHRISTIAN CHURCH.

SACRED ANIMALS. Belief in the sacredness of certain animals goes back into the distant past, and is still found amongst many primitive peoples. To them, some animals seem much more powerful and a great deal wiser than human beings, and therefore able to bring blessing or misfortune to men. These ideas have led to a great variety of beliefs and rites in connexion with sacred animals.

Primitive people live in a way which is much closer to the animals than our mode of life, gathering or hunting food and living much in the open, as animals do. Naturally they feel that some of their animal neighbours are somewhat

British Museum

SACRED FIRE SNAKE

Aztec carving

like themselves. And they express this in myths and stories, in which animals behave like human beings and men turn into animals or animals into men. These very ancient ideas linger on in some of our FAIRY-TALES (q.v.) and myths, such as the swan-maiden legend—a story of girls transformed into swans, told amongst people in many places all over the world. In many of these stories an animal talks human language, like Balaam's ass (Numbers xxii. 28), and is regarded as wiser in some ways than men.

Stone Age men painted animals, such as deer, bison, and wild boar on the walls of caves, sometimes depicting weapons sticking into them. Their purpose, probably, was to increase magically the number of these animals and achieve success in hunting them. As a hunter, primitive man learned to respect animals which could outwit or kill him, and when he was successful against them, he believed that he had been aided by supernatural powers. But primitive people, who are impressed by the strength or craftiness of an animal, often go on from this to think of it as having greater and stranger powers than it actually has. Very often they do not know the real cause of quite simple things, and so they think, for instance, that because frogs appear with the rain, therefore the frog is a rainmaker, or that when a bird, such as the swallow, appears in spring, it has brought the spring. If they see a frightened hare dash out of the corn as they reap the last sheaves, they suppose it to be the corn spirit. The ancient Egyptians may have come to believe in the jackal god of the dead, Anubis, because they sometimes saw jackals stealing away from the tombs; and no doubt the beetle was regarded by them as a sacred insect, because it was seen emerging from the ball of dried dung in which the egg had been laid—thus appearing to be life from the dead.

Men worship and regard as sacred things which may do them harm, as well as things which seem to bring them prosperity, and they treat them very carefully lest they should be aroused to do evil. Animals are amongst the strange things of this kind. A snake, for instance, appears mysterious as well as dangerous. People often exaggerate the powers of things they fear or which mystify them. Animals, therefore, are believed to have supernatural powers or to be themselves supernatural beings, requiring to be appeased with sacrifices or other forms of reverence.

Ashmolean Museum

ANUBIS

Egyptian jackal god of the dead. Sculpture from Tutankhamen's tomb, XVIIIth Dynasty

Sometimes these ideas result in the belief that it is wrong to kill certain animals. Thus, in some Indian bazaars, the monkeys are a great nuisance, for nobody dares to kill them when they boldly steal food. Some peoples believe in a mysterious connexion between their various groups and certain animals, which goes back to the creation of the world. Such animals, called totem animals, are usually not killed or eaten by the group named after the totem animal. An Australian aborigine, belonging to the frilled lizard clan, regards this creature as sacred and calls it 'father' (*see* TOTEMISM).

There are, however, many animals which have to be killed for food or in self-defence, and people feel that they ought to apologize to them or in some way appease their spirits, lest they avenge themselves on those who kill them. So the hunter often has to observe TABOO (q.v.) to prevent evil, supposed to be caused by the animal spirits, from befalling him. The Ainu of northern Japan and some Siberian tribes slaughtered bears and feasted on them, but always took the precaution of performing various ceremonies, so that the bears' spirits would not seek revenge.

Reverence may be shown to animals in other ways besides worship. Amongst Mongolians, for example, the tiger is spoken of with a specially respectful name. In Ancient Babylonian and other carvings there are human figures with animals' heads. It is thought that these represent dancers or people taking part in ceremonies with animal masks. There is a Stone Age picture of what is believed to be a magician wearing horns on his head, and many primitive people have magical dances in which they imitate animals.

See also FOLKLORE.

SACRED BOOKS. 1. Among the earliest sacred writings known to us are the spells and prayers which were inscribed on the walls of burial-chambers in the pyramids of Egypt, about 2600 B.C. These are called the Pyramid Texts. Some 600 years later, in Egypt, another collection of religious texts occurred on the lids and sides of coffins, and these may be considered the direct ancestors of yet a third collection—the *Book of the Dead*—which, from the later period of Egyptian civilization to the Roman period (about 1580 B.C. to A.D. 300), was frequently copied out on papyrus, or inscribed upon the walls of tombs.

In Greece, in the pastures of Thessaly, probably before 1000 B.C., songs were sung in which were woven vague memories of ancient wars and of the gods who were thought to have had their home on Mount Olympus. During the next three centuries, after the songs had greatly increased in number, they were finally put together and, in this form, have been handed down to us as the poems that bear the names of Homer and Hesiod. At that time the Greeks had no other sacred books, and so the Homeric songs—the *Iliad*, the story of the Trojan war, and the *Odyssey*, the tale of the wandering hero (Odysseus) on his return from Troy—became virtually the 'Bible of Greece'.

2. HINDU SACRED BOOKS. The oldest sacred books in the world are the collection of hymns known as the *Rig-Veda*, which were put together in India between 1500 and 1000 B.C. in honour of the nature-gods whom the Aryan-speaking peoples brought with them when they first entered the Punjab about 1500 B.C. (*see* INDIAN CIVILIZATIONS, Section 2). The term *Veda* means knowledge or wisdom, and the Hindus believe that these hymns are inspired songs, which were revealed to the seers as magical words of power, like the Egyptian texts. The *Rig-Veda* is about five times larger than the book of Psalms in the Old Testament, and contains 1,028 hymns grouped into ten books, for recitation by the priests at the sacrifices. The tenth book is much later than the rest, and contains more profound thought. It is believed that the Vedic hymns had been handed down from father to son in the families of the seers who composed them, and their contents were kept secret and never written down at the time of their composition.

Later, a number of instructions in matters of ritual were added to the hymns for the guidance of the priests or Brahmans, and these are called the *Brahmanas*. Since divine power was in the sacred words, the words had to be uttered quite correctly by the priests, otherwise the spell would be broken. Between 800 and 600 B.C., hermits began to try to find a way to escape altogether from the world, which they regarded as evil, by bringing their souls into tune with the divine soul of the universe. They began to break away from the old Vedic beliefs about nature gods and magical spells, and became seekers after the absolute, eternal, divine principle, which is also the world-soul into which every individual spirit is merged (*see* GOD). This 'secret Doctrine' was set forth in the *Upanishads* —a word meaning 'sitting close to' or getting into communication with the inner meaning of life. These beliefs took a great variety of forms, and there are some 250 *Upanishads*, many of which represent different Hindu schools of thought about 'Brahman' as the world soul (*see* HINDUISM).

3. BUDDHIST SACRED BOOKS. These doctrines, however, did not satisfy GAUTAMA, the Buddha (q.v. Vol. V) (born about 560 B.C.), who, as a result of his remarkable spiritual experience, which is called his 'enlightenment', discovered what he and his followers believed to be the true solution of the problem of existence and the mystery of pain and sorrow. The oldest books that tell of his life and teaching were not completely put into writing until about 500 years later. Very likely they go back in the oral memory of the Buddhist community much farther than this, and some of the materials from which they were formed may have come from the

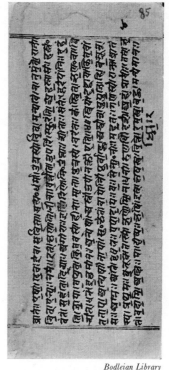

Bodleian Library

PAGE FROM THE RIG-VEDA
From a 17th-century MS.

first disciples of the Buddha, perhaps even from his own lips. But how much of these scriptures, called the *Tripitaka* or 'Three Baskets of Tradition', goes back to his time we cannot be certain. They were written in Pali, the dialect of the common people of north-west India, and contain twenty-nine subdivisions, ranging in length from 10 to 1,839 pages. Only some of them have been translated into English, but, when the text is complete, it will probably occupy 10,000 pages. Besides these authorized scriptures, there is also a large quantity of Buddhist literature in Sanskrit; but none of the writing claims to be a divine revelation, because in Buddhism there is no idea of a personal God who discloses Himself to man. Nevertheless, both in Hinduism and Buddhism a devotional movement arose in course of time, in which God was thought to have descended to earth in human form, as Krishna or one of the Buddhas. The story of these 'descents' is told in the great Hindu *Bhagavad Gita*, 'the Song of the Blessed One' (Krishna), and in the Buddhist *Lotus of the True Law* (*see* BUDDHISM).

4. CHINESE SACRED BOOKS. In China and Japan the sacred books are mainly 'the records of ancient matters', as one of them is called by the Japanese, in which the history of the nation is traced back to the mythical 'age of the gods'. The Chinese venerate the words of good rulers and wise men, because they are believed to have been raised up by Heaven to rule and teach men how to live well. One of these great teachers, CONFUCIUS (q.v. Vol. V), collected the literature of China and put it into four books, which have ever since been the *Classics* of the Chinese. These are *The Book of History*, *The Book of Poetry*, *The Book of Ceremony*, and *The Book of Changes*. The only work that Confucius wrote himself was a short history of his state of Lu, which is the fifth of the *Classics*. The rest are accounts of the traditional history of China, rules of behaviour and worship, folk-songs, hymns, and a book of the Sayings of Confucius, known as the *Analects*. Another Chinese wise man, Lao-Tzu, thought to have been born some 50 years earlier (*c.* 607 B.C.), is the supposed author of a short but important book of wisdom. The writer of this book expresses his belief that the 'Way of Heaven' or *Tao* is the divine order that runs through everything, and that if one lived quietly and acted according to this principle, one would be happy and blessed (*see* CHINESE RELIGION).

5. ZOROASTRIAN SACRED BOOKS. We must turn, however, to Zoroastrianism, Judaism, Christianity, and Islam to find sacred books which are believed to contain a divine revelation through the written words of scripture. Thus, the *Gathas* or Psalms of the *Avesta*, the Zoroastrian Bible, are thought to contain the records of the visions and revelations of the great prophet of Persia (who lived about 600 B.C.). In fact, only seventeen of those that remain go back to his time. The rest of the Avestan sacred books are later hymns in praise of angels and ancient heroes, and accounts of ceremonial rules concerning purifications and protection against demons (*see* ZOROASTRIAN).

6. HEBREW SACRED BOOKS. In Palestine, after the return of the Jews from exile in Mesopotamia in 538 B.C., the leaders of the community collected the ancient writings and, as is explained in the article on the BIBLE, divided them into three groups—the Law, the Prophets, and the Writings.

Besides these authorized sacred books, which make up what is known as the 'canon', or official scriptures, the Jews had other religious documents, described as *The Apocrypha*, portions of which, in addition to the canonical books, are appointed to be read in Christian churches. Some of these, such as *The Wisdom of Solomon* and *The Wisdom of Jesus, Son of Sirach* (*Ecclesiasticus*), are full of very beautiful literature. The books of the *Maccabees* describe the great struggle of the Jews for liberty in the 2nd century B.C., which played an important part in preparing the way

Bodleian Library
PAGE FROM THE ANALECTS OF CONFUCIUS
One of the earliest printed copies. Sung Dynasty, *c.* 10th century A.D.

for the events described in the New Testament (*see* JUDAISM).

In 1947 an interesting discovery was made in Transjordan. A dog belonging to an Arab disappeared into a cave near the Dead Sea and when its master followed it he found jars filled with manuscripts written in an unusual script. A further search in the district brought to light another ten of these so-called Dead Sea Scrolls. Those originally discovered include part of the text of the book of Isaiah, a commentary on the prophecies of Habakkuk, a number of quotations from other parts of the Old Testament and from later Jewish writings, together with an account of the rules of a Jewish sect that lived on the shores of the Dead Sea, about 150 B.C.–A.D. 70. What is probably the latest scroll, the commentary on the first two chapters of Habakkuk, seems clearly to reflect events about A.D. 70 when the Romans captured Jerusalem. The scrolls show that a standard Hebrew text then existed, hardly different from that drawn up by the 10th-century-A.D. guild of scholars known as Massoretes, except that they added vowel-points and accents to the consonants to ensure correct pronunciation. Several more scrolls have recently been found.

7. CHRISTIAN SACRED BOOKS. As Jesus left no written records, the accounts of His life, work, and teaching have come down to us in the form of narratives (i.e. Gospels), collected from various sources during the second half of the 1st century A.D. It is commonly thought by scholars that some of His teaching was written down in the form of a lost document (now called Q) that was known to the writers of the first three Gospels and from which they borrowed some of their material. To this they added stories about Jesus, His sayings and accounts of His mighty works, reserving for detailed treatment the sequence of events during His last few days on earth, from Maundy Thursday evening until Easter Morning (*see* BIBLE).

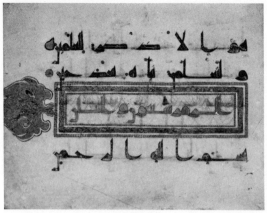

PAGE FROM THE KORAN
12th-century MS.

All the books of the New Testament were written in Greek, some fifty fragments of early Greek manuscripts having been discovered in recent years. The famous *Codex Sinaiticus*, for example, dates from the early 4th century, and there is a fragment of *St. John's Gospel* which is thought to have been written before A.D. 150. The Coptic Museum in Cairo has a collection of manuscripts which, after having been locked up in a suitcase for the past 10 years, are now being studied by scholars. Among them are a number of alleged sayings of Jesus occupying twenty pages, which are said to have been recorded by St. Thomas. Although these are called 'The Gospel of St. Thomas', they are not linked together in the form of a story, such as we find in the four Gospels printed in the New Testament. There is no account, for example, of the Crucifixion or the Resurrection, and they certainly were not written by the apostle St. Thomas. Besides this document there are several other interesting manuscripts in the collection, which include versions of a so-called 'secret revelation' of St. John, written between A.D. 130 and 140. It has been translated by an English scholar. Most of the rest of the collection of 48 writings are thought to have been the work of Gnostics, a Christian sect that flourished in the 2nd century A.D. When scholars have finished investigating these, we may expect some very interesting results which will throw new light on early Christianity.

8. ISLAMIC SACRED BOOK. The *Koran* (Qur'an), the 'Bible' of ISLAM (q.v.), is believed by Muslims to contain the words of Allah dictated to MU-HAMMAD (A.D. 570–632) (q.v. Vol. V) in Arabic from a book kept in Heaven. Some Muslims think, however, that, while the teaching was revealed to the Prophet, the language was his own. The Koran consists of many stories borrowed from the Old Testament, later Jewish writings, and the Christian apocryphal Gospels. But it is generally believed by Muslims that the revelation given to Muhammad has superseded the truth given in the Bible. Since these revelations describe things that the Prophet could not have learnt or known unless Allah (God) had revealed them to him, they are regarded as 'miraculous'. So the Koran is for Muslims the most sacred book in the world, containing, as they firmly believe, the last word of God to mankind.

SACRIFICE. The name given to the chief act of worship in most religions. It is the making of an offering to a divine being, in supplication for those who are making the offering. The sacrifice, however, can have a variety of purposes. Its purpose may be to establish a communion—that is, a joining of man and his god together in a very close bond of union. Its purpose may be to restore a relationship that has been broken by some improper act on the part of man (whether committed deliberately or accidentally) with harmful consequences. This driving away of evil, or covering it up with purifying blood, often forms an important element in the ritual or ceremony. In some religions sacrifice may be an act of thanksgiving for blessings received. The highest offering of all is the giving of self on behalf of others.

In sacrifice of the communion type a sacramental meal is very often held, in which the worshipper, in order to receive spiritual strength and power, partakes of food and drink which is filled with the divine life of the god. Before receiving this gift, the priest usually offers to the god the life-giving blood of the victim—for primitive people believe that the gods need new life, just as they need it themselves. Looked at from this point of view, sacrifice becomes of vital importance for the well-being of mankind and the world; for, unless the gods are kept healthy and vigorous, they will not be able to bestow their gifts on man. Victims, therefore, are slain on the altar so that the setting free of their lives may produce more life on earth, as well as to drive away evil, expel death, and restore the bond that has been broken by sin. The two chief objects of the ritual of sacrifice are the making of (*a*) an act of communion, (*b*) an act of reparation and amendment for some wrong committed, either by an individual or by the community. Behind both of these intentions is the same desire, namely to enter into closer and more beneficial relations with the source of all strength and power, and to remove everything that hinders and spoils this relationship, so important for the well-being of mankind.

To bring this about the victim has to be somehow identified with the god, so that his life is the same as the divine life. In the ancient civilizations and in many savage tribes the king was regarded as a god, living on earth as a man, or at least having a divine life different from that of anyone else. By his supernatural powers he controlled the forces of nature. If he became old or weak, the people believed that the crops might fail. To prevent this calamity, kings were often killed before they lost their full strength. Thus, they were required to give their own lives as a kind of sacrifice on behalf of the community over which they ruled, in order to renew the vitality of nature. But various attempts used to be made to find a substitute for the royal victim. For instance, a strong and healthy prisoner of war might be made into a mock king for a time (generally a year), and then, at the end of his period of office, he would be sacrificed at the altar instead of the real sovereign.

This custom was prevalent in central America among people like the AZTECS (q.v.), and relics of it are to be found in most of the ancient civilizations, where human sacrifice was very common. Nevertheless, since the practice has always been against the natural instincts of man, there has been a tendency to replace human beings by animals on the altar, as in the story of the offering of Isaac in the *Book of Genesis*. Among the Hebrews it seems that at one time human sacrifice was practised, and then, no doubt, the divine command of the God of Israel, 'the first-born of thy sons shalt thou give unto me', recorded in *Exodus* (xxii. 29), was carried out quite literally. The numbers of skeletons of children found in the foundations of buildings in Palestine suggest that infants were often offered as sacrifices to strengthen the walls of houses and cities. The Feast of the Passover appears to commemorate a general massacre of first-born; but this grim event came to be cele-brated every spring by the offering of a lamb or kid instead of human beings (Exod. xii; Deut. xvi. 1–8). The blood was then smeared on door-posts to drive away the forces of evil, which were supposed to be very active at that season of the year. For much the same reason, in the autumn a goat was slain, and its life-blood was sprinkled on the high priest, the sanctuary, and the whole congregation of Israel, while a second goat, the scapegoat, was sent into the desert, laden with the burden of the guilt of the nation, to carry it to a demon of the wilderness, called Azazel (Lev. xvi).

Thus, the institution of sacrifice centred in the idea of securing fresh life and driving away evil. As it has developed from these very crude beginnings, it has taken over other meanings, but they are all based on this general belief. For example, when the slaying of the first-born was no longer required among the Hebrews, they were allowed to pay a sum of money as an act of 'redemption' (i.e. buying back the victim that would have been offered) (Num. xviii. 15–16; Lev. xxvii. 27 f.; Ezek. xliv. 30). In this way the idea arose of paying 'tithe', or a tenth part of the first-fruits, in support of a sanctuary (Amos iv. 4; Lev. xxvii. 30, 32 f.). These offerings were made to the god or to his representative the king and were, therefore, holy (i.e. set apart), like the actual victim. But as soon as sacrifice became regarded as a gift of goods or money or the produce of the fields, it lost some of its earlier meaning, and it became very much easier for a rich man to buy off his sins by paying a sum of money than by making a real act of sacrifice.

In Christianity this conception is lifted on to a higher spiritual plane, when God is represented as offering Himself to take away the sins of mankind and to bring the human race into a new and closer relationship with Him. Thus, according to Christian beliefs, Jesus, as the Incarnate Son of God, laid down His own life in a supreme act of sacrifice to draw all men to God. To give oneself for the sake of others is the highest form of love, and this is what Christ did on the Cross (John xv. 13). So the outpouring of His life's blood represents the climax of sacrifice in both its aspects of renewing life and removing evil. This has been commemorated ever since in the central act of Christian worship, called the Eucharist or Holy Communion; although there are different views about the way in which the death of Christ is 'shown forth' in this service.

At first, it was mainly an act of thanksgiving before God for the blessing of Redemption. Later, it became more particularly a memorial of the offering on the Cross, repeated day by day at the altars on earth as an atonement for sin. Under the appearance of bread and wine Christ sacrifices Himself, as it were, in the same way that He offered Himself on Good Friday; and so the Mass became regarded as an act of propitiation to make God well disposed towards man. To some people this medieval view seemed to lay too much stress on the Eucharist as an act of sacrifice complete in itself, rather than as a memorial of what Christ had done Himself once and for all; and so, after the Reformation, the Eucharist was celebrated chiefly as a Communion service, in which Christians received the Body and Blood of Christ to refresh their souls. More attention now, however, is being paid to the sacrificial side of the rite, and it is generally agreed that in 'the Breaking of the Bread' (as the service was originally called by the Apostles) a memorial is made of the sacrifice of the death of Christ.

See also Religion; Sacrament.

SAGA, *see* Vol. XII: Saga.

SAHARAN PEOPLES (North Africa). **1.** The Mediterranean lands of North Africa have been the scene of many migrations, settlements, and conquests from prehistoric to very recent times. The Phoenicians, Greeks, and Romans colonized parts of the coast. The Arabs conquered these Mediterranean lands and converted the inhabitants to Islam (q.v.). Later, they were conquered by the Turks who, in turn, were driven out by the French in 1830.

South of the Mediterranean coast-line is the Sahara Desert (q.v. Vol. III), the largest desert in the world. It includes plains of hard sands, rock-strewn plateaux cut by dried-up water-courses, and series of mountain-ranges. Where large depressions occur in the desert, underground water often comes to the surface, and oases are formed where date-palms, fruit, vegetables, and millet can be grown. Some oases are small, but in many enough food can be grown to support a large number of people. The oasis of Taflit, in Morocco, for example, has a population of 50,000 people.

The north-west coastal region has a series of high mountain ranges, the Atlas mountains,

running from east to west, with a narrow coastal plain 80–160 km wide. Here, the climate is like that of southern Europe, with hot, dry summers and mild, rainy winters. In this region there are two main groups, the Berbers, who practise agriculture in the fertile river valleys, and for the most part live in permanent villages, and the Arabs (q.v.), most of whom are nomads, who live primarily off their livestock, moving from one place to another in search of fresh pastures for their flocks. The people of the Sahara, who are Muslims, with a few exceptions, are either Arabic speaking or Berber speaking; French is also spoken on the coast.

2. The Berbers. They are mostly agriculturalists, tradesmen, or nomads. The towns and villages of the agriculturalist Berbers have narrow streets with high flat-roofed houses (made of mud and stones) on both sides. Certain Berber communities combine farming with pastoralism; they plant their crops in the lowlands, and then move up into the mountains, taking their sheep and goats. There they live in tents, and when the harvest is ripe they come down again to their villages. Some Berbers who live in the Sahara oases raise dates, millet, vegetables, and fruits on land which they pay for not in rent but

Mansell

A BERBER HORSEMAN

on a sharecropping basis. There are also tradesmen who own, or work in, small shops in towns or markets, using their skills as leather workers, jewellers, weavers, or potters.

The Kabyles are fairly typical of the Berbers as a whole. They form a confederation of tribes in Algeria, Tunisia, and a few oases of the Sahara. They live in villages which are autonomous; a number of villages form a tribe, and a union of tribes forms a federation. Each village is made up of *kharouba*—that is, groups composed of a number of families. The village is governed by a *jamā'a*, a council of adult men

AN ARAB ENCAMPMENT IN THE SAHARA

Mansell

which meets once a week. It settles disputes within the village, the elders (heads of families and influential men) taking the principal part in the discussions. Each council elects a chief—generally a wealthy man from one of the leading families. Today the chief acts as the liaison with the government. The villages are also divided into two groups, known as *sofs*, at the head of which are rich and influential men. Members of a *sof* help one another in times of difficulty and when labour is needed for harvesting or house-building.

The villages are isolated and often built in inaccessible parts of the mountains for protection against raiders. Each family lives in one house. Descent is reckoned in the male line and most of the men have only one wife, though some have several. Ties between kinsmen are strong—a man's kinsmen used to be considered liable for crimes committed by him.

The Kabyles are an agricultural people, but, except in the river valleys, they have to cultivate poor soil. They keep sheep, oxen, donkeys, and poultry. They have two important crops, figs and olives, which are grown for local consumption and for sale. Another source of cash is the money sent to villagers by those who are working in towns. Nowadays young men leave the villages to seek employment in towns because of the poor opportunities in the villages. Moreover, educated Kabyles, both men and girls, are now to be found in the towns.

The Kabyles are good craftsmen. The women do some of the work on the land, and they also make pottery, weave, and embroider. Their jewellery work, some of it in silver enriched with coral, is excellent, and they wear ear-rings, necklaces, bracelets, anklets, and brooches.

Markets (*suqs*) play an important part in the economic and social organization of North African peoples. In some places large annual fairs are held, where goods from all parts of North Africa, the Sahara, the Sudan, and Morocco are exchanged. Most tribal groups hold weekly markets, and in these markets can be found traders in cottons and silk, sellers of groceries and fruit, grain merchants, and dealers in cattle and sheep.

3. THE ARABS. Typical nomadic Arab peoples are found farther east. Some are still true nomads, such as the camel-owning tribes, the Kababish and the Kawahla of north-west Kordofan in the Sudan. Others, like the Baqqara people who also inhabit Kordofan, are cattle-owning. The nomadic Arabs generally look down on the settled peoples, both Arab and Berber, just as the settled peoples, in their turn, dislike the nomadic way of life. Each Arab tribe is under the control of a head *shaikh*, and is made up of a number of groups, each with its own *shaikh*. Heads of tribes are responsible to their govern-

Paul Popper

EGYPTIAN *FELLAHEEN* WORKING ON IRRIGATED LAND BESIDE
A CANAL

ment. Generally, the position of *shaikh* is hereditary, though sometimes he is elected by the men
of the group. Descent in these tribes is reckoned
in the male line, and kinsmen co-operate in
economic and social activities. The Arab nomads
move in a regular cycle, each tribe within its
own particular territory.

4. NEGROES AND TUAREG. Many of the oases
of the Sahara are inhabited by negroid peoples—
the Haratin, for example, who are descended
from slaves; but most of the central Sahara is
inhabited by TUAREG (q.v.). The Haratin, who
have a low social status, are to be found in the
southern part of the Sahara where they work
mainly as sharecroppers in the agricultural
centres. The Tuareg are a camel-owning people
who were formerly feared as raiders of settlements and of caravans crossing the western
Sahara. Besides being nomads subsisting mainly
on camels, sheep, and goats, the Tuareg undertake caravan trading and some carry on agriculture. Tuareg men wear veils, without which they
cannot be seen in public; but the women do not
wear veils and they take part in public life. Both
the negro population and the Tuareg are
Muslims, and they speak various dialects of a
Berber language, *Tamaheq*.

5. TIBU. This is a distinct people who occupy
the Tibesti highland area farther east and south
of the Libyan Desert. They are Muslims and are
more negroid in appearance than the other
peoples of the Sahara. Most of the Tibu are
pastoral nomads. They keep camels, sheep, and
goats, moving their flocks from one place to
another following available pasture and water.
But some Tibu and other settled peoples in the
oases of the Sahara practise agriculture. Their
most important plant is the date-palm, which
supplies them with both food and wood. Many
Tibu nomads own palm groves to which they
return each year. The Tibu society is ranked in
the following order: nobles, vassals, smiths and
artisans, negroid serfs, and slaves. Caravan trade
is based mainly on the export of goats, salt, and
dates which are exchanged chiefly for millet,
cotton cloth, tea, and sugar, and for manufactured articles.

6. NILE VALLEY PEOPLES. The Nile valley was
the centre of ancient EGYPTIAN CIVILIZATION
(q.v.). In the 7th century A.D. it was overrun by
the Arabs who introduced the Islamic religion.
Modern EGYPTIANS (q.v.) are an intermixture of
ancient Egyptians, Arabs, and Turks. In the
Northern Sudan the inhabitants are an intermixture of the indigenous population with Arabs.
Those living in the Nile valley are mostly farmers
who occupy villages near the river. The soil of
the Nile valley is fertile and is irrigated either by
controlled flooding, as in Egypt, or by mechanical
pumps as in Northern Sudan. Apart from subsistence crops, including cereals and vegetables,
cash crops are also grown; in Egypt the principal
cash crop is cotton, and in Northern Sudan the
cash crops are citrus fruits, mangoes, and dates.

See also ARABS; ISLAM.
See also Vol. III: SAHARA DESERT; NILE VALLEY.
See also Vol. IV: AFRICAN LANGUAGES; ARABIC LANGUAGE.

SAINT. In the New Testament the word Saint
is used as meaning followers of Christ—people
made holy by their faith. Gradually the word
came to mean selected Christians of outstanding
holiness and courage. In A.D. 155 Polycarp,
bishop of Smyrna, was martyred: his people
buried him, and then gathered together every
year to celebrate 'the birthday of his martyrdom'.
This is the first example of the veneration of the
relics of a saint, and the keeping of a Saint's
Day. In the 4th century, when the Roman
Empire accepted Christianity, the custom of
venerating saints developed, because the idea of

paying honour to those who had suffered in the early struggles of the Church appealed to the people. The tendency to exaggerate the honour paid to saints led one Church authority to explain, 'We do not *worship* the saints, but venerate them as men of God.'

In the Early Church, when Christianity was brought to a new country, the missionaries sometimes turned the temples of the old religion into churches, and transferred heathen festivals to the honour of the saints. In this lay the danger that the saints might be worshipped as the local heathen god had been worshipped—a state of affairs little different from polytheism, and quite contrary to Christian teaching.

In the Middle Ages relics (or reputed relics) of saints established in shrines were visited by pious people on PILGRIMAGES (q.v.). The countries of Christendom each began to adopt a patron saint, generally someone connected with their history. The patron saint of Ireland, St. Patrick, was the missionary who brought Christianity to Ireland in the 5th century. St. David of Wales was a 6th-century archbishop of Caerleon. The adoption of St. Andrew for Scotland is less obvious. According to tradition the Apostle St. Andrew preached to the Scythians, and so became Russia's patron. There was a legend that a Greek bishop was directed by a vision to fetch a relic (an arm) from St. Andrew's grave in Constantinople. The bishop's ship was wrecked on the Scottish coast, and he landed and founded the Church and town of St. Andrews. A more likely reason is that a missionary went from an English church of St. Andrew in A.D. 732 to convert the Picts, and called the church which he founded by the name of his own church. St. George was martyred in A.D. 303 in Asia Minor. The Crusaders brought home stories of his aid in their battles; and this led to his being adopted in the 13th century as the English patron saint. His day, 23 April, is kept as the English national day.

Cities adopted a special saint as guardian, and so did trades and professions. Particular saints were thought of, generally as the outcome of a tradition or legend, as caring for man's welfare in some particular way. St. Christopher is the guardian saint of travellers, St. Nicholas cares for children, St. Anthony helps people who have lost things, St. Hubert looks after animals, and St. Blaise cares for those who have sore throats. People gave their children saints' names with

R. P. Howgrave-Graham

ST. LAWRENCE

The saint is holding the gridiron on which he was flayed. Figure from King Henry VII's Chapel, Westminster Abbey

the idea that the saint would look after the welfare of the child. The saint on whose day the child was born was considered as the child's patron saint.

Martyrdom was the usual qualification for becoming a saint. A new saint only becomes officially recognized or canonized in the Roman Catholic Church after very thorough investigation by the Congregation of Rites, and an official announcement by the Pope. A revised calendar of Saints' days was issued by the Vatican in 1969 with many changes, including the omission of forty-six saints' names formerly recognized. The veneration of saints plays an important part both in ROMAN CATHOLICISM and in the ORTHODOX EASTERN CHURCH (qq.v.). In Roman

Catholic churches there are generally many images of saints and side chapels dedicated to them. In an Orthodox Eastern Church icons—pictures of saints, painted or in mosaics—take the place of images and are considered sacred. In both churches prayers to God are often made through the mediation of saints. The Protestant churches hold that Christ is the only Mediator between man and God; and at the time of the Reformation there was a strong move against the veneration of saints.

See also INDEX, p. 113 (SAINTS).

SALVATION ARMY. This Christian organization preaches simply and persuasively the doctrine of salvation—that is, that a man needs to be saved from sin and to feel in his heart that God has saved him because he has repented. It is a movement with a strong missionary urge to save sinners, and sets about its task in a very practical way. Salvationists say that a man who is hungry and homeless is not likely to be interested in his spiritual needs until he has got food and shelter. They therefore lay great emphasis on social work, varying it from country to country according to the needs of the people. They run many different institutions, including hostels for homeless people, for students, for alcoholics, for unmarried mothers, and for old people; hospitals, orphanages, and maternity homes; and inquiry offices for lost and missing people.

The founder, William BOOTH (q.v. Vol. V), began preaching in street meetings in the East End of London in 1865, and quickly made converts to his Christian Movement. He had been a METHODIST (q.v.). In 1878 he re-named his movement the Salvation Army, and re-modelled it on the military lines suggested by the title. He became the first 'General', and the elected head of the Army still has this title. The members are called 'soldiers'. The full-time workers within the movement are highly-trained 'officers' who receive very little pay. There have always been women preachers as well as men. The first one was the founder's wife, Mrs. Catherine Booth, who was an excellent speaker, able to command large audiences. The *War Cry* is the official 'newspaper' of the Army. Music has always been very important in their worship; their brass bands and 'songsters' have long been familiar in British streets, and their 'pop group', the 'Joy Strings', has pleased many radio listeners

in the 1970s. The movement has spread over most of the world, but its international head-quarters is still in London.

SARACENS, *see* CRUSADES.

SARDINIANS, *see* Vol. III: SARDINIA.

SATAN. 1. Satan is the name that has been given by Jews and Christians to the chief spirit of evil and the great enemy of God and man. Sometimes he is known in a more general sense as the Devil, while Muslims call him Iblis. As he has many names, so he has a long history behind him, which goes back to the idea of a struggle between good and evil that has been going on ever since the world began. This conflict takes many forms, and we find examples of it in myths and fairy stories all over the world: the bad spirit engages in a fight or tussle of some kind with the champion of the friendly and helpful powers, who usually in the end defeats his wicked adversary.

2. THE DEVIL IN ANCIENT EGYPT. Ancient Egypt had long been divided into two kingdoms perpetually at war with each other; and the people were accustomed to live in a fertile oasis watered by the river Nile, and surrounded by a terrible desert. The distinction, therefore, between good and evil was a natural idea to them, and it found expression in their myths in the shape of two opposed forces—Set, around whose figure evil in its various forms had collected, and Osiris, the author of all life, who was connected with the life-giving Sun. Set murdered his brother Osiris, and became the model of the Devil as prince of the powers of darkness. The Egyptians, for instance, thought that Set tried to prevent the sun from rising in the sky at dawn; and as the enemy of mankind, they represented him as a huge serpent-dragon, having under his command all the fiends of the underworld. Night by night the never-ending fight between light and darkness went on, and in the changes in the seasons from winter to spring the same battle was fought between Set and Horus, the son of Osiris (*see* EGYPTIAN MYTHS).

3. THE DEVIL IN ANCIENT PERSIA. If the original idea of the Devil is seen most clearly in the Egyptian Set, it was in Persia that the picture of this struggle between good and evil reached its height in the imagination of the ancient

Mansell

SET, THE EGYPTIAN DEVIL

the Creator, Ahura Mazdah. Unlike Satan in Christianity or Islam, the Druj was thought to have under his control a crowd of demons, or *daevas*, whom he had actually himself created, together with harmful creatures such as serpents, wolves, locusts, ants, and vermin. Men of diabolical character, disease, magic, witchcraft, and similar evils were thought to be his agents—so that there were really two creations and two creators, one exercising his powers for good, and the other for ill (*see* ZOROASTRIAN).

4. THE JEWISH IDEA OF SATAN. It was probably under the influence of these Persian ideas that the Jewish conception of Satan took shape. At first, however, the 'Satan' in the Old Testament was regarded as one of the servants of God who, as a divine agent, was permitted to bring evil upon Job to test this righteous man (Job i. 6 ff.). Next, he is represented as the accuser of Israel as a nation (Zech. iii. 1 ff.), and is made responsible for leading David astray (1 Chron. xxi. 1). From being 'the Adversary' and 'tempter', he very soon became thought of as an evil spirit; and then, after the exiles returned from their captivity in Babylon, and Persian ideas had begun to spread in Palestine, he was transformed into the Devil, on the model of the Druj. Belief in evil spirits had been very prevalent among the Hebrews in ancient times, as among other Semitic people; and these included strange monsters, such as the winged serpents, the satyrs, ghouls, and a great mythical dragon called Leviathan. The serpent, who had long been regarded as the enemy of mankind, was a powerful 'demon of the waste' with almost divine knowledge (cf. Gen. iii. 1; Isa. vi). Therefore, when the world was supposed to be full of demons organized under the leadership of the Prince of Darkness, it was the serpent who was held responsible for having brought evil into creation by deceiving Eve in the Garden, although this was not the original meaning of the story in Genesis. But once the Satan and the serpent had been transformed into the Devil, the leader of the powers of evil was called by a great many different names, such as Lucifer, a fallen angel of light, Beliar (or Belial), Asmodeus, a Persian demon, and in the New Testament Beelzebub, an ancient god of flies. In later Jewish writings he was sometimes spoken of as a fallen angel, or as the great Prince in Heaven who came to earth to mislead the human race, and as an angel of death to take away their

world. There the central idea of religion was the warfare of the two opposed forces, who divided between them all the helpful and harmful powers in heaven and on earth, in nature and amongst men, as well as in the animal and vegetable kingdoms. Over and above these stood the good God called Ahura Mazdah. He alone had made the universe and he controlled it, but on a somewhat lower plane good and evil were arrayed against each other, represented by two primeval twin spirits, Good Thought (Spenta Mainyu) and the Lie (Angra Mainyu), with their respective followers. In course of time the twin spirits under one supreme God developed into a single author of evil, Ahriman or the Druj, who fought against, but was not as powerful as,

A MEDIEVAL SATAN AND DEVILS

Illumination from *Le Livre de la nostre Seigneur*. French, 15th century

souls. Nowhere, however, was he said to be on the same level as God, and it was always believed that he and all his works would be destroyed. Then God would finally triumph (*see* JUDAISM).

5. THE CHRISTIAN IDEA OF THE DEVIL. Since the first Christians were Jews, they had been taught to think like Jews before they became followers of Christ and members of the Church. But while many believed that sin came into the world through the Devil in the guise of the serpent tempting Eve in the Garden of Eden, actually Christ Himself says nothing about this in His teaching. He is recorded as having described Satan as the tempter of mankind, and He spoke as though some diseases were caused by demons taking possession of human beings. Indeed, the whole world was like a field in which an enemy had sown tares among the wheat—a mixture of good and evil, the work of God spoilt by the Devil. But if Satan was 'the ruler of this world' (John xii. 31), Jesus had conquered him

by resisting his temptations (Matt. iv. 1–12). In the last book of the New Testament, a striking picture is drawn of a war in heaven between God and his angels and 'the old serpent, the devil'— the deceiver of the whole world—and his hosts, in which Satan was cast out (Rev. xii. 7 ff.). At length he will be bound for a thousand years, imprisoned in the abyss or 'bottomless pit' (i.e. hell), and finally destroyed in a lake of fire and brimstone (Rev. xx. 2, 10). Borrowing the images and language of the late Jewish writers, the early Christians were expressing their own beliefs and hopes. Christ, they were convinced, had defeated the powers of evil, and although for a time Satan had been loosed and allowed to persecute the saints and martyrs, in the end his kingdom will be overthrown, and Christ and His Church will reign triumphantly for ever (*see* CHRISTIANITY).

6. SATAN IN ISLAM. In ISLAM (q.v.) the power of evil, called Iblis, is represented in the Muslim scriptures, the Koran, as an angel who was driven from heaven because he refused to prostrate himself before Adam when man was first created, believing that God (Allah) alone should be worshipped. But although Iblis is pictured as such a staunch upholder of monotheism (*see* GOD), he hates the human race, and therefore he has always tried to beguile men into serving other and false gods to their destruction. He cannot, however, compel the faithful to give up their faith. A man first becomes unfaithful, and then Iblis deprives him of the power to believe the truth about Allah. Among the other enemies of all that is good, Muslims recognize two persons in particular. One is Pharaoh king of Egypt, and the other Dadidjah the Anti-Christ, who will be destroyed at the second coming of Christ. Each of these three is said to work miracles; but, unlike Iblis, Pharaoh and the Anti-Christ claim to be divine.

See also RELIGION; GOD; HELL.

SAXONS, *see* BRITISH PEOPLES.

SCANDINAVIANS, *see* SWEDES; NORWEGIANS; DANES.

SCOTS. The name Scots belonged originally to the Irish, some of whom settled in mainland Argyll during the troubled period after the Romans withdrew from Britain. At that time, most of the inhabitants of the area now known as

Scotland spoke a language or languages closely akin to modern Welsh. The language of the Scots was Gaelic, and soon afterwards speakers of an Old English dialect established themselves in the area south of the Forth estuary. This dialect eventually developed into Lowland Scots. The use of the two new languages spread rapidly through the indigenous population, while political power came to be concentrated more and more in the hands of the Gaelic-speaking Scottish royal line.

By the late 12th century, the term 'Scot' meant 'inhabitant of the geographical area north of a line from Tweed mouth to Solway', and the connection with Ireland had been almost forgotten. The language of the Lowland Scots spread at the expense of Gaelic, and, since the 18th century at least, Gaelic had been unknown to the majority of Scots. Speech, however, still distinguishes Scot from Englishman and others.

The Celtic ancestry of many of the Highlanders has given them the romantic, poetry-loving qualities of other Celtic peoples, while the harshness of Scotland's climate and the poverty of her soil have developed in later settlers in the Lowlands a spirit of dogged endurance. Before the Norman conquest of England, Gaels, Norsemen, Danes, Angles, Saxons, and Flemings, all at one time raided Scotland, and many stayed to settle. Mary Queen of Scots brought a number of French in her court, when she returned from France in 1561; and Spaniards, shipwrecked on Scotland's rocky coasts when the Spanish Armada was fleeing from Drake, stayed to make Scotland their home. Englishmen, too, have crossed the border. Yet, whatever their origin, people born and bred in Scotland, or even remotely of Scottish descent, are intensely proud of their native traditions.

Throughout their history the Scots have shown a tough determination not to be mastered by their more powerful English neighbours. In the 13th century when EDWARD I (q.v. Vol. V) attempted to unify the whole of Great Britain, he met with stout opposition from the Scots. In the wars that followed, William WALLACE and Robert BRUCE (q.v. Vol. V) emerged as heroes of Scottish independence. A second attempt to draw the two nations closer together was made by Henry VII of England, when he married his daughter Margaret to James IV of Scotland. Two generations later, the rival claims to the English throne of Henry's grand-

J. Allan Cash

A PIPE BAND AT BRAEMAR GAMES, ABERDEENSHIRE

daughter ELIZABETH I and his great granddaughter, MARY QUEEN OF SCOTS (qq.v. Vol. V), caused grave unrest which ended only with the execution of the Scottish queen. When Elizabeth I died in 1603, Mary's son, James VI of Scotland, succeeded her. He became James I of England.

Though the two countries were now united under Stuart kings, they had separate parliaments until 1707, in which year, by the Act of Union, the parliaments were united, and Scotland sent members to Westminster. After the accession of the Hanoverians, the old spirit of Scottish nationalism flickered briefly in the risings of 1715 and 1745, when attempts were made to put a Stuart back on the throne of Great Britain. But though Charles Edward STUART (q.v. Vol. V), the hero of 1745, was a brilliant and romantic leader, he failed to gain the support of the whole nation. The Union had, in fact, become more than a political convenience. Today, Scotland's national interests are guarded by the SCOTTISH OFFICE, her legal system is maintained in SCOTTISH LAW, and her democratic traditions are assured by SCOTTISH EDUCATION (q.v. Vol. X). With these safeguards

L. & M. Gayton

CULROSS, FIFESHIRE

to her independence, Scots are content to be citizens of the United Kingdom.

Presbyterianism (*see* CALVINISM) is the official religion of the country. Its stern tenets, and the uncompromising spirit of John KNOX (q.v. Vol. V), the great Scottish reformer of the 16th century, have left a lasting impression upon the national character, for much of the sincerity and courage of a Scot comes from his religion. Scotland, however, is not entirely Protestant. Today, nearly a sixth of the population is Roman Catholic.

This nation has made a distinguished contribution to literature, to the sciences, and to political thought; and EDINBURGH (q.v. Vol. III) and the three older Scottish universities have long been the home of sound scholarship. The poets and novelists, Sir Walter SCOTT and R. L. STEVENSON, were both Scots. James HUNTER, the father of modern surgery, David HUME, the philosopher, and Adam SMITH, the

political economist, were all born north of the Border. The Scots are great travellers and pioneers in undeveloped countries—and David LIVINGSTONE, one of the greatest of all explorers, was born in Lanarkshire (qq.v. Vol. V).

Two distinct types of people are to be found in modern Scotland. The Highlander is usually quick-witted, well-mannered, courteous, and gentle in speech. To understand him it is necessary to understand the significance of the clan— a significance which continues in a modified form to this day. A clan in Scotland is a family grouping of those bearing the same name. The chief is the head of the family, and the relationship between chief and clansman is that between the head of the family and a brother or son, not that between master and man. The Lowlander is less impetuous than the Highlander, more thrifty, and less communicative, but once his confidence has been won he is both friendly and hospitable. In the past 200 years he has lived, for the most part, in the toil and grime of coal-mines, iron and steel works, and big factories. This industrial Scotland has produced James WATT, who gave us the first efficient steam-engine, and James Keir HARDIE (q.v. Vol. V), the founder of the Independent Labour Party.

Until fifty years ago, there was little brick or timber building in Scotland, for Scottish building is traditionally of the plentiful local stone. In all parts of the country crofters and farm-labourers lived in low cottages, originally thatched, but later roofed with slates or tiles. In the cities a very large proportion of the population lived in flats, or tenements as they are usually called. And in Edinburgh there still stand tenements eight to ten storeys high, built round courts more than 200 years ago. They used to be the town houses of the Scottish nobles, and many of them bear the name of a former inhabitant.

Deer-stalking and grouse-shooting have brought many visitors to Scotland, and the 'gillie' (gamekeeper) is a particularly well-known and popular Highland character. Golf and fishing are national pastimes, 'soccer' and rugby are played as in England, and in the north-west men play SHINTY (q.v. Vol. IX), which resembles a very violent type of hockey. Then in summer in many villages and towns there are Highland games, sometimes associated with the annual gathering of a particular clan. At these games Scottish dances are performed by individual dancers and teams of dancers to the rhythm of the bagpipes. There are running and jumping contests and a special Scottish contest called tossing the caber. There are competitions in bagpipe-playing: it is said that to appreciate the 'pipes' it is necessary to have Scottish blood —indeed, there is hardly a Scot who will not confess to being stirred by the sound of the pipes.

Special days of festivity in Scotland are St. Andrew's Day, Hogmanay (New Year's Eve), and the birthday of Robert Burns (25 January); Burns' well-loved poetry has many of the characteristics of the Scots. Their romantic imagination is deeply rooted in the simple life and in the awareness of unworldly human values —'A man's a man for a' that'.

SCYTHIANS, *see* RUSSIANS.

SEMITES. These are people who all speak languages which belong to the family of SEMITIC LANGUAGES (q.v. Vol. IV). According to Hebrew tradition, as set out in Genesis, the Semites are descended from Shem, son of Noah; but, in fact, the Genesis account includes peoples whose languages were not Semetic, and excludes others whose languages definitely were. Where the Semites originally came from is not known for certain, though it may have been Arabia. The main Semitic languages are Hebrew, Phoenician (very much like Hebrew), Aramaic (the language spoken by the Jews at the time of our Lord), Assyrian (which includes Babylonian), Arabic, and Ethiopic. Most of the peoples speaking these languages live in western Asia or north-east Africa, though the JEWS (q.v.) have spread very widely over Europe and America.

See also BABYLONIANS; ASSYRIANS; HEBREWS; PHOENICIANS; HITTITES; ARABS; ABYSSINIANS.

SERBIANS, *see* YUGOSLAVS.

SHINTO. Japanese religion is of three main sorts: Pre-Buddhist, Buddhist, and Christian. BUDDHISM (q.v.) entered Japan from China, possibly as early as the 5th century, but it did not get a permanent footing there until the first half of the 6th century. China, then probably the most advanced country in the world, had an immense influence on Japan.

But Japan had a native religion before that. Probably it was in many ways not unlike the religion of China before CONFUCIUS (q.v. Vol. V), or like the religion of ancient Greece—a belief in many gods and many lords. After Buddhism was introduced, and indeed more or less in opposition to Buddhism, the native beliefs were gradually unified into one system, which the Japanese called Shin-to, 'the Way of the Spirits'.

It is possible to distinguish three types of Shinto—first, the old Shinto which goes back long before European influence began; second, the government-sponsored state Shinto of this century, which was a revival of the old Shinto but with certain differences (it used to but does not now receive government aid); third, the sect Shinto, which is not under government control, and takes various forms, some showing apparent Christian influence.

From A.D. 540 until towards the end of the 16th century Buddhism was very strong in Japan. It influenced Shinto, and most Japanese, like many Orientals, found no difficulty in enjoying the consolations of both religions. But

I.S.E.F., Tokyo

SHINTO PRIESTS

Shinto includes the belief in a large number of minor gods and goddesses besides the great Sun-goddess. Some of these are fairly important *kami* or gods; others are little more than small bogies, of whom there may be millions; others, again, are unpleasant little animals like fox-gods, or female demons, who torment those who displease them.

Shinto shrines are often of great simplicity and beauty, and fit well into the landscape. Their shape is rather like that of the Hebrew tabernacle and, like it, they have two parts, an outer court and an inner or holy of holies. Shinto worship consists in keeping on good terms with the *kami*, and the Shinto priests also do a good business in consecrated objects, which are believed in as lucky charms. Vows are made and sacrifices offered to the various divinities. There are also pilgrimages to sacred spots (*see* FUJI YAMA, Vol. III).

Christianity was brought to Japan in the 16th century by Jesuit missionaries, and more recently American protestant missionaries have converted many Japanese. The Christian community is still small, but its numbers have increased since the war.

Christian teaching has had a considerable influence on sect Shinto. Sect Shinto consists of a number of different groups, rather like Nonconformist churches in England. Most of them accept the usual Shinto ideas, but add others, such as the healing of the sick. Indeed, one sect believes in the idea of One Good God—so great a development from the ordinary Shinto beliefs that some have thought it to be modelled on the teaching of the Bible; though it is also possible that it may be independent, like the movement of Zarathustra in early Persia (*see* ZOROASTRIAN).

After the Second World War, when Japan was occupied by the U.S. Army, Shinto was declining, and the Emperor, on 31 December 1945, publicly renounced the idea that he was a divine being, descended from the Sun-goddess. He declared his intention to abandon ancient superstitions and to rule as the constitutional monarch of a democratic state.

The Ise Grand Shrine, which is the shrine of the Emperor's ancestors, is a central point of Shinto. The Emperor keeps the ancient practice of making formal visits to this shrine to inform the ancestors of momentous events. A small replica of the shrine is kept within the Palace grounds, so that when the Emperor cannot make

between 1700 and 1841, and again in 1870, nationalist revivals led to anti-Buddhist riots, with the slogan 'abolish Buddhism and down with the monks'. This violence died down after 20 years, and today Buddhism in Japan seems as much alive as ever, though state Shinto, at any rate up to the defeat of Japan in 1945, has seemed equally alive.

The central idea of state Shinto seems to be that the Divine Spirit in nature, which is thought of in feminine terms, has produced the Japanese people as a strong race, with a divine origin and a great destiny. This idea used to be expressed by saying that the Sun-goddess, Amaterasu, is the original Mother of the line of Mikados (Emperors), so that the Emperor is a divine being. It also follows, said the Japanese, that since all human beings are the offspring of nature, whatever they think and do must be natural, and therefore right. In consequence, there is no such thing as 'wickedness in the sight of God'. Whatever is, is right, and mankind stands in no need of redemption. This was a very useful belief for unscrupulous Japanese leaders, and a comforting one for the people who had to obey them. Not everyone in Japan believed that the Emperor was a god, but the belief was taught in State schools, and fostered among the masses for political purposes.

the journey to Ise he can make a symbolic visit to the replica. Since 1950 there has been some revival of Shinto, but not with the same government control. It still has a hold over the hearts of the Japanese people. To people of the West, it appears rather similar to what Roman religion was like under the early Empire.

See also JAPANESE.

SIBERIAN PEOPLES.

1. These are the inhabitants of an immense territory, about twenty times as great as France and nearly twice as large as the United States of America. But the number of people who inhabited this area in 1970 was still comparatively small—probably around 20,000,000. Most of these are colonizers from European Russia and are not the natives of Siberia with whom we are concerned here. The real peoples of Siberia consist of small groups, varying from the largest, the Yakuts, numbering about 296,000 and dispersed in the Yakut Autonomous Soviet Republic, over an area equal to two-fifths of Europe, down to the small group of Koryaks (now called Nymylany) in the extreme north-east, of whom there are probably less than 8,000. These peoples of northern Asia have led for many generations the life of reindeer herders and of fishers, and most of them have been isolated in small, scattered groups. Many accept Christianity, others follow a kind of BUDDHISM (q.v.) called Lamaism, and some small groups practise a pagan religion called Shamanism.

2. THE YAKUTS. This is a Russian name: the inhabitants call themselves *Sakha* or *Uriankhai Sakaalar*. They settled in Siberia towards the

Novosti

HOW A YAKUT STORES DRINKING WATER

end of the 14th century, driving northwards the Yukagirs, Tungus, Lamuts, and others. They probably came from the Central Asian steppes or from beyond Lake Baikal; they are of Turki origin, with much Mongolian blood; they have high cheek-bones, slanting eyes, and black hair; their language belongs to the Turkic family.

They were conquered by Russian Cossacks in the 17th century and made to pay tribute in furs called *yasak*. This was changed in the 18th century to heavy taxes in cash; in addition, they had to provide transport for goods going overland to the far north-east or by boat along the rivers. They were offered relief from taxation if they accepted Christianity, and, consequently, by the middle of the 19th century most Yakuts were Christian. They also accepted Russian names and in this way some obtained Russian civic rights.

Formerly, they were a nomadic horse-breeding tribe and they retain customs from this way of life, such as drinking *kumiss* (mare's milk). Their cliff drawings are of horses and reindeer, hunting, and trapping. They introduced horses and cattle in the region where they now live; reindeer-breeding has been of secondary importance except in the Arctic north. Agriculture has only been developed recently.

THE PEOPLES OF SIBERIA

Novosti

TUNGUS GIRL MEDICAL STUDENTS AT TURA

The provision of food to last through the long winters, which may have 70° of frost, is the main problem in the life of the Yakuts. Many used to die during very severe spells, and whole reindeer herds were sometimes wiped out. Trapping and hunting foxes, squirrels, and wild reindeer were vital occupations, since fur skins are what the Yakuts exchanged for stores to keep them through the winter. Yakutsk, on the river Lena, is the centre of trade in the short, hot summer. The people arrive from everywhere, mainly in boats. Food is delivered frozen—milk is sold in round slabs. Meat, fish, and vegetables are not only preserved but sometimes eaten still frozen.

The Yakuts keep only small reindeer herds, and so often have to hunt wild reindeer. It is important to try to check the fall in numbers of wild reindeer brought about by wasteful hunting. Fishing is also an important occupation. Salting and storing is still partly carried on in primitive ways. How to keep cows alive in winter is a serious problem. Long log cowsheds are built

with wooden floors to protect the cattle from hoof-rot. The Yakuts themselves used to live at one end of the barn, in a square room with a fireplace in the centre but with no wooden floor. One of the government measures for improving conditions of life was a decree ordering the separation of the human dwelling-place from the animal shelter.

The Soviet Government after forming the Yakut A.S.S.R. in 1922, introduced reforms in the holding of land, which were resisted by the traditional headmen, the *toions*. As in the rest of the Soviet Union, collective farming was introduced and the people encouraged to give up a nomad life and to settle. Russian wooden houses were built in place of the primitive abodes, built partly below ground to keep out the winter cold. New ideas were introduced to increase the cultivated land, in spite of the permanently frozen subsoil, and potatoes and vegetables appeared. As well as the main industry of fur-trapping, fresh gold-fields have been discovered and coal and iron are also mined. Much of this work has been done by convict labour, as the indigenous population was not sufficient or suited to the work. It is difficult to arrange education for remote and isolated communities. Though the population was formerly nearly all illiterate, many can now read and write, Yakut being the first language, and Russian the second. As many of the children will be trappers and hunters when they grow up, they are taught to develop keen sight and hearing, and new ways are being tried to make sure that school lessons do not make the children fit less well into their surroundings and way of life.

3. THE BURYAT MONGOLS inhabit the other Autonomous Soviet Socialist Republic in Siberia, in a mountainous land south and east of Lake Baikal, one of the biggest freshwater lakes in the world. Less than half the inhabitants of Buryat Mongolia, are Buryats, most of the rest being Russian settlers. The Buryat Mongols are related to the Mongols of Outer Mongolia and were converted to Buddhism by Mongolian lamas during the 18th century. The majority used to be stock-breeders and fishermen, a nomadic people living in *yurta* (felt tents). Most of them have been settled by the Soviet Government, mainly in collective farms, though many return to tent life in summer, when they move their herds to summer pastures. Hay and fodder crops now prevent the losses among the herds which used

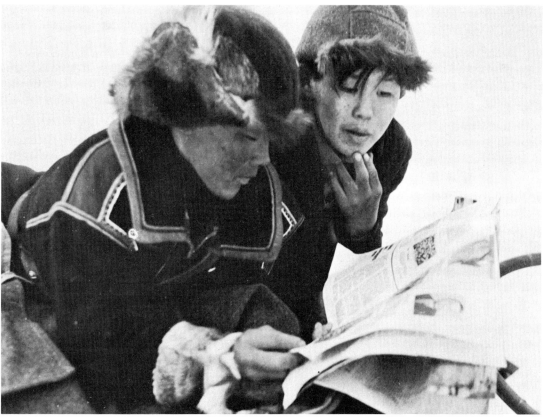

Novosti

REINDEER BREEDERS RECEIVE MOSCOW NEWSPAPERS

to follow a hard winter. Since 1923 new industries have been built up, such as the locomotive works in the capital Ulan Ude. Since 1941 new industrial regions have been developed, and these have attracted more settlers. Trapping, particularly of squirrel and sable, is still an important industry, and a State breeding farm for sable has been established. The Buryats live in less isolated conditions than other Siberian peoples since they are near the Trans-Siberian railway (*see* RAILWAY SYSTEMS, Vol. IV). Education is spreading, though the Buryats have not easily fitted into the industrial occupations which the Russian settlers have brought. Air transport is important in the opening up of these distant areas.

4. OTHER SIBERIAN PEOPLES. The other peoples of Siberia are far less numerous than the Yakuts and Buryats; they live in areas difficult of access and change their old ways of life very slowly. The main groups live in National Regions in the north and east near the Amur river.

The Ostyaks and Voguls share a National Region: the Ostyaks (now called Khanty) number about 21,000 and live on the right bank of the river Ob; the Voguls (now called Mansi) number about 7,600 and live on the eastern slope of the Urals. Many live in tents and huts and hunt, fish, and breed reindeer. Formerly they used to move over many hundreds of miles, going in the summer to the vast, treeless regions of the tundra, and returning to the pine forests in the early autumn in search of feeding grounds for their reindeer. Fishing is mainly for the older men; they sell their catch to government trading-posts. Some medical help, education, and radio services are now reaching them.

Some branches of the small group of Samoyed (now called Nentsy) live in these regions, some in the northern tundra between the Urals and the Yenisei river, some on the tundra between the Yenisei and the Khatanga river. They are mostly settled and keep horses and cattle but no reindeer.

The Tungus tribes, originally a Manchu people, migrated at some unknown time from the Manchu country to Siberia. They are now spread all over eastern Siberia in small groups. Their modern national name is Evenki; they dwell mainly in the northern forests, and they live by deer-breeding, hunting, and fishing. Reindeer skins are used for tents. The fur supplies blankets, caps, and boots; blouses and trousers are made out of reindeer skins. They used to trade fur and fish for liquor—with disastrous results; but this is now forbidden, and all trading is done through co-operative teams.

The Yukagir, who live in the remotest parts of Yakutia, represent the remnants of a very early migration north. Before the arrival of the Russians they were numerous, but are now nearly extinct, and those that remain have inter-married with the Evenki. Their language, which is now little spoken, is not related to any other known language except possibly the Chukchee and Koryak. They were nomadic deer-breeders, and their herds numbered thousands. They trained a few reindeer to pull their sledges. They traded the ivory from mammoth tusks found in the tundra. In the very far north reindeer cannot live, since there is no fodder, and here the people depend on dogs who, like the men, feed on fish. Apart from ivory, their only article of exchange is the skin of the white fox, and on the success of the hunt depends the purchase of tea, sugar, tobacco, and ammunition for the winter. The Yukagir are baptised, though they preserve some of their old Shamanist customs.

The Chukchee (now called Luonavetlany), Koryak (now called Nymylany), and Kamchadal live on the far north-east coast. They resemble the most western North American Indians in the structure of their language and in their fishing and hunting methods. The Chukchee—who number about 14,000—live in the extreme north-east peninsula. Some breed reindeer, others live by the sea and hunt seals and walrus. They distrust interference in their way of life, and medical help and education are still in the pioneer stage. The Koryaks are also divided between Reindeer and Maritime Koryaks and number about 7,500. Salmon is their chief food, but they love tea, and the tongue of the deer is a prized delicacy. The Kamchadal live in the south of the Kamchatka peninsula. Few speak their original language, but use dialects which show a strong Russian influence. They are a settled people and live in little Russian houses in small villages on the banks of a river, which they fish. In the centre and north of Kamchatka live the Lamut, a branch of the Evenki, who hunt and breed reindeer. In contrast to the Koryaks, they ride the reindeer and use them, as well as dogs, as draught animals.

On the island of Sakhalin and on the mainland opposite live the small Ainu and Gilyak (now called Nivkhi) tribes. They are rather apart from the other Siberian peoples and have always been excessively nervous of contact with strangers. They have changed their living places frequently, following the migrating fish.

See also Vol. IV: TURKIC AND FINNISH LANGUAGES.

SICILIANS, *see* ITALIANS. *See also* Vol. III: SICILY.

SIKHISM. This is a new religion which developed in India during the 16th and 17th centuries A.D. out of the contrast between HINDUISM and ISLAM (q.v.). Its origin is as follows. A certain young orthodox Hindu called Nanak, born in 1469, and living near Lahore in the Punjab, became dissatisfied with his ancestral religion and interested in Islam. He set to work to learn Persian, and then read various Muslim writings. But the new faith failed to meet his needs completely; so he developed one of his own, which took what he felt was best from both Hinduism and Islam, and which, in particular, rejected the Hindu idea of caste, and the inferiority of women to men. Nanak taught the equality of all human beings, and the uselessness of extreme self-torture (*see* ASCETICISM), and he advised the eating of meat and family life and marriage as the normal state for all. On the other hand, he urged temperance and simplicity, and forbade his followers the use of alcohol and tobacco. They were to rise early and take cold baths before morning prayer. All this sounds to us very familiar; and if Nanak had given up believing in the many Hindu gods and goddesses, he would have been rather like a Jew or a Puritan Christian in his religion. Indeed, at the beginning of the 20th century, one of the members of his movement, the famous Sundar Singh, actually crossed over to Christianity. There were, however, limits to Nanak's own reforms. He seems to have accepted the Hindu beliefs of his day about the various deities, except

Paul Popper

A SIKH SOLDIER

rebuilt two years later). He also collected a volume of hymns, to which he added some of his own composition, and these form the Sikh sacred book, known as the *Granth Sahib* or Master-Book.

At this point a remarkable development occurred. Hitherto the Sikhs had been a religious, not a political, community, and they had not been persecuted. But in 1606 a new and intolerant Muslim Emperor, a Mogul called Jehangir, succeeded his very liberal-minded father Akbar as ruler of north India. He tortured Arjun till he died, with the result that the Sikhs came to the conclusion that they would have to fight for freedom of worship and thought if they were to survive as a separate religious body. By this time they had already become a numerous and highly disciplined community. The threat to their freedom knit them more closely together, and strict military training, in addition to their abstemious habits, soon made them into a formidable army. For over fifty years they held their own successfully against the Muslim Emperors. Then the Mogul Emperor imprisoned the ninth *guru*, Teg Bahadur, for having dared to invite him to forsake Islam in favour of Sikhism. The *guru* was executed—a second martyr—and thereafter the Sikhs, under Govind, the tenth *guru*, became literally a nation of warriors, a people apart in the midst of the Mogul Empire. Before he died Teg Bahadur uttered a curious prophecy, that the Mogul Empire would fall, and that a Christian army would come from Calcutta and join forces with the Sikhs; and something like this actually happened towards the end of the 18th century.

The Sikhs still survive in modern India. During the British period they were initially at war with the forces of the East India Company. Later, they were highly valued for their martial prowess and made a significant contribution to the Imperial army. They fought in both world wars. In independent India they have lost none of their cultural identity, and even when they emigrate, they are willing to make great sacrifices to preserve it. The membership in the 1961 census was given as nearly 8 millions, four-fifths of these in the Punjab, with a steady rise in numbers from 1901 onwards. For some years after the partition of India most of the Sikhs lived in a series of states called PEPSU (Patiala and East Punjab States Union), but in 1956 this political unit was merged in the present Punjab.

that he regarded them all as inferior to the one Supreme God, the idea of which he took from Islam. He invented a costume for himself, partly Hindu, partly Muslim, and travelled forth as a wandering preacher, using especially hymns as a means of teaching his doctrine.

Nanak journeyed all over India and Ceylon, and some say that he even went as far as Mecca. But most of his followers came from the people of his homeland, and this may explain, to some extent, the later development of the Sikh community. When he died in 1538, he appointed a successor who was called by the ordinary Hindu title of *guru*, which means spiritual teacher. He was succeeded by a second *guru*, who invented a special alphabet, and in this, which was used to express a dialect of Punjabi, called *Gurumukhi*, the sacred books of the new movement were written down. The followers of Nanak called themselves Sikhs, which simply means 'disciples'. The first four *gurus* were specially chosen, but after that the office became hereditary. The fifth *guru*, Arjun, was responsible for establishing Nanak's religion as an institution. He built the celebrated golden temple at Amritsar (which was destroyed in 1762 but

Although most of the recruits for the Sikh army have come from the fighting tribes of the Jats, the Sikh movement is perhaps a unique example of a political unit, developed solely by religious influence, without the unifying power of common blood, in which the members have grown alike in appearance and manners. Supposing that the QUAKERS of Pennsylvania or the MORMONS of Utah in America (qq.v.) were to have grown into distinct peoples by strict inter-marriage among themselves, and were to have adopted a distinctive costume and spoken a separate dialect of English, that would have given us something like what has happened in the case of the Sikhs.

See also INDIAN PEOPLES.

SINHALESE, *see* CEYLONESE.

SKY-GOD. Many gods are in some sense sky-gods, while others are connected solely with the Underworld. Gods are often connected with the sun or the moon, the rain or the thunder. They live somewhere in the sky, and come down to earth from time to time in the guise of men or birds or even clouds. Many peoples, however, believe in a supreme god, who lives in the sky and never comes down at all—who, in fact, takes very little interest in the affairs of men. It is supposed among such peoples that, after creating the world, he retired to the sky, leaving the world to look after itself, or to be looked after by inferior gods. Gods of this type are probably the reflection of the kind of divine king who per-formed, once a year, the creation rite, and for the rest of the time remained shut up in his palace. This kind of god is not found among peoples whose kings were more active, such as the Greeks and Norsemen (*see* GODS OF GREECE AND ROME; NORSE MYTHS).

See also RELIGION; GOD.

SLAVS. These include most of the peoples now living in eastern Europe and speaking languages which have a common origin. Slav-speaking peoples first came into Europe, probably from Central Asia, at a very early date, and settled at various times in the countries where they are now known as RUSSIANS, BULGARIANS, POLES, CZECHO-SLOVAKS (including the Slovaks and Moravians), and YUGOSLAVS (including Serbs, Croats, Mon-tenegrins, and Slovenes) (qq.v.).

See also Vol. IV: SLAVONIC LANGUAGES.

SLOVAKS, *see* CZECHOSLOVAKS.

SLOVENES, *see* YUGOSLAVS.

SOUTH AFRICANS. 1. HISTORY. The area which is now the Republic of South Africa was settled as far back as we can trace by the HOTTENTOT and BUSHMEN peoples (qq.v.). At least 500 years ago, and certainly earlier in some areas, Bantu-speaking peoples moved down from the North. They were divided into two main groups of tribes, the Sotho—including the Basuto, Pedi, and Tswana, who settled in the more arid north and west; and the Nguni—including the Zulu, Swazi, and Xhosa, who settled in the more fertile south-eastern regions. European settlers first came to the Cape in the second half of the 17th century, under the auspices of the Dutch East India Company. They enslaved the Hottentots, murdered and drove off the Bushmen, and soon began to push back the Xhosa peoples on their eastern flank.

In 1806 the British captured the Cape during the course of the Napoleonic wars because they were concerned about the security of their sea route to India. The abolition of the SLAVE TRADE (q.v. Vol. VII) and the relatively more liberal treatment of the Africans by the British antagonized the predominantly Dutch farmers known as the Boers, particularly in the Eastern Cape. In 1836 a number of them trekked into the interior, beyond British control, to establish independent republics where they would be free to maintain (in their words) 'proper relations between master and servant'. This movement, known as the 'Great Trek' led them to set up republics in the Transvaal and the Orange Free State under leaders such as Paul KRUGER (q.v. Vol. V). They had to fight the warlike ZULU (q.v.) who were later completely defeated by the British.

In 1870 diamonds were discovered in Kim-berley, and in 1886 gold was found in the Transvaal. The British leaders, Cecil RHODES (q.v. Vol. V) and Milner, were convinced that Britain's position in Africa depended on con-trolling this vast mineral wealth. Consequently Britain declared war on the Boer republics, defeating them by 1902 and bringing them under British rule (*see* SOUTH AFRICAN WAR, Vol. X). Then, in spite of much bitterness, the Boer leaders worked well with the British to bring about unity. In 1910 the Union of South Africa

HOUSE ON RHODES' FRUIT FARM, BOSCHENDAL, CAPE PROVINCE

was formed, consisting of the Cape Colony, Natal, the Transvaal, and the Orange Free State. In fact, the people of Dutch descent, the Afrikaners, dominated the new Union because their greater numbers gave them more voting power. The non-whites had no voting power at all. In 1961 the Union broke away from the British Commonwealth and became a republic. The population of the Republic (1972) was: Whites 3,779,000; Africans 14,893,000; Coloureds 1,996,000; Asians 614,000.

2. THE AFRIKANERS. The Great Trek, the Boer Republics, and the Boer War created a nation within the white population, with its own language evolved from Dutch, its distinctive rural and Calvinist character, and a belief in the destiny of the Afrikaner 'Volk' to maintain domination of South Africa. Under SMUTS (q.v. Vol. V) many Afrikaners were persuaded to share the government with the richer and more urban English-speaking peoples; but a new Afrikaner Nationalist party grew in resolution and strength until, in 1948, it won power, which it has exercised ever since. It is committed to maintain White minority control, and under the leadership of President Verwoerd, it developed its policy of 'Apartheid', or racial separation. This involves the granting of limited self-governing rights to the Black majority who live in the small 'bantustans', areas which constitute about 13 per cent of the whole country. More than two-thirds of the Black South Africans work in 'White' areas, where their treatment has aroused the censure of most of the world. Their wages are on average under one-fifth of White wages, but only White workers have the right to strike. Africans in the White areas have virtually no political rights, and are liable to be expelled from their homes at any time.

3. THE ENGLISH-SPEAKING SOUTH AFRICANS. These comprise rather over 40 per cent of the white population. They include British, and also Jewish, Greek, and Portuguese settlers, and form a majority in most cities. They have dominated the financial centres and controlled mining, commerce, and industry, as well as the professions, though the Afrikaners have greatly increased their economic power under the Nationalist government. They are less extreme in their racial policies, but they have tended progressively to accept the central policies of the Nationalist government, though they are anxious about their economic effects.

4. THE AFRICANS. By far the largest part of the population is Bantu-speaking (*see* SOUTHERN

THE CAMPANILE AT PORT ELIZABETH WHICH COMMEMORATES
THE LANDING OF ENGLISH SETTLERS IN 1823

Satour

AFRICANS). When the Europeans first came, the Africans were divided into a number of tribes, and the successive White governments have endeavoured to maintain the tribal divisions, and to ensure that the tribal chiefs obey their orders. Today over a third of the Africans live and work in the cities where, in enforced segregation, a new African way of life has emerged. The Africans have never meekly accepted White control; at first they fought as organized tribes; and then, as these were repressed, in political organizations, which became more militant as the Nationalist party systematically tightened its domination. The 1960s, which began with the massacre of unarmed Africans at Sharpeville, saw a series of attempted counter-attacks by the African National Congress and the Pan-African Congress. The government ruthlessly suppressed them, and imprisoned their leaders.

5. THE CAPE COLOUREDS. In way of life these are a sub-group of the Afrikaners and are the result of racial interbreeding over the centuries. But, on account of their colour, they do not have a vote in the national elections, and are confined to relatively poorly-paid jobs below the 'colour-bar'. They live mainly in the Western Cape, but have been expelled from their traditional homes in Cape Town and other areas in furtherance of the government's ideal of racial segregation.

6. THE INDIANS. The bulk of the Indian population are descendants of labourers who were brought to South Africa in the second half of the 19th century to work in the sugar plantations of Natal. Most of them are still poor labourers in Natal, but some Indian traders later entered the country and prospered. These have now been expelled from the main trading centres, and all Indians are required to live in special ghettos outside the major cities.

In keeping with the policy of Apartheid, all residential, educational, and recreational facilities are racially segregated. Government expenditure on White facilities is far greater than that on facilities for all non-Whites, who constitute more than four-fifths of the population. Also Whites only can take part in national politics. The control of the government is ruthlessly maintained, and with the vast economic resources at its disposal, a modern and efficient system of racial domination continues to flourish, despite the hostility of most of the world's governments, and the development of independent African states in the rest of the continent.

See also SOUTHERN AFRICANS.
See also Vol. III: SOUTH AFRICA.

SOUTH AMERICANS, _see_ ARGENTINES; BOLIVIANS; BRAZILIANS; CHILEANS; COLOMBIA, PEOPLES OF; ECUADOR, PEOPLES OF; PARAGUAYANS; PERUVIANS; URUGUAYANS.

SOUTHERN AFRICANS. The black African population of South Africa is about 15 millions (1972), Rhodesia has about 5 million black Africans, Lesotho 1 million, Botswana, Swaziland, and Namibia (SWA) about half a million each. These people come from a number of tribal groups with local differences in their culture and language, but nearly all of them speak languages of the Bantu family and have a broadly similar way of life and traditions. Many consider themselves 'de-tribalized' and travel from their traditional areas to work in factories, mines, and modern plantations; many are Christians.

In South Africa they are divided by the government into 'national units', and have 'homelands' allocated to them as part of the policy of Apartheid (separate development for different races). For example the Transkei is for

J. Allan Cash

A XHOSA WOMAN, SOUTHERN AFRICA

the Xhosa people, Lebowa for the North Sotho, and Kwazulu for the Zulus (q.v.). The plan is for the 'homelands' to be self-governing, but the South African government will keep control over defence and security. The 'homelands' or 'bantustan' policy is also being extended to Namibia (South West Africa), but South Africa's right to administer the country is now disputed internationally. In Rhodesia, many Africans oppose the white government established by the U.D.I. in 1965 (*see* Rhodesians), and in Angola and Mozambique many are fighting the Portuguese government which regards the countries as part of Portugal. Swaziland, Lesotho, and Botswana are independent countries populated largely by Swazi, Sotho, and Tswana peoples.

In the past most southern African peoples depended on the products of their own farming. Women grew crops of maize, sorghum, and pumpkins, while the men looked after herds of cattle, sheep, and goats. Further north, in Angola and southern Zambia, for example, cassava and yams are grown. The Herero people of Namibia traditionally depend entirely on cattle, and grow no crops. Hunting, especially for antelopes, was important in the past. Some peoples, such as the Lozi (Barotse) of southern Zambia are fishermen, while others of South Africa and Botswana avoid fish.

Traditional African settlements are generally groups of round huts which, in many societies, were built by the women. Each hut is equivalent to a room, and it is the group of huts together which makes up a home. The *kraals* of the Zulu are scattered over the country, but the Sotho people live in large concentrated groups of up to about 20,000.

The groups are traditionally ruled by their

chiefs, who generally had councils of elders to advise them. The chiefs of some peoples, such as the Swazi, Xhosa, and Zulu, often had great personal power. When rival leaders quarrelled, a group sometimes seceded under a new chief, as for example, when Mzilikazi quarrelled with the great Zulu leader Shaka and led a group of people away northwards in the 1830s. Mzilikazi's followers conquered the Shona people of what is now Rhodesia and founded the Ndebele (Matabele) nation. Another great individual leader of those times was Moshoeshoe (Moshweshwe), who, by skill in war and diplomacy, established the beginning of the modern state of Lesotho.

The men of some of the peoples, particularly the Sotho, Pedi, and Tswana, are organized into age-sets. All the young men of a similar age are formed into a set at an INITIATION CEREMONY (q.v.) and then act as a unit, for example in war, or in building a chief's *kraal*, or providing a levy of cattle. Shaka's age-regiments among the Zulu were not allowed to farm or marry during their military service. This type of organization was adopted by peoples such as the Tsonga of southern Mozambique who were influenced by the expansion of the Zulu peoples in the 1820s and 1830s.

Polygamy was common amongst most southern African peoples before Christianity came to them. The man and his family also had to give a bride price, *lobola* (generally a number of cattle, and now sometimes money) for the bride's family. This was a kind of security for the marriage. It could provide support for the bride if her husband did not look after her properly, and was returnable to the husband if the woman failed in what was expected of a wife.

Many of the traditional religious beliefs concerned the power of the spirits of dead ancestors (*see* ANCESTOR WORSHIP). The spirits were believed to control harvests, weather, disease, and success or failure in war, so they had to be propitiated with sacrifices of cattle and other animals—particularly white goats. Some of the traditional rulers, such as the 'Rain-Queen' of the Lovedu people of the Transvaal, owed their power to their close contact with the ancestors. The 'Rain-Queen' was also believed to be able to bring rain. The Venda of the Transvaal, and the Shona of Rhodesia both had a cult of Mwari, a being who was both a rainmaker and an oracle.

The earliest surviving inhabitants of southern Africa were the Khoikhoi (Hottentot) and San (Bushman) peoples. People who spoke a Bantu language and used iron came later—archaeologists now believe such people have lived in parts of the Transvaal for more than 1,000 years. Clashes with white settlers began in the 18th century, as the Africans moved south-westwards and met Europeans spreading from the Cape. The 19th century was a period of migrations and wars, both between the African peoples, and between the Africans and Europeans. The Mfengu people, now of the Transkei and Ciskei, actually helped the European forces during the 'frontier war' of 1835, and were rewarded with land taken from the Xhosa. The Xhosa continued to resist the whites for about 100 years, and the Zulus won some victories over Europeans; but by 1900 most of the peoples of southern Africa were under European and colonial government.

See also AFRICA; BUSHMEN; HOTTENTOTS; ZULU.
See also Vol. IV: AFRICAN LANGUAGES.

SOVIET CENTRAL ASIAN PEOPLES. 1.

These peoples live in a large area which geographers have called the heartland of Eurasia. It stretches from the Caspian Sea in the west to the Chinese province of Sinkiang in the east: to the north lie European Russia and Siberia, and to the south lie Iran (Persia) and Afghanistan, and beyond that India. Since time immemorial various peoples and cultures have met, clashed, and mixed there. Conquerors have come and gone—the Greeks under Alexander the Great (329 B.C.), the Arabs (7th century), the Mongols (13th and 15th centuries), and the Russians (19th century). Across

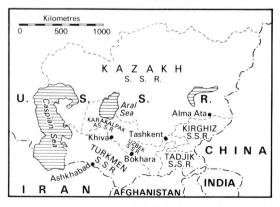

SOVIET CENTRAL ASIA

this region lie the earliest trade routes between the East and the West.

The peoples of this area are for the most part Mongolian by race and speak TURKIC LANGUAGES (q.v. Vol. IV). Their religion they owe to the Arab invaders: in particular, the more settled people were fanatical Muslims, mainly of the Sunnite Sect (*see* ISLAM), and their women were subjected to very severe restrictions. The nomad people, however, were much less strict.

The main part of the population is still rural. The long-settled agricultural people live near the oases, river valleys, and at the foot of mountains. Most of the former nomadic people have now become settled, though many still graze their herds at different seasons on pastures long distances from their villages. With the arrival of the Russians in the 19th century, nomadic life was weakened, for the colonizers settled on the more fertile lands and pushed the nomads into the barren parts. Since the revolution of 1917 the settlement of nomads has been carried out much more quickly, and now nomad life has almost disappeared, though some of its customs remain. Since 1955 more colonization from European Russia and intensive ploughing up of former grazing lands has been carried out by the government.

The principal indigenous peoples of Soviet Central Asia are the Kazakhs, the Kirgiz, the Tadjiks, the Uzbeks, the Turkmen, and the Karakalpaks. There are also Uigurs and Jews.

2. THE KAZAKHS, sometimes called the Kirgiz-Kazakhs, are of Mongol blood and speak a Turkic language, earlier called Chagatai. They were originally nomad stock-raisers; but today the majority are no longer nomads, although many still live, at least in spring and summer, in their felt tents called *yurta*. Since wood is scarce, they use dried dung for fuel. There are about 5,300,000 Kazakhs, making up less than half the total population of the KAZAKH SOVIET SOCIALIST REPUBLIC (q.v. Vol. III). Their country is enormous, but much of it lacks water. In the north are good grain districts, recently greatly expanded; the foothills round the capital Alma Ata (City of Apples) are rich in orchards. The Kazakhs never willingly accepted Russian colonization and domination; risings in the 19th century were followed by a revolt and emigration to China in 1916, in protest against conscription to serve in an auxiliary corps. The Kazakhs suffered particularly from the measures in 1931–2

S.C.R.

A KIRGIZ HUNTER WITH HIS GOLDEN EAGLE

of the Soviet Government to settle them quickly on collective farms.

3. THE KIRGIZ. South of Kazakhstan lie the better-watered highlands of the KIRGIZ SOVIET SOCIALIST REPUBLIC (q.v. Vol. III), bordering with Sinkiang, and believed by many scientists to have been the birthplace of the human race. The Kirgiz and Kazakhs have much in common in language, customs, and mode of life. They are often distinguished as the Kara-Kirgiz (Black Kirgiz) or Mountain Kirgiz. As nomad people they cherished freedom, and travelled for scores of miles in search of new pastures. They are now chiefly sheep and cattle breeders, their livestock playing an important part in the economy of the Soviet Union. Their food is produced by their cattle, sheep, and horses: mares give about nine quarts of milk daily, and from the fermented mare's milk the frothing and slightly intoxicating drink *kumiss* is made. The Kirgiz are fond of poetry and unwritten folklore: it is only since 1920 that the Kirgiz language has developed a written form. Kirgiz women, like the nomadic or semi-nomadic Kazakh women, enjoyed a good deal of freedom. They were not veiled, and occupied a fairly important position in the general life of the community. The Kirgiz S.S.R., formed in 1924, has over 1,500,000 inhabitants.

Novosti

TASHKENT: UZBEK CHILDREN AT SCHOOL

4. THE TADJIKS. South-west of Kirgizia, in the highlands bordering on Afghanistan, lies the Soviet Social Republic of TADJIKISTAN (q.v. Vol. III), formed in 1924, and the smallest of the Central Asian republics. The Tadjiks (Persian, *Taj*, crown) have strong ties with their Sunnite Muslim co-religionists in Afghanistan, and are fanatical in religious observances, neither eating meat nor drinking mare's milk. They are an Iranian race. Their language belongs to the Aryan family, and they are the only Central Asian people who speak a non-Turkic language. The Tadjiks were, until the 16th century, the main population of these Central Asian regions, but from that time on they had to submit to other races. They have long been settled and industrious agriculturalists, pursuing farming and sheep-breeding, horticulture, silkworm-breeding, and, now increasingly, cotton growing. Social changes, especially those improving the position of women, were not accepted easily. The

Tadjiks possess a rich folklore and an old traditional Persian literature; there are beautiful manuscripts with fine Persian miniatures. With the spread of modern education much Russian and other European literature has been translated into the Tadjik language, and one of the favourite plays in Stalinabad, the capital, is Shakespeare's *Othello*.

5. THE UZBEKS. To the north-west of Tadjikistan, in the river valleys, lies the Soviet Socialist Republic of UZBEKISTAN (q.v. Vol. III). It has a population of 12,000,000, of which about 66 per cent are Uzbeks. The capital, Tashkent, is the centre of most of the republic's industries, and is surrounded by very fertile irrigated lands. Well over half of the Soviet Union supply of cotton is grown in Uzbekistan. The Uzbeks are related to the Kirgiz, but are a very mixed people. Their name means 'master of himself' (*Uz*, self; *Beg*, master). They are passionately fond of their freedom, and partisans, named

Basmachi, resisted Soviet control for about 10 years. The Uzbek S.S.R. was created in 1925, out of the semi-independent states, called *khanates*, of Bokhara and Khiva, whose rulers, or khans, were overthrown. The Uzbeks adhered to Muslim customs; women were veiled and kept within the home. Resistance to change was strong and the Soviet Government did not risk forbidding women to hide their faces. Though the younger generation have abandoned veiling, there had been violent opposition, including murder by relatives of girls who had broken with tradition. The ancient cities of Bokhara and Samarkand are in Uzbekistan; the former particularly was a centre of Muslim learning in the 13th and 14th centuries, and they both possess beautiful tombs, notably that of TAMBURLAINE (q.v. Vol. V), and mosques decorated with coloured tiles. Many dwelling houses are still built of sun-baked clay. They are small and dark but are quickly constructed, need no timber, and are said to withstand earthquakes. Since 1959 the town population of Uzbekistan has increased by about 250,000 and new towns have appeared. Though perhaps most of the people in the towns are newcomers to the area, local peasants have taken an important part in the move from the country to the towns.

6. THE TURKMEN. To the south-east of the Caspian and north of Persia and Afghanistan is the Soviet Socialist Republic of TURKMENISTAN (q.v. Vol. III). The country is very arid, so that though it is the second largest republic of Central Asia it contains little over 1,200,000 inhabitants. A vast irrigation scheme, with a long canal from the Amu Daria, has been under construction since 1950. The Turkmen (or Turkomen) are closely related to the Kirgiz and Uzbeks. They are divided into numerous tribes and represent a mixture of various types—Turki in the north and Persian in the south. Persian blood came into Turkmenistan from slaves kidnapped in former times. The Turkmen speak different Turkic dialects; they are Muslims, but not fanatical, and their womenfolk always enjoyed a considerable amount of freedom. Before the days of Russian control their main occupation was raiding, in which their very good physique and strong horses gave them great advantages. They regarded labour as degrading and, when they were not on one of their 'expeditions', they passed their time drinking tea and telling stories. Under Russian

J. Allan Cash

AN ELDERLY TADJIK

influence much has been done to reclaim land by irrigation and to exploit the raw materials—oil, coal, chemicals, and cotton. Rug-weaving and dyeing, for which the Turkmen were renowned, have been encouraged, and Ashkhabad, the capital, is still the centre of the rug industry.

7. THE BOKHARA JEWS are said to be descendants of Israelites brought to these regions about 600–700 B.C. as prisoners of the kings of Assyria and Babylon. Their position among the Muslims has been difficult. They lived under many restrictions: they had to live in separate quarters; they could ride only donkeys instead of horses and mules; they were forbidden to wear the turban—instead they wore a high fur-trimmed cap; and they might only wear ropes as girdles. Their main occupation was the dyeing of native silk. They speak a dialect called Sart, which differs little from the Uzbek language. The name *Sart* was generally used for town-dwelling natives, to distinguish them from *Kazakh* (wanderer). About 103,000 Jews live in Uzbekistan.

8. In the years of economic planning by the government (since 1930) considerable progress has been made in developing the resources of these countries. Railway communications have been increased, large irrigation schemes have been undertaken, and non-ferrous metal and machine-building industries have been developed. The population of these five republics has grown faster since 1959 than the average growth of population for the U.S.S.R. as a whole. By 1970 it reached 23,000,000. A formerly illiterate population can read and write. Higher and technical education has developed steadily. Each of the republican capitals has at least one university; the earliest, the University of Tashkent, was founded in 1918, and now has over 20,000 students of various races. It includes big Medical and Agricultural schools. Several universities work in two languages, one of which is always Russian. National music and dancing have been encouraged, and the people take an active part in the direction of their local affairs; though, as elsewhere in the Soviet Union, the real authority rests with the Central Government in Moscow.

The importance of Central Asia and of its inhabitants is likely to increase in the future.

See also RUSSIANS; SIBERIAN PEOPLES.

SPANIARDS. It is difficult to talk in a general way about the 33,000,000 (1973) inhabitants of Spain, because their land is one with very strong regional differences. These affect the character of the people, as well as the look of the country; there is, for instance, little in common between the cautious, stubborn inhabitants of the damp, grey moorlands of Galicia in the north-west and the lively peasants who work in the paddy-fields and orange-groves round Valencia in the east. Moreover, many different races have settled in different parts of Spain, and, until the end of the 15th century, the country was divided into four separate kingdoms, each with its own separate ways of life—ways which have been partly preserved down to modern times.

Many people base their idea of Spaniards on the Andalusians of southern Spain. But the Andalusians are much less reserved, and more passionate, than most Spaniards; and their towns and villages of whitewashed houses, each with its inner courtyard, gay with geraniums and flowering shrubs, are not at all typical of most of the country. More characteristic of the nation are the Castilians who live on the enormous, high, tableland of central Spain, where the winters are very cold, and the summers hot and rainless. The Castilian has always been famous for the austerity and simplicity of his life, and for his individualism. The pride of

Spaniards makes them rather touchy with each other, but they are polite and hospitable to strangers, as long as they are treated as equals. The spirit of Spain, like that of the Spanish countryside, is strong, direct, and impressive, but rather gloomy. Spaniards like to think of themselves as very realistic, but their taste also runs to the ornate and the extravagant. This is shown in SPANISH ART and SPANISH LITERATURE (qq.v. Vol. XII). Spain is a Roman Catholic country, and the Church has always played a large part in Spanish life.

The prehistoric inhabitants of Spain were the Iberians, who probably came from Africa. Some scholars think they were closely connected with the Basques, who live in the western Pyrenees, and still preserve their ancient language. Later, Celtic tribes from the north settled in northern and eastern Spain alongside the Iberians. They were followed by Phoenicians and Greeks, who set up colonies in the south and along the Mediterranean coast. Next, as Hispania, Spain became an important part of the Roman Empire. Many traces of Roman occupation survive, especially in Merida, Tarragona, Segovia, and Itálica—near Seville; and the basis of modern Spanish civilization is Latin. After six hundred years of Roman rule Spain was conquered by the Germanic Visigoths, who taught Spaniards something of Germanic law and custom. The Visigoths were incompetent rulers, and the Visigothic kingdom was easily conquered in 711 by the MOORS (q.v.). For several centuries the Moors ruled nearly all Spain, and they were not finally conquered by the Christians until 1492. The Spanish Moors were tolerant, and highly civilized, and they influenced the life of Christian Spaniards in a great many ways. The SPANISH LANGUAGE (q.v. Vol. IV), with its many Moorish words, reflects this influence. MOORISH ARCHITECTURE (q.v. Vol. XII) has left its most splendid traces in the palaces of Granada and Seville, and in the mosque (now cathedral) of Cordoba. The music and customs of the Spanish people, particularly in the south and east, have been much influenced by Moorish traditions. The Jews were also a powerful force in medieval Spanish life.

In the 16th century, thanks to good luck and to the bravery and skill of her explorers, sailors, and soldiers, men such as COLUMBUS, CORTES, and PIZARRO (qq.v. Vol. V), Spain acquired a vast empire in Central and South America and

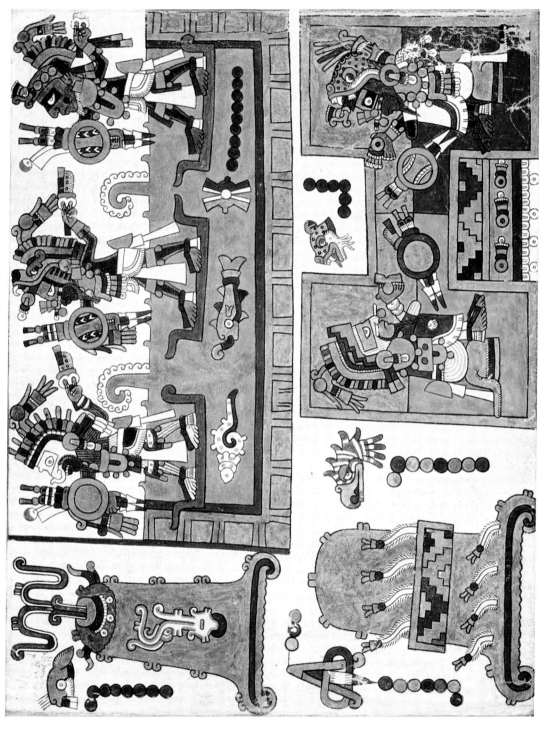

A PAGE FROM THE ZOUCHE (NUTTALL) CODEX, AN ANCIENT MEXICAN BOOK
PAINTED ON DEERSKIN

This page is part of the story of a chief called Eight Deer. At the top he is seen with two other warriors in boats and below he is exchanging gifts with another chief. On the left are the symbols of a smoking volcano (above) and a town, with date glyphs beside them

A NARROW STREET IN TOLEDO

became the most powerful country in Europe. But in the 17th century a rapid decline began. This decline was partly concealed for a time, by the luxury of the Spanish court as depicted in the paintings of VELAZQUEZ (q.v. Vol. V), and the brilliance of the Golden Age of Spanish Literature. By the time Spain was invaded by the armies of Napoleon, she had become a backward and bigoted country, though Spaniards put up a long and spirited resistance to the invader. Later, the country began to progress slowly, though handicapped by frequent outbreaks of revolution and civil war. The worst of these was the civil war of 1936-9, in which hundreds of thousands of Spaniards were killed.

In recent years industry has made notable advances, particularly in the north of Spain, and in the north-east where the industrious and go-ahead Catalan-speaking people live. Road, rail, and air communications have been greatly

improved. Spain has for long suffered extreme shortage of electric power, but the output was almost doubled between 1964 and 1971. The north is rich in minerals, especially coal, and a third of a million workers are employed in mining and metallurgical industries.

But Spain is mainly an agricultural country. She not only feeds herself but also exports fruits and wine. More land is devoted to livestock than to agriculture, mainly sheep, cattle, goats, and pigs. But while half the working population toil on the land, fewer than a third own any. In most of Spain the peasants live together in remote towns and villages, brown, grey, or red like the surrounding countryside, and walk to work in the fields or pastures. In recent years great efforts have been made to modernize agriculture and improve the lot of the land-workers by establishing co-operatives, and introducing mechanization, fertilizers, and improved seeds. But the peasant's life still contrasts strongly with the cultured social existence enjoyed in cities such as MADRID (q.v. Vol. III).

The traditional national sport of BULL-FIGHTING (q.v. Vol. IX) now attracts less interest than football, but the *torero* (bull-fighter) is still a national hero. Spaniards of all the different regions still prefer the characteristic rhythms of their own music, songs, and dances. The best time to hear them is on the occasion of the grape, corn, or olive harvests, when every town or village has its festival and Spaniards are at their gayest.

Twenty-four million foreigners a year now spend their holidays in Spain, enjoying sea and sunshine, beautiful cities and art treasures, picturesque countryside, and Spanish cuisine. Tourism has become an important Spanish industry.

See also BASQUES. See also Vol. III: SPAIN; INDEX, p. 155. See also Vol. IV: SPANISH AND PORTUGUESE LANGUAGES.

SPARTANS. The Spartans lived in the city of Sparta in the Peloponnese in ancient Greece. Sparta had been a centre of art and poetry, but the protracted effort she sustained to conquer and retain the surrounding lands led to a total change in her character. She became a military state to the exclusion of all ordinary cultural interests, a fate fortunately not suffered by any other Greek state. The Spartan citizens, always very restricted in numbers, devoted themselves exclusively to military training. They were forbidden to have anything to do with business and trade, which was carried on by their subject states who paid taxes to them. All the manual work and the cultivation of the soil was done by slaves. Sparta itself was not a beautiful city with fine buildings like Athens, but consisted of a group of straggling villages looking like a large military camp.

The training of a Spartan youth was very severe. There was no place for the weak and sickly. Delicate babies were not allowed to live. The youth of Sparta lived a communal life under strict discipline until they were thirty years of age. Their training aimed to develop powers of endurance, courage, and strict obedience, and they passed through a series of tests until they were considered fully qualified. Intellectual education played a very small part. Spartan girls, also, were trained in gymnastics, and the same high standards of endurance and courage were expected from them. Women played an important part in the life of the community.

Sparta grew to be a very strong military power, and the main rival to Athens in Greece. As a result of the Peloponnesian Wars she had become, by 404 B.C., the greatest power in Greece. Her rigid military organization and despotic rule, however, were much hated, so that, after some thirty years, her rivals united to overthrow her, and in 371 B.C. she was defeated in battle by the Thebans. The numbers of Spartans began to decline: in 480 B.C. there had been some 8,000 Spartan citizens, by 371 B.C. only 2,000 were left, and by 242 B.C. there were said to be only 700.

The word 'Spartan' is now used to indicate the courageous endurance of physical hardship. In most ways the Spartan way of life, and in particular their rivalry with Athens, was very harmful to Greek prosperity; but such examples of their soldiership as that of the heroic defence of the pass of Thermopylae against the Persians in 480 B.C. by King Leonidas and his Spartan army have won the admiration of later generations.

See also GREEK CIVILIZATION.

SPELLS AND CHARMS. In performing MAGIC (q.v.) the words which accompany the actions are very important, and magic is nearly always accompanied by words. These words may be called spells, charms, or incantations. Spells usually mean words having the power to impose a curse, to bewitch, enchant, and work evil by magic. 'Charm' is sometimes used of evil magic, but is usually meant to counteract evil, to cure illness, oppose witchcraft, and bring good fortune. Objects, as well as forms of words, are sometimes spoken of as 'charms'. 'Incantation' may mean the words uttered in a musical fashion for good or evil magic, and is used when a magician chants in an act of creative wonder-working.

To realize the importance of words in magic-making, we must remember that simple people think of words as very powerful things. A person's name, for instance, may be regarded as a part of him, just as much as his hand or leg. Indeed, sometimes it is thought to be his soul— as if the important part of him were a kind of name-substance. If a sorcerer then wishes to do harm to a person, he tries to learn his name, because he thinks thereby to obtain power over him. Thus the spells of Finnish wizards begin, 'I know thy birth'. For this reason it is a very common practice for names to be kept secret. Sometimes even a man's wife will not know his real and secret name. He has an 'ordinary name' for everyday use.

A curse is supposed to carry harm directly to the victim, and is not simply a way of expressing ill will towards him; many spells are curses, and are accompanied by actions representing the evil which the person wishes to fall on his victim. The witch or sorcerer acts on the belief that words are so full of power that to say what you wish to happen causes it to happen—just as he or she thinks that by acting a calamity to someone you bring it to pass. Although a magical spell is supposed to have power in itself to cause harm, yet quite often the names of demons or other spirits are brought into it to add to its effectiveness. Thus magical and religious notions become mingled. So also charms for some good purpose become rather like prayers, when the name of some divinity is invoked in them. Sometimes a spell is used by the sorcerer to compel a spirit to do his will. Here are a few examples of spells and charms:

A Hindu sorcerer used to kill a red-headed lizard saying, 'I am killing so-and-so'. An old Russian charm against fleas, bugs, and beetles is as follows: 'Fleas, bugs, beetles, and all such creatures, behold, I come to you as a guest; my body as bones; my blood as pitch; eat moss but not me. My word is sure. Key. Lock. Amen.

Amen. Amen.' In these the sorcerer relies on the words of the charm or spell and the magical actions to do their work, without the aid of spirits. The following words from the ancient Babylonian records are used by a man who believed his enemy had made a figure of him, to bewitch him; a prayer rather than a charm.

Those who have made images of me, reproducing my features,
Who have taken away my breath, torn my hairs,
Who have rent my clothes, have hindered my feet from treading the dust,
May the fire-god, the strong one, break their charm.

Some of the charms used by the ancient Egyptians against snake-bite were stories about gods, repeated because they were believed to have magical power. A person making magic may simply tell a story, including in it what he wants to happen. In New Guinea a man who wishes his taro plants to grow well says, 'Once upon a time a man laboured in his field and complained he had no taro shoots. Then came two doves flying. They had devoured much taro, and they perched on a tree in the field and during the night vomited up all the taro. Thus the man got so many taro shoots that he was even able to sell some of them to other people.' This native's wish had become a day-dream, and the day-dream had become a charm.

Since words are believed to be charged with power, sorcerers use spells or charms to give objects of one kind or another special magical qualities. When a Russian shopkeeper or merchant was doing badly in business, he used to go to a sorcerer and ask for his help. This man got some honey and said a charm over it: 'As the bees swarm around this honey, so let the purchasers flock to this merchant because of his wares.' To make the charm complete, the merchant smeared himself with the honey. The ancient Egyptians had a spell for curing bad eyesight. The spell was said over honey, mixed with the brain of a turtle, and then the eyes were anointed with this mess.

A natural step from using spoken words in charms was to write them down, and so have them handy all the time to keep off evil influences. Such charms are all the more useful as, in many countries, it is believed that a curse may float about for years, waiting for an opportunity to alight on the unfortunate person. These inscriptions were carried about in lockets, and so come into the class of 'amulets'—objects

Pitt Rivers Collection
AN ENGLISH GIRL'S LOVE CHARM
Putty figure of a man in a box with rose-buds

worn to keep off evil and bring good fortune. A Tibetan charm to counteract cooking smells in the kitchen, which the gods might dislike, consisted of the character for 'cow' wrapped in hedgehog skin. One Egyptian charm had to be written with myrrh and put in the mouth of a dead cat. It ended up '. . . the sacred Ianiee ien aeo eieeieiei'. These meaningless syllables were supposed to convey the secret name of a god, and so bring him under the sorcerer's power. A magician, who published a book on magic in 1606, gave the spells in code. They were deciphered more than a century later, and were found to consist of commands to spirits to appear and do his bidding.

A very famous charm, supposed to cure fevers and dating from the 2nd century A.D., consists of the word Abracadabra written thus:

ABRACADABRA	or thus	ABRACADABRA
ABRACADABR		BRACADABR
ABRACADAB		RACADAB
ABRACADA		ACADA
ABRACAD		CAD
ABRACA		A
ABRAC		
ABRA		
ABR		
AB		
A		

People will use nonsense in a spell, and think it all the better magic because they do not understand it. There was a belief that a person upon whom a spell had been cast could escape from it by saying it backwards, thereby, as it were, unwinding it. On the other hand, some witches' spells in Europe consisted of prayers said backwards; but the witch-cult in England and especially on the Continent was a form of devil worship rather than sheer magic (*see* WITCH-CRAFT).

In Christian countries heathen charms became something between charms and prayers. A Scottish cure for a sprain consisted of tying a black thread with nine knots around the limb and saying:

> The Lord rade
> And the foal slade;
> He lighted
> And he righted,
> Set joint to joint,
> Bone to bone,
> And sinew to sinew.
> Heal, in the Holy Ghost's name!

Originally, this charm, without the Christian references, was used for curing a lame horse, and was connected with the story from Norse mythology of how Baldur's foal was cured by Odin with spells. In later times people, using it to cure human injuries, did not worry about the mention of a foal being out of place in it.

Many Scottish charms are intended to counteract other spells which were supposed to be dangerous. To all magic there is a counter-magic, and so certain charms are believed to neutralize spells. The MAORIS (q.v.) used to say when a curse had been called down on someone:

> Great curse, long curse,
> Great curse, binding curse,
> Come hither, sacred spell!
> Cause the curser to lie low
> In gloomy night.

In the same way that a magician is supposed to have power over a person if he knows his name and birth, so he has power over certain objects believed to be full of magical quality if he knows their origin. When Väinämöinen, the hero in the beautiful Finnish epic, *Kalevala*, wounds himself with his axe, and is unable to staunch the bleeding, he goes to an old man who, by repeating the origin of iron and chanting other charms, is able to heal him.

Prayer is quite distinct from spells and charms although, as we have seen, charms and prayers may be confused together. In prayer, a person humbly seeks blessing, but does not believe he can command or control the divinity to whom he prays.

See also FOLKLORE; MAGIC.

SPIRITS. Many peoples, both primitive and civilized, think of spirit as the animating or life-giving principle in man and in nature, which shows itself in growth, movement, reproduction, and other signs of vitality, such as breathing. Breath, in fact, has often been regarded as the essence of life or soul, so that when an organism ceases to breathe, its soul is thought to have gone out of the body, departing with the last gasp. Souls and spirits are closely connected, and in all probability the idea of the soul is derived from the idea of the spirit. A very widespread and probably very old idea of man is of a person made up of a body and a life-principle or soul with an independent existence of its own. This, it was supposed, leaves the body when the latter is asleep, and its adventures are recalled in dreams. Sometimes it spends longer times away from its natural abode, and then the body is in a state of trance. Finally it departs one day for good, and that means the death of the body.

When man first began to think of himself as made up of two parts, the one physical, the other spiritual, he seems to have regarded every other living or moving thing in the same way.

Royal Geographical Society
A MEDICINE MAN IN ZAÏRE COMPOUNDING CHARMS

So he peopled the whole of nature with spiritual beings, good and evil, whom he held to be responsible for everything that happens in the universe, making them behave in much the same way as himself, although they belonged to the other world. They had supernatural powers, and could help or oppose him in all the affairs of his daily life (*see* NATURE WORSHIP).

In course of time, he began to think of gods with dominion over certain departments of nature. He conceived of a god of the woods— a Silvanus, as the ancient Romans called the impish deity who presided over the woodlands and in his kindlier moments looked after the interests of hunters and farmers. Similarly, he thought of the winds as under the control of a single divinity, such as Aeolus, who in Greek mythology is said to have kept the winds in a leathern bag, and let them out from time to time to lash the sea into fury. Thus, departmental gods of this kind were just part of the general animation of nature, that is, spiritual beings animating the natural objects or forces in which they were believed to dwell.

Besides these spirits and gods belonging to a different order from mankind, there are the souls or GHOSTS (q.v.) of dead men who, after death, live a life of their own, without their bodies, and are always liable to visit their old haunts on earth. Although these are generally invisible, they often appear in human form, looking as they used to when on earth, like the ghost in *Hamlet*: for the primitive mind thinks of the soul as the flimsy image of the body. On the whole, these visitations are regarded with fear and apprehension, because ghosts at best are uncanny, and always liable to bear a grudge against the living. Even to this day, many people are afraid to walk through a churchyard at night, or go into a room where a corpse is lying in its coffin. However, ghosts which are thought to be able to foretell the future, are sometimes deliberately called back to earth, as in the case of Saul's visit to the woman with 'the familiar spirit', the witch at Endor (1 Sam. xxviii. 8 f.).

If more attention has been paid to harmful than to helpful spirits, this is because man is inclined to take the good for granted and to seek chiefly for causes and remedies for his misfortunes. Therefore, he attributed to evil spirits or to black magic the ills of life that beset him— sickness, calamity, and death—and so imagined

British Museum

THE DEATH OF ST. GUTHLAC

The soul, escaping from the saint's mouth, is borne to heaven by angels. The Guthlac Roll, 12th-century MS. (B.M. Harley Roll Y. 6., f. 13)

himself surrounded by a host of demons ready to trip him up at any moment. He saw them actively at work in thunderstorms, avalanches, hurricanes, earthquakes, drought, plague, pestilence, and famine—in fact in any catastrophe. He believes that some are devils who have always been evil spirits, citizens of the underworld; others are the disembodied ghosts of persons who have died a sudden or violent death, and hover about in the air or in the dark recesses of the forests to wreak vengence on luckless mortals whom they happen to meet, or who they believe were responsible for their death.

This side of the picture can be easily exaggerated, for, while man is undoubtedly always on the look out against the attacks of unseen powers, and takes special precautions at critical seasons of the year or at crises in his own life, in fact the majority of spirits are thought of as neither good nor evil. It is always when they are neglected, provoked, or offended that these neutral beings become hostile, and the forces of evil are opposed by those whose purpose is to help man. Examples of guardian spirits are found in ancient Roman religion, where the homestead was under the care and patronage of the household spirits and gods, such as Vesta, the spirit of the hearth, Janus, the spirit of the door, and the Lares, the spirits of the home and

Royal Geographical Society
HUTS FOR THE SPIRITS OF THE DEAD
Zaïre

the fields. In China, also, the ancestors looked after their own people, and the spirits guarded the road, the gate, the path, the door, and the kitchen (*see* CHINESE RELIGION).

Moreover, in Rome, not only the house and the fields, but every man was supposed to have his own guardian spirit, or Genius, and every woman her Juno. In Egypt a spiritual helper called the *ka* was assigned first to the Pharaoh and then to everybody, to be his companion and guide all the days of his life, and at death to prepare a place for him in the next world. This same idea recurs in the Christian belief in guardian angels (*see* ANGEL). So we see that spirits are by no means always regarded as harmful and evilly disposed towards human beings and the world. On the contrary, an important part of their work has been supposed to be of a kindly and friendly nature, and only when they are not properly treated do they become vicious.

See also FAIRIES.

SPIRITUALISM is the name given to the practice of communicating, or attempting to communicate, with the spirits of the dead. Though the name is modern, the practice is very ancient. Witch-doctors and medicine-men in primitive societies have believed that they could get into touch with departed spirits. A well-known instance is that recorded in 1 Samuel xxviii, where Saul consulted the woman of Endor in order to speak with the dead prophet Samuel. The practice is said to have been forbidden in Israel even in those early days—certainly a passage in Isaiah (viii. 19-20) shows that the great prophets disapproved of it. The Jewish repugnance to Spiritualism was maintained by Christianity. Witches and wizards have always been regarded as being in league with the devil, and in times of fear and unrest they were often hunted out and persecuted (*see* WITCHCRAFT).

The qualities possessed by these ancient communicants with the spirit world were those we now call psychic, and there can be little doubt that they were similar to those possessed by the modern medium. The difference lies in the use made of them. In 1848 three sisters, Fox by name, living at Hydesville, New York State, heard mysterious rappings in their home. One of them devised a simple code which, the girls asserted, was answered by rappings in such a way as to prove that they were made by an intelligent being. The news of these happenings caused a great sensation; and from them the modern spiritualistic movement had its origin. Hitherto most Christians had believed that spirits were only invoked to do harm, and that they were evil—which explains the fear and hatred felt towards those who invoked them. Now, however, it was proclaimed that the spirits were good, or at least as good as ordinary people on earth. They dwelt, not with the devil in hell, but in lands far better than this world; and they were continually progressing. An inquirer could find his friends and relations among them, ready and anxious to give proof that they had survived death. It is still the claim of spiritualists that this proof can be supplied to all who seek it. Whether the proof is sufficient is a matter of dispute. A number of eminent men, including Sir William Barrett and Sir Oliver Lodge, have believed that it is; but the majority are sceptical.

The spiritualist movement has taken two directions, one scientific and the other religious. In England the Society for Psychical Research was founded in 1882. Its investigations include, not only communications with the dead, but such kindred subjects as the seeing of visions and the hearing of voices, telepathy or thought-transference, as well as GHOSTS (q.v.), haunted houses, and uncanny movements of furniture. It seems clear that such things happen; but more than sixty years' investigation has failed to discover any laws by which they can be explained or controlled. That mediums have access, in varying degrees, to knowledge beyond the ordinary is certain; but how that knowledge comes to them is still a mystery. The balance of evidence, however, is in favour of supposing it to proceed from some deep activity of the human mind, rather than from the spirits of the dead.

It has been suggested that there exists a vast reservoir of life, from which all creatures partake, and in which all experience and knowledge is stored. Tiny insects, which are close to this original source and only slightly differentiated from it, gather from it all the knowledge they need for their short earthly existence. As the scale of life rises, in animals and at last in man, a new power develops—the power of thinking. This comes to its height in human self-consciousness and reason; and for man, reason is the proper and normal guide to knowledge. But the old direct instinctive channels are not entirely closed; and in some persons, perhaps in all persons at some times, flashes of knowledge come through them, either spontaneously, as in visions, or after artificial stimulation, as when the medium goes into a trance. People who are continuously susceptible to these influences from the beyond are called psychic. In some of them the personality appears to split up and form two, three, or occasionally many personalities, with different characters, speech, and knowledge. It is through such people that the messages, which Spiritualists claim to come from the dead, have proceeded.

When Spiritualism is spoken of, it is generally the religious movement which is meant. The impulse to make psychic communications the basis of a new religion comes from the natural longing to know what has become of our loved ones who have died. This longing was very evident after each of the two World Wars of the 20th century. Spiritualist churches arise wherever a few people can gather together and procure a medium. Messages from the departed are confidently given to all who ask for them. The messages are generally very poor in quality, and concerned for the most part with trivial matters. But when inquirers are in distress through bereavement, they are, in general, not too critical in examining any message which brings them comfort.

The late Sir Arthur Conan Doyle became a Spiritualist, and wrote a book entitled *The New Revelation*, in which he claimed that Spiritualism was the true religion which must now supersede all others. In this book, and in the works of Mr. J. A. Findlay (of which *The Psychic Stream* is the most important), the creed of Spiritualists is set forth. They believe in the Fatherhood of God and the brotherhood of man, doctrines taken from Christianity. Some regard Jesus Christ as the Son of God; others proclaim him to be one of a series of high spirits who have temporarily left the other world to help men on earth. All deny the Atonement; for they insist that man rises by his own efforts, and that no one could bear the sins of another. The next world is conceived as a series of spheres or regions, rising one after another until the final heaven, the abode of God, is reached. Through these, the souls after death travel in a continuous progression, though at different rates. The weakness of Spiritualism as a religion is that it is based on an interpretation of psychic happenings which is, to say the least, doubtful. From a Christian point of view, it tends to obscure God by concentrating attention on the spirits of the departed.

STOICISM, *see* ASCETICISM. *See also* Vol. V: ZENO.

STONEHENGE. This great prehistoric monument on Salisbury Plain is one of the most remarkable and puzzling of our British antiquities, for the Bronze Age stone-circles elsewhere in Britain or on the Continent (to which it otherwise seems clearly related) are not constructed in this way—with horizontal lintels carried on uprights of carefully tooled stone.

The main features of Stonehenge are as follows: a not very large ditch and bank cut in the chalk encloses a circular area, about 104 metres across; there is a gap in the ditch on the northeast to which a wide 'avenue', marked out by a double line of small ditches 18 to 21 metres apart, leads from the direction of the river Avon. Nearly in the middle of this avenue, just outside the gap in the enclosing circular ditch, is a large standing stone (the Heel Stone). The main standing structure of Stonehenge is within the circular area enclosed by the ditch, and is arranged in this way: on the outside, nearest the ditches, there is a circle 30 metres in diameter, of large stone-uprights of grey sandstone, with continuous lintels of large carefully-shaped stones bridging them across on top. Next comes a

STONEHENGE

Aerofilms

circle of smallish stones of bluish-green stone; inside this come two 'horseshoe' settings, one formed by five enormous pairs of sandstone (sarsen) uprights with lintels, and the other formed by more of the bluish stones, also arranged in a horseshoe shape set inside the first horseshoe. In the curve of the horseshoe is a flat oblong slab. Many of the stones have now fallen or have been destroyed; but this plan can be seen quite well.

Excavations carried out to discover the date and the history of the construction of Stonehenge revealed that, almost certainly, Stonehenge was built in three main stages.

Stonehenge I belonged to the late Neolithic period (about 2500 B.C.) and consisted of the bank and ditch within which was found a circle of 56 pits, dug for ritual purposes and deliberately refilled. Human cremations had been put into some of them, and were found elsewhere nearby.

Stonehenge II dated from the Beaker period (within a century or so of 2000 B.C.) and was marked by the first use of blue stones, brought from the Presely Mountains in Pembrokeshire some 320 km away as the crow flies. They were probably brought mainly by sea and river routes, namely up the Bristol Channel, up the Bristol Avon, down the Wylye, and up the Wiltshire Avon to Stonehenge. The stones, not dressed to shape, were apparently intended to be set up in a double circle on the line of the present single blue stone circle, but the scheme was never finished. The double circle had an entrance aligned with the midsummer sunrise, and to Phase II also belongs the 'avenue' and probably the little circular ditch round the Heel Stone.

Stonehenge III was probably built in three stages during the period stretching from about 1500 to 1400 B.C. It was in some way connected with the powerful Bronze Age dynasty which ruled in Wessex and buried its dead near Stonehenge. Carvings of axes and a dagger on the Sarsen stones support this argument. The first stage in the building of Stonehenge III must have begun with the removal of the blue stones from the site. The huge sandstone (sarsen) stones were brought from north Wiltshire in the AVEBURY (q.v.) region, dressed to shape, and set up in their present form. Then, in the second stage, some of the blue stones were carefully dressed to shape and set up, probably in an oval setting more or less on the site of the present blue stone horseshoe, and having two pairs of lintelled stones. Holes which were dug but never used suggest that the remainder of the blue stones were to have been set up in a double ring outside the sarsen circle, but during the third stage of Stonehenge III the blue stones were set up instead in their present arrangement of a single circle and a horseshoe, with the lintels from the older structure now used as uprights.

See also MEGALITHS; RELIGION, PREHISTORIC.

SUDANESE, see AFRICANS; ARABS; NILOTIC PEOPLES. *See also* Vol. III: SUDAN; INDEX, p. 156.

SUMERIANS. Before the end of the 19th century the very existence of the people whom we now call Sumerians was unknown; but excavations have now proved that, earlier than the already well-known Semitic civilizations of the BABYLONIANS and the ASSYRIANS (qq.v.), there had existed for many centuries, in the fertile delta of the Euphrates and the Tigris, in what is now Iraq, a people whose language and culture were quite different from that of the Babylonians and Assyrians. We have now enough knowledge to form a fairly accurate picture of this, the most ancient civilization of Mesopotamia.

The origin of the Sumerians is still an unsolved problem. Their language does not belong to the Semitic family of languages nor is it related to any known ancient language. It is likely that the Sumerians entered south Mesopotamia originally either from Persia or perhaps from the islands and western shores of the Persian Gulf. Once arrived, they adapted for their own use an existing pictographic system of writing, soon modified into CUNEIFORM WRITING (q.v. Vol. IV), and absorbed into their own language many names of places and gods used by their predecessors. In a relatively short period of time they achieved a high level of civilization focused on the city of Uruk, *c.* 3500 B.C. From the marshy shores at the head of the Persian Gulf, northwards for about 550 km through the alluvial plain of the Tigris and Euphrates, they established a series of independent city-states. At times some of the city-states were united in loose allegiance to a par-

Giraudon

PORTRAIT OF GUDEA, GOVERNOR OF LAGASH
Sumerian sculpture 2170 B.C., in the Louvre

ticularly energetic and powerful leader. Extensive trade across land and sea linked them to Persia and India in one direction, to Egypt and Turkey in the other.

The period of Sumerian greatness lasted from 3500 B.C. to the fall of the Third Dynasty of Ur about 2030 B.C.—or a little later according to some scholars. During this long period there were many changes and a great deal of development. We shall deal with the civilization of the Sumerians under the three main heads— Organization of Society; Religion; and Arts and Crafts.

A. ORGANIZATION OF SOCIETY. What we know about the early social pattern of the Sumerians we have gathered from the various collections of laws which have survived. The famous Code of Hammurabi (described in the article of Babylonian civilization) was drawn up about 1785 B.C., and was based on earlier bodies of Sumerian law and custom, collected and set in order by Hammurabi's orders. But even earlier collections of Sumerian legal decisions have been found, and from these we can tell that the family was the Sumerian social unit, and the father was the head of the family. Landed property was the most important factor in holding the family together, and the need of securing an heir made it sometimes allowable for a Sumerian to have more than one wife. Adoption of children was also a frequent practice. The wife enjoyed a high degree of independence; she had her own property, and had the right of inheritance to her husband's estate.

There were three main classes in Sumerian society. The highest class included all government officials, soldiers of the regular army, and the priests. The second class consisted of the free-men who were merchants, farmers, and craftsmen. In the third class were found the slaves, whether born in the house or captured in battle. Between these different classes important legal

THE RUINS OF THE PALACE AT KISH, IN AKKAD   *Prof. S. Langdon*

distinctions existed. Offences against members of the highest class were punished much more severely than those against members of the lower orders. It is probable that this caste system was of military origin, since war was a very important factor in Sumerian society, and the Sumerians were far ahead of their neighbours in military technique.

The normal political unit was the small city-state, ruled over by a priest-king who had the title of *Ensi*. In the early days of Sumerian history the country was largely marsh and swamp, in which islands of cultivated land had been created by irrigation ditches, canals, and dams. These settlements developed into city-states. As more and more of the marsh was reclaimed, various cities sought to bring their neighbours under their own control, and so arose the succession of dynasties—Kish, Erech, Ur, Isin, and so forth—each being named after the city which had, at that time, acquired the leadership in Sumer. But even under rulers such as the Semite Sargon of Akkad, who brought the whole of Sumer under his sway and became the centre of a series of legends, the cities continued

to rule their own inhabitants and the out-lying farmers and cattle-breeders. The irrigation system had to be kept in repair, and this required the continual control and oversight of the *Ensi* and his officials. Documents show how carefully all matters relating to the land and its needs were watched over and regulated by the central authority. All mortgages, sales, and transfers of landed property were registered; a tenant or owner who farmed his land badly, or neglected to keep his section of the irrigation system in repair, might be heavily fined, or even be de-prived of his holding and reduced to slavery. In general, the Sumerians had reached, in these very ancient times, when our own country was still inhabited by primitive savages, a quite remarkably complete and efficient social organization.

B. THE RELIGION OF SUMER. From the earliest times of which we have any knowledge, each of the great cities of Sumer had its own special god, whose temple, called *e. gal*, or 'the great house', was the centre of the religious and civil life of the city. The great Mother-goddess, Innina, had her temple at Erech, in which has been found the earliest form of Sumerian writing yet known. En-lil, at first the god of wind and streams, and later the god of the dry land, had his temple at Nippur, the most central point of Sumer and Akkad. A Sumerian god of great importance was Ea, the god of the deep, who was regarded as the lord of wisdom and the inventor of all magic spells and incantations. His special seat was Eridu, the oldest of Sumerian cities. Ea's son Marduk, at first the god of the unimportant town Babilu, or Babylon, became, later, when Babylon rose to be the capital city, the chief god of the country, and the hero of the Babylonian myth of Creation (see BABYLONIAN MYTHS).

All these gods had their consorts, their sons and daughters, and their various attendants, and the temple buildings in which they lived, attended by a large staff of priests, were very elaborate and magnificent. The chief god of the city was regarded as the owner of the land, so that all those who worked on it were his tenants, and bound to bring a fixed proportion of the fruits of the land to the temple, as rent to the god. The earliest tables from the temple at Erech give a record of these temple dues.

The central feature of Sumerian religion was the great New Year festival, held in all the great cities, either in the spring or in the autumn. It lasted for twelve days, and the gods of the smaller places came into the great cities Erech, Nippur, or Babylon, as the case might be, to take part in the proceedings. The purpose of the various rituals performed at the festival was to secure a good new year, that is, a new year of fertility and prosperity for the whole community. The most important features of the ritual were (a) the killing and bringing to life again of the god, (b) a ritual combat between the god and a monster of dragon form, in which the god was victorious, and (c) a sacred marriage between the god and the goddess of the city. These ritual acts were performed by the king and the priests, mainly in the great open court of the temple buildings, or on the great temple tower, called a *ziggurat*, which was the most striking feature of Sumerian temple buildings (see RITUAL).

Another important feature of Sumerian religion was the universal belief in evil spirits. Pictures of these creatures have come down to us, and suggest the horrible fantasies of a nightmare. One class of priests had the special duty of performing rituals and incantations to protect individuals against the attacks of such evil spirits.

The Sumerians thought that all kinds of diseases were caused by evil spirits, and they used rituals in addition to medicines in the treatment of disease. We even have a tablet containing a ritual and its accompanying incantation for the cure of toothache.

C. SUMERIAN ARTS AND CRAFTS. We have seen that, when the Sumerians arrived in the Tigris–Euphrates delta, they already possessed an advanced civilization. Their early pottery, decorated with beautiful geometric designs and of graceful shapes, is clearly the work of a highly artistic people. They were skilled sculptors, and their work in gold and jewellery has hardly ever been surpassed. They had invented a special kind of inlay with shell and lapis lazuli. They had the potter's wheel, and knew the use of the drill for hollowing out pots and vases from alabaster. They were skilled builders, depending mainly on clay bricks for their material, since stone and wood were not to be found in the delta and had to be imported. Much of their inventive genius was devoted to the arts of war. They had invented or brought with them the war-chariot, a four-wheeled armoured car drawn by asses. Long before the Macedonians had thought of it, the Sumerians had discovered the advantages of the phalanx in attack—a phalanx in action is shown on the famous monument, known as the Stele of the Vultures, representing the victory of an early Sumerian king, Eannatum. They were fond of music, and one of the most

British Museum

QUEEN SHUB-AD'S HARP
Sumerian, 3rd millennium B.C.

beautiful objects found in the excavation of the ancient city of Ur was the very elaborate harp of Queen Shub-ad, adorned with a bull's head and inlaid with shell and lapis lazuli mosaic. The writing material used by the Sumerians was the clay tablet. The earliest form of writing was picture-writing, done with a reed pen on the soft clay. The tablet was then baked and was practically indestructible. Hence, the immense amount of written material of priceless value which has survived and has made possible the reconstruction of the civilization of this most interesting people (*see* WRITING, HISTORY OF, Vol. IV).

See ANCIENT CIVILIZATIONS; BABYLONIAN CIVILIZATION. See also Vol. XII: SUMERIAN ART.

SUN-GOD. The sun has been an object of worship from very early times: it has often been supposed to be a man, either sailing in a boat or driving in a chariot across the sky. These are very odd ideas, for the sun does not look at all like either of these things. For example, the Egyptian sun-god, who has various forms and names, is often represented as a hawk-headed man sitting in the centre of a boat with quite a large crew, and this boat was supposed to be the sun sailing along the heavenly river. The Egyptians could never have thought that the sun really looked like that; and so they must have, in imagination, transferred to the heavens the picture of the king, disguised as the sun-god, sailing down the Nile.

But the sun-god is more often thought of as a charioteer. This was so in Greece, where Helios drove the chariot of the sun across the heavens every day (see illus., p. 333). One day he lent the chariot to his son Phaethon, who drove it so near the earth that the latter was in danger of being burnt up. Then Zeus, the king of the gods, slew Phaethon, and the sun returned to its course.

The ancient Teutonic tribes also believed in the chariot of the sun; but with them the sun was feminine, so that the chariot was driven by a maiden. A famous sun-cult was that of the heretic king of Egypt, AKHNATEN (q.v. Vol. V), who suppressed the old gods, and worshipped only the solar disk. This cult was suppressed soon after his death. Another was that of Mithras, the Unconquered Sun, who was worshipped by the Roman legions (*see* MITHRAISM).

See also RELIGION; GOD.

SUPERSTITIONS, *see* FOLKLORE.

SUTTEE (sometimes spelt *săti*). This was the practice whereby, in India, a Hindu widow was expected to remain faithful to her husband even after death, and to be burnt or buried alive with him. It was abolished in 1829 by Lord William Bentinck, Governor-General of India, who carried a Regulation through the Council of State making those who aided and abetted the practice responsible for a 'culpable suicide'.

See also HINDUISM.

SWAHILI, *see* EAST AFRICANS.

SWEDES. We first hear of the Swedish people as the Svear, a group of tall, long-headed people, living on both sides of Lake Mälar. This Nordic or Teutonic tribe, which had originally migrated from Central Asia, gave its name to the whole country, Sverige, the English version of which is Sweden. These people in the 6th century B.C. were traders in amber, fur, and iron, and were known to the Romans as Suiones. In the 9th and 10th centuries A.D. they joined with the Norwegians and Danes in attacks on Western and Eastern Europe and were known as the Northmen, Norsemen, or Vikings ('the men of the long ships'). Under their leader Rurik the Swedes built a trading post beside Lake Ladoga in north Russia from which they spread southwards, conquering the wild Slav tribes, and founded settlements at Novgorod and Kiev. Out of these settlements grew up the great Russian state.

In the 15th century Sweden was joined with Denmark under the same king; the connexion ended in 1521. Under GUSTAVUS ADOLPHUS (q.v. Vol. V) she became the greatest power in north Europe. This famous military leader, known as the 'Lion of the North', held his court as far south as Munich in Bavaria; but his successors lost all that he had conquered. The last king of the royal family which had ruled Sweden for 300 years had no heir, so in 1810, at the wish of the people, he adopted Jean Bernadotte, one of Napoleon's marshals, and it is from him that the present Swedish Royal Family is descended.

Swedes, of whom there are over eight million (1973), are tall and strongly built. In central Sweden the people are truly Nordic in appearance, with heads longer than they are broad, straight, long noses, fair hair, and blue eyes. But

Camera Press

STOCKHOLM AT CHRISTMAS: THE ANNUAL NOBEL PRIZEGIVING TAKES PLACE IN THE CONCERT HALL (*left*)

to the north and south the people are shorter and darker. In the far north live a few LAPPS (q.v.). About 90 per cent of the population live in the southern half of the country.

There are a great many forests in Sweden, and so most of the farms and country-houses are made of timber, often painted with mineral paint to prevent dry-rot. At the last census (1965) 10 per cent of the labour force was engaged in agriculture and 2 per cent in forestry. The dairy farmers belong to a co-operative, a system which, as in New Zealand, is used for production as well as for distribution. The Swedes are proud of the way they have conquered their harsh and difficult country, making the most of their farms, forests, and mines.

Even more impressive is Sweden's swift and confident emergence as an industrialized nation. In the 19th century the Swedes began to exploit their mineral ore and forests for steelmaking and sawmilling. Their traditional exports—timber, paper, pulp, iron ore, iron, and steel—are still important, but today the emphasis has shifted from raw materials to manufactured goods, which now account for two-thirds of the total trade and include motor-vehicles, textiles, chemicals, machinery, electrical goods, and ships.

Three-quarters of the total population live in towns and villages, about half of which are small with between 200 and 500 people. Swedish builders have been innovators: they built in Stockholm blocks of houses arranged in zigzag fashion so that the windows of one do not overlook those of another; and they pioneered the construction of prefabricated houses for the rapidly expanding urban population. Many of the buildings, especially in the smaller towns, are made of timber. The town planning is good, and much of the architecture fine.

The Swedes are proud of their past, and preserve its records in many excellent local museums and libraries. In the remoter parts of central Sweden you still find old customs, though traditional costumes are now little seen except in the Nordiska Museet (Nordic Museum) at Stockholm, which also has examples of woodcarving and other rural crafts.

Their famous men include LINNAEUS, the 18th-century botanist; SWEDENBORG, scientist and philosopher (1688–1772); STRINDBERG, the 19th-century dramatist; and NOBEL, the inventor of dynamite and originator of the Nobel Prize (qq.v. Vol. V). They have always been great travellers and explorers; Dr. Sven Hedin journeyed through unknown Central Asia, and Adolf Nordenskjöld was the first to master the North-East Passage.

In 1813 Per Henrik Ling founded the Central Gymnastic Institute in Stockholm, and his ideas on physical culture spread throughout the world. Because of their long, snow-bound winter nearly everyone in Sweden can ski, whilst in summer the young men and women spend their holidays camping, swimming, canoeing, and sailing. The Royal Swedish Yacht Club is the largest in the world.

The Swedes maintain that they are the most democratic people in Europe. Although the country has always been a kingdom, the Swedes never forget that, by a law passed in A.D. 900, the people have the right 'to make or break the King'. They enjoy a high standard of living. Every child goes to school, and a high proportion of those who leave upper-secondary school at the age of 19 go on to attend universities such as Lund or Uppsala.

See also Vol. III: SWEDEN; INDEX, p. 156.
See also Vol. IV: GERMANIC LANGUAGES.

SWISS. A Swiss postage stamp has on it the word Helvetia instead of Switzerland. Helvetia was the land of the Helvetii, a Celtic tribe which invaded the southern part of Gaul, now France, in 58 B.C. They were defeated by JULIUS CAESAR (q.v. Vol. V), and they returned to their towns and villages, carrying with them the influence of Roman culture, which dominated their lives for several centuries. About A.D. 445 Helvetia was invaded from the north by Germanic tribes, who in the course of the following eight centuries were divided and ruled by many overlords. In 1291 three of the Cantons, or provinces, of Helvetia—those known as the Forest Cantons—joined together to form an alliance and to fight and defeat their Austrian overlords. This event is connected with the legend of William TELL (q.v. Vol. V). One of these Forest Cantons was called Schwyz, and from this came the names Switzerland and Swiss. Neighbouring districts joined the Forest Cantons in their struggle against the Austrians and, when in the 15th century independence was won, these districts remained united with the original Cantons, although they kept their own languages, customs, and ways of religious worship. This was the origin of the Swiss form of Federal Government, and is also the

J. Allan Cash

SWITZERLAND: DAVOS, IN THE SERTIG VALLEY

and grazes his cows in fields of wild flowers and, in the winter, goes about his business on skis. But in fact, nearly a quarter of the Swiss population of over six millions lives in the few big towns, where they make, among other things, the textiles, the clocks and watches, the machines and locomotives, the chocolate and condensed milk, which are the best-known products of Switzerland. They are a sturdy, hard-working, and practical people, who combine an intense love of their own country with a power of getting on well with people of other countries. Swiss hotel-keepers are found in almost every part of the world: indeed hotel-keeping, especially in the winter-sports resorts, is an important industry in their own country.

Her central position and the fact that she remained neutral in the two great international struggles of this century have made Switzerland a favourite meeting-place for great international gatherings. The International Postal Union grew from a conference held at Berne. The International Committee of the Red Cross grew from a conference at Geneva. The red cross itself, on a white ground, was chosen as the Society's emblem in compliment to the Swiss, whose national flag is the same sort of cross, but in white upon red. The League of Nations used to have its headquarters in a great Palace of the Nations in Geneva, where the International Labour Organization also has its headquarters. The European Headquarters of the United Nations is also in Geneva.

See also Vol. III: SWITZERLAND; INDEX, p. 156.

reason why four languages—French, German, Italian, and Romansch—are spoken.

Switzerland is a Confederation, or Federal State. Each of its twenty-two cantons has its own courts of justice, its own parliament, and its own educational system. Changes in federal or cantonal laws have to be submitted to the electorate for approval. Besides electing their own government the voters also elect their judges and teachers; they vote on the building of hospitals, schools, and churches. Every Swiss may speak his own language and write it to his government, and he may follow his own religion. The Central Government is by a Federal Assembly, with two Houses, and a Federal Council of seven members that meets in BERNE, the capital (q.v. Vol. III). The President is elected by the Assembly and holds office for one year. He is the President of the Swiss Federal Council, and while holding this office also has the title of President of the Confederation.

The type of Swiss best known to the foreigner used to be the peasant and the farmer, who lives in a wooden chalet under the shadow of the Alps,

E. O. Hoppé

A SWISS MAKING MUSICAL BOXES

SYRIANS AND LEBANESE. These people live in a land which holds such a key position between East and West that few great events of history have by-passed them. Both SYRIA and the LEBANON (q.v. Vol. III) have been part of the empires of the Egyptians, the Assyrians, the Persians, the Romans, the Muslim Arabs, the Turks, and finally the French (administered under a League of Nations Mandate). From about the 16th century B.C., on the coast of Syria, there grew up the great merchant city-states of the PHOENICIANS (q.v.). On the cliff walls north of Beirut there is a series of carvings and inscriptions recording the passage of armies along the coast of Syria in the course of thirty-three centuries. Syria has been involved in many great European wars, from the CRUSADES (q.v.) to the First and Second World Wars. Her people have hardly ever, until recently, been real masters of their own house. They gained legal independence from France in 1941, and now Syria and the Lebanon are independent states. Together they equal about the size of England and Scotland, with a joint population of about seven millions—four and a half million Syrians and more than two million Lebanese. Many Syrians and Lebanese live abroad, particularly in West Africa and North and South America, and when they get rich they send a good deal of money home.

It is not surprising that a people with such a history should be of a very mixed racial type. Arab blood as a whole predominates; but there is a considerable element descended from the ancient peoples of Syria, and in later times Armenians, Kurds, Turks, Turkmen, and Europeans have mixed with the population. Two-thirds of the people are engaged in agriculture, stock-raising, and horticulture; but the remainder live in towns such as Beirut, Aleppo, and Damascus (which has been called the oldest city in the world). The life of the peasants in the country is precarious and hard, made doubly insecure, until recently, by regular raids of nomadic tribes of BEDOUIN (q.v.). The peasants therefore tend to overcrowd the towns, and this raises economic and social problems, for there is not enough industry to absorb them. The standard of living in the overcrowded towns as well as in the country is very low. The dwellings in the countryside are primitive—cottages in the shape of beehives made of mud-brick, others made of wattle, and others partly of stone with flat roofs. There are also more than a quarter of a million Palestine refugees, most of them living in great poverty in camps near the big towns.

About half the population of Lebanon is Christian. (The Maronites have existed from the early days of Christianity.) The rest belong to the various Muslim sects (*see* ISLAM). The Syrians are nearly all Muslims, the majority being of the Sunnite community. About 13 per cent are Christians.

Those Muslims that are not Sunnite belong to the Shiah sect (also known as *Meta wilah*); and these are further split into three separate communities—the Druzes, the Alawis, and the Ismai'ilis—each with a particular form of unorthodox Shi'ism. Each of these groups has from the 9th century developed local traditions and characteristics, and they have not always been purely religious groups, but also secret societies with political aims.

The Druzes broke away from Orthodox Islam and fled from Egypt to Syria in the 11th century. There is now a strongly organized community, some 70,000 in the Lebanon and about 85,000 in Syria. As the result of strife among the different factions of the Druze nobility many Druzes settled in the Jebel Druze district, where they make up almost all the population. They cling tenaciously to their distinctive customs and their own laws, distrusting Christians and other Muslims, and resenting government interference, although Druzes have often been cabinet ministers. In 1841 there was a civil war between Druzes and Christians, and in 1860 many Christians were massacred. The quarrel was not only over religion, but was largely a conflict between Christian peasants and Druze landlords. Several times expeditions had to be sent against them, and in 1925–6 the French had great difficulty in subduing a Druze revolt.

The Alawis (or Nasaris) are, like the Druzes, hardly Muslims at all, their religious liturgy being largely Christian in origin. They differ from the other minorities in possessing no land-owning class, but are almost all peasants (*fella-heen*) and labourers. There are almost half a million of them, divided into tribes and sects. Sometimes they have risen to high positions in the armed forces and by this means managed to control governments in Syria.

The Ismai'ili broke off from the Shiahs in the 8th century. They are a compact community of about 24,000, living in the Syrian province of

A QUIET STREET IN DAMASCUS

Camera Press

130,000 in all, came into Syria at the end of the 19th century to escape from Turkish persecutions and massacres, and again in 1939, when their region was transferred to Turkey. They are mostly townspeople, craftsmen, and traders. About 4,000 Assyrians fled from Iraq in 1933 and were settled with League of Nations assistance in Jazirah, and have now become an integral part of the Syrian state. There are about 200,000 Kurds, followers of Islam, many of whom have been in Syria for a long time, though some are recent arrivals. The Kurds have a tribal organization, and many of them live a nomad life. They have a strong nationalist movement, aiming at a Kurdish state. There are about 30,000 Turkomans, and 20,000 Circassians who came into Syria from Circassia to escape Russian domination. There is also a very small group called the Yazidis, who follow an ancient secret religion and speak a dialect of their own. All these peoples speak non-Arabic languages.

Apart from these non-Arabic-speaking minorities the main unifying factor of the Syrians and Lebanese, whether Christian or Muslim (including about 30,000 Jews), is the Arab language. Under the French administration a strong sense of nationalism grew up, and the old animosity between Maronites and Muslims has grown less —in fact, in 1946 the President of the Syrian Republic with its Muslim majority was a Christian Arab, while since independence the Lebanese have agreed that the President should always be a Maronite Christian and the Prime Minister a Sunni Muslim. Although Syria and Lebanon have had their quarrels (sometimes the frontier between the two countries has been closed and no trade allowed to pass it), their people are united by fear of a strong new neighbour, ISRAEL (q.v. Vol. III). Israel occupied parts of Syria near Damascus after the 1967 Arab-Israel war, and on many occasions Israeli armies and aeroplanes have made raids into the Lebanon to destroy Palestinian strongholds there.

See also Vol. III: SYRIA; INDEX, p. 156.

Hama: they mix very little with others, and resent outside interference. They owe religious allegiance today to the Aga Khan.

Among the Christians the most important are the Maronites, of whom there are about 750,000, the majority living in the Lebanon. Their name comes from a 5th-century bishop, St. Maro. They became Catholics in the 11th century during the Crusades, and are now one of the biggest communities which, while acknowledging the supremacy of the Pope, retain their own (Syriac) liturgy and customs. During the 9th century most of them moved into Lebanon in order to seek safety in the mountains. As well as Maronites there are members of the ORTHODOX EASTERN CHURCH (q.v.), the Armenian and Assyrian Churches, groups of Jacobites and members of the NESTORIAN CHURCH (q.v.), and some Roman Catholics and Protestants.

Besides these religious groups there are many racial minorities. The ARMENIANS (q.v.), some

T

TABOO. When Captain Cook during his voyage to the Pacific Ocean visited the Polynesian island of Tonga in 1777, he found that anything that was forbidden was described as *tabu*. In nearby islands he discovered that this Polynesian word could include a variety of meanings, but was applied in all cases where things were not to be touched. The person of a chief, a corpse, or a newly-born infant were all tabu, because they were regarded as 'dangerous. in a supernatural sense and so must not be lightly approached, being set apart from common use or contacts. These early travellers introduced the word into English (spelt 'taboo'), and they used it to refer to persons, places, and events having these 'dangerous' supernatural qualities—such as a warrior, a divine king, a dead body, a shrine, a particular day of the week or season of the year, the name of a god, or a magic word.

The Bible offers many examples of taboos: for example, after touching the Ark of the Covenant in Israel, Uzzah is said to have been struck dead (2 Sam. vi); and Jonathan only narrowly escaped with his life when he ate honey, after his father, Saul, had placed a taboo on eating during a battle (1 Sam. xiv: 24, 27). The severe penalties suffered by those who broke the rules concerning the observance of the Sabbath as a taboo day are an example of the same principle, as is also the attitude towards Sunday that was adopted after the Reformation in northern Europe.

Taboos may, therefore, surround a great variety of objects and institutions that are regarded as sacred. Some objects, such as a corpse or a newly-born baby, are in themselves awe-inspiring. Others acquire supernatural qualities because of their social position or special activities (powerful chief, king, or priest, mourners, warriors, man-slayers), or because of their sacred associations (the Jewish Sabbath and the Christian Sunday). Finally, a person or thing may be set apart for religious purposes by an act of consecration, as when a church is dedicated, a king anointed and crowned, or a priest ordained. In all these ways persons, places, and objects are given a 'ritual status' in society, and so are hedged round with taboos.

It would be a mistake to dismiss all this as mere primitive superstition of no value. Taboo may play an important part in defining what is lawful and what is unlawful, or in protecting people from food-borne diseases, or in forbidding actions that would be harmful to good social relations between members of a community. Furthermore, taboo emphasizes the importance of an event such as a birth or a death. The total effect, in short, is to bind individual men, women, and children into an orderly society, in which each has his or her proper place and part to play for the well-being of the group as a whole.

The rules and regulations demand effort, discipline, and obedience, and represent the crude beginnings of a moral sense of right and wrong. The unforgivable sin is to do anything that is likely to bring ill luck on oneself, because ill luck is catching and therefore to be avoided at all costs, like any other contagious plague. The worst crime of all is to fail in the duty of being a good tribesman, and therefore the strictest taboos are those connected with the laws against incest (i.e. marriage between near relatives). If human beings are to live together in unity, peace, and concord, there have to be adequate controls such as the institution of taboo affords.

See also RITUAL.

TAMILS, *see* INDIAN PEOPLES; INDIANS, VILLAGE LIFE; CEYLONESE.

TAOISM, *see* CHINESE RELIGION.

TARTARS (Tatars). The word means 'inhabitants of hell', and is the name loosely given to nearly six million inhabitants of Russia, the descendants of the Turkic and Mongolian people of Tartary in Central Asia east of the Caspian, who invaded Europe in the 13th century. The Tartar invaders were led by Batu, grandson of the Mongol Emperor, GENGHIS KHAN (q.v. Vol. V). The majority of them were Muslims of Turkic origin (*see* TURKIC LANGUAGES, Vol. IV).

finally halted when the great Khan Ogatai died, in his capital at Karakorum, and their leaders had to go back to elect another Khan. Quarrels broke out among them and the colossal empire fell to pieces.

But the Tartars of the Golden Horde (called so because of the golden colour of the tent of Batu, their leader), who had established themselves in the south-eastern steppes of Russia, broke away from the Mongols, and for 200 years exercised a crushing despotism over Russia—a tyranny which had a serious effect upon the history of that country. It was not until 1380 that a Russian Prince, Dimitri Donskoi, defeated a great Tartar army at the battle of Kulikovo. Although the power of the Golden Horde was not yet broken, belief in their invincibility was gone; they were growing weaker and disunited and, before the end of the century, Russia was freed from their yoke.

By the 19th century the Tartars were well settled in the Russian empire and were modernizing their way of life.

TASMANIANS. When the Dutch navigator Abel Tasman (q.v. Vol. V) discovered the island of Tasmania in 1642, it was inhabited by a primitive people, developed in isolation from the Australian aborigine, and differing from him both physically and in way of life.

There were about 2,000 of the Tasmanian Aborigines, nomadic food-gatherers, with no means of cultivating or storing food. They lived in small bands of up to fifty people, building simple shelters of bark and sticks when they stopped to camp. Their rudimentary tools consisted mainly of digging sticks, throwing sticks, sharp quartz cutters and scrapers, and wooden spears. They had no boats, fishing equipment, or pottery. Their language differed from group to group, with four main branches, and perhaps two dozen dialects.

When the British colonized Tasmania, they found the Aborigines troublesome. They drove them to one part of the island, massacred huge numbers of them, and deported others to nearby islands. Others went as wives with sailors and whalers from boats that stopped to take on fresh water and food. The last pure-blooded Tasmanian died in 1876.

In the 18th century, French and British ships visited Van Diemen's Land, as Tasman had called it; but no determined settlement was made

British Museum

TARTAR HORSEMEN

Chinese painting of the Sung Dynasty, 13th century A.D.

The great Mongol empire of Genghis Khan spread from Persia to China. An army of some half-million well-trained, swift, and hardy horsemen carried everything before them, devastating the land they conquered, and causing unbelievable human suffering and slaughter. Between 1223 and 1245 they overran Russia, Moravia, Silesia, Hungary, and Bulgaria. Fortunately for Europe they could not sustain their power so far from their headquarters in lands which they had so ruthlessly ravaged. Their advance was

until 1803 when a party of officers and convicts was sent from New South Wales. Tasmania was to be the high-security gaol for the Australian convict colonies. Escaped prisoners, men convicted of particularly brutal crimes, and those who rebelled against the system in New South Wales were sent to the island, where rugged mountain terrain and shark-infested waters made escape impossible.

In 1825 Van Diemen's Land gained political independence from New South Wales, with its own governor and limited legislative rights. In 1853 it was re-named Tasmania, and in 1855 transportation ceased, and a responsible representative government was set up. Tasmania federated with the other states in 1901 to form the Commonwealth of AUSTRALIA (q.v. Vol. III).

Apart from fruit-growing (particularly apples), tourism, and dairying, Tasmania has a huge forestry and paper-milling industry; crude oil comes from Bass Strait, and there is vast hydro-electric development to meet the demand of the electro-metallurgical industry. Shipping, particularly of bulk metal, is of considerable importance, and there are profitable mines producing copper, tin, tungsten, iron pyrites, gold, silver, and other minerals.

TEMPLE. A temple is a holy place set apart for the worship of a particular god or spirit or of a number of gods. The solemn rites or ceremonies, held in honour of the divine being to whom it is dedicated, are usually performed by special people—priests or priestesses and their assistants—in a consecrated space in front of the inner shrine or chamber where the image of the god is enthroned. The word 'temple' was originally a Latin word meaning an enclosure set apart for divination by augurs; but later it was the name given to the 'house of god', the place where the image is kept, and eventually to any sacred building set apart for religious worship.

At first shrines were no doubt simple structures, as they are among primitive people today. In the Old Stone Age some of the earliest sanctuaries of the human race seem to have been in the dark recesses of caves, where paintings and engravings represented animals upon which man depended for his food. As civilization developed, and more labour and materials became available, sanctuaries were built of huge stones. The most elaborate temple of this kind still standing in Europe is STONEHENGE (q.v.) on Salisbury Plain, and similar sanctuaries are to be found in many parts of the world, especially along and near the sea-coasts in Brittany, the Spanish Peninsula, on both sides of the Mediterranean Sea, and in Asia Minor.

In Mesopotamia the most conspicuous feature of the Babylonian temples was a mound, shaped like a flat-topped pyramid, rising in seven terraces. This was situated in the centre of the temple-area, and was approached by the steps or an upward path, and there was a shrine at the top (cf. Gen. xi). The idea of pyramidal temples was developed by the SUMERIANS (q.v.), who first brought civilization to Mesopotamia. They furnished the sanctuary with a couch and a holy table. In the great Babylonian temples, later on, there was a long outer hall opening into a smaller one—the holy place—where the image stood in an inner shrine which was entered by the priests alone. As the priests also ruled the city there was, adjoining the sanctuary, a large number of buildings used for the training of priests and for carrying on the general administration and economic life of the city. The temple, therefore, became the civic as well as the religious centre of the community (*see* BABYLONIAN CIVILIZATION).

In Egypt pharaoh after pharaoh added more and more columns to the enormous temple of the Egyptian god, Amon Re, at Karnak. One of these columns, the pillar we know as 'Cleopatra's needle', is now to be seen on the Thames Embankment in London. Some of the later kings built new temples in much the same style as those which had been erected on the banks of the Nile a thousand years earlier. Other kings restored and enlarged these old temples. Thus Egypt became a land of complex sanctuaries and gigantic royal tombs, the remains of many of which have survived to this day.

As can be seen from the stories of the Patriarchs in the book of Genesis before the time of Moses, the Hebrew places of worship generally consisted of sacred stones, trees, caves, mountains, or wells, regarded as the abodes of the god, where he manifested himself. It was at such a spot that Jacob is said to have spent the night on his way to his uncle Laban, and had his dream about the ladder reaching from earth to heaven (Gen. xxviii, 10–12).

When the Israelite tribes returned to the desert after their escape from Egypt, the God

Griffith Institute

THE RUINS OF THE TEMPLE OF LUXOR, EGYPT, BUILT IN THE 18TH DYNASTY
A series of courts and colonnades led to a dark, columned sanctuary

of Israel was worshipped at the holy mountain called Horeb or Sinai; but, apparently, only their leader Moses was allowed to visit his God there. For the rest of the people a tent was set apart in the camp, surrounded by a space called the 'holy place'. When the Israelites took possession of Palestine they appear to have carried with them a portable shrine, the Ark of the Covenant, which contained a number of sacred objects thought to have been collected in the desert. The sanctuaries already in existence in Palestine consisted of regular enclosures, surrounded by walls and open to the sky. Within the enclosure stood lines of six or eight upright stones, with a grotto or cave for the god on one side, and on the other a space reserved for the worshippers. For a time the Israelites used these shrines; but in the reign of Solomon a temple was built on the old sacred hill called Sion at Jerusalem. Solomon's temple was built by foreign workmen, and was probably on the plan of temples in Egypt and Phoenicia (*see* p. 218). It had two stone pillars, known as Jachin and Boaz, standing at the porch, like those at the entrances to temples in Syria and Egypt. The outer court corresponded to the space in Egyptian temples between the entrance and the impressive hall, with its great columns supporting a roof. The hall led by a flight of steps to the inner shrine of the image of the god, with its lamps, pomegranate,

date-palm, and bull designs.

The Greeks built rectangular temples in marble and stone, with an inner shrine for the image of the god, the altar, and the treasury. Their temples were smaller than those of the Egyptians and Babylonians, but they were beautifully proportioned and were surrounded by graceful columns. One of their finest temples is the Parthenon, built of marble, and situated on the Acropolis at Athens, where the earliest citadel stood (*see* illustration, Vol. XII, opp. p. 17). This is a small building measuring 68 by 30 metres, but of wonderful proportions, with magnificent sculptures representing incidents from the siege of Troy, battles of the gods, and other incidents from the myths and festivals, as well as queer creatures such as centaurs and giants. Within the shrine with its wooden ceiling was a statue, 13 metres high, of the goddess Athena, the patroness of the city. Greek temples, in fact, were primarily houses for the sacred image of a god, to which a large open space called a *temenos* was added. But they were not places where large congregations assembled, and public business was transacted, as in Egypt and Babylonia. So little were they used that they were generally kept locked.

For practical purposes the large centres of worship were the places where the will and commands of the gods could be discovered by

Greek Information Office

THE THESEUM OR TEMPLE OF HEPHAESTOS, ATHENS

means of oracles, such as dreams, casting lots, interpreting signs, &c. (*see* DIVINATION). The chief of these was the Delphic Oracle where, at the shrine of the god Apollo, it was possible to get an answer to almost any inquiry from the priestess who was always in attendance to consult the oracle, very much as in Israel people resorted to the Ark when they wanted to know what their God would have them do. So great was the fame of Delphi that inquirers came to consult Apollo from all over Greece, Asia Minor, and the Roman Empire. There were several other similar centres, at one of which sick folk slept in the sanctuary of Aesculapius, the god of medicine, to receive miraculous cures through dream oracles. As at Lourdes in France today, cures were carefully tested, recorded, and published, so that the fame of the shrine attracted patients from distant cities (*see* PILGRIMAGES).

In the religion of Ancient Rome the *templum* was a sacred place without a roof, dedicated to a god, who was consulted by oracles at a tent within the enclosure. Later, when the Romans adopted the gods and worship of the Greeks and Etruscans, they built temples similar to theirs, with a central chamber for the image. Some were oblong in shape, others circular. At first (about 510 B.C.) they were erected on the Capitoline hill at Rome in the Etruscan style, in honour of Jupiter, Minerva, and Juno. Since the gods were thought to have human needs, every new god who was introduced into the capital had to be given a proper home (*see* ROMAN ART, Vol. XII).

In India for a long time worship was conducted in the open air and it was not until the use of stone in architecture was introduced under Buddhist influence in the 3rd century B.C. that great temples were built (*see* INDIAN ART, Vol. XII). In the north there are few large temples, though they often contain a number of small shrines in which the worshippers pay their devotions to one or other of the Hindu gods or goddesses. In the south some are very large with a collection of courts and buildings. Hindu worship, however, is not congregational as in Christian churches, and so the temples are not designed for crowds except in some of the great temples in the south. Simple offerings of fruit, grain, and flowers are made to the images of the god Vishnu, and his 'incarnations' Krishna and Rama, and to the block of stone known as the *lingam*, encircled by a stone ring which is the symbol of Shiva, while to the goddess Kali goats sometimes are sacrificed. These sacred objects, in the shrines, are treated as the divinities themselves because they are regarded as their embodiments.

In China, as in India, the earliest religion had no temples, and it seems that here also their introduction was due to Buddhism. When they came into vogue they followed much the same general plan in the three religions—Confucianism, Taoism, and Buddhism—with porches, or halls, and antechapels containing a table for offerings with lamps, vases of flowers, and images (*see* CHINESE RELIGION). But the principal act of worship was held at the great Altar of Heaven on the north side of Peking at midsummer and at the smaller Altar of Earth in the south of the capital at the winter solstice, when the Emperor sacrificed on behalf of the nation with an elaborate ritual handed down from very ancient times.

In Japan the SHINTO (q.v.) temples are small wooden structures with a thatched roof modelled on the plan of dwelling-houses, thought to be the abode of the gods. Those who visit them stand outside to make their offerings and prayers. The Grand Imperial Shrines for the worship of the Mikado are much more extensive, standing in large grounds with a PAGODA (q.v. Vol. XII). In ISLAM (q.v.) worship is confined to the recitation of the sacred scriptures in the MOSQUES (q.v. Vol. XII).

See also GOD; PRIEST; RITUAL.

TEUTONIC KNIGHTS, *see* KNIGHTS, ORDERS OF.

THAI. The south-east Asian kingdom, Thailand, was known as Siam until 1939, and its nationals were called Siamese. The Thai people are by far the largest and most important component of the 36 million population, forming about 85 per cent. Chinese and Malays are the two most numerous minorities, and they retain much of their national character, although most of them have Thai nationality.

The king was an absolute monarch until 1932, when a revolution limited his powers to those of a constitutional monarch. Since then there has been a series of political changes. The 1968 constitution provided for democratic government, with a Senate and a House of Representatives, and a Prime Minister appointed by the King. In November 1971, however, the National Executive Council, led by the former Prime Minister, suspended the constitution and took over the administration of the country. A new constitution has yet to be proclaimed. The administration is effected through thirteen ministries. For local administration the country is divided into seventy-one provinces, each further subdivided into successively smaller units, namely districts, communes, villages.

Local units are important, for Thailand is a nation of villages, with a few small towns and one very large city of 3 million people, BANGKOK, the capital (q.v. Vol. III). More than four-fifths of the people live in long-established villages with 300 to 3,000 inhabitants. The population is well distributed over the country except in Southern, or peninsular, Thailand, which is mountainous with narrow valleys running down to the coast on both sides. Para-rubber is the important crop in this region (*see* RUBBER, Vol. VI).

The Thai are slight in build, of medium height, with black hair, olive skin, and broad faces with well-defined cheek bones. In country districts, both men and women wear the *panning*, a length of cloth wound round the waist; but women also wear a scarf wound round the upper part of the body. In Bangkok, and the other towns European clothes are usually worn.

The Thai are a cheerful, friendly people and hospitable to visitors. They are Buddhists, professing the Hinayana School of BUDDHISM (q.v.) derived largely from the ancient Buddhist centres of Sri Lanka. With its stress on the need to gain merit, it is a central influence on the character of the people. Only the family is of equal importance. The Buddhist temple is the centre of social life in the rural community.

Most of the farmers own their own land. Nearly 80 per cent of the workers are engaged in agriculture, forestry, and fishing. The most important products are rice grown in the central lowland area; rubber from the south; and timber—especially teak—from the forests of the

Information Service of Thailand

THE GOLDEN BUDDHA, WAT TRIMITR, BANGKOK

north. The fish from the long coasts and from the 'fish-farming' in the paddy-fields provide an important part of the rice-based diet. The tropical fruits include mangoes, pineapples, and oranges. The most important minerals are tin and wolfram from which tungsten is made; but there are many other minerals, including coal, gold, and sapphires.

The artistic talent of the Thai people is most notably expressed in theatre, song, and dance. The half a million tourists a year and shoppers the world over prize the beautiful Thai silks, nielloware, woodcarving, jewellery, silverware, and lacquer for which Thailand is famous.

See also Vol. III: THAILAND; INDEX, p. 157.

THEOSOPHY is a term made up of two Greek words, *theos* 'God', and *sophia* 'wisdom', used to describe a philosophy claiming to attain to a knowledge of God by spiritual insight, direct intuition, or special methods. Thus certain spiritual exercises may be adopted to produce a state of consciousness in which knowledge of God beyond the powers of reason can be attained.

In India, since before the rise of Buddhism in the 5th century B.C., Hindu mystics have engaged in intense meditation, breathing exercises, and a very carefully worked-out technique to gain a direct knowledge of 'divine wisdom' by intuition and insight (*see* HINDUISM). Modern theosophists attach a great deal of importance to this aspect of the system, and try to find out what these Hindu thinkers were looking for in their search for 'God-wisdom' or 'God-knowledge'.

Some such search has appeared in most of the higher religions. In the 2nd century A.D. a half-Christian system flourished known as Gnosticism in which a *gnosis*, or higher knowledge of God, could be gained by a mystical enlightenment, helped often by mysterious rites and practices. Again, between the 9th and 13th centuries A.D., some Jews sought secret wisdom about the nature of God and His relation to the world under the name of Cabbala ('that which is received'). Certain Scriptural words and numbers were supposed to have a 'deeper meaning'.

The outstanding medieval European theosophists were Meister Eckhart (*c.* 1260–1327), and Jakob Boehme (1575–1624) who became known as 'the Theosophist'. Both started as Christian thinkers, but sometimes came near to making God the divine principle permeating all things rather than the Creator. Boehme, who had been brought up as a Lutheran in Germany, wrote in the *Aurora* or *Morning Redness* what he believed had been revealed to him. His doctrines brought upon him many years of persecution but had a considerable influence on later theosophy.

In the 19th century theosophy became established as a clearly defined system of belief and practice. In 1875 the Theosophical Society was founded in New York by a Russian, Madame H. P. Blavatsky, who had learnt the methods in a brotherhood in Tibet, and an American Colonel Henry Steele Olcott. From the United States it spread throughout the world. An Englishwoman, Mrs. Annie Besant (1847–1933), became its second president and devoted her life to its interests, working often in India and America. Modern theosophy has been strongly influenced by Indian mystical ideas, in particular, the doctrine of reincarnation. Mrs. Besant has described its three aims as (1) 'to form a nucleus of the Universal Brotherhood of Humanity, without distinction of race, creed, sex, caste, or colour; (2) to encourage the study of Comparative Religion, Philosophy, and Science; and (3) to investigate unexplained laws of Nature and the powers latent in man'. Today the Society is organized into forty-four National Societies distributed throughout the world.

TIBETANS. The Tibetans are a Mongoloid race, akin to the Burmese and, more remotely, to the Chinese and Mongolians. Their language is fundamentally monosyllabic like Chinese but since the 7th century A.D. they have adopted a phonetic script of Indian origin and their whole culture has been deeply influenced by their Indian neighbours, from whom at the same time they adopted the Buddhist religion. Until 1950 Tibet was an independent state ruled by its chief priest, the Dalai Lama, and his advisers. China had long claimed suzerainty over Tibet and even kept a garrison in Lhasa, the capital, in the 18th and 19th centuries, but the country was too remote and communications too difficult for her to establish effective control. The development of internal airlines and the building and improving of roads has now made such control possible and the Chinese government in Peking now regards Tibet as an integral part of the Peoples' Republic of China.

The country consists chiefly of vast arid uplands 3,000 m above sea-level at the lowest. The Himalayan range forms the southern border with India while the Chinese frontier is also mountainous. Thus Tibet has for centuries been a remote, almost inaccessible, country whose distinctive way of life was preserved virtually unchanged until the onset of Chinese control in 1950.

Because of its dryness and altitude it is hard to make a living from the soil, and unwillingness to divide an already limited property may account for an unusual form of marriage which sometimes occurs (known as polyandry), by which a woman may take two or more brothers as joint husbands. The great central and northern highlands are too cold for crops or even trees to grow; so the people are all herdsmen and are always on the move. The herdsmen live in tents— long, low constructions of black felt, moored securely against the fierce, ever-present winds. They eat meat, butter, and cheese, and drink great quantities of tea flavoured with rancid butter—a man will commonly drink up to fifty cups of tea in a day. In the more sheltered and better-watered valleys and plains, where the plateau falls away, towards India on the south and China on the east, cultivation is possible, and there are villages and towns, fields of barley, and orchards of apricots, peaches, and pears.

Women in Tibet enjoy more freedom and a greater voice in affairs than in most oriental countries. Tibetan children have a hard, but by no means a dreary life, for the Tibetans as a race are a fun-loving, merry people, fond of sports, open-air games, singing, and dancing, and especially of theatrical entertainments, which are performed by troupes of actors travelling through the country. They possess a rich FOLKLORE (q.v.), which spread among the people by professional storytellers, many of whom can neither read nor write.

Yet they have all been deeply influenced by their religion, which they refer to as Tibetan Religion (*bod-chos*). They are in fact, however, the direct inheritors of the whole later Indian Buddhist tradition. From the 7th century on they set about translating all the Buddhist literature available in India and Nepal, subsequently arranging it into a great canon of two parts—the *Kanjur*, consisting of revealed teachings, and the *Tenjur*, consisting of the commentaries and treatises of Indian masters. They gradually developed their own literature, which is now most extensive and consists of histories, biographies, works on philosophy and morality, collections of legends, and religious poetry. They print most of their books from large hand-cut wooden blocks, but manuscripts are still often copied by hand. As in early medieval Europe the monasteries were the centres of learning and of the arts, and in the 16th century one newly constituted monastic order, known as the 'Virtuous' (*dge-lugs-pa*) and popularly as the Yellow Hats succeeded with the support of the Mongolians in gaining political power. Since that time the Grand Lama of this order became the virtual ruler of Tibet. About one-fifth of the population of Tibet followed a religious calling, and although there were always some who belied their professions, ambitious prelates, preying charlatans, and easy-going ignoramuses, yet many of the lamas and monks cherished Buddhist sanctity and learning.

Besides the religious, there was a class of wealthy and powerful nobles. Some were descendants of the kings who ruled in Tibet before the days of lama government. Others sprang from the near relations of each successive Grand Lama. When the Dalai Lama died, his soul passed,

MUSICIANS AT A MONASTERY IN OLD TIBET

according to Tibetan belief into the body of a new-born boy, who might be the son of the highest or lowest in the land. The fortunate child—who could be recognized by certain bodily marks—then had to be found, and a royal baby-hunt ensued, supervised by the abbots of the principal monasteries. On the last occasion, just before the outbreak of the Second World War, the search lasted for nearly three years before the child was discovered and duly installed on the pontifical throne at Lhasa. This Dalai Lama later fled into India with large numbers of refugees after an unsuccessful revolt against the Chinese in 1956. Now small groups of Tibetans preserve their old way of life and their Buddhist religion, as far as possible, abroad. But Tibet itself is being reorganized on the pattern of China's system of communes and work-teams. Schools, hospitals, factories and woollen mills have been built, hydro-electric schemes developed to provide power and to irrigate arid land, and new crops and stock-breeding methods introduced, while Mao Tse-tung Thought and Marxist-Leninism have taken Buddhism's place as official ideologies.

See also Vol. III: TIBET.

TOTEMISM. The name comes from the word *ototeman*, which, in the dialect of the Ojibwa tribe of North America, means 'his brother-sister-kin'. The curious phrase suggests that totemism has something to do with people living together in social groups, in a very close relationship with one another.

In many parts of the primitive world—among native tribes in North America, Australia, and Africa, in the Melanesian islands of the Pacific Ocean, and in the hills and jungles of India and Sri Lanka—the people believe that a social group of common descent depends for its origin and identity on an intimate and exclusive relation that exists between all its members and a certain animal or plant, or occasionally an inanimate object, which is regarded as the supernatural ancestor or ally, i.e. the totem. This is often symbolized in the totem-pole (*see* Colour Plate opp. p. 288). All who belong to the particular group call themselves by the name of the totem, and adopt it as their badge—very much as boy scouts call themselves Peewits, Wolf-cubs, Foxes, and so on. Indeed, it was upon totemism that Baden-Powell based this feature in the organization of his great movement, as a sort of brotherhood of youth, though he gave the primitive custom a very different meaning and purpose.

So close is thought to be the relationship between those who belong to a totemic clan that the members of the group generally regard themselves as blood relations, through their common relationship with the 'elder brother', the totem. For this reason they are often forbidden to marry each other, and have to seek a partner outside their own clan—a practice that is known as 'exogamy', or 'marrying-out'. But in some cases it is quite the opposite: a tribe is divided into groups which have to marry within particular sections of the community. But, however the organization is arranged, totemism is a system of grouping people together through descent from a common supernatural ancestor connected with some aspect

Australian Information Bureau

AUSTRALIAN ABORIGINES IN CEREMONIAL DRESS WITH THEIR TOTEM POLE

of nature. On this social side it deals largely with marriage rules and relationship grouping. In its other aspect (i.e. on the religious side) it is mainly concerned with the food-supply and other human needs, through ceremonies believed to maintain order and well-being in both society and the universe. The species of animals or plants called totems are often those that are used for food, or at any rate are edible; but so great is the 'reverence' for them that members of the clan which is associated with a particular totem are often forbidden to eat it, except, perhaps, very sparingly once a year as a kind of sacramental meal. Such a rite is, in fact, the native equivalent of a 'communion service' (*see* SACRAMENT), since, by eating the sacred species solemnly in this manner, they believe they are strengthened and renewed, because they receive its life.

Some native tribes of Australia carry out rites and ceremonies, especially connected with the totems and their ancestors, at certain spots, to stir up the vitality of the species and make it become abundant. These ceremonies, in fact, reproduce what the people believe that the ancestors of the tribe did at the dawn of creation when, as the Australian Aborigines believed, they gave each group its country, its laws and customs, duties, and responsibilities. But the members of the clan do not perform their rites of increase to benefit themselves, since they are

not allowed to eat their totem freely when, as a result of their endeavours, it becomes plentiful. They do, however, get the advantage of the 'increase' rites of neighbouring clans. Therefore, totemism represents a form of collective effort, carried out by the people in a ceremonial manner for the benefit of the community as a whole— and this involves co-operation, foresight, the team spirit, and leadership. This makes for solidarity between local groups, just as the system of kinship and marriage rules prevents jealousy and strife, by forbidding courtship, marriage, and inbreeding among people who live at close quarters.

Some psychologists have suggested that the practice of exogamy, or 'marrying out', began by a jealous father expelling his sons when they grew up, in order to keep their sisters for himself as wives. According to this theory, totemism arose when the brothers, having joined forces and killed their father, were struck with remorse at their foul deed, and showed their sorrow by treating with great respect the animal (now become the totem) which represented their slain father, and refusing to marry the women they had tried to secure by their crime. But this theory is not very likely, for there is no evidence that anything of this kind ever really happened in the past in any human community; and certainly it does not occur in primitive society today.

Totemism is also connected with the worship of ancestors, especially in Africa, and with ideas about the transference of souls from one body to another. In exercising control over growth in nature and the rainfall, it linked man's environment with the laws and organization governing society. It is hardly likely that a set of beliefs with so many different elements has a single origin; but in its many forms it has played an important part in bringing together the order of nature and of society into a single system, in which the individual and the group each has its proper function for the well-being of mankind as a whole.

See also ANCESTOR WORSHIP; TABOO.

THE SACK OF TROY
Painting from an Attic vase, 5th century B.C.

TROJANS were inhabitants of ancient Troy (Ilium), which was situated in the north-west corner of Asia Minor (Turkey). Troy started as a little Late Stone Age village of sun-baked bricks, situated on a hill-top on the Trojan Plain. It was probably founded by traders about 3000 B.C. By 2500 B.C. it had developed into a wealthy, fortified, commercial town, prospering, most likely, on trade in tin brought from eastern Europe by the Danube. It was many times conquered and destroyed, but always recovered its prosperity. Altogether, nine successive cities were built on the hill, each upon the ruins of its predecessor, over a stretch of some 3,000 years.

About 1500 B.C., when the Trojans were at the height of their power, the sixth city of Troy was a splendid rival to Knossos, the Minoan (Cretan) city across the Aegean Sea. It is not likely, however, that the Trojans ever reached anything like the brilliance of the MINOAN CIVILIZATION (q.v.): indeed, it is not certain that they even possessed the art of writing. The successor of this city was laid in ruins by the Greeks in about 1200 B.C. The heroic tales of the Greek siege of this seventh city have survived in Homer's epic poem, the *Iliad*.

The Trojan war with Greece on 'the ringing plains of windy Troy' and the legends of the famous Helen of Troy have been favourite subjects for literature ever since. Stories of the Greek Achilles and Agamemnon and the Trojan Hector and Aeneas, as well as the story of the wooden horse of Troy, are familiar to most people.

All remains of the nine cities of Troy had, in the course of hundreds of years, become buried under a great mound, on which the Turks cultivated cornfields. In 1870 a German, called Schliemann, began to excavate this mound. In course of time, he and his successors dug through the remains of all nine cities, one below another, until they reached the original bare hill-top.

TUAREG. These people, who inhabit an extensive area of the Sahara Desert in North Africa, are mainly pastoral nomads, though some practise agriculture. Tuareg country ranges from comparatively fertile savannah in the south to barren desert in the north, where the nomadic Tuareg live in or near mountainous regions. The nomads subsist mainly on their livestock—camels, sheep, and goats. The farmers cultivate millet, wheat, barley, guinea corn, and vegetables, and have permanent garden plots and grow various kinds of fruit trees and date-palms.

In physical appearance the Tuareg belong to the Mediterranean stock, with some Negroid admixture, particularly in the south. They are Muslims and speak various dialects of a Berber language, *Tamaheq*; some also speak ARABIC (q.v. Vol. IV). They have a type of writing which is geometric in appearance. A distinctive custom is that men veil their faces: the name Tuareg means 'People of the Veil'. The veil is an indigo cotton cloth wound round the head to form a turban, and then over the mouth and nose, with a slit in front of the eyes.

There are over a quarter of a million Tuareg people, consisting of a number of tribes or federations. The most important groups are the people of Ahaggar, the people of Azjer, the people of Air, and the Ifoghas. Each tribe, with its sections, has its own territory and a chief who is assisted by deputies and a council. A man usually takes his tribal membership from his mother but, due to Arab influence, a man inherits property and office from his father. Thus a chief should be succeeded by his son, but a sister's son may inherit the chieftainship, property, and landrights if he is considered better fitted. The pastoral Tuareg live in camps comprising a number of tents made of matting or goat-skin. The agricultural Tuareg live in settlements in huts made of mud or stone.

The political organization of these tribes is based on three classes: the nobles who have the authority and provide chiefs; the vassals who pay tribute to the nobles for pasturage rights; and the slaves who look after animals, do domestic tasks, and cultivate some land for which they pay by part of the crop. These classes do not usually intermarry, but if they do so, the children generally acquire the father's status. Women go unveiled and enjoy a better status relative to their men than do many Muslim women. A man usually has only one wife, who is often his mother's brother's daughter, or his father's sister's daughter.

The Tuareg have camels, sheep, goats, and cattle, and the settled Tuareg have horses too. Camels, sheep, goats, salt, and agricultural produce are the chief items of caravan trading. Camels are the most important possession, and their number denotes a person's status. They provide milk, meat, hides, and transportation, and they are used in payment of bridewealth.

The Tuareg undertake woodwork, pottery,

Mrs. T. Muir

TUAREG TRIBESMEN

basketry, and skin and leather-work, and they make weapons and ornaments. Blacksmiths are an important class in Tuareg society since they perform many of the above crafts. A characteristic decoration for their ornaments, weapons, and wooden camel saddles is the 'Agades' cross which has five points and is surmounted by a circle.

See also SAHARA, PEOPLES OF.

TUMULI, *see* BARROWS AND CAIRNS.

TURKS. Turkic-speaking peoples inhabit not only Turkey but territories which extend eastward from the Aegean Sea in an unbroken line for some 6,400 km right into outer China. They stretch into Russia, east of the Caspian, northwards as far as, and beyond, the Trans-Siberian railway, and southwards to the mountains of northern Persia, Afghanistan, and Tibet. There are over 60 million Turks in the world today, about 36 millions of whom live in Turkey. A few millions inhabit northern Persia, Afghanistan, the Balkan states, and Cyprus; the remainder live in the U.S.S.R.

It is often said that the Turks are related to the MONGOLS (q.v.), and certainly the two peoples have been in close contact at certain periods in the past; but, although the structure of their language is similar, their vocabularies

Turkish Embassy

CARPET-MAKING AT ISPARTA, TURKEY

are different (*see* TURKISH AND ALLIED LANGU-
AGES, Vol. IV). The Turks of Anatolia and
Azerbaijan rarely show any Mongolian characteristics, but the Turkmen east of the Caspian
possess unmistakably the flat Mongolian features
(*see* SOVIET CENTRAL ASIAN PEOPLES).

Except for Yakut and Chuvash, which stand
apart from the rest, the Turkish dialects do
not greatly differ. They consist of three main
divisions: (1) South-western, including Osmanli,
the language of Turkey, Azeri, spoken in Russian
and Persian Azerbaijan, and Turkmen; (2)
North-western, including the speech of the
Tartars, Kazakhs, and Kirgiz; (3) South-eastern,
the chief representative being Uzbek. In Turkey
the Latin script has been used since 1928; in
the eastern regions either the Russian (Cyrillic)
or the Arabic script (*see* ALPHABET, Vol. IV).
Under the Turkish Republic there has been a
drastic campaign to purify the language by
ridding it of Arabic and Persian borrowings.

Chinese historians record that before A.D. 600
Turkish tribes, migrating westward, had reached
the shores of the Caspian Sea and settled there.
In the 8th century they came into the dominions
of the ARABS (q.v.), for whom they fought as

mercenaries, often rising to rule their masters.
In the 10th century they were converted to
ISLAM (q.v.). In 1055, under the leadership of
the Seljuk family, they seized Baghdad, and
then successfully invaded the Eastern Roman
Empire, whose capital was at Constantinople.
In Asia Minor they established the kingdom or
Sultanate of Rum, and the Seljuk Sultans of
Rum were great builders and famous patrons
of the arts.

In the 13th century the Mongol conqueror
GENGHIS KHAN (q.v. Vol. V), at the head of a
powerful army of Mongols and Turks, swept
right across Asia and even raided Anatolia.
Among the Turks who opposed the raiders was
a small band soon to become famous under the
name of the Osmanli or Ottoman Turks, after
their first Sultan, Osman I (*c.* 1299-1324). By
the middle of the 14th century the Ottomans had
established themselves as the dominant Turkish
power in western Asia. One by one the strongholds of the Eastern Roman or Byzantine
Empire fell into their hands until, in 1453,
Constantinople itself was captured by the Sultan
Mohammed II, and the BYZANTINE EMPIRE
(q.v.) came to an end.

For the next hundred years the Ottoman
Empire continued to spread. The Sultan's
armies, particularly the famous corps of Janis-
saries, appeared to be almost invincible. They
overran a large part of eastern and southern
Europe, and for a time threatened the whole
continent. During the reign of SULEYMAN THE
MAGNIFICENT (q.v. Vol. V) (1520-66) the empire reached the height of its power. It included
the territories now known as Anatolia; all the
Arab states; Egypt and North Africa; Bulgaria,
Rumania, and Yugoslavia; Hungary and a
part of Poland; Greece and all the Aegean
Islands; the Crimea and the Sea of Azov;
Georgia and Russian Azerbaijan (*see* INDEX,
map. p. 53).

By the end of the 17th century the decline of
the Ottoman Empire had begun, and during
the long period of decline, Turkey's most powerful and relentless enemy was Tsarist Russia.
For 300 years the two empires were inter-
mittently at war; and it was largely fear and
distrust of Russia which prompted the Turkish
leaders to throw in their lot with Germany in
1914. The defeat of Germany and her allies at
the end of the First World War in 1918 brought
about the final collapse of the Turkish Empire.

Indeed, had she not produced at this critical moment a leader of outstanding ability, she would probably have ceased to exist as a sovereign independent state.

That leader, Kemal ATATÜRK, (q.v. Vol. V), Turkey's soldier-stateman, became the founder of the new Turkish Republic. He accepted the loss of the non-Turkish provinces, but, by a series of brilliant military and political moves, succeeded in liberating the Turkish homelands, Thrace and Anatolia, from the Greek invaders and the occupying forces of the Allies.

Having freed his country, he proceeded to introduce a series of sweeping reforms. He overthrew the Sultanate, and established a Republic with himself as President. He set about to modernize the schools, to improve the position of women, and to introduce a Western system of law, abolishing the laws based on the Koran, the sacred book of Islam. He brought about the adoption of the Western calendar and the Latin alphabet in Turkey, and he developed the railway system and reorganized the methods of irrigation, farming, industry, and banking. Among other things he abolished the red fez, or Turkish cap—a matter of some psychological importance, for the fez, more than anything else, distinguished the Turk in appearance from the European.

Atatürk could hardly have carried through all these reforms in the Turkey of that time by democratic means. At the time of his death in 1938 the Republic was, in fact, a dictatorship. Nevertheless, no name in the long and picturesque history of Turkey is more revered by his countrymen than that of Kemal Atatürk, for no Turk can ever forget that he saved his country from disaster. His reforms, which aroused such bitter controversy, have long since been accepted as the foundations of the new Turkey.

Atatürk was succeeded by a wise and cautious statesman, Ismet Inönü, who gradually evolved in Turkey a 'Western' form of democracy and unselfishly ensured a peaceful transfer of government to the opposition when the Democratic Party won the general election in 1950. The new government embarked on a vigorous programme of agricultural and industrial expansion, regardless of how this was to be paid for. Turkey's foreign debt increased, with a resulting fall in the value of the currency, which in turn meant a steep rise in the cost of living and discontent among wage-earners. Adnan Menderes,

Camera Press

THE CAVE DWELLERS OF CAPPADOCIA

High up in this volcanic rock at Ortohisar early men made cave dwellings. Modern men have built houses into the mountain-side and added mud walls

the Prime Minister, concentrated on retaining the support of the three-quarters of the population who lived by agriculture and were relatively unaffected by rising prices. On 27 May 1960 officers and cadets overthrew his government, which they saw as having betrayed Atatürk's reforms for the sake of the peasant vote. He and two of his ministers were hanged after being found guilty of undermining the Constitution. The officers, however, did not cling to the power they had seized; they held elections in October 1961 and normal civilian government was resumed.

The great changes brought about by the Republic are at present more obvious in the towns than in the country. Life in the towns has been revolutionized by the emancipation of women and the abolition of polygamy (the custom of having more than one wife). In the country, although the people's dress and the houses have not altered a great deal, and although most farms are still small peasant holdings, conditions are changing. Modern methods of farming are being introduced. Education at all levels is free, compulsory, secular, and mostly co-educational. More and more schools are being built, and the outlook of the younger generation is increasingly Western. In the eastern regions, on the borders of Iraq and Persia, there are still tribes that lead a semi-nomadic and pastoral life moving into the hills in summer and back to the valleys in winter. The Kurdish tribes, who once lived this kind of life, have largely settled down. They are a warlike Muslim people who speak an Indo-European language, and whose home-lands are divided among Turkey, Syria, Persia, Iraq, and Afghanistan. The Kurds in Turkey number about a million and a half. Their hopes of winning an independent country for themselves, and their disapproval of Atatürk's policy of breaking the political power of Islam, led them to rise in rebellion in 1925, 1930, and 1936. Since then, however, the Kurdish areas of Turkey have been peaceful, and the Kurds have taken their place as citizens of the Republic.

There is complete liberty of worship in Turkey, the constitution is democratic and elections are free. Women have had the vote and have been able to stand for election to the Grand National Assembly (Parliament) since 1934. In 1952 Turkey became a full partner of the North Atlantic Treaty Organization, and in 1964 an associate member of the European Economic Community. The main problem at the end of 1972 was how to implement the economic and social reforms which the country needed to complete her development into a prosperous and flourishing democracy.

See also ISLAM.
See also Vol. III: TURKEY, ISTANBUL; INDEX, p. 158.

U

UGANDA, PEOPLES OF, *see* EAST AFRICANS.

UNICORN. Belief in the fabulous animal, the unicorn, grew up in the days when little was known about the animals of the world, apart from the common European animals. A Greek writer called Ctesias was the first to tell of it. He said that in India there lived a kind of white ass which had a red, white, and black horn on its forehead; and that drinking cups made of this horn prevented poisoning. Roman writers, who got most of their information about animals from the Greeks, also mention various one-horned animals. Possibly Ctesias saw carvings in stone of animals in profile, and thought they had only one horn, or he may have been given some vague information about the Indian rhinoceros.

When the Old Testament was translated into Greek and Latin and later English, the word for 'wild ox' was translated 'unicorn' (Deut. xxxiii. 17). So a set of new ideas became connected with the fabulous animal. A Roman writer, Aelian, who wrote in Greek, had recorded that it was marvellously gentle to the female; and from this the notion arose that the

THE UNICORN
Bodleian Library
Marginal drawing from the Ormsby Psalter, English *c.* 1290 (MS Douce 366)

usually ferocious animal would follow a maiden and put its head on her lap. In 61 B.C. a rhinoceros was brought to Rome, and eventually the ideas about the unicorn became attached to this beast. Centuries later MARCO POLO (q.v. Vol. V) wrote, 'They are not of that description of animals which suffer themselves to be taken by maidens, but are quite of a contrary nature.' By Shakespeare's time some people were doubtful if they existed: in *The Tempest* (Act III, Sc. iii. 22) Sebastian, astonished by Prospero's magic, says, 'Now I will believe that there are unicorns.' However, even in 1801 an article was written arguing that unicorns existed.

The belief that the unicorn's horn prevents poisoning persisted in France until 1789, when articles, supposed to be made of the horn, were used for testing the king's food for poison. Some of these were made of rhinoceros horn. In China rhinoceros horn is still supposed to have various marvellous properties.

The idea that the lion and unicorn are rivals is not very old. It is mentioned in Spenser's *Faerie Queene* (ii. 15). The unicorn appeared on gold coins of King James III of Scotland and, later, the two were incorporated in the Scottish Royal Arms. At the Union the unicorn took its place on the left-hand side of the British Royal Arms, with the lion facing it.

See also FABULOUS CREATURES.

UNITARIAN. A Unitarian thinks that the CHRISTIAN CHURCH (q.v.) has made Christianity too complicated, and believes that God could be more simply and clearly understood by using human reason. He is called a Unitarian because he questions the doctrines of the Trinity. He worships God the Father only, and is thus to be distinguished from a Trinitarian who worships God the Father, Son, and Holy Ghost. A Unitarian seeks earnestly to follow the moral teachings of Christ, whom he regards as a man with a divine message. He believes that Christ came to teach men how to live better, rather than that he came to die for men's sins.

At the Reformation some Italian exiles in Switzerland, who held these views, separated themselves from the Protestant communities who followed LUTHER and CALVIN (see Vol. V), and later Unitarian Churches were founded in Poland and Transylvania. Congregations still exist in Hungary and Rumania.

In England in the 18th century some Non-

conformist congregations led by Joseph PRIEST-
LEY (see Vol. V) professed Unitarian beliefs and
declared Christ to be a man. Because Unitarians believe that a man's reason should guide
his faith, they early realized that the search
for truth was a Christian duty. For the same
reason they have always tried to persuade
Christians to show greater tolerance towards
each other's beliefs. During the 19th century
Unitarians played a prominent part in social
and educational reform, and were particularly
active in encouraging the education of women.

There are 260 congregations of Unitarians and
Free Christian Churches in the United Kingdom
and 1025 in the United States.

UR, *see* SUMERIAN CIVILIZATION.

URUGUAYANS. The full name of Uruguay in
South America is the Eastern Republic of the
Uruguay River. This describes not only its position, but also one of the most important factors
in its history: for Uruguay came into existence
as a buffer-state between Argentina on the west
and Brazil on the north. It used to be called the
Banda Oriental (Eastern Bank) and its people
still refer to themselves as *Orientales*.

In the colonial period, when South America
was divided between the Portuguese Empire
(which afterwards became Brazil) and the
Spanish Empire, the Eastern Bank lay as a
wedge of no-man's-land between them on the
south, just as the Guianas did on the north. It
was colonized by both nations; but at length the
Spaniards prevailed, and the Eastern Bank
became part of the Spanish Viceroyalty of the
Rio de la Plata (*see* ARGENTINES).

When the independence movement began in
South America during the Napoleonic Wars,
the struggle over the Eastern Bank broke out
afresh. While the colonists of Buenos Aires were
fighting for their independence against Spain,
the colonists of the Eastern Bank were fighting
for their independence against Buenos Aires.
At the same time the Portuguese invaded the
country from Brazil and tried to annex it. For
nearly twenty years Uruguay was a battleground, until, in 1828, Argentine and Brazil
signed a treaty recognizing it as a free and
independent state.

But still Uruguay did not know peace. It
suffered partly from Argentine aggressions and
partly from civil wars; and during these troubles
GARIBALDI (q.v. Vol. V) and his famous Italian
legion of 'Red-Shirts' fought for the freedom of
Uruguay before returning to Europe to win the
freedom of their own country. From 1830 to
1903 there were only three of Uruguay's presidents who were not either assassinated or forced
out of office or involved in revolution.

After 1903, however, Uruguay became one of
the most prosperous and progressive of the
South American states and, indeed, of the
world. Like Argentina, it attracted many settlers
from abroad, the majority being Italians and
and Spaniards. The population is wholly of
European descent, the Indians having all died
out, and Spanish is the language of the country.

Uruguay made outstanding progress in political and social reforms. Its educational system,
its free medical services, its old-age pensions,
its poor relief, its laws protecting the welfare of
children and regulating the wages and hours
of work of the workers and farmers, are among
the most advanced of any country in the world.
The great statesman who began this policy of
social welfare was Batlle y Ordonez, who was
president in 1903-7 and 1911-15. His object
was 'the easing of human suffering', and his
motto was: 'Modern industry must not be
allowed to destroy human beings.' He also
inspired a new constitution which, he hoped,
would make it impossible for future presidents
to become dictators. In this last wish he was
successful, but in the last 20 years Uruguay's
economy has been unable to keep up with the
demands placed on it, and the political atmosphere has got worse. There have been outbreaks
of terrorism.

The capital of Uruguay is MONTEVIDEO (q.v.
Vol. III), a fine city on the Rio de la Plata
nearly opposite Buenos Aires, and one of the
great ports of the world.

Although Uruguay is one of the most progressive and socialistic countries in the world, it
is still pastoral, not industrial. The Uruguayan
ideal is not the worker in the city, but the
gaucho or cowboy, rounding up the cattle on the
pampas, picturesquely dressed in loose trousers
with tight cuffs at the ankles, a soft hat, and a
long wool *poncho* or blanket.

See also Vol. III: URUGUAY; INDEX, p. 159.

V

VANDALS. These were a people of Germanic origin, racially allied to the GOTHS (q.v.). They worked their way from eastern Germany westwards and, at the beginning of the 5th century, had reached Spain, where many settled in Andalusia. A few years later a Roman governor of North Africa, who was in disgrace in Italy, invited them to North Africa. Their great leader Graiseric soon fell out with the governor and completed his domination over the country by capturing Carthage in A.D. 439. After this, the Vandals built a powerful fleet, and became, in spite of the Romans, the leading sea-power in the Mediterranean for nearly 30 years. In 455 they invaded Italy, captured and looted Rome, and retired again to their rich lands in North Africa.

They became demoralized by the easy living in Africa, and were finally overthrown in 533–34 by Belisarius, a great Roman general. After this they disappeared from history. Their possession of the richest Roman corn-bearing provinces in North Africa had made it necessary for the Romans to concentrate on fighting them at a time when barbarians were invading the north. In consequence the Romans had to withdraw their garrison from Britain, and in course of time from France also.

From them we get the word 'vandalism', a wanton destruction of beautiful or sacred things. They were probably no more guilty than other invading barbarians; but no doubt the epithet grew because of the persecution of Christians carried out by Gaiseric and his son.

VATICAN, *see* ROMAN CATHOLIC CHURCH.

VEDDA (of Sri Lanka). The earliest conquerors of Sri Lanka were the Vedda, a small, dark-skinned folk, now fast dying out. The Sinhalese and Tamils (*see* CEYLONESE) drove them from the best lands as early as the 6th century. They are slender, with small heads, deep-set dark eyes, and long black wavy hair, generally worn loose. Most of the Vedda have learnt from their Sinhalese neighbours to keep cattle, grow vegetables and grain, and they have adopted from them social and religious customs and language. But there are a few families, the so-called 'Rock Vedda', who still follow a very primitive way of life, depending for food on wild game, and on tubers, wild fruits, and the honey of wild bees, which is their favourite food.

Though the Vedda know how to build huts, they are cave-dwellers by preference. They sleep on skins or even on bare rock. A fire is always kept smouldering nearby to frighten away bears and elephants. Little children wear no clothes. Boys and men wear a strip of cloth tucked fore and aft into a string round the waist. The girls and women wear very little more.

The women dig up yams and tubers, while the boys go with their fathers to shoot wild game with bows and arrows or, nowadays, with cheap

British Museum

A VEDDA FAMILY AT THE MOUTH OF THEIR CAVE

guns. They also collect honey. A fierce wild bee builds a single comb under ledges of rock precipices. At night the Veddas climb down a ladder made of canes tied together till they reach the level of the comb, then smoke out the bees with burning bunches of green leaves, break off the comb with a wooden fork or arrow, and drop it into a deerskin bag. They eat the comb, grubs and all; but they drain some of the honey to exchange for cotton, and axe- and arrow-heads. The pedlars shout from about half a kilometre away until a Vedda brings honey or dried flesh, to exchange for trade goods.

The Vedda are simple, cheerful people, fond of song and dance. Women are the equals of men; each man has only one wife and guards her jealously. They seldom rebuke their children, and often spoil them. The children's only education is imitation of their elders, and they marry at an early age. The proper marriage for a boy is with his father's sister's daughter. The boy calls on her father with a present of honey and dried flesh. If his proposals are welcome, the girl ties a waist string of her own making round his waist. That is the marriage ceremony, and they are henceforth man and wife. The husband will never part with his waist string, and if it wears out his wife must make him another. Religious customs consist mainly in offerings to the spirits of ancestors, and prayers and dances to ensure their good will (*see* ANCESTOR WORSHIP).

See also Vol. III: CEYLON (SRI LANKA).

VENEZUELANS. Venezuela means 'little Venice', the name given by the Spaniards to the first Indian village they discovered on the shores of this South American country. The Caribbean coast was the first part of the American mainland sighted by Columbus in 1498, and it became known as 'the Spanish Main', i.e. mainland. It lay in the centre of the vast Spanish Empire, and, together with Colombia and Ecuador, formed part of the viceroyalty of New Granada. English pirates preyed upon Spanish galleons as they plied to and fro across the Atlantic. The Orinoco Valley was the scene, moreover, of the strange Indian legend of *El Dorado*, the Gilded King, whose supposed wealth lured Sir Walter Raleigh on his hapless expeditions in 1595 and 1617.

Early in the 19th century Venezuela became the centre from which the great democratic

Camera Press

OIL PROVIDES VENEZUELA'S WEALTH

nationalist leaders MIRANDA and BOLIVAR (qq.v. Vol. V) sought to overthrow the tyranny of Spain. It declared its independence in 1811, and finally won its freedom ten years later as part of Bolivar's Union of Greater Colombia. It broke away from this Union in 1830 and became an independent republic. A long and stormy period of revolutions and dictatorships followed, but Venezuela now has a democratic constitution with a President and a National Congress elected by the people. Though the population includes a few Spanish whites and a few Indian tribes, it is mostly of mixed Indian and European blood; there is also an admixture of African blood, which comes from descendants of the negro slaves brought over from West Africa. Many Europeans have settled in the country in recent years.

With the growing prosperity brought by Venezuela's foreign-owned oil companies, and the development of her natural resources, a considerable improvement in the education and general well-being of her people is rapidly taking place, though the contrast between the rich and poor is more extreme than elsewhere in Latin America.

See also AMERICAN INDIANS, CENTRAL AND SOUTH.
See also Vol. III: VENEZUELA; INDEX, p. 160.

VIKINGS, *see* DANES; NORWEGIANS; SWEDES.

VIETNAMESE. Vietnam is the principal country of what was once French Indo-china. It stretches for over 1600 km, southwards from China, and includes the river deltas of the Song Koi and the lower Mekong and a narrow strip of lowland between the mountains and the sea. The Vietnamese people live almost entirely in the deltas and lowlands, whilst many smaller tribes, sometimes known generally as the Moi, occupy the uplands. The country has been divided into two parts since 1954, and has for many years been disrupted by warfare between the two, in which the United States has played a prominent part. Since 1965 intensive American bombing has caused much damage in both north and south. The war has done much, too, to change Vietnamese society. In the north, a Communist revolution has transformed the social system since the end of French colonial rule. In the south, change has been more the result of instability and civil war than of deliberate planning.

The Vietnamese originally occupied only the northern half of the country which, for a thousand years down to about A.D. 900, was ruled by China who exerted a strong influence on their language and culture. Nevertheless, they preserved their separate character as a people, and from the 10th century until the French conquest after 1858, Vietnam was an independent country with its own identity. During the centuries of independence, the Vietnamese expanded southwards. By the year 1470, they had conquered an ancient Hindu-Buddhist kingdom called Champa, in Central Vietnam; and be-

tween about 1650 and 1800 they annexed the Mekong delta area, province by province, as a result of wars with Cambodia. South Vietnam is thus a newer country than the north, rather less traditional and also less densely settled. For centuries the Tongking Delta has been over-populated, whereas parts of the Mekong delta are still underpopulated. In time of peace, the South exported rice. The population of the whole country is now nearly forty millions, and continues to grow.

Traditionally the most important Vietnamese religion has been ancestor-worship and the veneration of all kinds of spirits. Until 1945 they had an emperor who was a spiritual as well as a political figure, and before the arrival of the French colonizers they were ruled by Confucian officials. Confucianism (*see* CHINESE RELIGIONS) has declined now, but Buddhism is still a flourishing religion; there are also about two million Christian Vietnamese.

Until the 20th century the vast majority of the people lived in rural villages. A majority are still village people, but since 1900 several important towns and cities have grown up, notably Hanoi and Saigon. The latter has over two million people, with many Chinese immigrants, and in time of peace is a major trading centre. In addition, there has been some industrial development, mainly in the north. The Vietnamese are adapting themselves to a changing world in which cities and industry will play a more prominent part, and many traditions will be left behind.

See also Vol. III: VIETNAM; INDEX, p. 160.

W

WALDENSIAN. A member of a small Christian community who call themselves Vaudois, in the Piedmontese Alps. In 1170 a merchant of Lyons in south France, called Peter Waldo, felt a call to accept a life of poverty and the work of simple preaching of the Gospel. This man and his followers—'the Poor Men of Lyons' had no wish to break from the Church, only to protest against its worldliness. Unfortunately, instead of recognizing them as an orthodox Order, the Church persecuted them as heretics, and they scattered over many parts of Europe. Some of these simple societies survived in the seclusion of the French and Italian Alps until the period of the Reformation. Then they threw in their lot with the Reformed Church, i.e. the CALVINIST (q.v.). They form now the Reformed Church of Italy, with a membership of about 30,000, not only in the Alpine valleys, but in many towns and villages outside. They have a ministry with a 4 years' theological training, a few schools, hospitals, orphanages, and they do a little missionary work in Africa.

See also CHRISTIAN CHURCH.

WALLOONS, *see* BELGIANS.

WELSH. The Welsh have remained a distinctly individual people, although their population is only some 2,724,000 (1971), and they are closely associated with a powerful neighbour. They differ from the English in appearance, language, and temperament, and have preserved these differences throughout the centuries. The reason for this is to be found in their origin and history.

The Welsh are the descendants of early Celtic settlers in Britain. These Celtic people were small and long-skulled, with dark hair and brown eyes. The modern Welshman has these physical characteristics, and his language, too, is Celtic. The Welshman is vivacious and hot-tempered, emotional, and sensitive, and easily moved to laughter or despair. Like all Celts, he loves music, especially singing, and the sound of words. Wales has produced many famous musicians and orators. From the earliest times the Welsh have resented English domination of their country. They used to resist the English with armed force on all possible occasions; but now the spirit of resistance is redirected in fostering their national culture.

The Roman, Saxon, and Norman invasions of England drove the Welsh into the western mountainous region which is now their home. Though the Romans under Agricola conquered North Wales and annexed the west coast in A.D. 77, the Welsh conducted very effective guerrilla warfare against them from hill-fortresses, and proved such turbulent neighbours that the Romans stationed a considerable part of their military power on the Welsh border in forts, such as those at Carleon and Chester. Later, the Saxons built a wall, called Offa's Dyke, to mark the boundary between Wales and England, and to prevent raids from the hills. William I established a number of barons on what were called the March estates bordering Wales, so that they should hold the Welsh in

J. Allan Cash

CORACLES ON THE RIVER TEIFI BELOW CILGERRAN CASTLE, PEMBROKESHIRE check and protect the border. South Wales was mainly conquered in the 12th century, but the mountain inhabitants of Snowdonia were not subdued till EDWARD I (q.v. Vol. V) built castles such as Caernarvon and Harlech round the coast, and, by a successful trick, got the Welsh to accept his son as Prince of Wales.

Under the leadership of OWEN GLENDOWER (q.v. Vol. V), a national hero whose deeds are celebrated in Welsh poetry, the Welsh made a last unsuccessful bid for independence in 1405. Under the Tudor kings, themselves descended from the Welsh royal line, there was peace; and by the Act of Union in 1536 Wales was joined politically to England. LLOYD GEORGE (q.v. Vol. V), a Welshman, as Prime Minister of Great Britain, led the country to victory in the First World War.

The Welsh now foster all the cultural aspects of their nationality by preserving their language, literature, and history. Almost all Welshmen can speak English, which they speak with a distinctive accent and turn of phrase; but Welsh is taught in all schools, and is becoming the medium of all teaching in an increasing number of them. The language is further kept alive by use in conversation every day throughout Wales. The National Eisteddfod, a gathering of bards attended by many thousands of ordinary people, meets each year and keeps alive the traditional songs and poetry. The universal love of music is expressed in singing; there are many excellent choirs, especially in the industrial regions, and choral and dramatic societies flourish even in small villages. Many Welsh writers, including Dylan Thomas, have enriched the literature of the English language with their stories, plays, and poems, and Welsh singers and actors have delighted London audiences.

The religion of the Welsh today is Nonconformist, for the most part METHODIST (q.v.). Their emotional temperament, easily moved by oratory, made them susceptible to the 18th-century religious revivalists. Their chapels are generally small and often rather bare; but they nearly always have an excellent choir, so that the beauty and fervour of the singing make up for the bareness of the building.

Most of the Welsh living in the region of the South Wales coalfield, and in the smaller industrial region of Flint and Denbigh in the north, are employed in mining and heavy industry. These districts have often been hard hit

J. Allan Cash

RAM SALE AT CAPEL CURIG

by economic depressions and unemployment, which may be the reason for the vigorous political nationalist movement.

Most of the interior of the country is mountainous with poor soil, suitable for little else than sheep-farming. The whitewashed farm-houses are clean and well managed; but living is hard, and many people have left the land to migrate to the south, in search of employment in industry. In the north-west slate quarries employ a few people, and the magnificent country of Snowdonia has encouraged a tourist trade.

The Welsh, though living in a country from which it is often hard to get a good living, yet never tire of singing the praises of their native land.

See also BRITISH PEOPLES; CELTIC CIVILIZATION.
See also Vol. III: WALES.
See also Vol. IV: WELSH LANGUAGE.
See also Vol. X: WELSH EDUCATION.

WEST AFRICANS. The vast area called West Africa stretches from the highlands of Cameroon in the East to Gambia and Senegal in the West: a distance of about three thousand km. Bounded to the South and West by the Atlantic Ocean, its northern limits are marked by the arid wastes of the Sahara. Across it flow two great rivers, the Senegal and Niger, and throughout much of its history the latter, navigable along most of its length, has provided a major route for the movement of people and trade. The landscape and climate of such a large area show many variations. In general the areas lying directly behind the coast receive most rain and are covered by thick tropical forest and bush. As one moves north from the coast, rainfall decreases, the country becomes more and more open, and the vegetation more stunted and sparse. In the fertile forest areas the people live by growing green bananas, coco-yam, cassava, and yams while in the drier North they cultivate yam and grains.

Although Europeans did not reach West Africa by sea until the 15th century, it is important to realize the area has a long and complex history going back many thousands of years. Archaeologists have discovered that the Nok people were living in Northern Nigeria before the time of Christ. From at least the 7th century A.D. onwards in the dry savannah lands there were great states such as ancient Ghana, Mali, and Kanem-Bornu. From these and other areas long-distance trade routes crossed and recrossed the Sahara to North Africa, the Mediterranean, and Arab lands. Along these routes camel caravans carried gold, ivory, and products of the forests, and brought back salt, metal, and cloth.

It was largely stories of great gold resources that attracted Europeans to West Africa and, from the 15th century, they set up small fortified trading posts along the coast. Besides trading for gold, especially on the Gold Coast, now Ghana, they sought ivory, pepper, and slaves. (It is from West African slaves that most American Negroes are descended.)

The Europeans shifted trade towards the coast, and the guns they exchanged for African products helped the development of forest states like Asante (*see* ASHANTI). But such developments came late in the history of the region: already over the centuries the West Africans had developed a wide variety of societies, religions, and philosophies. Their political systems ranged from elaborate centralized kingdoms, using cavalry forces, to small chiefless societies based mainly on kinship ties. Although most groups had a belief in a distant Creator God, they often combined this with the worship of lesser gods and with ANCESTOR WORSHIP (q.v.). Islam and Christianity are now deeply rooted in the region, sometimes alongside older beliefs. But perhaps the most outstanding feature of these complex and varied civilizations is the great quantities of superb sculpture they produced. The art of people such as the Yoruba or Dogon represents some of mankind's greatest achievements.

During the 19th century Europeans, using superior weapons and resources, seized control of most of West Africa. They divided the area up into colonies and introduced new industries, crops, and schools, and also built many roads and railways. Great material and educational progress resulted in some areas. Yet the Colonial period, seen in the perspective of West Africa's long past, was a brief one, and by the late 1960s nearly all areas had regained their independence and become nations in their own right.

See also AFRICANS.
See also Vol. III: AFRICA; GAMBIA; GHANA; NIGERIA.
See also Vol. IV: AFRICAN LANGUAGES.
See also Vol. XII: AFRICAN ART.

WEST INDIANS. The ancestors of the West Indians were mostly West African; others came from Spain, Britain, France, Holland, and later from India and China. None of these people lived in the Caribbean, or even knew of its existence, before Columbus sailed across the Atlantic from Spain in 1492. The inhabitants he met there were AMERICAN INDIANS (q.v.)— the Arawaks in the big western islands, and the Caribs in the eastern chain of islands. As the Spaniards moved in to settle on the fertile lands, the Arawaks and Caribs were forced to retreat to the mountains. A lot of them were killed, others died of new diseases. Today less than a hundred survive in Dominica, and nowhere else.

Most West Indians are black; a very small proportion are white. There are large groups of Indians, small numbers of Chinese, and a great number of people of mixed ancestry. Many black and coloured West Indians know of a white grandfather or great grandfather in their family tree. The prime minister of Jamaica, Michael Manly, has an English mother, Jamaican father, Irish grandfather. The motto of Jamaica is Out of Many, One People.

Europeans started settling in the Caribbean islands in the 16th century because the land was fertile and there they could grow crops that were rare and expensive in Europe. Spanish farmers and labourers grew tobacco, cotton and sugar in Cuba, Hispaniola, Puerto Rico, and Jamaica. In the early 17th century little groups

J. Allan Cash

GRENADA: FISHERMEN ON THE GRAND ROY BEACH

of French, English, and Dutch landed on the smaller islands of the eastern Caribbean, hacked down the dense tropical undergrowth and scrub, and cultivated fields of tobacco. The labourers were poor British and French men who hoped that after 7 years' grinding work in the sun they might get a bit of land of their own and work it. Some succeeded, others failed. The settlers found that they could get a better price for sugar than for tobacco, so gradually they turned their land over to growing cane. Sugar canes require a lot of labour; and the canes have to be processed into sugar in mills. The wealthier farmers bought up the smallholdings, imported more labourers, and developed large plantations.

There was always a shortage of labour, and first the Spanish, then the British and French, bought Africans and transported them as slaves across the Atlantic until the SLAVE TRADE (q.v. Vol. VII) was abolished in 1807. Slavery ended in the British Caribbean in 1833, in the French colonies in 1848, and in Cuba in 1886. Many slaves left the plantations, and the planters had to look elsewhere for labour. The Dutch intro-

duced Javanese into Surinam. Portuguese, Chinese, and Indians came to Trinidad and Guyana where today they are the largest racial group.

West Indians are descended from all these peoples, slave and free. There were always more European men than women in the islands, and children were born of African mothers and white fathers. A coloured middle class grew up, slightly apart from both whites and blacks, and intermarried among themselves. They became the shopkeepers, estate overseers, clerks, and later merchants and office workers.

The blacks had come from different West African societies, many hundreds of kilometres apart. The conditions of slavery made it impossible for them to live in their former way. Families were broken up, and most traditional customs lost. As they spoke dozens of different languages, they had to find a common language —Spanish in Puerto Rico, Cuba, Hispaniola; French in Haiti, Guadeloupe, Martinique; English in Jamaica (which the British seized from Spain in 1655) and in the Eastern Caribbean islands.

Some of the islands were fought over by the European powers and changed hands several times in the course of the 18th century. St. Lucia finally became English-owned in 1804, and by then French was the dominant language. A dialect of French developed in St. Lucia and the other French islands, and was mingled with African words and grammatical forms into a new form of the language, known as Creole or patois. Jamaicans speak a language which is mainly English in vocabulary, but has some African forms and words (such as unu for you).

So a few elements of African languages do survive in West Indian talk. Folk stories, like the Anancy spider stories, have been passed down through oral traditions and the songs, music, and dance of the Caribbean peoples still echo the music and dance of West Africa.

See also AMERICAN INDIANS, CENTRAL AND SOUTH.
See also Vol. III: WEST INDIES.

WITCHCRAFT. This takes many different forms in various parts of the world; but it always involves the belief in MAGIC (q.v.). Witchcraft may be good or evil, though we usually think of it as evil. It may be performed by single individuals or by groups. Different kinds of magic-

TWO WITCHES DISCOVERED
Woodcut from Matthew Hopkins, *Discoverie of Witches*, 1647

makers may be called magicians or sorcerers, or witch-doctors in Africa, or shamans among the Eskimos, Siberian tribes, and North American Indians. The shaman goes into a kind of fit or trance, and is believed to be possessed by a spirit when he is performing magic. In the British Isles 'witches' usually signify women who work evil magic; men witches are called magicians or wizards. In England in times past, and to this day in Scotland, we hear of 'black' and 'white' witches who may be either men or women, but usually women. Black magic is evil, but white is good and has the power to counteract evil magic.

The witch of European FAIRY-TALES (q.v.) is a sinister old woman who practises magic arts, using SPELLS (q.v.) and incantations to cause people harm. She dances round a cauldron in which she brews enchanted broth, from horrible ingredients:

> Fillet of a fenny snake,
> In the cauldron boil and bake;
> Eye of newt and toe of frog,
> Wool of bat and tongue of dog,
> .   .   .   .   .
> And now about the cauldron sing,
> Like elves and fairies in a ring.
> *Macbeth*, Act IV, Sc. i.

She flies about at night on a broomstick, wearing the traditional 17th-century hat, and can change herself or other people into animal form.

Witches, unlike ELVES or FAIRIES (qq.v.), were thought to be real people possessed by the devil or given over to his service. In the past many people were tortured and executed on the charge of being witches; as recently as 1722 such a woman was executed in Scotland.

It was from shortly before the middle of the 15th century to the end of the 17th century that the fear of witches was greatest in European countries, and they were hunted down most unmercifully. Witnesses at their trials said that they anointed their bodies with some substance which enabled them to fly through the air; and that they had animal 'familiars', such as cats and hares, into whose shape they could transform themselves; and that at witches' 'Sabbaths' groups of thirteen gathered in 'covens' to dance in a ring at night, and worship a horned god who was the devil. Accused people might confess to such doings because they were frightened, or not quite sane. Until recently, in many parts of Europe, very ancient magical practices were carried out in the belief that they would make the crops and herds prosper. It is possible that people who carried on this kind of fertility magic in the Middle Ages were called witches by persons who were afraid of them.

Most witch-doctors and sorcerers, in addition to doing particular people harm or good, concern themselves with making rain or otherwise altering the weather. One indication that witches in Europe were connected with a fertility ritual is that they were believed to be able to raise storms. One of their methods was to throw a cat into the sea, after performing magical rites. Another was to float a small dish in a larger dish full of water: by upsetting the small dish, they were supposed to be able to sink a ship. Like all magic-makers, witches believed that, by doing something resembling what they wanted to happen, they could cause it to happen, even at a great distance.

Witches also believed that practices, generally regarded as doing good and bringing blessing, could be made to bring harm by being done the wrong way round. So they used to make prayers into spells by saying them backwards. In good ritual images are made as a help to worship; in witchcraft they are made in order to be pierced or destroyed, so that the persons they represent may suffer.

To counteract witchcraft, people sometimes try to make the same kind of witchcraft against it. Thus a record from Babylonia says:

A witch hath bewitched me,
A sorceress hath cast her spell upon me.
. . . .
I have made a figure of the man or woman who
   hath bewitched me.

Evidently he pierced or melted the image to revenge himself on the witch or sorceress. People in the British Isles also made figures of wax or clay to bring harm to other people.

British Museum

A WITCH AND HER FAMILIARS
Drawing from the Fairfax MSS., 1621

The belief in witches is strongest where people are not educated enough to understand how disasters come about. If they are suddenly taken ill, they imagine that someone has bewitched them. If the weather is not suitable for the crops, they believe certain people know how to change it. As people learn what causes disease, or weather conditions, the belief in witchcraft tends to die out. Nobody need regret this, as it was responsible for a great deal of cruelty.

See also FOLKLORE; MAGIC; SPELLS AND CHARMS.

XY

XHOSA, *see* SOUTHERN AFRICANS.

YAKUTS, *see* SIBERIAN PEOPLES.

YOGA, *see* HINDUISM, Section I.

YUGOSLAVS. This name means Southern
Slavs, and it is used for the three branches of
the same Slav family—the Serbs, Croats, and
Slovenes—which, together with large Albanian
and Magyar minorities, and some smaller ones,
inhabit Yugoslavia. The Slavs invaded the
Balkans in the 7th century, and settled mainly
in the mountainous areas, where they lived by
hunting. Gradually they came down to the
lowlands and began to cultivate the soil. After
some quarrels among themselves, and after

Yugoslav Embassy

BIRTHPLACE OF PRESIDENT TITO

wars and negotiations with Byzantium, the
Serbs set up an independent kingdom named
Raška, which was ruled for nearly 200 years by
the Nemanjid dynasty and by the mid-14th century dominated most of the Balkans. The
Emperor, Dušan, who was crowned at Skoplje,
now in modern Macedonia, established a Code
of Law, encouraged commerce, and endowed a
number of beautiful monasteries.

After Dušan's death the Serbian Empire was
weakened, and by the middle of the 15th century
practically the whole of Serbia, Bosnia, and
Herzegovina came under Turkish rule. The less
powerful medieval state of Croatia in the north
had become part of the Kingdom of Hungary,
while Slovenia in the north-west was a province
of the Austrian Empire. The Republic of Venice
seized most of the eastern shore of the Adriatic
in order to protect her shipping, and built or
developed the beautiful cities of the Adriatic—
Split, Dubrovnik, Zadar, and others. Only the
heroic Montenegrins maintained their independence. For over 400 years the Serbs were subject
to Turkish overlords, but clung to the Orthodox
Church. In Bosnia and Herzegovina, however,
many became Muslims; and the Croats and
Slovenes were Roman Catholics.

In the 19th century the Serbs, after two major
rebellions, were successful in driving out the
Turks; and after the First World War and the
collapse of the Austro-Hungarian Empire, the
Serbs, Croats, and Slovenes were at last united
into the one kingdom Yugoslavia. More than
500 years of separation, however, under rulers
with widely differing cultures, had made the
three main peoples so different in outlook and
way of life that the problem of welding them
together into a united country has not been
easy. Most Yugoslavs speak 'Serbo-Croat', but
Slovene is a slightly different language. The
west of the country used the Latin alphabet,
the Serbs used the Cyrillic alphabet, and, as a
result, only well-educated Serbs and Croats read
each other's books and newspapers. Each cherished their old traditions: the Serbs prided
themselves on their valour and statecraft, the
Croats on their culture, and the Slovenes on
their civilization and efficiency. These differences
created political and economic strains which the
Kingdom of Yugoslavia never managed to
resolve.

The Second World War brought a bitter
renewal of civil strife in which, quite apart from

Yugoslav Embassy

A TRADITIONAL DANCE

casualties incurred in fighting German and Italian invaders, nearly a million Yugoslavs lost their lives. Of the resistance movements, only the Communist-led Partisans, with the slogan 'Brotherhood and Unity', made a broad appeal to all nationalities in Yugoslavia. After the war, the discipline of a Communist régime and its successful opposition to Russian Communist imperialism in 1948 brought a measure of unity to this much torn people. More recently, however, as local authorities have gained more power to manage their own affairs tension has revived, particularly between Serbs and Croats.

Before the Second World War the majority of Yugoslavs were peasants. Both men and women in the villages used to wear beautiful local costumes, while folk-songs and dances flourished everywhere. Some of the dances were extremely elaborate—for instance, the medieval sword dance on the island of Korčula. Women did heavy manual work in the fields and provided the crews for the cumbersome sailing craft which brought fruit and vegetables from the islands. Something of this still survives, but with the rise of industry since the war nearly a third of the population has left the villages and moved to the towns. Many Yugoslavs, too, have emigrated to North and South America, particularly Chile, and to Australia. In recent years large numbers have also found work in the countries of western Europe.

See also Vol. III: YUGOSLAVIA; INDEX, p. 160.
See also Vol. IV: SLAVONIC LANGUAGES.

Z

ZENANA. This word is more correctly spelt 'Zanana', and is in origin allied to the Persian word for woman, i.e. *zan*, plural *zanan*. It is the name given in India and Pakistan to the portion of a house reserved for the women. The Muslim custom of keeping women shut up in a harem (or zenana) was widely adopted in India by the richer Hindus. It did not exist among Hindus in south India; but in the north it was considered a sign of respectability, and was prevalent only among the upper 'classes'.

See also CASTE; HINDUISM; INDIAN PEOPLES, PAKISTANI.

ZIONIST, *see* JEWS.

ZODIAC, *see* ASTROLOGY. *See also* Vol. III: CONSTELLATIONS.

ZOROASTRIAN. Zarathustra, who is perhaps better known under the Greek form of his name, 'Zoroaster', was a Persian prophet, who was born about 600 or more years before Christ. Very little is known of his actual history. He seems to have been of priestly rank, was married, and had a daughter. We possess five poems, called *Gathas*, which are almost certainly genuine compositions of his. From these poems we deduce that he came into public life at a time when there was tension between the Persians and some wandering invaders from central Asia, probably Mongols, who were raiding Persia and carrying off cattle. Zarathustra, like Moses seems to have begun as a champion of his oppressed fellow countrymen; but after a time he showed that his greatest interest was in urging them to be more faithful to one true and holy God (whom he calls Ahura Mazda), and to give up polytheism, or the worship of many gods. The Persian king, Darius, recognized Zarathustra's reforming movement, and ordered the

old religion to be given up. His successor, Xerxes, not only suppressed the old religion, but tried to force Zarathustra's faith upon his subjects. This attempt did not succeed and, after some sixty years, much of the earlier polytheism returned, and a system was established under the name of Zarathustra, which contained some of the very features which he had most opposed. Zarathustra claimed that he was trying to bring the Persians back to a still older and purer faith from which they had fallen away. It is rather doubtful, however, whether such a faith had really ever existed.

From then onwards the religion of Persia continued to be Zoroastrian in name right up to A.D. 700 when, as a result of the great Arab conquests, ISLAM (q.v.) entered in. Before this date there were efforts to convert the country to Christianity. Another Persian reformer, Mani, about A.D. 252, also tried to make a new religion out of a mixture of Christianity and old oriental science; but he was flayed alive by order of the Persian king. During the 3rd century A.D. the Persian Empire was becoming a formidable rival to the Roman Empire. The Persian rulers tried to identify the religion of Zoroaster with patriotism; and as they meant to overthrow the Roman Empire, so they meant to establish Zoroastrianism as the supreme religion on earth. They persecuted most of the Christians, who looked to Rome for protection; but they protected NESTORIAN Christians (q.v.), since they had broken away from the main Church and therefore were dissociated from Rome. Finally, when the Muslim Arabs conquered Persia in the 7th century A.D., most of the inhabitants of Persia became Muslims, though some of the followers of Zoroastrianism migrated to India, and formed there the community now called PARSEES (q.v.). Parsee is only a modification of the word Persia. The modern Persian Church is the result of 19th-century Christian missionary activity (*see* PERSIANS).

The teaching of Zarathustra himself and the beliefs of Zoroastrians are not entirely the same. It is not safe to suppose that any great teacher taught exactly the same doctrine all his life, because the thought of a great teacher develops. Zarathustra probably began by believing in a number of gods. It seems, however, that by the end of his life he had become a convinced and ardent monotheist, and believed in the goodness and holiness of one God—a God engaged in a continual struggle against evil. Man's life, he said, ought properly to be spent in serving the good God loyally and in sharing his struggle. Zarathustra did not deny the existence of other superhuman beings; but he came to think of them as lower than Ahura Mazda himself, and as merely of the rank of angels. He taught the doctrine of a last judgment, and of heaven and hell, and he may have believed in some kind of heavenly redeemer. Later generations added some stories about him which remind us of many in the Gospels—such as that he was virgin-born, that attempts were made to kill him when a child, and that he was tempted in the wilderness by Angra Mainyu, the Lord of Evil. How much of this was copied from Christianity, and also how much Zarathustra's own teaching influenced the Jews at an earlier date during their captivity in Babylon, we cannot be sure. Certainly, after the conquest of Babylon by the Persian king, Cyrus, the Jews came into contact with the Persians.

After Zarathustra, when Persian religion recovered some of its old features, a tribe called the Magi made itself indispensable as a priesthood. Indeed, these Magi seem to have become a sort of sacred caste, not unlike that of the Brahmins in India. They started the custom of exposing the dead to vultures. This derived from the belief that death was caused by a malignant spirit, who must be prevented from harming the living by a very quick disposal of the body of the dead person. The quickest way of destroying the body was either by fire or by letting carrion birds devour it. Fire being sacred, and therefore not to be used for this purpose, the dead body was exposed to vultures. This practice still exists among the Parsees in India, where it is attended with much ceremony. The Magi also practised the interpretation of dreams and the pseudo-science of ASTROLOGY (q.v.); and it is said that they sacrificed a wolf periodically to the powers of evil.

Whatever Zarathustra may himself have thought and taught, these later Magi and their disciples thought of the world as almost exactly like a great game of chess, in which there was, so to speak, a black king (or Lord of Evil) who was about equal in power to the white king (or Lord of Good). This is what is called Dualism. Yet it is doubtful whether anyone was ever a complete Dualist; even the Magians taught that Good would in the end win, and they had also

calculated the date of this future victory, which is said to be A.D. 2398.

See also PERSIAN CIVILIZATION.

ZULU. This African Negro tribe is made up of southern Bantu people who live chiefly in Zululand, the coastal region of South Africa, south and east of the Drakenberg mountains in north Natal. They are generally strong, well-built people, with fine figures and upright bearing.

Formerly Zululand was divided among a number of small tribes; but these were conquered and united by a chief named Chaka in the early 19th century. He organized a fighting force, which was a terror to the surrounding country for a number of years, but which united the Zulu and enabled them to offer stiff resistance to white incursions. In 1879 the Zulu army was routed by the British forces, and the military power of the Zulus came to an end.

The traditional interests of the Zulu lie in cattle and fighting. Cattle are the means by which a man can gather and display his wealth. Fines in the courts are payable by means of cattle, and marriages are arranged by handing over cattle to the family of the bride. Many religious and magical beliefs are associated with them, and men spend much of their lives just looking at their cattle, admiring them, and talking about them. The Zulus live in *kraals*—

Harold Scheub

A ZULU STORYTELLER .

homesteads with cattle pens in the middle of a ring of huts. These huts are round, dome-shaped structures built of saplings stuck into the ground.

Marriages, as among most African cattle peoples, are arranged through payment of *lobola*, that is, cattle paid to the father of the bride either by the bridegroom himself or more often contributed by his father or near relations—for it is rare for a young man to have enough cattle of his own. The cattle are not kept by the bride's father, but are shared out among close relatives.

In a Zulu family the children help their parents in their everyday activities. The boys help in looking after the goats of the kraal and in driving away birds from the growing crops. Girls nurse younger children, fetch firewood and water, grind corn, sweep out the huts, and help in cooking. Girls play with small clay and wooden dolls, boys with models of oxen. The boys also have friendly fights with other boys, and learn how to throw stones to kill wild animals or birds, and to shoot with bows and arrows.

Formerly, when the boys grew up, they were formed into regiments as warriors of the king. They lived apart in military kraals, and were not allowed to marry until the king gave his permission. They acted as police, messengers, or as a labour corps, and helped to look after the king's cattle. A regiment (or *impi*) numbered 800–1,000 men and had its own war-cry and regimental songs. Their older weapon was the long spear (the assegai), but Chaka used to make his men use the short stabbing-spear, because it forced them to come to grips with the enemy at close quarters. The warriors also had knob-kerries (short sticks with knobbed heads) and shields of strong hide. The different regiments had shields of different colours. Much of this military life survives today in ceremonial.

While the young men were undergoing their military service, the care of the cattle remained in the hands of the older men and the boys; and the women looked after the fields. Cultivation was simple, and wasteful of the soil. The chief food of the Zulus was milk drunk sour, millet and maize, and vegetables such as pumpkins, peas, and beans.

The chiefs still hold very important positions in Zululand. A chief succeeds to his position by hereditary right, either as the eldest son of the chief's principal wife, or as his nearest male relative. The Zulu king still controls all the chiefs, and has to be approached with very great ceremony. He represents the nation at the annual festivals and in the war rites, and also in relation to their ancestral spirits, who are believed to watch over the whole of Zululand. He is in charge of all the magic that affects the nation—magic for rain-making and success in war (*see* MAGIC). He also decides important law cases, and hears appeals from the chiefs' courts. He has a council of chiefs and close relatives to advise him. The king receives from the people many gifts of cattle, beer, and grain; but, in return, he is expected to look after his regiments and to help his people in time of famine. For two generations, these Zulu officials have effectively been controlled by the white government of South Africa, but they continue where possible to assert the interests of their people.

The chief religion of the Zulus is ANCESTOR WORSHIP (q.v.)—a man worships his own ancestors in the male line, and at feasts and beer-drinking a small libation is always poured out for the ancestors. They also believe in a power which shows itself in rain, thunder, and lightning (*see* NATURE WORSHIP).

See also SOUTHERN AFRICANS; EAST AFRICANS.
See also Vol. IV: AFRICAN LANGUAGES.